TIGHT FISTS OR OPEN HANDS?

TIGHT FISTS OR OPEN HANDS?

Wealth and Poverty in Old Testament Law

David L. Baker

William B. Eerdmans Publishing Company
Grand Rapids, Michigan / Cambridge, U.K.

© 2009 David L. Baker
All rights reserved

Published 2009 by
Wm. B. Eerdmans Publishing Co.
2140 Oak Industrial Drive N.E., Grand Rapids, Michigan 49505 /
P.O. Box 163, Cambridge CB3 9PU U.K.

Printed in the United States of America

14 13 12 11 10 09   7 6 5 4 3 2 1

Library of Congress Cataloging-in-Publication Data

Baker, D. L.
Tight fists or open hands?: wealth and poverty in Old Testament law / David L. Baker.
p.   cm.
Includes bibliographical references and indexes.
ISBN 978-0-8028-6283-9 (pbk.: alk. paper)
1. Wealth — Biblical teaching. 2. Poverty — Biblical teaching.
3. Bible. O.T. — Criticism, interpretation, etc. 4. Jewish law.
5. Law, Ancient.   I. Title.

BS1199.W35B35   2009
221.8′3625 — dc22
                                    2009010684

www.eerdmans.com

Contents

Preface — xiii

Abbreviations — xvi

1. Introduction — 1
   1.1 Ancient Near Eastern Laws — 1
      a. Sumerian — 3
      b. Babylonian — 4
      c. Hittite — 5
      d. Assyrian — 5
   1.2 Old Testament Laws — 6
      a. Decalogue — 7
      b. Book of the Covenant — 8
      c. Holiness Code — 9
      d. Deuteronomic Laws — 10

PROPERTY AND LAND

2. Property Rights — 15
   2.1 Theft — 16
      Exod 20:15; 22:1-4; Lev 19:11a, 13a; Deut 5:19

	a. Ancient Near East		16
	b. Decalogue		20
	c. Book of the Covenant		22
	d. Holiness Code		24
	e. Conclusion		26
2.2	Coveting		28
	Exod 20:17; Deut 5:21		
	a. Ancient Near East		28
	b. Decalogue		30
	c. Conclusion		33
2.3	Lost Property		36
	Exod 23:4-5; Deut 22:1-4		
	a. Ancient Near East		36
	b. Book of the Covenant		38
	c. Deuteronomic Laws		40
	d. Conclusion		42
3.	**Property Responsibilities**		**44**
3.1	Owner Liability		44
	Exod 21:28-36; Deut 22:8		
	a. Ancient Near East		45
	b. Book of the Covenant		46
	c. Deuteronomic Laws		51
	d. Conclusion		52
3.2	Negligent Damage		57
	Exod 22:5-6		
	a. Ancient Near East		57
	b. Book of the Covenant		59
	c. Conclusion		61
3.3	Care of Property		62
	Exod 22:7-15		
	a. Ancient Near East		62
	b. Book of the Covenant		66

4. Ancestral Land — 75

- c. Conclusion — 71

4.1 Jubilee — 76
Lev 25:8-17, 23-34
- a. Ancient Near East — 77
- b. Holiness Code — 79
- c. Conclusion — 95

4.2 Boundaries — 97
Deut 19:14
- a. Ancient Near East — 97
- b. Deuteronomic Laws — 99
- c. Conclusion — 101

4.3 Military Service — 102
Deut 20:5-7
- a. Ancient Near East — 102
- b. Deuteronomic Laws — 104
- c. Conclusion — 106

MARGINAL PEOPLE

5. Slaves — 111

5.1 Chattel Slaves — 112
Exod 21:16; Lev 25:44-46; Deut 24:7
- a. Ancient Near East — 112
- b. Exodus and Deuteronomy — 116
- c. Holiness Code — 118
- d. Conclusion — 119

5.2 Slave Abuse — 121
Exod 21:20-21, 26-27
- a. Ancient Near East — 121
- b. Book of the Covenant — 122
- c. Conclusion — 129

5.3 Fugitive Slaves	130
Deut 23:15-16	
a. Ancient Near East	130
b. Deuteronomic Laws	132
c. Conclusion	134
6. Semi-Slaves	**136**
6.1 Temporary Slaves	136
Exod 21:2-6; Deut 15:12-18	
a. Ancient Near East	136
b. Book of the Covenant	138
c. Deuteronomic Laws	143
d. Conclusion	148
6.2 Concubines	150
Exod 21:7-11; Deut 21:10-14	
a. Ancient Near East	150
b. Book of the Covenant	152
c. Deuteronomic Laws	155
d. Conclusion	157
6.3 Bonded Labourers	159
Lev 25:39-43, 47-55	
a. Ancient Near East	159
b. Holiness Code	160
c. Bonded Labour and Temporary Slavery	166
d. Conclusion	173
7. Other Vulnerable Groups	**175**
7.1 Resident Aliens	176
Exod 22:21; 23:9; Lev 19:33-34; 24:22; Deut 24:17-18	
a. Ancient Near East	177
b. Biblical Terminology	178
c. Book of the Covenant	182
d. Holiness Code	184

e. Deuteronomic Laws	186
f. Conclusion	187
7.2 Widows and Orphans	189
Exod 22:22-24; Deut 24:17-18	
a. Ancient Near East	189
b. Book of the Covenant	191
c. Deuteronomic Laws	192
d. Conclusion	193

JUSTICE AND GENEROSITY

8. Just Lawsuits	199
8.1 Witnesses	201
Exod 20:16; 23:1-2; Deut 5:20; 17:6; 19:15-21	
a. Ancient Near East	201
b. Decalogue	202
c. Book of the Covenant	204
d. Deuteronomic Laws	205
e. Conclusion	208
8.2 Impartiality	209
Exod 23:3, 6-7; Lev 19:15; Deut 16:18-19a	
a. Ancient Near East	209
b. Book of the Covenant	209
c. Holiness Code	212
d. Deuteronomic Laws	213
e. Conclusion	214
8.3 Bribery	215
Exod 23:8; Deut 16:19b-20	
a. Ancient Near East	215
b. Book of the Covenant	217
c. Deuteronomic Laws	219
d. Conclusion	220

9. Shared Harvests — 223

9.1 Sabbatical Year — 223
Exod 23:10-11; Lev 25:1-7, 18-22
- a. Ancient Near East — 224
- b. Book of the Covenant — 226
- c. Holiness Code — 228
- d. Conclusion — 231

9.2 Gleaning — 232
Lev 19:9-10; 23:22; Deut 24:19-22
- a. Ancient Near East — 233
- b. Holiness Code — 234
- c. Deuteronomic Laws — 235
- d. Conclusion — 237

9.3 Triennial Tithes — 239
Deut 14:28-29; 26:12-13
- a. Tithes in the Ancient Near East — 239
- b. Tithes in Biblical Law — 241
- c. The Triennial Tithe — 245
- d. Conclusion — 247

9.4 'Scrumping' — 248
Deut 23:24-25
- a. Deuteronomic Laws — 248
- b. Conclusion — 250

10. Generous Loans — 252

10.1 Interest — 253
Exod 22:25; Lev 25:35-38; Deut 23:19-20
- a. Ancient Near East — 253
- b. Book of the Covenant — 257
- c. Holiness Code — 258
- d. Deuteronomic Laws — 262
- e. Conclusion — 264

10.2 Security	266
Exod 22:26-27; Deut 24:6, 10-13, 17b	
a. Ancient Near East	267
b. Book of the Covenant	269
c. Deuteronomic Laws	271
d. Conclusion	273
10.3 Debt Relief	275
Deut 15:1-11	
a. Ancient Near East	276
b. Deuteronomic Laws	278
c. Conclusion	283
11. Fair Trade	**286**
11.1 Holidays	287
Exod 20:8-11; 23:12; Deut 5:12-15; 12:12, 18; 16:11, 14; 26:11	
a. Ancient Near East	287
b. Decalogue	288
c. Book of the Covenant	291
d. Deuteronomic Laws	292
e. Conclusion	294
11.2 Wages	296
Lev 19:13b; Deut 24:14-15	
a. Ancient Near East	296
b. Holiness Code	297
c. Deuteronomic Laws	298
d. Conclusion	299
11.3 Weights and Measures	299
Lev 19:35-36; Deut 25:13-16	
a. Ancient Near East	299
b. Holiness Code	301
c. Deuteronomic Laws	302
d. Conclusion	303

12. Conclusion	**305**
12.1 Biblical Law in Its Ancient Near Eastern Context	306
a. Similarities	306
b. Differences	307
12.2 Theological and Ethical Implications	310
a. Property and Land	310
b. Marginal People	311
c. Justice and Generosity	313
d. Postscript	315
Bibliography	316
Index of Subjects	369
Index of Foreign Words	381
Index of Scripture	383
Index of Ancient Near Eastern Laws	397
Index of Authors	400

Preface

The magnitude of the problem of wealth and poverty at the beginning of the third millennium can hardly be overstated. In Indonesia, where I lived for many years, it is impossible to ignore the contrast between the opulence of the super-rich and the destitution of those who own nothing apart from the rags they wear. Seventeen thousand islands provide vast natural resources, while the gentle climate and fertile land should ensure that all have at least enough to eat. Nevertheless, most Indonesians struggle to provide the bare essentials for their families because of the ongoing effects of feudalism, colonization, international debt, domestic corruption, mismanagement of resources, religious conflict, and a series of natural disasters. I used to think that things were much better in Britain, where people could earn a fair wage without excessive differentiation between the 'haves' and the 'have-nots', and the state ensured that even those without employment would have their basic needs supplied. But now more and more people are homeless or in serious debt, despite the fact that an increasing number are enjoying unprecedented levels of luxury. It is an oversimplification to categorize the West (or the North) as rich and the East (or South) as poor, since there are desperately poor people in countries like America and Britain, while quite a few of the world's billionaires are Asian. In almost every corner of the globe, the gap between rich and poor is growing.

It seems to me axiomatic that a Christian response to this problem should be based on a sound understanding of the Bible and a realistic view of how things actually are today. Living with one's eyes open in the 'Two-thirds World' does not permit a simplistic prosperity theology; on the other hand, liberation theology's 'preferential option for the poor' emphasises certain biblical texts and downplays others. The Old Testament both affirms the good things of this world and condemns those who monopolise them for their own benefit. We are told that God blesses his people in tangible ways and judges those who deprive others of their legitimate rights to material possessions. It is not so much that God takes the side of the poor in their struggle against oppressors as that his concern is justice for all, whoever they may be. Both prosperity theology and liberation theology contain elements of truth, but both tend to focus on particular aspects of biblical teaching and ignore others. I believe we can learn from both, while trying to bring together the teaching of the whole Bible into a balanced, holistic theology.

Books have been published on various Old Testament texts and topics, such as Leviticus 25, Deuteronomy 15, Amos, oppression, social justice, property rights, land, and debt-slavery. There are several academic studies of wealth and poverty in wisdom literature and some semi-popular works which cover the whole Bible. To the present, however, there has been no thorough study of wealth and poverty in Old Testament law. I believe this is much needed, since an understanding of the law is fundamental for interpretation of the whole Old Testament. The present study is intended to fill this significant gap in Old Testament scholarship and also to lay a foundation for more popular works that consider the relevance of these laws to everyday life in the twenty-first century.

The heart of the book is a new translation and exegetical study of all the biblical laws concerned with wealth and poverty. Laws on the same topic are discussed together, giving consideration to similarities and differences between the Decalogue, Book of the Covenant, Holiness Code, and Deuteronomic Laws. These laws are placed in the wider context of ancient Near Eastern law, so that it becomes clear which attitudes are distinctively biblical and which are held in common with other civilised peoples. Each section has an extended conclusion which summarises the main points, considers intertextual relationships with other parts of the canon, and gives some pointers to the significance of the laws for today's world. The title of the book is derived from Deut 15:7b-8a — 'You shall not be hardhearted or tight-fisted toward your poor brother. Rather, open your hand generously to him.'

I wish to record my gratitude to all who have helped to bring this work to completion. My interest in this subject dates back to 1980, when I taught a module on the Old Testament teaching about wealth and poverty in a Master of Theology programme at the Asian Theological Seminary in Manila, at the invitation of Dr. Chester Wood. I followed this up by giving lectures, leading seminars, and writing papers in Indonesia during the next two decades and benefited from interaction with students and colleagues in that country. In 2001 I returned to England and was grateful that my responsibilities as deputy warden at Tyndale House, Cambridge, allowed me a substantial amount of time for research and writing. It also provided the opportunity for informal discussions with other researchers over morning coffee.

I am particularly grateful to Professor Alan Millard of the University of Liverpool, who has read the whole manuscript, and Professor Graham Davies of the University of Cambridge, who has read several chapters. Both have made valuable suggestions for improvement. Others who have given input and encouragement include Professor Gordon McConville, Dr. John Nolland, Dr. Bruce Winter, and Dr. Christopher Wright.

Most important of all, my wife, Elizabeth, has given continual support and companionship, without which this book would never have seen the light of day. She has also read the whole manuscript at various stages of the writing process, making many helpful comments concerning both content and style. I dedicate the book to her.

DAVID L. BAKER
Trinity Theological College, Perth
February 2009

Abbreviations

Ancient Near Eastern Laws

AI	*Ana ittišu* tablet 7, incl. Sumerian Family Laws (ca. 2300-2076 B.C.)
CH	Laws of Hammurabi (ca. 1750 B.C.)
EAS	Edict of Ammi-saduqa (ca. 1646 B.C.)
HL	Hittite Laws (ca. 1650-1500 B.C.)
LE	Laws of Eshnunna (ca. 1770 B.C.)
LL	Laws of Lipit-Ishtar (ca. 1930 B.C.)
LRO	Laws about Rented Oxen (ca. 1800 B.C.)
LU	Laws of Ur-Namma (ca. 2100 B.C.)
LX	Laws of X (ca. 2050-1800 B.C.)
MAL	Middle Assyrian Laws (ca. 1450-1250 B.C.)
NBL	Neo-Babylonian Laws (ca. 700 B.C.)
RU	Reforms of Uru-inimgina/Uru-kagina (ca. 2350 B.C.)
SLET	Sumerian Laws Exercise Tablet (ca. 1800 B.C.)
SLHF	Sumerian Laws Handbook of Forms (ca. 1700 B.C.)

Biblical Texts and Versions

BHS	Biblia Hebraica Stuttgartensia (2nd ed., 1983)
ESV	English Standard Version (2001)
KJV	King James Version [Authorised Version] (1611)
LXX	Septuagint
MT	Masoretic Text
NAB	New American Bible (1969)
NEB	New English Bible (1970)

Abbreviations xvii

NIV	New International Version (1984)
NJB	New Jerusalem Bible (1985)
NJPS	New Jewish Publication Society Translation (1989)
NRSV	New Revised Standard Version (1989)
REB	Revised English Bible (1989)
RSV	Revised Standard Version (1952)
RV	Revised Version (1885)
TB	Alkitab Terjemahan Baru [Indonesian New Translation] (1974)
TEV	Today's English Version [Good News Bible] (1976)
TNIV	Today's New International Version (2005)

Journals, Series, Reference Works, Symposia

AB	Anchor Bible
ABAW	Abhandlungen der Bayerische Akademie der Wissenschaften, Philosophisch-Historische Klasse.
ABD	*The Anchor Bible Dictionary*, ed. David Noel Freedman (6 vols.; New York: Doubleday, 1992).
ABR	*Australian Biblical Review*
ABRL	Anchor Bible Reference Library
ADD	*Assyrian Deeds and Documents Recording the Transfer of Property: Including the So-Called Private Contracts, Legal Decisions and Proclamations Preserved in the Kouyunjik Collections of the British Museum, Chiefly of the 7th Century B.C.*, ed. C. H. W. Johns (4 vols.; Cambridge: Deighton, Bell, 1898-1923); vol. 4, ed. A. S. Johns.
AfO	*Archiv für Orientforschung*
AfOB	Archiv für Orientforschung Beiheft
AGJU	Arbeiten zur Geschichte des antiken Judentums und des Urchristentums
AJBI	*Annual of the Japanese Biblical Institute*
AJSL	*American Journal of Semitic Languages and Literature*
AJT	*American Journal of Theology*
ALGHJ	Arbeiten zur Literatur und Geschichte des hellenistischen Judentums
AnBib	Analecta biblica
ANET	*Ancient Near Eastern Texts Relating to the Old Testament*, ed. James B. Pritchard (3rd ed.; Princeton: Princeton University Press, 1969).
AOAT	Alter Orient und Altes Testament
AOS	American Oriental Series
AOSTS	American Oriental Society Translation Series

ARE	*Ancient Records of Egypt: Historical Documents from the Earliest Times to the Persian Conquest,* ed. James Henry Breasted (5 vols.; Ancient Records, 2nd series; Chicago: University of Chicago Press, 1906-07).
ARM 1	*Correspondance de Šamši-Addu et de ses fils,* ed. Georges Dossin (Archives royales de Mari 1; Paris: Imprimerie Nationale, 1950).
ARM 8	*Textes juridiques,* ed. Georges Boyer (Archives royales de Mari 8; Paris: Imprimerie Nationale, 1958).
ArOr	*Archiv Orientální*
AS	*Assyriological Studies*
ASAW	Abhandlungen der Sächsischen Akademie der Wissenschaften, Philologisch-historische Klasse
ASOR	American Schools of Oriental Research
AT	*The Alalakh Tablets,* ed. Donald J. Wiseman (Occasional Publications of the British Institute of Archaeology at Ankara 2; London: British Institute of Archaeology at Ankara, 1953).
ATD	Das Alte Testament Deutsch
AuOrSup	Aula Orientalis Supplementa
AUSS	*Andrews University Seminary Studies*
BA	*Biblical Archaeologist*
BAR	*Biblical Archaeology Review*
BASOR	*Bulletin of the American Schools of Oriental Research*
BAT	Die Botschaft des Alten Testaments
BBB	Bonner biblische Beiträge
BBET	Beiträge zur biblischen Exegese und Theologie
BBR	*Bulletin for Biblical Research*
BDB	*A Hebrew and English Lexicon of the Old Testament,* ed. Francis Brown et al. (Oxford: Clarendon, 1907); repr. with corrections 1957.
BETL	Bibliotheca Ephemeridum Theologicarum Lovaniensium
Bib	*Biblica*
BibInt	*Biblical Interpretation*
BIW	The Bible in Its World
BibS(F)	Biblische Studien (Freiburg im Breisgau)
BJS	Brown Judaic Studies
BN	*Biblische Notizen*
BO	*Bibliotheca orientalis*
BRS	Biblical Resource Series
BRev	*Bible Review*
BSac	*Bibliotheca sacra*
BSOAS	*Bulletin of the School of Oriental and African Studies*
BT	The Bible Translator
BTB	Biblical Theology Bulletin

Abbreviations

BWA[N]T	Beiträge zur Wissenschaft vom Alten [und Neuen] Testament
BWL	*Babylonian Wisdom Literature,* ed. W. G. Lambert (Oxford: Clarendon, 1960).
BZ	*Biblische Zeitschrift*
BZAW	Beihefte zur Zeitschrift für die alttestamentliche Wissenschaft
CAD	*The Assyrian Dictionary of the Oriental Institute of the University of Chicago,* ed. Ignace J. Gelb et al. (21 vols.; Chicago: Oriental Institute, 1956-).
CAH	Cambridge Ancient History
CahRB	Cahiers de la Revue biblique
CANE	*Civilizations of the Ancient Near East,* ed. Jack M. Sasson (4 vols.; New York: Scribner's, 1995).
CBQ	*Catholic Biblical Quarterly*
CC	Continental Commentaries
CDA	*A Concise Dictionary of Akkadian,* ed. Jeremy A. Black et al. (SANTAG Arbeiten und Untersuchungen zur Keilschriftkunde 5; Wiesbaden: Harrassowitz, 1999).
Comm	*Communio*
COS	*The Context of Scripture,* ed. William W. Hallo (3 vols.; Leiden: Brill, 1997-2002).
CTA	*Corpus des tablettes en cunéiformes alphabétiques découvertes à Ras Shamra-Ugarit de 1929 à 1939,* ed. Andrée Herdner (Mission de Ras Shamra 10; Paris: Imprimerie Nationale, 1963).
CTJ	*Calvin Theological Journal*
CurBS	*Currents in Research: Biblical Studies*
DCH	*The Dictionary of Classical Hebrew,* ed. David J. A. Clines (projected 8 vols.; Sheffield: Sheffield Academic, 1993-).
DERANE	*Debt and Economic Renewal in the Ancient Near East,* ed. Michael Hudson and Marc van de Mieroop (Institute for the Study of Long-Term Economic Trends and the International Scholars Conference on Ancient Near Eastern Economies Series 3; Bethesda, MD: CDL, 2002).
DOTP	*Dictionary of the Old Testament: Pentateuch,* ed. T. Desmond Alexander and David W. Baker (Downers Grove/Leicester: Inter-Varsity, 2003).
DOTT	*Documents from Old Testament Times,* ed. D. Winton Thomas (Edinburgh: Thomas Nelson, 1958).
EncJud	*Encyclopaedia Judaica,* ed. Cecil Roth et al. (16 vols.; Jerusalem: Keter, 1972).
ErIsr	*Eretz-Israel*
ETCSL	*The Electronic Text Corpus of Sumerian Literature,* ed. Jeremy A.

	Black et al. (Oxford: Oriental Institute, 1998-2006; http://etcsl.orinst.ox.ac.uk).
EvQ	*Evangelical Quarterly*
EvT	*Evangelische Theologie*
ExAud	*Ex Auditu*
ExpTim	*Expository Times*
FAT	Forschungen zum Alten Testament
FB	Forschung zur Bibel
FRLANT	Forschungen zur Religion und Literatur des Alten und Neuen Testaments
GKC	*Gesenius' Hebrew Grammar,* ed. E. Kautzsch and A. E. Cowley (2nd ed.; Oxford: Clarendon, 1910; trans. from German, 28th ed., 1909).
GTA	Göttinger theologischer Arbeiten
HALOT	*The Hebrew and Aramaic Lexicon of the Old Testament,* ed. Ludwig Koehler et al. (5 vols.; Leiden: Brill, 1994-2000; rev. trans. from German, 1967-96).
HANEL	*A History of Ancient Near Eastern Law,* ed. Raymond Westbrook (2 vols.; Handbook of Oriental Studies, Section One: The Near and Middle East 72; Leiden: Brill, 2003).
HAR	*Hebrew Annual Review*
HBT	*Horizons in Biblical Theology*
HKAT	Handkommentar zum Alten Testament
HOTTP	*Preliminary and Interim Report on the Hebrew Old Testament Text Project* (5 vols.; New York: United Bible Societies, 1979-80).
HSM	Harvard Semitic Monographs
HSS	Harvard Semitic Studies
HTKAT	Herders Theologischer Kommentar zum Alten Testament
HTR	*Harvard Theological Review*
HUCA	*Hebrew Union College Annual*
ICC	International Critical Commentary
IDB	*The Interpreter's Dictionary of the Bible,* ed. G. A. Buttrick (4 vols.; Nashville: Abingdon, 1962).
IDBSup	*The Interpreter's Dictionary of the Bible: Supplementary Volume,* ed. Keith Crim (Nashville: Abingdon, 1976).
IEJ	*Israel Exploration Journal*
IJT	*Indian Journal of Theology*
ILR	*Israel Law Review*
Int	*Interpretation*
IOS	*Israel Oriental Studies*
ITQ	*Irish Theological Quarterly*
JAOS	*Journal of the American Oriental Society*
JBL	*Journal of Biblical Literature*

JBQ	*Jewish Bible Quarterly*
JCS	*Journal of Cuneiform Studies*
JEA	*Journal of Egyptian Archaeology*
JESHO	*Journal of the Economic and Social History of the Orient*
JETS	*Journal of the Evangelical Theological Society*
JHI	*Journal of the History of Ideas*
JJP	*Journal of Juristic Papyrology*
JJS	*Journal of Jewish Studies*
JLA	*Jewish Law Annual*
JLR	*Journal of Law and Religion*
JNES	*Journal of Near Eastern Studies*
JNSL	*Journal of Northwest Semitic Languages*
JPOS	*Journal of the Palestine Oriental Society*
JPS	Jewish Publication Society
JQR	*Jewish Quarterly Review*
JSOT	*Journal for the Study of the Old Testament*
JSOTSup	Journal for the Study of the Old Testament, Supplement Series
JSS	*Journal of Semitic Studies*
JTS	*Journal of Theological Studies*
KAI	*Kanaanäische und aramäische Inschriften,* ed. Herbert Donner and Wolfgang Röllig (3 vols.; Wiesbaden: Harrassowitz, 1962-64).
KAT	*Kommentar zum Alten Testament*
KD	*Kerygma und Dogma*
KTU	The Cuneiform Alphabetic Texts from Ugarit, Ras Ibn Hani and Other Places, ed. Manfried Dietrich et al. (2nd enlarged ed.; Abhandlungen zur Literatur Alt-Syrien-Palästinas und Mesopotamiens 8; Münster: Ugarit, 1995).
LAPO	Littératures anciennes du Proche-Orient
LD	Lectio divina
Leš	*Lešonénu*
LHB/OTS	Library of Hebrew Bible/Old Testament Studies
MBPF	Münchener Beiträge zur Papyrusforschung und antiken Rechtsgeschichte
NCB	New Century Bible
NEA	*Near Eastern Archaeology*
NEchtB	Neue Echter Bibel
NIB	*The New Interpreter's Bible,* ed. Leander E. Keck et al. (Nashville: Abingdon, 2006).
NIBCOT	New International Biblical Commentary on the Old Testament
NICOT	New International Commentary on the Old Testament
NIDNTT	*New International Dictionary of New Testament Theology,* ed. Colin

	Brown (3 vols.; Grand Rapids: Zondervan/Exeter: Paternoster, 1975-78) (rev. trans. from German, 1967-71).
NIDOTTE	*New International Dictionary of Old Testament Theology and Exegesis,* ed. Willem A. VanGemeren (5 vols.; Carlisle: Paternoster/Grand Rapids: Zondervan, 1997).
OBO	Orbis biblicus et orientalis
OBT	Overtures to Biblical Theology
OCD	*The Oxford Classical Dictionary,* ed. Simon Hornblower and Antony Spawforth (3rd ed.; Oxford: Oxford University Press, 1996).
ODCC	*The Oxford Dictionary of the Christian Church,* ed. F. L. Cross and E. A. Livingstone (2nd ed.; Oxford: Oxford University Press, 1983).
OIP	Oriental Institute Publications
OLA	Orientalia lovaniensia analecta
OLP	*Orientalia lovaniensia periodica*
OLZ	*Orientalische Literaturzeitung*
Or	*Orientalia*
OTA	*Old Testament Abstracts*
OTL	Old Testament Library
OTS	Old Testament Studies
OtSt	*Oudtestamentische Studiën*
PAAJR	*Proceedings of the American Academy for Jewish Research*
PEQ	*Palestine Exploration Quarterly*
Presb	*Presbyterion*
PRU 3	*Le palais royal d'Ugarit 3: Textes accadiens et hourrites des archives est, ouest et centrales,* ed. Jean Nougayrol et al. (Mission de Ras Shamra 6; Paris: Imprimerie Nationale, 1955).
PRU 4	*Le palais royal d'Ugarit 4: Textes accadiens des archives sud (Archives internationales),* ed. Jean Nougayrol (Mission de Ras Shamra 9; Paris: Imprimerie Nationale, 1956).
PRU 5	*Le palais royal d'Ugarit 5: Textes en cunéiformes alphabétiques des archives est, ouest et du petit palais,* ed. Charles Virolleaud (Mission de Ras Shamra 11; Paris: Imprimerie Nationale, 1965).
PRU 6	*Le palais royal d'Ugarit 6: Textes en cunéiformes babyloniens des archives du grand palais et du palais sud d'Ugarit,* ed. Jean Nougayrol (Mission de Ras Shamra 12; Paris: Imprimerie Nationale, 1970).
QD	Quaestiones disputatae
RA	*Revue d'assyriologie et d'archéologie orientale*
RB	*Revue biblique*
RBL	Review of Biblical Literature
RevQ	*Revue de Qumran*
RHPR	*Revue d'histoire et de philosophie religieuses*
RHR	*Revue de l'histoire des religions*

RIDA	*Revue internationale des droits de l'antiquité*
RSO	*Rivista degli studi oriental*
RThom	*Revue thomiste*
RTL	*Revue théologique de Louvain*
RTR	*Reformed Theological Review*
SAA 6	*Legal Transactions of the Royal Court of Nineveh, Part I: Tiglath-Pileser III through Esarhaddon,* ed. Theodore Kwasman and Simo Parpola (State Archives of Assyria 6; Helsinki: Helsinki University Press, 1991).
SAA 14	*Legal Transactions of the Royal Court of Nineveh, Part II: Assurbanipal through Sin-šarru-iškun,* ed. Raija Mattila (State Archives of Assyria 14; Helsinki: Helsinki University Press, 2002).
SAAS	State Archives of Assyria Studies
SBAW	Sitzungsberichte der Bayerischen Akademie der Wissenschaften, Philosophisch-Historische Klasse
SBL	Society of Biblical Literature
SBLSBS	Society of Biblical Literature Sources for Biblical Study
SBLBSNA	Society of Biblical Literature Biblical Scholarship in North America
SBLDS	Society of Biblical Literature Dissertation Series
SBLSP	*Society of Biblical Literature Seminar Papers*
SBLSymS	Society of Biblical Literature Symposium Series
SBLWAW	Society of Biblical Literature Writings from the Ancient World
SBS	Stuttgarter Bibelstudien
SBT	Studies in Biblical Theology
ScrHier	Scripta Hierosolymitana
SDANEL	*Security for Debt in Ancient Near Eastern Law,* ed. Raymond Westbrook and Richard Jasnow (Culture and History of the Ancient Near East 9; Leiden: Brill, 2001).
SDIO	Studia et documenta ad iura orientis antiqui pertinentia
Sem	*Semitica*
SHBC	Smyth & Helwys Bible Commentary
SJLA	Studies in Judaism in Late Antiquity
SOSup	Symbolae osloenses, Supplement
SÖAW	Sitzungsberichte der österreichischen Akademie der Wissenschaften in Wien
STDJ	Studies on the Texts of the Desert of Judah
StPatr	Studia Patristica
SWBA	Social World of Biblical Antiquity
TA	*Tel Aviv*
TB	Theologische Bücherei
TDOT	*Theological Dictionary of the Old Testament,* ed. G. Johannes

	Botterweck and Helmer Ringgren (17 vols.; Grand Rapids: Wm. B. Eerdmans, 1977–; trans. from German, 1970–)
Text	*Textus*
TGUOS	*Transactions of the Glasgow University Oriental Society*
Them	*Themelios*
ThSt	Theologische Studiën
ThTo	*Theology Today*
TJ	*Trinity Journal*
TOTC	Tyndale Old Testament Commentaries
TS	*Theological Studies*
TSAJ	Texts and Studies in Ancient Judaism
TUAT	Texte aus der Umwelt des Alten Testaments
TynBul	*Tyndale Bulletin*
TZ	*Theologische Zeitschrift*
UBS	*UBS Translator's Handbooks* (Paratext 6 Distribution Ed.: United Bible Societies, 2003).
UF	*Ugarit-Forschungen*
VAB	Vorderasiatische Bibliothek
VE	*Vox evangelica*
VT	*Vetus Testamentum*
VTSup	Supplements to Vetus Testamentum
WBC	Word Biblical Commentary
WD	*Wort und Dienst*
WMANT	Wissenschaftliche Monographien zum Alten und Neuen Testament
WO	*Die Welt des Orients*
WTJ	*Westminster Theological Journal*
ZA	*Zeitschrift für Assyriologie*
ZABR	*Zeitschrift für altorientalische und biblische Rechtsgeschichte*
ZAW	*Zeitschrift für die alttestamentliche Wissenschaft*
ZTK	*Zeitschrift für Theologie und Kirche*

Chapter 1

INTRODUCTION

1.1 Ancient Near Eastern Laws

It is fascinating to delve into the rich and diverse cultural world of the ancient Near East, the context in which the ancient Israelites lived and formulated their laws. Among the many documents discovered by archaeologists, there are six major and ten minor collections of laws, bequeathed to us by the Sumerians, Babylonians, Hittites, and Assyrians.[1] Unfortunately, there are no comparable laws from Egypt or Canaan, though other documents have survived which give us some insight into the legal traditions of these neighbours of Israel.[2] When quoting the laws and other documents, I use the translations from *The Context of Scripture (COS)* unless otherwise stated.[3]

---

1. My grouping and dating of the laws generally follows Roth (1997), who assumes the 'middle chronology'. I treat them in chronological rather than geographical order. Sources for the law collections are given in footnotes below.

2. The Demotic legal code from Egypt is much later. On Egyptian law, see Lurje (1971); Mattha and Hughes (1975); Redford (2001); Jasnow (2003a; 2003b; 2003c; 2003d); Manning (2003); Porten (2003). On legal texts from Ugarit, see Rowe (1999).

3. Apart from the indispensable collections of texts in *ANET* and *COS*, sources for other legal documents include *ADD*; ARM 1; ARM 8; *AT*; SAA 6; SAA 14; Johns (1904); Kohler and Ungnad (1913); Schorr (1907-10; 1913); Koschaker (1928); Leemans (1960b); Postgate (1976); Beckman (1999). Further sources of nonlegal materials include *ARE; BWL; CTA; DOTT; ETCSL; KAI; KTU; PRU* 3; *PRU* 4; *PRU* 5; *PRU* 6; Cowley (1923); Gordon (1949b); Falkenstein and von Soden (1953); Gordon (1959); Caquot (1974); Beyerlin (1975); Seux (1976); Faulkner and Andrews (1985); Caquot (1989); Dalley (1989); Kovacs (1989); Davies (1991; 2004a); Foster (2005); Lindenberger (2003); George (1999); Black et al. (2004); Glassner (2004); Dobbs-Allsopp et al. (2005).

The nature and purpose of the ancient Near Eastern laws has been debated at length by scholars.[4] We should not assume that they served the same function as modern laws, designed to provide authoritative sources for use in law courts. A number of rulers considered it important to have laws compiled and inscribed on monuments, and some of these laws were copied and recopied in later centuries. One reason for doing this may have been royal propaganda, judging by prologues and epilogues to several Sumerian and Old Babylonian law collections which praise the author as 'king of justice' and recount his wonderful deeds. Several student exercises containing laws have been found, which suggests that scribes and officials were expected to study law. On the whole, the collections are more like textbooks than normative legislation, and the copies may have been for the use of educators rather than lawyers. Probably the laws were intended to record precedents as a basis for considering subsequent cases, but how far they were followed in practice is hard to tell.

For the purpose of this book, it is enough to affirm that the extant law collections show the existence of legal traditions in the ancient Near East. Local communities would have had their own traditions and procedures, and there was a good deal of common law too. Some of these legal traditions, and possibly a few of the actual laws, would have been familiar to the compilers of the Old Testament laws and are therefore of interest in understanding biblical law in its wider context. Since virtually all the ancient Near Eastern laws in question are earlier than those in the Old Testament, even on the most conservative dating of the Pentateuch, it is clear that any borrowing that may have taken place was on the part of the biblical writers.[5] I discuss this possibility in more detail in connection with some of the individual laws, for example the classic case of the goring ox.[6]

---

4. See Landsberger (1939); Mendenhall (1954: 32-34); Finkelstein (1961: 100-104; 1981: 14-16); Cardascia (1969: 23-52); Wiseman (1973: 9-10); Bottéro (1982); Westbrook (1985a; 1989; 2003b: 12-21); Eichler (1987); Otto (1994a: 160-63); Renger (1994); Fitzpatrick-McKinley (1999: 82-108); Walton (2006: 287-302); and esp. Lévy (2000).

5. For a comprehensive and up-to-date history of ancient Near Eastern law, see *HANEL*. On the comparison of ancient Near Eastern and biblical law, see David (1950); Paul (1970); Boecker (1976); Finkelstein (1981: 14-20, 39-46); Phillips (1984: 101); Westbrook (1988b); Walton (1989: 69-92); Malul (1990); Greengus (1992; 1994); Lafont (1994); Miller (1995); Wright (2003; 2006c); Heger (2005); Wells (2006); Strenge (2006). On broader issues relating to the social, economic, and cultural context of the ancient Near East, see *CANE*; Contenau (1954); Silver (1985); Postgate (1992); Snell (1997; 2005); Averbeck, Chavalas, and Weisberg (2003); Walton (2006).

6. See below, 3.1.d.

Introduction 3

In assessing the significance of these law collections, and the other ancient Near Eastern documents which have been discovered, it is important to realise that this extant material is probably a relatively small part of the written material which once existed. Some documents would have been destroyed when they were no longer needed, for example when a debt was cleared or because they were no longer of interest; and many others have been lost in the sands of time. Moreover, the vast majority of everyday events and situations were never recorded at all. Two consequences follow from this. First, we must be wary of drawing conclusions from lack of evidence because, as has often been said, 'absence of evidence is not evidence of absence.' Second, even when there is evidence of a specific event or situation, it does not necessarily prove that this event or situation was common. It might have been recorded because it was unusual — as present-day newspapers tend to focus on matters of interest to readers rather than those which are typical or important — or it might simply be that this is what happens to have been found.[7]

a. Sumerian

The oldest major law collection is the Sumerian Laws of Ur-Namma (LU), also known as Ur-Nammu.[8] Originating from Ur about 2100 B.C., the prologue and thirty or so laws are preserved on three incomplete tablets.

From the city of Isin, almost two centuries later, we have the Laws of Lipit-Ishtar (LL).[9] Lipit-Ishtar reigned 1934-1924, and his laws are known from more than a dozen manuscripts, consisting of a prologue, about forty laws, and an epilogue.

Apart from these two major collections of laws, six other Sumerian documents contain laws:

- Reforms of Uru-inimgina (RU), also known as Uru-kagina, from Lagash (ca. 2350)[10]

---

7. On the role of accident in providing our knowledge of the ancient Near East, see Millard (2005). Note also the comment of Yaron (1988: 275) on the unsystematic character of the laws, which means that the absence of a prohibition is not evidence that something is allowed.
8. *ANET* (523-25); *COS* (2.153); Borger (1982: 17-23); Roth (1997: 13-22).
9. *ANET* (159-61); *COS* (2.154); Driver and Miles (1955: 306-7); Borger (1982: 23-31); Roth (1997: 23-35).
10. *COS* (2.152); Kramer (1963: 79-83, 317-23); Cooper (1986: 70-74).

- *Ana ittišu* tablet 7 (AI), the first section of which is sometimes called the Sumerian Family Laws, a scholastic text probably from Isin (ca. 2300-2076)[11]
- Laws of X (LX), a fragmentary text of unknown provenance, probably dating to 2050-1800[12]
- Laws about Rented Oxen (LRO), a student exercise from Nippur (ca. 1800)[13]
- Sumerian Laws Exercise Tablet (SLET), a student exercise of unknown provenance (ca. 1800)[14]
- Sumerian Laws Handbook of Forms (SLHF), a compendium of laws of unknown provenance (ca. 1700)[15]

b. Babylonian

The first major collection of laws from Babylonia is the Laws of Eshnunna (LE).[16] It consists of sixty laws, written in Akkadian and originating from the city of Eshnunna (ca. 1770 B.C.). Apart from some damage to the heading, the laws are well preserved on two almost complete tablets, plus a student exercise tablet with several extracts.

Best known of all the law collections is the Laws of Hammurabi (CH), often termed the Code of Hammurabi, from which its conventional abbreviation derives.[17] Hammurabi was the sixth ruler of the First Dynasty of Babylon, and his laws were compiled toward the end of his forty-three-year reign (ca. 1750). It is by far the longest of the Mesopotamian collections, with a substantial prologue and epilogue and nearly three hundred laws. The most complete text of the laws is inscribed on a black stone stela which now stands in the Louvre, but many other manuscripts of the laws have been preserved, which were copied and recopied in succeeding centuries.

---

11. Driver and Miles (1952: 25-26; 1955: 308-13).
12. Roth (1997: 36-39).
13. Roth (1997: 40-41).
14. *ANET* (525-26); Roth (1997: 42-45).
15. Roth (1997: 46-54).
16. *ANET* (161-63); *COS* (2.130); Szlechter (1954); Borger (1982: 32-38); Eichler (1987); Yaron (1988); Otto (1989); Roth (1997: 57-70).
17. *ANET* (163-80); *COS* (2.131); *DOTT* (27-37); Kohler et al. (1904-23); David (1950); Driver and Miles (1952; 1955: 1-304); Wiseman (1962); Borger (1982: 39-80); Bottéro (1982); Roth (1997: 71-142); Richardson (2000); Strenge (2006).

Two other Babylonian law collections should also be mentioned:

- Edict of Ammi-saduqa (EAS), formerly known as the Babylonian Seisachtheia, probably issued in the first year of his reign (1646), which was the last in a series of edicts by the successors of Hammurabi[18]
- Neo-Babylonian Laws (NBL), just fifteen laws from a much later period (ca. 700), possibly from Sippar[19]

c. Hittite

In the ruins of Hattusha, the capital of the Hittite kingdom, thousands of cuneiform tablets have been discovered, including many copies of the Hittite Laws (HL).[20] Two hundred clauses cover a range of matters in considerable detail. The four earliest copies were written in the Old Hittite period (ca. 1650-1500 B.C.), and the rest in the Middle and New Hittite periods (ca. 1500-1180). An ongoing process of revision is apparent, for example in clauses which mention a former penalty of forty shekels replaced by one of twelve shekels (§§81, 94; cf. §§57-59, 63, 67-69, 91-92). One of the New Hittite copies revises some clauses of the older laws, while others simply modernise the language.

d. Assyrian

The most important of the Assyrian law collections is the Middle Assyrian Laws (MAL), dating to the fourteenth century.[21] Over a hundred of the laws are known from a series of tablets excavated in Assur, containing eleventh-century copies of the originals.

There are two other extant collections of Assyrian laws, but they do not deal with matters related to wealth and poverty, so are simply mentioned here for completeness:

18. *ANET* (526-28); *COS* (2.134); Driver and Miles (1955: 319-23); Kraus (1958; 1984); Finkelstein (1961).
19. *ANET* (197-98); *COS* (2.133); Driver and Miles (1955: 324-47); Borger (1982: 92-95); Roth (1997: 143-49).
20. *ANET* (188-97); *COS* (2.19); Neufeld (1951); Borger (1982: 96-123); Hoffner (1997); Hoffner in Roth (1997: 213-40).
21. *ANET* (180-88); *COS* (2.132); Driver and Miles (1935: 4-373, 380-453, 457-511); Cardascia (1969); Borger (1982: 80-92); Roth (1997: 153-94).

- Old Assyrian Laws, only fragments of which survive (ca. 2350-2100 B.C.)[22]
- Middle Assyrian Palace Decrees, also known as the Harem Edicts, containing regulations about the behaviour of palace personnel (ca. 1363-1076)[23]

Although no collection of laws has survived from the Neo-Assyrian period, a great deal of information on legal practice is available from documents in the State Archives of Assyria (791-612) and other archives.[24]

1.2 Old Testament Laws

Four biblical law collections have a significant amount of material on wealth and poverty: the Decalogue, Book of the Covenant, Holiness Code, and Deuteronomic Laws. For each topic of this book, relevant laws in the four collections are discussed in canonical order, and I also refer to other legal and literary materials when relevant. Whenever the laws and other Old Testament texts are quoted in this book, I make my own translation from the Hebrew.[25] Biblical references follow the verse numbering conventional in most English translations, on the assumption that those who know the original language will be aware of the differences and can make necessary adjustments.

I follow a canonical approach to the laws, seeking to understand them in their biblical rather than their historical context.[26] While a historical approach might also be illuminating, it has two major difficulties. First, as with the other ancient Near Eastern laws, the origin and purpose of the biblical laws are still matters of debate. Their historical context is relevant to their interpretation only if it can be established that they arose out of and were designed to address specific historical situations. Second, scholars are more divided than ever on the dating of the laws and the historicity

22. Driver and Miles (1935: 1-3, 376-79, 455-57).
23. Roth (1997: 195-209).
24. *ADD*; SAA 6; SAA 14; Kohler and Ungnad (1913); Postgate (1976).
25. My translation aims to represent the original as closely as possible without becoming unintelligible or ungrammatical. Where practical I have used inclusive language, but sometimes it has seemed less clumsy to use third person singular masculine pronouns, following the Hebrew, rather than substitutes such as 'one' or 'person'.
26. Cf. Soss (1973); McConville (2006); Wright (2006b).

of the materials which may provide their historical context, so such a historical approach would at best yield tentative results. In any case, the results would not necessarily be more useful than those yielded by a canonical approach. Unlike prophecy, which is often closely related to historical events, law has a much looser connection with history.

The canonical context is clearly important, however, since it provides clues concerning the way the compiler[s] of the Pentateuch intended readers to understand the laws. It is also the primary context in which people through the ages have understood or misunderstood, and applied or ignored, these laws. It remains a good starting-point for interpretation today, both by those who consider these texts as authoritative sources for contemporary law and ethics and by others who are simply interested in what they might have to say of lasting value about human affairs. How far this canonical meaning coincides with that intended by the 'original' authors of the laws is a separate question that I will not attempt to answer here.[27]

a. Decalogue

The first and most fundamental of all the biblical law collections is the Decalogue or Ten Commandments, recorded in Exodus 20:2-17 and Deuteronomy 5:6-21. As I have argued elsewhere,[28] there is good reason for considering these laws to date to the time of Moses. It is possible that some of the present laws have been expanded from an earlier shorter form, and probable that the Deuteronomic version is later than the one in Exodus. The consistent apodictic style in the second person singular is unusual in the Old Testament and unknown elsewhere in the ancient Near East. Its comprehensive scope also marks it out from all the other law collections.

---

27. For further discussion of biblical law, see Alt (1934); Noth (1940); Daube (1947; 1973); Rabast (1949); Gemser (1953); Mendenhall (1954); Gevirtz (1961); Gerstenberger (1965); Liedke (1971); Bright (1973); Patrick (1973; 1985; 1989); Weinfeld (1973); Gilmer (1975); Boecker (1976); Wenham (1978a; 1978b); Sonsino (1980; 1992); Jackson (1989b; 2000); Crüsemann (1992); Greengus (1992); Kaiser (1992); Brin (1994); Levinson (1994); García López and Fabry (1995); Fitzpatrick-McKinley (1999); Watts (1999); Falk (2001); Otto (2001); Frymer-Kensky (2003). On the relationship between law and ethics, see Bailey (1963); Falk (1992); Otto (1994c); Wenham (1997); Wafawanaka (2000); Rodd (2001: 50, 107); Lalleman (2004); Wright (2004a: 281-326).

28. Baker (2005b: 5-9).

In its two biblical contexts, the Decalogue is addressed to Israel, as individuals and as a community, by God himself. It may in fact be understood as the constitution of the people of God. After a brief historical prologue, stating the basis of Israel's relationship with God, there is a list of the primary obligations laid upon her for maintenance of that relationship. These obligations are divided into two groups of five, the former concerned mainly with love for God and the latter with love for human beings. Thus the Decalogue is foundational for the life of the people, as shown also by many allusions to its ethical guidelines in later biblical texts.[29]

b. Book of the Covenant

Almost immediately following the Decalogue in Exodus is a collection of laws that is conventionally termed the 'Book of the Covenant' (cf. Exod 24:3, 7). In this canonical context they are introduced as 'judgements' (מִשְׁפָּטִים, often translated 'laws', 'rules', or 'ordinances') which Moses is to set before the people (21:1; cf. 20:22; 24:3). This explicitly distinguishes them from the Decalogue, which is presented as direct words of God (20:1). The structure of the collection may be seen as follows:

- prologue, including instructions for worship (20:22–21:1)[30]
- first section of laws (21:2–22:17)[31]
- second section of laws (22:18–23:12)
- epilogue, including instructions for worship (23:13-33)[32]

---

29. For further discussion of the Decalogue, see Baker (2005b; 2005d) and the literature cited there; also Keszler (1957); Reventlow (1962); Fohrer (1965); Jepsen (1967); Hamel (1969); Carmichael (1985b; 1992); Segal and Levi (1985); Braulik (1991); Olson (1994); Jackson (2000: 197-202); Marshall (2003); Brown (2004); Hossfeld (2004); Kuntz (2004); Braaten and Seitz (2005); Frevel, Konkel, and Schnocks (2005); Aaron (2006).

30. Most scholars identify the divine command to Moses in 20:22 as the beginning of the unit, and it is often assumed that the laws begin in v. 23. However, the new introduction in 21:1 suggests that the laws proper begin in 21:2 and the instructions for worship at the end of ch. 20 are to be seen as part of the prologue, linking the theophany and the laws.

31. A few scholars suggest the first section ends at v. 20 (e.g. Halbe 1975: 421) or v. 27 (e.g. Otto 1988b: 9-10).

32. Many scholars view 23:20-33, containing divine promises and exhortations to obedience, as the epilogue. However, there is already a brief conclusion in 23:13, followed by further instructions for worship (vv. 14-19) before the epilogue proper. Some scholars treat vv. 10-19 as a unified section on worship, but this overlooks the fact that the instructions about sabbath and sabbatical years in vv. 10-12 are concerned with the social benefits of these insti-

The style of the laws is consistently casuistic in the first section, then predominantly apodictic in the second.

All of the Ten Commandments except the prohibition of blasphemy and coveting reappear in the Book of the Covenant, in different words and often in more detail. The death penalty is generally prescribed for breaking them, except in the case of theft, and murder is differentiated from accidental killing so that only the former is a capital crime. There is general agreement that the Book of the Covenant is earlier than either the Holiness Code or Deuteronomic Laws, with a range of dates suggested between the Mosaic period and the monarchy.[33] Whatever the date of compilation, it is likely that many of the individual laws are older, and some may even be pre-Mosaic. It is also possible that there has been some Deuteronomic editing of the collection.[34]

c. Holiness Code

The second part of Leviticus is commonly called the 'Holiness Code', and is thought to have constituted a separate collection of laws from the 'Priestly Code' in the earlier part. Although most scholars mark the boundaries of this collection as chapters 17–26, it is arguable that it begins at chapter 18.[35] Two of the most distinctive features of the collection are absent from chapter 17: the characteristic refrain ('I am the LORD [your God]') and the key term 'holy' (קדשׁ). Also, the prologue in 18:1-5 and conclusion in 26:46 clearly mark chapters 18–26 as an entity, at least from a ca-

---

tutions, not even mentioning the idea of sabbath as a holy day, and are separated by the 'conclusion' of v. 13 from the cultic instructions of vv. 14-19.

33. *Pace* Van Seters (2003), who dates it to the exilic period. For critiques of Van Seters's proposal, see Levinson (2004); Otto (2004).

34. In a major study that became available to me only after the completion of the present work, so that I have been unable to take account of it here, Jackson (2006) argues that the *Mishpatim* of Exod 21:1–22:16 are to be understood as wisdom laws. For further discussion of the Book of the Covenant, in addition to the works already cited, see Jepsen (1927); Morgenstern (1928); Cazelles (1946); Mendenhall (1954); Lewy (1957); Vesco (1968); Paul (1970); Childs (1974: 440-96); Hanson (1977); Durham (1987: 305-37); Otto (1989; 1993a; 1994a; 1994c: 18-104); Schenker (1990); Schwienhorst-Schönberger (1990); Osumi (1991); Carmichael (1992); Crüsemann (1992: 109-200); Marshall (1993); Morrow (1994); Patrick (1994); Sprinkle (1994); Westbrook (1994c); Jackson (1995); Houtman (1996: 72-283; 1997); Knight (2000); Rothenbusch (2000); Wright (2003; 2006c); Wells (2006).

35. Hoffmann (1905: 469); Kilian (1963: 169-79); Wenham (1979: 7).

nonical perspective. In any case, whether or not chapter 17 is part of the Holiness Code is only of marginal interest in the present book, since none of the main texts studied occur in this chapter.[36]

The relative dating of the Holiness Code and Deuteronomic Laws remains a matter of disagreement. As is well known, in the nineteenth century the classic Documentary Hypothesis displaced the traditional view of Mosaic authorship as the dominant view of pentateuchal origins. For a century or so critical scholarship worked with the assumption that the Priestly writings, including the Holiness Code, formed the latest of the major sources of the Pentateuch, written during or after the Babylonian exile. This view is still held by many scholars, such as Otto who sees the Holiness Code as the work of the final editor of the Pentateuch, designed to harmonise the earlier laws.[37] There never was unanimity on this, however, and the opposition of Kaufmann (1961) has since been taken up by a good many others, who have argued that the Priestly writings — including the Holiness Code — are preexilic, and quite possibly pre-Deuteronomic or even premonarchic.[38] I do not attempt to address wider questions of dating here, but simply note that in the texts studied for the purpose of this book there is more evidence of the Deuteronomic Laws adapting material from the Holiness Code than the other way round.[39]

d. Deuteronomic Laws

The fourth collection of biblical laws important for the topic of this book is that found in Deuteronomy 12–26. The extent of this collection is almost

---

36. Differently again, Milgrom (2000: 1332-34) treats ch. 27 as the conclusion of the Holiness Code. However, ch. 27 lacks the characteristic refrain, 'I am the LORD', and the list of blessings and curses in ch. 26 suggests that the law collection ends here (cf. Exod 23:20-33; Deut 27–28). Both chs. 17 and 27 concern cultic matters, and their placement at the beginning and end, outside the main collection of laws, may be seen as parallel to the structure of the Book of the Covenant.

37. Otto (1994b; 1994c: 233-56; 1999b); cf. Nihan (2004); Stackert (2007).

38. Weinfeld (1972a: 179-89; 2004); Hurvitz (1974; 1982); Milgrom (1976b; 1991: 3-13; 2000: 1361-64); Haran (1978: 5-12); Japhet (1978); Zevit (1982); Knohl (1995: 220); Joosten (1996: 203-7); Wenham (1999); cf. Blenkinsopp (1992: 58-97).

39. The same conclusion is reached by Braulik (1995; 1996) in a study of various texts from Deuteronomy 19–25 in relation to their parallels in Leviticus. For further discussion of the Holiness Code, apart from the works already cited, see Reventlow (1961); Cholewiński (1976); Hartley (1992: 247-475); Grünwaldt (1999); Ruwe (1999); Crüsemann (1992: 277-327); Milgrom (2000; 2001).

universally agreed. It is also clear that in their canonical context the speeches of Moses in chapters 1–4 and 5–11 form an extended introduction to the laws, while the blessings and curses in chapters 27–28 and confirmation of the covenant in chapters 29–30 form a conclusion.[40] The identification of the Deuteronomic Laws with the book discovered in the eighteenth year of Josiah's reign (622 B.C.), which became the legal basis for his reform, is highly likely. It is often assumed on this basis that it was compiled in the seventh century, but that does not necessarily follow. Apart from those who maintain its traditional attribution to Moses,[41] several scholars argue that Deuteronomy originated earlier in the monarchy or in the premonarchic period.[42]

It has been suggested that the Deuteronomic Laws are structured on the basis of the Decalogue, and there may be an element of truth in this, though attempts to relate all the material to one or other of the Ten Commandments seem to overpress the point.[43] Others have pointed to thematic links with biblical narratives[44] and affinities with wisdom literature.[45] While all these intertextual relationships are of interest, most important for our present purposes is the relationship of the laws in Deuteronomy to those in the Book of the Covenant. As mentioned above, most would agree that the Deuteronomic collection is later, and that some of its laws are intended as revisions of the earlier collection.[46] There is no consensus concerning its relationship to the Holiness Code but — so far as the laws discussed in this book are concerned — there are several cases where the Deuteronomic version appears to be an expansion of a shorter law in Leviticus.[47]

40. Olson (1994) divides the material slightly differently, considering chs. 12–28 as the 'statutes and ordinances' and chs. 29–32 as the confirmation of the covenant.

41. E.g. Kline (1963); Segal (1967: 75-102); Craigie (1976: 24-29).

42. E.g. Welch (1924); Thompson (1974: 47-68); Ashmore (1995: 118-49); Tigay (1996: xix-xxiv); McConville (1998: 276-81; 2002a: 34-36). There are also a few who reject the connection with Josiah's reform and believe the book to be later still (e.g. Kennett 1920).

43. E.g. Kaufman (1979); Braulik (1991); Olson (1994: 62-125); Biddle (2003: 197-392).

44. Esp. Carmichael (1974; 1985b); cf. Christensen (2001; 2002).

45. E.g. Malfroy (1965); Weinfeld (1972a: 244-319).

46. E.g. Otto (1993b; 1994a: 192-96; 1995b; 1996b); Levinson (1997).

47. See below, 9.2.c; 10.1.d; 11.2.c; 11.3.c. This does not necessarily mean that the Deuteronomic compiler had the Holiness Code available to him. It could simply be that both Leviticus and Deuteronomy refer to the same principle in the written or unwritten legal tradition of ancient Israel, and the latter expands it more than the former. For further discussion of the Deuteronomic Laws, in addition to the works already cited, see Driver (1902: iii-xix); Merendino (1969); Choleswiński (1976); Crüsemann (1992: 201-75); Otto (1994c: 175-219; 1999a); Patrick (1995); Vermeylen (1997); McConville (2002b); Fretheim (2003); Levinson (2005b).

PROPERTY AND LAND

Chapter 2

PROPERTY RIGHTS

The ownership of property is of fundamental importance in most societies, as shown by the cruel penalties for infringing property rights thought necessary in ancient Assyria and Babylonia and the obsessive materialism of postmodern Western society, to give just two examples. Although there are always some people who choose an ascetic lifestyle, they have never been in the majority, nor does the Bible as a whole encourage this. The Rechabites and John the Baptist were respected for their discipline, but neither Old nor New Testament tells others to follow their example. On the contrary, property is seen as a good thing to be enjoyed and used responsibly, as in the idyllic picture of Israelites living in peace, 'all of them under their vines and fig trees' (1 Kgs 4:25; cf. 2 Kgs 18:31; Mic 4:4; Zech 3:10). In fact, even the nomadic ideal did not mean a complete refusal to own property, for Abraham was wealthy by the standards of his time (Gen 13:2) and his nomadic lifestyle did not prevent him purchasing a cave to bury his wife (Genesis 23).[1] The same was true of Jacob (Gen 32:5; 33:19). The New Testament also acknowledges the right to own and enjoy material things (1 Tim 6:17), so long as it is accompanied by a generous attitude toward others (v. 18). The communal ownership practised in the early days of the Jerusalem Christian fellowship (Acts 4:32-37) was voluntary (5:4) and apparently not repeated in other New Testament fellowships.

Nevertheless, although property is not considered a bad thing in itself, the dangers of materialism are frequently pointed out (e.g. Deut 8:17-18; Ps 52:7; Matt 6:24; Luke 6:24-25; 12:16-21; 1 Tim 6:9-10; Rev 3:17) and the will-

---

1. Cf. Westbrook (1971b).

ingness to give up material goods in the pursuit of a higher good is commended (Luke 6:20-21; 18:18-30). In fact, the biblical understanding of ownership is more like stewardship than the absolute right of disposal over something. God is recognised as the ultimate owner of the land (Lev 25:23), and wealth is divine gift rather than human achievement (Deut 8:17-18). Thus, real estate is a sacred trust to be kept in the family and passed on to descendants, and the produce of the land is intended not only for the benefit of the owner but to be shared with others.[2] On this view, property is intended to be a resource for the common good, with an emphasis on responsibility and compassion rather than possession and power.[3] This does not mean renunciation of all individual property rights, but it does mean that members of the covenant community should have a radically different approach to property ownership from that common in a world where 'what you have is who you are'.

2.1 Theft

The most common infringement of property rights is theft. The seriousness of this offence is indicated by its extensive treatment in the ancient Near Eastern laws and its inclusion in the biblical Decalogue.

a. Ancient Near East

Regulations about theft are found in many of the ancient Near Eastern laws. The oldest are two clauses in the Laws of Lipit-Ishtar:

> If a man enters the orchard of another man and is seized there for thievery, he shall weigh and deliver ten shekels of silver.
> If a man cuts down a tree in another man's orchard, he shall weigh and deliver twenty shekels of silver. (§§9-10)

The first regulation is also found in the Laws of Eshnunna, extended to cover fields and houses and adding that if the theft takes place at night then the punishment will be death (§§12-13). Compensation of ten silver

---

2. These matters will be discussed at length below: ch. 4 (ancestral land) and ch. 9 (shared harvests).
3. Brueggemann (1975); cf. Waterman (1982); Sacks (1999: 22).

shekels is also decreed for theft of a boat (LE §6). The second regulation also occurs in the Laws of Hammurabi, but with a higher penalty of thirty silver shekels (§59).[4]

The Laws of Hammurabi are generally much stricter than the earlier law collections, demanding capital punishment for robbery (§§21-22) and compensation by the local authorities if the robber is not arrested (§§23-24). However, it appears that the possibility of composition (i.e. payment of an agreed sum in lieu of the stipulated penalty) is not ruled out, since one clause allows for tenfold restitution, or thirtyfold in the case of temple or royal property, and insists on the death penalty only if the thief is unable to pay this sum (§8).

Looting also counts as theft and is to be punished ruthlessly:

> If a fire breaks out in a man's house, and a man who came to help put it out covets the household furnishings belonging to the householder, and takes household furnishings belonging to the householder, that man shall be cast into that very fire. (CH §25)

The culprit in this case may have justified his action as a reasonable reward for helping to extinguish the fire, but the law still considers it an infringement of property rights.

Several laws deal with indirect theft, for example:

> If a man should purchase . . . anything . . . from a son of a man or from a slave of a man without witnesses or a contract — or if he accepts the goods for safekeeping — that man is a thief, he shall be killed. (CH §7)
>
> If the buyer could not produce the seller who sold [the lost property] to him or the witnesses before whom he made the purchase, but the owner of the lost property could produce witnesses who can identify his lost property, then it is the buyer who is the thief, he shall be killed; the owner of the lost property shall take his lost property. (CH §10; cf. §§9, 11-13; LE §40)

According to the first law, a person who obtains property illegally from someone within a household, such as a minor or a slave, is guilty of theft. According to the second law, a purchaser of stolen goods who is unable or

---

4. Whether this concerns damage or theft is uncertain, but it seems likely that someone who went to the trouble of felling a tree would take away the wood, which was a valuable commodity in Babylonia (cf. Driver and Miles 1952: 160-62).

unwilling to identify the thief is reckoned to be the thief. In both cases the death penalty applies. A receiver of goods stolen from the temple or palace is liable to the death penalty as well as the thief (CH §6).

A much lighter penalty is decreed for stealing agricultural implements, namely compensation of three or five shekels of silver (CH §§259-60). It is possible that this case refers to an unauthorised loan rather than theft,[5] though the usual Akkadian verb for stealing is used *(šarāqu)*. An employee who is corrupt, resulting in the loss of his employer's property, is punished severely but not by death (CH §§253-56, 265).[6]

The Middle Assyrian Laws contain several clauses dealing with theft by women, generally penalised by death or mutilation (§§A1, 3-6), for example:

> If a man is either ill or dead, and his wife should steal something from his house and give it either to a man, or to a woman, or to anyone else, they shall kill the man's wife as well as the receivers [of the stolen goods] . . . (§A3)
>
> If . . . a slave . . . should receive something from a man's wife, they shall cut off the slave's . . . nose and ears; they shall restore the stolen goods; the man shall cut off his own wife's ears. But if he releases his wife and does not cut off her ears, they shall not cut off [the nose and ears] of the slave . . . , and they shall not restore the stolen goods. (§A4)[7]

On the other hand, the punishment for a man who steals (§§B14-15; C5, 8; F1), receives stolen property (§C9), or is involved in corruption (§§C10-11; F2) is relatively lenient, generally consisting of a beating plus restitution.[8]

The most detailed treatment of theft is found in the Hittite Laws. There are more than fifty clauses which specify precise penalties for theft, which vary depending on what is stolen and — in some cases — the status of the thief. For example:

---

5. Cf. Driver and Miles (1952: 449-50).

6. For a detailed commentary on the clauses concerned with theft in the Laws of Hammurabi, see Driver and Miles (1952: 80-105, 108-11, 444-53) and Jackson (1975c). The Sumerian Laws Handbook of Forms, dated half a century after the Laws of Hammurabi, treats theft more leniently, with two brief clauses specifying compensation of twice the value in the case of stolen boats and pigs (§3:10-15).

7. Note that both the thief and the receiver of the stolen goods are to be punished, and if the punishment is waived it must be waived for both of them (cf. CH §129; HL §198).

8. On theft in the Middle Assyrian Laws, see Driver and Miles (1935: 17-29, 330-34); Cardascia (1969: 303-5, 310-15, 319-20); Lafont (2003: 553-55).

> If anyone steals a bull — if it is a weanling calf, it is not a 'bull'; if it is a yearling calf, it is not a 'bull'; if it is a two-year-old bovine, that is a 'bull'. Formerly they gave thirty cattle. But now he shall give fifteen cattle: five two-year-olds, five yearlings and five weanlings. He shall look to his house for it. (§57)
>
> If they seize a free man at the outset, before he enters the house, he shall pay twelve shekels of silver. If they seize a slave at the outset, before he enters the house, he shall pay six shekels of silver. (§93)

Multiple restitution is required for stealing of animals, varying from fifteenfold for a bull to threefold for an ox or horse (§§57-70). A different rule applies in the case of pigs or bees, where a monetary payment is required, the amount depending on the circumstances (§§81-85, 91-92). Monetary compensation also applies in the case of stolen plants, trees, clay, birds, or implements (§§101-4, 108-10, 113, 119-26, 129-33, 142-43), while stolen bricks or foundation stones are to be replaced twofold or fivefold, respectively (§128). If a door should be stolen, the thief is liable for any consequential loss in the house as well as compensation of forty silver shekels (§127). Burglary or attempted burglary is punished by a monetary payment, in addition to full restitution, the figure depending on the status of the offender: twelve shekels for a free man, six shekels plus mutilation for a slave (§§93-97). The only instance of the death penalty is for theft of a bronze spear from the palace (§126).[9]

---

9. No laws on theft are known from the Neo-Sumerian period, but some information is available from other documents (Lafont and Westbrook 2003: 220-21). On the Middle Babylonian period, see Slanski (2003b: 516-18). Although no law collection survives from Nuzi, reports of legal cases indicate that penalties for theft were less brutal than in the Babylonian and Assyrian laws but nevertheless severe: generally multiple restitution or substantial damages (Gordon 1936; Zaccagnini 2003: 612-13). On Alalakh, see Rowe (2003a: 715). On the Neo-Babylonian period, see Oelsner, Wells, and Wunsch (2003: 962-65). In the absence of law collections from ancient Egypt, incidental information suggests that the penalty for theft from individuals was multiple restitution, while theft from temples or royal tombs was a very serious crime resulting in severe beating, mutilation, enslavement, or death (Černý 1937; Lurje 1971: 154-60; Jasnow 2003a: 281; 2003b: 344-45).

b. Decalogue

You shall not steal.

Exod 20:15//Deut 5:19

The simplicity of the eighth commandment[10] is unparalleled in all the ancient Near Eastern laws on theft. On the one hand, it leaves open the question of what sanctions should be applied to those who break the commandment. On the other hand, it has a universal application, as it is addressed to the whole people of God without distinction of status. The Hebrew uses the second person singular form, which is often used in the Old Testament for the whole nation but at the same time indicates the personal responsibility of each individual Israelite to obey.

The verb 'steal' (גנב) is found forty times in the Old Testament, and the related nouns 'thief' and 'stolen object' another nineteen times, in narrative, law, wisdom, and prophecy. Generally the object is a material thing or an animal, but it can also refer to a person in the sense of kidnapping (Exod 21:16; Deut 24:7; cf. Gen 40:15) or taking someone away for their own safety (2 Sam 19:41; 2 Kgs 11:2; 2 Chr 22:11). There are also various figurative senses, such as to steal someone's heart (2 Sam 15:6; cf. 19:3; Job 4:12; 21:18; 27:20; Jer 23:30). The word may be distinguished from 'take/seize' (לקח) and 'rob/take by force' (גזל) by the element of secrecy, though there is not a rigid distinction.[11] In any case, we should not make too much of this, in view of the uniformly brief form of the commandments in the second section of the Decalogue. One of the three verbs had to be chosen, and it is likely that it was intended to express the whole semantic range covered by the English words 'steal', 'rob', 'seize', and 'take by force'.

A distinctive interpretation of this commandment was proposed by Alt (1949), who argued that it was originally concerned not with material possessions but rather with the stealing of free Israelites, that is kidnapping, with the object of selling or enslaving them (as in Exod 21:16 and Deut 24:7; cf. CH §14; HL §19).[12] This is related to Alt's understanding of the tenth commandment as not merely a desire to acquire someone else's

---

10. This is counted as the seventh commandment in the Roman Catholic and Lutheran traditions. On the different numbering systems, see Baker (2005d: 6-8).

11. Hamp (1974); cf. Jackson (1972: 1-19); Westbrook (1988b: 15-38).

12. A similar understanding of the eighth commandment is found in rabbinic literature, though Alt does not refer to that (Gottstein 1953; Petuchowski 1957; Jackson 1972: 148 n. 5).

possessions but action towards that end,[13] so effectively the same as stealing, which led him to this interpretation of the eighth commandment. Phillips (1970: 130-32) also considers the eighth commandment to refer to 'man-stealing' on the basis of his view that the Decalogue forms ancient Israel's criminal code and all the offences listed therein were punishable by death, whereas it is clear that ordinary stealing is not a capital offence in Old Testament law. Quite a few scholars were convinced by this view,[14] but many others have rejected it.[15] A detailed rebuttal is unnecessary here, since Jackson (1971) and others have already provided that, so suffice it to say that in my opinion the eighth commandment is deliberately broad in scope, including all kinds of action that deprive other people of property which is rightfully theirs. In the ancient Near Eastern context this would include stealing chattel slaves, whose legal status is property, and possibly also kidnapping a free person, thus taking them away from their home and family. However, although kidnapping is clearly a serious crime, as the two texts which mention it make clear, it was probably not common enough to justify a separate place in the Decalogue.[16]

Clines (1995: 42) suggests that prohibition of theft is in the interests of the rich, who have possessions they want to hold on to, whereas McConville (2002a) points out that it is particularly important for the protection of the poor, who have only limited property which is necessary for survival (cf. 2 Sam 12:1-6). Brueggemann (1994) reflects on some of the wider implications of the eighth commandment, warning against interpreting it as a mere defence of private property — which is not always justly acquired — and pointing to some of the inequities of the modern world, where economic structures within and between nations make robbery an institution and ensure that some people are fabulously rich while others are permanently poor.[17]

13. On which, see below, 2.2.
14. E.g. Noth (1959); von Rad (1964a: 59); Craigie (1976); Wehmeier (1977); Lochman (1979: 119-22); cf. Sivan (2004: 188-207).
15. E.g. Hyatt (1971); Jackson (1971); Hamp (1974); Klein (1976); Mayes (1979); Durham (1987); Wright (1990: 134-38); Weinfeld (1991); Houtman (1996); Tigay (1996); Harrelson (1997: 113-16); Propp (2006).
16. On kidnapping, see below, 5.1.b.
17. Slightly differently, Gnuse (1985b: 5-9) argues that the eighth commandment does not serve to protect private property, because important possessions belong to the community and — ultimately — to God. So the focus of the commandment is on the appropriation of communal possessions for private use and is designed to protect persons, especially the poor, rather than property.

c. Book of the Covenant

When someone steals an ox or a sheep, and slaughters it or sells it, he shall restore five oxen for an ox, and four sheep for a sheep.

If a thief is caught breaking in [at night] and is beaten to death, it is not murder. If it happens after sunrise, it is murder.

He shall make full restitution, but if he has nothing, he shall be sold [as a slave to pay] for his theft. If the stolen [animal] — whether ox or donkey or sheep — is found alive in his possession, he shall restore twofold.

Exod 22:1-4 [Hebrew 21:37–22:3]

Several translations rearrange the material, since verses 3b-4 seem to follow naturally from verse 1 (e.g. NRSV, REB, TEV), though others follow the order of the Masoretic Text (NIV, NJB, ESV).[18] It may be that verses 2-3a are a later insertion,[19] but if so it was very early since there is no manuscript evidence for a different order.[20] Perhaps it is the equivalent of a footnote or parenthesis, which ancient writing had no standard method of marking.[21] It seems best therefore to retain the order of material in the text, but to provide paragraph breaks as above for clarity. The text as it stands deals with the more important issue of possible loss of human life during a robbery before the details of material compensation and includes protection for the life of the thief, something unknown in other ancient Near Eastern laws.

The basic punishment for theft in the Book of the Covenant is multiple restitution: four- or fivefold in the case of an animal that has been slaughtered or sold (cf. 2 Sam 12:6), twofold if the animal is found alive in the possession of the thief and can be returned to its owner (cf. Exod 22:7, 9). In either case, it is implied that action is taken only when there is clear evidence of the offence, either proof of sale (v. 1) or possession of the animal (v. 4).[22] Philo (*Laws* 4:11-12) suggests that the higher restitution for an

---

18. Some scholars (e.g. Paul 1970: 86; Jackson 1972: 49) make a distinction between stealing animals (vv. 1, 3b-4) and burglary (vv. 2-3a), but this overlooks the fact that in Palestine animals were regularly kept in the lower part of the house overnight and could well be the object of burglary (cf. Canaan 1933: 41-42, 70; Stager 1985: 12-15; Tigay 1995: 373-74).

19. So Cassuto (1951: 282).

20. Wenham (1971: 101) argues for the originality of the MT order on form-critical grounds. For a survey of various studies of the literary history, see Houtman (1996).

21. Paul (1970: 110 n. 1); Finkelstein (1981: 39); Sprinkle (1994: 130-34).

22. Daube (1947: 89-96; followed by Jackson 1972: 41-42) argues for a development in

ox was because it was a beast of burden, used for ploughing and threshing, and therefore more crucial to the ancient economy than a sheep.[23]

If the thief is unable to pay this restitution, he is to be sold as a slave (v. 3b).[24] The enslavement is for the purpose of making restitution, which implies that the slave is to be freed as soon as he has provided service equivalent in value to the stipulated amount. In any case, debt-slavery in Israel was limited to a maximum of six years, as emphasised at the beginning of the Book of the Covenant (Exod 21:2).[25] Nothing is said about multiple restitution in this case, and Sprinkle (1994: 132-33) suggests that only a rich thief would be expected to pay this, whereas a poor thief is punished sufficiently with the loss of his freedom for the length of time it takes to pay his debt. This is an attractive idea, but the fact that multiple restitution is not specified does not prove it was not assumed. Philo (*Laws* 4:2-5) assumes that double restitution will be paid, as in most other cases of theft, while mentioning that the thief will have the normal right to freedom in the seventh year.

The owner of a property which is burgled does not have the right to kill the burglar, though if the burglary occurs at night this may be excused, presumably because of the need for self-defence (vv. 2-3a; cf. Job 24:14, 16). During the day, the owner can more easily call for help and can see the intruder clearly and thus identify him to the authorities, so there should be no need for violence. This may be compared with a clause in the Laws of Eshnunna (§13) which stipulates that a burglar caught in the day must pay compensation of ten silver shekels, whereas he is to be executed if the burglary took place at night.[26] However, it should be noted that the biblical law exonerates the house-owner only if he kills the intruder on the spot and does not stipulate capital punishment for the offence.[27] In fact, the

---

the law between these verses, but this is unconvincing since the Laws of Hammurabi (which are much older than the Book of the Covenant) refer to both kinds of evidence in succeeding clauses (CH §§9-10) and either is sufficient for administration of the death penalty. Cf. Westbrook (1988b: 111-28), who argues on the basis of a comparison with other ancient Near Eastern laws that the text provides an 'orderly and logical presentation of the law of theft'.

23. For various other explanations of the difference, see Sarna (1991); Sprinkle (1994: 134-35).

24. Note the contrast with CH §8, where a thief unable to pay the stipulated restitution is put to death.

25. On which, see below, 6.1.

26. Propp (2006: 241) gives further parallels from Greece, Rome, and the Bedouin.

27. Cf. Schoneveld (1973).

d. Holiness Code

> *You shall not steal . . . You shall not defraud or rob your neighbour.*[29]
>
> Lev 19:11a, 13a

Leviticus 19:11a is identical to the eighth commandment, except that it uses the second person plural form whereas the latter is phrased in the singular. Verse 13a develops the same idea — after an interlude on lying and false oaths (vv. 11b-12) — with two further verbs: 'defraud' and 'rob', both in the singular.[30] One example of such oppression of a neighbour is given in the second half of the verse: 'You shall not hold back the wages of a daily worker till the next morning'.[31]

As often in the Pentateuch, 'neighbour' refers to a fellow member of the people of Israel rather than necessarily someone who lives nearby (cf. vv. 17-18; Exod 2:13; 20:16-17; 21:14; Deut 4:42; 23:24-25). However, the use of the word 'neighbour' does not mean that these prohibitions are *only* concerned with treatment of fellow Israelites, for verses 33-34 make clear that resident aliens should be treated in a similar way.

These three simple apodictic prohibitions are all that is said about theft in the Holiness Code, but there is a longer passage on the subject earlier in Leviticus which may be mentioned here:

> When anyone sins and is unfaithful to the LORD, by deceiving a neighbour about a deposit or security, or by robbery, or by defrauding a neighbour, or by finding lost property and lying about it — and swearing falsely regarding any of the various things that one may do and sin-

---

28. Capital punishment is required by biblical law in the case of kidnapping (Exod 21:16; Deut 24:7), which in Hebrew is literally 'stealing a person', because that is considered an offence against a person comparable to murder and adultery. On kidnapping, see below, 5.1.b.

29. The object 'your neighbour' is placed after 'defraud' in Hebrew (lit. 'You shall not defraud your neighbour and you shall not rob [him/her]'), but it also implicitly refers to 'rob' and so is placed in the final position in my translation.

30. The Hebrew verbs are עשׁק ('defraud, oppress, take advantage of') and גזל ('rob, take by force').

31. On which, see below, 11.2.

ning thereby — when he/she[32] sins and is therefore guilty [in any of these ways], he shall return what was taken by robbery or by fraud or the deposit that was held in trust, or the lost property that he had found, or anything else about which he had sworn falsely. He shall repay in full and shall add one-fifth [of the value] to it, giving it to its owner on the day he realises his guilt.[33] And he shall bring his guilt offering[34] to the Lord, a ram from the flock, without blemish and of the proper value, [bringing it] to the priest as a guilt offering. Then the priest shall make atonement for him before the Lord, and he shall be forgiven, for any of the things he did that made him guilty. (Lev 6:2-7 [Hebrew 5:21-26])

The initial offence is general, including various kinds of direct and indirect theft, but the case is specific, that is, someone has committed such an offence and sworn falsely that he is not guilty (cf. Exod 22:10-11). The reference to swearing innocence implies that the thief has been under suspicion but not proved guilty, so it seems that the text is referring to a case where the thief himself realises his guilt and decides to make good, as also in the related law of Numbers 5:5-8. The penalty, 120 percent restitution plus a guilt offering, is apparently lower than in the Book of the Covenant, perhaps taking account of the repentance of the thief and to encourage voluntary surrender.[35] However, the value of a ram would be considerable, and the total penalty may be as much or even more than the double restitution stipulated in Exodus.[36]

Interestingly, the guilt offerings prescribed in the preceding verses are explicitly for unintentional sins (Lev 5:14-19), and the same applies to the sin offerings which precede those (4:1–5:13). Further, Numbers 15 distinguishes between unintentional sins, which may be dealt with by sacrifice

---

32. In the rest of this passage the third person singular will be translated 'he' (cf. ESV; NIV; NJB; NJPS), which is the literal form in Hebrew, though the meaning is inclusive and would certainly have been intended to apply to women as well as men. NRSV translates all the verbs as though they were in the second person singular ('you') to avoid this problem, while TNIV uses the third person plural ('they').

33. Cf. NRSV; REB. Other possible translations are 'presents his guilt offering' (NIV; cf. TB) or 'is found guilty' (TEV).

34. So NRSV; NIV. REB translates 'reparation offering' (also Hartley 1992; Milgrom 2004) and TEV 'repayment offering'.

35. Cf. Wenham (1979); Hartley (1992); Sprinkle (2003).

36. Jackson (1972: 171-80) argues that בערכך ('of the proper value') means that the offering is to be equivalent in value to the stolen property, so the total cost to the thief is actually 220 percent — higher than in the Book of the Covenant.

(vv. 22-29), and intentional sins, for which there is no remedy (vv. 30-31). So why is atonement allowed here for sin that was both intentional and made worse by denying it under oath? Milgrom (2004) suggests that the repentance of sinners reduces their intentional sin to the level of an inadvertence, thus making it eligible for sacrificial expiation.[37] The precondition is restitution to the owner, which demonstrates the sinner's acknowledgement of wrongdoing and willingness to put things right with neighbour as well as with God (cf. Matt 5:23-24). Certainly the Old Testament often emphasises the mercy of God towards repentant sinners, including those who have committed serious and deliberate offences (e.g. Exod 34:6-7; 2 Sam 12:13; 2 Chr 33:10-13; Psalm 51).

e. Conclusion

In comparison with the extensive coverage of theft in the ancient Near Eastern laws, the biblical laws seem to treat the subject very briefly. That does not mean it is a trivial offence, for it is prohibited in the Decalogue as one of those actions which fundamentally disrupt the life of the people of God. The basic principle, 'You shall not steal', is also repeated with slight variations in the Holiness Code. But the Old Testament does not trouble to define all the many kinds of theft and appropriate punishment (as done by the Hittite Laws), and just two sections give guidelines by dealing with sample cases. The Book of the Covenant specifies punishment and compensation in the common cases of stealing animals and burglary, while Leviticus 6 is more concerned with how a thief may not merely put things right with the person from whom he stole but also must obtain the forgiveness of God. The Deuteronomic Laws make no direct mention of theft at all, though there is a good deal of social legislation concerning property rights and responsibilities.[38]

There is also legislation for various kinds of indirect theft, which will be dealt with separately below: for example, taking possession of lost property (ch. 2.3) or property which has been entrusted for safekeeping (ch. 3.3), theft of land by moving boundary markers (ch. 4.2), and theft in business by charging interest on loans (ch. 10.1) or using false weights and mea-

---

37. See Marx (1988) for a different explanation.
38. Theft is mentioned frequently in the Psalms and Prophets, e.g. Ps 35:10; 50:18; 62:10; 69:4; Jer 7:9; Ezek 18:7, 12, 16, 18; Hos 4:2; Mic 2:2; Zech 5:3-4.

sures (ch. 11.3). The taking of spoil in war is not considered to be theft (Deut 2:35; 3:7; 20:14), except in the case of holy war (חרם, Josh 7:11, 21), which involves theft from God rather than from other human beings.

The penalties prescribed for theft in the Bible are much more humane than in most ancient Near Eastern laws, and never involve mutilation, beating, or death.[39] Rather, a property offence is paid for in terms of property, by multiple restitution. In this the biblical laws are comparable to the Hittite Laws, though the rate of restitution is significantly lower: fivefold for an ox (cf. tenfold in HL §63) and fourfold for a sheep (cf. sixfold in HL §69). If the original animal can be returned to its owner, double restitution is considered sufficient (cf. threefold in HL §70[40]). Neither in the Bible nor in the other laws is such payment to be understood as a 'fine' in the modern sense of a penalty paid to the state, but rather as compensation paid to the person who has suffered a loss by theft.

Another notable feature of the biblical laws in comparison with ancient Near Eastern parallels is that one rule applies for all. Some other laws stipulate different punishments depending on the status of the thief (e.g. HL §§93-99) or the owner of the stolen property (e.g. CH §8). The Middle Assyrian Laws also differentiate between offences by men and by women, with harsher penalties for the latter. There are no such distinctions in biblical law, and even the king is subject to the law (Deut. 17:18-20) and expected to respect the property rights of his citizens (cf. 1 Kings 21). This would have been a revolutionary idea in the ancient world, where rulers tended to regard the property of their people as their own.[41] Samuel warns Israel that kings tend to behave in this way (1 Sam 8:11-17), while affirming that he himself is innocent of such theft (12:1-5).

Several issues are dealt with in the ancient Near Eastern laws but not in the Bible. For example, in the Laws of Hammurabi, receiving stolen goods is considered equivalent to theft (§6); likewise, to be in possession of someone else's goods without proof of purchase can lay someone open to a charge of theft (§§7, 10). In the case of a robber not being caught, the city and governor are responsible for compensating the property owner who has suffered a loss (§23) or his family if he is killed during the robbery

---

39. Greenberg (1960: 13-20) contrasts the severity of biblical law in dealing with homicide, ruling out composition between the murderer and next of kin, with its relative leniency in dealing with property offences. See also Finkelstein (1981: 37-41).

40. So Hoffner (1997), though some interpreters believe that the Hittite Laws only require double restitution in this case (e.g. Paul 1970: 85-86).

41. Landes (1998: 31-36); Sacks (1999: 14-15); cf. Gnuse (1985b: 60-65).

(§24). Looting is a serious offence (§25), as is stealing in the course of employment (§§253-56). We have no way of being sure whether these principles also applied in ancient Israel, but they may well have been known and accepted there too. In the absence of evidence to the contrary, we may tentatively assume that to be the case.

To sum up, two implications may be drawn from the biblical laws on theft. First, as made clear by the prohibition of theft in the Decalogue, repeated in the Holiness Code, the ownership of property is a God-given right and responsibility, so that to deprive someone else of their property is a serious offence and not to be tolerated within the covenant people. Second, as shown by the relative leniency of the regulations in the Book of the Covenant and Leviticus compared with parallel regulations in other ancient Near Eastern laws, the Bible places a much higher value on human life than on material possessions, so that property offences are punished less severely than offences against the life and dignity of other human beings such as murder and adultery.

2.2 Coveting

As we have seen, to deprive someone else of their property by means of theft was unacceptable behaviour for the Old Testament people of God, as it was also for other ancient Near Eastern peoples. However, there is one text — the Decalogue — which goes much further than prohibiting actual theft, for the tenth commandment is concerned with the very desire to possess things. Exactly what is meant by 'You shall not covet' needs to be clarified, but there is no doubt that it is relevant to the right to own property and attitudes towards property belonging to other people.[42]

a. Ancient Near East

None of the ancient Near Eastern laws refer to coveting, except one clause in the Laws of Hammurabi which mentions coveting goods in a burning house and taking them (§25). Even there it is not said that coveting would have been a problem in itself if it had not led to theft.

---

42. This section includes some material from a previously published article of mine (Baker 2005c), which is used here with kind permission of the publisher.

In nonlegal materials, however, there are various references to coveting. The Akkadian Shamash Hymn (or Hymn to the Sun God) mentions it briefly:

A man who covets his neighbour's wife
Will [. . .] before his appointed day[43]

In an Assyrian confession of sins, the penitent admits: 'I lifted my face to your extensive possessions, to your precious silver went my desire'.[44]

Coveting is considered foolish in Egyptian wisdom literature, such as the Instruction for Merikare.[45] It is also mentioned in the 'Negative Confession' in the Egyptian Book of the Dead. This text includes a declaration of innocence before a tribunal of forty-two gods, and to the third god the deceased claims:

O Beaky, who has come forth from Hermopolis, I have not been envious.[46]

Other declarations in this text range from murder and robbery to winking and blabbering, so the inclusion of coveting here does not necessarily mean it was considered a serious wrongdoing.

A treaty between the Hittite king Mursili II and his vassal Kupanta-Kurunta of Mira-Kuwaliya requires, 'You shall not desire any border district of Hatti',[47] which is similar in form to the tenth commandment. No doubt the suzerain was concerned with potential seizure of territory rather than simply the desires of the vassal, as is made explicit in the subsequent clause, so the prohibition was directed against both wanting and attempting to take land.[48] Such desire combined with action is also implied in one of the Amarna letters, where Abdihiba of Jerusalem reports

43. Lines 88-89. *COS* does not include this section of the hymn, so I have quoted it from *BWL* (130-31); cf. Foster (2005: 631).

44. Text in Ebeling (1916: 297; 1919: no. 45:12-13); trans. by Moran (1967: 547); cf. Seux (1976: 207).

45. Lines 40-41 (*COS*: 1.35). Cf. Instruction of Ptah-hotep, lines 300-315 (*ANET*: 413) and Eloquent Peasant, lines 165, 290-93 (*ANET*: 409).

46. Ch. 125 (*COS*: 2.12, p. 61). *ANET* (35 §B3) translates '. . . I have not been covetous'. Clause 41 may also refer to coveting, but its meaning is uncertain: 'O Serpent-Whose-Head-Is-Erect, who has come forth from the cavern, my possessions have not increased except by my own property' (*COS*: 2.12, p. 62).

47. Part of §10; see Beckman (1999: 76); cf. Mendenhall (1954: 30).

48. Moran (1967: 546).

to the Egyptian king that 'Milkilu does not break with the sons of Lab'aya and the sons of Arzayu, in order to covet the land of the king for themselves'.[49]

A Phoenician inscription from Karatepe pronounces a curse on someone who covets a city, using the same Semitic word as in the tenth commandment:

> Now if a king among kings or a prince among princes,
> if a man, who is a man of renown . . . ,
> if indeed he shall covet this city, and shall tear away this gate . . . ,
> if from covetousness he shall tear [it] away —
> if from hate or from evil he shall tear away this gate
> then shall Ba'al Shamem and El, creator of the earth . . .
> erase that kingdom, and that king, and that man who is a man
>   of renown.[50]

Here too it is clear that an external act is involved, not just covetous thoughts, and the additional verb 'tear away' is used to make this explicit.[51]

b. Decalogue

> *You shall not covet your neighbour's household: you shall not covet your neighbour's wife, or his male or female slave, or his ox or donkey, or anything else of your neighbour's.*
>
>   Exod 20:17

> *You shall not covet your neighbour's wife; and you shall not desire your neighbour's house, his field, or his male or female slave, his ox or donkey, or anything else of your neighbour's.*
>
>   Deut 5:21

---

49. Letter 289:5-8. Text in Knudtzon (1915), trans. by Moran (1967: 547).

50. The Azatiwada Inscription, lines iii.12-iv.1 (*COS*: 2.31). For the original text, with translation, see *KAI* (no. 26); Gordon (1949a: 111-12).

51. Cf. Alt (1949: 334 n. 1); Marcus and Gelb (1949: 120); Moran (1967: 544). For a comparative study of covetousness and desire in Egyptian and biblical wisdom literature, see Shupak (1993: 105-16).

Property Rights

The tenth commandment[52] consists of a double prohibition.[53] In Exodus the verb 'covet' is repeated, whereas in Deuteronomy a pair of synonymous verbs is used: 'covet' and 'desire'.[54] These two verbs also occur elsewhere in parallel (e.g. Gen 3:6; Prov 6:25 and Ps 45:11; Ps 68:16 and 132:13-14) and are very close in meaning. Both are used in positive and negative contexts, and both are commonly used with reference to human desire but can also be used of the divine.

Apart from the use of these different verbs, there are two interrelated differences between the canonical versions of the tenth commandment:

- change of order between 'house[hold]' and 'wife'
- addition of the word 'field' in Deuteronomy[55]

In Exodus 20, the Hebrew word *bayit* (בית) means 'household' and includes all a man's possessions that are of economic significance (cf. Gen 7:1; Deut 11:6).[56] The main contents of the household are specified in decreasing order of importance: wife, slaves, working animals, and material things. While the wife might be coveted because of sexual attraction (cf. Prov 6:25 and the Shamash Hymn), the primary motive for coveting in this context is probably her economic significance. The dowry is capital which

---

52. The text printed above is considered by most Jews and many Christians to be the tenth commandment, following a tradition that goes back as far as Philo and Josephus. The Roman Catholic and Lutheran Churches divide the text in two, counting 'You shall not covet the household of your neighbour' as the ninth commandment and 'You shall not covet the wife of your neighbour, etc.' as the tenth. The latter numbering also follows an ancient tradition, going back to Clement of Alexandria and Augustine, but it is less satisfactory in terms of form and content and I will assume the former arrangement here. See further discussion in Baker (2005d: 6-8).

53. It has been suggested that the present forms were expanded from an original shorter form, perhaps because this was one of the commandments with which the covenant community had difficulty and therefore needed more detail, like the second to fifth commandments (Durham 1987). On attempts to reconstruct the 'original' form of the Decalogue, see Baker (2005b: 11-14).

54. The Hebrew verbs are חמד and אוה. For a detailed discussion of these verbs, see Baker (2005c: 7-13).

55. I am assuming here that the Deuteronomic version is later than that in Exodus (see Baker 2005d: 14-16). The Septuagint harmonises these differences, so that the form in Exodus is the same as in Deuteronomy, and also uses the same word to translate both חמד and אוה. It also adds 'or any of his livestock' after 'ox or donkey', probably influenced by Deut 5:14.

56. Cf. Jepsen (1967: 295); Durham (1987); Houtman (1996); Propp (2006).

the wife brings to the marriage,[57] and Proverbs 31:10-31 emphasises the major role of the Israelite wife in the family economy.[58]

In Deuteronomy 5, the word *bayit* means 'house' rather than 'household'. It is transposed with the word 'wife' and follows the second verb. The effect of this is to create two parallel clauses, rather than a summary clause followed by a detailed list as in Exodus. The first clause prohibits coveting a neighbour's wife, while the second clause prohibits desire for his house or field, male or female slave, ox or donkey, or any other of his possessions. The addition of 'field' makes three pairs and a concluding phrase, a total of seven items (cf. Gen 39:5; 2 Kgs 8:3, 5; Isa 5:8; Mic 2:2 for the pairing of 'house' and 'field'). Thus the two clauses forbid the coveting of family and property, 'the kernel of a man's existence'.[59]

It has been suggested that the change in order of the words 'house-[hold]' and 'wife' is due to the higher status of women in the thought of the Deuteronomic editors.[60] Moran (1967) disputes this, arguing that the last part of the commandment reflects a traditional type of list of possessions in the ancient Near East, especially Ugarit, so the version in Deuteronomy could be as old as that in Exodus. Whatever the precise social status of women may have been in ancient societies, a man's wife is not included in such lists of possessions because neither in Israel nor at Ugarit was she regarded as a saleable item. Concerning the lists in the two forms of the tenth commandment, 'what the items have in common is not that they are pieces of property, but that they are typical of what may be the object of a neighbor's coveting'.[61]

The key issue for interpretation concerns whether the tenth commandment prohibits desire for the property of other people, or action to obtain what is desired, or both. Some of the rabbis and later Jewish inter-

---

57. E.g. Gen 31:14-16; Josh 15:16-19; 1 Kgs 9:16; cf. Vasholz (1987); Westbrook (1991; 2003b: 60-62); Matlock (2007: 303-4).

58. Children are noticeably absent from the list. This may be because their function in a family is not primarily economic and they are not so likely to be objects of coveting. Another possible reason is that children do not belong in this list of possessions because they have not been purchased (Propp 2006). According to Cassuto (1951), the list of things to be coveted numbers seven, as in the list of those who are prohibited from working on the sabbath. This may be true in terms of form, but not with respect to content if my interpretation of בית as a summary term is correct.

59. Weinfeld (1991).

60. E.g. Phillips (1983: 6); Weinfeld (1991). There may be some truth in this, but Wright (1990: 90-92) points out the weaknesses in Phillips's extreme version of the theory.

61. Wright (1990: 197).

preters argued that it does not simply forbid desire but acting on that desire. A similar view of the tenth commandment as concerned with action, not just intention, was proposed in the nineteenth century and defended by various twentieth-century scholars,[62] though rejected by others.[63] On this theory, the verb 'covet' means not just an emotion but also the action which results from that emotion. Various texts are adduced in support, where it is argued that not merely a desire but attempted or actual acquisition is implied. As a result, the tenth commandment is understood to be much more concrete in application than it appears at first sight, at least to the modern reader, and rather similar in meaning to the eighth commandment (and, in the case of coveting a neighbour's wife, much the same as adultery). Because of this, Alt (1949) took the further step of reinterpreting the eighth commandment as kidnapping, that is, stealing people rather than objects.[64]

This theory is to be rejected, as I have argued in detail elsewhere.[65] The tenth commandment is concerned primarily with thoughts and intentions, unlike the earlier clauses of the Decalogue which focus on action and — in the case of the ninth commandment — words.

c. Conclusion

As shown above, coveting is mentioned only once in ancient Near Eastern laws, though the concept is found in other literature. It seems that it was considered a bad thing, but only an actionable offence if accompanied by taking a forbidden object. Apart from the Decalogue, Old Testament law also makes little reference to coveting, never in the Book of the Covenant or Holiness Code, and rarely in Deuteronomy. The second 'sermon' of Moses contains the warning, 'You shall not covet the silver and gold on them and take it for yourself, lest you be ensnared by it, for it is an abomination to the LORD your God' (Deut 7:25), while the Deuteronomic Laws use the word 'desire' several times in a neutral sense but never to denote coveting.

Rofé (1985b: 54-65) believes four Deuteronomic laws to be interpretations of the tenth commandment, namely Deuteronomy 19:14; 23:24; 23:25;

---

62. E.g. Meier (1846: 70-74); Herrmann (1927); Alt (1949); von Rad (1964a).
63. E.g. Jacob (1923: 166-78); Volz (1932: 54-55); Moran (1967); Hyatt (1971); Jackson (1971).
64. Cf. above, 2.1.b.
65. Baker (2005c: 13-20).

and 24:10-11. However, although offences such as moving a boundary stone may occur because of covetousness, neither of the key terms meaning 'covet' or 'desire' is used in any of these texts. In fact, the only specific biblical law on coveting is the tenth commandment, in its two forms, which is therefore unique among all the laws of Israel and the ancient Near East.

All sorts of interpretations of the tenth commandment have been suggested. Particularly popular has been the idea of the rabbis, and also various nineteenth- and twentieth-century scholars, that the commandment refers not merely to desire or covetous thoughts but to action with the intention of acquiring another person's property. However, most scholars have now recognised the weakness of this theory.

The shape of the Decalogue is significant.[66] It begins with a general clause demanding exclusive allegiance to God, then provides eight rules concerning serious offences which disrupt a person's relationship with God and neighbour, and ends with a final clause about attitude to one's neighbour. Other laws decree capital punishment for infringing six of the first seven commandments (Exod 21:12, 15, 17; 22:20; 31:14-15; Lev 20:9-10; 24:16, 21; Deut 17:2-7; 21:18-21; 22:22),[67] and lesser punishments for breaking the eighth and ninth commandments (Exod 22:1-4; Deut 19:16-21), but none in the case of the tenth. However, that does not mean it is unimportant or in need of reinterpretation. Since the tenth commandment concerns intention rather than action, it would hardly be practical to take people to court for breaking it.

It seems the tenth commandment was deliberately formulated to indicate the importance of thoughts — alongside words (as in the ninth commandment) and deeds (as in most of the others) — in the life of the people of God. Most of the commandments are relatively easy to keep, if one wants to, and if it were not for the tenth it would be easy for someone to conclude that they were perfect (cf. Luke 18:21[68]). Thoughts are extremely important, not merely because good or bad thoughts can lead on to words and deeds which affect other people, but because God is concerned with the whole of

---

66. Cf. Baker (2005d).

67. The punishment for making an image is not specified, but it was certainly considered a very serious offence (cf. Exod 20:5-6; 32:1-35; Deut 27:15) and probably would have resulted in capital punishment too.

68. 'I have kept all these since my youth'. It is interesting that the selection of commandments Jesus mentions in Luke 18:20 does not include the tenth, and the young man's answer might have been different if it had. The ensuing conversation certainly indicates that material possessions had an excessive importance in his life.

life, including those parts which are invisible to other people (cf. Gen 6:5; 1 Sam 16:7; Psalm 139; Jer 1:5; John 2:24-25; Rom 8:27). Wrong thoughts are wrong in themselves and therefore to be avoided, whether or not they become known to others through visible actions. There is no provision in the laws for human punishment, because such punishment can only justly be carried out when there is adequate proof of an offence, which is impossible in the case of the tenth commandment. Nevertheless, the people of God are encouraged to be satisfied with nothing less than perfection (cf. Matt 5:48), whether or not there are sanctions to enforce obedience.

The particular concern of this commandment in relation to wealth and poverty is to discourage greed and exploitation (cf. Mic 2:1-2; also Isa 5:8, which expresses the same idea without using the word 'covet') and to advocate gratitude and contentment (cf. Deut 8:10-14; Ps 62:10; Prov 30:7-9; 1 Tim 6:6-8; Heb 13:5). For example, the methods used by the wealthy to acquire land at the expense of smallholders may not have been technically illegal, but they were fundamentally unacceptable in the people of God, stemming from ambitions that were clearly opposed to the tenth commandment.[69] Thus the purpose of the tenth commandment is 'the safeguarding of access by all members of the human community to the basic requirements for a productive and satisfying life',[70] a deliberate reaction against the Canaanite economic system where a small proportion of the population controlled the majority of the goods produced.

Coveting is not simply wrong in itself. It is also dangerous, because it is often the first step towards breaking other commandments: lust leads to adultery, the desire for material things leads to stealing, and so on. A similar understanding of human nature is expressed in the New Testament (Matt 15:19; 1 Tim 6:10). Wright (2004a: 162) sums it up with reference to economics:

> The guiding ethos of Old Testament economics could be said to be summed up in the tenth commandment: 'You shall not covet.' Addressed in the second person singular to the individual, and including among its specific objects a neighbour's economic assets, this fundamental commandment locates the source of all sinful forms of economic growth where they truly originate — the greed of individual human hearts.

---

69. Wright (1990: 139); cf. Premnath (1988).
70. Ceresko (1988).

The commonest motivation for breaking almost any of the commandments is greed or self-interest, whereas the nature of the covenant community requires that members focus their attention not on self-fulfilment but on the worship of God and service of neighbour.[71]

2.3 Lost Property

The nineteenth-century saying 'Finders keepers, losers weepers' reflects an attitude commonly found in society. Compilers of ancient Near Eastern laws, however, gave no approval to such opportunism. Nor did biblical compilers offer theirs. To the contrary, they affirmed the obligation of a finder to respect the rights of owners of lost property by helping them recover it.[72]

a. Ancient Near East

To be in possession of lost property is a serious offence, according to the Laws of Eshnunna, tantamount to stealing:

> If a military governor, a governor of the canal system, or any person in a position of authority seizes a fugitive slave, fugitive slave woman, stray ox, or stray donkey belonging either to the palace or to a commoner, and does not lead it to Eshnunna but detains it in his house and allows more than one month to elapse, the palace shall bring a charge of theft against him. (§50)

The same principle is found in the Laws of Hammurabi, which stipulate capital punishment for possession or sale of lost property, and also for falsely accusing someone else of having lost property in their possession (§§9-13). The law elaborates in detail the procedure for establishing the truth of the matter in such cases, insisting on the calling of witnesses and formal identification of the property in a temple.[73]

---

71. For further reflection on the relevance of the tenth commandment in today's world, see Wallace (1965); Bothwell (1982); Reno (2005).

72. This section is substantially the same as a previously published article of mine (Baker 2007a) and is used here with permission of the publisher.

73. For a detailed study of these clauses, see Driver and Miles (1952: 95-105).

The Hittite Laws also insist that lost property be returned to its owner and consider failure to do so the same as theft:

> If anyone finds implements, [he shall bring] them back to their owner. He [the owner] will reward him. But if [the finder] does not give them [back], he shall be considered a thief. (§45)
>
> If anyone finds a [stray] ox, a horse, [or] a mule, he shall drive it to the king's gate. If he finds it in the country, they shall present it to the elders. [The finder] shall harness it [i.e. use it while it is in his custody]. When its owner finds it, he shall take it according to the law in full, but he shall not have him [the finder] arrested as a thief. But if [the finder] does not present it to the elders, he shall be considered a thief. (§71)[74]
>
> If oxen enter [another man's] field, and the field's owner finds [them], he may hitch them up for one day until the stars come out. Then he shall drive them back to their owner. (§79)

There are several more related rules. Clauses §§60-62 prescribe stiff penalties for someone who finds a bull, stallion, or ram and castrates it. In §86, a property owner is exonerated from responsibility if he kills a pig who wanders onto his property, though he must return the carcass to its owner. A rather different approach is taken in §66, however, which entitles an owner to retrieve his stray animal from someone else's property without accusing the other person of theft. In this law the property owner is not required to take the initiative in returning the animal.[75]

---

74. A later version of the laws combines §§45 and 71 into one regulation, omitting the mention of reward and adding a penalty of threefold compensation for unlawfully keeping lost property, which was standard for theft (§XXXV).

75. §72 stipulates that, if an ox is found dead on someone's property, the property owner is to pay twofold compensation. It might be assumed from the context (following §71) that this stipulation refers to lost property, but such a punishment would be most unfair to the property owner unless he was responsible for the death. Even in the case of a rented ox that dies, the renter only gives simple restitution, so the double restitution required here suggests that this law is concerned with theft (cf. §73). On some of the Hittite laws concerning lost property, see Haase (1957).

b. Book of the Covenant

When you come upon your enemy's ox or donkey straying, be sure to take it back to him. When you see the donkey of someone who hates you lying down under its burden, you shall not leave it [there];[76] *be sure you help him restore it.*[77]

Exod 23:4-5

The Book of the Covenant assumes the basic principle underlying the Babylonian and Hittite laws, that lost property should be returned to its owner, but goes significantly further by stipulating that this applies even if the owner is one's enemy (v. 4). The word 'enemy' (איב) can mean either a personal enemy, belonging to one's own people, or an enemy nation.[78] Clearly the former is intended here (cf. 1 Sam 18:29; 1 Kgs 21:20). In the context, it may refer to someone with whom one has a legal conflict, since the preceding and following verses deal with lawsuits.[79]

A supplementary clause (v. 5) then expands the point by requiring the faithful Israelite to give assistance when an enemy's donkey falls and cannot get up again (cf. Deut 22:4) or lies down and refuses to budge even though it is capable of doing so (cf. Num 22:27). The meaning of the Hebrew is uncertain, but probably there is a play on words between two homonyms. The common verb 'leave' (עזב) is used in the first part of this sen-

---

76. This is the probable meaning of the Hebrew (so NIV; cf. Durham 1987), understanding the word לו to refer to the animal. It could also refer to the owner, as in RSV ('you shall refrain from leaving him with it') and Huffmon (1974: 274, 'you shall desist from leaving [it] to him'). All these translations assume this difficult clause to be part of the apodosis (consequent clause of conditional sentence). Alternative interpretations, taking it to be part of the protasis (conditional clause), are found in NRSV ('and you would hold back from setting it free'), Houtman (1996, 'and you would be unwilling to help him'), and REB ('however unwilling you may be to help').

77. For the meaning of v. 5b, see discussion below. Several alternative translations are mentioned in the notes. Some older scholars emended עזב in the second part of the sentence to עזר, 'help' (see Cooper 1988: 21), but there is no manuscript evidence for this, nor any insuperable difficulty about understanding MT, so such emendation has generally been considered unnecessary.

78. Ringgren (1971a: 214).

79. As pointed out by Noth (1959). There has been extensive debate as to whether this text is a later insertion in the present context, since its form and content are different from the preceding and following laws (see Childs 1974; Durham 1987; Cooper 1988: 2 n. 5; Marshall 1993: 154-55; Sprinkle 1994: 178-82). However, this question does not significantly affect the understanding of the text itself and will not be discussed here.

tence, and it is suggested that a rare homonym is used in the second part of the sentence.[80] The homonym is thought to mean 'restore, put in order' (cf. Neh 3:8, 34), 'arrange',[81] or 'strengthen'.[82] This sense is supported by the Septuagint (συνεγερεις) and the parallel law in Deuteronomy 22:4, and followed by many modern translations (e.g. NRSV, NIV, REB).[83]

The law on beasts of burden is combined with that on lost property because it embodies a similar concern for the welfare of other members of the Israelite covenant community, particularly in relation to problems with their livestock. If someone loses an animal, their neighbour should help them recover it. If a beast of burden is in distress or refuses to work, the neighbour should help the owner to get it moving. The latter principle is distinctively biblical and there is nothing comparable in the other ancient Near Eastern laws.

---

80. So Huffmon (1974: 274); Halbe (1975: 430 n. 26); Durham (1987); Margalit (1987: 394-97); Talmon (1989: 108). This rare verb עזב is thought to derive from Ugaritic and Arabic ʿdb.

81. Cassuto (1951).

82. HOTTP.

83. Williamson (1985b) disputes the existence of the homonym, arguing that there is only one verb עזב but here it has an unusual meaning, namely 'release' (cf. Job 20:13). Thus he translates the sentence as in RV margin: 'If thou see the ass of him that hateth thee lying under his burden, and wouldest forbear to release it for him, thou shalt surely release it with him'. Cf. Dietrich (1986); Gerstenberger (1986); Sprinkle (1994: 178, 180-81). Similarly BDB, while acknowledging the homonym in Neh 3:8, considers עזב in Exod 23:5 (also Job 9:27; 10:1; 20:13) to be the common verb, with the meaning 'let loose, set free, let go', suggesting the translation: 'thou shalt by all means free it (sc. the beast) with him'.

Cooper (1988) agrees with Williamson that the common verb עזב is used in both parts of the sentence, but believes that it has its ordinary meaning 'leave' (cf. Frymer-Kensky 2003: 1037). So he translates as follows: 'When you see your enemy's ass crouching under its load, and you would refrain from leaving it, you must leave the animal alone.' If this is correct, there is a contrast between the cases of the wandering animal (v. 4, which should be returned) and the animal that is lying down (v. 5, which must not be interfered with). It follows that the second clause merely forbids taking advantage of an enemy when his animal is resting or in difficulty, rather than encourages a positive act of love. While this translation is possible linguistically, it goes against a tradition of interpretation that goes back to Deuteronomy (22:4) and Philo (*Virtues* 116–17) and it has not been widely accepted by scholars.

Differently again, NJPS understands both occurrences of עזב in this verse to be the rare homonym, with the meaning 'raise', translating: 'When you see the ass of your enemy lying under its burden and would refrain from raising it, you must nevertheless raise it with him' (cf. Sarna 1991).

c. Deuteronomic Laws

You shall not see your brother's ox or his sheep going astray, and ignore them; be sure to take them back to your brother. And if your brother [does] not [live] near to you or[84] you do not know him, then you shall bring it to[85] your own house, and it shall be with you until your brother claims it, then you shall give it back to him. You shall do the same with his donkey, and you shall do the same with his clothing, and you shall do the same with any of your brother's lost property which he loses and you find. You may not ignore them.

You shall not see your brother's donkey or his ox fallen on the road and ignore them; be sure to help him lift [it] up.

Deut 22:1-4

As in the Book of the Covenant, two principles are combined in the one text: the returning of lost property (vv. 1-3) and helping someone get their beast of burden onto its feet (v. 4).[86]

The word 'brother', as distinct from 'enemy' in Exodus 23:4-5, focuses the Deuteronomic version of the text on behaviour towards fellow Israelites,[87] though it does not thereby permit taking advantage of others outside the covenant community. The word is clearly emphatic, being used six times in the four verses, reminding the hearer of that mutual responsibility which is part of being the people of God. Another distinctive feature is the phrase 'You shall/may not ignore them' (vv. 1, 3, 4). Literally this means to 'hide yourself [from] them', so that you are not seen, in order to avoid having to take the action that would be expected of someone who has *seen* someone else's need (vv. 1, 4; cf. Isa 58:7). Similar anticipation of possible reactions is found elsewhere in Deuteronomy, with its sermonic approach to law (e.g. 15:9, 18).[88]

---

84. So NRSV; NIV; TEV; but REB translates 'and' (cf. TB).

85. Lit. 'inside'.

86. Scholars are agreed that Deut 22:1-4 is based on Exod 23:4-5, not vice versa (e.g. Driver 1902; Braulik 1995: 11-12; Tigay 1996).

87. In this context 'brother' refers to a fellow Israelite (TEV; cf. REB) rather than a neighbour (NRSV), as becomes clear in the next verse. Obviously it is not limited to blood brothers, since the possibility is envisaged that the person may not be known. This is in fact the commonest use of the word in Deuteronomy (e.g. 15:3-12; 17:15; 18:15; 19:18; 23:19-20; 24:7, 14; 25:3). Cf. Neufeld (1955: 402): 'the whole of Israel comprises one family, one paternal house and therefore all its members are brothers.' See also Ringgren (1971b).

88. Tigay (1996).

The basic principle of returning lost property in verse 1 is the same as that in Exodus, though the wording is quite different. In addition to the distinctive features already noted, the form is apodictic rather than casuistic, the animals specified are ox and sheep (instead of ox and donkey), and a different Hebrew word is used for 'stray' (cf. Ezek 34:4, 16, which refers to the Deuteronomic version). Verses 2-3 elaborate on the basic principle, concerning cases of the owner being far away or unknown (v. 2) and extending it to all kinds of possessions (v. 3, the same range being specified as in Exod 22:9). In the case of the owner not being contactable, the finder is expected to bring the lost animal to his own house, where it would be kept on the ground floor with his own cattle (cf. Gen 24:31-32; Judg 19:21; 1 Sam 28:24).[89] At first sight, this seems to lay open a person to the charge of taking possession of lost property, a possibility which is forestalled in the Hittite Laws (§71) by instructing the finder to report the find to the local authorities before taking custody. However, in a closely knit society like Israel, such a find would scarcely be a private matter, and if the finder made the situation known to his neighbours from the beginning then there would be no need for such suspicion. This custody would last 'until your brother claims it' (v. 2; cf. 1 Sam 9:3-20; Ezek 34:6, 8, 10, 11). Presumably, if no claim is made, the property would remain in the house of the finder, but the rule stops short of giving the finder the right to consider unclaimed lost property as his own.

Concerning the second point (v. 4), there are several differences from the version in Exodus which simplify and clarify the law:

- Exodus is ambiguous as to whether or not the donkey is in distress; Deuteronomy makes it clear that the animal has fallen.
- In Exodus the first clause is casuistic in form, while the second is syntactically ambiguous and could belong to either the protasis or apodosis;[90] in Deuteronomy the whole is transformed into apodictic form.[91]
- The verb that has provoked so much scholarly debate (עזב) is replaced by the unambiguous 'lift up' (הקים), a word more appropriate for a fallen animal.

---

89. See Canaan (1933: 41-42, 70); Stager (1985: 12-15); Tigay (1995: 373-74).
90. See n. 76.
91. So NRSV, though NIV and REB incorrectly translate it as case law.

As in the law about lost property, the word 'enemy' is replaced by 'brother' and there is a warning not to 'ignore' the situation. Also, Exodus specifies just one kind of animal while Deuteronomy mentions two.

It appears that Deuteronomy broadens the law of Exodus, though it does not really change the meaning significantly. Rather, it is a matter of making explicit what is implicit in the earlier law and clarifying ambiguities. Exodus deals with the ox or donkey of a personal enemy, Deuteronomy with any animal or clothing or other lost property belonging to a fellow Israelite. Exodus is simply giving examples of lost property, and the fact that only two kinds of animal are specified does not mean people are entitled to help themselves to other animals or property that are lost. Also, Exodus surely does not intend to limit such concern to enemies: if an enemy is to be helped in this way, all the more so a brother or sister. Several of the other changes in Deuteronomy serve to make clear what is unclear in Exodus.

d. Conclusion

'Am I my brother's keeper?', Cain asks God (Gen 4:9). Of course that is not a genuine question in the context, nor does the answer Cain receives tell us much about care of siblings. Nevertheless, it is an implicit question in many other parts of the Bible, and the answer given is a resounding 'Yes'. The biblical texts discussed above are just two examples. They are not primarily concerned with the welfare of animals,[92] though the Old Testament does show such consideration elsewhere,[93] but with the welfare of the owner of the lost property. (The animal itself may actually prefer wandering to being kept in a pen, and lying down to trudging along under a heavy load![94]) Though they occur in law collections — the Book of the Covenant and the Deuteronomic Laws — these texts are not so much laws as exhortations to positive action on behalf of one's 'brother', that is, a fellow member (male or female) of the Israelite covenant community. It is expected that a member of the community will take the initiative to help others, whether or not they deserve it, as expressed by the principle in the Holiness Code of loving one's neighbour

---

92. *Pace* Crüsemann (1992: 261).
93. See below, 11 n. 1.
94. Cf. Huffmon (1974: 274); Durham (1987).

as oneself (Lev 19:17-18; cf. Job 31:29; Prov 24:17; 25:21; Jer 29:7; Matt 5:44; Luke 10:25-37).[95]

Love is not legally enforceable, and if someone chose to ignore this principle and let an animal continue to stray or lie under its burden, it is unlikely that they would be taken to court. This may be compared with Anglo-American common law, where there is no legal obligation to rescue or give assistance to someone in danger or distress, unlike maritime law which obliges a ship's captain to help anyone found at sea and in danger.[96] A passerby may have a legitimate reason for not stopping to help someone (e.g. inability to help or unawareness that help is needed) and 'to establish a law requiring such kindness would result in an avalanche of litigation between people who had troubles and those passers-by whom the people with troubles think should have stopped but, for reasons of their own, did not'.[97]

The problem, however, is not simply that people 'pass by on the other side' when others suffer misfortune (cf. Luke 10:31-32), but that some actually take advantage of the circumstances to their own benefit. Cattle were of great value in the ancient world, and someone might well be tempted to take possession of a lost animal if its ownership was unknown. Finders keepers? Clearly not. To do this would be equivalent to stealing (cf. Exod 22:9; Lev 6:2-7[98]). The ancient Near Eastern laws expect the finder of lost property to take reasonable steps to return it, if the owner is known, and otherwise to report the matter to the authorities. In the case of a lost animal, the finder is responsible for taking care of the animal until it can be returned. The parallel texts in Exodus and Deuteronomy agree with this principle and go beyond it. Far from acquiescing to opportunism, they encourage Israelites to look for opportunities to help other members of the covenant community, even enemies.[99]

---

95. Cf. Wolff (1973: 188-91). For a detailed study of the love of enemy in the Old Testament, with particular reference to the law concerning the enemy's donkey, see Barbiero (1991).
96. Huffmon (1974: 275).
97. Sprinkle (1994: 186).
98. On which see above, 2.1.d.
99. On lost property in Jewish law, see Albeck (1972); Broyde (1995); Ominsky (n.d.).

Chapter 3

PROPERTY RESPONSIBILITIES

As shown in the previous chapter, one of the concerns of ancient Near Eastern and biblical law is to protect property rights. However, property ownership carries not only rights but also responsibilities. For example, owners are responsible for making sure that their property does not cause harm to other people or property belonging to them. And everyone, whether or not they own property, is expected to be careful not to damage other people's property, either deliberately or by negligence.

3.1 Owner Liability

Theft refers to direct action to take someone else's property, just as murder refers to the taking of another person's life. By 'owner liability', I refer to liability for loss of life or property caused indirectly by something a person owns and for which that person is therefore responsible. Whereas theft and murder are intentional, such indirect loss normally takes place unintentionally, perhaps even without the knowledge of the owner of the animal or inanimate object which was the immediate cause of the incident. Lack of intention or lack of knowledge do not, however, mean the owner is free of responsibility.

a. Ancient Near East

The classic treatment of owner liability concerns the case of a goring ox, as expressed by three clauses in the Laws of Eshnunna:

> If an ox gores another ox and thus causes its death, the two ox-owners shall divide the value of the living ox and the carcass of the dead ox.
>
> If the ox is a gorer and the ward authorities so notify its owner, but he fails to keep his ox in check and it gores a man and thus causes his death, the owner of the ox shall weigh and deliver forty shekels of silver.
>
> If it gores a slave and thus causes his death, he shall weigh and deliver fifteen shekels of silver. (§§53-55)

The same rules apply in the case of a dog who bites a man or slave causing his death, though nothing is said about the case of one dog killing another, perhaps because dogs were not considered to be of great value (§§56-57). The Laws of Hammurabi also deal with the subject of oxen that gore people to death, prescribing monetary compensation in the case of an ox that is known to be vicious and whose owner has been warned but has not taken steps to control it (§§251-52: thirty shekels for a free man; twenty shekels for a slave), but otherwise exonerating the owner (§250). The Hittite Laws try to prevent such things happening by making it a criminal offence to allow a bull outside its pen (§176a; cf. §57).[1]

One more clause in the Laws of Eshnunna refers to owner liability, concerning the case of a collapsing wall:

> If a wall is buckling and the ward authorities so notify the owner of the wall, but he does not reinforce his wall and the wall collapses and thus causes the death of a free man[2] — it is a capital case, it is decided by a royal edict. (§58)

The punishment of the owner is more severe than in the cases of the vicious ox or dog, perhaps because animals have minds of their own so their behaviour can be unpredictable and difficult to control, whereas the col-

---

1. A bull is defined as a plough ox, ram, or he-goat in its third year which is capable of breeding. Cf. Goetze (1966).

2. The translation 'free man' is taken from *ANET*, whereas *COS* has 'member of the *awīlu*-class'. Yaron (1988) translates literally, 'son of a man' (cf. Westbrook 1988b: 57-58). The word *awīlu* in Akkadian means 'man' or 'gentleman', referring to a free citizen as distinct from a serf or slave.

lapse of a wall is entirely the responsibility of its owner if it is obviously in a dangerous condition and he has not repaired it.[3] Again on the subject of walls, the Laws of Hammurabi decree:

> [If . . . a man] declares [to the owner of a rundown house], 'Reinforce your scalable wall; they could scale over the wall to here from your house,' or to the owner of an uncultivated plot, 'Work your uncultivated plot; they could break into my house from your uncultivated plot,' and he secures witnesses — if a thief [breaks in] by scaling the wall, the owner [of the rundown house shall replace anything which is lost by] the scaling; if [a thief breaks in by access through the uncultivated plot], the owner [of the uncultivated plot] shall replace anything [which was lost . . .]. (CH § gap e; cf. LL §11)[4]

b. Book of the Covenant

The main treatment of owner liability in Old Testament law is found in Exodus 21, covering three closely related topics:

- an ox that kills a person — one basic rule, four supplementary clauses (vv. 28-32)
- an uncovered pit that causes the death of an animal — one basic rule (vv. 33-34)
- an ox that kills another ox — one basic rule, one supplementary clause (vv. 35-36)

An Ox That Kills a Person

When an ox gores a man or a woman to death, the ox shall be stoned and its flesh shall not be eaten, but the owner of the ox shall be clear.[5]

---

3. Finkelstein (1981: 22). A related issue is that of faulty construction. This is referred to in CH §§229-33, which make a builder liable for severe punishment if a house he built collapses and causes loss of life, and require compensation in the case of loss of property, but this is not *owner* liability.

4. For further discussion of owner liability in LE and CH, see Driver and Miles (1952: 170-72, 441-44); Haase (1967: 12-26); Yaron (1988: 291-303); Otto (1989: 109-35).

5. I.e. free from liability.

But if the ox has had the habit of goring in the past and its owner has been warned but has not kept it [under control],[6] then it kills a man or a woman, the ox shall be stoned and its owner shall be put to death as well. [However,] if a ransom is allowed for him,[7] he may redeem his life[8] by paying whatever is required of him. Also, if it gores a son or a daughter, [its owner] shall be dealt with according to this rule. If the ox gores a male or female slave, [its owner] shall pay thirty shekels of silver to their master and the ox shall be stoned.

Exod 21:28-32

The basic rule is that when an ox kills someone, the ox is to be stoned and its flesh not eaten, but the owner is clear of liability. This rule is supplemented by four clauses which clarify specific matters. If the ox is a *habitual* gorer and the owner has been warned, then the owner is subject to capital punishment. However, the owner may be allowed to *ransom* his life by a monetary payment. The same rule applies in the case of a *minor* being

---

6. LXX (followed by Vulgate and Josephus) reads 'but has not destroyed it', and on the basis of this it has been suggested that the Hebrew verb be emended from שמר ('keep') to שמד ('destroy') both here and in v. 36 (cf. BHS). Jackson (1975b: 121-30; cf. 141 n. 135) discusses the difficulties of understanding MT at this point. The verb שמר could mean that the owner of a goring ox was warned to 'keep' the ox penned up (so NIV; TEV), but this meaning is unusual in legal texts, and to do this would render the ox useless as a working beast. Alternatively it could mean that the owner was warned to 'watch' the ox so that it does not cause harm to others, which fits with usage of the verb elsewhere, but this would scarcely be practical since even if a full-time guard was employed they would not have the strength to restrain a vicious ox. So Jackson argues that LXX has understood the text correctly, pointing out that the most realistic option for the owner was to cut his losses by slaughtering the beast for its flesh and hide, at the same time protecting himself from liability in the case of a further offence in the future. The warning to destroy the ox would presumably be advisory rather than compulsory, but should an owner ignore it and the ox subsequently take someone's life, he would no longer be in a position to claim freedom from liability.

However, the parallel ancient Near Eastern laws point to the accuracy of MT. LE §54 expects the owner of a vicious ox to keep it under control, and CH §251 adds that its horns should be blunted, while HL §176a says that any bull should be kept in a pen. The verb שמר ('keep, watch, guard, look after') is quite broad in meaning, and its use here simply indicates that the owner of an ox is responsible for looking after it and ensuring it does not harm others. According to Greenberg (1986: 10 n. 19), LXX reflects a later Jewish interpretation of the law and should not be regarded as based on a more accurate text than that followed by MT. I have therefore followed MT in my translation above.

7. It is not specified under what conditions this would be allowed, but see further below (n. 10).

8. So most translations and commentaries, though NRSV translates: 'the victim's life'.

killed, whereas in the case of a *slave* being killed, monetary compensation is to be paid to the master. In all cases the ox is to be stoned.

There are several points of interest here:

- The stoning of the ox and taboo on eating its flesh (cf. Gen 9:5-6) is unparalleled in other ancient Near Eastern laws.[9]
- Owner liability applies if the ox is known to be vicious and the owner has been warned, resulting in capital punishment.
- There is a possibility of avoiding the death penalty by ransom, presumably at the discretion of the victim's family or the local authorities,[10] which is never allowed in the Bible in cases of intentional homicide (cf. Num 35:31).[11]
- There is no distinction between the life of a man or woman, boy or girl.[12]
- Capital punishment does not apply if the ox kills a slave, but monetary compensation is payable and the ox is to be stoned.[13]

---

9. On this, see van Selms (1950); Driver and Miles (1952: 443-44); Greenberg (1960: 15); Jackson (1975b: 108-21); Finkelstein (1981: 26-29); Fensham (1988); Westbrook (1988b: 83-88); Schwienhorst-Schönberger (1990: 132-36); Wright (1990: 162-63); Sprinkle (1994: 123-28).

10. Houtman (1996: 174) assumes that the family will make the decision about a possible ransom and suggests that they may do so either because they are sorry for the guilty owner or because the payment of a sum of money is to their advantage. Sarna (1991) also thinks the ransom would be determined by the family, comparing with v. 22, but at the same time he notes a tradition in Targum Jonathan that it was fixed by the court. In principle the ransom is intended as redemption of the ox-owner's life, not as compensation to the victim's family, though in practice there would be a fine line between the two since the family stand to benefit financially from the arrangement. On ransom and atonement in this context, see Sprinkle (1994: 117-19) and Houtman (1996: 176-78).

11. Cf. Greenberg (1960: 13-20). See Jackson (1975e: 41-50) for a critique of Greenberg's view, and the latter's response (Greenberg 1986: 9-17).

12. Cf. Paul (1970: 83); Finkelstein (1981: 32-36). In contrast, the Mesopotamian laws only refer to the death of a man. This is also an implicit repudiation of the ancient Near Eastern practice of vicarious punishment, e.g. if a jerry-built house collapsed and killed a son of the householder, then the son of the builder was to be killed rather than the builder himself (CH §230; cf. §§116, 210). The practice is repudiated explicitly in Deut 24:16.

13. This combination of penalties may indicate the ambiguous status of the slave: on the one hand, he is considered to be the property of his owner, who therefore requires monetary compensation; on the other hand, he is a human being, so that the death of the ox is required (Paul 1970: 83). At first sight the compensation of thirty shekels seems high, since in other laws a slave is valued at only fifteen (LL §13; LE §55) or twenty (CH §§116, 214, 252; cf. Gen 37:28) shekels, while thirty shekels is compensation for the death of a free man (CH §251). However, all those sums date to the eighteenth century or earlier, whereas docu-

The basic position on owner liability is similar to that in the Laws of Eshnunna and Hammurabi, where the owner is considered liable for the death only if the ox is a known gorer and if the owner has been warned, but the penalty prescribed is much greater. Monetary compensation was normal in the other ancient Near Eastern laws, but capital punishment is the standard here.[14] Even in the case of nonliability, the biblical law requires destruction of the ox and a taboo on eating its flesh (v. 28), which is a considerable loss to the owner, whereas the Laws of Hammurabi simply say that there is no basis for a claim (§250).

An Uncovered Pit That Causes the Death of an Animal

When someone removes the cover of a pit, or digs a pit and does not cover it, and an ox or donkey falls into it, the owner of the pit[15] shall make restitution,[16] paying compensation to its owner, and the dead animal shall be his.[17]

Exod 21:33-34

Whether the owner digs a pit and fails to provide a cover, or provides a cover and someone else leaves it open, the owner is held responsible for the death of an animal who falls into the pit. However, no punishment is required, just compensation for the actual loss, which is the difference in value between a live and dead animal. The question arises, why is the owner always liable in this case, even if someone else actually leaves the pit open? Perhaps it is due to the difficulty of proving who left a pit open,

---

ments from Alalakh and Nuzi indicate the price of a slave in the fifteenth century to be twenty-five or thirty shekels (Mendelsohn 1955: 68; Kitchen 2003: 344-45), which is closer in time to the origin of the biblical law in the fifteenth or thirteenth century (according to biblical chronology).

14. See Jackson (1975b: 127-30); Finkelstein (1981: 29-32); Wright (1990: 163-64).

15. The owner of the pit is held responsible for the accident, even if someone else uncovered it. This is clear in the Hebrew text, in spite of TEV, which implies that the person who uncovers the pit is responsible, whether or not he is its owner.

16. Hebrew שלם ('restore, make whole, make good [the loss], make restitution'). Several versions translate the verb as 'pay back' or 'repay', but this is less satisfactory than 'restore' or 'make restitution' since its reference is almost always to compensation in kind rather than a monetary payment (thirteen times in Exod 21:36–22:15, the only exception being the present text (cf. Daube 1947: 134-44).

17. I.e. the owner of the pit.

unless there happen to be witnesses, so it is more practical to make the owner liable for any death that occurs as a result of the pit being there, thus making him responsible for ensuring that it is covered at all times. Although there is no exact parallel to this law, the principle that an owner is liable for death or loss resulting from property that is inadequately maintained is found in several ancient Near Eastern laws (LE §58; CH §§53, gap e).

An Ox That Kills Another Ox

When someone's ox gores his neighbour's ox to death, then they shall sell the live ox and divide the money, and they shall also divide the dead animal. [But] if it is known that the ox has had the habit of goring in the past and its owner has not kept it [under control],[18] then he shall make full restitution — ox for ox — and the dead animal shall be his.

Exod 21:35-36

This part of the law on the goring ox is separated from the first, perhaps deliberately to emphasise that loss of property is a far less serious matter than the loss of a person's life.[19] In this case the owners of the two oxen share the loss equally, a principle almost identical to that in the Laws of Eshnunna (§53).[20] However, the biblical law adds a further clause, specifying that if there is evidence the ox has been in the habit of goring and its owner has not taken adequate steps to keep it under control, then the owner of the goring ox is to make good the loss by providing a live ox to replace the dead one, while being allowed to keep the latter for himself. It is

---

18. See n. 6.

19. Finkelstein (1981: 36-39). Daube (1947: 85-89) argues, less convincingly, that this is a later addition to the group of laws and was therefore placed at the end. For a detailed discussion of the structure, see Sprinkle (1994: 105-15).

20. The Book of the Covenant requires the owner of the goring ox to sell the animal and share the proceeds, whereas the Laws of Eshnunna do not exclude the possibility that he might keep the animal and give half its market-price to the owner of the dead ox as compensation (Yaron 1988: 291 n. 124; Schwienhorst-Schönberger 1990: 151-52; Houtman 1996), though Jackson (1975b: 131-32) considers this unlikely. In any case, it is clear that the loss is intended to be shared equally between the two owners, even though in practice the exact loss each one suffered would depend on the value of their respective oxen (cf. Jackson 1975b: 132-35).

not stated what is to happen to the gorer in this case, but presumably it would be killed and sold, with the proceeds kept by its owner. The law thus makes the owner of the goring ox liable to compensate the other owner for his loss, if the ox's vicious tendencies were known and its owner had not taken preventative measures, but does not require any additional punishment. This is radically different from the previous case of an ox killing a human being, where compensation is irrelevant because human life cannot be given a monetary value (except in the case of a slave). In that case punishment is essential, involving both the destruction of the ox and — in the case of culpable negligence — the death of the owner.[21]

c. Deuteronomic Laws

> *When you build a new house, you shall make a parapet for your roof, so that you will not be liable*[22] *if anyone falls from it.*
>
> Deut 22:8

The flat roof of a Palestinian house would be used for various purposes — storage, worship, relaxation, and sleeping (e.g. Josh 2:6; 1 Sam 9:25; 2 Sam 11:2; Neh. 8:16; Jer 19:13; cf. Acts 10:9) — so this law makes a houseowner responsible for safety precautions, specifically for the construction of a safety wall round the edge of the roof to stop people from falling to the ground. The underlying principle of owner liability is found in several ancient Near Eastern laws and in the Book of the Covenant, though there is no exact parallel to this law. Its brevity leaves two matters unclear:[23]

- Would a houseowner be liable to charges for not having a parapet on the roof, on the basis of contravening building regulations, or only in the case of an accident?
- In the case of an accident, would a death be treated as homicide and result in capital punishment, as in the case of the collapsing wall or goring ox where there was proof of negligence by the owner?

---

21. The law of the goring ox has been the object of extensive scholarly discussion. In addition to the works already cited, see Otto (1989: 135-60; 1991b: 147-64); Schenker (1990: 61-66); Rothenbusch (2000: 319-35); Wright (2004b).

22. Lit. 'bring bloodguilt on your house'.

23. Cf. Wright (1990: 164-65).

Probably the implication of the second part of the law is that liability only applies if someone falls from the roof, so this is an advisory measure rather than a law which automatically attracts a penalty if contravened. Almost all the other biblical and ancient Near Eastern laws on liability deal with cases where actual damage or death has occurred, the Hittite law on keeping a bull penned up being the only exception, and in this last case a roaming bull is of much greater danger to society than an unfenced roof. So it seems likely that a houseowner who ignored the rule would receive no more than a warning, unless there was an accident. On the second matter, most scholars believe a fatal fall from a rooftop would be regarded as homicide on the part of the owner,[24] though Daube (1961: 251) doubts that either a court or the victim's family would really take such an attitude. It is difficult to be certain, but there would not be much point in including the law unless it was intended to be effective, and its presence in the statute book would give an adequate basis for the family or community to press charges, particularly if it could be shown that the absence of a parapet was a contributory factor in causing the fall. If that was the case, the reference to liability (lit. 'bloodguilt') suggests that there would be punishment, quite possibly capital.

d. Conclusion

The laws discussed above deal with just a few cases of owner liability, but they are sufficient to give a fairly clear understanding of how the matter was viewed in ancient Israel and Mesopotamia, at least by the compilers of the laws,[25] though they do not answer all the questions we might wish to ask. Actual occurrences of oxen goring people or other oxen to death were apparently quite rare, judging by the paucity of references to such incidents in the tens of thousands of cuneiform legal documents which have been discovered.[26] So, the fact that the possibility attracts such detailed attention in three major law collections suggests this case is recorded as a textbook example, to illustrate a principle which would apply in a variety

---

24. E.g. Phillips (1970: 94), who uses the term 'constructive murder'; Craigie (1976), 'manslaughter'; Tigay (1996) and Christensen (2002), 'criminal negligence'.

25. How far these laws reflect actual legal practice in these ancient societies, and how closely they relate to specific social settings, is a complicated issue which cannot be discussed here. For just one perspective on the matter, see Finkelstein (1981: 42-46).

26. Cf. Finkelstein (1981: 21). The one clear example is an account of a lawsuit from Nuzi (*COS:* 3.121).

of real-life cases. In fact, we may assume that all the cases are presented as examples, to provide guidelines for the administration of justice, because none of the law collections is remotely comprehensive.[27] For instance, the Laws of Eshnunna deal with oxen, dogs, and walls but not with pits or houses. The Book of the Covenant focuses almost entirely on oxen, with a short interlude on pits, and the Deuteronomic Laws include just one sentence on rooftops.

It is evident that there are both similarities and differences between the Old Testament laws and those in other ancient Near Eastern law collections, but how far this similarity is due to dependence of one on the other is debatable. The Laws of Hammurabi were presumably well known in Mesopotamia, judging by the number of copies that have been found, but there is no evidence that they were known elsewhere. The Laws of Eshnunna originated in a relatively small kingdom, and it appears even less likely that these were known by the compiler of the Book of the Covenant, though the closest similarity with any of the biblical laws is in fact found there (LE §53). David and van Selms consider the biblical laws to be independent, whereas Jackson and Malul argue for a connection.[28] According to van Selms, the mention of the ox in all three law collections could be coincidental, since it was such a common animal in the ancient Near East, while Malul argues that the specific circumstances, which would have occurred infrequently in real life and are hardly ever documented outside the laws, suggest a common literary tradition as the link between the laws. Malul also notes the uniqueness of the legal principle that an owner's liability for a goring ox depends on a prior warning, which is found in these three law collections but nowhere else in ancient law systems. Yaron and Fensham attribute the similarities to common Near Eastern legal traditions and practices, while Wright and Levinson argue for direct knowledge of the Mesopotamian laws on the part of the biblical writer.[29] All in all, it seems clear that there is a link between the biblical laws on owner liability and those from Mesopotamia, though whether this is due to direct literary knowledge or a common legal heritage is uncertain.

27. Daube (1961: 257) suggests that ancient law collections tend to regulate 'matters as to which the law is dubious or in need of reform or both' (cf. 1973). So the fact that the biblical laws deal with indirect damage, but not simple direct damage, does not mean that the latter was allowable but that it was a straightforward matter that communities were used to dealing with and did not need a written law.
28. David (1950); van Selms (1950); Jackson (1975b); Malul (1990: 113-52).
29. Yaron (1966; 1988: 293-94); Fensham (1978); Wright (2003); Levinson (2004: 289-90).

Two main categories of liability are distinguished in the laws: that where one person's property causes loss of someone else's property and that where it causes loss of human life. The principles relating to *loss of property* may be summarised as follows:

- In the case of ox killing ox, the law in the Book of the Covenant is similar to that in the Laws of Eshnunna, providing for the two owners to split the loss; however, if the owner of the goring ox has been negligent (by not taking steps to control his ox even though it has a previous history of goring), the biblical law requires him to bear the full loss whereas Eshnunna does not make this distinction.
- In the case of a wall being left in bad condition or a plot of land being left uncultivated, and after due warning to the owner of the wall or land that this neglect is causing a security problem for his neighbour, the Laws of Hammurabi make the owner of the wall or land in question liable for any resulting loss if there should be a break-in.
- In the case of an open pit causing the death of an animal, the Book of the Covenant requires the owner of the pit to make good the loss.

In every case the owner of the animal or structure which caused the loss is required to compensate the owner of the property which has been lost or damaged, but in no case is any punishment stipulated. In other words, the owner of property — animate or inanimate — is responsible for ensuring that his property does not cause harm to other property; nevertheless, in the event of an incident he is not considered a criminal but simply has to make good any losses. A corollary is that the victim does not make any profit out of the incident. Specifically in the case of one animal killing another, where the animal has a mind of its own and its behaviour is not entirely predictable, the owner of the killer is only required to give partial compensation (splitting the loss with the other owner) unless it can be shown that he has been negligent in not anticipating such an incident.[30]

It is apparent that the Old Testament laws concerning liability for loss of property are broadly similar to other laws in the ancient Near East, but when it comes to liability for *loss of life* there are considerable differences.[31] In the nonbiblical laws, the position is as follows:

30. Cf. Finkelstein (1981: 36).
31. Cf. Greenberg (1960: 13-20); Paul (1970: 79-83).

- In the case of an ox killing someone, where the ox has a previous history of goring and its owner has been warned to keep it under control, the Laws of Eshnunna and Hammurabi require monetary compensation to be paid by the owner (presumably to the victim's family), the actual sum varying between the laws and depending on the status of the victim.
- In the Laws of Eshnunna there is also a clause concerning killer dogs, with identical penalties as in the case of oxen.
- In the Laws of Hammurabi there is also a clause freeing the owner from liability if the ox does not have a history of goring and no warning has been given.
- The Hittite Laws refer briefly to the matter of vicious animals, treating it much more strictly by making it a crime to keep a bull outside a pen, whether or not there is an incident.
- In the case of a wall collapsing and killing someone, where the wall was in visibly bad condition and its owner had been warned to repair it, the Laws of Eshnunna require capital punishment for the owner.

In the biblical laws, the principles are rather different:

- In the case of an ox killing someone, where the ox has a previous history of goring and its owner has been warned to keep it under control, the Book of the Covenant requires stoning of the ox and capital punishment for the owner.
- Further clauses in the Book of the Covenant provide for the possibility of the owner redeeming his life by means of a payment, and for monetary compensation if the victim is a slave, but the ox is still to be stoned.
- The Book of the Covenant also frees the owner from liability if the ox does not have a history of goring and no warning has been given, but the ox is still to be stoned.
- In the case of someone falling from the flat roof of a house, which has not been provided with a parapet, the Deuteronomic Laws make the owner liable for any death or injury which may occur.

The most significant differences concern liability for death caused by an ox or other vicious animal. The primary concern of the Mesopotamian laws is economic, so they specify compensation by the owner to the victim's family for their loss. Apart from that, there is no punishment for either the owner or the ox itself. In contrast, the biblical laws are concerned first of all with bloodguilt, because human life is of inestimable value (cf. Gen 9:5-6). So the ox is to be stoned in all cases and the owner sentenced to death if there is evidence of culpable negligence. The only way to avoid this is by payment of a ransom, understood not as compensation to the family but as redemption of the ox-owner's life.

To sum up, there is a clear distinction in Old Testament law between offences against property and offences against persons. The former are dealt with by compensation in the form of property or money, never by physical punishment or death.[32] The latter are treated with much greater severity, though punishment must be in proportion to the crime committed, as stated by the law of talion ('an eye for an eye . . .', Exod 21:23-25; Lev 24:19-20). This distinction applies to both direct offences (theft, murder, etc.) and indirect ones caused by negligence (owner liability for animals or structures which cause harm to other people's property or loss of human life). The general principle is that someone who owns property is held responsible for injury, damage, or death caused by that property, though in the case of an animal it is necessary to prove negligence on the part of the owner before a case can be brought. In the case of loss or damage to other property, the owner is required to make monetary compensation but is not punished; in the case of death, the owner's life is forfeited — with some exceptions — and if an animal is involved, then its life is also forfeited.[33]

32. Cf. above, 2.1.e.

33. The law of the goring ox has had a significant influence on European, British, and American legal history, as shown by Finkelstein's studies of animal trials and the deodand (1973; 1981: 48-85). During the Middle Ages, it was apparently common in continental Europe to try to punish animals for injury or death caused to human beings. English law developed in a different direction with the institution of the deodand (lit. 'given to God'), whereby an animal or object which had caused the death of a person was forfeited to the Crown as the representative of God. In theory the idea was that the object itself be given over to the church or for charitable use, but in practice it was usual for the value of the animal or object to be assessed and that sum paid as a fine to the king. As Finkelstein points out (1981: 81), the execution of homicidal animals may be understood as a literal implementation of the law of the goring ox whereas the deodand was a transformation of the law based on a distinctive perception of sovereignty and its prerogatives. Animal trials largely died out with the Enlightenment, though occasional examples of the practice have been documented in modern times, especially in the United States. The deodand was abolished in England in 1846 and replaced by a law covering damages for wrongful death. However, Finkelstein (1973) believes that this was not the end of the principle lying behind the deodand and explores its post history in relation to forfeitures by the state in various countries and the Western notion of sovereignty. See also Jackson (1978).

3.2 Negligent Damage

The previous section was concerned with responsibilities pertaining to ownership of property, including laws which make an owner liable for loss of life caused by vicious animals or unsafe structures, if he has been negligent in not anticipating and preventing such an incident. Next we move on to the closely related matter of responsibility with respect to the property of others, beginning with the matter of damage caused by negligence. Here the issue is not primarily one of ownership, but that a person whose negligence permits damage to occur is held responsible for compensating the person who suffers loss as a result of the incident.

a. Ancient Near East

Three main categories of negligent damage are covered in ancient Near Eastern laws, namely that caused by flooding, grazing, and fire.[34]

The oldest law on *flooding* is a short clause in the Laws of Ur-Namma, which states:

> If a man floods [?] another man's field, he shall measure and deliver nine hundred *sila* of grain per one hundred *sar* of field.[35] (§31)

Much more detail is found in the Laws of Hammurabi.[36] There it is laid down that a person who neglects to reinforce the irrigation canal embankment of his field, so that the canal floods and causes damage to someone else's grain, is liable to replace the lost grain, and if he is unable to do so then he and his property are to be sold to compensate the owners of the grain (§§53-54; cf. NBL §3). Compensation for negligence is also due if someone floods his neighbour's field in the process of irrigating his own (CH §§55-56; cf. SLHF §4:35-41).

The next two clauses of the Laws of Hammurabi deal with unauthorised *grazing* in fields by sheep and goats. The basic rule is as follows:

---

34. HL mentions two other situations that may involve an element of negligence: a dog that devours lard (§90) and someone who sows seed on land that has already been sown (§§166-67). Cf. Haase (1967: 26-38).
35. In metric terms, this is approximately 2,500 litres per hectare.
36. For a commentary, see Driver and Miles (1952: 150-54).

If a shepherd does not make an agreement with the owner of the field to graze sheep and goats, and without the permission of the owner of the field grazes sheep and goats on the field, the owner of the field shall harvest his field and the shepherd... shall give in addition six thousand *sila* of grain per eighteen *iku* [of field][37] to the owner of the field. (§57)

The shepherd has to compensate the owner of the field at a rate double that which applies in the case of flooding (cf. §56). Apparently it was usual in Babylonia to graze sheep on agricultural land during part of the year, which could be beneficial to the crop, so the issue here is not the grazing in itself but the fact that it takes place without the permission of the landowner.[38] If grazing takes place later in the season, however, after the official termination of pasturing, it is a much more serious offence since it is too late for the owner to replant the crop and so the loss is greater. In this case the negligent shepherd has to take over responsibility for the damaged field until harvest and at that time pay compensation to the owner, at a rate three times higher than in the former case (§58). There is a similar law on grazing in vineyards in the Hittite Laws (§107).[39]

The Hittite Laws do not refer to flooding, but contain several clauses concerning *fire*. A house or shed that burns down must be rebuilt by whoever who started the fire, and if the shed was being used for storing straw, then he is also responsible for feeding the shed owner's cattle until the following spring (§§98, 100). If the fire was started by a slave, his owner is responsible for compensation, and the slave's nose and ears are also to be disfigured (§99). In the case of negligent burning of vines or fruit trees, the person who ignited the fire is to pay monetary compensation and also do necessary replanting (§105). A slightly different rule applies in the case of a burnt field, where the person responsible is to give a good field to the owner of the burnt field for him to harvest and takes over the burnt field himself for the rest of that agricultural year (§106).

---

37. In metric terms, this is approximately eight hundred litres per hectare.
38. Cf. Theophrastus, *Enquiry into Plants* 8:7.4; Driver and Miles (1952: 154).
39. For further discussion of the grazing laws, see Driver and Miles (1952: 154-57); Haase (1967: 20-38).

b. Book of the Covenant

When someone grazes[40] *[his livestock in] a field or vineyard, and he lets the livestock stray and graze in someone else's field,*[41] *he shall make restitution [from] the best*[42] *[produce*[43]*] of his*[44] *field or vineyard.*

40. So NIV; cf. LXX; NRSV; TB; TEV. A homonym of the verb בער means 'burn', as in v. 6, so REB translates 'When a man burns off a field or a vineyard and lets the fire spread so that it burns another man's field'; this meaning is supported by the Palestinian Targum (Teicher 1951; Schelbert 1958; Kahle 1959: 205-8; Heinemann 1974). However, most scholars consider the meaning 'graze' to be correct here (e.g. Pedersen 1920: 404-5, 535; Cassuto 1951; Childs 1974; Jackson 1976; Schwienhorst-Schönberger 1990: 187-92; Houtman 1996), as do BDB and *HALOT,* perhaps with a stronger sense such as 'devour' or 'ravage' as in Isa 3:14 and 5:5 (cf. Fensham 1981; Sarna 1991). Durham (1987) combines the two meanings, understanding the verb to mean 'burn, consume' but with reference not to fire but to animals who are allowed to roam freely and so devastate the harvest; similarly, Sprinkle (1994: 140-41) thinks it probable that there are not two roots בער but just one, meaning 'consume' and having a semantic range large enough to cover the action of fire on wood and cattle on vegetation. Aejmelaeus (1987: 82-83), followed by Propp (2006), tentatively suggests emendation to בעה 'destroy', citing 4QpaleoExod^m in support, but it seems unnecessary to emend MT when it is perfectly intelligible as it stands.

41. The Samaritan text and LXX add at this point: 'he shall make restitution from his [own] field, according to the produce [expected]; and if it is the whole field [which his livestock have] eaten, [then]'. NIV, NRSV, and TEV follow MT; REB is based on the longer text, but does not follow the LXX translation of בער as 'graze' (cf. previous note). Childs (1974) considers the longer text to be original, arguing for a distinction between partial damage (in which case restitution is to be made according to the usual yield of the damaged field) and total damage (in which case there is no way of calculating what the yield of the field would have been, so restitution is to be made from the best of the offender's own field); but most interpreters consider it to be a later expansion (e.g. Bickerman 1956; Rabinowitz 1959; Durham 1987; Sarna 1991; Houtman 1996).

42. The noun מיטב means 'best part' (e.g. Gen 47:6, 11), in which case the sense 'from' is presumably implied, though B. Jackson (1976) understands it as the construct form of the noun טוב (*tub,* 'good things') with the preposition מי ('from'; cf. Peshitta).

43. It seems likely that the law intends the lost crops to be replaced with other crops — of the highest quality, to ensure satisfactory compensation — so the meaning 'produce' is implied. Some interpreters understand the word מיטב literally as the best part of the field itself (cf. Rabinowitz 1959), but to give land as compensation for lost crops would be out of character with the other laws on liability and neglect which stipulate adequate restitution rather than punitive damages.

44. I take 'his' to refer to the owner of the livestock, indicating that restitution must be made from the best-quality crops he has available, though Paul (1970: 87-89) and Sprinkle (1994: 142) think that it refers to the expected yield of the most productive part of the neighbour's field or vineyard.

> *When fire breaks out*[45] *and spreads through thornbushes and consumes stacked grain, or standing grain, or the whole field, the one who kindled the fire shall make full restitution.*
>
> Exod 22:5-6 [Hebrew 22:4-5]

The only reference to negligent damage in Old Testament law is in this pair of clauses on damage to crops caused by straying livestock and fire, the same two issues dealt with in the Hittite Laws (§§105-7) but in reverse order. Flooding is not mentioned, perhaps because irrigation was not such an important part of agriculture in Palestine as in some other parts of the ancient Near East.[46] There has been extensive scholarly debate on the text and translation of these verses (see footnotes), but I see no convincing reason for departing from the Masoretic Text and its traditional understanding as translated above. There has also been discussion about possible reasons for grazing and burning,[47] but this is not really relevant here since the point of the law is simply to make clear that when the owner of crops suffers loss due to someone else's negligence, the latter is responsible to make restitution.

It is possible that there is a slight penal component in the first clause, in that the owner of the straying animals is to make good the loss from the *best* of his own produce, and this could be because the owner of the sheep is considered more negligent in this case than when a fire gets out of control.[48] A shepherd might even do this deliberately, to obtain free grazing for his flocks, and this appears to be the implication of the wording in the Laws of Hammurabi. In this case it would be a form of theft.[49] On the other hand, the variation of language between grazing in the first field or vineyard and grazing in the other person's field may suggest that the former is intentional and the latter unintentional.[50] In any case, it would be

---

45. Talmon (1981: 519) suggests emending תצא 'go out' to תצת 'kindle', on the grounds that elsewhere the phrase אש תצא is always preceded or followed by a noun with the preposition מן or one of its short forms (e.g. Lev 9:24; 10:2). However, this replaces one problem with two new ones: the phrase תצת אש is never used at all in the Old Testament, whereas תצא אש is common; and the qal form of תצת is elsewhere always preceded or followed a noun with the preposition ב, which it is not in the present text, and has a transitive rather than intransitive meaning. So the suggested emendation is no improvement syntactically over MT.

46. Cf. Driver and Miles (1952: 150-54).

47. E.g. Jackson (1976); Marshall (1993).

48. Daube (1947: 152 n. 69); Sarna (1991).

49. Sprinkle (2003: 843).

50. Sprinkle (1994: 141).

difficult to measure the quality of lost crops and to prove whether or not the unauthorised grazing was deliberate, so it is more likely that the rule about the best produce is intended to ensure that the owner of the damaged field gets adequate compensation rather than to penalise the owner of the animals. Also, a spreading fire cannot be considered purely accidental and almost certainly involves some degree of negligence. Although the law is not concerned with intentional burning of fields (as in Judg 15:5; 2 Sam 14:30), anyone who ignites a fire — especially in an arid country like Palestine — should be aware of the potential danger and must surely take responsibility for consequential damage just as much as the owner of straying livestock.[51]

c. Conclusion

Negligent damage is closely related to owner liability, especially in the case of livestock who stray into someone else's field and graze there. In the case of fire and flood, the person who carelessly allowed the damage to take place does not 'own' the fire or flood, but he is still responsible for the results of his action or inaction. As we have seen, negligent damage — like owner liability — is dealt with by compensation rather than punishment:

- The Laws of Hammurabi and other laws stipulate that in the case of *flooding* caused by negligence which results in damage to crops, the person responsible is to make good the loss.
- The Laws of Hammurabi and Hittite Laws provide for compensation to the owners of fields or vineyards if their crops are ruined due to unauthorised *grazing* by sheep and goats, the amount payable depending on the loss sustained.
- The Hittite Laws deal with negligent damage to buildings, fields, and vineyards by *fire*, stipulating that whoever started the fire must compensate the owner for straw or crops destroyed and do any necessary rebuilding (in the case of houses or sheds) and replanting (in the case of trees).
- The Book of the Covenant deals briefly with the matters of *grazing* and *fire*, stipulating full restitution by the negligent party to the one who has suffered loss.

51. On rabbinic interpretations of Exod 22:5 (Hebrew v. 4), see Jackson (1974).

Clearly the biblical laws on negligent damage follow the general principles of ancient Near Eastern law, providing for adequate compensation but nothing more. Neither punitive damages nor profit on the part of the injured party would be appropriate in this case.

3.3 Care of Property

The common circumstance of one person being entrusted with someone else's property — whether for safekeeping, borrowing, rental, or in the course of employment — can be viewed quite differently in different cultures and by different people. For example, I know that if I lend a book to one person, it will be returned promptly and in good condition. Someone else may return the book damaged — or not at all. Another difference in perspective on this matter concerns whether loans are made freely or with the expectation of payment, and there are a whole range of assumptions and practices here. The entrusting of goods to another for safekeeping is not so common today as it appears to have been in ancient times, apart from keeping money and valuables at a bank, though we may still put possessions in storage if we move abroad or between leaving one house and occupying another.[52]

a. Ancient Near East

The ancient Near Eastern laws pay considerable attention to the matters of safekeeping, rental, and employment.

On *safekeeping*, the Laws of Eshnunna read as follows:

> If a man gives his goods to someone[53] for safekeeping, and he then allows the goods which he gave to him for safekeeping to become lost — without evidence that the house has been broken into, the doorjamb scraped, the window forced — he shall replace his goods for him.
>
> If the man's house has been burgled, and the owner of the house in-

---

52. This section is substantially the same as a previously published article of mine (Baker 2006a) and is used here with kind permission of the publisher.

53. The word *napṭaru* is a class designation, denoting a person with certain privileges, which is difficult to translate since there is no exact equivalent in English (cf. *CAD*: 11.324-25; Landsberger 1968: 98-99; Finkelstein 1970: 252-54; Kraus 1976; Yaron 1988: 351; Westbrook 1994b). It is transliterated without translation in *COS*. I have translated it with the generic 'someone', which is adequate for the present purpose though less than precise.

curs a loss along with the goods which the depositor gave to him, the owner of the house shall swear an oath to satisfy him at the gate of [the temple of] the god Tishpak: 'My goods have been lost along with your goods; I have not committed a fraud or misdeed'; thus shall he swear an oath to satisfy him and he will have no claim against him. (§§36-37)

The division of responsibility is clear: if there has been a burglary, the owner of the goods bears the loss; otherwise the keeper has to do so. In the Laws of Hammurabi, the matter is dealt with rather differently. Two clauses deal with storage of grain, stipulating an annual granary rental of one sixtieth[54] of the grain stored and twofold restitution in the case of loss (§§120-21). If property entrusted to someone for safekeeping is stolen due to lack of security in the house, then the householder has to replace the lost goods (§125). The importance of witnesses and a contract is emphasised, making clear that if property is given for safekeeping without at least one of these, then there is no basis for a claim (§§122-23). If someone denies having received goods for safekeeping and there are witnesses to prove that he is lying, he has to make twofold restitution (§124). Conversely, someone who falsely claims that his property has been misappropriated is to be fined twofold what he claimed was lost (§126).

There are detailed regulations about *renting* animals, boats, and agricultural land. In the case of injury to a rented ox, the renter normally has to give monetary compensation to the owner (LL §§34-37; CH §§247-48; LRO §§1-5; SLHF §6:11-15). If a rented ox dies or is lost or seriously injured, it is to be replaced with another of comparable value (CH §§245-46; SLET §10; SLHF §6:23-31; cf. LRO §6), though the renter is exonerated from responsibility if the animal is killed by a lion (CH §244; LRO §§7-8; SLET §9; SLHF §6:16-22, 32-36) or a god (CH §249). The Hittite Laws deal with the matter slightly differently, stipulating that if someone breaks the horn or leg of an ox, then he must replace it with an ox in good condition and take the injured ox for himself, unless the owner prefers monetary compensation (§74). Other injuries to animals are to be compensated by a payment of cash or grain (§§77-78), and in the case of death or loss the person renting the animal has to replace it, even if it was devoured by a wolf, unless the animal has died suddenly of its own accord so that it is believed the death has been divinely caused (§75).[55]

---

54. So *COS*, though Driver and Miles (1952: 234) understand it to be one thirty-sixth.
55. Rental is only specifically mentioned in §§76 and 78, but §§74-78 are a series of re-

Several laws cover the renting of boats, stipulating that the person renting a boat which sinks or is lost due to negligence or deviation from the agreed route has to replace it (LL §5; LE §5; CH §236; SLHF §§4:42-5:11, 5:21-26; cf. SLET §3) or — for lesser damage — give monetary compensation (CH §238; SLHF §5:12-20). If a hired boatman negligently causes a boat to sink or loses its cargo, he has to make good the loss (CH §237).[56]

There are also various laws on renting fields and orchards, beginning with two clauses in the Laws of Ur-Namma:

> If a man violates the rights of another and cultivates the field of another man, and he [the squatter] sues [to secure the right to harvest the crop, claiming that] he [the owner] neglected [the field] — that man [the squatter] shall forfeit his expenses (§30).[57]
>
> If a man gives a field to another man to cultivate but he does not cultivate it and allows it to become wasteland, he shall measure out 720 *sila* of grain per 100 *sar* (§32).[58]

Presumably the reason for the second clause is that the owner of agricultural land is entitled to a share of the crop, in lieu of rent, and the tenant is not excused from this obligation if he fails to cultivate the land (cf. CH §§42-44, 62-63). The Laws of Lipit-Ishtar and Hammurabi lay down principles for dividing the crop, while also stipulating penalties for unsatisfac-

---

lated clauses and it seems likely that this is the primary concern in the other clauses as well, though Fensham (1978: 289) thinks the earlier ones refer to borrowing. The meaning of §76 is not entirely clear, but it appears to say that if someone requisitions an ox, horse, mule, or ass for public use and it dies, then the person who requisitioned it should return the dead animal to its owner and pay the rent (cf. Hoffner 1997: 82, 94).

56. In the case of collision of two boats, the captain of an upstream boat which sinks a downstream boat has to replace the lost boat and its cargo (CH §240; SLHF §5:27-31), whereas no compensation is required if a downstream boat sinks an upstream boat (SLHF §5:32-36). Boats might be rented on a daily basis, with payment in silver (CH §§275-77), or annually, in which case the rent would be paid at the end of the year in grain (SLHF §5:37-44).

57. An alternative translation of the second part of the clause is: 'and he (the owner) sues (against the squatter), but he (the squatter) reacts in contempt — that man (the squatter) shall forfeit his expenses' (cf. *ANET*, where it is numbered as §27). Either way, the law upholds the owner's right to the produce of his field and the squatter forfeits his agricultural expenses (e.g. purchase of seed, rental of animals and equipment). It goes without saying that he forfeits the crop too (*ANET*: 525 n. 26).

58. In metric terms, this is approximately two thousand litres per hectare.

tory work by the tenant (LL §§7-8; CH §§60-61, 64-65).[59] Finally, there are three clauses concerning storm and flood damage to fields:

- If the owner's share has already been given to him when the damage occurs, the cultivator bears the loss to any remaining crops in the fields and makes good any damage to the field and dykes (§45).
- If the owner's share has not yet been given to him, the cultivator and owner share the loss, dividing the remaining grain in the previously agreed proportions (§46).
- If the cultivator wishes to cultivate the field the following year to make good his own losses, the owner of the field must allow him to do so (§47).

Concerning *employment,* the laws mention several cases of people whose work necessitates the care of property, though there is no systematic treatment. If a guard is negligent in his work, resulting in the house he is guarding being broken into, capital punishment is required by the Laws of Eshnunna (§60). If clothes left at a laundry are lost, the launderer must replace them with others of equal value, whereas if it is proved that he has sold them then he is to be treated as a thief (MAL §M3). If tools are damaged, they are to be replaced (HL §144).

A shepherd is responsible for livestock entrusted to him, and has to make good any losses (CH §§262-64). Exceptions to this rule are made in the event of an epidemic breaking out or a lion attacking a sheepfold, in which case the shepherd is not held responsible; but if sheep fall sick due to the shepherd's negligence then he has to make restitution to their owner (§§266-67). In the case of a shepherd abandoning a sheep to a wolf,[60] the Hittite Laws allow the owner to take the meat while the shepherd keeps the sheepskin (§80).[61]

---

59. The Laws of Lipit-Ishtar specify that a tenant farmer who leases a date orchard should keep 10 percent of the crop (§7), whereas according to the Laws of Hammurabi a tenant who has planted and cultivated a field as a date orchard over a period of four years is entitled to divide the yield equally with the owner from the fifth year on (§60). In the case of a tenant taking on a ready-planted orchard, he is to receive one third of the yield in payment for his work (§64).

60. The clause could also mean 'snatching a sheep from a wolf' (cf. Hoffner 1997: 85, 195).

61. For further discussion of the care of property in the Laws of Eshnunna and Hammurabi, see Driver and Miles (1952: 136-44, 157-64, 233-45, 429-41, 455-61); Otto (1988a: 4-16; 1989: 78-98); Yaron (1988: 247-51).

b. Book of the Covenant

Three aspects of the care of property belonging to other people are dealt with in Exodus 22:

- goods entrusted for safekeeping (vv. 7-9)
- animals entrusted for safekeeping (vv. 10-13)
- borrowed or rented animals (vv. 14-15)

On the basis of rabbinic interpretation, Cassuto (1951) distinguishes the safekeeping of articles and animals as unpaid and paid custody, respectively.[62] The latter is paid because it involves a considerable amount of work, effectively acting as shepherd. That is possible, though the extra work involved in keeping animals would be offset to some extent by their usefulness. In any case, the text uses identical language in both cases and does not refer to payment in either, so we cannot be sure that this was the intention of the author.

Goods Entrusted for Safekeeping

When someone gives to his neighbour silver or goods for safekeeping, and they are stolen from that person's house, the thief — if caught — shall restore twofold. If the thief is not caught, the owner of the house shall be brought to God,[63] [64] *[to determine] whether or not he has laid hands on his neighbour's property. In every case of disputed*

---

62. Cf. Sarna (1991).

63. So ESV; NJB; NJPS; NRSV; REB; RSV; cf. LXX; TB; TEV. Two alternative translations of האלהים have been suggested. KJV and NIV have 'the judges' here and in Exod 21:6 (cf. Targum Onqelos; Ehrlich 1908: 348), but there is no parallel elsewhere to support such a translation (cf. Chirichigno 1993: 236-38; Houtman 1996: 116). Gordon (1935) translates it literally as 'the gods' (cf. Draffkorn 1957; Houtman 1996), understanding it to refer to 'household gods' (תרפים), following a suggestion of Schwally (1891). While this is a legitimate translation linguistically, and if the law has been taken from a stock of ancient Near Eastern laws it might have meant that in a different context, the present context in Exodus rules out such an interpretation here (cf. Loretz 1960; Vannoy 1974; Fensham 1976: 264; Chirichigno 1993: 232-36; Sprinkle 1994: 145-46; Propp 2006).

64. LXX inserts here 'and take an oath', so TEV translates the final clause of the sentence: 'and there he must take an oath that he has not stolen the other one's property.'

ownership[65] *involving an ox, donkey, sheep, clothing, or any lost property about which someone says, 'This is it',*[66] *the case of both [parties] shall come before God;*[67] *the one whom God*[68] *declares guilty shall restore twofold to his neighbour.*

Exod 22:7-9 [Hebrew 22:6-8]

The first aspect of care for other people's property dealt with in the Book of the Covenant is the theft or loss of goods entrusted to a neighbour (i.e. another member of the people of Israel) for safekeeping. A simple procedure is laid down for dealing with such a case:

- If a robbery has taken place and the thief can be found, he is to make twofold restitution, as normal in cases of theft (v. 7).[69]
- If not, the owner of the house where the goods have been kept is to be brought 'to God' to establish whether or not he is guilty of taking the goods (v. 8).

The expression 'to God', also used in Exod 21:6, probably means that the keeper is to be brought to a recognised place of God's presence, a sanctuary or place of theophany (cf. Josh 24:1; 1 Sam 14:36).[70] This is confirmed by the similarity of this stipulation with clause 37 of the Laws of Eshnunna, quoted above.[71] Exactly what would happen at the sanctuary is not certain. Most likely the keeper would be made to swear a solemn oath, thereby risking divine judgement if it is false.[72] Such an oath is referred to in v. 11 (cf. Lev 6:2-

---

65. So NRSV; cf. Holladay (1971); NJB; TB; TEV. The Hebrew word is פשע, elsewhere translated 'transgression' (BDB) or 'crime' *(HALOT)*. Other suggested translations here are 'misappropriation' (NJPS; REB; Paul 1970: 89); 'illegal possession' (NIV); 'embezzlement of property' (Houtman 1996).

66. So NJPS; Childs (1974); Durham (1987); cf. 'This is mine' (NIV; NRSV). Jackson (1972: 239-40) suggests the translation 'This is he', so that the statement identifies the offender rather than the property, which is possible linguistically but fits the context less well than 'This is it/mine.'

67. See n. 63.

68. See n. 63. Here the accompanying verb is plural in form, which is unusual when אלהים means 'God' — though not unprecedented (e.g. Gen 20:13; 31:53; 35:7) — so there is a stronger argument at this point for NIV's translation 'the judges' (cf. Vannoy 1974).

69. Cf. above, 2.1.c.

70. Durham (1987: 313); Chirichigno (1993: 238-40).

71. Cf. Fensham (1959).

72. This is made explicit in LXX and TEV; see nn. 64 and 80.

5; 1 Kgs 8:31-32).[73] This also seems to be the meaning of 'establish his grain before the god' in a similar regulation in the Laws of Hammurabi, though there it is the owner rather than the keeper who has to take the oath.[74] Another possibility is that the object of the exercise is to seek an oracle of God, perhaps through the priest at the sanctuary who would use the sacred lots (*urim* and *thummim*) to settle the matter.[75] In either case the summons to appear 'before God' at the sanctuary might sometimes be sufficient to make a wrongdoer reluctant to cooperate, thereby revealing his fault.

The last part of the law expands on this point with a general principle concerning disputed ownership (v. 9). If two people claim ownership of the same animals or goods, then the matter is to be decided 'before God' and the guilty party is treated as a thief, making twofold restitution to the other (cf. v. 4; CH §§120, 124, 126).

Animals Entrusted for Safekeeping

When someone gives to his neighbour a donkey, or ox, or sheep, or any other animal for safekeeping; and it dies or is injured or is captured, without anyone seeing it; an oath by the LORD[76] *shall decide between the two of them, that the one has not laid hands on his neighbour's property. The owner shall accept this,[77] and the other need not make restitution. But if in fact it has been stolen from*

---

73. This meaning is supported by Alt (1934: 91-92), Paul (1970: 90), Cole (1973), and Sprinkle (1994: 146-48). Cf. Num 5:11-31, where an oath of innocence is supplemented by a grain offering and the administration of 'water of bitterness', and Zech 5:3-4, concerning divine judgement on those who swear false oaths. The passage in Numbers shows some similarity to the ancient Near Eastern practice of ordeal, and some scholars have argued that the present text refers to a kind of ordeal (see references cited by Jackson 1972: 237 n. 1). However, there is no evidence that this was used in Israel for theft.

74. CH §120; cf. §§23, 126, 240 (cf. Driver and Miles 1952: 235).

75. So Budde (1899: 34); Kittel (1925: 99-100); Durham (1987); Westbrook (1994a: 391-93). Alternatively, it might mean that the case would be brought to a law court where judges were authorised to decide such cases in the name of God (cf. Cassuto 1951: 267, 286; Marshall 1993: 135-36), in which case the NIV translation ('before the judges') would correctly convey the intention of the text, though by means of a paraphrase rather than a strict translation (cf. n. 63).

76. I.e. an oath in the name of the LORD, as in 2 Sam 21:7 (cf. 1 Sam 20:42) and 1 Kgs 2:42-43.

77. I.e. the oath, according to most interpreters, though Sprinkle (1994: 145 n. 1) argues that the owner accepts the carcass of the animal.

him,⁷⁸ *he shall make restitution to its owner. If on the other hand it has been torn to pieces [by a wild beast], he shall bring it as evidence;⁷⁹ he need not make restitution for the torn animal.*

Exod 22:10-13 [Hebrew 22:9-12]

The Book of the Covenant now deals with the case of death, injury, or loss of an animal entrusted to a neighbour for safekeeping. As in the case of inanimate property, the central issue is to determine whether or not the keeper is to be held responsible for the incident. Three possibilities are provided for.

First, if the animal dies, or is injured, or is taken captive, and the keeper has done nothing to harm it but has no witnesses who saw the incident, then he is to take an oath of innocence and be freed from responsibility for the loss (vv. 10-11). In this case it is not required that he be brought 'before God' (to the priests in the sanctuary), though witnesses would presumably be required for the oath. A guilty person would not lightly take an oath swearing his innocence in a society where the judgement of God was taken very seriously.⁸⁰

Second, if the animal has been stolen, the keeper is to make restitution to the owner (v. 12). This could be referring either to a thief stealing the animal from the house where it was in safekeeping or the keeper himself stealing it.⁸¹ The fact that simple restitution is required suggests the former to be correct, since multiple restitution would be expected if the keeper were guilty of theft (cf. vv. 7-9).

The distinction between the capture of an animal referred to in vv. 10-11 (in which case the owner bears the loss, so long as the keeper swears his innocence) and the theft referred to in v. 12 (in which case the keeper bears the loss) is not entirely clear. Probably the former is concerned with an en-

---

78. The word 'him' is ambiguous and could refer to either the keeper (in which case the thief is a third party, so NIV; REB; TB) or the owner (in which case the keeper himself is the thief, so NAB). NRSV and TEV omit 'from him', leaving the ambiguity.

79. This translation assumes the word עֵד to be the noun *'ēd* (as in MT), meaning 'witness' (cf. Exod 20:16; 23:1) and equivalent to 'evidence' in the present context (so NIV; NRSV; REB; TEV). LXX and Vulgate assume it to be the preposition *'ad*, meaning 'to', so the sentence becomes: 'he shall bring him [i.e. the owner] to the torn animal, and he need not make restitution'. Fensham (1962a) argues tentatively for the originality of the latter reading, but although it makes good sense — perhaps better than the Hebrew — MT is perfectly intelligible and there is insufficient textual evidence for emending it (cf. le Déaut 1972).

80. On oaths, see Price (1929); Horst (1957); Lehmann (1969).

81. Cf. n. 78.

emy raid (cf. 1 Chr 5:21; 2 Chr 14:15; Job 1:15, 17), which could not reasonably be prevented, whereas the latter is ordinary theft made possible by lack of security or negligence.[82]

Third, if the animal has been killed by a wild beast, the keeper is to bring the remains as evidence and is then free of liability for the loss (v. 13; cf. Amos 3:12). There is no need for restitution in this case, as also stipulated by the Laws of Hammurabi concerning lion attacks on rented animals or sheep in the care of a shepherd (§§244, 266). In the light of this, Laban's terms for Jacob's care of his flocks — making Jacob bear the loss of sheep and goats killed by wild beasts — were harsher than the requirements of both Mesopotamian and biblical law (Gen 31:38-39). Likewise, David's prowess as a shepherd, rescuing sheep from lions and bears, is all the more notable (1 Sam 17:34-35).

Borrowed or Rented Animals

When someone borrows [an animal] from his neighbour and it is injured or dies, while its owner is not present, he shall make full restitution. [But] if its owner is present, he need not make restitution; [and] if it is rented, [the loss] is covered by its rental charge.[83]

Exod 22:14-15 [Hebrew 22:13-14]

Finally, the law mentions briefly the injury or death of an animal borrowed or rented from a neighbour, with three rules:

- If the owner is not present at the time of the incident, the borrower is responsible for making restitution to the owner (v. 14).

---

82. Cf. Cassuto (1951); Sprinkle (1994: 151); Houtman (1996).

83. Alternative interpretations of the final clause are possible if שכיר ('hired, rented') is understood to refer to the borrower rather than the animal (cf. Exod 12:45; Lev 19:13). On this basis the text could be translated: 'if he is [a] hired [worker], [the loss] will come out of his hire' (i.e. will be deducted from his wages, so Geiger 1857: 191-92; cf. Cole 1973; Sarna 1991) or 'if he is [a] hired [worker], [the loss] is covered by his hire' (i.e. the risk is included in the agreed wages; cf. Crüsemann 1992: 165). Yet another interpretation is proposed by Lipiński (1992: 132-33), that שכיר refers to the owner of the animal who accompanies it as the hired driver (cf. LE §3; CH §271). Any of these is grammatically possible, but it is more likely in the context that the word refers to the animal (Driver and Miles 1952; Childs 1974: 449; Durham 1987; Houtman 1996; Propp 2006).

- If the owner is present, the owner bears the loss (v. 15a).
- If the animal is rented, rather than borrowed, the owner bears the loss (v. 15b).

Unlike the rule for safekeeping of animals (vv. 10-11), where no restitution is required so long as the keeper takes an oath of innocence before the Lord, the rule for borrowing does require the keeper to make restitution (v. 14). The difference is probably because safekeeping is for the benefit of the owner, whereas borrowing is a favour granted by the owner, and so a greater degree of responsibility is expected of the borrower than the keeper. 'Since he has full use of the animal without any payment, he also has full responsibility'.[84]

If, however, the owner is present, then it is assumed that he will be in charge of the situation and he is considered responsible in the case of accident. Also, if the animal is rented rather than simply borrowed, the rental charge is calculated to allow for the element of risk and the owner bears the loss in the case of death or injury. The last clause could mean either that the owner receives payment for the entire period agreed for rental of the animal[85] or simply payment up to the incident in question.[86] If the former is correct, then the loss is shared between the two parties, whereas in the latter case the loss would be entirely that of the owner.

c. Conclusion

The Decalogue, Holiness Code, and Deuteronomic Laws do not contain any legislation on the care of other people's property, and the only reference in biblical law outside the Book of the Covenant is in Lev 6:2-7, a passage already discussed above because it also deals with theft.[87] Here it is stipulated that someone who deceives a neighbour about property deposited with him for safekeeping, by swearing falsely about it, must return the neighbour's property plus an additional 20 percent of its value and also make a guilt offering to the Lord. The penalty is exactly the same as for theft, because it is of course theft, done in a roundabout way.

---

84. Paul (1970: 94 n. 4).
85. Ehrlich (1908: 354).
86. Cassuto (1951); Sprinkle (1994: 155).
87. Ch. 2.1.d.

To sum up, there are four main categories of care for other people's property in ancient Near Eastern and biblical law:

- safekeeping — mentioned in the Laws of Eshnunna and Hammurabi, and the Book of the Covenant
- borrowing — only in the Book of the Covenant[88]
- rental (animals, boats, fields) — extensive coverage in ancient Near Eastern law but only brief mention in the Bible
- care of property in the course of employment — only in ancient Near Eastern law

None of the law collections is comprehensive in its coverage, but the materials available give a fairly clear picture of the division of responsibility in the case of loss or damage to such property.

In most cases the same principles apply for safekeeping, borrowing, rental, and employment. The basic rule is that a person who cares for property — whether it is an animal, boat, field, or inanimate object — is responsible for loss or damage. The following exceptions are noted:

- In the case of burglary in a house where property has been deposited for safekeeping and the thief cannot be found, the keeper may be freed from responsibility (LE §37; Exod 22:7-9, though cf. v. 12), unless lack of security in the house provided easy access for the thief (CH §125).
- In the case of an animal being killed by a wild beast, the keeper is not held responsible (LRO §§7-9; CH §§244, 266; SLHF §6:16-22, 32-36; Exod 22:13; though HL §75 differs on this point).
- In the case of circumstances beyond the keeper's control, such as the sudden death of an animal (CH §249; HL §75; cf. Exod 22:10-11), or an epidemic (CH §266), or an enemy raid (Exod 22:10-11), the keeper may be freed from responsibility.
- In the case of storm or flood damage to unharvested fields, the owner and cultivator share the loss equally (CH §46).
- In the case of injury or death of a borrowed animal where the owner is present, the owner bears the loss (Exod 22:15a).
- In the case of injury or death of a rented animal, the owner bears the loss (Exod 22:15b).

---

88. HL §§74, 75, and 77 could refer to borrowing or rental, but the latter is more likely in the context (see n. 55).

Generally, simple restitution is required, though double restitution applies in the case of deliberate wrongdoing. If a keeper attempts to deceive an owner by denying he has received property for safekeeping or an owner falsely claims that his property has been misappropriated, this is equivalent to theft and is punished by double restitution (CH §§124, 126; Exod 22:9).[89] In the case of a house break-in facilitated by the negligence of the guard, the guard is to be put to death (LE §60).

In most respects the biblical laws on care of others' property are consistent with those found elsewhere in the ancient Near East, though the specific exceptions to the basic rule differ to some extent and the lack of exact parallels means we cannot compare all the details. The matter of renting boats would not have concerned landlubbers like the Israelites, nor was renting land part of their socio-economic system. While there are no laws concerning terms of employment in the Old Testament, the principle of responsibility for goods entrusted to an employee is clear in the examples of Jacob and David mentioned above,[90] though it is unlikely that a guard whose negligence allowed a break-in would have been executed.

The Laws of Hammurabi specifically require witnesses and a contract to bring a successful claim for loss (§§122-23), whereas according to Exod 22:10-11 an owner must accept an oath of innocence with respect to the injury or loss of an animal in safekeeping in the absence of witnesses to prove what happened. Although witnesses and contracts are not explicitly mentioned in the other laws on care of property, that does not mean such proof was considered unnecessary. As a basic principle of justice, the importance of witnesses is made very clear in the Bible.[91] The apocryphal story of Tobit recounts the use of a contract for a deposit of ten silver talents (Tobit 1:14; 4:1, 20; 5:1-3; 9:3-7).

The most significant difference is that the ancient Near Eastern laws make detailed provision for *renting*, whereas the parallel clauses in the Book of the Covenant are concerned with *borrowing*. There is no mention of borrowing in the ancient Near Eastern laws, while the only biblical mention of renting is a brief supplement to the law on borrowing (Exod 22:15b). It is noteworthy that this supplement makes the owner bear the

---

89. The rules in Lev 6:2-7 are rather different. The Laws of Hammurabi also stipulate double restitution in the case of loss of grain (§120), perhaps because grain cannot be easily or quickly stolen without the knowledge of the keeper, so that — if this should happen — the keeper is assumed to have connived at the offence.
90. Ch. 3.3.b.
91. See below, 8.1.

loss if a rented animal is injured or dies, whereas according to other ancient Near Eastern laws the renter bears the loss unless the circumstances are completely outside his control. So the biblical law tends to favour the poor who rent rather than the rich who own. The facts that the rental terms are weighted against the owner, and that the emphasis is on borrowing rather than renting, suggest that the very idea of rental was frowned on in Israel. It seems that here we have an Israelite distinctive, whereby a member of the covenant community is expected to help another member in need by lending an animal without making a profit, just as he or she is expected to lend money without interest to a needy person.[92] The focus of the ancient Near Eastern laws is commerce (rental); the biblical laws emphasise compassion (borrowing). The former are more concerned with protecting the rights of owners, whereas the latter are more concerned with supplying the needs of those without property.

---

92. See below, 10.1.

Chapter 4

ANCESTRAL LAND

In almost all societies, the most important kind of property is land. It may be owned communally or individually, and transfer of ownership may take place by inheritance, sale, gift, or seizure. The details vary between agricultural and industrial economies, between rural and urban areas, but the essence is the same: land is the key to security and prosperity. Even in jungles and deserts, where boundaries are invisible and there is no trading in real estate, inhabitants have tacit agreements concerning rights to hunt and sources of water.

Ancient Israel was no exception to this general principle, but it did have a distinctive view of landed property. According to the promises of Genesis (e.g. 12:1-9; 15:7-21; 28:13-15) and the preaching of Deuteronomy (e.g. 1:8, 21, 25; 7:12-16; 8:1-10; 28:1-14), the land of Canaan was God's gift to the descendants of Abraham. This is referred to repeatedly in the various law-collections (e.g. Exod 20:12; 23:20-26; Lev 20:24; 25:2, 38; 26:3-12; Deut 5:16; 12:1, 8-12; 15:4-6; 26:1-3) and is implemented in practical terms by the division of the promised land among the tribes and clans of Israel (Numbers 26; 32–36; Josh 1:2-6; 13–21). It is not simply a theological issue concerning the origin of the land, whereby Old Testament theology might be compared with the myths and traditions of other nations.[1] It is also an

---

1. There are one or two texts which suggest that other ancient Near Eastern nations may have believed their land to be divinely given, e.g. "Udmu was given of 'Ilu, [it is] a present of the father of mankind' in the Kirta Epic (*COS*: 1.102, p. 335; *CTA*: 14 iii 135-36). The Moabite Stone describes Moab as the land belonging to Kemosh (line 5) and implies that he determines who lives there, though does not actually say he gave it to the Moabites (*COS*:

economic issue, because it involves the principle of inalienability of ancestral land (e.g. 1 Kgs 21:3) and the responsibility of redeeming land which has been unavoidably sold (e.g. Ruth 4:1-9; Jer 32:7-10), in contrast to attitudes in other ancient Near Eastern nations where land was treated as a saleable commodity.

Ephron the Hittite, for example, sells burial land to Abraham (Genesis 23), the sons of Hamor sell a plot of land near Shechem to Jacob on which he erects an altar (Gen 33:18-20), Araunah the Jebusite sells his threshing floor to David (2 Sam 24:18-25), and Shemer sells the hill of Samaria to Omri (1 Kgs 16:24). Sale of land is no problem to these non-Israelites, because it is understood simply as a commercial transaction. However, there is no record in the Old Testament of any Israelite selling land outside his extended family, and Naboth refuses to do so even at the demand of the king (1 Kgs 21:1-4). Archaeological evidence confirms this contrast, with records of the buying and selling of land in Canaan and other parts of the ancient Near East, but none where the parties involved are Israelite.[2] When the Shunammite woman leaves the country because of Elisha's prediction of famine, she does not sell her land but returns seven years later to reclaim it together with the harvests yielded in her absence (2 Kgs 8:1-6; cf. Naomi in the book of Ruth).

This understanding of ancestral land is at the heart of the Old Testament law of Jubilee and is also the basis for the law concerning boundary marks and one of the clauses in the law on military service — the three matters that will be covered in this chapter.[3]

4.1 Jubilee

According to Old Testament law, every seventh day was a sabbath and every seventh year a sabbatical, as will be discussed below.[4] In addition, after

---

2:23). However, it appears that the idea of land as a divine grant was much less prominent in the surrounding nations than in Israel (Block 2000: 93-111).

2. Bess (1963: 2-21); Postgate (1976: 22-25); Wright (1990: 56). For examples of land sales at Ugarit, see COS (3:103-6); for Mesopotamia, see COS (3:115, 133C).

3. On the Old Testament understanding of land, see von Rad (1943); Diepold (1972); Davies (1974); von Waldow (1974); Ohler (1979); Strecker (1983); Gnuse (1985b: 53-85); Davies (1989); Wright (1990: 1-131; 2004a: 76-99); Janzen (1992); Weinfeld (1993); Habel (1995b); Joosten (1996: 137-92); Johnston (2000); Brueggemann (2002); McKeown (2003).

4. See below, 9.1; 11.1; cf. 6.1; 10.3.

seven cycles of seven years there was to be a jubilee year. I will consider the jubilee at this point, before the other holy days and years, because of its particular focus on the restoration of alienated ancestral land to its original owner. But first, it will be helpful to set it against its ancient Near Eastern background.

a. Ancient Near East

The only ancient Near Eastern law which is comparable to any part of the Old Testament law of jubilee is found in the Laws of Eshnunna:

> If a man becomes impoverished and then sells his house, whenever the buyer offers it for sale, the owner of the house shall have the right to redeem it. (§39)

This shows some concern for the plight of someone who is forced to sell his house and limits the freedom of the buyer in terms of selling it on to others, but there is no guarantee that the seller will ever get his property back unless the buyer chooses to put it on the market and the original owner has the resources at that point to redeem it. It is not stated whether the right of redemption applies only when the property is first offered for sale or continues through successive purchasers if the original owner is unable to redeem his property at that time. Neither is it clear whether the price of redemption is determined by the original sale, which might well be at a discounted rate in view of the seller's difficulty, or the current market value. These alternative possibilities are significantly different in the extent to which they give real help to an impoverished person who wishes to reclaim his property. Assuming the law was intended as a serious measure to alleviate poverty, it is likely that the owner had a continuing right to redeem the house, because otherwise it would be possible to arrange a fictive sale immediately after the first one with the sole purpose of denying the original owner the right of redemption. It also seems likely that the original sale price would apply at the time of redemption, because otherwise the law would offer the original owner little advantage over anyone else who might wish to purchase the house at the current market value when it was offered for sale.[5]

---

5. For further discussion of these issues, see Westbrook (1985b); Yaron (1988: 232-34).

The right of redemption is mentioned in a text from the Old Babylonian archive at Tutub (modern Khafajah, in Iraq):

> Whenever he [Kalarum] will acquire money of his own, he may redeem the field.[6]

Another Babylonian text records the case of Arad-Sin, who made the following complaint in court:

> The field, which I acquired from my father's house, have Ibku-Sala and his brother, the sons of Šamaš-Nasir, sold for money to the merchant Ibni-Ramman.[7]

The text then recounts the decision of the judges that the field be restored to Arad-Sin. This might mean that the court recognised the right of a descendant to regain possession of family land which had been sold to someone else, although it could simply be a case of fraudulent sale of land by someone who did not own it. The possibility of property being redeemed appears to underlie a number of Babylonian sale documents which specifically exclude the seller or his family from making future claims on sold property.[8]

Apart from the question of redemption, there is a Mesopotamian parallel to the idea of jubilee in the royal decrees for the establishment of *andurāru* ('freedom, liberation') and *mīšaru* ('justice, equity'), which were proclaimed from time to time by kings who wanted to show favour to their people, particularly on accession to the throne.[9] These decrees included such measures as remission of debts, liberation of slaves, return of lands and houses to their rightful owners, and amnesty for prisoners. I discuss them further below, in the section on debt relief (10.3.a).

An even older text which reflects a concern for the rights of ordinary citizens to own land, and thus has some connection to the idea of Jubilee, is the twenty-fourth-century Reforms of Uru-inimgina.[10] It refers to the

---

6. Text no. 82. See Harris (1955: 96-97); cf. Yaron (1988: 233-34).

7. Trans. by Leggett (1974: 65-66, 319) from the text originally published by Meissner (1893).

8. Clay (1938: 25); Leggett (1974: 66-67).

9. Cf. Neufeld (1958); Lemche (1976); Weinfeld (1990); Hudson (1999); Simonetti (2000); Milgrom (2001: 2167-69, 2241-42); Bergsma (2007: 20-26).

10. The last king in the first dynasty of Lagash, one of the city-states of ancient Sumer, who is also known as Uru-kagina and ruled ca. 2351-42 B.C. (*COS*: 2.152, p. 407). I have used

accumulation of large tracts of land in the hands of a privileged few, specifically rulers together with their wives and children:

> The ruler's estate and ruler's fields, the estate of the woman's organization and fields of the woman's organization, and the children's estate and children's fields all abutted one another.

As a measure to limit the growth of such large estates, Uru-inimgina promulgates an ordinance giving individuals the right to refuse the sale of land if they feel the proposed terms are unfair:

> When the house of an aristocrat adjoins the house of a king's retainer,[11] and the aristocrat says to him, 'I want to buy it from you'; whether he lets him buy it from him, having said to him, 'Pay me the price I want! My house is a large container — fill it with barley for me!' or whether he does not let him buy it from him, that aristocrat must not strike at him in anger.[12]

b. Holiness Code

The Old Testament law of jubilee is found in Leviticus 25, interspersed with laws concerning the sabbatical year (vv. 1-7, 18-22) and loans (vv. 35-38).[13] First, three main subjects are dealt with:

- the fiftieth year — a holy jubilee (vv. 8-12)
- the great return and its implications for land prices (vv. 13-17)
- the basic principle of land ownership (vv. 23-24)

Then there is a detailed treatment of sale and redemption, in three paragraphs covering:

---

the translation of Cooper (1986: 71-72) since *COS* does not include the sections relevant to the present discussion. For another translation, together with commentary, see Kramer (1963: 80-83, 317-22).

11. Sumerian *shublugal*, a free worker given a field by the king or a master in compensation for labour (Cooper 1986: 72). Cooper transliterates the Sumerian word without translation, but I have followed Kramer (1963: 319) by translating it as 'king's retainer'.

12. For other possible ancient Near Eastern antecedents to the jubilee legislation, see Bergsma (2007: 27-36).

13. On the sabbatical year, see below, 9.1; on loans, see 10.1.

- general principles (vv. 25-28)
- city houses (vv. 29-31)
- Levite cities (vv. 32-34)

Finally, the jubilee is referred to in connection with two special cases:

- slaves and bonded labourers (vv. 39-43, 47-55)
- land dedicated to the LORD (Lev. 27:16-24)

It is possible to discern a three-stage descent into poverty in these texts.[14] First, a farmer in difficulty is forced to sell part of his land to cover his debts and provide food for his family (vv. 25-28). Second, things get worse and the farmer is helped by a more wealthy Israelite who gives him interest-free loans, probably with his remaining land as security so that he effectively becomes a tenant farmer under the authority of his creditor (vv. 35-38). Third, the tenant can neither repay his loans nor support his household and eventually becomes a bonded labourer in the household of his creditor (vv. 39-43). A variant of the third stage is if he becomes a bonded labourer with a resident alien rather than a fellow Israelite (vv. 47-55). At each stage of the process, the laws seek to alleviate the suffering of the impoverished farmer and eventually to ensure the restoration of his ancestral land.[15]

The Fiftieth Year — A Holy Jubilee

You shall count for yourself seven weeks of years, seven years seven times, so that the days of the seven weeks of years give you forty-nine years. Then you shall send out [people to blow] the trumpet loudly in the seventh month, on the tenth of the month; on the Day of Atonement, you shall send out [people to blow] the trumpet in all your land. And so you shall hallow the fiftieth year, and you shall proclaim freedom in the land for all its inhabitants; it shall be a jubilee for you

---

14. Speiser (1960: 36-39); Japhet (1978: 75); Wright (1990: 121-23); Chirichigno (1993: 323-28); Milgrom (2001: 2191-93; 2004: 299-302); cf. Schenker (1998); Bergsma (2007: 84).

15. A similar process of impoverishment in a different context is recounted in the story of Joseph in Egypt (Gen 47:13-26). Carmichael (1999; 2006: 122-38) interprets the whole idea of the jubilee cycle as a deliberate contrast to the Egyptian plan for famine relief which resulted in the enslavement of the people to the pharaoh.

[all]: you shall return each one to his property, and each one to his clan[16] *you shall return.*[17] *That fiftieth year shall be a jubilee for you [all]: you shall not sow, and you shall not reap the after-growth, and you shall not harvest the unpruned vines. For it is a jubilee, it shall be holy to you; from the field you shall eat its produce [directly].*

Lev 25:8-12

Two distinctive words are used in this text, namely 'freedom' (דרור) and 'jubilee' (יבל). The first word is related to *andurāru* ('freedom, liberation') in Akkadian and in the Old Testament means 'freedom' or 'liberation', particularly in the context of the jubilee year (v. 10; cf. Isa 61:1; Jer 34:8; Ezek 46:17).[18] The second word is generally thought to originate from the sheep's horn trumpet that was sounded to announce the jubilee year, on the Day of Atonement (v. 9).[19]

After seven cycles of seven years (v. 8), the fiftieth year is designated as a sort of 'supersabbatical' (v. 10). In that year freedom is to be proclaimed for all inhabitants of the land,[20] and land which has changed hands is to be

---

16. Gottwald (1979: 315) points out that in anthropological terminology 'clan' commonly refers to an exogamous group with communal land ownership, quite unlike the Israelite משפחה, and suggests the translation 'protective association of extended families'. Wright (1990: 48-49), followed by Milgrom (2001: 2175), accepts Gottwald's point but proposes 'kin group' as a more succinct translation. Andersen (1969) suggests 'phratry'. However, as Wright himself agrees, the word 'clan' is a convenient shorthand to denote the intermediate level in Israelite social structure between 'tribe' and 'family'. (In fact all three terms had distinctive meanings in ancient Israel, not synonymous with their modern equivalents.)

17. The Hebrew text repeats 'you shall return', creating a chiastic (symmetrical) structure for this last clause. TEV understands the two elements of the clause to refer respectively to restoration of land and freedom for slaves: 'all property that has been sold shall be restored to the original owner or his descendants, and anyone who has been sold as a slave shall return to his family'.

18. For further discussion, see North (1975); Olivier (1997a); Lefebvre (2003: 98-100).

19. In fact, the word שופר is used for the trumpet in Lev 25:9 rather than יבל, but the two words seem to be synonymous. Cf. Exod 19:13; Josh 6:4-13; Joel 2:1, 15. An alternative etymology is proposed by North (1980), who links it with the verb יבל ('lead back, lead forth', Isa 55:12; Jer 31:9). This suggestion is supported by the translation of יבל in LXX as αφεσις ('liberation'), and Josephus also gives its meaning as 'freedom'. In any case, whatever its etymology, the primary reference of יבל here is to the Israelite observance of the fiftieth year (v. 10).

20. This does not include foreign slaves purchased on the slave market (vv. 44-46, on which see below, 5.1). In contrast to the sabbath day and sabbatical year, which apply to everyone without exception, the jubilee year is specifically for the people of Israel (cf. 'for you' and 'to you' in vv. 11-12).

returned to its original owner. As in the sabbatical year, no sowing and reaping is to take place during the jubilee year, though people are free to glean and eat what grows of itself (vv. 11-12). The distinctive characteristic of the jubilee, however, is the restoration of land to the owner designated by God when Israel took possession of the promised land.[21]

This regulation apparently means that two sabbatical years are to be observed in succession (the 49th and 50th years), which raises the question of whether it would be feasible for the land to remain unplanted for two successive years. One suggestion is that the jubilee year is in fact the forty-ninth year, which by inclusive reckoning from one jubilee to the next is called the fiftieth year.[22] Inclusive reckoning, which counts the first and last element in a period of time, was certainly common in ancient Israel (e.g. Lev 23:15-16, where the seven-week period between Passover and Pentecost is described as fifty days; John 20:26, where 'eight days' is the inclusive reckoning for a week) and is found in some modern languages too (e.g. a fortnight in French is *quinze jours,* 'fifteen days').

Another suggestion is that the fiftieth year is an intercalary 'year', inserted in the calendar to harmonise the lunar year with the solar year, and its length is just forty-nine days (cf. the 'seven weeks' of v. 8).[23] Its function would be comparable to the additional day inserted every leap year in the Julian calendar. This interpretation might be supported by the fact that the jubilee begins on the tenth day of the seventh month (v. 9), not at the beginning of the year, though there are other possible reasons for that.[24]

On the other hand, Milgrom (2001: 2248-51) adduces agricultural evidence to argue that there would be no problem in principle about leaving the land fallow for two years, and the real difficulty in implementing the law would be resistance by the rich and powerful whose interests would be adversely affected. (There might well be resistance also from ordinary peo-

---

21. Schaeffer (1922: 68-98); Ginzberg (1932: 369-74).

22. Advocates of this view include Kugler (1922: 17-22); North (1954a: 109-34); Noth (1962); van Selms (1976); Hartley (1992: 434-36); Chirichigno (1993: 317-21); Paterson (1994); and Lefebvre (2003: 154-66).

23. E.g. Zeitlin (1962: 216-18); Hoenig (1969); Wenham (1979).

24. Milgrom (2001: 2164-65). Yet another suggestion is made by Kaufman (1984: 284 n. 1), who thinks the jubilee was not a year but a proclamation, made at the beginning of the seventh sabbatical year. And Gnuse (1985a: 47) mentions the possibility that the jubilee was a liturgical year, beginning with the seventh month of the seventh sabbatical year and overlapping with the following year (which was also the first of the new jubilee cycle).

ple who were struggling to make ends meet and were unable to store up food in advance to provide for the fallow years.) Moreover, even though there is evidence that regular fallow years would have been beneficial for agriculture in Palestine, perhaps as often as every other year,[25] sabbatical rest is not presented in the laws as an agricultural measure. Rather, the significance of the sabbatical and jubilee years is primarily in the theological realm, and those who keep the law are assured that God will provide for their needs (vv. 18-22). If 2 Kings 19:29 (= Isa 37:30) is referring to a jubilee year, it would support the view that the jubilee was intended to be observed separately from the seventh sabbatical year.

If the jubilee is the year after the seventh sabbatical, the question arises whether this would make a fifty-year cycle ([7x7]+1) or whether the jubilee is treated as the first year of a new cycle so that the next sabbatical occurs six years later, making a forty-nine-year cycle from one jubilee to the next (fifty years by inclusive reckoning).[26] The latter seems more likely and would mean that the seven-year cycle of sabbatical years is not disrupted, just as the weekly cycle of sabbaths is not disrupted by other holidays.[27] In any case, even if the method of reckoning is uncertain, there is no lack of clarity about the social measures which are to be taken in the jubilee year nor about its theological meaning.[28]

---

25. Hopkins (1985: 200-202).

26. The rabbis generally understood it to be a fifty-year cycle, though a forty-nine-year cycle was suggested by Rabbi Judah (Wacholder 1973: 154; North 2000: 26; Milgrom 2001: 2250). Recently Kawashima (2003) has argued for the former and Bergsma (2005; 2007: 88-91) for the latter.

27. Support for this may be derived from the forty-nine-year cycles attested at Qumran and in the *Testament of Levi* (cf. Beckwith 1980; 1996: 218-34; Glessmer 1991) and the evidence for seven-year cycles (but not fifty-year cycles) in the Second Temple and rabbinic periods (Wacholder 1973).

28. I do not discuss here the dating of the jubilee legislation. Many scholars believe it to come from Israel's early period, probably before the monarchy (e.g. Schaeffer 1922: 93-95; Jirku 1929: 178; van der Ploeg 1951: 169-71; Stein 1953: 164; North 1954a: 191-212; Lewy 1958; Wenham 1979: 318; Hartley 1992: 427-30; Wright 1992a: 1028; Fager 1993: 25-34; Weinfeld 1995: 177; Bergsma 2007: 53-79), though some date it to the eighth century (Knohl 1995: 204-18; Milgrom 2001: 2241-45) and others towards the end of the Old Testament period (e.g. Ginzberg 1932: 381; de Vaux 1961: 176-77; Westbrook 1971a: 38-52, 55-57; Gnuse 1985a; Robinson 1991; Amit 1992: 55-59; Lefebvre 2003: 331-32). Neufeld (1958) considers the idea to be of great antiquity (pre-Israelite) but sees the specific context in an attempt to revive this ancient idea after the division of the monarchy as an expression of the nomadic ideal supported by the prophets.

The Great Return and Its Implications for Land Prices

In this year of jubilee, you shall return, each one to his property. And when you sell[29] [land][30] to your neighbour, or buy from your neighbour, do not oppress[31] one another. According to the number of years since the jubilee, you shall buy [land] from your neighbour; according to the number of years [remaining] for produce, he shall sell to you. If there are many years, you shall increase its price, but if there are few years, you shall reduce its price; for it is the number of crops produced that he is selling you. You shall not oppress one another, but fear your God; for I am the LORD your God.

Lev 25:13-17

The principle that property which has changed hands is to return to its original owner in the jubilee year is repeated in v. 13 and supplemented by an explanation of the implications of this law for land prices during the intervening years (vv. 15-16). It effectively means that land in ancient Israel was not really sold at all, but simply leased until the jubilee year. There is no word in Biblical Hebrew to denote 'leasing' as distinct from 'buying' and 'selling', but the context shows clearly that this is what is intended.[32] The basis for calculating the value of the land is the amount of produce expected rather than simply its area, since it is really a series of crops which are bought rather than the land itself.

---

29. On the translation of מכר as 'sell' and קנה as 'buy', see below, n. 32.

30. Lit. 'sell a sale', but in the context it is clear that sale of land is intended, not other items.

31. The hiphil of ינה generally means 'oppress' (BDB; *HALOT*; *DCH*), but it could also be translated 'cheat' (NRSV), 'take advantage of' (NIV), 'exploit' (REB), or 'deal unfairly [with]' (TEV) in this context.

32. In fact, the Hebrew words קנה ('buy') and מכר ('sell') are quite broad in meaning, respectively covering the ideas of 'acquire, buy, redeem' and 'deliver, hand over, transfer, sell' (*DCH* 5:271-73; Falk 1967; Lipiński 1982; 1984; 1990). The transfer of ownership does not always involve monetary compensation (e.g. 1 Sam 12:9; 1 Kgs 21:20, 25; Ruth 4:10; Prov 4:5; 23:23; Isa 11:11). If the meaning 'buy' or 'sell' is intended, the verb is often supplemented by the explanation 'for money/silver' (e.g. Gen 17:12; Exod 12:44; Lev 22:11; Deut 21:14; Amos 2:6). The transfer of ownership may be temporary or permanent, so the concept of leasing is also included. My translation of the text here is deliberately literal, aiming to use consistent English equivalents for Hebrew words wherever possible. While קנה could generally be translated 'acquire', there is no one English equivalent to מכר that will fit all the laws. So I have retained the conventional translations 'buy' and 'sell' and explained the nuances of meaning in the notes or text as necessary.

The members of the covenant community are twice forbidden to oppress each other in this matter by taking advantage of a neighbour's difficulties for personal benefit (vv. 14, 17). On the contrary, they should fear God, a contrast which makes a close link between fear of God and care for the poor (cf. Lev 19:14). To prohibit taking advantage of each other does not of course give Israelites permission to take advantage of those outside the community, for the present context is only concerned with the community issue of inherited land. The verb 'oppress' (ינה) is used in other laws and prophetic texts with reference to oppression and exploitation of anyone who is poor and needy, including orphans, widows, resident aliens, and fugitive slaves (Exod 22:21; Lev 19:33; Deut 23:16; Jer 22:3; Ezek 18:7, 12, 16; 22:7, 29; 45:8; 46:18).

The Basic Principle of Land Ownership

The land shall not be sold in perpetuity,[33] for the land is mine; you are [like] resident aliens or tenants[34] with me. And throughout the land [which] you [hold as] property, you shall provide for redemption of land [which is sold].

Lev 25:23-24

Here we come to the heart of the matter. God himself asserts his claim as ultimate owner of the land occupied by Israel (v. 23; cf. Josh 22:19; 1 Kgs 8:36; 2 Chr 7:20; Ps 10:16; 85:1; Isa 14:2, 25; Jer 2:7; 16:18; Ezek 36:5, 20; Hos 9:3; Joel 1:6; 2:18).[35] His gift of the land is not an unconditional grant, but more like a long-term lease or loan. This means that the people of Israel are like tenants or stewards, who are free to live and work in the land but do not have abso-

---

33. Lit. 'unto annihilation'. The word is generally understood to mean 'in perpetuity' (RSV) or 'permanently' (NIV; cf. TEV), though Hogg (1926) renders it 'without right of redemption'. A similar formula is used in legal documents from Ugarit, referring to a transfer made in perpetuity, e.g. *PRU* 3 (nos. 15.136, 16.131, 16.137, 16.246); the first is also in *COS* (3.109). This was first pointed out by Rabinowitz (1958) and developed further by Loretz (1962); cf. Huehnergard (1987: 171-72).

34. Or 'temporary residents'. The two nouns may be understood as a hendiadys in this verse, which Milgrom (2001: 2187) translates simply as 'resident aliens'. For further discussion, see below, 7.1.b.

35. God is, of course, owner of the whole earth, according to Old Testament theology (Exod 19:5; Deut 10:14; Ps 24:1; 50:12), and has also apportioned land to other nations (Deut 32:8), but the present text focuses simply on his ownership of this particular land.

lute rights of disposal over it (cf. 1 Chr 29:15; Ps 39:12; 61:4; Heb 11:13). The phrase 'with me' may point to God as protector of those who live on his land, affirming the security of the Israelites and their divinely given right to a share in the land.[36] Nevertheless, the conditional nature of the land grant is made explicit by the threat of expulsion if Israel does not keep God's laws (Lev 18:24-30; 20:22-23; 26:14-39; cf. Josh 23:14-16).

The word 'property' (אחזה) is used repeatedly in Leviticus 25 (vv. 10, 13, 24-25, 27-28, 32-34, 41, 45-46). On the one hand, it is associated with God's ownership of the land (Josh 22:19) and, on the other, with his gift to the descendants of Abraham (Gen 17:8). Its meaning overlaps with 'inheritance' (נחלה), and in some texts the two words are used interchangeably (e.g. Num 32:5, 18, 19, 20; 35:8; cf. Ezek 44:28).[37] In other texts there may be a distinction, especially between the Holiness Code and Deuteronomic Laws: in the former, 'property' denotes Israel's conditional holding of the land, whose true owner is God; in the latter, 'inheritance' denotes a possession, given by God to Israel.[38] Nevertheless, Deuteronomy — like Leviticus — reminds Israel that continued enjoyment of the blessings of the promised land is conditional on faithfulness to the God who gives it to them as an inheritance and warns them graphically that unfaithfulness will lead to the gift being revoked (e.g. Deut 8:11-20; 28:15-68).[39]

This view of land has a parallel in the Middle Assyrian period, when it seems all land belonged theoretically to the king, who conceded it to individual owners in return for their service *(ilku)* but received it back if a direct line of succession failed.[40] In the Nuzi tablets there is also a ban on the sale of patrimonial land, apparently based on a feudal system in which all land belonged to the king and was held as a grant or fief by his subjects. They had no right to transfer it to anyone other than a direct male relative, though it seems the law was regularly circumvented by the legal fiction of

---

36. Wright (1990: 64).

37. On these two terms, see Horst (1961); Gerleman (1977); Lipiński (1986b); Koopmans (1997); Wright (1997); Block (2000: 75-82); Lefebvre (2003: 100-2).

38. Milgrom (2001: 2171-73). On the Deuteronomic theology of the land, see Miller (1969).

39. Gerleman (1977) and Fager (1993: 89) argue that אחזה does not refer to the promised land as a whole but specifically to agricultural land and that the jubilee is therefore agrarian legislation concerning the source of food and basis of survival. If this is correct, it would explain why houses within the walled cities are not covered by the jubilee law. However, this distinction is doubtful (Milgrom 2001: 2171-73).

40. So Postgate (1971), who refers to MAL §§A45 and B6 as well as various other texts. The same applied to some but not all land at Ugarit (*COS*: 3.107-10, cf. 103-6).

'sale-adoption', in which real estate was negotiated by adopting a buyer as one's son.[41] So in Israel, Yhwh is king and thus owner of the land, and he grants his people the right to live and work there, but not to treat it as a saleable commodity.

If in exceptional circumstances ancestral land does have to be sold, provision must be made to ensure that such a sale is only a temporary measure, equivalent to a lease, and the land is in due course returned to its rightful [human] owner (v. 24). This is done by means of redemption, which is explained in the next three sections of the text.

Sale and Redemption: General Principles

When your brother[42] becomes poor,[43] and [has to] sell some of his property, his next-of-kin[44] shall come and redeem what his brother is selling.[45] Or if the man has no redeemer, but [later] prospers and finds sufficient means to redeem it, he shall calculate its value for the years [since it was sold], and refund the balance to the man to whom he sold [it]; then he may return to his property. But if he does not find sufficient means to recover it, what was sold shall remain in the

---

41. Steele (1943: 14-15); cf. Greenberg (1972). Further parallels to this understanding of land are suggested by Milgrom (2001), such as the status of sacred cities in Mesopotamia which were considered to be the property of their gods (p. 2187) and the principle in several parts of the ancient Near East that divine lands may not be sold (p. 2189).

42. I.e. a fellow-Israelite; cf. Lev 10:6; also Deut 22:1-4 (see above, ch. 2, n. 86). Cf. Lefebvre (2003: 179-83). An eighth-century bowl from Beth Shemesh is inscribed with the word אחך ('your brother'); Barkay (1991; 1992) suggests that it may have been intended to collect contributions for the support of the poor.

43. ימוך, an unusual word to describe poverty (used also in vv. 35, 39, 47; and elsewhere only in 27:8).

44. Lit. 'near redeemer'. The word אליו ('to him') probably refers to the nearness of the redeemer, in which case its meaning is included in the term 'next-of-kin', and this is understood by most translations (cf. Lev 21:2-3; Num 27:11). However, an alternative translation is possible if אליו is taken with the verb בא ('come'): 'his next-of-kin shall come to him' (cf. Buhl 1897: 738; 1899: 62).

45. The noun ממכר (lit. 'something which is sold') is often translated here as 'what [his brother] has sold' (e.g. NIV; NJB; NRSV; REB), but it could equally be 'what [his brother] is selling' or '... was going to sell' (Buhl 1897: 738; 1899: 62); this fits the context better, as will become clear in the discussion below. This is also supported by the verb ומכר earlier in the verse, which is a consecutive perfect and more naturally translated 'has to sell' than 'has sold'.

> hands of its purchaser, until the year of jubilee; in the jubilee it shall be released, and [the original owner] shall return to his property.
>
> Lev 25:25-28

Land which has to be sold because of financial difficulty should be redeemed by the closest member of the family (vv. 24-25), and if that does not happen the person who sells the land retains the right to redeem it himself later on if he becomes able to do so (vv. 26-27).[46] But if neither of these provisions succeeds in restoring the land, it must return to its original owner in the jubilee year (v. 28). An indication of the order of responsibility within the family for redeeming the property of a relative who has fallen on hard times is given later in the chapter, with reference to redemption from slavery: first a brother, second an uncle or cousin, then any blood relative in the clan (vv. 48-49). This order is virtually the same as that used to determine the right to inherit property in the absence of a son or daughter (Num 27:9-11).

There are two ways to interpret the first sentence of this law. Many translations (see n. 45) understand it to mean that in the case of hardship someone may sell their ancestral land to anyone who is willing to buy it, and it is then the responsibility of the next-of-kin to redeem the land as soon as possible, to keep it within the original owner's family. However, it can also be understood to mean, as implied by my translation above, that the next-of-kin is expected to come and buy the land directly from the impoverished relative. The latter is clearly the case in the example of land redemption reported in Jeremiah 32, where Jeremiah buys the land from his cousin and there is no prior sale to a third party. It is also supported by verses 26-27 of the present passage, which specify how the price of redemption is to be calculated if the original owner is later in a position to redeem sold land. This contrasts with verse 25, which does not mention such calculation, presumably because the redeemer buys the land directly and thus pays the full purchase price. Concerning Ruth 4, the other Old Testament example of land redemption, it is likely that Elimelech had sold the land before emigrating to Moab, since he left at a time of famine and would have needed any cash that could be realised to cover the expenses of the journey and to rent land or find other means of survival in a foreign country.[47] Apparently this sale

---

46. On redemption of land in ancient Israel, see Westbrook (1971c; 1985b); cf. Milgrom (1995).

47. Naomi clearly returns to Bethlehem as a poor widow rather than as a landowner, or

was made outside the family, and the narrative is concerned with how Naomi recovers it for the family with the help of Boaz.[48] In any case, the two interpretations of Leviticus 25:25 are not mutually exclusive, and it may be the law allows for both possibilities:[49]

- If possible, someone who has to sell his land will prefer to do so to a relative, and the next-of-kin has an obligation to buy if able to do so.
- If that is not possible, the land is sold to someone else who is willing to buy on the understanding that at any point it may be redeemed by the family.

Another question concerns the implications of redemption. Does land which has been redeemed return to its original owner immediately or become the property of the redeemer until the jubilee? Some scholars assume the former, since otherwise the impoverished person would be no better off than if his land was in the possession of any other buyer;[50] others argue for the latter, considering that the primary object of redemption is not to give aid but to ensure that ancestral land remains within the extended family.[51] In the first example mentioned above, it is explicitly stated that Jeremiah purchases the land of Hanamel for himself and keeps the title deeds (Jer 32:7-14), and there is no indication that he then returns the land to his cousin. In the

---

she would not have sent Ruth out to glean (Ruth 2:2; cf. 1:21). The main problem with this understanding is Ruth 4:3 (cf. v. 5a), which appears to say that Naomi is selling the land at this point, at least in many English translations (NIV; NJB; NRSV; REB; cf. TEV). In fact, the verb מכרה is a perfect form and could more accurately be translated 'has sold', which would fit with the land having been sold before the departure to Moab (Westbrook 1971c: 65-67; Brichto 1973: 14-15). It is still unclear why the text says that Naomi rather than Elimelech sold it, though Westbrook explains this in terms of the narrative technique of the passage. An alternative possibility is to understand מכרה here as Naomi's surrendering her right to redeem the land, which she is unable to do because of her poverty, and appealing to her dead husband's next-of-kin to do this for her (Gordis 1974: 252-56; Bush 1996: 199-215; cf. Schneider 1982).

48. There may be an extrabiblical parallel in a recently discovered ostracon containing the plea of a widow with no sons to recover land belonging to her late husband (*COS:* 3:44; Bordreuil, Israel, and Pardee 1996; 1998; Shanks 1997; Lindenberger 2003: 108-11; Davies 2004a: no. 99.008; 2005: 161-62; Dobbs-Allsopp et al. 2005: 567-73), but the authenticity of this inscription is doubtful (Eph'al and Naveh 1998; Rollston 2003: 145-47, 158-73, 183-84).

49. Cf. Rudolph (1962: 63-64).

50. E.g. Noth (1962); Leggett (1974: 92-95); Levine (1989); cf. Hartley (1992).

51. E.g. Pedersen (1920: 83-89); Daube (1956: 272-73); de Vaux (1961: 167); Wright (1990: 120-24); Milgrom (2001: 2195; 2004: 300); cf. Yaron (1960); Hubbard (1997).

second example, redemption of Elimelech's ancestral land is linked with marriage to Ruth and the continuation of Elimelech's line so that there will be an heir to the land (Ruth 4:3-12).[52] It is possible that, having redeemed the land, Boaz returns it to Naomi for her use, but verses 8-9 suggest rather that he keeps it himself, while no doubt ensuring that her needs are supplied. The fact that Boaz is obliged to give the first opportunity to buy the land to the nearer relative (cf. 3:12-13), who declines to do so only when he realises that the purchase includes marriage to Ruth, may also imply that the purchase is beneficial to the redeemer and not pure charity.

On the whole, it seems more likely that the redeemer would keep the title to the land until the jubilee, since otherwise there would be no incentive for him to make the purchase apart from care for a relative. (If such care was a priority to him, he would have done better to take action earlier to help the relative in need with a gift or loan rather than waiting until he was so desperate that he had to sell his land.) Probably someone who had sold their land to next-of-kin would become dependent on them for support, perhaps continuing to work the same land and enjoy at least some of its produce. In any case, the principle of inalienability of ancestral land is served by keeping it within the extended family, which would serve to discourage land speculation[53] and make more likely that the land will actually be restored to the original owner or his heirs at the Jubilee than if it was sold on the open market.

Sale and Redemption: City Houses

When someone sells a dwelling-house [in] a walled city, [he] retains the right of redemption for a full year after its sale; during that time he has the right of redemption. If it is not redeemed before a full year has passed, a house in a walled city shall belong in perpetuity[54] to the purchaser and his descendants; it shall not be released in the ju-

---

52. There is clearly a connection with the institution of levirate marriage (Deut 25:5-10), though the narrative does not match the law in all the details (Rowley 1952; McKane 1963; Westbrook 1971c: 63-68; Bush 1996). The birth of Ruth's first child Obed is greeted by neighbours with the words, 'A son has been born to Naomi' (4:17); but in the genealogy at the end of the book, Boaz is counted as the father of Obed rather than Elimelech or Mahlon (4:20; also 1 Chr 2:12).

53. Cf. Eichrodt (1959: 96-97).

54. See above, n. 28.

> bilee. But houses in villages which do not have walls around them shall be considered as open country; there is [always] the right of redemption, and in the jubilee they shall be released.
>
> Lev 25:29-31

There is one exception to the rule that land which has changed hands is to return to its original owner in the jubilee year: in a walled city, a house and the land on which it stands can only be redeemed in the first year after it has been sold, and it becomes the permanent property of the purchaser if not redeemed in that time (vv. 29-30). The jubilee law was intended to protect the interests of ordinary people for whom ancestral land was the primary source of sustenance. Apart from theological reasons for holding on to their part of the promised land, they would be reluctant to part with it for practical reasons of survival and only in case of serious hardship would a sale of land be likely to take place. An urban situation would be quite different, however, with a mixture of Israelite traders, officials, soldiers, and non-Israelites, as well as farmers whose fields were located nearby or who were rich enough to own a second home in the city (cf. 1 Kgs 4:7-19; 9:19; 20:34). Such a population would be relatively mobile and a housing market would be appropriate. In these circumstances people might well buy and sell property for convenience or in the course of business, without necessarily being in great need, and the law allows this to take place. Unlike v. 25 (and also vv. 35, 39, 47) there is no mention here of poverty, and it seems the sale of a city home is viewed simply as a business transaction.[55]

In a village, however, the original owner of a house always has the right of redemption and the house is automatically returned in the jubilee year, just as for land in open country (v. 31). Villagers live and work on the land, and it is primarily their interests which are protected by the jubilee rather than those of urban communities. That is not to say that the Old Testament as a whole has a rural bias, however. There are other laws which show concern for people in the cities — for example, relating to slaves,

---

55. Pedersen (1920: 88) suggests that the reason for the fortified cities having different laws is that they are 'something new and strange in Israelitic life and do not depend upon the old Israelitic ideas of kindred and property'. From a slightly different perspective, Noth (1962) argues that ancient Canaanite city law was followed in the former Canaanite cities and the year's delay before the sale became irredeemable was a small concession to Israelite custom. See also Boecker (1976: 92); Wright (1990: 44 n. 1, 125); Hartley (1992); Joosten (1996: 156); North (2000: 73-84); Milgrom (2001: 2198). For detailed studies of the city in ancient Israel, see Frick (1977) and Fritz (1995).

lawsuits, loans, and fair trade (on which see below) — and Deuteronomy in particular gives a great deal of attention to city life.

Sale and Redemption: Levite Cities

As for the cities of the Levites, there is a perpetual right of redemption for the Levites concerning the houses in the cities which they hold. And whatever is [not] redeemed [by] the Levites[56] — a house sold in[57] a city which they hold — shall be released in the jubilee; because the houses in the cities of the Levites are their property among the people of Israel. But the pastureland around their cities shall not be sold; because it is their property for ever.

Lev 25:32-34

The city-house exception does not apply in Levite cities, because those cities are the only land they possess (vv. 32-33; cf. Num 35:1-8; Joshua 21; 1 Chr 6:54-81). The Levites retain a perpetual right of redemption over their city houses, while the pastures surrounding the cities are not to be sold at all, even on a short-term basis (v. 34; cf. Ezek 48:13-14).

Ancient Israelite cities were surrounded by common land, often used for pasturing flocks,[58] and it is clear from Joshua 21:2-3 that such pastureland around the cities allocated to the Levites is reserved for their use. The Levites are not allowed to own land (Num 18:20, 23b-24), and so do not engage in agriculture, but they do have livestock and need access to pastures (Num 35:2-5; Josh 14:4). So the pastureland around the Levite cities is held in common for this purpose and no individual Levite has the right to buy or sell it.

---

56. Lit. 'And whatever is redeemed from the Levites' (cf. NRSV), the meaning of which is rather unclear. In the context a negative would be expected, which is supplied by the Vulgate and followed by BHS and REB. I have tentatively adopted this text in the translation above. Attempts to translate the text as it stands result in a rather free translation, e.g. 'So the property of the Levites is redeemable' (NIV); 'which any of the Levites may exercise', understood as the conclusion to the previous sentence (Hartley 1992); 'whoever of the Levites redeems [should know that]' (Milgrom 2001: 2202-3). See also Möller (1978).

57. So LXX, followed by many modern translations, also suggested by BHS; MT has 'and'.

58. Barr (1984); Portugali (1984); Milgrom (2001: 2203-4); Lefebvre (2003: 216-18).

Two Special Cases

Bonded Labourers Apart from the restoration of property, the Jubilee laws provide for the release of Israelites who have become bonded labourers. These provisions are found in verses 39-43 and 47-55 and will be discussed below (6.3). In this context there is also a reference to ancestral land:

> Then he shall leave your [service], together with his children; and he shall return to his own clan, and go back to his ancestral property. (Lev 25:41)

However harsh the economic circumstances, no one may be forced to give up their personal freedom or their family inheritance on a permanent basis.

Land Dedicated to the LORD In Leviticus 27 there is a regulation about ancestral land which has been dedicated to the LORD, that is, handed over to the priests so that its produce may be used for maintenance of the temple:

> If someone dedicates part of his ancestral land to the LORD, its valuation[59] shall be according to its seed [requirements[60]]: fifty shekels of silver per homer[61] of barley seed. If he dedicates his field from the year of jubilee, its valuation will apply [in full]. But if he dedicates his field after the jubilee, the priest shall calculate for him the [price in] silver according to the [number of] years remaining, until the [next] year of jubilee; thus its valuation shall be reduced. If the person who dedicates the field wishes to redeem it, he shall add a fifth to its valuation and it shall revert to him. (Lev 27:16-19)

A person who makes such a dedication retains the right of redemption, at a 20 percent premium over the priestly valuation. Presumably the redemp-

---

59. Lit. 'your valuation'. On the term ערכך, see Hartley (1992: 73 n. 15.b).

60. So the majority of translators and commentators (NIV; NJPS; NRSV; RSV; TB; Harrison 1980; Hartley 1992; Milgrom 2001: 2382), though a few understand it to imply 'yield', i.e. the quantity of barley produced by the field (NJB; de Vaux 1961: 168; Wenham 1979).

61. The size of a homer is uncertain. According to Powell (1992), it was between 100 and 200 litres, though other estimates put it higher than that (e.g. 220 litres, NIV; 450 litres, NJB). Several translations give values in kilograms, which is confusing since it is a measure of capacity, not weight.

tion price continues to decrease until the jubilee year (cf. 25:15-16), at which point it becomes nil and the land returns to its original owner (cf. 25:10, 28). Such a dedication does not therefore affect the general principle of restoring ancestral land in the jubilee, but there is one exception:

> If he does not redeem the field, and if he had sold the field to someone else, it can no longer be redeemed. When the field is released in the jubilee, it shall be holy to the LORD, like a devoted field; it shall become the property of the priest. (Lev 27:20-21)

There has been considerable debate over the meaning of this rule,[62] but Milgrom (2001: 2383-85) has convincingly argued that it refers to a field already sold by the owner before it is dedicated to the sanctuary. In this case, the sanctuary receives no benefit in the short term, since the land is in someone else's possession, and the purpose of the dedication can only be that the owner intends the land to become priestly property at the jubilee instead of reverting to him. Nevertheless, before the jubilee, it is still possible for the original owner to redeem the land, if he is able and willing to do so twice: from the present holder and also from the sanctuary.

Finally, another possible scenario is mentioned:

> If it is a bought field, which is not part of his ancestral land, that he dedicates to the LORD, the priest shall calculate for him the amount of its valuation until the year of jubilee; and he shall pay its valuation as of that day,[63] a holy gift to the LORD. In the year of jubilee the field shall return to the one from whom it was bought, to whom the property belongs in the land. (Lev 27:22-24)

In this case it is not the original owner who makes the dedication, but the purchaser. Redemption by the purchaser is possible during the period leading up to the jubilee, and in the jubilee year the land returns to its original owner. No one has the right to dedicate someone else's ancestral land permanently to God.

---

62. See Wenham (1979); Hartley (1992).
63. So NJPS; NRSV; REB; Milgrom (2001: 2387). Others take the meaning to be 'on that day' (e.g. ESV; NIV; Wenham 1979; Hartley 1992; cf. TEV; NJB).

c. Conclusion

The essence of the jubilee is that everyone is entitled to receive back their ancestral land, if for any reason it has changed hands, and bonded labourers are to be freed without redemption payment so that they can return to their own family and land. Such measures were not unprecedented in the ancient Near East, but the idea of observing them on a recurring basis every fifty years appears to have been distinctive to Israel. Mesopotamian kings instituted reforms from time to time and showed favour to their subjects if it pleased them, but the people of Israel were expected to take measures to promote social justice and equality at the times appointed in the law, whether or not it was convenient or politically advantageous.[64]

There is one significant exception to the jubilee law, in that houses in non-Levite walled cities are not returned to their original owner in the jubilee year. In the cosmopolitan society of the cities, with a mix of Israelites who do not live off the land and resident aliens who are outside the land inheritance laws, it would not be realistic to apply the same principles as in the rural areas. Even so, the seller retains the right to redeem a sold house for a year after the sale, and Levites have a perpetual right of redemption — plus restoration at the jubilee — since the cities and surrounding pasturelands are all the property they have.

A corollary to the law concerns the situation when a landowner dies without leaving any sons (Num 27:1-8). In this case a daughter is entitled to inherit the land, but she must marry within her own tribe (36:1-12), so that her portion of land does not become the property of another tribe (v. 7). For if a female heir were to marry outside her tribe, the land she inherited would become the property of her husband's tribe and not be restored in the jubilee year (vv. 3-4). The jubilee law effectively means that land in ancient Israel was not to be sold, but simply leased until the jubilee year. If someone became poor and was forced to 'sell' his land, it would be returned to that person or their family by the fiftieth year at the latest. There is a theological basis for this: the land belongs to God (Lev 25:23). He has given it to his people Israel, but they live there as temporary residents, not absolute owners.

It may seem that the regulations for the jubilee year are unrealistic from an economic point of view.[65] The biblical writers themselves antici-

---

64. Cf. Hallo (1977: 5-16).
65. Houston (2006: 194-202) addresses the apparent impracticality of the law by argu-

pate that some will object to such radical legislation (Lev 25:20; cf. Deut 15:9). Radical improvements to the situation of the poor cannot happen without loss on the part of the rich, because levelling is necessary if all people are to have enough. In spite of the claims of prosperity theology, faithfulness to God does not necessarily lead to wealth in this world. Nevertheless, the regulations for the holy years are accompanied by a promise applicable in this world, that those who keep them will be blessed by God with security (v. 18) and an adequate harvest (v. 19). This promise is elaborated in Leviticus 26:3-13 and Deuteronomy 28:1-14.[66]

Whether or not the jubilee year was observed in ancient Israel is uncertain. The historical books do not mention it, except perhaps in 2 Kings 19:29. But the jubilee was only to be celebrated every fifty years, so there would be no reason to mention it unless a particular event took place during the jubilee year, and only then if that fact was considered significant.[67] In the prophetic writings, apart from Isaiah 37:30 (= 2 Kgs 19:29), there are three references: Ezekiel 46:16-18 (about the future, not Ezekiel's own time), and Isaiah 58 and 61.[68] These texts indicate knowledge of the idea of Jubilee, but do not prove that the law was actually kept. In fact, other prophetic texts denounce the rampant accumulation of estates by the wealthy (e.g. Isa 5:8-10; Mic 2:1-4), which would not have been possible if the jubilee was being observed regularly. Apparently sabbatical years were not kept consistently during the monarchy (Lev 26:34-35, 43; 2 Chr 36:21), and it is likely that the same applied to the jubilee. Even after the exile, in spite of the social levelling that resulted from the destruction of the kingdoms and

---

ing that its object is to teach justice rather than enforce detailed regulations. It is intentionally utopian in character, and this is the key to understanding its importance. It provides a vision of justice, to inspire and challenge, within the framework of the agrarian life of ancient Judah.

66. On prosperity theology, see Moo (1988); Jackson (1989b); Herlianto (1992); Ro (1996); Hattu (2002); Alcorn (2003); Perriman (2003).

67. Cf. Hartley (1992: 429).

68. On the idea of jubilee in the last two texts, see Baker (1998: 51-53); cf. Zimmerli (1970); *pace* O'Brien (2001), who rejects the link between Isaiah 61 and the jubilee. Osborne and Stricher (1999: 75-91) discuss Isaiah 61 in the context of their study of the jubilee year, since there are similarities in its vision, but do not think the author is deliberately referring to Leviticus 25. The term דרור (vv. 8, 15, 17, 17) is also used in Jeremiah 34, but it would seem that the sabbatical year is intended there, or perhaps an extraordinary measure outside the cycle of holy years. Bergsma (2007: 149-294) discusses these and several other possible allusions to the jubilee in historical and prophetic texts and also in the Pseudepigrapha and at Qumran.

decades of life far from home, the rich were oppressing the poor (Neh 5:1-5). Nehemiah took various measures to deal with this, including the restoration of ancestral land which had been mortgaged (vv. 11-12).[69]

It is probable that the jubilee year was not observed regularly, at least from the eighth century onwards, and as a result the gap between rich and poor grew steadily wider. Nevertheless, the values enshrined in the institution were not completely forgotten. The prophets reminded Israel that the land was a sacred inheritance, given by the Lord God to his chosen people, and castigated those who amassed an unfair share of its wealth for themselves by exploiting the poor and needy. And at least one prophet used images from the jubilee in challenging his hearers to make radical changes to their lifestyle (Isaiah 58) and in looking forward to the messianic age (Isaiah 61).[70]

4.2 Boundaries

Whether land was treated as a sacred inheritance or a saleable commodity, the marking of boundaries between one person's land and that of another was clearly important for harmonious living among neighbours.

a. Ancient Near East

The oldest extant law on boundaries is in the Hittite Laws, where it is stipulated that if anyone violates the boundary of a neighbour's field the neighbour is entitled to compensation in land — plus one sheep, ten loaves, and a jug of beer — and the field is to be reconsecrated (§168). The following clause adds that if a violation of boundaries occurs when buying land, presumably unintentionally, the buyer is required to offer an appropriate prayer to settle the matter (§169). In both cases it is assumed that land boundaries have been divinely appointed and an offence must there-

---

69. For further discussion of the observance of the jubilee year, see Neufeld (1958: 119-24); Baker (1998: 50-51); Fried and Freedman (2001); Loewenberg (2001: 107-10).

70. For theological reflections on the relevance of the Jubilee in the modern world, especially in relation to the turn of the millennium, see Ringe (1985); Ucko (1997); Baker (1998: 55-63); Brubacher (1999); de Chirico (1999); Kinsler and Kinsler (1999); Schweitzer (1999); Lowery (2000); Moloney (2000); Goldingay (2002); Tidball (2005: 292-304); Wright (2006a: 289-323). Cf. Galvão (1994).

fore be dealt with not merely by restoration of the boundary and compensation to the human owner but also by prayer to the god.[71]

There is more extensive treatment of the subject of boundaries in the Middle Assyrian Laws, beginning with the following:

> If a man should incorporate a large border area of his comrade's [property into his own] and they prove the charges against him and find him guilty, he shall give a field 'triple' that which he had incorporated; they shall cut off one of his fingers; they shall strike him one hundred blows with rods; he shall perform the king's service for one full month. (§B8)[72]

Clearly this is a very serious offence, punished by multiple restitution, physical mutilation, severe beating, and forced labour. The next clause is similar, dealing with appropriation of smaller border areas and stipulating a slightly less severe punishment (§B9). After this there are regulations concerning digging a well, building a permanent structure, planting an orchard, and making bricks in someone else's field (§§B10, 12-15), all of which are lesser offences.[73]

An important nonlegal text dealing with boundary markers is the Egyptian Instruction of Amenemope. Chapter 6 begins as follows:

> Do not move the markers on the borders of fields,
> Nor shift the position of the measuring-cord.
> Do not be greedy for a cubit of land,
> Nor encroach on the boundaries of a widow.[74]

The potential offender is then warned of divine judgement, and others are encouraged to look out for such oppressors of the weak and take appropriate action to stop them. The falsifying of boundaries is also one of the transgressions listed in the Akkadian Shurpu incantations.[75]

Numerous examples of inscribed stone monuments, often supposed

---

71. Cf. Hoffner (1997: 216).

72. Translation from Roth (1997: 178-79). Cf. Driver and Miles (1935: 433), who translate: 'If a man has encroached upon the great boundary of his neighbour . . . , he shall give (up) a third as much field as that upon which he has encroached.'

73. §§B19-20 deal with similar subjects, but the text is damaged and it is impossible to reconstruct it with certainty (cf. Driver and Miles 1935: 302, 438-41; Roth 1997: 181-82). For a detailed discussion of encroachment on neighbouring property in the Middle Assyrian Laws, see Driver and Miles (1935: 302-9); Cardascia (1969: 276-86).

74. COS (1.47 §7.11-15).

75. §2.45 (Beyerlin 1975: 132).

to be ancient boundary stones or landmarks (*kudurru*s), have been found in Mesopotamia.[76] A study of 'ancient kudurrus' from the third millennium shows that these documents deal with acquisition of land and that they were kept in temples to put them under the protection of the gods and to ensure accessibility by the public to land titles.[77] Further, a recent investigation of later monuments, dating from the fourteenth to the seventh centuries B.C., concludes that they are properly termed *narûs* ('stone monuments') and were placed in temples rather than on field boundaries.[78] No doubt there were also boundary markers at strategic points on the land which would correctly be termed *kudurru*s, but these are likely to have been made of wood or rough stone and have not been preserved like the finely crafted entitlement *narû*s.[79]

b. Deuteronomic Laws

> *You shall not move your neighbour's boundary marker,*[80] *established by those who come first*[81] *into your inheritance which you are to inherit, in the land which the* LORD *your God is giving you to possess.*
>
> Deut 19:14

Without roads and maps to define boundaries, a farmer struggling to survive could well be tempted to help himself to a little more land to support his family by means of the simple device of shifting a boundary marker when no one was looking. Even a prosperous farmer might be tempted to extend his property if he thought he could get away with it, and it seems this sort of land grabbing was common in the eighth century B.C. (Isa 5:8;

---

76. Oppenheim (1964: 123, 159); cf. King (1912).
77. Gelb, Steinkeller, and Whiting (1991: 23-24).
78. Slanski (2003a); cf. Hurowitz (1997: 1-4).
79. Cf. *CAD* (8.495-96; 10.2: 113-14; 11.364-67); Slanski (2003a: 32, 55, 59-61). On violation of boundaries in Greek and Roman law, see Driver (1902).
80. The word גבול ('boundary, border, territory') is used here to denote a 'boundary marker' or 'landmark'.
81. Cf. McConville (2002a). This translation fits the canonical context, as part of Moses' preparation of the Israelites before they enter the promised land. Several translations mix the tenses here, leading to a confusion of contexts; e.g. 'fixed by the men of former times' (REB) appears to be addressed to those who have long been in the land, whereas the next phrase ('in the holding which you will occupy in the land') appears to be addressed to the Israelites on the plains of Moab. For ראשנים with the meaning 'ancestors', cf. Lev 26:45.

Mic 2:2). So the moving of boundary markers is categorically forbidden in this law, for unauthorised extension of boundaries amounts to stealing and neither rich nor poor are entitled to take land belonging to others. The land was allocated to the people of God when their ancestors first entered the promised land, and their descendants do not have the right to change these divinely ordained allocations. No human punishment is stipulated for breaking the law, though later in the book there is a warning of divine judgement: 'Cursed be anyone who moves his neighbour's boundary marker' (Deut 27:17). The use here of the theological term 'inheritance' (נחלה), together with its root verb 'inherit' (נחל), is a reminder that land issues concern not only human beings but also God, the land-giver.[82]

The only biblical reference to a specific landmark is in the covenant between Jacob and Laban, where Jacob sets up a stone as a pillar (Gen 31:45, 49) and Laban makes a pile of stones (vv. 46-48). The two together serve to mark the boundary between their lands (vv. 51-52). A ceremony takes place in which both the pillar and the pile are given names, oaths are made, and a sacrifice offered. This covenant is of international importance, as it establishes the boundary between what will become the countries of Israel and Aram/Syria, and it does not necessarily follow that ordinary field boundaries would have been marked in this particular way.

The boundary law may have been placed at this point in Deuteronomy because of verbal links with the preceding verses: the Hebrew word translated 'boundary marker' (גבול) is also found in verses 3 and 8 (with the meaning 'territory'), and the word 'inheritance' (נחלה) is also in verse 10.[83] There may also be a link with the Decalogue, as several scholars have suggested:

- Biddle (2003) treats it as part of the section of Deuteronomy that explicates the *sixth* commandment (murder), arguing that 'stealing can be killing' if poor people are deprived of their means of agricultural production.
- Brown (1993) and Christensen (2001) relate it to the *eighth* commandment (theft.)[84]

---

82. Wright (1990: 129); cf. Lipiński (1986b); Wright (1997).

83. Cf. Carmichael (1967: 198-200; 1974: 113-14), who argues that both Deut 19:1-13 and 19:14 presuppose the historical traditions relating to the allocation of the land in Deuteronomy 1–4, and 'those who come first' (19:14) is a reference to the events described in that passage. (גבל is used six times and נחל eighteen times in Deuteronomy 1–4.)

84. Jackson (1975a: 244) and Houtman (1996: 64) also treat the moving of landmarks as a form of theft.

- Rofé (1985b) interprets it as one of four Deuteronomic laws which illustrate the *tenth* commandment (coveting), pointing out the linguistic similarity of this one in particular with Deut 5:21 (negation, imperfect verb, direct object, 'your neighbour').[85]

These suggestions are not mutually exclusive, for the Decalogue provides basic principles which are developed in the detailed law collections, and there is no reason why this law should not be based on several of the commandments.

c. Conclusion

The law on boundary markers is unique in the Old Testament legal collections but has several parallels in the ancient Near East. The essence of the offence is the same — the violation of land boundaries — but the form is quite different. The Hittite and Middle Assyrian laws are casuistic in form and prescribe severe penalties for infringement, depending on the circumstances, and according to the former the offender also incurs divine displeasure. In contrast, the Deuteronomic Law takes the form of a brief apodictic prohibition together with a historical and theological explanation. It is characteristic of biblical law to view the problem from the perspective of the covenant community, reminding the people that the land on which they live is a divine gift rather than an intrinsic right, and requiring them to maintain the ancestral boundaries according to the law of God rather than manipulate them according to the law of the jungle.

The integrity of boundaries is also referred to quite frequently in the biblical wisdom literature. Like Amenemope, Proverbs warns the reader not to move ancient landmarks (Prov 22:28[86]) and threatens those who exploit the weak in this way with the judgement of God (23:10-11; cf. 15:25).

---

85. Tigay (1996) follows Rofé in this, pointing to Mic 2:2 as confirmation of the point.

86. The language of law and wisdom are very similar here:

| 'You shall not move your neighbour's by those who come first'. (Deut 19:14) | boundary marker, | established |
| 'You shall not move an ancient by your ancestors'. (Prov 22:28) | boundary marker, | made |

Weinfeld (1972a: 265-67) and Rofé (1985b: 58-60) argue persuasively that Deuteronomy draws on the wisdom tradition here rather than the converse.

Job refers to the removal of landmarks as typical of the wicked in their oppression of the poor and needy (Job 24:2-4), and the prophet Hosea takes up a similar theme (Hos 5:10).

4.3 Military Service

The relevance of military service to the theme of this book may not be immediately obvious, but there is one aspect which is of particular interest here, namely the question of what happens to a soldier's land if he is taken prisoner by the enemy or dies in battle.

a. Ancient Near East

There is quite extensive treatment of this matter in the Laws of Hammurabi. They are particularly concerned with property held by soldiers[87] as a royal grant, linked with an obligation of service to the crown.

First, the responsibility to obey orders is emphasised, and the death penalty prescribed for a soldier who refuses to go on a royal campaign or pays someone else to go as his substitute. In this case his estate passes to the one who informs against him (§26; cf. §33).

Second, if a soldier is taken captive while on duty, any field or orchard which has been granted to him in respect of his service may be given to another. The recipient takes on the service obligation together with the land, but if the original property holder later returns, then both land and obligation are to be restored to him (§27). The soldier's son has the first option to take on this privilege and responsibility (§28), unless he is too young to do so. In this case, a third of the land is to be given to his mother as a resource for his maintenance (§29).

Third, if a soldier absents himself and another person takes possession of his property and performs the associated service obligation for three years, the former loses his right to reclaim the property (§30). But if he re-

---

87. The laws apply to both *rēdû* and *bā'iru*. The former term is generally agreed to denote an ordinary foot soldier; the latter means lit. 'fisherman' *(COS)* or 'hunter' (Richardson 2000: 158) but in this context denotes a soldier of some sort, perhaps enlisted to provide food supplies for the armed forces. The conditions of service are the same as for other soldiers. Possible dynamic translations are 'commissary' *(ANET)* or 'commando' (Millard, private communication). For more details, see *CAD* (2.31-33).

turns after one year, he still has a claim on the property and a responsibility to complete the service (§31).

Fourth, if a soldier is taken captive while on royal service but is redeemed by a merchant and enabled to return home, then the merchant is to be reimbursed. This should be done by the person he redeemed if he has funds available, and if not, by the local temple, and if that is also not possible, by the palace. In any of these cases the soldier does not lose his land or house (§32).

Fifth, buying and selling of fields, orchards, or houses belonging to a soldier is strictly forbidden (§§36-37, 41), and property which is linked to a service obligation may not be passed on to a wife or daughter nor used to settle another obligation (§§38-39). (A merchant may, however, sell property which has a service obligation, so long as the buyer takes on that obligation, §40.)[88]

The only other ancient Near Eastern law on soldiers' property is a clause in the Middle Assyrian Laws (§A45) which details action to be taken in the event of a soldier being taken captive. If the soldier's wife has no father-in-law or son to support her and her husband holds a field and house as a royal grant, it seems she is entitled to mortgage the property to provide an income to live on and may continue to live in the house for two years, after which she is expected to marry again. If her first husband later returns, he retains the right to reclaim his wife and to redeem his property, at the price for which it was mortgaged; but if he dies abroad, then the right to reallocate the property reverts to the king, the ultimate owner of all land.[89]

---

88. This understanding of the relevant clauses in the Laws of Hammurabi is based on the translation of Roth (1997: 85-89). Somewhat different translations are given by Driver and Miles (1955: 20-27, 161-68) and Richardson (2000: 50-57). For further discussion of the rights and duties of crown tenants in these laws, see Driver and Miles (1952: 111-27).

89. This interpretation of the law follows Driver and Miles (1935: 256-66, 412-15), Cardascia (1969: 217-26), and Roth (1997: 170-71). A somewhat different interpretation has been proposed by Postgate (1971: 502-8). For detailed discussion of the issues, see the aforementioned works.

b. Deuteronomic Laws

Then the officials[90] shall speak to the people,[91] saying,

'Is there anyone who has built a new house but not yet started to live in[92] it? Let him go back to his house, otherwise he may die in battle and another man will start to live in it.

'Is there anyone who has planted a vineyard but not yet enjoyed [its fruit]? Let him go back to his house, otherwise he may die in battle and another man will enjoy it.

'Is there anyone who has betrothed[93] a wife but not yet married her? Let him go back to his house, otherwise he may die in battle and another man will marry her.'

Deut 20:5-7

This text forms part of the Deuteronomic rules of warfare (Deuteronomy 20). Three categories of people are exempted from military service, in each case because they have begun something of great importance but not yet

---

90. So NRSV; NJPS; Rofé (1985a: 33); Christensen (2001); McConville (2002a); cf. 'scribes' (NJB). The translation 'officers' (NIV; REB; TEV) is confusing, since they are not the actual commanders of the troops (see v. 9). Cf. the use of שטרים in Deut 1:15, where it is also distinguished from the commanders; in 16:18, where it is parallel to judges; and in 29:10 (Hebrew v. 9) and 31:28, where it is together with elders.

91. I have translated the word עם according to its usual meaning 'people' (cf. TEV 'men'), rather than 'army' (NIV, NEB) or 'troops' (NRSV). In the canonical context, the whole people of God is theoretically the army, and the object here is to select those who will actually go to war, who might then be described as 'troops'.

92. The verb חנך is commonly translated 'dedicate' (e.g. NIV; NJB; NRSV; REB; TEV), but Rankin (1930: 27-33) and Reif (1972) have shown that it actually means 'begin, inaugurate, initiate, train', both in the Old Testament and later Hebrew. I have therefore translated it in the present context as 'start to live in' (cf. Craigie 1976; Dommershausen 1977; Tigay 1996; Naudé 1997; Christensen 2001; McConville 2002a). There is no indication in the Old Testament that private houses were dedicated to God, and the parallel term relating to vineyards in v. 6 (translated here 'enjoyed [its fruit]') actually means 'desacralise' (cf. Lev 19:23-25; Jer 31:5), the exact opposite of 'dedicate' (cf. Tigay 1996). The parallel phrase in Deut 28:30 simply says: 'You shall build a house, but not live in it'.

93. NRSV and TEV translate 'engaged', NIV and REB 'pledged', and NJPS 'paid the bride-price'. What took place was something much stronger than a modern engagement, at least in Western culture, and would have included payment of the bride-price (מהר) to the woman's father (cf. Gen 24:53; 34:12; 1 Sam 18:25; 2 Sam 3:14), so I prefer the translation 'betrothed' (RSV). Once betrothed, the couple were legally bound to each other, even before the marriage was consummated (cf. Deut 22:23-24).

completed the process. In relation to the subject of the present chapter, the planting of the vineyard most obviously concerns the land, but the other two are closely related since houses are built on land and children are essential if ancestral land is to be passed on to the next generation. Housing, agriculture, and marriage are fundamental to the life of the people of God in the promised land, and this law makes clear that the demands of war do not necessarily take priority over the responsibilities of everyday life. They have been promised 'rest' (מנוחה) in the land and should be able to enjoy that in peace (Deut 3:20; 12:9-10; 28:7-14; contrast v. 65).[94] We should note, however, that Deuteronomy 20 is primarily concerned with wars where Israel is the aggressor rather than defensive wars, and it may have been assumed that in the case of the latter everyone would automatically take part to protect their properties and families.[95]

The length of time a person is to be exempted from military service on the grounds of house-building is not stated, but it appears that in the case of planting a vineyard it could be up to five years, and in the case of marriage the exemption would last for the time of betrothal plus a further year. According to Leviticus 19:23-25, fruit trees are not to be harvested in the first three years, and the produce of the fourth year is set apart for 'rejoicing in the LORD', so it is only in the fifth year that the produce of the tree becomes available for the one who planted it. Deuteronomy 24:5 gives a year's exemption from war after marriage, probably to allow time for the first child to be conceived and born, thus ensuring the continuity of the family.[96]

Two further texts throw light on this passage. Among the many curses for disobedience to the LORD in Deuteronomy 28, there are three which constitute the precise opposite of the happiness made possible by the exemptions from warfare: the engaged man will lose his fiancée, the person who has built a house will not live in it, and the person who has planted a vineyard will not enjoy its fruit (v. 30).[97] And in Jeremiah's letter to the exiles in Babylon, he encourages them to settle down and avoid further con-

---

94. See Carmichael (1974: 118-28) for an exposition of this idea in relation to various other biblical passages.

95. On rabbinic discussions concerning the application of this law, see Gurewicz (1958); Rofé (1985a: 33-34); Tigay (1996: 379 nn. 12, 14).

96. Cf. Carmichael (1974: 122-23). On the importance of continuing the family line, see the law of levirate marriage (Deut 25:5-10).

97. On the relationship between such 'futility curses' and the exemptions from military service, see de Bruin (1999); McConville (2002a: 318-19); Nelson (2002: 250).

flict with their conquerors, referring to the same three matters: building houses and living in them, planting gardens and eating their produce, and taking wives and having children (Jer 29:5-6).[98] It is evident in both texts, as also in the exemptions from military service, that three of the most vital blessings bestowed on the people of God are a house (in which to live), land (for sustenance), and marriage (for continuation of the family).

c. Conclusion

The Old Testament's generous attitude to exemption from military service is related to its emphasis on willing participation (Judg 5:2; cf. vv. 17, 23) and the conviction that success in warfare depends more on divine presence than human effort (Deut 20:1-4; cf. Judges *passim*, esp. 7:1-8). People with certain responsibilities in relation to ancestral land — in particular those who are in the process of building houses, planting vineyards, and getting married — are not to be prevented from fulfilling them by enlistment in the armed forces. These idealistic principles were not always applied in practice, as we learn from the total mobilisation of 1 Kings 15:22, where 'none was exempt' from Asa's summons; but in later days Judas Maccabaeus is recorded as having followed the letter of the law, even in a defensive war with vast forces arrayed against the Jews (1 Maccabees 3:56).[99]

While such exemption is not completely unknown in the rest of the ancient Near East,[100] their laws have a quite different concern, namely to

---

98. On the relationship between Deut 20:5-10 and Jer 29:5-7, see Berlin (1984).

99. Segal (1967: 80) points to the idealistic nature of the laws of warfare as an indication of their early origin, arguing that 'it is inconceivable that a late post-Mosaic writer could have shown such a total disregard of the actual course of events of Israel's conquest and settlement of Canaan as recorded in the books of Joshua and Judges.'

100. The extant laws do not include exemption from warfare, though it is occasionally mentioned in nonlegal texts. In the Sumerian poem 'Gilgamesh and Huwawa' (also known as 'Gilgamesh and the Land of the Living'), Gilgamesh summons to war fifty men who are unattached, allowing those with family responsibilities to go home (lines 50-53; *ANET*: 48; George 1999: 152). Such exemptions are also implied by a passage in the Ugaritic Kirta Epic (also known as the 'Legend of King Keret'), where even those normally excused from military service are expected to go on this occasion, including only sons, invalids, and newly-weds (lines 96-103, 184-91; *COS*: 1.102). The relationship between this text and Deut 20:5-7 is discussed by W. Herrmann (1958). There is also a Babylonian text which refers to the tragedy of dying before consummating a marriage, referred to by Tigay (1996: 188), citing an unpublished doctoral dissertation by Shaffer (1963). In contrast, one of the Mari letters demands

ensure proper handling of royal property held in conjunction with an obligation of service, in the event of the capture or death of the property holder. The Laws of Hammurabi stipulate that the authorities may transfer the land and obligation to someone else, normally the holder's adult son if he has one, on the understanding that they will be returned to the original holder if he should later return home safely. Although the details in the Middle Assyrian Laws differ from those of Hammurabi, the underlying principle of royal ownership is the same, for the wife of a captured soldier has the right to use her husband's property for two years, but she is then expected to remarry and the property reverts to the crown.

Clearly land is a fundamental issue in the ancient Near Eastern laws on military service, including those of the Old Testament, but there are significant differences in how the land is understood. According to the laws of Old Babylonia and Middle Assyria, land belongs ultimately to the king and may be granted to his subjects in return for specific obligations of service, but in the event of failure to render that service — whether deliberately or due to capture in battle — the land reverts to the crown. Although it is possible that exemption from service was granted occasionally on compassionate grounds, the laws do not specify this but rather emphasise the absolute duty of a soldier to obey orders. Provision is made for a soldier's family in the event of his captivity or death, and his right affirmed to reclaim the land granted to him (together with its associated service obligation) if he returns home alive. According to the laws of the Old Testament, however, ancestral land is the gift of God to his chosen people, which has been allocated equitably to all of them, and is to be enjoyed and cared for, then passed on to one's descendants. This sacred inheritance is of inestimable value, so that in some circumstances responsibilities relating to the land take precedence even over the duty to serve king and country.

---

total mobilisation, without exception: 'If the king goes on an expedition, everybody down to the youngsters should immediately assemble. Any sheikh whose men are not all assembled commits a sacrilege against the king even if he leaves only one man behind!' (Oppenheim 1967: 96-97).

MARGINAL PEOPLE

Chapter 5

SLAVES

Three main social classes can be distinguished in the Old Babylonian period:

- elite citizens or freemen *(awīlu)*, including priests, nobility, officials, merchants, and landowners
- subordinate citizens or serfs *(muškēnu)*, including craftsmen, shepherds, labourers, and tenant farmers, who worked for the state or for private landowners but had no land of their own
- chattel slaves (*wardu,* male; *amtu,* female), considered to be the property of their owners, including foreign captives and slaves purchased in markets or born in their master's house

A similar class structure is found in Babylonia at other times, and in neighbouring countries. Within this system, the terms 'free' and 'slave' are relative in meaning, since no one has absolute freedom, and some slaves have considerable power and wealth. All subjects of a king are considered his 'slaves', even though they are 'free' citizens; and even the king himself may be described as a 'slave' with respect to his emperor or god. In some contexts, the term 'slave' could refer to any hierarchical inferior.[1]

In Israel, however, there is no social stratification — at least in theory — because all Israelites are free and every tribe, clan, and family has land

---

1. On social stratification in ancient Sumer, see Cripps (2007); on the Old Babylonian period, see Diakonoff (1987); Westbrook (2003b: 376-85); on Pharaonic Egypt, see Lorton (1995: 351-52); on Hittite Anatolia, see Hoffner (1995: 565-66); on Neo-Assyrian society, see Radner (1997: 198-200); on Babylonia in the 7th to 4th centuries B.C., see Dandama[y]ev (1984: 456-68, 585-661); on the classical period, see Finley (1973: 62-94).

allotted to them during the settlement period.² (Only the priests and Levites are not allotted land, and they are compensated for this by other privileges.) If hard times should result in the loss of ancestral land, it is to be returned to its original holder at the jubilee. Even the king is subject to the law and is not to exalt himself above other members of the community (Deut 17:18-20). The commonest Hebrew word for 'slave' (עבד) means literally a 'worker' (cf. Exod 20:9), unlike the Akkadian *wardu,* which means 'one who has come down' in social position.³ Nevertheless, there are people at the margins of Israelite society who effectively form a lower class, especially chattel slaves, temporary slaves and bonded labourers, concubines, widows and orphans, and ethnic minorities. These 'marginal people' form the subject of this chapter and the following two chapters.

5.1 Chattel Slaves

First, I will consider the laws relating to chattel slavery in the Old Testament in the context of the ancient Near East. From a legal point of view, a chattel slave may be distinguished by his or her status as property, over whom a master has right of disposal. This definition is not rigid, however, since household heads have considerable rights over their dependants even though the latter are free citizens; and slaves have some human rights and responsibilities which limit the power of their masters.⁴

a. Ancient Near East

It seems that the number of chattel slaves in the ancient Near East was less than in Greco-Roman society, though in both cases they constituted a mi-

---

2. On the social structure of ancient Israel, see de Vaux (1961: 68-79); von Waldow (1970); Gottwald (1979: 235-587; 1993); Long (1982); Thiel (1985); Rogerson (1986); Martin (1989); Mayes (1989); Chirichigno (1993: 139-42); Bendor (1996); Sneed (1999b); Younker (2003).

3. Driver and Miles (1952: 223).

4. There are several substantial works on slavery in the ancient Near East and in the Old Testament, especially Mendelsohn (1949; 1962); Bakir (1952); Riesener (1979); Cardellini (1981); Dandama[y]ev (1984; 1992a; 1992b). See also Contenau (1954: 14-25); de Vaux (1961: 80-90); van der Ploeg (1972); Wolff (1973: 192-205); Ringgren, Rüterswörden, and Simian-Yofre (1986); Powell (1987); Carpenter (1997); Radner (1997: 195-248); Haas (2003); Westbrook (1995a; 2003b: 40-44); Wilcke (2007: 53-58). On the Greek and Roman world, see Westermann (1955); Finley (1960). On early Christianity, see Glancy (2002).

nority of the population.⁵ The actual condition of slaves varied greatly: some were allowed to marry, own property, and hold responsible jobs; others were cruelly exploited and treated as little more than animals. They belonged to private households, temples, or the palace, and were used as domestic servants, messengers, or in agriculture, industry, and construction.⁶

There were various sources of slaves: prisoners of war, foreign slaves trafficked by merchants, children sold or abandoned by their parents, and desperate people who sold themselves because they could find no other means of survival.⁷ Once such people became slaves, their children would be slaves too, so a slaveowner could rely on a continual supply of labour. Another possible way of obtaining slaves would be kidnapping, but this is specifically forbidden in the Laws of Hammurabi (§14) and Hittite Laws (§§19-21), to be punished by severe penalties.⁸ In principle, no citizen could be enslaved against their will and no dependant without the permission of their head of household, except in the case of punishment for crime (e.g. CH §54; cf. Exod 22:3).

Like other property, chattel slaves could be transferred between owners as a gift or legacy, or by means of trade.⁹ Several clauses in the Laws of Hammurabi address the buying and selling of slaves. If a slave develops epilepsy within a month of sale, the buyer is entitled to return the slave for a full refund (§278), and the seller has to take responsibility if a claim arises contesting the legality of the sale (§279; cf. NBL §6).¹⁰ Slaves were also hired out, and hire contracts often include a clause providing for compensation if the slave runs away, fails to work, or develops epilepsy.¹¹

If someone buys a slave abroad, but on returning home someone else identifies the slave as their property, the original owner has the right to

---

5. Dandama[y]ev (1984: 215-19, 648, 652, 660); Greengus (1995: 477); cf. Mendelsohn (1949: 119-20); Westermann (1955: 5-12, 28-34, 84-90).

6. Mendelsohn (1949: 64-74, 92-117); Dandama[y]ev (1984: 235-397, 469-584).

7. For further details, see Mendelsohn (1949: 1-33); Dandama[y]ev (1984: 103-11).

8. The terms translated 'kidnap' or 'abduct' are the ordinary words for 'steal' in the respective languages, as also in similar laws in the Bible (Exod 21:16; Deut 24:7), since kidnapping is of course a kind of theft. See Driver and Miles (1952: 105) for discussion of the Babylonian law, and Hoffner (1997: 179-80) for the Hittite one.

9. Dandama[y]ev (1984: 207-14). On the value of slaves in ancient law, see Lindgren (1995).

10. Cf. Mendelsohn (1949: 38-40); Driver and Miles (1952: 478-82); Greengus (1997: 2-7); Radner (1997: 174-79).

11. *CAD* (2: 206); Mendelsohn (1949: 59-62); Oelsner (2003: 930-31); cf. Sumerian Family Laws (AI §A7).

claim the slave back (CH §§280-81). The rule of §279 (which makes the seller responsible for any claim) cannot be applied here, because the seller is in a foreign country and not subject to Babylonian law, so a different procedure is set out. If the slave is a native of the home country, the buyer is to return the slave to the original owner without payment; if the slave is a foreigner, the buyer is to be compensated at cost price by the owner. Presumably the reason for the distinction is that the buyer should establish the legal status of a slave originating from his own country before completing the purchase, whereas he cannot be expected to do that if the slave is a foreigner. A Babylonian slave in a foreign country might well have run away or been stolen from his owner, in which case the finder should return him, not take possession of him (cf. LU §17; CH §§17, 32; HL §§22-23a). The slave is expected to show loyalty to his original owner in these circumstances, and if he does not do so is punished by the removal of an ear (CH §282).[12]

There are several other laws which deal with irregular sales of slaves. Someone who buys a slave is considered a thief if he cannot establish the identity of the seller (LE §40) or has no witnesses or contract to verify the purchase (CH §7).[13] It is also a serious offence to sell someone who is not a chattel slave, but is residing in a house as a temporary slave or pledge or for some other reason (MAL §§C2-3).[14]

There are a number of regulations in the ancient Near Eastern laws concerning the marriage of slaves. A particular concern is the status of children born to a marriage between a slave and a free person (especially LU §5; CH §§175-76; HL §§31-32).[15] It is assumed that the children of a

---

12. For a detailed discussion of these clauses, see Driver and Miles (1952: 482-90).

13. The role of witnesses is illustrated in an Egyptian lawsuit over a Syrian slave, in which a woman is accused of using another woman's property to purchase a slave (*COS:* 3.10). The defendant denies the accusation, pointing out that the transaction had been made 'in the presence of the authorities' and making an oath of innocence, but the accuser brings six witnesses to support his case. Various contracts for the sale of slaves have been discovered, e.g. Sumerian contracts from the third millennium B.C. (*COS:* 3.133A, B; Mendelsohn 1949: 34-38) and numerous Neo-Assyrian contracts (*COS:* 3.111-12, 114; SAA 6: nos. 1-9, 39-41, 48-59, 85-92, 96, 244, 246, 289, 341-48; SAA 14: nos. 3-6, 8-10, 12-14, 16-21, 56, 240-47, 264, 337). On contracts in the Neo-Babylonian and Persian periods, see Dandama[y]ev (1984: 181-206).

14. On temporary slaves, see below, 6.1.a; on human pledges, see 10.2.a.

15. For further discussion, see Mendelsohn (1949: 55-58); Driver and Miles (1952: 353-56); Westbrook (1988a: 66-68; 1998: 224-27). On slave marriages in the Neo-Babylonian period, see Dandama[y]ev (1984: 406-14). For an example of a marriage between an Elephantine Jew and an Egyptian slave girl, see Porten (1968: 203-13).

slave couple are themselves slaves (cf. LE §§33-35; HL §33). According to the Hittite Laws, when a slave marries a free woman without paying a bride-price, she becomes a slave for a period of two to four years (§§35, 175);[16] but if a bride-price is paid, both the slave and the free person retain their respective social status (§§34, 36).[17]

Slave women were distinguished by the lack of a veil, as were prostitutes, and the Middle Assyrian Laws prescribe very heavy penalties for disobeying this law or turning a blind eye when it is disobeyed by others (§§A40-41). According to these laws, the veil is to be worn by all married women and widows, concubines when accompanying their mistress or if their status is formally upgraded to that of a wife, and upper-class single women; while others are strictly forbidden from wearing it. Isaiah 47:1-2 implies that the custom of veiling was standard in Babylonia too.[18]

The laws provide very little information about the manumission of chattel slaves. If manumission is to be granted, it applies on an individual basis, according to the Laws of Ur-Namma, so that if a male slave is freed it does not follow that his wife is freed too (§4). The Edict of Ammi-saduqa provides for the release of temporary slaves and human pledges (§20), but not home-bred slaves (§21). From other sources we know that the commonest methods of manumission were release by adoption and by purchase. In the former case, a slave would be adopted by a master as son or daughter on condition that the slave supported the master until his death and then was freed from any further obligation. In the latter case, either the slave or a relative would pay an agreed sum of money for the release. However, in practice such manumission seems to have been quite rare.[19]

---

16. *COS* (2.19); cf. Hoffner (1997: 186).

17. According to Neufeld (1951: 10-11) and Hoffner (1997: 42, 185), though Hoffner's translation in *COS* is rather different. Cf. Westbrook (1998: 225-26).

18. For a detailed discussion of these clauses, see Driver and Miles (1935: 126-34).

19. Mendelsohn (1949: 78-84); Driver and Miles (1952: 225-30); Dandama[y]ev (1984: 438-55, 648-49). There is a Neo-Assyrian contract for the redemption of a slave (*COS*: 3.113), and a few slave sale contracts allow for the possibility of redemption (e.g. SAA 6: nos. 1, 132, 197, 257; SAA 14: nos. 20, 67, 243). Two contracts stipulate the payment required for redemption, which is considerably higher than the purchase price (SAA 6: nos. 197, 257). Cf. *CAD* (1.1: 115-16).

b. Exodus and Deuteronomy

Both the Book of the Covenant and the Deuteronomic Laws prohibit kidnapping, the main purpose of which would be to enslave a person or sell them as a chattel slave to someone else. (Kidnapping for political reasons or to demand a ransom does not seem to have been common in the ancient Near East.) I will discuss this brief law first, in its two versions, before looking at the rather different law on chattel slavery in Leviticus.

In the Book of the Covenant the law is part of a sequence dealing with capital crimes (vv. 12-17), all related to the Decalogue:

Whoever kidnaps a person and sells him, or [if the person] is found in his possession,[20] *shall be put to death.* (Exod 21:16)

The word translated 'kidnap' is actually the Hebrew verb denoting theft, so this is a particular instance of the eighth commandment (Exod 20:15).[21] Joseph uses the same word when he tells the cupbearer in Egypt that he has been 'stolen out of the land of the Hebrews' (Gen 40:15). Because kidnapping is an offence against a person rather than property, it is punished more severely than ordinary theft — by the death penalty.[22]

No one has the right to deprive another person of their freedom, whether to sell them as a slave or to hold them against their will. When an animal is stolen but still in the thief's possession, the punishment is less severe than if it has been slaughtered or sold (Exod 22:1, 4), perhaps because there may be reason for doubt about the thief's intention and the animal cannot answer for itself. But anyone who holds a free person captive against their will is clearly in the wrong, and the person concerned can testify to the circumstances if required, so no leniency is required.[23]

---

20. So most translations and commentaries, though the syntax of the clause is slightly awkward and other translations are possible. Cole (1973) suggests 'and is caught with the money in his hand'; Westbrook (1988b: 119) suggests 'and he in whose possession he is found' (i.e. both the kidnapper and the buyer are to be punished). Daube (1947: 95), who accepts the standard translation, suggests the clause is an interpolation to close a loophole whereby a kidnapper who has not yet sold the person would be excused the death penalty. A possible Akkadian parallel to the expression is cited by Paul (1970: 66).

21. Some scholars suppose that the eighth commandment itself is concerned with kidnapping, but this supposition is to be rejected (see above: ch. 2.1.b).

22. See above, 2.1.e. Cf. Paul (1970: 65).

23. Houtman (1996).

The Deuteronomic version restates the law of Exodus, with two clarifications and a theological explanation:

When a person is caught kidnapping a brother, one of the people of Israel,[24] *and treats him as a slave*[25] *or sells him, that kidnapper shall die, and [so] you will purge the evil from your midst.* (Deut 24:7)

First, it is clarified that the law is concerned with the kidnapping of a fellow-member of the covenant community. The Mishnah assumes that this is also intended in Exodus (*Sanhedrin* 11:1; cf. LXX), and in the context of the Book of the Covenant this is probably the primary concern. Those who have been freed by God from slavery in Egypt must never be enslaved again (cf. Exod 20:2; Lev 25:39-43; Deut 15:15). There would not be many opportunities for kidnapping foreigners, in any case, apart from in war, when it was assumed that defeated enemies would be killed or enslaved.[26] Although kidnapping foreigners in peacetime is not specifically prohibited, the absence of a prohibition does not amount to permission. The exhortations concerning the rights of resident aliens indicate that this would also be considered wrong, even if not a capital crime (e.g. Exod 22:21; 23:9; Lev 19:33-34; 24:22; Deut 24:17-22).[27]

Second, the death penalty is limited by Deuteronomy to a kidnapper who enslaves someone, whether for their own use or to sell to someone else (cf. Rabbi Judah in *Mishnah Sanhedrin* 11:1), whereas the wording of Exodus could be understood to mean that possession of someone is a capital crime in itself, regardless of whether enslavement can be proved. In practice, in the tightly knit society of ancient Israel, a kidnapper would be unlikely to keep someone in their possession for long, or try to sell them to another Israelite, but would probably sell them abroad as soon as possible

---

24. Lit. 'stealing a person, from his brothers, from the people of Israel'.

25. The verb התעמר is found only here and in Deut. 21:14. I have translated it 'treat as a slave' (as ESV; NIV; cf. NJB; NJPS; NRSV; TEV), which is also the traditional Jewish understanding, both here (*Mishnah Sanhedrin* 11:1; *Sifre* 273) and in Deut. 21:14 (Josephus, *Antiquities* 4:259; Philo, *Virtues* 115; *Sifre* 214). Others suggest 'deal tyrannically with' (BDB; cf. REB; Driver 1902; Thompson 1974) or 'treat as a commodity' (Nelson 2002; cf. *HALOT*; David 1951; Hulst et al. 1960: 16; Christensen 2002). Alt (1952) argues that it refers to the action of someone who claims power of disposal over another, on the basis of a cognate noun in Ugaritic.

26. See below, 5.1.d.

27. Cf. HL §§19-21, which specify different punishments for kidnapping, depending on the nationality of the person concerned.

(cf. Gen 37:25-28), thus also depriving them of the benefits of living in the covenant community.

The theological explanation is that this is necessary 'to purge the evil from your midst,' a characteristic formula of Deuteronomy that is regularly used in connection with capital punishment (cf. 13:5; 17:7, 12; 19:13, 19; 21:21; 22:21, 22, 24).[28]

c. Holiness Code

> *The slaves[29] you may have, male and female, [are to come] from the nations around you; from them[30] you may buy male and female slaves. And you may also buy children[31] of temporary residents living with you, and members of their clans who are with you, who have been born in your land; and they may become your property. You may bequeath them to your children after you as inherited property, you may treat them as slaves in perpetuity; but as for your brothers, the people of Israel, you shall not rule over one another with harshness.*
>
> Lev 25:44-46

This is the only biblical law which specifically permits chattel slavery, though several others assume its existence. However, even this law is not designed to encourage it, but rather to limit it to those who are outside the covenant community of Israel. Only two categories of people may be slaves: residents of other countries (v. 44) and temporary foreign residents in Israel (v. 45). The latter group is probably to be distinguished from 'resident aliens', who have rights comparable to those of poorer Israelite citizens.[32]

---

28. There is a similar sentiment in the epilogue to the Laws of Hammurabi, which makes it clear that any future king is expected to observe the same principles of justice, and 'eradicate the wicked and the evil from his land' (lines xlviii.91-92).

29. The Hebrew is singular, but has a collective meaning in the context.

30. The preposition מִ ('from') probably has a partitive meaning here (cf. n. 31), so that the sentence permits buying foreigners as slaves, rather than slaves from foreigners.

31. Understanding the preposition מִן to have a partitive meaning, as in v. 25 (so Hartley 1992; cf. NJPS; REB; TB; TEV) and v. 44. The word בני may be intended as a collective term referring to the temporary residents themselves rather than their children, in which case the translation would become: 'you may also buy some of the temporary residents' (cf. NIV; NRSV).

32. See below, 7.1.

The law permits only buying slaves, not kidnapping; so it concerns the acquisition of those who are already slaves, or are offered for sale by their families, not the forcible enslaving of free people. Such slaves may be owned as property[33] and passed on to others (v. 46a). These verses are really little more than a clarification of verses 39-42, which emphatically prohibit slavery for Israelites, and end by reaffirming that point (v. 46b).[34]

d. Conclusion

The existence of chattel slavery was taken for granted in the ancient Near East, both by the free population and by the slaves themselves. There is no trace of ideological condemnation of the institution as such nor of demands for its abolition.[35] War captives were often enslaved, but kidnapping free citizens was illegal. Slaves were bought and sold, given and inherited, and their children became slaves too. The legal status of a slave was property rather than person, but not entirely without human rights. Usually chattel slaves remained in bondage throughout their lives, though there are a few examples of manumission.

Turning to the Old Testament, we see that chattel slavery is still taken for granted.[36] Abraham is recorded as having many slaves, either born in his house or bought with his money (Gen 14:14; 15:3; 17:12, 13, 23, 27). Prisoners of war taken by Israel become slaves (Gen 34:29; Num 31:7-12; Deut 20:10-14; cf. Isa 14:2), though this is not allowed in the case of the Canaanites, for whom total destruction is prescribed (Deut 20:15-18).[37] In fact the destruction is far from total, and there are several references to the subjugated local population becoming slaves or made to do forced labour (Josh 9:23; 16:10; 17:13; Judg 1:28-35; 1 Kgs 9:15-21; cf. Gen 9:25). It is apparently normal for Israelites to buy slaves too (Exod 12:44; Lev 22:11; cf. Eccl 2:7), and international trafficking of slaves is also mentioned (Ezek 27:13; Joel 3:3, 6; cf. Amos 1:6, 9; 1 Maccabees 3:41; 2 Maccabees 8:10-11). Gideon

---

33. Hebrew אחזה, used only here with reference to persons (Milgrom 2001: 2230).

34. On vv. 39-42, see below, 6.3.b. According to Milgrom (2000: 1694-95; 2001: 2214), Lev 19:28b also prohibits Israelites from becoming slaves, but this interpretation is questionable.

35. Dandama[y]ev (1992a); cf. Finley (1973: 68).

36. For discussion of hermeneutical issues relating to the Bible's acceptance of slavery, see Swartley (1983); Giles (1994); Barclay (2007).

37. According to Deut 21:10-14, Israelites are allowed to take captured girls as concubines. This text will be discussed below, 6.2.c.

and Ziba are mentioned as owning a significant number of slaves (Judg 6:27; 2 Sam 9:10). Slaves constitute about 15 percent of the postexilic community (Ezra 2:64-65).

There are relatively few biblical laws concerning chattel slavery compared with the extensive treatments in other ancient Near Eastern laws.[38] The main principles are that free citizens must not be kidnapped and made slaves (Exod 21:16; Deut 24:7), and only non-Israelites may be treated as slaves at all (Lev 25:44-46). In general it seems Israelites did not enslave fellow-members of the covenant community, in accordance with these laws, and this is specifically stated in the case of Solomon (1 Kgs 9:22).[39] Northern Israel took slaves from the people of Judah after their defeat in battle, but set them free again when reprimanded by a prophet of the LORD (2 Chr 28:8-15). Inevitably Israelites became slaves in foreign countries from time to time, such as Samson in Gaza (Judg 16:21) and the servant of Naaman's wife (2 Kgs 5:2), though when Nebuchadnezzar deported the Judeans to Babylon it seems they were not enslaved en masse.

However, although slavery was not abolished in ancient Israel, the laws move in the direction of ameliorating the condition of slaves. This may be seen in several laws that will be discussed below, especially those on slave abuse (ch. 5.2), fugitive slaves (ch. 5.3), and the right of slaves to worship and take holidays (ch. 11.1). Humane treatment is also emphasised in the laws on semi-slaves: temporary slaves (ch. 6.1), concubines (ch. 6.2), and bonded labourers (ch. 6.3).[40] If put into practice, laws such as these would serve to limit the worst effects of slavery and ensure that even slaves have basic human rights.

Tragically, in spite of its progressive abolition as a legal institution during the past two centuries, slavery itself has survived until the present day. It takes many different forms such as debt bondage, contract slavery, and forced prostitution. In a few countries, such as Mauritania and the Sudan, traditional chattel slavery continues as well. Altogether, it has been es-

---

38. Greengus (1997) discusses this, arguing on the basis of parallels with rabbinic literature that some of the ancient Near Eastern laws were known and accepted in ancient Israel, even though they did not find their way into the Hebrew Bible.

39. Although we are told Solomon keeps the letter of the law by not enslaving Israelites, he uses them for forced labour, which causes a good deal of resentment (1 Kgs 5:13-14; 11:28; 12:4, 18). In some circumstances Hebrews could become semi-slaves (e.g. Exod 21:2-11; Deut 15:12-18), and this will be discussed below, ch. 6.

40. There are also a few laws in which slaves are treated merely from the perspective of their value as property (e.g. Exod 21:21, 32).

timated that there are twenty-seven million slaves at the beginning of the twenty-first century, more than at any other time in history.[41] The number would be far greater if it included two hundred million child labourers, and countless women and men working for a pittance in exploitative factories and plantations, or sacrificing their personal dignity to work in the sex trade, whose only choice is between degrading employment and grinding poverty. Although my concern here is not to discuss these modern problems, I mention them to guard against the erroneous assumption that the subject of slavery is of purely historical interest and that today's world is more civilised and kind.

5.2 Slave Abuse

As mentioned above, even slaves had some human rights in the ancient Near East, though they were limited compared with those of free citizens. For example, a number of laws were designed to protect slaves from abuse.

a. Ancient Near East

There are several references to slave abuse in the Mesopotamian laws. The Laws of Lipit-Ishtar stipulate that anyone who strikes a slave woman, causing a miscarriage, must give monetary compensation, at one sixth of the rate applicable in the case of a free woman (§§d, f). If a man deflowers another man's slave woman, the Laws of Eshnunna demand that he pay substantial compensation and clarify that he does not thereby gain any right of ownership over her (§31). According to the Laws of Hammurabi, someone who blinds the eye or breaks the bone of a slave has to pay half the slave's value (§§199, 220), while someone who kills a slave has to replace the slave or pay twenty shekels of silver (§§116, 214, 219; cf. 213). Similarly, if a man's ox is known to be dangerous but he fails to take safety precautions

---

41. Bales (1999); cf. UNHCHR (1991); Jermyn (2002); Britannica (2003a; 2003b); Anti-Slavery International (2005). A report of the ILO (2005) gives a rather lower figure of 12.3 million, though emphasises that this is a minimum estimate. For examples of slavery, see Huggler (2006). According to a recent United Nations report (UNODC 2006), human trafficking takes place all over the world today, with 127 countries of origin (mainly developing countries), 137 destination countries (mainly in the industrialised world), and 98 transit countries.

and it kills a slave, monetary compensation is payable (§252).[42] In each case the punishment is less than for the same injury to a free person (§§196-98, 209-12, 251).

The most detailed treatment of slave abuse is in the Hittite Laws. Someone who kills another person's slave has to replace him with two slaves of his own (§2), unless it is an accident, in which case one slave is to be given (§4). Monetary compensation is required for injuries, with different amounts for blinding an eye or knocking out a tooth (§8), breaking an arm or leg (§12), biting off a nose or tearing off an ear (§§14, 16), and causing a miscarriage (§18). In most cases the punishment is half of that required in the case of an equivalent injury to a free person (§§1, 3, 7, 11, 17). Later versions of some laws differentiate between deliberate injuries and accidents (§6), and between injuries which cause permanent and temporary handicaps (§11).

In all these cases, it may be assumed that compensation is paid not to the slaves themselves but to their masters, since it is the master who is considered to have suffered a loss by damage to his property. Related to this, it should be noted that these laws do not protect slaves from abuse by their own masters, though it would normally be in the interest of masters to avoid permanently injuring or killing their own slaves. In fact, the laws are not designed to protect slaves at all, but to protect masters from loss if their slaves are injured or killed by others.[43]

b. Book of the Covenant

In a section of the Book of the Covenant dealing with various kinds of violence (Exod 21:12-27), there are two rules about slave abuse, which cover beating (vv. 20-21) and permanent injury (vv. 26-27). It is striking that both rules concern abuse by the slave's own master, which is quite unprecedented in ancient Near Eastern law, as shown above.[44]

There has been considerable scholarly debate about the kind of slaves

---

42. For discussion of this clause, and similar clauses in other ancient Near Eastern laws, see above, 3.1.a.

43. There are a few references to punishment of slaves, which seem cruel by modern standards but may possibly have been intended to restrain the fury of masters and give some protection to slaves by setting a limit to punishment for certain offences (e.g. CH §§205, 282; MAL §A44). See Chirichigno (1993: 145-46); Westbrook (2003c: 383).

44. Cf. Paul (1970: 69); Boecker (1976: 162); Wright (1990: 241); Sarna (1991).

intended here, whether [foreign] chattel slaves[45] or [Hebrew] debt-slaves[46] or slaves in general.[47] The context suggests that these laws are designed to supplement those on homicide (vv. 12-14) and injuries (vv. 15, 18-19, 22-25), which are concerned primarily with free members of the covenant community. Since the legal status of a slave is somewhere between that of a person and property, it cannot be assumed that the preceding laws automatically apply to slaves, so these supplementary laws clarify the situation. A master is not free to treat his slave as mere property but is obliged to respect the slave's dignity as a human being, though the law is not quite the same as for a free person. The primary reference is probably to chattel slaves, who would be at the greatest risk of abuse since they were generally of foreign origin and would have no family in the vicinity to protest or to avenge them. This is confirmed by the expression 'the slave is his property' (v. 21b[48]) and is clearly what is meant in the case of a slave gored to death by an ox (v. 32). It is difficult to be sure whether 'Hebrew' debt-slaves (v. 2)[49] would be covered by the laws on free persons or those on slaves, since their status is between the two.

Beating

When a man beats his male or female slave with a stick, and the slave dies from the beating,[50] he shall certainly be avenged.[51] But if

---

45. Greenberg (1962b: 738); Sarna (1991); Chirichigno (1993: 148-85).

46. David (1950: 162); Driver and Miles (1952: 223); Cardellini (1981: 258-68, 343-47).

47. Mendelsohn (1962: 388); Boecker (1976: 162).

48. Some scholars have argued that v. 21b is a later addition to the law (e.g. Boecker 1976: 161), but even if that is the case it would seem the editor understood the law to concern chattel slaves.

49. On which, see below, 6.1.

50. So Durham (1987); lit. 'under his hand'. Other possible translations are 'as a direct result' (NIV), 'immediately' (NRSV), 'on the spot' (REB; TEV; Childs 1974).

51. This is almost certainly the literal meaning of the clause נקם ינקם in this context; cf. NJPS; Cazelles (1946); Paul (1970: 69); Liedke (1971: 48); van der Ploeg (1972: 78-80); Greenberg (1986: 11); Chirichigno (1993: 162); Peels (1995: 69); Houtman (1996). However, instead of 'he [i.e. the slave] shall certainly be avenged', most English translations have 'he [i.e. the master] shall certainly be punished' (e.g. NIV; NRSV; REB; RSV; TEV; cf. NJB; Durham 1987). Admittedly the idea of vengeance raises theological and ethical questions to modern ears, but there is no philological reason for translating the verb in this way. Lipiński (1986a: 2) suggests emending the vowels of MT to read *noqem yinnaqem* ('an avenger shall

the slave stays [alive][52] *a day or two, he is not to be avenged,*[53] *for he is his property.*[54]

Exodus 21:20-21

Beating with a stick or rod is the standard method of discipline for children and others (Prov 10:13; 13:24; 19:25; 22:15; 23:13-14; 26:3; cf. 2 Sam 7:14). In the Deuteronomic law it is limited to forty strokes (Deut 25:3); here the master is to use his discretion but does not have the right to kill his slave. In fact, it would make no sense to punish slaves so severely that they become permanently disabled or die, since the master would lose their labour and their resale value would be reduced, but angry masters do not always behave rationally. So the law insists that masters be sensitive to the physical condition of their slaves and administer punishment accordingly. If they misjudge the situation and the slave dies, they are to be punished. Thus the law provides some protection for slaves from cruel treatment by their masters.

Two exegetical issues arise at this point: the nature of the contrast between verses 20 and 21; and the kind of punishment implied by the term 'avenge'. First, it has been suggested that the contrast between verses 20 and 21 lies in the distinction between intentional and unintentional killing, in other words between murder and manslaughter (as in vv. 12-14).[55] However, it is unlikely that a master would deliberately kill a slave, since he would be depriving himself of his own property (cf. v. 21b). Also, murderers have much more efficient methods of killing than beating with a stick (cf. Num 35:16-18). If the question of intention is crucial here, why is that not stated explicitly as it is in verses 13-14, and also at length in Numbers 35:16-28 and Deuteronomy 19:4-5, 11-13? It is more probable that the law intends to punish a master who fails to restrain his anger in administering discipline and ends up killing a fellow human being (v. 20), while giving him the benefit of the doubt if the slave dies later, since it is then conceiv-

---

take vengeance'), understanding the niphal as a reflexive (which is the normal usage) rather than a passive. The Samaritan Pentateuch has מות יומת ('he shall certainly be put to death') as in v. 12.

52. The verb עמד means 'stand, stay', and is generally understood here to mean 'stay alive, survive' (NJB; NJPS; NRSV; REB; cf. TEV), though NIV has 'get up' (cf. Chirichigno 1993: 174). See further discussion below.

53. See n. 51.

54. I.e. '[the slave] is [the master's] property [lit. 'money']'.

55. Noth (1959); Vesco (1968: 258); Boecker (1976: 161); Peels (1995: 72).

able that something other than the beating was the cause of death (v. 21).[56] In any case, the master suffers the loss of the slave, so does not go entirely without punishment.

It is also possible, as suggested by Chirichigno (1993: 173-77) on the basis of comparison with verses 18-19, that verse 21 does not envisage the slave's death at all but simply a severe beating. The slave is badly injured and may be in danger of death, but nevertheless survives and is able to get up again.[57] In that case it would follow that the master has the responsibility of caring for the slave until he or she is well (cf. v. 19), 'for the slave is his property' (v. 21b). The expression 'day or two' probably refers to a minimum period and does not exclude the possibility that the slave may recover and live for much longer than that.[58]

Second, although elsewhere the term 'avenge' generally implies the death of the person concerned, several scholars argue that a lesser penalty is envisaged in this law.[59] It is pointed out that the formula 'he shall certainly be put to death' (מות יומת; vv. 12, 15, 16, 17) is absent here, suggesting that execution is not envisaged. This is also supported by the different punishments for the injury or death of a slave compared with the injury or death of a free person in verses 26-27 (cf. 23-25) and 32 (cf. 28-31), which make it unlikely that a master would be condemned to death for the killing of a slave since that would make the offence identical with the killing of a free person.[60] Since the actual penalty is not stated, it is assumed that this would be left to the discretion of the judge.

---

56. So Houtman (1996). Daube (1961: 248-50) points to the need for caution where legal consequences are attached to a deed. In this case, a master might well beat his slave frequently. If the master was still liable to punishment when a slave died some time later, it could mean that any death might be linked to the most recent beating, whether or not that was the actual cause (Phillips 1970: 87-88; Greenberg 1986: 12). Less plausibly, Cassuto (1951) argues that even if the beating is the primary cause of death, the master does not actually kill the slave. A lighter punishment (loss of the slave) is appropriate for indirectly causing death, since the master also has human rights and his life must be protected too. This may be compared with vv. 29-30, where capital punishment for allowing a vicious ox to gore someone to death may be commuted for a ransom payment, whereas in the case of murder this is explicitly ruled out (Num 35:31-33).

57. As mentioned above (n. 52), עמד could be translated as 'get up' instead of 'stay [alive]', which would fit well with this interpretation.

58. Cf. the 'two or three witnesses' in Deut 19:15, which does not exclude the possibility of there being four or more witnesses (cf. Jackson 1975f: 161).

59. Driver (1911); Childs (1974); Marshall (1993: 120); Houtman (1996).

60. A further argument adduced by Childs (1974) is that this law is in the section on injury, not manslaughter, but this point has little weight since v. 29 returns to homicide.

Jackson (1975e: 45) suggests that a monetary payment would be required, but does not explain who would be entitled to receive such a payment. Payments in ancient Near Eastern and Israelite law are normally intended as compensation to the injured party, not fines paid to the state, and in this case it would be impossible to pay to the dead slave and inappropriate to pay to the master since the latter is the offender. Since most slaves were foreigners, it is unlikely they would have family at hand who could receive compensation; and in any case there would be no legal right to compensation because the person had been surrendered to another family as a slave, thereby losing rights in their own family. Also, when monetary payments are required, the amount is generally specified (e.g. 21:32-36; 22:1-4).

It seems more likely that the death penalty is intended, which is quite remarkable in that the life of a slave is put on a level with that of a free Israelite. The term 'avenge' (נקם) in the Old Testament usually implies the death of the offender, and an indeterminate punishment would more naturally be expressed by a general expression like 'call to account' (פקד) rather than the specific term for vengeance.[61] The very old interpretation of the Samaritan Pentateuch understands the law to require capital punishment, and this is certainly the traditional Jewish understanding. The head of a household has considerable power over its members — including his wife, children, and slaves — but this does not extend to the right of determining life and death. Only God has that right (Gen 2:7; Deut 30:15-20; 32:39; Eccl 12:7), so to beat a slave to death would be criminal homicide. The principle of life for life applies to the killing of any human being, slave or free (Gen 9:5-6; Exod 21:12; Num 35:30-31).

Many scholars think the law refers to blood vengeance, carried out by the 'redeemer of blood' appointed by the family (e.g. Num 35:19; Deut 19:6, 12).[62] However, in spite of the apparent similarity of the two concepts, such blood vengeance is not in fact expressed in the Bible by the term 'avenge'.[63] Vengeance is taken by Israel, and occasionally individuals, on enemies (e.g. Num 31:2-3; Josh 10:13; Judg 11:36; 15:7) or by God on disobedient nations (e.g. Lev 26:25 re Israel; Num 31:3; Isa 34:8; 47:3 re other nations). The only

---

61. Wright (1990: 241-42); cf. Sprinkle (1994: 100-101); Peels (1995: 72-73).

62. E.g. Merz (1916: 97); Horst (1956: 61); Liedke (1971: 48); Boecker (1976: 162); Lipiński (1986a: 4); Schwienhorst-Schönberger (1990: 71). On blood vengeance, see also de Vaux (1961: 10-12); Greenberg (1962a); McKeating (1963). This procedure may be implied in vv. 12-14, though not in vv. 15-17.

63. Chirichigno (1993: 165).

use of the term in a legal context apart from the present law is Leviticus 19:18, where vengeance is forbidden. There are in fact very few actual examples of blood vengeance within the covenant community, and David is a notable example of refusing vengeance when he spares the lives of Saul and Shimei (1 Samuel 24; 26; 2 Sam 16:5-14; 19:18-23). In any case, blood vengeance by the family is irrelevant for foreign slaves who have been captured in war, bought on the slave market, or born in the home, so it could only be applied in the case of Hebrew slaves. Rather, the law requires justice for a murdered slave, expressed by the idea of vengeance and implying the death penalty, probably to be carried out by the civil authorities.[64] This may be compared with the case of an anonymous murder in Deuteronomy 21:1-9, where the elders, judges, and priests have the responsibility of investigating the matter and taking appropriate action.[65]

According to biblical theology, ultimately it is only God who has the right of vengeance (Deut 32:35, 41, 43; Ps 94:1; 99:8; cf. Rom 12:19), so the sanction here may be understood as divine judgment on the offender.[66] Nevertheless, while it is conceivable that such judgment might be administered directly by an 'act of God' (cf. Gen 4:10, 15; Exod 22:22-24; Num 21:5-

---

64. Cf. Noth (1959); Phillips (1970: 88); Greenberg (1962b: 738); Sarna (1991); Peels (1995: 74, 76; 1997). Greenberg (1986: 13-14) suggests the usual formula (מות יומת) is absent because a slave does not have family to avenge his blood in the 'normal way', so נקם ינקם refers to death by an extraordinary procedure. Differently, Peels (1995: 75-76) suggests that different terminology is used because the usual formula would focus on the perpetrator, whereas the use of נקם focuses attention on the victim (i.e. the slave). Despite being his master's property, a slave is not a thing but a person, and the master must not think he can do as he pleases because there is no blood avenger around to take action (contrast vv. 12-14). Yet another interpretation is proposed by Westbrook (1988b: 89-100), in the light of CH §116 which demands vicarious punishment in the case of a debt-slave's death. From this Westbrook argues that v. 20 is concerned with the death of an Israelite debt-slave and נקם is a technical term for vicarious punishment, meaning that if the debt-slave is another man's son, then a son of the murderer is to be executed, etc. He also argues that v. 21b means 'it [i.e. the revenge] is his money [i.e. the debt]', so that if the slave dies after a few days he forfeits his claim on the debt for which the person concerned was enslaved. While Westbrook's interpretation of v. 21b would make good sense in the case of Hebrew debt-slaves, I have argued above that they are probably not the main focus of this law. Moreover, it is unlikely that vicarious punishment is intended, since it is specifically forbidden in the goring ox case (v. 31), just a few verses later (cf. Deut 24:16). For further critique of Westbrook's interpretation, see Peels (1995: 74-75); Houtman (1996: 158-59).

65. Cf. Lev 20:2, 4 where it is 'the people of the land' who are responsible for carrying out the death penalty.

66. Cf. Lipiński (1986a: 4); Chirichigno (1993: 165).

6), it is more likely that the present law envisages it taking place indirectly through those with God's authority in the community.[67]

Permanent Injury

> When a man strikes the eye of his male or female slave and destroys it, he shall let the slave go free [as compensation] for the eye. And if he knocks out the tooth of his male or female slave, he shall let the slave go free [as compensation] for the tooth.
>
> Exod 21:26-27

The law on beating covers the possibilities that the slave will either die or recover fully. A third possibility is that a slave may suffer permanent bodily injury at the hands of his or her master, and two specific cases of this are addressed by the law of verses 26-27. The law follows and supplements the *lex talionis* ('law of retaliation') in verses 23-25,[68] whereby punishment is administered in proportion to the offence committed by inflicting a similar injury on the offender (cf. Lev 24:18-20; Deut 19:21; CH §§116, 196-97, 200, 229-32; MAL §§A50, 52). That law is concerned with injuries to free citizens, and gives eight examples: life, eye, tooth, hand, foot, burn, wound, stripe. Here just two examples are mentioned (eye and tooth), one much more serious than the other, but it may be assumed that the intention is to cover other injuries to slaves as well. Possibly the word-pair defines the upper and lower limits for application of the law: injuries as serious as causing blindness and as slight as knocking out a tooth.[69] A master is expected to respect a slave's humanity and dignity, and his right to exercise discipline does not extend to maiming or mutilation (contrast CH §282).[70]

---

67. On the vengeance of God, see Swartzback (1952); Mendenhall (1973: 69-104); and the critique of Mendenhall's thesis by Pitard (1982).

68. The use of תחת ('for') with each injury is identical in both laws. On Exod 21:23-25, see Paul (1970: 70-77); Jackson (1975d); Loewenstamm (1977); Westbrook (1986); Van Seters (1999); van Staalduine-Sulman (2006). On the *lex talionis*, see further below, 8.1.d.

69. Sprinkle (1994: 95-96).

70. A rather different interpretation of the law is proposed by Osumi (1992), who sees vv. 24-27 as a unity. On this basis, he argues that v. 25 refers to the punishment of a slave and that the law as a whole is designed to apply the talion principle to treatment of slaves. Thus he concludes that a slave who has suffered any of the injuries listed in vv. 24-25 is to be released. However, this would effectively rule out corporal punishment for the discipline of

From a modern perspective, it may seem inadequate to simply grant freedom to a slave who has been permanently injured without punishing the master responsible. Nevertheless, the ruling of the Book of the Covenant compares very favourably with the Laws of Hammurabi, where a master is compensated for injury to his slave by a third party but nothing at all is said about compensation for the slave (§199). Here the master himself is punished for abuse of his slave, because he forfeits a valuable piece of property, and the slave actually benefits much more than if the *lex talionis* were applied. Even for a relatively minor injury like loss of a tooth, a slave is entitled to freedom. 'The cost of an eye or a tooth to the master might deter brutality, but emancipation changes fundamental social relations'.[71]

Laws do not enforce themselves, and it is unlikely that a master unscrupulous enough to maim his slave would immediately turn round and grant the slave's freedom. So the question arises as to whether the community is expected to notice what has happened and take punitive action, or whether slaves have the right to take their masters to court for maltreatment. Although it is possible that a citizen might feel sufficiently concerned for someone else's slave to risk the wrath of his neighbour by reporting him to the authorities, it is more likely that this law implies the right of slaves in Israel to take legal action against their masters (cf. Job 31:13-15).[72] Thus it is another indication of Old Testament law treating marginal people as human beings, with many of the rights accorded to full members of the covenant community.

c. Conclusion

The laws on slave abuse in the Book of the Covenant are unique in considering such abuse in terms of human rights rather than property rights. Elsewhere in the ancient Near East a slave is treated as property, and the laws concerning abuse are designed to compensate the master for loss or damage to his property. In the Old Testament, however, the laws emphasise that slaves are to be treated as persons — even if not on quite the same level as free citizens — and masters are to be punished if they kill or cause permanent injury to slaves.

---

slaves, contradicting vv. 20-21 which implicitly allow it, so it is less likely than the interpretation I have outlined above.

71. Brueggemann (1994).
72. Wright (1990: 243-49); cf. Phillips (1973: 358).

Apart from the two laws discussed here, there are two other Old Testament laws which touch on the abuse of slaves. First, if an ox gores a slave to death, the law specifies monetary compensation to the master and the death of the ox (Exod 21:32).[73] Second, there is a law concerning sexual relations with a slave woman who is designated for another man (Lev 19:20-22), which allows the matter to be settled with a guilt offering; unlike the Deuteronomic law on sexual relations with a free woman who is engaged (Deut 22:23-27), where the death penalty is required.[74] In both laws the slave is considered more than mere property, but still of lower status than a free person.

The wisdom literature contains various references to humane treatment of slaves (e.g. Job 31:13-15; Prov 30:10; cf. Sirach 33:29-31), as well as warnings against pampering them (Prov 29:19, 21; cf. Sirach 33:24-28). It is aware that all too often the powerful exploit the weak (Eccl 8:9), but there is no sense of need for a social revolution (Prov 19:10; 30:21-22; Eccl 10:5-7). In the world to come, however, there will be no distinction between slave and free (Job 3:19).

5.3 Fugitive Slaves

One of the main issues faced by a slaveowner is how to stop slaves from running away, and most of the ancient Near Eastern law collections touch on this problem.

a. Ancient Near East

The oldest law is in the Laws of Ur-Namma, stipulating a reward for anyone who returns a fugitive slave from another city:

> If [a slave or] a slave woman . . . ventures beyond the borders of [his or] her city and a man returns [him or] her, the slave's master shall weigh and deliver [x] shekels of silver to the man who returned [the slave]. (§17)

---

73. On which, see above, 3.1.b.
74. A similar distinction is found in other ancient Near Eastern laws on sexual relations with an engaged woman: monetary compensation if she is a slave (LE §31), capital punishment if she is free (LE §26; CH §130). On Lev 19:20-22, see Wenham (1979); Hartley (1992); Milgrom (2000: 1665-77).

The Laws of Lipit-Ishtar (§§12-13) deal with the case of a male or female slave who runs away from their master and finds refuge within the same city, requiring the man who provides refuge in his house to compensate the slave's master. Similarly, the Hittite Laws stipulate a scale of rewards for returning fugitive slaves, depending on how far they have run (§§22-23a), and a monetary penalty for harbouring such a slave (§24). However, someone who retrieves a slave from an enemy country is allowed to keep him (§23b).[75]

The most stringent regulations on this subject are in the Laws of Hammurabi. Capital punishment is the penalty for enabling a slave to escape through the main city gate (§15) or harbouring a fugitive slave (§§16, 19). In the latter case, one who keeps another person's slave is guilty of theft (cf. LE §§49-50), which is a capital crime according to Hammurabi. A reward is to be paid to anyone who returns a fugitive slave to his master (§17). If a fugitive slave is caught and refuses to identify his master, he is to be surrendered to the palace authorities for investigation of the circumstances (§18). If a fugitive slave escapes after being caught, the captor has to swear an oath of innocence to free himself from a charge of negligence or collusion in the matter (§20).[76]

In order to make it more difficult for slaves to run away, they were often made to bear fetters, shackles, or a 'slave-mark' (LE §§51-52; CH §146).[77] The nature of the slave-mark *(abbuttu)* is uncertain, but it seems that it was either a distinctive hairstyle,[78] or a mark which was branded, incised, or tattooed in the flesh.[79] It is considered a very serious offence to re-

---

75. For discussion of these clauses, see Hoffner (1997: 180-81).

76. For discussion of these clauses, see Driver and Miles (1952: 105-08). It seems the death penalty for helping slaves to run away was discontinued in the Middle and Neo-Babylonian periods (Mendelsohn 1949: 62-63; Oelsner, Wells, and Wunsch 2003; Slanski 2003b: 517).

77. Akkadian *kannu, maškanu, abbuttu*. For the meaning of these terms, see *CAD* (8:156; 10.1:372; 1.1:48-50); Yaron (1988: 162-65, 349-50); Westbrook (2003c: 382-83). On shackling of slaves, see Dandama[y]ev (1984: 235-38). Gurney (1949: no. 2) records the fastening of a copper chain round the waist of a slave.

78. *CAD; COS;* Rowe (2003a: 707).

79. Mendelsohn (1949: 42-50); Driver and Miles (1952: 306-09, 421-25); Dandama[y]ev (1984: 229-34, 475). Mendelsohn and Dandama[y]ev also give evidence for marking slaves with a tag hung on a chain round the neck, wrist, or ankle. The mark would generally identify the slave's owner, though in some cases it would be a symbol of a god such as a star. Several Aramaic documents refer to marking slaves with their owner's name or other identification (*COS*: 3.68; Porten 1968: 204-5; Lindenberger 2003: 22, 47, 94). In Pharaonic Egypt, both distinctive hairstyles and branding were used to distinguish slaves (Bakir 1952: 68, 98).

move the slave-mark without the consent of the slave's master (CH §§226-27). According to the Sumerian Family Laws (AI §A1), a father is entitled to mark a rebellious son in this way and sell him as a slave.

One of the Hittite Laws specifies punishment for a rebellious slave (§173b), but masters do not generally need laws to tell them to punish their slaves, and any fugitive slave who was caught and returned would expect a thorough beating, if not worse.[80] A letter from Mari reports that a master gouged out the eyes of a slave who had run away, and the same punishment is mentioned in several contracts from Nuzi.[81] From the Neo-Sumerian period, there are examples of a promissory oath being used to discourage fugitive slaves who have been recaptured from running away again.[82]

Various extradition treaties with clauses concerning international fugitives have been found, from as early as the third millennium.[83] Further examples are known from Alalakh[84] and Ugarit,[85] between Egypt and the Hittites,[86] between the Hittites and Amurru,[87] and the third Sefire inscription.[88]

b. Deuteronomic Laws

> *You shall not give up a slave to his master, who comes to you [for protection] from his master. Let him stay with you, in your midst, in the place he chooses in one of your towns, wherever suits him best; you shall not oppress him.*
>
> Deut 23:15-16 [Hebrew 23:16-17]

---

80. CH §282 is not primarily concerned with punishing fugitive slaves, but deals with a specific situation as set out in the preceding two clauses (Driver and Miles 1952: 488-89).

81. Westbrook (2003c: 383); Zaccagnini (2003: 586). An Aramaic letter orders unspecified punishment for a group of fugitive slaves (Lindenberger 2003: 88).

82. Lafont and Westbrook (2003: 200). On fugitive slaves in the Neo-Babylonian period, see Dandama[y]ev (1984: 220-28).

83. Between Ebla and Abarsal, and between Akkad and Elam (Cooper 2003: 248).

84. E.g. *AT* (nos. 2:22-32; 3; cf. 101) = *COS* (2.128; 2.129); cf. Rowe (2003a: 707-8).

85. E.g. *PRU* 4 (17.238, pp. 107-8; 17.369A, p. 52; cf. 18.114, p. 108); cf. Hoftijzer (1991: 197).

86. *ANET* (200-203); cf. Bakir (1952: 89). There is also an Egyptian letter which recounts the pursuit of runaway slaves (*ANET*: 259; *COS:* 3.4).

87. *COS* (2.17B: lines A ii.38′-iii.33). On Hittite treaties, cf. Beckman (2003: 762).

88. *COS* (2.82: stele 3: lines 4b-7a, 19b-20); cf. Greenfield (1991).

Now for something completely different! Deuteronomy provides one of the most striking contrasts between Old Testament law and other ancient Near Eastern laws by prohibiting what is elsewhere a fundamental obligation (v. 15).[89] Members of the covenant community are not to return fugitive slaves to their masters, but must provide them with hospitality and a safe refuge (v. 16a). What in Babylon is a capital offence, in Jerusalem is to be an opportunity for kindness and generosity. Like other marginal people, fugitive slaves could very easily be oppressed, but this is forbidden to the people of God (v. 16b). Oppression of the weak is forbidden in Israel, whether of ethnic minorities (Exod 22:21; Lev 19:33; Jer 22:3), orphans and widows (Jer 22:3; Ezek 22:7), the poor and needy (Ezek 18:7, 12, 16; 22:29), neighbours (Lev 25:14, 17), or ordinary people (Ezek 45:8; 46:18).

The main exegetical issue in this short text is the identity of the slaves who are to benefit from the law. Mendelsohn suggests that the law is intended to help Hebrew slaves who flee from slavery in foreign countries, while Weinfeld thinks it refers to Israelite slaves who flee from oppressive masters, wherever they may be.[90] However, Mendelsohn's view is based on a misunderstanding of clauses §§280-81 in the Laws of Hammurabi,[91] and there is no indication in Deuteronomy that this law is concerned only for Israelite slaves.

In fact, for several reasons, it is much more likely that the primary concern is for foreign slaves who flee to Israel for refuge (cf. Isa 16:3-4).[92] First, the slave is invited to choose a suitable place of refuge in Israel (v. 16a), which suggests he or she has no natural home or family to go to. Israelite slaves who deserted their masters would presumably return to their own clan for protection. Second, the expressions 'in your midst' (cf. 13:1; 16:11; 17:2) and 'in one of your towns' (cf. 15:7; 17:2) are apparently addressed to Israel as a whole and imply the slave had previously been outside the country. If a domestic fugitive were envisaged, it would be more

---

89. The nearest parallel in the ancient world to this biblical law is the practice of granting of temporary asylum for slaves at certain temples, to enable disputes to be resolved or possibly to facilitate the transfer of the slave to a different master (Westermann 1955: 17-18, 39-41; Greenfield 1991; Tigay 1996: 215). In contrast, the biblical law offers permanent asylum in any part of the country.

90. Mendelsohn (1949: 63-64); Weinfeld (1972a: 272 n. 5).

91. Cf. Driver (1952: 482-87).

92. Cf. Driver (1902); de Vaux (1961: 87); von Rad (1964a); Loewenstamm (1971: 252); Thompson (1974); Boecker (1976: 86); Craigie (1976); Mayes (1979); Gnuse (1985b: 26-28); Tigay (1996); McConville (2002a).

natural for the law to be formulated in terms of a slave fleeing from one town to another. Third, if the law was intended to refer specifically to Israelites, it would be normal to indicate that with the use of a term such as 'brother' (cf. 15:7, 12; 22:1-4; 23:19; 24:7; 24:14) or 'neighbour' (cf. 15:2; 19:14; 24:10). Fourth, the laws make clear that Israelites are not allowed to enslave each other, except on a temporary basis to settle a debt — with freedom guaranteed after six years — or by a voluntary choice on the part of the slave to become a permanent member of the master's family.[93] It seems improbable that the law is designed to undermine the economic system by giving debt-slaves permission to default on their commitment and leave their master's service whenever it suits them, or to help slaves who have committed themselves for life to change their mind. Fifth, the law has much more point if it is designed to help those who have become slaves against their will, that is chattel slaves, who would generally be foreigners.[94] Sixth, this law may be seen as part of an effort to maintain the distinctiveness of Israel as a holy nation, bound only by their covenant with God (cf. Deut 6:4-9; 7:2, 6, 9-11) and therefore unwilling to engage in extradition treaties with other nations.

Nevertheless, although the law seems to be concerned primarily with fugitive slaves from abroad, the principle of providing refuge for such people might be extended to specific instances of slaves within the country who flee because of maltreatment (cf. Sirach 33:31). If foreigners in need of protection should be given assistance, the same would surely be true for local people as well.

c. Conclusion

The Deuteronomic law giving protection for fugitive slaves is unique in the ancient Near East, as elsewhere it is considered a serious offence to help such a slave. The other laws focus on maintenance of the status quo, defending the rights of slave owners to keep their property; this law focuses on the slave as a person, emphasising compassion for someone in distress. Clearly this echoes Old Testament traditions which portray Israel's origin as a people who have fled from slavery in Egypt, and who therefore should be sympathetic to others in a similar position. As God has shown his

---

93. See below, 6.1.
94. Cf. above, 5.2.b.

mercy to them, so they must be merciful to others. Slavery is not outlawed in the Old Testament, but its laws clearly move in the direction of weakening the institution and reducing the number of people held as slaves.[95]

It is striking that the fugitive slave is given the opportunity to choose a place to live in the land of Israel. The verb 'choose' is common in Deuteronomy (occurring 31 times), but almost always with God as subject. God chooses his own place to dwell (12:5, 11, 14; etc.), whereas the Israelites are expected to live in the portion of land allotted to their clans (Numbers, Joshua). Apart from the challenge to choose between life and death in Deuteronomy 30:19, it is only in this law that human beings are offered a choice. It is characteristic of Old Testament law that the beneficiaries are not the elite but those at the margins of society. David and Solomon must live where they are told, but asylum seekers can choose their place of residence.

There are several references to fugitive slaves in the Old Testament narrative books, from Hagar (Gen 16:6) to the 'many slaves breaking away from their masters' during the reign of Saul (1 Sam 25:10). On one occasion David finds an Egyptian slave of an Amalekite, who cooperates with him on condition he swears not to hand him over to his master (1 Sam 30:11-15). The inhumanity of the master in question is clear from the fact that he had abandoned the slave when he fell sick (v. 13). In 1 Kings 2:36-46 Shimei is prepared to risk his life to recover two slaves who have fled to the Philistines.[96] The outstanding New Testament example of a fugitive slave is Onesimus, and it is notable that Paul follows the Old Testament precedent of nudging gently in the direction of abolishing slavery rather than promoting an immediate social revolution (Phlm 8-21[97]; cf. 1 Cor 7:21-23; 12:13; Gal 3:28; Col 3:11, 22; 4:1).[98]

---

95. Mendelsohn (1949: 63) suggests that if just this one law had been fully implemented, it would have brought slavery in Palestine to an end. This cannot be sustained, however, since the law is concerned primarily with foreign slaves who flee to Israel for refuge, as demonstrated above.

96. Tigay (1996: 387 n. 57) suggests that this text implies an extradition treaty between Israel and the Philistines, but that is by no means certain.

97. On which, see Feeley-Harnik (1982: 116-25); Piattelli (1987).

98. For a wide-ranging study of flight and freedom in the ancient Near East, see Snell (2001).

Chapter 6

SEMI-SLAVES

Although biblical law does not permit Israelites to enslave other members of the covenant community, there are certain people whose status falls somewhere between that of a free person and that of a chattel slave. In this chapter I discuss three main kinds of 'semi-slave': temporary slaves, concubines, and bonded labourers.

6.1 Temporary Slaves

Temporary slavery is distinct from chattel slavery, because it is entered into for a limited period of time to repay a debt, whereas chattel slavery is a permanent status in which owners have an absolute right of disposal over their slaves.[1]

a. Ancient Near East

From time to time subordinate citizens would incur debts that they were unable to repay, in which case they would be forced to surrender a member of their household or even themselves to work for the creditor or a merchant until the debt was paid.[2] The debtor effectively became a

---

1. On chattel slavery in the ancient Near East and the Old Testament, see above, ch. 5. For a detailed study of debt-slavery (temporary slavery) in the Old Testament, against the background of the ancient Near East, see Chirichigno (1993).

2. Mendelsohn (1949: 5-18); Dandama[y]ev (1984: 157-80).

slave, but only on a temporary basis. In the Laws of Lipit-Ishtar we read as follows:

> If a man's slave contests his slave status against his master, and it is proven that his master has been compensated . . . two-fold, that slave shall be freed. (§14)

This suggests that debtors were released after having provided service equivalent to twice their debt, presumably to cover repayment of capital together with accumulated interest. According to the Laws of Hammurabi, the standard duration of temporary slavery was three years:

> If an obligation is outstanding against a man and he sells or gives into debt service his wife, his son, or his daughter, they shall perform service in the house of their buyer or of the one who holds them in debt service for three years; their release shall be secured in the fourth year. (§117)[3]

Such temporary slaves could become free sooner if they found a way to repay their debt or in the event of a general remission of debts, though both of those eventualities would be quite rare.[4] It is uncertain how far the three-year rule was applied in practice, and it is very possible that some temporary slaves ended up in long-term or permanent slavery.[5] By the Neo-Babylonian period, however, the economic climate in Mesopotamia was considerably better and the sale of free citizens into temporary slavery had become rare.[6]

On the face of it, temporary slavery might be seen as a necessary evil, providing a way for debtors to become solvent again when all other possibilities had been exhausted. However, a number of studies assess the situation much more negatively. Finley and Cornell discuss *nexum*, a voluntary debt-bondage arrangement known in early Rome, raising the question of

---

3. The next two clauses add that the time limit does not apply in the case of a chattel slave being surrendered to settle the debt (§118), and that if a man surrenders a concubine who has borne him children then he retains the right to redeem her by repaying the loan in cash at a later date (§119). For a fuller discussion of the three clauses, see Driver and Miles (1952: 217-19); Chirichigno (1993: 67-72).

4. See below, 10.3.a. Cf. Hallo (1995). SLHF §2:1-13 describes a manumission ceremony, but does not indicate the basis for the slave obtaining his freedom (cf. Driver and Miles 1952: 225-30).

5. On the question of whether CH §117 was enforced, see Hallo (1995: 88-90).

6. Dandama[y]ev (1984: 177-80).

why lenders would make loans to poor peasants who might well be unable to repay them.[7] They suggest that the possibility of default was not only accepted but may in fact have been the primary motivation of the creditor. In other words, while receipt of interest would be a welcome benefit for wealthy businessmen making loans, even more important than this was the prospect of obtaining long-term dependent labour by those who proved unable to repay their loans. Likewise in ancient Babylonia, according to Steinkeller (2002), loans were made primarily in the hope of acquiring the labour and/or land of the debtor. The reason for charging interest was not so much to make a profit on the investment as to increase the amount of the debt to a point where it could not be repaid. One piece of evidence in favour of this supposition is the survival of so many loan documents. It was customary for creditors to hold the documents during the period of the loan and then destroy them on repayment, thus ensuring that the creditor had no further claim on the debtor. The documents which have survived would therefore appear to represent loans that were never repaid, in which case it is likely that these debtors became permanent slaves of the creditors.[8]

b. Book of the Covenant

The key passage in the Book of the Covenant dealing with temporary slaves is Exodus 21:2-6.[9] Three matters are covered:

- freedom in the seventh year (v. 2)
- wives and children (vv. 3-4)
- voluntary extension (vv. 5-6)

---

7. Finley (1981); Cornell (1989: 329-34; 1995: 281-83).

8. From eighteenth-century Alalakh, there is a receipt for the purchase of a debt-slave with an exclusion clause stating that she is not to be released even in the event of a general release (*COS*: 3.100). A Neo-Assyrian contract for the sale of a daughter to settle debts stipulates such heavy penalties for revocation of the transaction that it effectively makes her a permanent slave (SAA 14: no. 85; cf. 162). A Demotic papyrus records a self-sale into slavery which is intended to be permanent from the outset (*COS*: 3.6).

9. On the form and structure of these laws, see Turnham (1987); Osumi (1991: 104-8); Chirichigno (1993: 196-99); Sprinkle (1994: 50-66). On the relationship between these laws and CH §117, see Chirichigno (1993: 218-26).

Freedom in the Seventh Year

When you buy[10] a [male] Hebrew slave, he shall serve six years; and in the seventh, he shall go free[11] without payment.

Exod 21:2

The exact meaning of the term 'Hebrew' (עברי), and its relationship to the people called *ḫabiru* in the ancient Near East, has been long debated.[12] It is often used in the Old Testament in a somewhat derogatory sense, generally by others referring to Israelites rather than by Israelites concerning themselves (e.g. Gen 14:13; 39:14, 17; 40:15; 41:12; Exod 1:15-16, 19; 2:6-7; 1 Sam 4:6, 9; 13:19-20; 14:11, 21[13]; 29:3; Jon 1:9). In the present context the word seems to denote an Israelite in financial difficulty who has to surrender himself or a family member as a limited-term slave to pay his debt (cf. Deut 15:12; Jer 34:9).[14]

Apart from the possibility of people being sold into slavery because of debt (cf. 2 Kgs 4:1-7; Neh 5:5; Amos 2:6), this could also happen as a punishment for theft, if the thief was unable to pay the multiple restitution required by law (Exod 22:1; cf. Gen 43:18; 44:4-17).[15] Either way, it is stipulated that an Israelite who is impoverished to the extent of becoming a

---

10. Falk (1967) and Lipiński (1990) propose the meaning 'acquire' for the verb קנה. However, I have retained the translation 'buy' in the literal translation of the text here, together with 'sell' for its antonym, מכר. On this, see above, ch. 4 n. 32; and below, ch. 6 n. 96.

11. Some commentators have suggested that the word חפשי should be translated 'freedman' (e.g. Paul 1970: 47; Cole 1973; Childs 1974; Wright 1990: 256), indicating a social status above slavery but still lower than that of a full citizen. Chirichigno (1993: 209-14) disputes this at length. There is no evidence for the existence of such a class in historical Israel (Lohfink 1977a). More likely it indicates restoration to full independence within the Israelite community (McConville 2002a: 262).

12. See Lewy (1939); Bottéro (1954); Greenberg (1955); Gray (1958); Weippert (1967: 63-102); Astour (1976); Loretz (1984); Na'aman (1986); Lemche (1992); Chirichigno (1993: 200-206, 275-78).

13. In 1 Sam 14:21 'Hebrews' appear to be distinguished from 'Israelites', perhaps because the derogatory term is applied to those who have sided temporarily with the Philistines. Elsewhere in 1 Samuel the two terms are equivalent in meaning.

14. Alt (1934: 93-96); Paul (1970: 45-47); Ellison (1973); Lipiński (1976); Childs (1974); Wright (1990: 253-59); Chirichigno (1993: 207-18); Pressler (1998: 154); Propp (2006). A similar meaning is evident in Deut 15:12 and Jer 34:9. Van Seters (1996: 540) suggests that this text is concerned with the purchase of a person who is already a slave, but this suggestion is refuted by Levinson (2006a). For other views, see Lemche (1975: 136-42); Weingreen (1976: 133); Riesener (1979: 115-35); Phillips (1984); Lowery (2000: 26-30); Bergsma (2007: 43-45).

15. This might be seen as an ancient equivalent to imprisonment, enabling someone who could not pay restitution to work off the debt over a fixed term (cf. Wenham 1979: 322).

slave of another Israelite may only be held for a maximum of six years before he is released. In other words, he is not a slave in the full sense of the word but enters into a contract for a limited period of time, rather like a bonded labourer (cf. Lev 25:39-43).[16] His social status is somewhere between that of a slave and that of a free citizen, as was the case with temporary slaves in Mesopotamia. Presumably the six years are to be counted from when the person begins to work for the master,[17] though the rule could also be understood to mean that all people in this category are to be released simultaneously in the sabbatical year, that is, every seventh year as observed on a national basis.

It is striking that a law which provides freedom for temporary slaves stands at the beginning of the Book of the Covenant, just as the Decalogue opens with a reminder that the people of Israel have been freed from slavery in Egypt.[18] The word 'Hebrew' (עברי) used here is also associated with the exodus (Exod 3:18; 5:3; 7:16; 9:1, 13; 10:3). The verb 'go' (יצא) is used both for the exodus and for the seventh-year release of slaves. The later laws on temporary slavery and bonded labour make specific reference to the exodus (Deut 15:15; Lev 25:42, 55).

Wives and Children

If he comes alone, he shall go alone; if he has a wife [when he comes], his wife shall go with him. If his master gives him a wife, and she bears him sons or daughters; the wife and her children shall belong to her master, and he shall go alone.

Exod 21:3-4

Temporary slaves are entitled to marry and have children, and becoming a slave or being released from that bond does not affect family rights (v. 3). However, if a slave's wife is the property of his master, then the master's right to ownership takes priority over the slave's right as a husband in the event of conflict between these rights (v. 4; cf. LU §4). This may sound harsh to modern ears, but the whole institution of slavery is harsh, and the principle here is consistent with the nature of that institution in the ancient Near East.

16. On which, see below, 6.3.
17. De Vaux (1961: 173); Craigie (1976: 238); Lemche (1976: 42); Chirichigno (1993: 224).
18. Cassuto (1951); Paul (1970: 52, 106-7); Cole (1973); Sarna (1991); Chirichigno (1993: 187-88); Sprinkle (1994: 62-65).

Masters might well provide their male slaves with wives, often foreign slaves, for the purpose of producing home-bred slaves, without there necessarily being any emotional bond.[19] If that is what is envisaged here, it would explain why the master is not expected to let the wife and children go when the male slave is granted his freedom. In practice, of course, the slave would be likely to develop an emotional bond with his wife and children, irrespective of the master's intentions in initiating the marriage.

It is also conceivable that the wife would be the master's daughter, as in 1 Chronicles 2:34-35.[20] Sheshan had no sons, so he gave his daughter in marriage to a slave, presumably so that they would stay with him to manage his property and care for him in old age, as a son and daughter-in-law would normally do. This is not an exact parallel, however, because Jarha was an Egyptian slave and probably did not have the right to leave after six years' service. There is also some similarity with the account in Genesis 29–31 of Jacob serving Laban twice seven years in order to marry his daughters, and the reluctance of Laban to let his daughters and son-in-law leave.[21]

Voluntary Extension

But if the slave says firmly, 'I love my master, my wife and my children; I will not go free,' then his master shall bring him to God:[22] *he shall bring him to the door, or to the doorpost, and his master shall pierce his ear with an awl, then [he shall be] his slave in perpetuity.*[23]

Exod 21:5-6

Finally, there is a surprise. The law envisages the possibility of a temporary slave choosing to stay with his master even though freedom has been offered to him (v. 5)![24] This implies that Israelite slaveowners treat their slaves

---

19. So Sarna (1991), referring to Gen 14:14; 15:3; 17:12, 13, 23, 27; Lev 22:11; Eccl 2:7; Jer 2:14.

20. For an extended discussion of this passage, see Japhet (1992).

21. Chirichigno (1993: 229); cf. Carmichael (1992: 79-87; 2000: 510-19). Another incomplete parallel is Eliezer (Gen 15:2-3), the slave who is to be Abraham's heir if he has no sons of his own, though he does not marry his master's daughter.

22. Cf. Exod 22:8. On the translation of this expression, see above, ch. 3, n. 63.

23. Cf. 1 Sam 27:12; Job 41:4. The same term (*'bd 'lm*) is found several times in the Kirta Epic, e.g. *CTA* 14 lines 55, 127, 139-40 (tr. in *COS:* 1.102, pp. 334-35). According to halakhic exegesis, this means until the death of the master or the jubilee, either of which brings release to slaves apart from the other rules (e.g. *Sifre* 122; cf. Tigay 1996).

24. The cynical view of Crüsemann (1992: 156), that this law is not really intended for

humanely, so that the condition of a slave in the family of a good master may be better than that of a poor free person without land as a source of sustenance.[25] This might be particularly relevant for someone unable to live independently, for example because of disability or old age, though in Israel's tightly knit society most people would have the option of returning to their families. The idea that a slave might *love* his master and prefer bondage to freedom is distinctively biblical, with no known ancient Near Eastern parallels.[26] The slave's love for his family is also a factor in the decision, of course, and it could be that one motive behind a master's gift of a wife would be to put pressure on the slave to stay permanently.

The ear-piercing ceremony is undergone in the presence of God, probably at the door of the sanctuary.[27] In this way it is confirmed publicly that the master has fulfilled his responsibility to release the slave at the end of the agreed period of service, and that the slave has freely chosen to continue in service.[28] It is possible that a ring or tag would be inserted into the pierced ear to brand the person as a perpetual slave,[29] making it more difficult to run away, though this seems inappropriate for someone who has voluntarily entered into slavery. Indentured servants in the ancient Near East were not required to be branded, and even some chattel slaves were excepted from the procedure, so it may be that the ceremony is purely symbolic and the ear would be left to heal.[30] The ear as the organ of hearing perhaps symbolises obedience, in this case to the head of the household of which the slave is to be a permanent member (cf. Ps 40:6-8).[31]

---

the protection of the slave but to facilitate the transition from temporary to permanent slavery, is unconvincing.

25. Noth (1959).

26. Lohfink (1977a: 117).

27. The expression 'bring him to God' probably refers to the sanctuary, and may have involved the taking of an oath, as in Exod 22:8-9 (on which, see above, 3.3.b). In that case, the door is presumably that of the sanctuary, as in LE §37 (Fensham 1959; Loretz 1960: 168-70; Durham 1987; Chirichigno 1993: 240-41). However, it is also possible that oath-taking at the sanctuary would be followed by ear-piercing at the house (cf. Driver 1911: 184), or that the whole ceremony was intended to take place in the home (Paul 1970: 50; Sprinkle 1994: 55-56; Houtman 1996). A third possibility is that the 'door' refers to the city gate (Ibn Ezra; cf. Propp 2006).

28. Falk (1959).

29. Mendelsohn (1962: 385).

30. Chirichigno (1993: 243).

31. Hoffmann (1913); Boecker (1976: 159); Sprinkle (1994: 55-56). For an extended discussion of this procedure in the light of ancient Near Eastern sources, see Hurowitz (1992).

c. Deuteronomic Laws

Deuteronomy also has a law on temporary slaves (15:12-18), which follows on directly from its legislation on debt relief.[32] It is based on that in the Book of the Covenant (Exod 21:2-6) but has significant differences and additions.[33] Four main aspects of the subject are covered:

- freedom in the seventh year (v. 12)
- generous provision for freed slaves (vv. 13-15)
- voluntary extension (vv. 16-17)
- promise of divine blessing (v. 18)

Freedom in the Seventh Year

When your Hebrew brother or sister[34] is sold[35] to you, and serves you six years, in the seventh year you shall let them[36] go free from you.

Deut 15:12

---

32. On which, see below, 10.3.

33. Most interpreters agree that the Deuteronomic law is later than that of Exodus and based on the former (e.g. Driver 1902; Horst 1930: 74-76; von Rad 1964a; Weingreen 1976: 133-39; Japhet 1978: 69-70; Cardellini 1981: 357-76; Lemche 1984; Lohfink 1996a: 149-65; Tigay 1996: 466; McConville 2002a; Levinson 2006b: 293-304). The main alternative view is that of Kaufmann (1961: 168), who considers the two to be 'independent crystallizations of Israel's legal-moral literature', while agreeing that the version in Deuteronomy is later than that in Exodus (cf. David 1948: 73; Boecker 1976: 180). A more radical — and unconvincing — theory is that of Loretz (1984: 139-61), van Seters (1996), and Sparks (1998: 245-50), who argue that the Exodus text is later than that of Deuteronomy. For a synopsis of the two laws, together with that on bonded labourers in Lev 25, see below, 6.3.c. On the setting and form of the Deuteronomic law, see Hamilton (1992b: 19-31); Chirichigno (1993: 256-63); Christensen (2001).

34. Lit. 'your brother, a Hebrew or Hebrewess'.

35. *DCH*, following Falk (1967) and Lipiński (1982; 1984), proposes the meaning 'deliver over/up' for the verb מכר, since it refers to transfer of possession, not necessarily by way of sale. In some contexts this is certainly more appropriate than 'sell', but I have retained the conventional translation here because a monetary transaction is involved, in that the poor person becomes a temporary slave in order to clear a debt. For further discussion of the Hebrew terminology, see above, ch. 4, n. 32. The niphal of מכר is usually passive in meaning, as is clear in Exod 22:1; Lev 25:23, 34, 42; 27:27, 28; Esth 7:4; Ps 105:17; Isa 50:1; 52:3. In the present text it could possibly be understood as the reflexive, 'sold himself/herself' (BDB; NIV; NJB; REB; TEV; McConville 2002a), but the majority translate it as the passive, 'is sold' (*HALOT*;

The law in Exodus is concerned with male slaves, though a few interpreters have suggested it might have been intended to include females in certain circumstances;[37] but the Deuteronomic law applies explicitly to both sexes (v. 12; see also v. 17b). In any case, regardless of whether it is implied in Exodus, Deuteronomy clearly envisages the possibility of a free woman being sold as a temporary slave, most likely because of debts incurred by her father or husband. The terms and conditions are the same for males and females: both are to work for a fixed term and then be released.[38]

There are three other differences from Exodus 21:2. First, the person concerned is described as a 'brother', a term regularly used to denote a fellow-member of the covenant community. In this context it emphasises that someone who has fallen on hard times and becomes a temporary slave should be treated as part of the extended Israelite family, not as an inferior being.[39] This term replaces the noun 'slave' in the earlier law, though the corresponding verb ('serve') is still used. Second, in Exodus the emphasis is on the action of the creditor, expressed by the verb 'buy'; whereas Deuteronomy focuses on the debtor, with the verb 'sold'. Third, reversing the emphasis, the release is described in Exodus from the perspective of the debtor, with the verb 'go'; but in Deuteronomy from the perspective of the creditor, using 'let go'. The former focuses on the right of the temporary slave to go free, the latter on the obligation of the master to grant freedom (cf. Exod 21:26-27).[40]

NJPS; NRSV; Driver 1902; Craigie 1976; Chirichigno 1993: 275-76; Schenker 1998: 31-32; Christensen 2001). Two other instances of the niphal in Neh 5:8 and Jer 34:14 are variously translated. Only in the law about bonded labourers in Lev 25:39, 47, 48, 50 is it necessary to translate the verb as a reflexive (on which, see below, n. 97).

36. Lit. 'him'.

37. E.g. Tigay (1996: 149). There is a supplementary law dealing with females in Exod 21:7-11, but this is concerned with girls sold as concubines, not temporary slaves, and will be discussed separately below, 6.2.b.

38. Phillips (1984: 56) suggests that the development of the law in Deuteronomy is due to the extension of legal responsibility to women, making the law of Exod 21:8-11 redundant and giving male and female slaves the same rights and privileges (cf. Driver 1902; Mayes 1979). However, although that may be the reason why Deuteronomy regulates both men and women becoming temporary slaves, it does not make Exod 21:8-11 redundant since this is dealing with a different situation, as discussed below (ch. 6.2; cf. Chirichigno 1993: 279-82).

39. On the word אח, see above, ch. 2, n. 87; also Hamilton (1992b: 34-40). This word is also used in the related passages in Lev 25:39 and Jer 34:9, 14, 17.

40. Mayes (1979) and Gnuse (1985a: 44) suggest that Deuteronomy intends all temporary slaves to be released simultaneously in the seventh year on a national basis, since all debts are remitted in that year (vv. 1-11). This would mean that slaves serve for a maximum

Generous Provision for Freed Slaves

And when you let them go free from you, you shall not let them go empty-handed. Provide generously for them — sheep, grain, and wine[41] *— giving to them as the* LORD *your God has blessed you. Remember that you were a slave in the land of Egypt, and the* LORD *your God redeemed you; that is why I am giving you this command today.*

Deut 15:13-15

Whereas Exodus 21:2 simply stipulates that the slave is to be freed in the seventh year 'without payment', Deuteronomy insists on open-handed generosity. Freed slaves are to receive a share of the produce which resulted from their work (vv. 13-14). Otherwise, it could easily happen that freed slaves would be worse off than before, since they would probably have no land of their own to grow crops and in any case it would take time to find a means of sustenance. So the master is encouraged to give the leaving slave severance pay, to express gratitude for service rendered and provide capital for life as a free person. The amount to be given is not specified, as it would be a contradiction in terms to legislate for generosity, which would then no longer be generosity but obedience to the law. 'As the LORD God has blessed you' implies that the master should give what he can afford, in proportion to his wealth (cf. 16:10, 17).[42]

The Deuteronomic version of the law is apparently designed to ensure that temporary slaves take advantage of the opportunity to become free at the end of the agreed period, if at all possible.[43] Moreover, it attempts to break the cycle of poverty that would otherwise quickly result in the freed person becoming a slave again.

Like several other laws in Deuteronomy, the command to free temporary slaves is based on the remembrance that God freed his people from

---

of six years, rather than a fixed period from when their service began as in Exodus. However, this does not fit with vv. 12 and 18 which state that slaves work for six years before release (cf. Jer 34:14); cf. Robinson (1988: 118-19).

41. Lit. 'from your flock, and from your threshing-floor, and from your wine-press'.

42. So Tigay (1996), who mentions that halakhic exegesis stipulates a minimum gift of thirty shekels, the price of a slave according to Exod 21:32. Such a gift would presumably be equivalent to the original debt, which would be generous indeed, but there is no indication that the text itself implies any specific amount.

43. Phillips (1984: 56-57).

slavery in Egypt (v. 15; cf. 5:15; 16:12; 24:18, 22). There is probably an allusion to the jewellery and clothing given by the Egyptians to the Israelites at the time of the exodus (Exod 3:21-22; 11:2-3; 12:35-36). This is supported by the word 'empty-handed' (ריקם) here and in Exodus 3:21; and by an unusual verb (עָנַק), which I have translated 'provide generously' but which literally means 'make a necklace'. There may also be an allusion to the account of Jacob leaving Laban after his twenty years' service (Gen 31:41-42), which uses the same pair of Hebrew words as in the present verse concerning Laban's intention — overruled by God — to let Jacob go empty-handed.[44]

Voluntary Extension

But it may be that [the slave] says to you, 'I will not go from you'; because he loves you and your household, because he is well off with you. Then you shall take an awl and put it through his ear into the door, and he shall be your slave in perpetuity. And you shall do likewise for your female slave.

Deut 15:16-17

As in Exodus, temporary slaves are to be given the option of staying in service if they wish, and the same rule applies here to both males and females. Nevertheless, the generous provision stipulated in the previous verses should ensure that slaves do not continue in that state simply because there is no realistic economic alternative, but only if they really want to do so. The ear-piercing ceremony is essentially the same in both laws, except that the requirement for the master to bring the slave 'to God' is omitted. In view of the centralisation of worship characteristic of Deuteronomy, it is likely that a ceremony at home is envisaged rather than at a local sanctuary.[45]

---

44. The Hebrew words are שלח and ריקם. This allusion is suggested by Daube (1963: 66-71); cf. Chirichigno (1993: 287-90); Carmichael (2000: 519-23). Cf. 1 Sam 6:3; Job 22:9.
45. Von Rad (1964a).

Promise of Divine Blessing

Do not consider it a hardship when you let them[46] go free from you, for they have served you six years at half the cost of a hired worker;[47] and the LORD *your God will bless you, in all that you do.*

Deut 15:18

The final sentence is unique to Deuteronomy. The underlying principle is that generosity to others will lead to divine blessing (cf. 14:29; 15:10; 23:20; 24:19). This complements the earlier principle in verse 14, that God's blessing provides the opportunity and motivation for generosity.[48]

There are two more probable allusions to the exodus in this verse. First, the verb 'let go' here and in verses 12-13 is often used in connection with the exodus (e.g. Exod 3:20; 4:21, 23; 6:1, 11; etc.). Second, the reference to considering it a hardship to free a slave may allude to the hardening of Pharaoh's heart which resulted in his refusing to free Israel (Exod 7:3; 13:15[49]). As mentioned in the preceding law on debt relief (Deut 15:7), prosperous Israelites are not to be hard-hearted towards poorer members of the community, lest they suffer the same fate as hard-hearted Pharaoh.[50]

Mendelsohn (1962: 388) suggests the Deuteronomic legislator was aware that the limit for debt service in Babylonia was three years (CH §117) and therefore stresses that the creditor has been amply compensated. Whether the biblical author knew the Laws of Hammurabi is debatable, but a biblical comparison indicates that six years' service is twice the standard period for a hired worker (Isa 16:14). The value of a chattel slave was twenty shekels according to the Laws of Hammurabi (§§116, 214, 252; cf. Gen 37:28), thirty shekels at Nuzi (cf. Exod 21:32), and forty shekels at

---

46. Lit. 'him'.

47. Cf. RSV; TEV; lit. 'double the hire of a hired worker'. NIV translates as follows: 'his service to you these six years has been worth twice as much as that of a hired hand' (cf. REB; McConville 2002a). NRSV has 'for six years they have given you services worth the wages of hired labourers', taking משנה to mean 'equivalent' instead of the usual 'double' (cf. Tsevat 1958; Craigie 1976; Mayes 1979; Tsevat 1994), but this is quite unjustified (Zakovitch 1974: 349-51; Phillips 1984: 65 n. 28; Lindenberger 1991).

48. Cf. Weinfeld (1972a: 307-13); McConville (1984: 16-18).

49. The root קשה ('be hard, consider a hardship') is used in these verses, as in Deut 15:18, though Exodus more often uses the root חזק (7:13, 22; 8:19; 9:12, 35) or כבד (7:14; 8:15, 32; 9:7, 34) for the concept of hardening the heart.

50. Lowery (2000: 33).

Ugarit.[51] It appears that wages for hired workers in the Old Babylonian period varied between six and fourteen shekels per year,[52] so three years' service would be roughly equivalent in value to the price of a slave. Assuming the debtor is sold at the standard price for a slave, six years' service to repay the debt means the creditor gets a worker at half the usual cost. This may be compared with §14 of the Laws of Lipit-Ishtar (quoted above), which refers to freedom being granted after repayment of a sum equivalent to twice the original debt. However, in that case the double payment would have been due to interest; whereas in Israel the charging of interest was forbidden.[53] This arrangement would therefore be all the more beneficial to the creditor, and he would have good reason not to consider it a hardship to grant the temporary slave his freedom.

d. Conclusion

Whereas chattel slaves normally continued in that status for life, temporary slaves had a limited term of service and may well have had better treatment. There are two references in the ancient Near Eastern laws to temporary slavery, both providing some protection for the slave: one stipulates freedom after twofold repayment of the debt (LL §14) and another after three years' service (CH §117).

As we have seen, temporary slavery is dealt with in Exodus 21 and Deuteronomy 15. While there are various similarities and differences between the two versions, as noted above, three major points are clear:

- Both laws stipulate that temporary slaves must be freed after six years' service, and Deuteronomy adds that they should be given generous provision to enable them to live independently and supports this with theological reasons.
- Both laws give temporary slaves the option of becoming permanent members of the household, and explain the procedure if they wish to do this, but the provision of capital stipulated in Deuteronomy may be intended to encourage the slave to choose freedom.

51. Mendelsohn (1949: 118); cf. Garelli (1969: 279). Cf. Lev 27:2-5; on which, see Wenham (1978c).

52. Driver and Miles (1952: 470-72); Chirichigno (1993: 225), on the basis of CH §§257-58, 261, 273. Cf. Meissner (1936: 37-38).

53. See below, 10.1.

- Exodus is concerned with males and explains the implications for their wives and children if they take their freedom, whereas Deuteronomy covers both males and females without mentioning the matter of marriage.

Against the background of freedom from slavery in Egypt, slavery is strongly discouraged in the covenant community. In exceptional circumstances, temporary slavery may be the only way out of a desperate situation, and this is permitted by Exodus and Deuteronomy so long as it is limited in term. However, the conditions of these temporary slaves are to be so favourable that they may end up loving their masters and possibly even choosing to stay indefinitely, after the expiry of the agreed term of service. If and when the slave is granted freedom, generous provision is to be provided to enable him or her to begin life again as a free person.[54]

Only one actual instance of temporary slaves being liberated is recorded in the Old Testament, towards the end of the monarchy, when Zedekiah made a proclamation of liberty for all Hebrew slaves (Jer 34:8-10). Apparently the seven-year law was not being kept (vv. 12-14), and the royal proclamation was intended to give everyone a new start, but it was not long before the slaveowners changed their minds and took their slaves back again (vv. 11, 15-16).[55]

It is now two centuries since the abolition of the slave trade by Britain, and chattel slavery is illegal in virtually all countries today. Unfortunately, however, this has not eliminated the desire of the powerful for cheap labour, and in many places this is still sourced by means of debt-slavery.[56] Euphemisms such as 'contract service' or 'bonded labour' may be used rather than the term 'slavery', but the reality is much the same. Worse still, such slaves often have little legal protection or likelihood of becoming free again. Their situation is not very different from that of temporary slaves in ancient Babylon and Rome, who were unable to pay their debts and ended up in permanent bondage.[57]

---

54. Cf. Philo, *Laws* 2:79-85.

55. On the release of slaves in Jer 34, see David (1948); Kessler (1971); Sarna (1973); also commentaries on Jeremiah. It is likely that the liberation of slaves is also implied by Neh 5:9-13 (cf. vv. 5, 8).

56. On debt-slavery in modern times, see Epstein (1962: 75); Ennew (1981); Anti-Slavery International (1996; [1998]); Steinkeller (2002: 112-13, 126).

57. Payer (1974: 52) and Rowbotham (1998: 137) use debt-slavery as a model to understand the relationship of indebtedness between nations in the modern world. As in the case

On a more positive note, the biblical limitation of temporary slavery to six years may be compared with modern bankruptcy laws, which are designed to deal with insolvency in as fair a way as possible, and may include setting a limit to the amount a debtor is required to repay.[58] Where such laws are applied, there is some hope that debtors may be able to successfully rebuild their lives.

6.2 Concubines

Another kind of semi-slave was the concubine, whose status was lower than that of a free wife but higher than that of a chattel slave. Both slaves and free women could be taken as concubines, so in the former case concubinage tended to raise the status of the woman compared with that of other female slaves, whereas in the latter case she had a lower status than an ordinary wife. In the case of a slave-concubine, her legal situation could be ambiguous if a conflict arose between family law (governing slaves as persons) and property law (governing slaves as chattels).

a. Ancient Near East

Monogamy was the norm in the ancient Near East, though it was acceptable for a married man to have a secondary wife or concubine.[59] In practice, this would be the exception rather than the rule since there would not be enough women available for everyone to do this, and it was rare for an adult man to remain single. Generally it was the rich and powerful who had more than one wife, though after a war the number of men might be significantly depleted so that polygamy and concubinage became more common.

Apart from working in the home and providing sexual companionship, a major role for a concubine would be to produce children, to in-

---

of individual debt slavery, the aim of which can be to keep the labourer permanently indentured by avoiding both the extremes of starvation and actually clearing the debt, so current economic systems offer little hope of poorer nations being able to break away from dependence on the wealthy nations.

58. Cf. Lowery (2000: 25).

59. Westbrook (1988a: 103-11); Jasnow (2003b: 323, 326); Lafont (2003: 538); Radner (2003: 895-96); Wilcke (2003: 160).

crease the work force in the household. Her children would not normally be heirs to the estate, though they could become heirs in certain circumstances. For example, the Laws of Lipit-Ishtar mention the possibility of a slave-concubine and her children being given their freedom by her master, while clarifying that her children do not share inheritance rights with the children of his legal wife (§25). However, if the wife dies and the master marries his concubine, then her children may have a share in the inheritance, though still not equal to that of the primary heirs (§26).

According to the Laws of Hammurabi, a concubine who has borne her master children and is then sold as a debt-slave may be redeemed by her original owner (§119), rather like a family member (§117), whereas other debt-slaves can be kept indefinitely or sold by the creditor (§118). By default, the children of a concubine are illegitimate, but a master may recognise them as his children and heirs, though still secondary in status to the children of his first-ranking wife (§170).[60] If he has not done this before he dies, the concubine and her children are to be freed, not passed on like property to the legitimate heirs (§171). So a concubine with children was in a better position than an ordinary slave, comparable to that of a secondary wife.[61]

Several clauses deal with the problem of a childless wife. She has the right to take the initiative in the situation, by providing her husband with a slave woman as a concubine, to bear children for her (CH §144; cf. Genesis 16; 30:1-13).[62] If she does not do this, the husband has the right to take a secondary wife (§145; cf. 1 Sam 1:1-3). In neither case does the concubine or secondary wife obtain a status equal to that of the first wife (§§145-46). If the concubine aspires to equality with her mistress, she is to be punished by marking her as a slave (§146), which implies that a concubine is normally of higher status than a slave. If the concubine produces children, the ownership rights of her mistress are limited and she can no longer be sold (§§146-47). Thus it seems the legal personality of the woman is split: she is a slave to her mistress but a concubine to her master.[63]

---

60. Westbrook (1998: 220-23, 233). For example, a cuneiform text (CT 8 37d) refers to a concubine who produces five sons, one of whom is adopted by the master as his son (Westbrook 1988a: 120).

61. There is also an Old Assyrian contract which gives some protection to a concubine even before becoming a mother (Westbrook 1998: 216-17).

62. This is also mentioned in an Old Assyrian marriage contract (*ANET*: 543) and an adoption contract from Nuzi (*ANET*: 220).

63. A cuneiform text (CT 8 22b) records the joint purchase of a slave by a husband and wife, lines 5-6 of which read: 'To Bunene-abi she is a wife, to Belessunu she is a slave' (West-

The status of a concubine in the Middle Assyrian Laws is also higher than that of a slave but lower than that of a wife. In general only free women are to wear a veil, and slaves must not be veiled, but an exception to the rule is a concubine accompanying her mistress (§A40). A man may decide to take his concubine as a legal wife, which is done by veiling her in the presence of witnesses (§A41).[64]

From Nuzi (Arrapha) there are contracts for the sale of a daughter as a slave-bride.[65] In contrast to the unconditional sale of children into slavery in Babylonia and Assyria, these give the girl some protection by guaranteeing that on reaching puberty she will be married and therefore not exploited as a prostitute. The designated marriage-partner varies, and can include the master or his son, another freeman, or a slave. There is also a Neo-Assyrian contract which records the sale of a daughter to settle debts in which she becomes the wife of the purchaser's son.[66] Cole (1973) suggests a parallel with an old Chinese custom of buying a young girl as future wife for a son. This custom avoids paying a higher bride-price at a later age, and ensures that she adapts to the family before becoming a daughter-in-law.

b. Book of the Covenant

When a man sells his daughter as a concubine,[67] she shall not go as the [male] slaves do. If she does not please her master, who has desig-

---

brook 1988a: 119). Cf. Driver and Miles (1952: 305); Westbrook (1998: 215, 234). There is also evidence of this practice from the Old Assyrian period (Westbrook 1998: 216; Veenhof 2001: 453).

64. Neufeld (1944: 83-88) argues that the word *esirtu* should be translated 'captive maid' rather than 'concubine', and also points to clauses in the Hittite Laws which he considers refer to marriage by capture. However, *CAD* (4: 336) and *CDA* (80) retain the translation 'concubine'.

65. Mendelsohn (1935; 1949: 10-12); Neufeld (1944: 75-76); cf. Driver and Miles (1935: 164-65); Paul (1969: 49; 1970: 52-53). Westbrook (1998: 218-19) disputes Mendelsohn's view that these texts provide a legal model for the law in Exod 21:7-11, arguing that they are concerned with marriage whereas Exodus is concerned with concubinage. However, he admits that in social terms the girl's condition may well have been little more than slavery, so in practice she was probably more like a concubine than a free wife.

66. SAA 14 (no. 161).

67. The word אמה is usually translated 'female slave' or 'maidservant', often paired with עבד ('male slave, manservant'), but in this context 'concubine' is more appropriate (cf. Gen 20:17; 21:10, 13; 31:33; Exod 23:12). It is used interchangeably with פילגש in Judg 19:1, 10, 19. For further discussion of the terminology, see Neufeld (1944: 121-24); Jepsen (1958); Cohen

> nated her for himself,[68] then he shall let her be redeemed; he has no right to sell her to foreigners[69] because he has treated her unfairly.[70] If he designates her for his son, he shall grant her the rights of a daughter. If he takes another [woman] for himself, he shall not reduce her food, clothing, and conjugal rights.[71] And if he does not do these three things for her, then she is to go free, without [payment of] money.
>
> Exod 21:7-11

Although in the Book of the Covenant this law follows directly from the law on temporary slaves discussed in the previous section, and at first sight the main difference is the gender of the person involved, it is actually concerned with something rather different. Whereas Exodus 21:2-6 focuses on free men or their sons sold as temporary slaves, to work off a debt and then return to their family, the present law is concerned with daughters sold by their fathers as concubines (v. 7).[72] No doubt the usual reason for doing

---

(1978-79); Riesener (1979: 76-83); Engelken (1988; 1990: 127-69); Reuter (1995); Schultz (1997a); Kessler (2002).

68. Assuming the *qere*, with LXX, Targum, Vulgate, and most modern translations (also Childs 1974; Durham 1987). If the *ketiv* 'not' is correct, the translation would become as follows: 'If she does not please her master, so that he does not designate her' (so Osumi 1991; Crüsemann 1992: 158). Wagenaar (2004: 224-25) accepts the *ketiv* but proposes emending יעדה to ידעה, so that the clause means 'who has not had intercourse with her', which makes good sense but has no manuscript support except possibly the Peshitta.

69. Lit. 'a foreign people'. Cf. Hoftijzer (1957); Phillips (1984: 59-60); van Seters (1996: 542). Cazelles (1946) suggests that in this context the expression refers to anyone outside the girl's own family, not simply non-Israelites (cf. Chirichigno 1993: 249; Wagenaar 2004: 227-28; Propp 2006). This would make good sense, but would be an unusual meaning for נכרי ('foreign'), though there are possible parallels in Job 19:15 and Ps 69:8 (Sarna 1991). Westbrook (1998: 219-20) argues for the literal meaning, since sale within the Israelite community would not result in the girl's family losing the right of redemption, but if she was sold abroad the purchaser would be unlikely to recognise her rights under Israelite law and she would probably become a chattel slave (cf. Neufeld 1944: 71). Van Seters (2007: 174) agrees, pointing out that if the law intended to prohibit sale to another Israelite, it would be sufficient simply to say that she should not be sold.

70. So REB; TEV; cf. NRSV. Other possible translations are 'broken faith with her' (NIV; NJPS; cf. NJB; TB; Childs 1974) and 'severed his relationship with her' (Durham 1987).

71. So most ancient and modern translations, though North (1955b), Paul (1969; 1970: 56-61), and Paradise (1997) make quite different proposals. For discussions of the various proposals, concluding in favour of the traditional translation, see Levine (1999); Baker (2007b: 91-92).

72. Cf. Childs (1974); Boecker (1976: 160); Durham (1987); Sarna (1991); Chirichigno

this would be financial difficulty, and the possibility of selling a daughter to a creditor is alluded to in Isaiah 50:1. In the present context, however, it is clear that the girl is intended as a concubine for the master or his son, not a temporary slave. She becomes a permanent member of their family, though retaining a right to freedom in some circumstances.

Three scenarios are anticipated and provided for. First, the master may intend to take the girl as a concubine but then change his mind, in which case he is not entitled to sell her on the slave-market but must allow her to be redeemed by her family (v. 8). She has already suffered unfair treatment because the original plan of concubinage has been cancelled, and this must not be compounded by selling her as a chattel slave. The right of redemption with respect to a concubine is also mentioned in the Laws of Hammurabi (§119), but the situations are quite different: Exodus deals with the redemption of a free woman sold as a concubine, whereas Hammurabi deals with a woman who is already a concubine and is sold as a debt-slave to another master.

Second, the master may designate her for his son as a concubine, in which case she is to be treated as a daughter-in-law (v. 9).[73] This does not necessarily mean that she is to be the son's wife rather than his concubine, but that she is considered part of the family, not a chattel slave whose role would be simply to work.[74]

Third, the master may take another concubine, in which case the first concubine still has rights to food, clothing, and conjugal relations (v. 10). If he is not prepared to grant her these rights, he must give compensation by granting her freedom without demanding payment (v. 11).[75] In other words, the master has broken the terms of the concubinage contract, which results in the ending of the contract and annulment of the debt which was the reason for selling the girl in the first place.[76]

(1993: 244-54); Sprinkle (1994: 51-52); Pressler (1998: 155-60); Westbrook (1998: 218-20, 235-37); Fleishman (2000); Jackson (2000: 193-97).

73. This scenario is presented as an alternative to the first, and does not imply that the woman might be designated to both the father and the son, which would be quite unacceptable (Lev 18:8, 15; 20:11-12; Amos 2:7). Cf. Crüsemann (1992: 157-58).

74. Westbrook (1998: 236).

75. The 'three things' most likely refer to the three rights mentioned in the previous verse (Cassuto 1951; Noth 1959; Durham 1987), though a few scholars see a reference to the three scenarios in vv. 8-10 (Sarna 1991; Chirichigno 1993: 252-53; Paradise 1997: 93-94).

76. Westbrook (1998: 236).

c. Deuteronomic Laws

When you go out to war against your enemies, and the LORD your God gives them into your hands and you take them captive, and you see among the captives a beautiful woman, and you desire her and take [her] for yourself as a wife: you shall bring her into your house, and she shall shave her head and pare her nails, and take off her captive's garb and live in your house, and mourn her father and her mother for a full month.[77] After that you may go in to her and become her husband, and she shall become your wife. But if it turns out that you are not pleased with her, and you end the relationship with her,[78] you shall not sell her for money. You shall not treat her as a slave,[79] because you have had conjugal relations[80] with her.

Deut 21:10-14

In ancient times it was common for prisoners of war to be made slaves (cf. Deut 20:14; Judg 16:21; 2 Chr 28:8-15). Like other spoil of battle, they would have been treated as property by whoever came into possession of them, so having the status of chattel slaves.[81] This text deals with a special case,

---

77. After the initial 'when' clause, this long sentence contains a series of eleven *waw*-consecutive clauses. My translation assumes that the first five are conditions and the remaining six prescriptions (cf. NJPS; TEV; Christensen 2002), though others locate the transition from condition to prescription after the fourth (NIV; REB; Craigie 1976) or sixth (NJB; NRSV; Pressler 1993: 10; McConville 2002a) clauses.

78. Or 'you shall let her go free' (NRSV; cf. NIV; REB; TEV). Lit. 'and you release her to herself'.

79. For other possible meanings of התעמר, which is found only here and in Deut 24:7, see above, ch. 5, n. 25.

80. There are various renderings of the last verb in the translations, such as 'you have dishonoured her' (NIV; NRSV), 'you have had your will with her' (REB), 'you have exploited her' (NJB; cf. NJPS; McConville 2002a), and 'you have humbled her' (Christensen 2002). These are all possible meanings of the piel form of ענה, the semantic range of which includes 'oppress, humble, violate, overpower', and if this meaning is to be understood here, the best translation would probably be 'you have violated her'. However, the word is also used to denote sexual intercourse, rather than rape, in Gen 34:2; Deut 22:24, 29; 2 Sam 13:12, 14, 22, 32; and Ezek 22:10-11. The rule that the concubine must not be sold as a slave is not based on compensation for abuse, but the fact that she has had a sexual relationship with her master and thereafter is reckoned as a member of the family — a secondary wife — rather than a chattel slave. Therefore I propose the above translation. This meaning is further supported by the use of ענה in Exod 21:10 (see above, n. 71). For a more detailed argument in favour of this translation, see Baker (2007b: 95-96).

81. Cf. above, 5.1.

however, in which a beautiful girl is taken as a concubine (vv. 10-11; cf. Num 31:17-18). As with the daughter sold as a concubine in Exodus 21:7-11, it is clear that the captured girl has a status higher than that of a chattel slave and is to be treated with respect and consideration. Three main points are made:

- She must first be allowed a period to mourn her parents and adjust to her new situation (vv. 12-13a).[82]
- Then she may become the wife or concubine of her captor (v. 13b).
- If he is dissatisfied with her, he may not enslave her but must let her go free (v. 14).

Like other Old Testament laws on war and marriage, this is not Christian ethics; but it is an improvement on the treatment received all too often by women in warfare, both ancient and modern. Not only is rape excluded, but the girl is allowed a full month of mourning before she is expected to become a concubine (cf. Num 20:29; Deut 34:8).[83] Whether the mourning for her parents is because they died in the war (cf. Deut 20:13), or because

---

82. The significance of shaving the head, paring the nails, and changing clothes is uncertain. Shaving the head can be a sign of mourning (Farbridge 1923: 233-39), and this is Josephus's understanding of the procedure (*Antiquities* 4:257-59), though it is forbidden for Israelites in Deut 14:1. Rabbinic interpretation suggests the rules were intended to discourage marriage with captives, by making the woman less attractive (Tigay 1996). Christensen (2002) comments: 'If the man can live with a wailing and relatively unattractive woman for a month and still want her as his wife, perhaps the marriage will last'. Much more likely is that the girl's act of discarding old clothes and removable parts of the body is intended to symbolise her purification, leaving her former life and becoming part of the covenant community (cf. Gen 35:2; Lev 14:8-9; Num 6:9; 8:7). There are two parallels in the Mari texts which support this view (ARM 1: no. 8 line 31; no. 75 lines 18-19; cf. du Buit 1959). This seems preferable to either of the other suggestions (cf. Mayes 1979; Pressler 1993: 12-13; Washington 1997: 349-50; Nelson 2002).

83. Thirty days of mourning were observed for Aaron and Moses, according to these texts, but just seven days for Joseph (Gen 50:10) and Saul (1 Sam 31:13), so this might be considered relatively generous. Washington (1997: 350-51) argues that the reason for specifying a full month before consummation is not related to mourning customs but to allow long enough for the woman's cycle to prove she is not pregnant, so that the paternity of any children subsequently born is not in doubt. Ellens (2008: 170-88) considers the production of legitimate progeny to be the primary interest of the text. It is possible that these were also considerations in the formulation of the law, but on a canonical reading of the text it is clear that the primary reason is to allow the woman time to 'mourn', presumably including recovery from trauma and adaptation to the Israelite community.

she will never see them again (cf. Ps 45:10), the girl's grief is to be respected and she should not be asked to provide pleasure for someone else during this time. And when in due course she enters into an intimate relationship with her 'husband', this enhances her status so that he cannot then change his mind and make her an ordinary slave instead (cf. Exod 21:8). If he does not want to continue the arrangement, he must at least grant her freedom (cf. Exod 21:11).

If that should happen, she would of course be in a very difficult situation, far from home. To make a long and dangerous journey back to her own country would probably not be a realistic option, so she would have to look for work or another concubinage. If neither was to be found, she would become dependent on charity.[84]

Westbrook (1998: 235) argues that this text is actually concerned with marriage, not slave concubinage. In his view, the captured girl initially has the status of a slave, but when married she becomes free. If later she is divorced, it might be expected she would return to being a slave again, but the law forbids the man to treat her as such and insists that in fact she leaves as a free person. His argument depends primarily on the terminology used in the text for marriage and divorce, but in neither case is it convincing.[85] I suggest a simpler scenario than that of Westbrook: the captured girl is potentially a slave, but in fact she becomes a concubine (semi-free), and if the concubinage is ended she gains her freedom.[86]

d. Conclusion

In ancient Israel, monogamy is the ideal (Gen 2:24; Exod 20:17; Deut 24:5; Psalm 128; Prov 5:15-19; 12:4; 18:22; Eccl 9:9; Mal 2:14), even though polygamy is not illegal and one law deals with inheritance rights in the case of a man having two wives (Deut 21:15-17). Polygamy and concubinage seem to be quite common in the patriarchal period (Gen 22:20-24; 25:6; 29:21-30; 36:2-3, 12; 1 Chr 7:14), but after that most marriages of commoners are monogamous. Three kings are reported to have numerous wives and concubines — in spite of the prohibition in the law of the king (Deut 17:17) —

---

84. On which, see below, chs. 7 and 9. If this was not forthcoming, she would probably turn to prostitution or end up selling herself into slavery after all.
85. For a refutation of Westbrook's argument, see Baker (2007b: 93-94).
86. On rabbinic interpretation of this text, see Elman (1997).

namely David (1 Sam 25:39-44; 2 Sam 5:13; 1 Chr 3:1-9), Solomon (1 Kgs 11:3), and Rehoboam (2 Chr 11:21).[87] Several references to multiple wives and to concubines relate to the period of the judges, specifically Caleb (1 Chr 2:18, 46, 48), Gideon (Judg 8:30-31), a Levite (Judges 19), and Elkanah (1 Sam 1:1-2).[88] Judges 21 recounts the capture of wives in war by the Benjaminites, but there is no reference to the law of Deuteronomy 21, and in the context the incident is presumably to be understood as an example of 'all the people [doing] what was right in their own eyes' (v. 25) rather than obedience to a divine commandment.

According to Judges 19:1-3, when the Levite's concubine leaves him and returns to her parents' house, he goes to get her back by persuasion rather than force. This suggests he values her as a person rather than property. Later on, however, his attitude towards her is quite despicable (vv. 25, 27-28), though no worse than that shown by his host and Lot towards their daughters (v. 24; cf. Gen 19:8a). While the reason for such an attitude may be explained in terms of the sacred duty of hospitality (Judg 19:23; cf. Gen 19:8b), the narrators certainly do not justify sacrificing the weak for the benefit of the strong in this way. The incident reflects an ambivalent attitude towards concubines, found also in the patriarchal narratives, which distinguishes them from both full wives and mere slaves.

Against the background of such male attitudes towards women, the biblical laws do not attempt to eliminate the institution of concubinage, but simply provide a degree of protection for girls who enter into it. First, if a daughter is sold as a concubine, she is to become part of the new family and enjoy some of the rights of a wife or daughter — depending on whether she is designated for the master or his son — though presumably not becoming equal with either (Exod 21:7-11). She is subject to the will of her master, instead of her father, but he does not have unlimited rights with respect to her. If he does not want to continue the relationship he may not sell her as a chattel slave but must allow her to return to her own family. Second, if a prisoner of war is taken as a concubine, she is to be treated with kindness and allowed an appropriate period of mourning before taking on her new role (Deut 21:10-14). As in Exodus, if her master wants to

---

87. Saul has a wife (1 Sam 14:50) and concubine (2 Sam 3:7), and 2 Sam 12:8 may imply other wives too, though the meaning of this text is uncertain. 1 Kgs 20:3 implies that Ahab has several wives. Joash has two wives (2 Chr 24:3). Apparently Zedekiah has several wives too (Jer 38:23).

88. Others are Lamech (Gen 4:19), Ashhur (1 Chr 4:5), Mered (1 Chr 4:17-19), and Shaharaim (1 Chr 8:8).

terminate the relationship, he does not have the right to treat her as a slave but must grant her freedom.

Clearly these laws are not directly transferable to life in the modern world. However, two things are worthy of note. First, although neither of the laws has a close parallel in the ancient Near East, they come from the same world and reflect a similar view of the status of a concubine. Nevertheless, there are some distinctive features. The reference to conjugal rights for the concubine in Exodus 21 is an indication that sex was not understood to be exclusively for the benefit of males in ancient Israel (cf. Song of Songs). Also, the kindness towards concubines advocated in the biblical laws, especially Deuteronomy 21, is an advance over the matter-of-fact treatment in those of Mesopotamia. Second, these laws focus on the doable rather than the desirable. In each case the lawgiver works in a context where concubinage is inevitable and he simply endeavours to ameliorate the condition of the weaker party involved. It is left to poets and prophets, not to mention the authors of the New Testament, to expound the benefits of faithful monogamy.

6.3 Bonded Labourers

Bonded labour may be similar in practice to temporary slavery, treated in the first section of this chapter with reference to the laws of Exodus and Deuteronomy, but in theory it is voluntary and the labourer is not a slave. I discuss it separately here, because the law on bonded labour in Leviticus is quite distinctive and emphasises specifically that it is *not* slavery.

a. Ancient Near East

There are no extant ancient Near Eastern laws which regulate bonded labour as distinct from temporary slavery.[89] Chirichigno (1993: 334) suggests that the arrangements for bonded labour in Leviticus 25:39-43 and 47-55 are similar to the way in which ancient Near Eastern temples and palaces maintained their subordinate citizens (serfs), but with the difference that these citizens were unlikely ever to own their land or gain their freedom.

89. On which, see above, 6.1.a.

Eichler (1973) has made a detailed study of indenture at Nuzi, as known from the personal *tidennūtu* ('indenture') contracts. Impoverished citizens would enter voluntarily into these contracts because of debt, and their status appears to have been that of bonded labourers. Some contracts specify periods of between two and fifty years, others are of indefinite duration. The status of the *tidennu* may be compared with that of *ḫabiru* in Nuzi service contracts, which was also somewhere between freedom and slavery since it was taken voluntarily.[90] However, the *ḫabiru* took this status not because of debt but because they were outsiders and had no alternative means of obtaining the necessities of life, and their status was lower than that of the *tidennu*. There is a close parallel between the *tidennūtu* contracts and the Old Babylonian *mazzazānūtu* ('being a pledge') contracts.[91]

There are various examples of destitute citizens selling themselves to obtain food and clothing: from Ur III and Larsa, the Old Assyrian period, and the Neo-Babylonian periods in Mesopotamia; and from Egypt in the seventh and sixth centuries BC.[92] In practice such an arrangement would be similar to slavery, though it seems the master's rights were more limited than in the case of a chattel slave. Sometimes the service was for a specific length of time, and sometimes it was specified that the person could not be sold to anyone else as a slave. In Media there was a custom whereby a poor person could become dependent on a rich person in order to obtain food, effectively as a slave, but retaining the right to leave his master at any time if he was poorly fed.[93]

b. Holiness Code

The biblical laws on bonded labour are part of the jubilee legislation in Leviticus 25. Two main sections deal with:

- Israelites serving Israelites (vv. 39-43)
- Israelites serving foreigners (vv. 47-55)

---

90. Eichler (1973: 47). For a fuller discussion, see Bottéro (1954: 43-70).
91. Eichler (1973: 48-101); cf. *CAD* (10.1: 233).
92. Dandama[y]ev (1984: 175-77 n. 21).
93. According to a report of Ktesias, preserved by Nicolaus of Damascus (Dandama[y]ev 1984: 177 n. 21).

Both sections are concerned with ensuring humane treatment for bonded labourers (vv. 39, 43, 53) and release in the jubilee year so that they can return to their ancestral property (vv. 40-41, 54). And both sections give the same theological rationale for the laws: the people of Israel belong to God because he freed them from slavery in Egypt, so they should not become slaves to anyone else (vv. 42, 55). The latter section also provides a somewhat detailed treatment of the right of redemption as applied to bonded labourers (vv. 47-52).

Israelites Serving Israelites:
Humane Treatment and Jubilee Release

And when your brother[94] becomes poor beside you[95] and 'sells'[96] himself[97] to you, you shall not make him serve as a slave. He shall be with you as a hired worker or temporary resident,[98] until the year of

---

94. I.e. a fellow-Israelite; cf. v. 25 (on which, see above, ch. 4, n. 42).

95. עמך is usually translated 'with you' (e.g. vv. 6, 35b, 36, 40), but in vv. 35a, 39, and 47 'beside' is more appropriate. NIV renders it 'among you', though this is problematic since the 'you' here is singular. Another possibility is 'under you' (NJPS) or 'under your authority' (Speiser 1960: 38-39; Milgrom 2001: 1938, 2205-6, 2208-9).

96. The translation 'sell' is not ideal, since a bonded labourer is emphatically not a slave. The verb could be translated 'indenture' here, and 'lease' when referring to land transactions earlier in the chapter (e.g. vv. 25, 33), but in some sentences it would still need to be 'sell' (e.g. vv. 23, 42), while in others it would be difficult to decide (e.g. v. 29, where it is uncertain at the beginning whether it will turn out to be a sale or a lease). In view of the literal character of my translation, I have preferred to use the translation 'sell' and 'sold' throughout. In the present context it should be understood figuratively (cf. Milgrom 2001: 2220), hence the inverted commas. On the semantic range of the Hebrew verb, see above, ch. 4, n. 32.

97. The niphal of מכר usually has a passive meaning, 'is sold' (see above, n. 35). Schenker (1998: 31-32), Milgrom (2001: 2219-20), and Lefebvre (2003: 270-74) argue that it should be understood passively here too, because if the reflexive had been intended it would have been more appropriate to use the hithpael, which is consistently reflexive in meaning (e.g. Deut 28:68). However, in the present context — as in vv. 47, 48, and 50 — the reflexive meaning is more likely, whether translated as 'sell oneself' (BDB; NIV; NJB; NRSV; REB; TEV; Wenham 1979; Hartley 1992; Chirichigno 1993: 329-31), 'give oneself over' (NJPS; cf. TB), or 'deliver oneself' *(DCH)*. Unlike a temporary slave who may be sold by others, a bonded labourer takes the initiative in the transaction (see below, 6.3.c).

98. According to Milgrom (2001: 2221-23), the two nouns 'hired worker' and 'temporary resident' form a hendiadys, which he translates 'resident hireling' (cf. Lev 22:10; 25:6; Exod 12:45).

> *jubilee he shall serve with you. Then he shall go from you, together with his children; and he shall return to his own clan, and go back to his ancestral property. For [the people of Israel] are my slaves, whom I brought out from the land of Egypt; they shall not be sold as slaves are sold. You shall not rule over him with harshness;*[99] *but fear your God.*
>
> Lev 25:39-43

As mentioned above (4.1.b), a three-stage descent into poverty is discernible in Leviticus 25. A poor brother has already mortgaged his land (vv. 25-28), and taken advantage of an interest-free loan (vv. 35-38), but is still in difficulty and has no resources left except his labour and that of his family. Verses 39-43 are concerned with the third stage of impoverishment, when he becomes a bonded labourer to another Israelite. If this should happen, the law makes clear, he is to be treated as an employee rather than a slave (vv. 39-40); and in the jubilee year he must be freed from that bond so that he can return to his clan and land (v. 41).

There is only one master to whom Israelites owe absolute loyalty as slaves — the LORD, who has redeemed them from slavery in Egypt and taken them to be his special possession (v. 42; cf. v. 55; also Exod 6:6-7; 19:4-6; Ps 74:2; Isa 43:1-3).[100] Just as the land belongs to God and must not be sold in perpetuity (v. 23), so the people belong to God and must not be sold in perpetuity. To put it a different way, this means that the poor person is not selling himself, but only his service for a specified period; just as land is not really sold but only a number of harvests.[101] Moreover, the Egyptian experience has taught the people of Israel what it is like to suffer harsh treatment as slaves (Exod 1:13-14; cf. Deut 15:15), and they are not to treat fellow members of the covenant community in this way (v. 43a; cf. v. 46; Ezek. 34:4). Rather than acting as masters who inspire fear in others, they should fear their own Master (v. 43b; cf. vv. 17, 36; 19:14).

This law is concerned primarily with a head of household, as is clear

---

99. So NRSV; Milgrom (2001); cf. NJB; TEV; Wenham (1979). Others translate the expression בפרך as 'ruthlessly' (NIV; NJPS; REB; Hartley 1992).

100. Exod 6:7 is just one example of the 'covenant formula' ('I will take you as my people, and I will be your God'), a distinctive expression of this divine-human relationship which is used or alluded to in many Old Testament texts (Baker 2005a: 22-23). The idea that Israel belongs to God is found elsewhere too, not always in connection with the exodus, e.g. Deut 32:36; Ps 100:3.

101. Japhet (1978: 84-86); Riesener (1979: 124); Milgrom (2001: 2217).

from the mention of children and ancestral property (v. 41). No separate provision for females is made here, since as a rule the head of a household in ancient Israel would be male. Nevertheless, two examples of women in this position are recorded in the historical books. First, there is a widow who is liable for the debts of her deceased husband (2 Kgs 4:1-7). Second, we are told of a wealthy woman who appears to have been in charge of her household even though her husband was alive (2 Kgs 4:8-10) and who later took responsibility for appealing to the king in connection with her land rights (8:1-6).[102]

Israelites Serving Foreigners

(1) Right of Redemption

And when a resident alien or temporary resident[103] with you prospers, while your brother becomes poor beside him, so he 'sells' himself to the resident alien [or] temporary resident with you, or to a member of the resident alien's clan, he shall have the right of redemption after he has 'sold' himself. One of his brothers may redeem him, or his uncle or his cousin may redeem him, or any blood relative in his clan may redeem him; or if he prospers, he may redeem himself.

He shall calculate with his 'buyer' [the time] from the year he 'sold' himself until the year of jubilee; and the price of his 'sale' shall be applied to the number of years, [so] it shall be [reckoned] as the term of a hired worker.[104] If there are still many years until the year of jubilee,[105] he shall pay for his redemption a proportionate amount

---

102. Cf. Abigail, who was not the household head but clearly had an influential role in its running (1 Sam 25).

103. Milgrom (2001: 2236) understands the two nouns 'resident alien' and 'temporary resident' as a hendiadys, which he translates 'resident alien' (cf. vv. 23, 35). However, the terms are similar in meaning but not quite identical (see below, 7.1.b). A similar pair occurs in v. 40: 'hired worker' and 'temporary resident' (on which, see above, n. 98).

104. Cf. NRSV; Hartley (1992); Milgrom (2001). Alternatively it could be translated 'and the price for his release shall be based on the rate paid to a hired worker for that number of years' (cf. NIV; REB; TEV; Hartley 1992). Differently again, Lefebvre (2003: 287-92) proposes 'selon le temps d'un salarié il sera avec lui' ('he shall be with him as the term of a hired worker'), so that the clause refers not to the calculation of an amount to be paid but to the conditions of service (cf. the similar clauses in vv. 40 and 53).

105. The explanatory phrase 'until the year of jubilee' is not actually provided in the Hebrew until v. 52, but I have transposed it here for clarity in English (cf. REB).

of his purchase price. And if [only] a few years remain, he is to make a calculation, [and] in proportion to the number of years he shall pay for his redemption.

Lev 25:47-52

An Israelite is permitted to become dependent on a foreigner or temporary resident (v. 47) only on the condition that he and his family retain the right of redemption (vv. 48-49). The financial implications of the bond are to be made clear from the beginning, so that the labourer and his family know how much would be required to redeem him at any time (vv. 50-52; cf. v. 16).

The order of responsibility for acting as redeemer is the same as for the right of inheritance (vv. 48-49; cf. Num 27:9-11). If the bondman should be redeemed by his family, it is probable that he would not immediately become free, but would live as a dependant of the redeemer until the jubilee and then return to his own land.[106] Until that point he would still be effectively a bonded labourer, but within his clan rather than a foreign household, and presumably the rules of verses 39-43 would apply. In general it is likely that conditions of service would be more favourable to the labourer within the family than outside.

Alternatively, a bonded labourer could become completely free if circumstances made it possible to accumulate capital to redeem himself, perhaps through inheritance or by means of private enterprise alongside the duties allocated by his master.[107] But unless land was available to him, or he had skills as a craftsman, it might still be difficult for him to live independently before the jubilee restoration.

The principle underlying the law on bonded labourers is the same as for the law earlier in the chapter which stipulates that land must be leased rather than sold (vv. 13-17, 23-28), and there are many verbal similarities between the respective laws.[108] In effect, the poor brother is selling his services for a period of years, and does not give his master ownership rights as would be the case for a slave.

Resident aliens are potentially vulnerable people (Lev 19:33), but they

---

106. Chirichigno (1993: 340-41); Milgrom (2001: 2236-37). The text does not state this explicitly, but it seems unlikely that a kinsman would be able to provide such substantial help on a purely charitable basis. This is supported by the parallel with land which is redeemed, and remains in the hand of the redeemer until the jubilee (see above, 4.1.b).

107. Cf. Mendelsohn (1962: 387); Milgrom (2001: 2238-39).

108. As Milgrom (2001: 2232-33) shows in his synopsis of vv. 48-55 and vv. 15-17, 23-28.

are to be given the same legal rights as Israelites (Lev 24:22) and so could prosper in some circumstances (cf. Deut 28:43).[109] There are several examples in the historical books, such as Doeg the Edomite (1 Sam 21:7), Uriah the Hittite (2 Sam 11:3), and Zelek the Ammonite (2 Sam 23:37). Two Akkadian documents from Nuzi mention Hebrews voluntarily becoming slaves of foreigners.[110] An example of Jewish people being sold to foreigners and then redeemed is recorded in Nehemiah 5:8, though the word 'buy' (קנה) is used rather than the technical term 'redeem' (גאל).[111]

(2) Humane Treatment and Jubilee Release

He shall be with him[112] as a worker hired from year to year, and you must see that [his master] does not rule over him with harshness.[113] And if he is not redeemed in any of these ways, then he shall go [free] in the year of jubilee, together with his children. For the people of Israel are mine, as slaves; they are my slaves, whom I brought out from the land of Egypt. I am the LORD *your God.*

Lev 25:53-55

This section closely parallels the law on Israelites serving Israelites (vv. 39-43). An Israelite who becomes dependent on a foreigner is to have the status of a bonded labourer, just as if the master was another Israelite (v. 53a; cf. v. 40a). His living and working conditions must be better than those of a slave (v. 53b; cf. v. 43a; also v. 46b). If possible he should be redeemed, as already stipulated in verses 48-52, but if not he must go free (יצא) in the jubilee year (v. 54; cf. vv. 40b-41). The final sentence dealing with the redemption of bonded labourers begins with the phrase 'for the people of Israel are mine' (v. 55a), echoing the basic principle underlying the re-

---

109. On laws relating to resident aliens, see below, 7.1. Levine (1989: 274) suggests that Lev 25:47-52 originated in the postexilic period, when the population was mixed and there was a greater likelihood of Israelites becoming indentured to foreigners, but Milgrom (2001: 2236) demolishes this theory, locating its origin in the monarchic period.

110. *ANET* (220).

111. For further discussion of redemption in relation to Lev 25:47-55, see Yaron (1959); Neufeld (1961); Leggett (1974: 68-71, 98-106); Hubbard (1991: 9-13).

112. I.e. the resident alien or temporary resident.

113. Cf. NIV; REB. Lit. 'he shall not rule over him with harshness in your sight'. Following a rabbinic interpretation, Milgrom (2001: 2239) understands this to mean that action is only to be taken if the master openly flouts the rule, and his privacy is to be respected (cf. Deut 24:10-11), but it seems unlikely that the law intends to permit harsh treatment of bonded labourers in private while forbidding it in public.

demption of land: 'for the land is mine' (v. 23). The theological basis for Israelites refusing to become slaves of other people is the exodus from Egypt, by which God freed (הוציא 'brought out', lit. 'made to go [free]') his people from human dominion and made them his own (v. 55b; cf. v. 42). And as the law on Israelites serving Israelites ends with the exhortation, 'fear your God' (v. 43b), so the law on Israelites serving foreigners ends with the refrain, 'I am the LORD your God' (v. 55c).

c. Bonded Labour and Temporary Slavery

The Problem

The relationship between the laws on bonded labour in Leviticus 25 and those on temporary slavery in Exodus 21 and Deuteronomy 15 has been discussed at length by scholars.[114] To facilitate comparison, I have drawn up a synopsis of the laws using my own translation (see table). There are about fifteen verbal similarities between Exodus and Deuteronomy, and several between Leviticus and Deuteronomy, but no significant verbal similarity between Exodus and Leviticus. Almost all scholars agree that the oldest law is that of Exodus, and it is probable that the Deuteronomic law is a deliberate revision and expansion of this predecessor. There is no consensus on the relative order of the laws in Leviticus and Deuteronomy, however, and whether the similarities are due to a direct literary connection or because both drew on a common stock of laws. Perhaps the most troublesome question is why Exodus and Deuteronomy stipulate that a slave is to be liberated in the seventh year after acquisition, whereas Leviticus provides for liberation only in the jubilee year. Fifty years is a long time, and someone who entered bonded labour soon after the jubilee might not live to be released.

---

114. The law concerning concubines in Exod 21:7-11 is also closely related, since a daughter might be sold as a concubine rather than as a temporary slave (on which, see above, 6.2). The status of a concubine appears to be somewhere between that of a slave and a wife, and she becomes a relatively permanent member of the creditor's family, though she may be granted freedom in some circumstances.

Synopsis of Laws on Temporary Slavery and Bonded Labour

Exodus 21:2-6	**Deuteronomy 15:12-18**	**Leviticus 25:39-43, 47-55**
<u>When</u> you buy a [male] <u>Hebrew</u> slave,	<u>When</u> your <u>Hebrew</u> *brother* or *sister* *is sold to you,*	And <u>when</u> *your brother* becomes poor beside you and *'sells' himself to you,* you shall not make him serve as a slave. He shall be with you as a hired worker or temporary resident; until the year of jubilee he shall <u>serve</u> with you. (vv. 39-40)
he shall <u>serve six years;</u> and <u>in the seventh,</u> he shall go <u>free</u> without payment. (v. 2)	and <u>serves</u> you <u>six years,</u> in the seventh year you shall let them go <u>free</u> from you. (v. 12)	
If he comes alone, <u>he shall go</u> alone; if he has a wife [when he comes], his wife shall go with him. If his master gives him a wife, and she bears him sons or daughters; the wife and her children shall belong to her master, and he shall go alone. (vv. 3-4)	And when you let them go free *from you,* you shall not let them go empty-handed. Provide generously for them — sheep, corn, and wine — giving to them as the LORD your God has blessed you. Remember that you were a *slave* in *the land of Egypt,* and the LORD your God redeemed you; that is why I am giving you this command today. (vv. 13-15)	Then <u>he shall go</u> *from you,* together with his children; and he shall return to his own clan, and go back to his ancestral property. For [the people of Israel] are my *slaves,* whom I brought out from *the land of Egypt;* they shall not be sold as slaves are sold. You shall not rule over him with harshness; but fear your God. (vv. 41-43)
But if the slave <u>says</u> firmly, 'I <u>love</u> my master, my wife and my children; <u>I will not go</u> free,' then his master shall bring him to God: he shall bring him to <u>the door,</u> or to the doorpost, and his master shall pierce <u>his ear</u> with <u>an awl,</u> then [he shall be] his <u>slave in perpetuity.</u> (vv. 5-6)	But it may be that [the slave] <u>says</u> to you, '<u>I will not go</u> from you'; because he <u>loves</u> you and your household, because he is well off with you. Then you shall take <u>an awl</u> and put it through <u>his ear</u> into <u>the door,</u> and he shall be your <u>slave in perpetuity.</u> And you shall do likewise for your female slave. (vv. 16-17)	And when a resident alien or temporary resident with you prospers, while your brother becomes poor beside him, so he 'sells' himself to the resident alien [or] temporary resident with you, or to a member of the resident alien's clan, he shall have the right of redemption ... (vv. 47-52) He shall be with him as a worker hired from year to year, and you must see that

Exodus 21:2-6	Deuteronomy 15:12-18	Leviticus 25:39-43, 47-55
		[his owner] does not rule over him with harshness. And if he is not redeemed in any of these ways, then he shall go [free] in the year of jubilee, together with his children. For the people of Israel are mine, as slaves; they are my slaves, whom I brought out from the land of Egypt. I am *the* LORD *your God*. (vv. 53-55)
	Do not consider it a hardship when you let them go free from you, for they have served you six years at half the cost of a hired worker; and *the* LORD *your God* will bless you, in all that you do. (v. 18)	

Three Theories

According to the classic documentary theory, Leviticus 25 is the latest of the three laws. It is seen as a reform, replacing the seventh-year individual release — which had proved too difficult to enforce — with a fiftieth-year universal release. At the same time it grants a higher status to the Israelite debtor, as a bonded labourer rather than a slave, and exhorts the master to treat the labourer kindly.[115] One of the problems with this view is that Leviticus 25 appears to be more idealistic than pragmatic, and there is little evidence that the jubilee was put into practice in ancient Israel. It seems unlikely, therefore, that Leviticus would have deliberately postponed the manumission of slaves from the seventh to the fiftieth year for the sake of expedience. Why would a six-year term of slavery be replaced by what would in many cases be bondage for life, with only an exhortation to leniency as compensation? Such a 'reform' would benefit only wealthy creditors, and does not fit the exilic or postexilic period (when Leviticus is supposed to have been written) when blame for the national disaster was cast on the failure to keep laws such as the release of slaves (Jer 34:17; cf. Lev 26:34-39).[116] Since the documentary theory was proposed, Mesopotamian precedents for the jubilee have been discovered, mostly dating from the early second millennium, which give strong support to the antiquity of the jubilee law.[117]

---

115. E.g. Wellhausen (1883: 116-20); Driver (1902: 185); de Vaux (1961: 83); Phillips (1970: 78); Cholewiński (1976: 232-50); Cardellini (1981: 347-56); Gnuse (1985b: 24-25).

116. Ginzberg (1932: 349, 389-90); Wright (1990: 250-51).

117. On the Mesopotamian precedents, see above, 4.1.a; and below, 9.3.a. Cf. Weinfeld

The late dating of Leviticus has been questioned by a significant number of twentieth-century scholars, beginning with Kaufmann, concluding that the Deuteronomic laws are later than those of Leviticus, though not necessarily dependent on them.[118] An analysis of the manumission laws by Japhet (1978) concludes that Deuteronomy 15 is dependent on both of its predecessors in subject matter and literary form, and is intended to replace them.[119] Milgrom (2001: 2251-57) agrees, arguing that Leviticus 25 abolishes the slave status for Israelites and therefore rejects the seventh-year manumission of Exodus 21 because it is no longer relevant. If an Israelite has to indenture himself, it must be as a 'resident hireling' (vv. 40, 53). A slave freed according to the law of Exodus might soon become enslaved again because he has no resources; whereas Leviticus insists that all ancestral land be returned in the jubilee, so the status quo is reestablished and all Israelites are on the same level again. Like Japhet, Milgrom believes that Deuteronomy 15 is later than Leviticus 25, and provides various linguistic arguments to support the case. That may be true, though the evidence is not conclusive in my judgement; but the associated view that Deuteronomy intends to reform the earlier laws is unconvincing, particularly with respect to Leviticus. For example, as Japhet herself admits, it is difficult to reconcile Deuteronomy's 'humane tendencies' with the retention of permanent bondage for Israelites, in contrast to Leviticus which rules this out and only allows foreigners to be held as permanent slaves.

Conservative scholars have tended to harmonise the laws, arguing that Leviticus assumes the seventh-year rule of Exodus and supplements it by stipulating that if the jubilee should come earlier then the slave must be released, since it is the universal year of freedom and no slavery can be allowed to continue.[120] This is an old solution, attested in Philo (*Laws* 2:122)

(2004: 60-63). Loewenstamm (1971: 251-52) rejects the reform theory because it does not suit 'the ancient character of the law of the Jubilee,' suggesting rather that the jubilee was observed only in northern Israel, while the Book of the Covenant was at first observed only in Judah; however, he offers very little evidence to support this suggestion.

118. E.g. Kaufmann (1961: 169, 318); Weinfeld (1972a: 179-89; 2004); Wenham (1979: 11-13); Milgrom (1991: 3-13; 2000: 1357-61); Bergsma (2007: 125-29, 136-38).

119. This conclusion is anticipated by Weingreen (1976: 133-39). Ginsberg (1982: 100) accepts Japhet's conclusions with respect to these laws, though he does not consider the Holiness Code as a whole to pre-date Deuteronomy. Kaufman (1985) and Levinson (2006b: 316-22), on the other hand, reject her arguments, concluding that Lev 25 is later than Deut 15. For a critique of Levinson, see Bergsma (2007: 138-42).

120. E.g. Keil and Delitzsch (1864: 464-65); Cole (1973); Harrison (1980); Sarna (1991). According to Keil and Delitzsch, slavery entered into voluntarily would be excepted from the

and the Mishnah (*Qiddushin* 1:2). However, it is problematic because according to verse 40 the service lasts until the jubilee, which would rarely be the case if six years of service were the norm; and according to verses 50-52 the price of redemption is calculated on the basis of years to the next jubilee, not the next seventh year. It is strange that there is no mention of the seventh-year rule in Leviticus, if that is indeed assumed, when earlier in the chapter the law of jubilee is clearly related to the older law on sabbatical years (vv. 1-12).

A Proposed Solution

None of these theories explains the relationship between these particular laws satisfactorily. The reason is quite simple: they all assume that the three laws are dealing with the same subject (manumission) and therefore have to explain why the rules are different. In fact, I suggest, it is possible to obtain a much more coherent understanding of the laws if it is accepted that Leviticus 25 is concerned with circumstances quite distinct from those envisaged in Exodus 21 and Deuteronomy 15. Several scholars have made proposals along these lines, especially Ellison, Wright, Chirichigno, Schenker, and Lefebvre, and I will incorporate some of the results of their research into my proposed solution to the problem.[121] There are two main circumstances.

First, Exodus 21 and Deuteronomy 15 legislate for the *temporary slavery* of a person identified as a 'Hebrew', in the latter text supplemented with the term 'brother [or sister]'. What kind of person is this?

Ellison and Wright argue that the term 'Hebrew' has a social rather than an ethnic meaning, referring to a landless person with no hope of ac-

---

jubilee release; whereas Hartley (1992: 433) believes that Leviticus is particularly concerned with the exception in the earlier laws, whereby a slave has the right to renounce his freedom and stay with his master for life (cf. Josephus, *Antiquities* 4:273). Such a slave and his family are to be released at the jubilee, which aims to restore all Israelites to the status of free citizens with their own land.

121. Ellison (1973); Wright (1990: 249-59); Chirichigno (1993: 200-218, 275-82, 328-43); Schenker (1998); Lefebvre (2003: 301-30). Another theory is that of Mendelsohn (1949: 88-89), who suggests that Exodus and Deuteronomy are concerned with defaulting debtors, whereas Leviticus is concerned with those who sell themselves into perpetual slavery. Wright (1990: 252-53) demonstrates the weakness of this theory. See also Hartley (1992: 430-33); Tigay (1996: 466-67); Milgrom (2001: 2223); Bergsma (2007: 142-45).

quiring land.[122] The only way for such a person to earn a living is as a hired worker, a hard life in which it is easy to fall into debt. If unable to repay a debt, he would be sold as a slave, or allow a child to be sold, for a limited term. Such temporary slaves are protected by these laws, especially Deuteronomy 15 which gives a new start to those who are freed (vv. 13-14). The question of redemption is not mentioned here, because a marginal person like this would be unlikely to have a wealthy family able to redeem him. He has no land to which he can return on release, so the possibility of continuing in service is also mentioned. This is a plausible scenario, and there may well have been people like this in ancient Israel. However, there is insufficient evidence to establish that the 'Hebrews' constituted a distinguishable social class, a 'landless and rootless substratum of society who lived by selling their services to Israelite households'.[123]

Probably closer to the mark is the proposal of Chirichigno that Exodus 21 and Deuteronomy 15 are concerned with Israelite debt-slaves, usually dependants who have been sold by their family. Unlike the situation depicted in Leviticus 25, no loss of land is involved, just an individual working off a family debt by means of temporary slavery. Similarly, Schenker considers these laws to deal with the temporary slavery of a single person, or someone who is married without sons and has not yet acquired the status of family head. Lefebvre agrees that the person envisaged is a family-member rather than the head, pointing out that this could also include someone who has sons but is still living in his father's house and has not yet become a family-head.[124]

In any case, it seems that these laws are designed to protect *individuals* who work as temporary slaves in order to pay off a personal or family debt. In practice, those 'sold' in this way would generally be weaker members of society, such as children of poor families (2 Kgs 4:1; Neh 5:5; cf. Isa 50:1), those without family to support them (e.g. widows and orphans[125]), and other poor people (Amos 2:6).

Second, Leviticus 25 deals with an Israelite *landholder* forced by poverty to mortgage it, then to go into the service of another landholder, to-

---

122. Cf. Alt (1934: 93-96).
123. Wright (1990: 258). Milgrom (2001: 2253) suggests that the term 'Hebrew' in Exodus may reflect an earlier use with wider social or ethnic connotations (as in Genesis), but argues that by the time of the Book of the Covenant it had lost any such meaning and denoted simply an Israelite. For further discussion of this term, see above, 6.1.b.
124. Cf. Chirichigno (1993: 223).
125. On widows and orphans, see below, 7.2.

gether with his wife and children.[126] It is emphasised that he is *not* to serve as a slave, but as a *bonded labourer* (vv. 39-40, 53). In this way he obtains a place to live and work until his land is returned in the jubilee year. Although he does not receive a wage, a bonded labourer is presumably entitled to certain contractual rights, perhaps including fixed working-hours and benefits such as food, clothing, and housing.[127] When he regains his freedom in the fiftieth year, he does not need the generosity of his master because he returns to his own ancestral land (vv. 41, 54).

These different circumstances are the basis for terms and conditions of service for bonded labourers, which are quite different from those for temporary slaves.[128] There are five interrelated points:

- Fifty years is the maximum term of service, not a requirement, and few would serve the full term.
- The purpose of the jubilee legislation is to restore all Israelites to their ancestral land, and sort out social inequalities, so if this is put into practice it should be many years after the jubilee before economic problems get to the point of people becoming bonded labourers again.
- Whereas Exodus and Deuteronomy regulate temporary slavery, Leviticus is not concerned with slavery at all, but with a way of providing for poor families until the time when their land is returned to them.
- In Leviticus there is no option of continuing as a slave beyond the jubilee, because a bonded labourer is not a slave in the first place.

126. Leggett (1974: 103) and Chirichigno (1993: 330-31) argue that the arrangement is voluntary, translating נמכר in v. 39 as the reflexive 'sells himself'; while Schenker (1998: 28-32) and Lefebvre (2003: 270-76) understand it to be unavoidable (passive, 'is sold'). However, in reality there would be little difference between the two. Legally it might well be a voluntary decision to enter into bonded labour, but if the only alternative was starvation it would effectively be unavoidable.

127. Chirichigno (1993: 333-34). On hired workers, see Driver and Miles (1952: 469-78); de Vaux (1961: 76); Warhaftig (1972); Dandama[y]ev (1984: 112-31); Lipiński (1992).

128. Schenker (1998: 33) suggests that a head of family works for a longer period to pay his debts, which is to the benefit of creditors because it gives better assurance that the debts will be paid in full, nevertheless the law retains the idea that bondage should be limited in length and avoids making debtors slaves in the strict sense of the word. So the law of Leviticus complements the manumission rules of the Book of the Covenant, which provided for individual release after six years of slave labour, by introducing a general release in the jubilee year. He believes the heavier economic burden of taking an entire family into a creditor's household would demand a longer period of service, though this is questionable since the shortage of labour in ancient times would make the presence of extra workers a benefit rather than a burden.

- From the perspective of Leviticus, the overarching concern is not the length of service but to ensure that ancestral land is eventually returned to its original owner, and the arrangements for bonded labour are designed to achieve this goal.

d. Conclusion

The Holiness Code bans slavery between Israelites, while allowing bonded labour or indenture. This law is concerned with landholders who lose their land and enter the service of others, together with their families, until their own land is returned at the jubilee. A major difference from indenture in other parts of the ancient Near East is that loans in Israel are to be interest-free and therefore it is a more realistic possibility to pay off a debt in this way. Elsewhere, high interest rates could often mean that indenture merely covered the interest payments on a loan and resulted in long-term or lifetime bondage for the unfortunate debtor.[129]

The biblical rules are somewhat different in the case of service to an Israelite (vv. 39-43) and to a foreigner (vv. 47-55), particularly concerning the right of redemption. In the former case, the bonded labourer is emphatically not a slave and so redemption is not necessary.[130] In the latter case, his status is also theoretically that of a hired worker (v. 53), though in practice it may not be very different from that of a slave. Foreigners may be reluctant to observe the Israelite prohibition of slavery, and so the terms for redemption are stipulated. It is also made clear that bonded labourers must not be treated harshly and are to be freed in the jubilee year.

One of the most important themes in the understanding of the jubilee year is freedom, and Ezekiel actually refers to it as the 'year of freedom' (Ezek 46:17). The people of Israel have been freed by the Lord God from oppression and slavery in Egypt, and thereafter must not be enslaved by anyone, because they are now divine property (Lev 25:38, 39, 42, 55). As a consequence, they are forbidden to oppress the weak within their own society (Exod 22:21–23:9) or to enslave fellow Israelites (Lev 25:39-43).[131]

However, the Old Testament does not provide a categorical condem-

---

129. Cf. Eichler (1973: 44-46). On loans with and without interest, see below, 10.1.

130. Cf. Milgrom (2001: 2216-17, 2223, 2253); contra Wright (1990: 255).

131. Milgrom (2000: 1694-95; 2001: 2214) argues that the prohibition of slavery is the reason for banning tattoos in the covenant community (Lev 19:28), because slaves were marked in this way, but the evidence he gives is far from conclusive.

nation of slavery in all its forms; this may be one reason why the opposition to Wilberforce in the nineteenth century included some who tried to justify the institution on the basis of the Bible. It seems that in this respect Old Testament law was realistic rather than idealistic. Rather than banning slavery completely, a step for which the world was not ready, the Israelite legislators tried to ensure that temporary slavery and bonded labour would be limited in term and humane in nature. If their laws were followed, it is arguable that fixed-term slavery and bonded labour in ancient Israel would be comparable to paid employment today, whereas freedom would be equivalent to self-employment and involve considerably more risk.[132]

The millions involved in debt bondage, contract slavery, and forced prostitution today are not helped much by the fact that slavery is illegal. These modern slaves often have little legal protection or likelihood of becoming free again. Their plight is almost certainly worse than that of temporary slaves and bonded labourers in ancient Israel. Two hundred years after Wilberforce, and two thousand years after Jesus who came 'to proclaim release to the captives' (Luke 4:18), it seems the step of abandoning slavery completely is something for which our world is still not ready.

---

132. Cf. de Vaux (1961: 85); Wenham (2000: 92 n. 52); Schluter (2005: 193-95).

Chapter 7

OTHER VULNERABLE GROUPS

Apart from slaves and semi-slaves, there were various kinds of marginal people in Israelite society. In this chapter I focus on three vulnerable groups which are often mentioned in legal texts: *resident aliens, widows,* and *orphans*. Deuteronomy generally groups all three together,[1] while Leviticus refers only to resident aliens and Exodus varies in its focus.

Further vulnerable groups mentioned in the laws — especially Levites, hired workers, and the poor — are discussed in the course of examining the laws in question rather than separately here.[2] However, it may be helpful at this point to explain briefly who they were.

Levites are distinct from the rest of the people of Israel: on the one hand because of their consecration to the service of God (Exod 32:29; Num 3:41, 45; Deut 10:8; 33:8-10); and on the other because they receive no allotment of land (Num 18:23b-24; 26:62; Deut 10:9; 18:1-2) except for the pasture surrounding their cities (Num 35:1-8; Lev 25:32-34). Because they have

---

1. Cf. Ps 94:6; 146:9; Jer 7:6; 22:3; Ezek 22:7; Zech 7:10; Mal 3:5. On this word pattern, see Miller (1980: 80-82); Krapf (1984); Lohfink (1996b: 7-9).

2. There were also other marginal people, for whom there are no specific laws of protection, such as infertile women (e.g. Gen 11:30; 25:21; 29:31; Job 24:21), divorced women (Lev 21:7, 14; 22:13; Ezek 44:22), defiled women and prostitutes (Lev 21:7, 14), illegitimate children (Judg 11:1), and refugees. On divorced women, see Otwell (1977: 115-23); cf. Instone-Brewer (2002: ch. 2). Levine (1999: 159) argues that divorced women are included in the laws on widows, but this is far from certain. There are various references to Israelites as refugees in other countries (e.g. Gen 27:41–28:5; Ps 42:6; 1 Sam 27:1-4; 1 Kgs 11:40; 2 Kgs 25:26; Jer 40:11-12; 43:5-7) and one to foreign refugees in Israel (Jer 50:28), but no laws relate specifically to their situation, apart from that on fugitive slaves (see above, 5.3). On other ancient Near Eastern laws relating to refugees, see Altman (2002).

relatively little land, they are to be supported by a share of the tithes and offerings of the people (Num 18:21-24; Deut 12:5-19; 14:22-29; 18:1-8; 26:12-13). This is probably implicit, too, in the instructions to include the Levites when celebrating the festivals, as well as the three marginal groups mentioned above (Deut 16:11, 14; 26:11).[3]

Hired workers would generally be landless people, dependent on the availability of employment and needing fair treatment by employers. In a predominantly agricultural society they would be much more vulnerable than landowners (1 Sam 2:5; Job 7:1-2; Jer 22:13; Zech 8:10; Mal 3:5). Often work would be seasonal (Ruth 2), or dependent on a major building project (2 Chr 24:12), or risky (Judg 9:4; 2 Sam 10:6; Jer 46:21). Judging by the prohibition on taking part in Passover (Exod 12:45), such workers may often have been foreigners.[4]

The *poor* are denoted in the laws by several Hebrew words.[5] These words do not denote a clearly defined social group, but simply refer to those in particular need of help from more prosperous members of the covenant community. Their situation is recognised in ceremonial laws which provide alternatives for those who cannot afford the stipulated sacrifices and offerings (e.g. Lev 5:7-13; 14:21-32).[6]

7.1 Resident Aliens

In many societies, there is a tendency for ethnic minorities to be marginalised, whether intentionally because of racial discrimination or unintentionally because minorities are less fluent in the dominant language and less aware of the appropriate cultural behaviour for acceptance and success within the host society. The Old Testament does not deal with racial discrimination and cultural marginalisation in general terms, but includes a number of laws designed to protect vulnerable individuals. These individuals are denoted by a distinctive Hebrew word, translated here as 'resident

---

3. For further discussion, see 4.1.b; 9.3; 11.1.d. Cf. Loewenstamm (1971: 247-49); Rehm (1992); Nurmela (1998); Garrett (2003).

4. For further discussion, see 11.2; cf. 3.3.b; 6.3.b; 9.1.c. Cf. Lipiński (1992); van Dam (1997); Falk (2001: 99-102).

5. Especially אביון ('poor, needy') and עני ('poor, humble, afflicted'), and occasionally דל ('poor, helpless') and מוך ('become poor'). On these words, see Botterweck (1970); Fabry (1974); Gerstenberger (1987); Pleins (1992); Domeris (1997).

6. For further discussion, see 8.2; 9.1; 9.2; 10.1; 10.2; 10.3; 11.2.

alien', which will be discussed in some detail after a preliminary survey of the relevant ancient Near Eastern material.

a. Ancient Near East

There appears to be relatively little concern for resident aliens in the ancient Near Eastern laws, compared with those of the Old Testament. Several Mesopotamian laws refer to a wife abandoned by a man who leaves his country to reside abroad, giving permission for her to remarry and denying the man the right to reclaim her if he should later return (LE §30; CH §136; cf. MAL §A36). However, very few specifically grant rights to foreign nationals who have come to live in the country. There is a brief clause in the Laws of Eshnunna, which includes *ubaru* ('foreigner, resident alien') among several classes of people who may not be exploited by an unscrupulous taverness (§41). The Edict of Ammi-saduqa includes Akkadians and Amorites, and some other foreign citizens, in its general remission of debts (§§3, 5, 6, 8, 20, 21). Several legal texts provide evidence of concern for widows and orphans,[7] and the poor in general, but do not mention resident aliens.

Of course the absence of such laws does not in itself prove that people in the ancient Near East were unsympathetic to the needs of foreigners who took up residence in peaceful circumstances. The Eastern tradition of hospitality would suggest the opposite.[8] The law collections are clearly not comprehensive, and no doubt many matters would be regulated by unwritten common law and custom. Sometimes a foreigner in Babylon would be granted special protection by a ruler, so acquiring the status of a resident alien with certain legal rights.[9] Without such protection, it would be very easy to end up as a slave. Likewise at Ugarit, resident aliens are considered members of the community and possess many rights and responsibilities as a result.[10] The Hittite Instructions to Commanders of Border Garrisons *(bel madgalti)* make provision for deportees who have been settled on the land, supplying them with winter food stores, seed for the spring, and livestock.[11]

---

7. On which, see below, 7.2.a.
8. Cf. de Vaux (1961: 10); Kooy (1962); Koenig (1992).
9. Westbrook (2003b: 37, 42; 2003c: 377, 380). On foreigners in Mesopotamia, see Cardascia (1958); Limet (1995); on Egypt, see Pirenne (1958).
10. Rowe (2003b: 723); cf. Vargyas (1995).
11. Column 3: lines 36-41; see von Schuler (1957: 49); COS (1.84); cf. Weinfeld (1977: 77). Likewise, the Hittite Instructions to Priests and Temple Officials refer to 'one entitled to the

Pedersen (1920: 41) draws a comparison with the 'neighbours' (περιοικοι) of Sparta, the original inhabitants of the Peloponnese who keep their freedom but are without political rights. The comparison may be valid for groups of Canaanites who are incorporated into Israelite society, like the Gibeonites, but this is the exception rather than the rule according to the conquest accounts and is of course contrary to the original plan. Weber (1921: 32-36) refers to resident aliens as 'metics' (μετοικοι), a term which denotes settlers from abroad incorporated into the social system of Athens as second-class citizens. Although there are some similarities, it would be precarious to draw conclusions about biblical interpretation on the basis of an Athenian institution which is far removed in time and place from the Old Testament.

b. Biblical Terminology

The identity of the 'resident alien' (גר) in different strands of the Old Testament has been the subject of much debate.[12] For the present purpose, I focus on the key points from texts containing this noun or its related verb 'reside [as an alien]' (גור), as a starting point for understanding the laws relating to this group of people.

First, there is a strong tradition that the ancestors of Israel lived in foreign countries at several points in their early history. Abraham, Isaac, and Jacob are described as aliens in connection with their residence in the promised land (e.g. Gen 17:8; 23:4; 28:4; 35:27; Exod 6:4). The same word-group is used to describe the status of the Israelites in Egypt (Gen 12:10; 15:13; 47:4; Exod 22:21; Lev 19:34; Deut 10:19; 23:7; 26:5; Ps 105:23; Isa 52:4) and other places of temporary residence abroad (Gen 20:1; 26:3; 32:4; cf. Exod 2:22; Ruth 1:1; 2 Kgs 8:1-2).[13] There is good reason to consider this tradition au-

---

protection due to a citizen' (column 1: lines 53-54), according to Beyerlin (1975: 181), which appears to mean a foreigner who has been granted asylum and corresponds to the resident alien in the Old Testament. However, COS (1.83) translates it rather differently as 'important (?) guest'.

12. See Pedersen (1920: 39-46); Weber (1921: 28-57); Sulzberger (1923); Meek (1930); Cazelles (1954: 126-37); de Vaux (1961: 74-76); Mauch (1962); Kellermann (1973b); Amusin (1981); Spina (1983); Cohen (1990); van Houten (1991); Bultmann (1992); Joosten (1996: 54-76); Rendtorff (1996); Konkel (1997); Ramírez Kidd (1999); Milgrom (2000: 1493-1501); Burnside (2001); Bennett (2002: 38-48); Knauth (2003); Krauss (2006).

13. In later times it is used once in connection with the exile in Babylon (Ezra 1:4), and frequently by Jeremiah with reference to the Judeans who migrate to Egypt after the fall of Jerusalem (42:15, 17, 22; 43:2; 44:8, 12, 14, 28; cf. 43:5).

thentic, since it is unlikely that a nation would invent a tradition that they were not the original inhabitants of the land to which they clung so closely.[14]

Second, the verb 'reside [as an alien]' is used with reference to Israelites in Canaan who reside outside their own tribal territory. The Levites, who are not allotted land of their own (Josh 13:14), live among the other tribes (Deut 18:6; Judg 17:7-9; 19:1).[15] Members of the northern tribes of Israel who reside in the south are classed as aliens (2 Chr 15:9; cf. Judg 19:16), as are the people of Beeroth who flee to Gittaim and take up residence there (2 Sam 4:3).[16] The Rechabites who attempt to preserve the ancient nomadic ideal by refusing to settle anywhere are described with the same terminology (Jer 35:7). In Job 31:32 the noun refers to an individual traveller who is provided with hospitality.[17]

Third, the resident alien is mentioned in legal texts alongside the Israelite, the latter being referred to as a 'native' (אזרח) of the land or a 'brother' (אח), particularly when it is emphasised that the same law applies to both (Exod 12:19; Lev 17:10-16; 18:26; 19:34; 20:2; 22:18; 24:16, 22; Num 15:13-16, 26, 29-30; 19:10; Deut 1:16; cf. Josh 20:9; Ezek 14:7). Resident aliens may celebrate Passover, so long as they are circumcised (Exod 12:48-49; Num 9:14; cf. 2 Chr 30:25), and offer sacrifices (Lev 17:8; Num 15:14). They are involved in covenant ceremonies (Deut 29:10-12; 31:12; Josh 8:32-35) and festivals (Deut 16:11, 14; 26:11), and expected to observe the sabbath (Exod 20:10; 23:12; Deut 5:14) and the Day of Atonement (Lev 16:29). For the present they do not own land — since none is available for sale — but in a future 'golden age' they will receive an inheritance together with natives of Israel (Ezek 47:22-23; cf. Isa 14:1). In these texts the Israelites are no longer aliens but natives; and the resident aliens are foreigners who have become integrated with Israel and are treated in many respects as members of the covenant community.[18] Nevertheless, the

---

14. Spina (1983). For recent studies of the authenticity of the exodus traditions, see Hoffmeier (1997); Davies (2004b).

15. Levites and resident aliens are listed together in the context of the triennial tithe laws (Deut 14:29; 26:12) and celebration of festivals (Deut 16:11, 14).

16. Beeroth is one of the Canaanite cities said to have made peace with Israel together with Gibeon (Josh 9:17), so these people might in fact be Canaanites rather than Israelites.

17. For examples of the tradition of hospitality to strangers, see Gen 18:1-8; 19:1-8; Judg 19:16-23.

18. The claim of Weber (1921: 33) that impoverished Israelites who lose their land become aliens is based on a misunderstanding of Lev 25:35 and cannot be sustained (cf. van Houten 1991: 38-41). On Lev 25:35, see below, 10.1.c. The theory of Cazelles (1954: 126-37) that after the exile the Samaritans were regarded as natives and those who returned from Babylon were referred to as aliens has been generally rejected by scholars (see Joosten 1996: 56

alien status of Israel is not entirely left behind — at least on the theological level — for the promised land is understood to be divine property where they reside as aliens and tenants (Lev 25:23; cf. 1 Chr 29:10-15; Ps 39:12; 119:19).

Fourth, the resident alien is to be distinguished from the 'foreigner' (נכרי[19]), which often has a negative connotation (e.g. Gen 31:15; Ps 144:7; Isa 2:6; 62:8), though the possibility is not excluded that one day even foreigners may join the people of God (Isa 44:5; 60:10; 61:5-7). A foreigner is someone who comes from another country and has no relationship to the Israelite tribal system and covenant community (Deut 17:15; 29:22; Judg 19:12; 1 Kgs 8:41). Apparently foreigners follow their own religion, since they are never included among those who take part in religious ceremonies and are specifically excluded from eating the Passover (Exod 12:43; cf. 48). They do not benefit from the seventh year remission of debts (Deut 15:3) or the facility of interest-free loans (Deut 23:20).[20] It seems the status of resident aliens is somewhere between that of natives and foreigners, and individual aliens may be incorporated into the community by becoming dependent members of an Israelite family, under the protection of the household head (cf. Exod 20:10; 23:12).[21]

---

n. 144). Vink (1969: 42-48) and van Houten (1991: 151-55) turn Cazelles's theory back-to-front, suggesting that the term 'alien' in the priestly laws refers to Israelites and Samaritans who have settled in Judah during the years of Babylonian domination and later join the restoration community formed by those who return from exile and consider themselves to be the true Israelites. Cohen (1990) believes that the aliens are nationals of northern Israel who move to the south, especially after the fall of Samaria. Bultmann (1992: 22, 35-93, 121-36) argues that the alien in Deuteronomy is an Israelite living an economically marginal existence in another part of Judah, in contrast to van Houten (1991: 77-108) who believes the Deuteronomic Laws consistently treat the alien as a non-Israelite (cf. Houtman 1996: 224). It is unnecessary to assess all these proposals in detail here, for they do not significantly affect the exegesis of the laws on the resident alien in the present book. For further discussion, see Joosten (1996: 55-58); Milgrom (2000: 1494-95, 1498-99); Patrick (2002).

19. Also בן־נכר. The word זר ('strange, foreign, unauthorised') sometimes has a similar meaning, especially in the prophetic writings (e.g. Job 19:15; Isa 1:7; 25:2, 5; 61:5; Jer 2:25; 5:19; 30:8; 51:51; Lam 5:2; Ezek 7:21; 11:9; 28:7, 10; 31:12; Hos 7:9; Obad 1:11; cf. Ps 69:8).

20. The rationale for this is discussed below, 10.1.d; 10.3.b.

21. Neufeld (1955: 388-94). According to Deut 14:21, an Israelite may not eat an animal that dies of itself, while this is allowed for both resident aliens and foreigners. The former are to be given the meat as charity, whereas the latter are given the opportunity to buy it. However, Lev 17:15 implies that resident aliens should avoid eating such meat. Burnside (2001: 42) explains the apparent contradiction by arguing that גר in Leviticus refers to the assimilating alien (while תושב refers to the nonassimilating alien), and Deut 14:21 refers to the nonassimilating alien (cf. Sparks 1998: 238-45).

Other Vulnerable Groups

Fifth, a number of texts mention the 'temporary resident' (תושב), which appears to be close in meaning to 'resident alien' though not quite synonymous.[22] Several times the two words are used together, either in parallel (1 Chr 29:15; Ps 39:12) or as a hendiadys (Gen 23:4; Lev 25:23[23]). Nevertheless, temporary residents are occasionally distinguished from resident aliens (Num 35:15)[24] and not permitted to celebrate Passover (Exod 12:45; cf. v. 48), which suggests that the temporary resident is less integrated into Israelite society than the resident alien. This would be consistent with usage of the two terms in the Holiness Code, where it is only the former who may be enslaved (Lev 25:45) and only the latter who is listed as a participant in worship (e.g. Lev 16:29; 17:8-9; 22:18) and given legal equality with the Israelite (e.g. Lev 24:16, 22).[25]

Sixth, a census of resident aliens records that they number 153,600 during the reign of Solomon, all of whom are conscripted to work on the temple and other building projects (2 Chr 2:17-18; cf. 1 Kgs 5:15-16; 1 Chr 22:2). In earlier days they are said to have worked as wood-cutters and water-carriers (Deut 29:11). These people seem to be Canaanites who have survived Israel's occupation of the land (Josh 9:21-27; 1 Kgs 9:15-21; cf. Josh 16:10; 17:13; Judg 1:28-35). It is also mentioned that a 'mixed crowd' joined the Israelites in the exodus from Egypt, who may later have been counted as resident aliens (Exod 12:38; cf. Lev 24:10; Num 11:4). A few individuals are known from the historical books, including the Amalekite who claims to have killed Saul (2 Sam 1:13) and Uriah the Hittite (2 Samuel 11).[26]

There is no single word in English that adequately covers the seman-

---

22. De Vaux (1961: 75-76); Kellermann (1973b: 448); Leggett (1974: 101 n. 64); van Houten (1991: 124-31); Joosten (1996: 73-74); Burnside (2001: 16); Lefebvre (2003: 54-71).

23. Also vv. 35 and 47, according to Kellermann (1973b: 448) and Milgrom (2001: 2187, 2207, 2236).

24. Kellermann (1973b: 448) and Milgrom (2001: 2187, 2207, 2236) regard the two words in Num 35:15 as a hendiadys. However, Lefebvre (2003: 237) points out that Num 35:15 has a separate preposition for each noun, so it is more likely that in the this text the words are intended to form part of a list: Israelite, resident alien, and temporary resident (cf. van Houten 1991: 130-31).

25. Sparks (1998: 251-53) points out that Lev 25:45 mentions 'temporary residents' who have been born in the land, and argues that the two terms are to be distinguished not so much in terms of permanency of residence as in degree of assimilation to the covenant community.

26. Although the word גר is not used in connection with Uriah, that would appear to be his status. His Yahwistic name suggests he is well integrated into Israelite society, and this is confirmed by his concern for the ark and abstinence from sexual intercourse during war (v. 11; cf. 1 Sam 21:4-5).

tic range of this Hebrew word (גר). 'Sojourner' (ESV; RSV) conveys the idea of temporary residence, but misses the hint of foreignness in the original and sounds quaint in modern English; while 'stranger' (KJV; NJPS) and 'foreigner' (TEV) are too general in meaning and say nothing about residence. One attractive suggestion is 'immigrant',[27] which covers quite a few cases but not that of Israelites who go to live in a different part of their own country, nor that of Canaanites who continue to live among the people of Israel. Another is 'refugee',[28] but this implies an element of compulsion that is not present in the Hebrew. To use current terminology, these people might be described as 'ethnic minorities', who have distinctive racial or cultural traditions and are vulnerable to exploitation or discrimination by dominant groups in the population.[29] This may be the best term when referring to groups, but unfortunately it has no convenient singular form. Therefore, in the absence of any entirely satisfactory substitute, I use the conventional scholarly translation 'resident alien', to denote a free person who resides outside their native country or region, being accepted by the host community and having certain rights but not regarded as a full citizen.[30]

c. Book of the Covenant

> *You shall not oppress*[31] *a resident alien, for you were resident aliens in the land of Egypt.*
>
> Exod 22:21 [Hebrew 22:20]

> *You shall not oppress a resident alien; you yourselves know how it feels to be*[32] *a resident alien, for you were resident aliens in the land of Egypt.*
>
> Exod 23:9

---

27. Spina (1983); Burnside (2001: 14); cf. Meek (1930); Bianchi (1979: 6-8).
28. Knauth (2003).
29. Cf. Bennett (2002: 45-46).
30. So NRSV; REB; cf. NIV; NJB; Leggett (1974: 101 n. 63); Wenham (1979); van Houten (1991); Hartley (1992); Houtman (1996); Joosten (1996: 54-73); Milgrom (2000); Rodd (2001: 166 n. 20).
31. A pair of words is used in Hebrew — ינה (hiphil) and לחץ — both of which mean 'oppress'. These terms are discussed further below.
32. Lit. 'know the soul of'.

In Exodus 22:21 the style shifts from the third person, used in most of the preceding clauses of the Book of the Covenant, to the second person. God[33] addresses his people directly, to tell them of his concern for vulnerable people in Israelite society and to warn them of dire consequences if they do not show a similar concern. Beginning with a law prohibiting oppression of resident aliens, the same style continues in verses 22-24 on widows and orphans, in verses 25-27 on the poor, and in most of the remaining clauses. A group of laws on the practice of justice in chapter 23:1-3, 6-8 is concluded with a second version of the law on oppression of aliens in verse 9.[34] Whether in everyday life (22:21) or at a court of law (23:9), oppression of ethnic minorities is quite unacceptable.

Both versions of this law consist of a divine command followed by a motivation clause, the latter referring back to Israel's own experience of oppression as resident aliens in Egypt (cf. Exod 3:9; Deut 26:7). In the second version, the divine command is abbreviated and the motivation expanded, so that it complements the first without changing its meaning. In both cases the divine command is addressed in the second person singular to the individual Israelite, while the motivation is worded in the second person plural, recalling the experience of the whole people. This contrast perhaps reflects the fact that most of those who hear the law will not have personally experienced life in Egypt, and can acknowledge it as part of their history only because they are part of the chosen people, whereas each of them individually can be expected to refrain from oppressing resident aliens in their own lives.

It is interesting to note the vocabulary of oppression in this law. There are two Hebrew verbs which are normally translated 'oppress': the first (ינה hiphil) is generally used in the context of Israelites oppressing the

---

33. That the speaker is God becomes clear in vv. 23-24 and 27.

34. Van Houten (1991: 45, 55), following a suggestion of Lohfink, sees the two versions of this one law as forming a frame *(inclusio)* to open and close a section on oppression of the weak and social justice (Exod 22:21–23:9). Cf. Lohfink (1991: 40-42); Schwienhorst-Schönberger (1990: 23, 29, 373); Crüsemann (1992: 182). If that is intended, however, it is only a rather general device because the section is not exclusively concerned with social issues (see 22:28-31) and there is a good deal of social concern outside this section, including the verses immediately following (23:10-12). Lewy (1957) suggests that Exod 22:21-27 and 23:1-9 once formed an ethical code alongside the Decalogue, originating from before the division of the monarchy, that was interpolated into the Book of the Covenant. While it is certainly not impossible that this material was once separate, there is no clear evidence that this was the case (cf. Durham 1987: 328). Sprinkle (1994: 166-68) divides the material differently again, treating v. 28 as a generalising summary for the preceding verses.

weak in their own society (e.g. Lev 19:33; 25:14, 17; Deut 23:16; Jer 22:3; Ezek 18:7, 12, 16; 22:7, 29; 45:8; 46:18); while the second (לחץ) generally refers to foreigners oppressing Israel (Exod 3:9; Deut 26:7; Judg 2:18; 4:3; 6:9; 10:12; 1 Sam 10:18; 2 Kgs 13:4, 22; Ps 106:42; Isa 19:20; Amos 6:14). In the present context, the first verb would seem more natural, and it is in fact used in Exodus 22:21. However, it is striking that it is supplemented with the second verb in this version of the law, and the second verb stands alone in Exodus 23:9. The message is clear: just as Israel has been freed from oppression in a foreign land, so Israelites must protect resident aliens in their own land from oppression. Nevertheless, although this word is often used in international contexts, the laws in the Book of the Covenant appear to be primarily concerned for individuals in need of protection rather than large ethnic minorities such as the Gibeonites and other surviving Canaanites.[35]

d. Holiness Code

There are many references to resident aliens in the Holiness Code, some of which are discussed elsewhere in this book, but the key points are expressed by two laws in chapters 19 and 24.

Social Equality

When an alien resides with you in your land, you shall not oppress him. The alien who resides with you shall be [treated] as the native among you; you shall love him as yourself, for you were resident aliens in the land of Egypt. I am the LORD *your God.*

Lev 19:33-34

This law is an expansion of the pair of laws in the Book of the Covenant discussed above (Exod 22:21; 23:9). The prohibition of oppressing a resident alien is repeated (v. 33), using the first of the two verbs in Exodus 22:21 (ינה hiphil), which generally denotes oppression of the weak within Israelite society. As in both versions of the Exodus law, the motivation is remembrance of Israel's own experience in Egypt (v. 34c). There are three significant additions:

---

35. Van Houten (1991: 52-53, 59-62).

- a principle that resident aliens should be treated as natives (v. 34a)
- a command to love resident aliens as oneself (v. 34b)
- a reminder that the law has divine authority, in the characteristic refrain of the Holiness Code (v. 34d)

In principle, the social status of resident aliens is the same as that of native-born Israelites. They are to be treated as natives and loved like neighbours (cf. v. 18). 'The injunction to love the alien is quite remarkable in the context of religious thought and practice in antiquity.'[36] The assumption that they will be loved in this way is even the basis for another law, according to which impoverished Israelites are to be treated like resident aliens (Lev 25:35).

Legal Equality

There shall be one law for you, [and] it shall apply to both the resident alien and the native-born; for I am the Lord *your God.*

Lev 24:22

This law is set in the context of a case of blasphemy by a half-Israelite (vv. 10-14, 23), perhaps considered a resident alien. The decision in this particular case and the supplementary instructions (vv. 15-22) make it very clear that in such matters there is no legal differentiation on the basis of ethnic origin. Verses 16-22 form a chiasmus or palistrophe (symmetrical pattern), beginning and ending with the principle of legal equality between natives and resident aliens.[37]

The principle of legal equality is repeatedly emphasised in the Holiness Code (Lev 18:26; 20:2; 22:18; 24:22), as well as by various other laws in Exodus (12:19, 48-49), Leviticus (16:29; 17:8-10, 12-16), and Numbers (9:14; 15:13-16, 26, 29-30; 19:10; 35:15). These laws give resident aliens both rights and responsibilities. On the one hand, they are to benefit from fair treatment and compassion on the part of their hosts; on the other hand, they are expected to participate in the life of the community in accordance with the law and are liable to be punished for wrongdoing. It is striking that most of the laws where the principle of equality is mentioned are con-

---

36. Blenkinsopp (1986: 366).
37. Wenham (1979); cf. Hartley (1992).

cerned with religious issues. Perhaps it was considered obvious that resident aliens would follow civil laws but less clear whether they needed to follow religious laws as well — thus the need to clarify the point.

Nevertheless, although resident aliens enjoy equal legal protection with Israelites, they do not have identical privileges and obligations.[38] The fundamental distinction is that they are bound by the prohibitive commandments, but not the performative ones. For example, observance of Passover is compulsory for Israelites but voluntary for resident aliens (Exod 12:47-48; Num 9:13-14), and only Israelites are mentioned in connection with the festival of Booths (Lev 23:42). The laws on slaughtering of animals in Leviticus 17 repeatedly emphasise that they apply to both Israelites and resident aliens, except in verses 3-7 and 11 where slaughtering is linked with sacrifice and only Israelites are mentioned. It seems the omission of resident aliens here is intentional, indicating that for them sacrifices are voluntary (cf. vv. 8-9), whereas the prohibition on eating blood applies to all (vv. 10, 12-14; cf. Gen 9:3-4) because it relates to the holiness of the land.

e. Deuteronomic Laws

> *You shall not pervert the justice [due to] a resident alien or orphan; and you shall not take a widow's garment as a pledge. Remember that you were a slave in Egypt, and the* Lord *your God redeemed you from there; that is why I am commanding you to do this.*
>
> Deut 24:17-18

As in Exodus 23:9, resident aliens are mentioned in the context of legal justice (v. 17a). The basic principles for just lawsuits have already been laid out in Deuteronomy 16:18-20 and 19:15-21,[39] and nothing new is added here. This brief law simply emphasises the importance of implementing the principles for the benefit of resident aliens, as is also made clear in the introduction to Deuteronomy:

> I charged your judges at that time: 'Hear [the disputes] between your brothers and judge fairly, between one person and [another, whether] a brother or a resident alien'. (1:16)

---

38. As pointed out by Weinfeld (1972a: 230-32) and Milgrom (2000: 1496-99).

39. On which, see below, ch. 8.

and mentioned again towards the end in the twelve curses on Mount Ebal:

> Cursed be anyone who perverts the justice [due to] a resident alien, orphan, or widow; and all the people shall say 'Amen!' (27:19)

The command to love resident aliens, following the divine example, is also set in a legal context:

> For the LORD your God is God of gods and Lord of lords, the great God, mighty and awesome, who does not show partiality and does not accept a bribe. He sees justice done for orphans and widows; and loves resident aliens, giving them food and clothing.[40] You also shall love resident aliens, for you were resident aliens in the land of Egypt. (10:17-19)

Like the Book of the Covenant (Exod 22:21; 23:9) and the Holiness Code (Lev 19:34), the Deuteronomic Law reminds Israel of its experience in Egypt as the primary motivation for showing compassion to vulnerable groups in its own society, beginning with the resident alien (24:18; cf. 5:15; 10:19; 15:15; 16:12; 24:22). At the same time it may be assumed that those who are protected by the law are expected to obey it as well (cf. 29:9-12; 31:12; Josh 8:32-35).

f. Conclusion

The exodus tradition made a lasting impression on the people of Israel, and resulted in a particular concern for ethnic minorities in their laws, unparalleled elsewhere in the ancient Near East.[41] Once upon a time the descendants of Jacob had been aliens in a foreign country. Over a period of centuries, they experienced a change of situation from a warm welcome to open hostility and ruthless exploitation. By God's mercy they were granted freedom and a land of their own; now they must be sympathetic to anyone else in a similar situation far from home. The Book of the Covenant, Holiness Code, and Deuteronomic Laws are unanimous in giving this as the primary motivation for protecting resident aliens within the covenant

---

40. 'Orphans', 'widows', 'resident aliens', and 'them' are all singular forms in Hebrew, but it is clear in the context that they refer to a general principle rather than a specific case, and so I have translated them as plurals.

41. For a study of the Torah that gives particular attention to the 'stranger' (resident alien), see van Wijk-Bos (2005: esp. 25-32, 133-36, 188-91, 195-202).

community. Kindness cannot be enforced — since it is hardly feasible to punish those who are unkind so long as they stay within the letter of the law — so the motive clause is of great importance in each of these laws.[42] (The effectiveness of such a historical motivation is another matter: it is not difficult to find examples of peoples who have suffered terribly and then turn to inflict similar suffering on others.)

The majority of resident aliens in Israel will have left their homes and moved to a new country or region because of hardship — famine or plague, oppression or war. Then they will have faced further problems such as learning a new language, cultural adjustment, and finding ways of making a living. In general they are counted among the poor (cf. Lev 19:10; 23:22), regularly mentioned together with widows and orphans, and also with hired workers (Deut 24:14). More often than not they are the recipients of charity, though occasionally they may prosper (Lev 25:47; cf. Deut 28:43). In many ways resident aliens are integrated into the covenant community; nevertheless, they remain marginal people in two important respects: they own no land and thus have no regular source of sustenance, and they have no family network to whom they can turn in a crisis. It would be convenient to ignore the needs of these people, but they are to be loved just like other members of the community (Lev 19:18, 34), imitating God's love for vulnerable people (Deut 10:17-19).

Resident aliens in Israel are mentioned as beneficiaries in several other laws which will be discussed below, including those on gleaning (9.2), the triennial tithe (9.3), holidays (11.1), and wages (11.2). They may also be implied in the sabbatical year law (9.1), which lists several beneficiaries including 'temporary residents' (Lev 25:6). Apart from laws relating to wealth and poverty, they are entitled to protection in the cities of refuge (Num 35:15; Josh 20:9). According to rabbinic counting, concern for strangers is mentioned thirty-six times in the Law, more frequently than the love of God, observance of the sabbath, circumcision, or theft.[43] And beyond the laws, the prophets repeatedly exhort the people of God to refrain from oppression of ethnic minorities (Jer 7:6; 22:3; Ezek 22:7, 29; Zech 7:10; Mal 3:5) and other vulnerable people (Isa 1:17, 23; 10:2; Jer 5:28; Ezek 16:49; Amos 8:4).

In ancient Israelite society, where the solidarity of the clan and secu-

---

42. On these motive clauses, see van Houten (1992). For further discussion of motivation in Old Testament law, see Gemser (1953); de Vaux (1961: 149); Doron (1978); Engelhard (1980: 17-23); Sonsino (1980); Chirichigno (1981); Gowan (1981); Watts (1999: 65-67).

43. Sprinkle (1994: 172).

rity of belonging to a kinship group were of the utmost importance, those outside this structure would be in particular need of protection. The laws dealing with resident aliens discussed above were designed to provide such protection. How far they were effective is difficult to tell. In modern Europe and America, family ties are much less significant than in the ancient East, or even the East today, but this change has not led to a ready acceptance of ethnic minorities at the grassroots level. There is no shortage of laws against discrimination, but racism continues to flourish and ethnic minorities are still vulnerable to exploitation in many parts of the world.[44]

7.2 Widows and Orphans

In the patriarchal societies of the ancient Near East, women and children who lost the head of their family were in a particularly vulnerable position. Widows and orphans are frequently paired in the Old Testament (e.g. Job 22:9; Isa 1:17, 23; Lam 5:3), often alongside other marginal people such as resident aliens (see above, n. 1), hired workers (Mal 3:5), Levites (Deut 14:29), divorced women (Lev 21:14; 22:13), and the poor in general (Job 24:3-4, 9; 29:12-13; 31:16-21; Isa 10:2; Zech 7:10).

a. Ancient Near East

The oldest ancient Near Eastern reference to concern for widows and orphans dates to the twenty-fourth century B.C., in the Reforms of Uru-inimgina:

> Uru-inimgina made a compact with the divine Nin-girsu that the powerful man would not oppress the orphan [or] widow.

A similar claim is made by King Ur-Namma, two and a half centuries later, in the prologue to his collection of laws:

> I did not deliver the orphan to the rich. I did not deliver the widow to the mighty.

---

44. On the status and welfare of immigrants in contemporary society, viewed in the light of biblical law, see Rosoli (1979); Moucarry (1988); Burnside (2001).

Likewise, one of the purposes of the Laws of Hammurabi, according to the epilogue, is:

> In order that the mighty not wrong the weak, to provide just ways for the waif and the widow.

In each case the emphasis is on justice rather than charity. The king considers it his responsibility to protect vulnerable people such as orphans and widows from potential oppressors, but never claims to act as their benefactor.[45]

Several law collections make stipulations concerning widows and orphans, mainly in connection with inheritance rights. Hammurabi stipulates that a widow is entitled to her dowry, a designated portion of her husband's estate, and to be allowed to live in her husband's house for the rest of her life, although she may not sell it (§§150, 171b-72a; cf. 176). She also has the right to remarriage, with various conditions concerning her first husband's estate (§§172b-74, 177). Similar principles apply in the Neo-Babylonian Laws (§§12-13). According to the Middle Assyrian Laws, a widow may return to her father's house (§§A25-26, 33), or marry again (§§A28, 34-35, 45), or stay with her husband's family and be supported by her sons, unless the husband has made alternative provision in his will (§A46). If a woman's husband is taken prisoner by an enemy, there are detailed provisions for her support for up to two years; and if he has still not returned after that time, she is declared to be a widow (§A45). In general, sons inherit their father's property, and a number of laws cover details relating to this (LL §§24-27, 31; CH §§167, 170-71a, 177; MAL §§A25-26, 28-29, 41; NBL §15). In many of these laws it seems that the rights of the male relatives are the primary concern rather than those of the unfortunate widow, but the latter is certainly not without rights.[46]

Apart from this legal material, there are a number of references to widows and orphans in hymns and other literature. A Sumerian hymn to

---

45. Cf. Havice (1978: 128-29).

46. For further discussion of these laws, see Driver and Miles (1935: 193-98, 212-40; 1952: 334-35, 350-58; 1955: 330-31); Havice (1978: 130-34); Roth (1991-93); cf. Hiebert (1989: 128, 134-35); Westbrook (2003a: 680-81; 2003b: 62). In a detailed study of a text concerning inheritance from Ur III Sumer, Owen (1980) argues that in this case the widow appears to have had the primary right of inheritance rather than the sons. For other legal material concerning widows, see *CAD* (1.1: 363).

Nanshe makes the king responsible to render judgement for orphans and widows.[47] An Akkadian hymn to Ninurta acknowledges him as protector of the weak and helpless, including orphans.[48] At Ugarit there are similar ideas. In the Aqhat Legend, Daniel is described sitting at the city-gate to judge the cases of widows and orphans; while King Kirta is reproached by his son for having failed to do this.[49]

The Eloquent Peasant from the Egyptian Middle Kingdom appeals to the high steward — whom he flatters as 'greatest of the great, leader of all that is and all that is not' — as 'father to the orphan, husband to the widow'.[50] King Merikare is advised by his father that in order to endure on earth he should do justice, two examples of which are not to oppress the widow, and not to expel an orphan from his father's property.[51] Amenemope advises not to 'encroach on the boundaries of a widow', and to allow a widow to glean without impediment.[52] Several pharaohs are portrayed as protectors of orphans and widows, including Mentuhotep, Amenemhet I, and Rameses III.[53]

b. Book of the Covenant

You shall not abuse any widow or orphan.[54] If you do abuse one of them, and they cry out to me, I will certainly hear their cry. My anger will rage, and I will kill you with the sword; and your wives will become widows, and your children orphans.

Exod 22:22-24 [Hebrew 22:21-23]

---

47. Lines 91-92 (*COS*: 1.162).

48. Lines 9-11; see Falkenstein and von Soden (1953: 315); Seux (1976: 315); Foster (2005: 711); cf. Ringgren (1982: 478). For further examples of hymns in which the god is praised for his concern for orphans and widows, see Havice (1978: 149-56).

49. *COS* (1.103 p. 346; 1.102 p. 342); *CTA* (17 v 7-8; 16 vi 33-34, 45-50).

50. Papyrus B1 lines 52-63 (*COS*: 1.43 p. 100); cf. the 18th Dynasty inscription of Intef the Royal Herald lines 17-18 (*ARE* 2: 229).

51. Lines 47-48 (*COS*: 1.35 p. 62).

52. Chapters 6, 28 (*COS*: 1.47 lines vii.15; xxvi.9-10).

53. *COS* (1.36 lines I.6-7); Fensham (1962b: 133); Hoffner (1972: 288-89); Havice (1978: 29-35); Ringgren (1982: 478). On widows in ancient Egypt, see also Galpaz-Feller (2008).

54. The Hebrew יתום ('orphan') is generally taken to mean a child without a father, regardless of whether the mother is still alive (e.g. Ringgren 1982), though Renkema (1995) argues that it refers to a child who has lost both parents.

Like the law on resident aliens which immediately precedes it, the law on widows and orphans is addressed to the people of Israel in the second person, with God referring to himself in the first person. A brief apodictic prohibition of abuse (v. 22) is followed by a warning that if abuse does occur and the abused cry to God, he will hear them (v. 23), be angry, and punish the abuser (v. 24).[55] The Hebrew of the warning is quite emphatic, with a series of three infinitive absolute verbs (abuse, cry, hear). A loving God will be angry when those he loves are harmed; and the punishment he inflicts will fit the crime, rather like the principle of talion (cf. Exod 4:22-23; 21:23-25).

A similar motive for keeping the law is found in Exodus 22:27, and Deuteronomy 15:9 and 24:15. At the time of the exodus, God is said to have heard the cry for help of the Israelites in Egypt (Exod 2:23-25; 3:7-8), and in the messianic age he will take action against various crimes, including oppression of the widow and orphan (Mal 3:5). When Israel was oppressed, God took up her cause; but if Israelites become oppressors, they will find themselves on the opposite side to God (cf. Prov 22:22-23). According to Proverbs, God is concerned to maintain the boundaries of land belonging to widows and orphans (15:25; 23:10-11), and in Psalm 68:5 he is called the 'father of orphans and protector of widows' (cf. Ps 10:14, 18; 146:9). In his address to the divine council, God demands justice for orphans and other needy people (Ps 82:3-4). The teaching of Jesus ben Sirach on prayer gives the assurance that God will not ignore the pleas of a widow or orphan who is wronged (35:13-20). There is an Egyptian parallel in the Eloquent Peasant, where the high steward is described as 'creator of justice, who comes at the voice of the caller'.[56]

c. Deuteronomic Laws

> *You shall not pervert the justice [due to] a resident alien or orphan; and you shall not take a widow's garment as a pledge. Remember that you were a slave in Egypt, and the* LORD *your God redeemed you from there; that is why I am commanding you to do this.*
>
> Deut 24:17-18

---

55. On the cry of the oppressed, see Boyce (1988: 41-42); Ben-Dov (2006).
56. Papyrus B1 lines 67-68 (*COS*: 1.43 p. 101); cf. Instruction of Ptah-hotep lines 264-76 (*ANET*: 413); Shamash Hymn lines 130-47 (*COS*: 1.117 p. 419).

Orphans and widows have a right to both justice (v. 17a) and compassion (v. 17b). The primary motivation, as often in the laws on compassion, is the memory that God delivered Israel from slavery in Egypt (v. 18). These verses have already been discussed above, with reference to resident aliens (7.1.e), and the clause about the widow's garment will be dealt with below under the topic of security (10.2.c).

The theological basis for care of widows and orphans in the Deuteronomic Laws is the nature of God. He is omnipotent and gracious, strong and loving, as emphasised in the introduction:

> The LORD your God is God of gods and Lord of lords, the great God, mighty and awesome, who . . . sees justice done for orphans and widows. (10:17-18a)

and those who fail to imitate him in the matter of justice are subject to a curse:

> Cursed be anyone who perverts the justice [due to] an . . . orphan or widow. (27:19)

d. Conclusion

It seems ancient Near Eastern peoples considered the protection of vulnerable people to be the divine will and expected their leaders to promote such values, though in practice the legal rights of widows and orphans were rather limited. The same was true of Israel, but Old Testament law is distinctive from the other law collections in its inclusion of several principles for their protection. As we have seen, the Book of the Covenant and Deuteronomic Laws emphasise that widows and orphans are not to be abused, nor exploited in the law court or in financial dealings. They are also beneficiaries of several other Old Testament laws, which will be discussed below, especially those on gleaning (9.2), the triennial tithe (9.3), and holidays (11.1).[57] In the New Testament, James sums up true religion as 'to care for orphans and widows in their distress, and to keep oneself unstained by the world' (1:27).

How far these laws and principles were put into practice in ancient Israel is hard to tell, but the impression we gain from the prophets is that it

---

57. For further discussion, see Baker (2009).

was not uncommon for widows and orphans to be abused by the powerful (Jer 7:6; 22:3; Ezek 22:7; Zech 7:10) and refused justice (Isa 1:17, 23; 10:2; Jer 5:28). They were not always poor (e.g. Abigail, 1 Samuel 25), but without their household head they were more likely than others to be exploited by the unscrupulous and so they needed special protection.

A widow in ancient Hebrew society had not only lost a husband, but as a result had lost her protector and source of sustenance.[58] It appears she had no inheritance rights and so would have been dependent on the goodwill of the community.[59] While some widows did own property, or at least had the use of it until their death (Job 24:3; Prov 15:25), others were almost destitute (1 Kgs 17:10-12).[60]

If a widow had no sons, she would be in an especially precarious position (2 Sam 14:4-7; 1 Kgs 17:20; cf. Luke 7:12). The law of levirate marriage (Deut 25:5-10) is primarily concerned with producing an heir for a man who dies without sons, to continue his line and inherit his land, and secondarily to provide for the needs of the childless widow.[61]

Bennett (2002) argues that the Deuteronomic Laws which appear to be for the benefit of widows, strangers, and orphans are in fact designed to promote the interests of the privileged classes who produced them.[62] His

---

58. Cf. de Vaux (1961: 53-55); Boecker (1976: 19); Otwell (1977: 123-31); Hiebert (1989); Toorn (1994: 134-40); Sparks (1998: 240 n. 46); King and Stager (2001: 53); Galpaz-Feller (2008).

59. Cf. Num 27:1-11; 36:6-9; Deut 21:15-17. This appears to be confirmed by an ostracon recording a widow's plea to recover land belonging to her late husband, which she claims as a favour rather than a right, but this text is probably a modern forgery (see above, ch. 4 n. 48). For a different view, arguing that women did inherit land in ancient Israel, see Osgood (1992).

60. Steinberg (2004) distinguishes between three terms: אלמנה denoting a widow with very limited economic resources, אשה־אלמנה (lit. 'widow woman') denoting a widow with an inheritance and sons, and אשת־המת (lit. 'wife of the dead man') denoting a widow with an inheritance but no sons (cf. Tavares 1987). The first term is used in all the laws concerning care of widows and orphans, as well as the wisdom literature and prophets, whereas the second is used in four historical texts (2 Sam 14:5; 1 Kgs 7:14; 11:26; 17:9-10), and the third in Deut 25:5 and Ruth 4:5. While the third term may well be used deliberately in the context of levirate marriage, the evidence for distinguishing the first two is rather slim. Be that as it may, Steinberg's study confirms that the term 'widow' in the laws refers to a woman in dire need due to lack of material resources and family support.

61. Cf. Gen 38:1-11; Ruth 1:8-11; 4:1-12; Matt. 22:24. For discussion of this institution in ancient Israel and neighbouring countries, see Driver and Miles (1935: 240-50); de Vaux (1961: 37-38); Coats (1972); Leggett (1974: 9-62); Westbrook (1977); Davies (1981); Pressler (1993: 63-74); Hoffner (1997: 226); Weisberg (2004); Matlock (2007); Ellens (2008: 249-67).

62. Sneed (1999a) holds a similar view.

argument is based largely on exegetical speculation and ideological presupposition, and I will not refute it in detail here.[63] Precisely the opposite position is argued by van Houten (1991: 67). She points out that the laws for protection of vulnerable people could not have not been formulated as a result of a struggle between competing interest groups, since they protect those outside one's extended family and community, people who would not have had the influence to arrange for laws to be produced for their own benefit. Van Houten's position appears to be much nearer the truth. Old Testament laws are not designed for the benefit of the lawgiver but for that of the covenant community to whom they are given, and this is clearly the case in the laws concerning resident aliens, widows, and orphans.[64]

---

63. For further discussion, see Houston (2004); Phillips (2004); Willis (2004); Jackson (2005).

64. Otto (1995a: 165-66) also rejects the idea that biblical laws were designed by priests to legitimate the behaviour of the upper class. He suggests a more appropriate approach based on that of Max Weber, who points out that intellectuals are not necessarily bound by a class standpoint. In Otto's view, it is more likely that these ethical programmes were the work of intellectual circles of priests who were concerned about social issues and wrote against their own class standpoint.

JUSTICE AND GENEROSITY

Chapter 8

JUST LAWSUITS

The desire for justice is as old as human society, ever since the beginning of sin and the first efforts to stop it from spreading (cf. Gen 3:14-24; 4:9-15, 23-24; 6:1-8; 9:5-6). Long before the time of Moses and the Hebrew prophets, King Ur-Namma of Sumer and Akkad concluded the prologue to his laws with the claim, 'I eliminated enmity, violence, and cries for justice. I established justice in the land.' In the other main collection of Sumerian laws, Lipit-Ishtar makes an almost identical claim, repeating it twice in the prologue and twice in the epilogue. Hammurabi refers to himself four times as the 'king of justice' (Epilogue lines xlvii 77; xlviii 7, 96; xlix 13), claiming by divine appointment to have 'established truth and justice as the declaration of the land' and thereby to have 'enhanced the well-being of the people' (Prologue lines v 14-24). We have no independent witnesses to establish whether ordinary people also viewed these reigns in such a positive light.

It is not feasible here to tackle the grand theme of justice in the Bible and its world, and it is hardly necessary since it has already been discussed at length by others.[1] Instead I focus on the question of just lawsuits, as

---

1. See Miranda (1971: 109-99); Boecker (1976); Marshall (1980); Epsztein (1983); Mays (1983); Adamiak (1985); Ateek (1989); Birch (1991); Hamilton (1992b); Reventlow and Hoffmann (1992); Mafico (1992); Gossai (1993); Bovati (1994); Habel (1995a); Irani and Silver (1995); Knierim (1995: 86-122); Weinfeld (1995); Westbrook (1995b); Malchow (1996); Niehr (1997); Schultz (1997c); Jackson (1998a); Nel (2000); Loewenberg (2001); Nardoni (2004); Wright (2004a: 253-80); Houston (2006). Some of these works also include reflection on the relevance of this ancient material for efforts to bring about justice in today's world. On the key Hebrew terms for justice and righteousness (משפט, שפט, צדק), see Johnson

dealt with in the laws of the Old Testament, against their ancient Near Eastern background. One of the biggest differences between the rich and the poor in both ancient and modern societies concerns access to legal redress for crime and injustice. Apart from the issues of extortionate fees, bribery, and intentional partiality, judges inevitably belong to the privileged classes and may unconsciously tend to favour their peers.

Lawsuits in ancient Israel were often dealt with by elders who sat at the gate of a town to discuss the affairs of the local community (Gen 23:10, 18; Deut 21:19-20; 22:15-21; 25:7-9; Job 29:7; Prov 31:23; Amos 5:10, 12, 15; Zech 8:16). Examples of legal proceedings at the gate are provided by the well-known stories of Boaz (Ruth 4:1-12) and Naboth (1 Kgs 21:8-14).[2] There were also professional judges (Deut 16:18; 19:17-18; 25:1-2; 2 Chr 19:5-8) to whom difficult cases could be referred by the elders (Deut 17:8-13; 2 Chr 19:9-11). In some cases elders and judges would work together (Deut 21:2-4). Priests and Levites were responsible for teaching the law (Deut 33:10; Jer 18:18; Mal 2:7) and might also be involved in the legal process (Deut 17:9; 19:17; 21:5; 2 Chr 19:8-11).

The highest human court of appeal would be the king as leader of the people (1 Sam 8:5; 2 Sam 8:15; 14:4-11; 15:2-6; 1 Kgs 3:9, 16-28; 7:7; 2 Kgs 8:3-6; Ps 72:1-2; Prov 16:10; 29:14; Jer 21:11-12; 22:15-16), following the pattern of Moses in earlier days (Exod 18:16, 22, 26; cf. Judg 4:4-5; 1 Sam 7:15-17). However, it is noteworthy that — unlike elsewhere in the ancient Near East where the king had absolute legal authority — the king of Israel was himself subject to the law of God (Deut 17:18-20; 2 Sam 12:1-14; cf. 1 Sam 19:4-5). Especially in cases where the evidence was inconclusive, appeal might be made to the judgement of God by means of an oath (Exod 22:7-11; Num 5:11-31; Deut 21:6-8; Judg 17:2; 1 Kgs 8:31-32) or the sacred lots (Exod 28:15, 30; Deut 33:8; Josh 7:10-20; 1 Sam 10:20-24; 14:38-42; Prov 16:33; 18:17-18; cf. Jon 1:7).[3]

Three specific matters relating to just lawsuits are addressed in Old Testament law: witnesses, impartiality, and bribery. The principles enunci-

---

(1984); Ringgren and Johnson (1989); Niehr (1995); Enns (1997); Reimer (1997); Schultz (1997b).

2. Thirteen more examples are listed by Falk (2001: 57).

3. For more detailed discussion of legal procedure in ancient Israel, see Köhler (1953: 149-75); de Vaux (1961: 150-58); Macholz (1972); Weinfeld (1977); Johnson (1984); Bovati (1994); Gertz (1994); Niehr (1995); Jackson (1998b); Falk (2001: 47-65); Frymer-Kensky (2003: 981-99); Heltzer (2004); Wright (2004a: 301-04). On legal procedure in Mesopotamia, see Jas (1996); Skaist and Levinson (2005: 11-81).

ated would apply at every level, though some of the laws may be more related to the context of the popular court (Exod 23:1-3, 6-8; Lev 19:15) and others to that of professional jurisdiction (Deut 16:18-20; 19:15-21).

8.1 Witnesses

a. Ancient Near East

It seems the use of witnesses to establish the truth in legal cases was widespread in the ancient Near East, and perjury was considered a very serious offence. The Laws of Ur-Namma include the following clauses:

> If a man presents himself as a witness but is demonstrated to be a perjurer, he shall weigh and deliver fifteen shekels of silver. (§28)

> If a man presents himself as a witness but refuses to take the oath, he shall make compensation of whatever was the object of the case. (§29)

According to Hammurabi, a false witness in a trial for a capital offence is liable to capital punishment (§§1-3), and a lesser punishment where the penalty for the crime is compensation in grain or silver (§4). The principle of talion applies in each case (cf. LL §17). Witnesses are also used to ensure the veracity of property and financial transactions in order to avoid a possible charge of theft (§§7, 9-11, 13, gap z, 106-7, 122-24; cf. HL §35) and to confirm that a warning has been given to someone whose wall is in a state of disrepair (CH § gap e).[4]

According to the Middle Assyrian Laws witnesses are called to prove charges of rape (§A12), slander (§A17), unauthorised wearing of a veil (§A40), and witchcraft (§A47). No doubt they would be used in other cases too, but the testimony of witnesses would be particularly important for offences such as these which cannot be proved after the event. (Unlike a case of theft, for example, where property may be found in someone's possession.)[5]

---

4. For detailed discussion of these clauses, see Driver and Miles (1952: 58-68, 82-85, 95-105, 170-71, 185-86, 196-98, 236-39); cf. Hoffner (1997: 190). On witnesses and perjury in the Old Babylonian period, see also Johns (1904: 85-87); Westbrook (2003c: 373, 423). On the Middle Babylonian period, see Slanski (2003b: 494). On the Neo-Babylonian period, see Oelsner, Wells, and Wunsch (2003: 923-34, 965).

5. For detailed discussion of these clauses, see Driver and Miles (1935: 36-41, 65-70, 118-

Although there are no extant laws from ancient Egypt and the Levant, there is considerable evidence concerning the role of witnesses in legal practice.[6] Apart from the laws, there are various references to perjury in ancient Near Eastern literature, including that of Egypt,[7] Assyria,[8] Babylon,[9] and the Hittites.[10] In every case it is considered a serious offence.

b. Decalogue

You shall not testify against your neighbour [as] a false witness.[11]

Exod 20:16//Deut 5:20

The ninth commandment is placed between those on theft and coveting, already discussed above (2.1; 2.2), perhaps because false accusation can often be a way of depriving someone else of their possessions (cf. Lev 19:11-13; 1 Kgs 21:7-10). 'Your neighbour' refers to a fellow member of the covenant community,[12] all of whom are bound by the Decalogue, though that does not mean it would be acceptable to give false testimony against a non-Israelite.

The original meaning of the ninth commandment is to be found in the legal context of ancient Israel, where it refers to false testimony in court. It is effectively the same as the modern offence of perjury (lying under oath), though there is no evidence that witnesses in Old Testament

---

34). On witnesses in the Old Assyrian period, see Veenhof (2003: 443-46). Many Neo-Assyrian legal documents include a list of witnesses, usually at the end (SAA 6: *passim;* SAA 14: *passim;* Postgate 1976: 9).

6. On Egypt, see Jasnow (2003a: 268; 2003b: 311, 346; 2003c: 110-11). On Alalakh, see Rowe (2003a: 696-97, 704-5). On Ugarit, see Rowe (2003b: 723).

7. E.g. the Prayer Stele of Nefer-abu to Ptah (Beyerlin 1975: 36) and Instruction of Amenemope, chs. 6, 11, 13 (*COS:* 1.47 lines vii.18, xiv.9, xvi.1).

8. E.g. Shurpu incantations, lines 14-19 (Beyerlin 1975: 132).

9. E.g. 'I Will Praise the Lord of Wisdom', line ii 22 (*ANET:* 596; Beyerlin 1975: 139).

10. E.g. the Prayer of Kantuzilis (*ANET:* 400; Beyerlin 1975: 168) and one of the state archive catalogues (*COS:* 3.38 line A ii 18).

11. The Hebrew word עֵד refers to the witness rather than the testimony, in spite of the traditional translation of this commandment as 'You shall not bear false witness' (ESV; NJPS; NRSV; RSV), and its equivalent in more modern language as 'You shall not give false testimony' (NIV) or 'You shall not give false evidence' (NJB; cf. REB). Cf. Simian-Yofre (1986); Propp (2006).

12. Childs (1974); Durham (1987); Brueggemann (1994); contra Cassuto (1951).

times took oaths before giving evidence.[13] Witnesses might be called by the prosecution (e.g. 1 Kgs 21:10, 13; Isa 43:10, 12) and the defence (e.g. Prov 14:25; Isa 43:9). In fact, in the absence of professional lawyers, a witness would often act as accuser (e.g. Ps 27:12; 35:11). In some cases forensic evidence could be produced (e.g. Exod 22:13; Deut 22:17), but generally the testimony of witnesses would be the main evidence in bringing a conviction and their responsibility to tell the truth would be correspondingly great.

Although the primary reference is to false testimony, the commandment has been understood from early days to cover other kinds of lying and deceitful speech as well.[14] In Leviticus 19, which recapitulates most of the commandments, the Israelite is told 'You shall not lie or deal falsely with one another' (v. 11b), followed immediately by a recapitulation of the third commandment on swearing falsely by the name of God (v. 12) and soon after by a prohibition of slander (v. 16). In the summary of the Decalogue in Hosea 4:2, false witness is broadened to become lying.[15]

Like the other negative commandments, the ninth does not simply prohibit a serious crime. It can also be understood positively as an affirmation of the fundamental importance of truthful speech (and writing) for the people of God, and indeed for society as a whole. This is expressed clearly in Psalm 15, where God welcomes 'those who walk blamelessly, and do what is right, and speak the truth from their heart' (v. 2). Similarly in Psalm 24, it is 'those who have clean hands and pure hearts, who do not lift up their souls to what is false, and do not swear deceitfully' (v. 4) who are blessed by God. Flattery and boasting are ruled out (Ps 12:3-4), as are slander, deceit, and lies (Jer 9:4-5).[16]

---

13. Phillips (1970: 143-44).

14. In the Deuteronomic version of the Decalogue, the term שקר ('false'; Exod 20:16) is replaced by שוא (Deut 5:20), which means literally 'vain', as in the third commandment. This may be intended to extend the meaning to any sort of evasive or worthless testimony (Durham 1987).

15. For a very thorough study of lying in the Old Testament, see Klopfenstein (1964).

16. See also Ps 50:19-20; Prov 6:17; 10:18-21; 12:6, 13-22; 13:3; 14:3; 18:6-8; 26:18-28; cf. Matt 5:33-37; 15:19; John 8:31-32, 44; Eph 4:25; Col 3:9; Jas 3:1-12.

c. Book of the Covenant

You shall not make a false statement;[17] you shall not join hands with the wicked, by acting as a malicious witness.[18] You shall not follow the crowd[19] in wrongdoing; and you shall not testify[20] in a lawsuit, diverting [from the truth] to follow the crowd, so as to pervert[21] [justice].

Exod 23:1-2

The primary context of these verses is the law court. The ninth commandment is expanded into four prohibitions, arranged in two pairs, addressed to ordinary members of the covenant community who may be called as witnesses, rather than to judges as in verses 6-8.[22] First, witnesses are not to make false statements, whether based on unsubstantiated hearsay or deliberate distortion of the truth (v. 1a). Second, they must withstand any pressure to cooperate with the wicked, who attempt to convict the innocent or free the guilty (v. 1b). The third prohibition is a general warning against following the trend towards falsehood rather than standing for the truth (v. 2a). In a traditional society like ancient Israel, it would be even more difficult to swim against the tide than it is in individualistic modern societies (cf. 1 Kgs 19:10; Jer 11:19). The final prohibition highlights the danger of being carried along by the majority with a more specific reference to giving testimony in legal proceedings (v. 2b). Perhaps it is on the basis of

---

17. Cf. Cazelles (1946). Or 'utter a false report' (RSV; cf. ESV; NIV; NRSV); or 'spread a false rumour' (cf. NJB; NJPS; REB; TEV; Childs 1974). The reference appears to be to slander, primarily in the context of legal proceedings.

18. So most translations, implying false testimony given against an innocent person (cf. Deut 19:16), though the expression could also mean false testimony for the benefit of a guilty person (cf. TEV; Durham 1987). Lit. 'witness of violence'.

19. So NIV; Durham (1987); alternatively 'the majority' (NJB; NRSV; REB; TEV; Childs 1974); lit. 'many'. Differently, NJPS has 'the mighty', a translation of רבים which finds some support in 2 Chr 14:11 and Job 35:9, and would make a nice balance with 'the poor' in the following verse, but is much less likely to be the intended meaning here (Childs 1974). The word means 'many' rather than 'mighty' in the vast majority of its occurrences in the Old Testament, and the two supporting texts are almost certainly much later than the Book of the Covenant.

20. Lit. 'answer'.

21. There is a play on words in the Hebrew between the qal and hiphil forms of נטה, translated here as 'divert' and 'pervert' respectively. Cf. Sprinkle (1994: 183).

22. Cassuto (1951); Frey (1957); Marshall (1993: 156); cf. Carmichael (1974: 97); contra Crüsemann (1992: 189); Houtman (1996).

verse 2 that the Mishnah instructs the youngest judge to speak first, so that he is not swayed by the majority opinion (*Sanhedrin* 4:2).

d. Deuteronomic Laws

The matter of witnesses is elaborated further in Deuteronomy. The laws aim to minimise the risk of injustice by stipulating a minimum number of witnesses to secure a conviction, and outline the procedure for dealing with a witness who is suspected to be false and the appropriate punishment for a proven false witness.

Minimum Number of Witnesses

On the testimony of two witnesses or three witnesses, the [guilty] person shall be [sentenced] to death;[23] *no one shall be [sentenced] to death on the testimony of a single witness.*

Deut 17:6

A single witness shall not testify against someone[24] *for any crime or any offence, concerning any sin which he may have committed; on the testimony of two witnesses, or on the testimony of three witnesses, a case shall be established.*

Deut 19:15

The role of witnesses in a tribal society would be even more important than it is in court cases today, where lawyers play a major role. In those days either the victim or a witness would have been the accuser. In order to protect people from false accusations, a minimum of two witnesses was required to convict someone of a crime.[25] The first version of the law relates to a case of

---

23. Lit. 'the person who is to die shall be put to death', referring to the capital case described in vv. 2-5.

24. Cf. REB; Craigie. Lit. 'One witness shall not arise against a man'. An alternative translation is 'One witness is not enough to convict a man' (NIV; cf. NJB; NRSV; TEV).

25. As Jackson (1975f) has shown, the expression 'two or three witnesses' is simply a way of saying 'at least two witnesses', and does not exclude the possibility of calling a larger number of witnesses if they should be available. Cf. NJPS; Tigay (1996). The expression may be compared with the 'day or two' of Exod 21:21, which denotes a minimum period of time (see above, 5.2.b).

apostasy, for which capital punishment is specified (17:2-5), and Numbers 35:30 makes a similar stipulation in connection with a trial for murder. The second version of the law extends the principle to all lawsuits. Of course, even this sensible rule can be misused if false witnesses are available to help pervert justice, as pointed out in Exodus 23:1-2 (see above) and exemplified in the trial of Naboth (1 Kgs 21:10, 13). In the latter case, the legal minimum of two witnesses was followed, but the requirement of truth-telling ignored — as also in the trials of Jesus (Matt 26:59-60), Stephen (Acts 6:11-14), and Susanna (Dan 13:28-41[26]). It appears that two or more witnesses were also used for the signing of legal documents (Isa 8:2; Jer 32:9-12).[27]

Dealing with False Witnesses

When a malicious witness comes forward to testify falsely against someone,[28] the two parties to the dispute shall stand before the LORD, before the priests and the judges who are [in office] at the time. The judges shall investigate thoroughly; and if the witness is a false witness, who has testified falsely against his brother,[29] then you shall do to him as he intended to do to his brother. So you shall remove the evil from your midst. The rest [of the people] will hear and be afraid; and no one will ever again do such an evil thing as this in your midst. You shall show no pity [in such a case]: life for life, eye for eye, tooth for tooth, hand for hand, foot for foot.

Deut 19:16-21

26. In the deuterocanonical Additions to the Book of Daniel.

27. Examples of the positive application of the principle of multiple witnesses are given in Matt 18:16; 2 Cor 13:1; and 1 Tim 5:19. For a detailed discussion of the law requiring two or more witnesses in Roman and Greek law, Judaism, and the New Testament, see Vliet (1958).

28. The meaning of this clause depends on whether סרה ('apostasy, rebellion, falsehood') refers to the offence or the testimony. Most scholars assume the former, translating it as 'apostasy' (NJB; cf. UBS; Craigie 1976; Mayes 1979), 'wrongdoing' (ESV; NRSV; RSV), or 'crime' (NIV; REB). The meaning 'apostasy' is supported by several texts (Deut 13:5; Isa 1:5; 31:6; Jer 28:16; 29:32) but is too specific for the present context, since apostasy carries the death penalty, whereas the range of penalties in v. 21 suggests that the law covers a range of offences. The meaning 'wrongdoing' or 'crime' is possible, but does not contribute to the point of the law which concerns the truthfulness of the witness rather than the nature of the offence. It seems likely, therefore, that סרה refers to the testimony rather than the offence, as שקר ('falsehood') does in the similar construction of v. 18 (cf. NJPS; McConville 2002a).

29. I.e. a fellow-Israelite.

If it is suspected that someone has given false testimony, there is to be a thorough investigation (vv. 16-18a; cf. 13:14; 17:4). This is to take place 'before the LORD' (v. 17), represented by the priests and judges, presumably at the central sanctuary (cf. 17:8-13).[30]

If the witness is proved to be false, he suffers the punishment intended for the accused (vv. 18b-19a, 21b; cf. CH §§1-4; LL §17). This follows the principle of talion, that is, punishment matching the crime in both kind and severity (cf. Exod 21:23-25; Lev 24:18-20; CH §§116, 196-97, 200, 229-32; MAL §§A50, 52). Although in this case no actual harm may have yet been done to the defendant, the malicious witness is punished on the basis of the harm he intended to inflict on his neighbour. Such punishment is designed to cleanse the community of evil (v. 19b; cf. 13:5b; 17:7b) and deter others from repeating the offence (v. 20; cf. 13:11).

Far from encouraging vengeance, as it is sometimes misunderstood, the *lex talionis* is a guarantee of justice. On the one hand, it limits vengeance and rules out punishment disproportionate to the offence (cf. Gen 4:23-24); on the other hand, by ensuring appropriate punishment for those who kill or abuse other human beings, it maintains the sanctity of life (cf. Deut 12:23; 21:8; 25:11-12).[31] The expression 'life for life, eye for eye, etc.' (v. 21b) should not be understood as a list of specific punishments but as a familiar formula to express the principle of punishment to fit the crime. The precise application of the principle would no doubt be decided by the judges in a particular lawsuit.

Weinfeld (1972a: 2) points out that the phrase 'show no pity' (v. 21a; cf. 7:16; 19:13) is used elsewhere in contexts where there is a danger of excessive leniency, because the guilty person is a relative or friend (13:6-9; 25:12). A similar point is made in Numbers 35, where the death penalty is compulsory for murder (vv. 16-21) and the possibility of a wealthy person buying their way out of punishment is specifically excluded (vv. 31-34; contrast MAL §§A10, B2).

---

30. So Driver (1902); Wilson (1995: 144-45, 173-77); contra Tigay (1996).

31. On the *lex talionis*, see Daube (1947: 102-53); Mikliszanski (1947); Diamond (1957); Phillips (1970: 96-99); Frymer-Kensky (1980); Carmichael (1985a); Crüsemann (1987); Otto (1991a; 1994c: 73-81); Nel (1994); Piattelli (1995); Haase (1997); Jackson (2002); cf. Shemesh (2005). See also above, 5.2.b.

e. Conclusion

A just legal system is essential to any healthy community, and attempts to undermine this are therefore punished severely, as is clear from various ancient Near Eastern and biblical laws. The importance of truthful testimony is further emphasised in psalms, wisdom, and prophecy (e.g. Ps 24:4; Prov 6:19; 12:17; 14:5, 25; 25:18; Jer 7:9). Great harm can be caused by false witnesses, as shown in the death of Naboth and the death of Jesus, to mention just two of the most notorious examples.

At the same time, it is irresponsible to avoid giving false testimony by substituting silence for speech. Witnesses may be reluctant to speak out if they know that what they say will be unwelcome (cf. Amos 5:10), so Leviticus makes it clear that members of the community have a duty to testify if they have seen a crime take place (5:1; cf. Prov 29:24). Wrongdoing is not to be covered up, even by just keeping quiet.

Members of the covenant community are expected to tell the truth in court — the whole truth, and nothing but the truth. It is further recognised that, even if human courts fail to discover the truth, nothing is hidden from the divine Judge and he can be relied upon to rectify injustice in due course (Ps 27:12-14; 69:4-33; 94:16-23; 96:13; Prov 16:1-5; 19:5, 9; 21:28; Eccl 3:16-17; Mic 3:9-12).

The Old Testament also affirms the importance of truth in other areas of public life, with particular condemnation of religious leaders who use their position to propagate lies (Jer 6:13-14//8:10-11; 23:9-40; Ezekiel 13) and pander to their audience with smooth talk (cf. Isa 30:9-11). Mendacity brings iniquity (Isa 5:18), and causes confusion by pretending to be virtue (v. 20). In connection with the subject of the present book, Isaiah 32:7 warns of villains who 'ruin the poor with lying words, even when the plea of the needy is just'. And for both rich and poor, one of the basic requirements for life in the presence of God is to speak the truth from one's heart (Ps 15:2).[32]

---

32. For reflections on truthfulness and falsehood in public life today, with particular reference to the ninth commandment, see Andrew (1963); Brueggemann (1997); Harrelson (1997: 119-23); Braaten (2005); Hütter (2005).

8.2 Impartiality

a. Ancient Near East

None of the extant ancient Near Eastern laws mentions the question of impartiality in lawsuits, though there are several references in other literature. For example, according to the Akkadian Shamash hymn, the wicked and just will appear together to face divine judgement.[33] There are Hittite instructions which set out principles for commanders of border garrisons in dealing with lawsuits, and these include a prohibition of favouritism:

> Let him not, however, decide [the case] for [his] superior [or] for [his] brother, his wife, or his friend.[34]

In Egypt, according to the Installation of the Vizier Rekhmire, 'the abomination of the god is partiality', so the vizier is charged to treat equally those he knows and those he does not know.[35]

b. Book of the Covenant

> *You shall not be partial to the poor in their lawsuits.*
>
> Exod 23:3

> *You shall not pervert*[36] *the justice [due to] the poor among you*[37] *in their lawsuits. Keep far from a false charge; do not condemn*[38] *the innocent and righteous, for I will not acquit the guilty.*[39]
>
> Exod 23:6-7

---

33. Line 56 (*ANET*: 388; *BWL*: 128-29).

34. Column 3: lines 25-26; see von Schuler (1957: 48); *COS* (1.84); cf. Weinfeld (1977: 77); Milgrom (2000: 1643). There is a similar prohibition in the military instructions of the Hittite king Tudhaliya (Weinfeld 1977: 76-77).

35. Lines 12-16 (*ANET*: 213; cf. Weinfeld 1977: 79). See also Instruction for Merikare lines 43-44 (*COS*: 1.35), Instruction of Amenemope chapter 20 (*COS*: 1.47 lines xxi.1-4), and Eloquent Peasant B1 lines 96-100, 148-49, 268-69 (*COS*: 1.43).

36. The root נטה ('divert, pervert'), used twice in v. 2, appears again here.

37. One or two scholars have suggested emendation of אבינך ('your poor') to איבך ('your enemy'), but there is no manuscript evidence for this and the text is perfectly intelligible as it stands (cf. Houtman 1996). Cassuto (1951) suggests that אביון here is not the common word

Some commentators have suggested emending 'and the poor' (ודל) in verse 3 to 'the great' (גדל).[40] In view of the Book of the Covenant's concern to protect the weak, the prohibition of partiality to the poor is no doubt surprising, but then the Bible often surprises its readers. When there are alternative manuscript readings from which to choose, the more difficult reading *(lectio difficilior)* is often chosen by textual critics on the basis that an editor is more likely to have smoothed out a difficulty than created one. All the more so here: there is no textual evidence at all for the easier reading and therefore no good reason to emend a perfectly intelligible text just because it says something unexpected.[41] This text may not be to the liking of those who claim that God is on the side of the poor, but it is perhaps intended to counteract such an oversimplified claim. It is more accurate to say that the biblical laws portray God on the side of justice, and that rules out partiality to either rich or poor (cf. Lev 19:15). While there is clear divine authority for defending the rights of the poor and needy, as mentioned frequently in the texts discussed in the present work, they are not freed from the obligation to keep the law themselves. Thus judges and witnesses must be strictly impartial, and compassion for the poor is no justification for doctoring the truth. Philo (*Laws* 4:72-77) comments:

> The lawgiver has filled nearly the whole of the law with precepts of mercy and humanity ... in order to enrich the poor on whom it is al-

---

meaning 'poor' but a homonym meaning 'adversary', making a triplet with 'your enemy' and 'someone who hates you' in the two preceding verses. It is an interesting suggestion, but the linguistic evidence is very weak. The large majority of interpreters understand the word in its usual sense. The expression 'your poor' may mean either 'the poor among you' (NJB), as in Deut 15:11; cf. Exod 22:25; 23:11, or 'the [poor] person who is dependent on you' (Houtman 1996; Houston 2006: 115); cf. Ps 72:2. The former seems more probable in this context.

38. Lit. 'kill, put to death'. Most versions translate the verb הרג literally, but it can also have a figurative meaning (cf. Ps 78:47; Prov 7:26), and a few commentators understand it thus, e.g. 'ruin' (Durham 1987) or 'cause great loss' (Cassuto 1951).

39. I use plurals for translating categories of people such as 'poor', 'innocent', and 'guilty', as common in English usage. The Hebrew uses singular forms here, so a literal translation would be: 'And you shall not be partial to a poor [person] in his/her lawsuit. . . . You shall not pervert the justice [due to] a poor [person] among you in his/her lawsuit. Keep far from a false charge; do not condemn an innocent [person] or a righteous [person], for I will not acquit a guilty [person].'

40. E.g. Noth (1959); McKay (1971: 316-17); Fabry (1974); Houston (2006: 114-15); cf. BHS.

41. Cf. Cazelles (1946); Cole (1973); Childs (1974); Durham (1987); Marshall (1993: 155); Brin (1994: 88); Sprinkle (1994: 180); Houtman (1996).

ways proper to have compassion except at the time of giving judgment, for compassion is due to misfortunes; but he who behaves wickedly with deliberate purpose is not unfortunate but unrighteous, and punishment is due to the unrighteous.

After an interlude on attitudes towards the property of enemies (vv. 4-5[42]), the law returns to matters of justice in court. Three further clauses prohibit:

- perverting the course of justice (v. 6)
- accepting a false charge (v. 7a)
- condemning the innocent (v. 7b)

The first clause is concerned particularly with protection of the poor from abuse of legal power, and so balances the prohibition of partiality to the poor in verse 3. The second clause uses the same word for 'false' as in the ninth commandment (שקר, Exod 20:16; cf. Deut 19:18), and is close in meaning to the prohibition of false testimony in verses 1-2 of the present chapter.[43] However, it is addressed to the judge rather than the witness, instructing him to have nothing to do with a charge which is clearly fraudulent.

The third clause elaborates the consequences of perverting justice by making false charges and showing partiality in judgement. In ancient Israel, where capital punishment applied to many crimes, to convict an innocent person would often have been to condemn them to death (cf. Lev 19:16; Deut 27:25). There is a brief motivation clause: 'I will not acquit the guilty' (v. 7c). This may be a warning to any judge who ignores this law, and plays fast and loose with the truth, that he will one day have to face the divine Judge (cf. Prov 17:15; Isa 5:18-23).[44] However, it could also be understood as an appeal to the judges of Israel to be cautious in their sentences. In the absence of conclusive evidence, it is better to acquit someone who may in fact be guilty than to condemn someone who may in fact be innocent, since God himself will ensure that justice eventually prevails (cf. 1 Kgs 8:32; Mal 3:1-5).[45]

---

42. On which, see above, 2.3.b.
43. Discussed above, 8.1.c.
44. Cassuto (1951).
45. Ehrlich (1908); Jacob (1945); Sarna (1991); cf. Houtman (1996).

c. Holiness Code

> *You shall not act corruptly*[46] *in judging [lawsuits]; you shall not show favouritism towards the poor, nor partiality towards the rich;*[47] *with righteousness you shall judge your fellow.*
>
> Lev 19:15

The essential points of this law for judges[48] are the same as those made in the Book of the Covenant, arranged here in a chiasmus of three prohibitions followed by a positive summary:

no injustice (v. 15a; cf. Exod 23:6-7)
    no favouritism to the poor (v. 15b; cf. Exod 23:3)
    no partiality to the rich (v. 15c; cf. Exod 23:6)
only justice (v. 15d).

Although the wording is quite different, several key terms are common to the two legal traditions: 'justice/judging', 'poor', 'partial[ity]', and 'righteous[ness]'.

A notable difference is the reference to 'face' here. Translated literally, the second and third clauses would read 'you shall not lift the face of the poor, and you shall not honour the face of the rich'. Honour and shame were probably key factors in Hebrew society, as they still are in many Asian cultures today.[49] As a result, the social system would be concerned with the preservation or loss of 'face', in the sense of reputation, dignity, and prestige. In such a context, it is remarkable that a judge is instructed to disre-

---

46. The word עול ('wrong, injustice, iniquity, corruption') is a synonym of 'falsehood' (Isa 59:3), 'wickedness' (Job 34:10; Hos 10:13), and 'deceit' (Ps 43:1). It is contrasted with 'righteousness' (Prov 29:27; Ezek 3:20; 18:24, 26; 33:13, 18; Zeph 3:5), 'justice' (Isa 61:8), 'good' (Ps 53:1), 'truth' (Mal 2:6), 'uprightness' (Ps 92:15; 107:42), 'blamelessness' (Ezek 28:15), and 'faithfulness' (Deut 32:4).

47. Cf. NJPS; Levine (1989); Milgrom (2000: 1643). Lit. 'great'. The word גדול may have been chosen here to create a play on words with דל ('poor'). It is also used to denote a rich person in 2 Sam 19:32 and 2 Kgs 4:8. The usual antonym of דל is עשיר ('rich'), e.g. Exod 30:15; Prov 10:15; 22:16.

48. Cf. Exod 23:6-7; Deut 1:16-17; 16:18-20. Rabbinic traditions interpret this law with respect to the judicial process (Milgrom 2000: 1642), and most modern commentators follow this view (e.g. Wenham 1979; Harrison 1980; Hartley 1992; Gerstenberger 1993; Paterson 1994), though a few consider it to apply to the wider community (e.g. Noth 1962; Bailey 2005).

49. Daube (1969); Bechtel (1991); Biddle (2003: 282).

gard the 'face' of a litigant who appears before him. However, while impartiality is the rule in a court of law, deference (lit. 'partiality') to the old is appropriate in everyday life (v. 32).

d. Deuteronomic Laws

> *You shall appoint judges and officers in all your towns, which the LORD your God is giving to you, to your tribes,[50] and they shall judge the people with righteous judgement. You shall not pervert justice, you shall not show partiality.*
>
> Deut 16:18-19a

In addition to the local courts of community elders, there are to be judges and other legal personnel (v. 18a). Their responsibility is to ensure that the processes of law are carried out fairly. This is emphasised in verse 18b by qualifying the verb 'judge' with the term 'righteous judgement',[51] summarising the principles enunciated in Exodus 23:6-7 and Leviticus 19:15.

The first three words of verse 19a in Hebrew ('You shall not pervert justice') are identical to the opening of Exodus 23:6, but they are not followed by a reference to the poor as in the earlier text. At this point Deuteronomy generalises the more specific regulation in the Book of the Covenant, though later it applies the principle to certain kinds of vulnerable people: resident aliens, orphans, and widows (24:17; 27:19; cf. Isa 10:2; Amos 5:12). The second person singular form strictly refers to the

---

50. Cf. the translation of von Rad (1964b: 78); *pace* most English versions, which take לשבטיך as part of the main clause, translating it 'according to your tribes' (ESV; RSV), 'for your tribes' (NJPS; cf. NIV; NJB), or 'throughout your tribes' (NRSV). That the expression refers to the divine gift of land rather than the human appointment of judges is supported by the omission of the clause concerning the gifting, including לשבטיך, in 11QT 51:11. This is the only occurrence of the noun שבט with a second person singular suffix, but it occurs with the plural suffix in Deut 1:13, 15; Josh 7:14; 23:4; 1 Sam 10:19. In Josh 23:4 it is linked with the gift of land, while Deut 1:13-15 is concerned with the appointment of officers, so the probabilities are finely balanced. Gertz (1994: 34) considers the double use of the preposition ל with an object to be syntactically problematic, and suggests that לשבטיך is a later addition to the text (cf. Rütersworden 1987: 14), a suggestion which is rejected by McConville (2002a). There is in fact similar syntax in Gen 27:37 (Morrow 1995: 164).

51. In Hebrew, שפט and משפט־צדק. A similar combination of שפט and צדק occurs elsewhere, for example Amos 5:24, with the first root denoting the practice of law and the second its proper basis.

people of Israel as a unit, who are responsible for appointing the judges (v. 18a),[52] but in practice the prohibitions in verse 19 are meant for the judges themselves.[53]

The rest of verse 19a states succinctly the principle of impartiality, using different terminology from both Exodus and Leviticus but without any significant change of meaning. This principle is of great importance in Deuteronomy, and is traced back to Moses' institution of the judicial system:

> I charged your judges at that time: 'Hear [the disputes] between your brothers and judge fairly, between one person and [another, whether] a brother or a resident alien. You shall show partiality in judgement: you shall hear both small and great alike. Do not be afraid of anyone, for judgement belongs to God.' (Deut 1:16-17a)

Impartiality is a fundamental characteristic of the God of Israel:

> The LORD your God is God of gods and Lord of lords, the great God, mighty and awesome, who does not show favouritism and does not accept a bribe. (Deut 10:17)

and therefore to be imitated by his people.[54]

e. Conclusion

The essence of justice in a law court is to establish the truth and to deal with the parties concerned in accordance with that truth. 'Justice is blind', it is said, and the traditional symbol of justice as a woman holding scales and sword is often depicted with a blindfold to indicate impartiality. While right and wrong are to be weighed before a verdict is reached, a judge is expected to disregard appearances, status, and prestige.

---

52. Milgrom (1983) argues that the king or other central authority appoints the judges, but this is doubtful for several reasons (see Tigay 1996: 373 n. 5).

53. LXX makes this explicit by using the third person plural as in v. 18b. Cf. McConville (2002b: 32-33); contra Tigay (1996).

54. On the imitation of God as a basis for ethics, see Exod 20:8-11; 31:12-17; Lev 19:2; 20:7, 26; 21:8; Deut 10:18-19; 15:13-15; cf. Matt. 18:23-25; 1 John 4:11. For scholarly discussion, see Tinsley (1960); Lindars (1973); Albeck (1985: 277-79); Nasuti (1986: 16-19); Birch (1995); Davies (1999); Rodd (2001: 65-76).

Although the principle of impartiality was known elsewhere in the ancient Near East, it receives much greater emphasis in the Bible and is the basis for specific laws in the Book of the Covenant, Holiness Code, and Deuteronomy. These laws are designed to benefit vulnerable members of society, since it is generally the rich and powerful who are in a position to influence judges and courts in their favour. Apart from the possibility of bribery, which will be discussed below (8.3), the elite may be influential because of their better education, smarter appearance, and greater self-confidence, as well as their potential as benefactors and ability to take revenge if a verdict is not to their liking. Nevertheless, while partiality towards the rich is outlawed, that does not permit partiality towards the poor (Exod 23:3, 6; Lev 19:15; Deut 16:19). The bottom line is 'justice, only justice' (Deut 16:20), to be applied impartially to each and every person, irrespective of their social and economic standing.

The same principle can be seen throughout the Bible. The ultimate source of justice is God, the impartial judge (Deut 1:17; 10:17; 2 Chr 19:7; Job 34:19; cf. Sirach 35:12-15), who expects those to whom he has delegated his power to implement his judicial policy (2 Chr 19:6; Ps 72:1-2; 82:2-4; Mal 2:9). The terminology for perversion of the course of justice used in the laws (Exod 23:6; Deut 16:19) reappears in historical and prophetic texts (1 Sam 8:3; Isa 10:2; 29:21; Amos 5:12; Mal 3:5). Proverbs cautions that partiality leads to the perversion of justice (18:5; 24:23-26; cf. 28:21; Sirach 4:22). And Lamentations assures the people that God is aware of injustice (3:35-36), encouraging them to 'return to the LORD' (v. 40) and appealing to him to take up their cause (vv. 55-66).

Similarly in the New Testament, the impartiality of God in judgement is fundamental (Acts 10:34; Rom 2:11; Eph 6:9; Col 3:25; 1 Pet 1:17; cf. Gal 3:28). Even Jesus' enemies acknowledge his practice of this principle (Mark 12:14//). It follows that impartiality is an important value for the everyday life of Christian believers (Jas 2:1-13).

8.3 Bribery

a. Ancient Near East

The only ancient Near Eastern law that appears to relate to bribery is in the Laws of Hammurabi, where a judge is prohibited from reversing his judgement after the end of a trial, and threatened with very serious penalties if he does (§5). The reason for this is not stated, but a major reason why a judge might change his mind would be if he had been bribed.[55]

In spite of the paucity of laws on the subject, it is clear from other literature that bribery was a common problem in the ancient Near East. There are references to legal proceedings for corruption, including bribery, in many places.[56] It is also a subject of reflection by wisdom writers. For example, the Babylonian 'Advice to a Prince' warns against various kinds of injustice, including accepting a bribe to obtain an improper conviction.[57] In Egypt, the Instruction of Amenemope advises judges: 'Don't accept the gift of a powerful man, and deprive the weak for his sake'.[58] Similarly, Hittite commanders of border garrisons are instructed to judge cases brought before them properly, and this specifically excludes taking a bribe.[59]

The Shamash Hymn includes the following pair of couplets:

> You show the roguish judge the [inside of] a jail,
> He who takes the fee but does not carry through, you make him
> bear the punishment.
> The one who receives no fee but takes up the case of the weak,
> Is pleasing to Shamash, he will make long his life.[60]

According to this translation, the second line refers to a judge who receives a legitimate fee but fails to deliver justice for the litigant. Beyerlin (1975: 103) understands the line differently, as a reference to a judge who commits injustice because he has received a bribe. It is difficult to be certain which is correct, because Akkadian does not make a clear distinction between fees, gratuities, presents, and bribes.[61]

---

55. For a detailed discussion, see Driver and Miles (1952: 68-79). The word *šulmānu* ('gift, bribe') occurs in MAL §L5, but the context is so fragmented that it is impossible to draw conclusions about the meaning of the clause.

56. For examples from Babylon, see Johns (1904: 318, 321); Schiffman (1998: 156); for Nuzi, see Westbrook (2003b: 29); for the Hittite kingdom, see Hoffner (1997: 4-5, 218); for Egypt, see Jasnow (2003b: 346); for Elephantine, see Lindenberger (2003: 63, 71).

57. Line 11 (*BWL*: 112-13).

58. Chapter 20 (*COS*: 1.47 lines xxi.3-4). The stele of Horemheb also includes an instruction to judges not to take bribes (Weinfeld 1977: 78).

59. Column 3: lines 26-28; see von Schuler (1957: 48); *COS* (1.84).

60. Lines 97-100 (*COS*: 1.117); cf. *BWL* (132-33); *DOTT* (110). There are further references to just lawsuits in lines 101 and 127.

61. Both *ṭātu* and *šulmānu* cover the whole semantic field. Cf. Finkelstein (1952); *BWL* (320); *CAD* (17.3: 244-47); *CDA* (413).

Just Lawsuits

Reciprocal gift-giving was fundamental in ancient societies, as it is still in many societies today, and so it is very plausible that litigants would make gifts to judges before or after they did their work, without necessarily intending to distort the legal process.[62] This is illustrated in three texts from Nuzi concerning a mayor who received fees from litigants but did not attend to their lawsuits.[63] Against this background, the dividing-line between legitimate gifts (e.g. fees and gratuities) and bribes (e.g. gifts intended to sway a judge or obtain something illegally) may be less clear than in modern Western societies.

b. Book of the Covenant

You shall not accept a bribe,[64] for a bribe blinds the clear-sighted,[65] and subverts the cause[66] of the righteous.

Exod 23:8

I have translated the key term here (שחד) as 'bribe'.[67] Although the basic dictionary definition is 'gift', it usually denotes a gift made in order to obtain something in return (quid pro quo), often with a negative connotation (e.g. 1 Kgs 15:19; 2 Kgs 16:8; Job 6:22; Prov 17:8; 18:16; 21:14; Isa 45:13;

---

62. Cf. Mauss (1950); cf. Goldberg (1984: 16-18).
63. Finkelstein (1952: 78-79).
64. Or 'gift' or 'fee' (see discussion below).
65. So ESV; NJB; NJPS; or 'those who see' (NIV; Houtman 1996; cf. LXX) or 'the discerning' (REB). Alternatively פקחים could be translated as 'eyewitnesses' (cf. Cazelles 1946). 'Officials' (NRSV; RSV) is an interpretation rather than a translation.
66. Understanding דברי here to mean 'case, cause', as in Exod 22:9; 24:14; Josh 20:4; 2 Sam 15:3; 1 Kgs 15:5; so ESV; NRSV; RSV; McConville (2002a: re Deut 16:19); cf. NJB; NJPS; TEV; Cazelles (1946); Childs (1974); Durham (1987); Houtman (1996). NIV translates the phrase literally as 'twists the words'; cf. LXX; Vulgate; REB; Sprinkle (1994: 178); Mayes (1979: re Deut 16:19); Christensen (2001: re Deut 16:19).
67. Following most modern translations. (LXX has δωρον ['gift'], and KJV translates it as 'gift'.) Several other words are used occasionally with the meaning 'bribe', e.g. בצע (Exod 18:21; 1 Sam 8:3; Prov 28:16; cf. Isa 33:15), on which, see Kellermann (1973a); Harland (2000); כפר (1 Sam 12:3; Prov 6:35; Amos 5:12), on which, see Lang (1983: 301-02); מתן/מתנה (Prov 15:27; 18:16; 19:6; 21:14; Eccl 7:7), on which, see Montgomery (2000: 139-40); שלמן (Isa 1:23), a cognate of the Akkadian *šulmānu* (cf. Greenfield 1967: 119); שלום (*shillum*, Mic 7:3). In the last two texts there may be a play on words with שלום ('peace'), which is a fundamental objective of legal justice according to Exod 18:23; Zech 8:16; cf. Ps 122:5-6; Isa 9:6-7 (Bovati 1994: 196 n. 69).

Ezek 16:33).[68] Occasionally it refers to fees paid to judges, which might be compared with modern legal expenses, but in these contexts too the payment is regarded negatively since judges in Israel are expected to fulfil their role without financial incentives (e.g. Isa 1:23; Mic 3:11). Presumably state-appointed judges would receive a salary, and local elders acting as judges would do so as part of their responsibility for leadership in the community, not as a way of supplementing their income.

As with the parallel terms in Akkadian,[69] biblical terminology does not distinguish rigorously between gifts, payments, and bribes. Nevertheless, in many cases, the straightforward meaning of this term is clearly 'bribe' (e.g. 1 Sam 8:3; Ps 15:5; 26:10; Prov 17:23; Isa 5:23; 33:15; Ezek 22:12). In the laws too, this translation seems appropriate, though if the translation 'gift' or 'fee' were used it would not materially alter the intention of the texts to prohibit all such payments. Bribes, gifts, and fees are equally unacceptable in the Israelite legal system, since any of them are likely to influence a judge in favour of a litigant who is able and willing to pay.[70]

This prohibition is probably addressed primarily to judges, like verses 6-7.[71] A judge's responsibility is to shed light on a case by means of a thorough investigation (e.g. Deut 13:14; 17:4; 19:18), elucidating what is obscure, so that the truth becomes clear and justice is seen to be done.[72] It is crucial, therefore, that the judge can see clearly and no one interferes with his vision (cf. Lev 20:4; Job 9:24). If such interference should happen — for example through bribery — the result will be subversion of justice, whether condemnation of the innocent or acquittal of the guilty.

---

68. Beyse (1993: 556-57). A similar usage to that in Kings is found in line 28 of the third Sefire inscription (*COS:* 2.82; *KAI:* 266, 271; Greenfield 1967: 119). On the texts from Proverbs, see Scherer (1997: 65-66); Montgomery (2000). Cf. the use of מתן ('gift') in Prov 18:16.

69. See above, 8.3.b.

70. Cf. Tigay (1996: 161).

71. Cf. above, 8.1.c; 8.2.c. However, if פקחים was translated 'eye-witnesses' instead of 'clear-sighted' (see above, n. 65), the focus would be on the witnesses.

72. For a study of the metaphor of light in relation to justice in the Old Testament, see Bovati (1994: 363-69).

c. Deuteronomic Laws

> *You shall not accept a bribe,[73] for a bribe blinds the eyes of the wise, and subverts the cause[74] of the righteous. You shall follow justice and righteousness;[75] so that you may live and possess the land, which the LORD your God is giving to you.*
>
> Deut 16:19b-20

This is the continuation of a section on good legal practice (Deut 16:18-20), the first part of which has already been discussed above (8.2.d). The whole section is carefully structured to emphasise the crucial importance of justice and righteousness for the people of God who live in the promised land:[76]

'[towns] which the LORD your God is giving to you'	v. 18a
'they shall judge (שפט) . . . with righteous judgement (משפט־צדק)'	v. 18b
'you shall not pervert justice (מִשְׁפָּט)'	v. 19a
'subverts the cause of the righteous (צדיק)'	v. 19b
'you shall follow justice and righteousness (צדק צדק)'	v. 20a
'[land] which the LORD your God is giving to you'	v. 20b

As the paragraph opens in verse 18 with a demand for judges to practise righteous judgement, it closes in verse 20 with an exhortation to make justice and righteousness their top priority.

The prohibition (v. 19b) is verbally identical to that in the Book of the

---

73. On the term שׁחד, see above, 8.3.b.

74. See above, n. 66.

75. צדק צדק is often translated 'justice, and only justice' (e.g. ESV; NRSV; RSV), which is not inaccurate for this emphatic doubled form (cf. GKC: §123e) but does not include the element of 'right' or 'righteous' which is also part of the meaning of this Hebrew root. In fact it is arguable that the latter meaning is dominant in the present text where צדק and צדיק are used alongside שׁפט ('judge') and מִשְׁפָּט ('justice'), as shown above. On this basis, I have translated the phrase as 'justice and righteousness', intended as a hendiadys to represent the meaning of this Hebrew term in English more fully than is possible with any single word. Another possibility, suggested by Morrow (1995: 171), is 'totally correct judgement', which combines the ideas of rightness and justice in an emphatic expression.

76. For more detailed analysis of the structure, see Morrow (1995: 164-72); Christensen (2001). Other examples of the combination of שׁפט and צדק are Lev 19:15 (see above, 8.2.c); Isa 9:6; 11:4; Amos 5:24.

Covenant, except that 'clear-sighted' is replaced by 'eyes of the wise', a change that accords with the wisdom interests of the Deuteronomist.[77] The two reasons given — blinding the wise judge and subverting the righteous cause — are really aspects of the same miscarriage of justice, expressed by means of parallelism, perhaps using the words of an ancient proverb.[78] That judges must be wise is emphasised from the beginning of the office in Israel (Deut 1:13; cf. Exod 18:13-26; Prov 8:15-16). Finally, there is a positive command to pursue justice (v. 20a; cf. 6:25; 24:13), because a just society is one that will endure (v. 20b; cf. 4:1; 5:33; 6:18, 24; 8:1; 30:19-20). Individual judges may not become rich through performance of their duties, but the covenant community as a whole will certainly prosper as a result.

The theological basis for prohibiting bribery is that God does not accept bribes (Deut 10:17; 2 Chr 19:7; cf. Sirach 35:12). On the one hand, this assumes the imitation of God as a basis for ethics;[79] on the other, it is based on the belief that human judges are acting in the name of God, and therefore obliged to follow divine principles of justice (Deut 1:17; 2 Chr 19:6). The seriousness of the matter is highlighted by its inclusion in the twelve curses that follow the Deuteronomic Laws:

> Cursed be anyone who accepts a bribe to shed innocent blood; and all the people shall say 'Amen!' (27:25)

d. Conclusion

It seems that while bribery was viewed negatively in the ancient Near East, the payment of fees and gratuities to judges was common and not considered improper unless the intention was to pervert the course of justice. As a result, the distinction between right and wrong in gift-giving could be somewhat blurred. In practice it would be relatively easy to get away with payment of a bribe, because if it became known both parties could claim that it was simply a gift.

---

77. Cf. McKay (1971: 320); Weinfeld (1972a: 245). Another small change is that the order of the first noun and verb is reversed, but this does not significantly affect the meaning, and cannot be represented in English translation without creating an awkward sentence in Exod 23:8 ('A bribe you shall not accept . . .').

78. Cf. Prov 17:23; Eccl 7:7; Sirach 20:29; so von Rad (1964a); Thompson (1974); Cairns (1986b).

79. See above, n. 54.

On this matter Old Testament law is quite distinctive from the laws of neighbouring countries in its categorical prohibition of all payments to judges by litigants. Justice and righteousness are fundamentally important for the life of the covenant community (Deut 16:20), and the legal system provided for maintaining these values should not operated on an economic basis. Wealthy people may be happy to pay officials, especially if they can expect efficient and favourable attention to their cases (Prov 17:8; 18:16; 19:6). But the poor are rarely in a position to pay for justice, and so are particularly vulnerable if a judge asks for a fee or is bribed by others (Isa 1:23; cf. Jer 5:28). Thus the prohibition of bribes and gifts to judges is crucial in order to ensure just lawsuits for the poor. Moreover, it has a theological foundation, in the belief that human judgements are made on behalf of the God of the covenant, and bribing God is out of the question (Deut 10:17; 2 Chr 19:6-7).

Apart from the explicit prohibitions in the Book of the Covenant and Deuteronomic Laws (Exod 23:8; Deut 16:19b), it is assumed throughout the Old Testament that bribery is unacceptable. Jethro advises Moses to appoint judges who hate dishonest gain (Exod 18:21). Later on Samuel is able to claim — and the people agree — that he has never taken a bribe (1 Sam 12:3-5), though his sons have a very different attitude (8:1-3). Psalms and wisdom writers note that a righteous person will refuse bribes (Ps 15:5; 26:10; Prov 15:27; cf. 28:16), whereas the wicked are readily corrupted (Prov 17:23; Eccl 7:7). And the prophets repeatedly condemn bribery, along with other forms of oppressing marginal people (Isa 5:23; 33:15; Ezek 22:12; Amos 5:12; Mic 3:9-11; 7:30).

The prohibition of judicial corruption, especially bribery, recurs frequently in later Jewish sources. Deuteronomy 16:18-20 is quoted in the Temple Scroll (11QT 51:11-16), and supplemented with the death penalty for disobedience (lines 17-18). Later the same law is applied to the just king (57:19-20).[80] Josephus also emphasises the pursuit of justice (*Antiquities* 4:214-18), advocating capital punishment for a judge who accepts a bribe (*Apion* 2:207).[81] Philo (*Laws* 4:62-66)[82] and the Mishnah (*Bekhorot* 4:6)[83] rule out not only bribes but any kind of payment to a judge. A similar principle is found in Islamic law.[84]

80. Cf. Swanson (1995: 139-40); Schiffman (1998: 157-62).
81. Cf. Schiffman (1998: 164-66).
82. Cf. Schiffman (1998: 162-64).
83. Cf. Bazak (1987: 27-32); Schiffman (1998: 166-73).
84. Gibb and Kramers (1961: 201).

In the New Testament, there are three records of actual or attempted bribery (Matt. 26:15; 28:12-15; Acts 24:26) but no specific teaching on the subject. It may be assumed that this was one of those matters where Old Testament principles were considered sufficiently clear and nothing more needed to be said.

Chapter 9

SHARED HARVESTS

Justice is fundamental to any civilised society, especially one where Almighty God is recognised as the source of justice and righteousness as in Israel (Deut 32:4; Job 37:23; Ps 89:14; Zeph 3:5). However, justice without generosity can be very hard-hearted. Wealthy people may have legal rights over much property, but do they have a moral right to hold on to it when others are starving? A corollary of the Old Testament conviction that the land belongs ultimately to God is that human beings do not have absolute rights of disposal over the produce of the land. They are intended to enjoy the harvest of cornfield, orchard, and vineyard, but never without the awareness that some are less fortunate than themselves and the willingness to share God's blessing with others. In this chapter I shall explore four aspects of the 'shared harvests' advocated by Old Testament law, beginning with the institution of the sabbatical year.

9.1 Sabbatical Year

Two distinctive Hebrew terms are associated with the seventh year in Old Testament law. The first (שׁבת) means 'rest' and is often associated with the sabbath or seventh day (cf. Gen 2:2-3; Exod 23:12). It is used seven times in Leviticus 25:2-6 in connection with the sabbatical year.[1] The second (שׁמט) means literally 'leave' or 'let go'. In Exodus 23:11 it is used about

---

1. On the term שׁבת, see North (1955a); Andreasen (1972: 94-121); Robinson (1980); Haag (1993); Bosman (1997).

land, which is allowed to rest by leaving it fallow in the seventh year. In Deuteronomy 15:1 it denotes the remission or 'letting go' of debts.[2] Before looking at the biblical texts in question, it will be helpful to view their ancient Near Eastern context.

a. Ancient Near East

None of the ancient Near Eastern laws legislate for a sabbatical year, nor any other regular fallowing of land, though we know that fallowing was common practice from early times. There are numerous references to fallowing in the State Archives of Assyria, generally in documents granting the right to use a plot of land for three or four crop years and an equal number of fallow years.[3] Concerning ancient Palestine, Turkowski (1969: 21-24) argues that in earliest times there was a one-field system and when the land was exhausted the farmer simply moved elsewhere. Later the land was divided into two, half cultivated and half fallow, which made a more stable social life possible.[4]

The question arises how a sabbatical year would fit in with this biennial fallowing, and two answers have been suggested. Feliks (1972: 375) believes the sabbatical was an extra fallow year, so the farmer planted a particular field just three times in seven years. Hopkins (1985: 191-95, 200-202) suggests that the farmer would have planted all his fields in the sixth year, to provide sufficient food during the sabbatical fallow, so that over a seven-year period the land usage would average out at half the fields planted and half fallow.[5]

---

2. On which, see below, 10.3. On the term שמט, see Wakely (1997d).

3. SAA 6 (nos. 146, 223, 226, 252, 268); SAA 14 (nos. 41, 44, 45, 118, 122, 346).

4. Cf. Hopkins (1987: 185). Later still the Romans introduced a three-field system of crop rotation, in which one field was planted with grain, and another with legumes, while a third was left fallow and used for pasturage, which also provided some animal manure. In the nineteenth century fallowing was stopped, and replaced by the use of manure and the planting of certain vegetables during what had been the fallow year. This didn't work well, however, so eventually the two-field system was reintroduced, but instead of alternating usage each year it was common to plant one field for three to seven years until it was exhausted, and then to plant the other.

5. In his detailed study of agriculture in Iron Age Israel, Borowski (1987: 143-45) makes no reference to the biennial fallow, and is apparently unaware of the research cited above which has advocated this. He assumes that the sabbatical year was the only fallow year practised in ancient Israel.

Shared Harvests 225

There are several references to seven-year periods in texts from Ugarit, and Gordon (1949b: 4-5; 1953) argues that they provide the background for the Old Testament laws concerning the sabbatical year. These periods are apparently related to agriculture, with some connection to the mythical conflict between the weather god Baal and Mot, the god of death.[6] One text refers to a seven-year period of abundance,[7] another to a seven-year drought.[8] There is also a reference to the god El's banishment of his wives and sons to the desert for a seven-year period, which is followed by the discovery of agriculture.[9] Two other ancient Near Eastern texts which mention seven-year famines are the Akkadian Gilgamesh Epic[10] and the Egyptian Famine Stela.[11] Interesting though these texts are, however, their significance for understanding the Old Testament institution of the sabbatical year should not be overestimated. First, Gordon (1949b: 4) overstates his case when he claims that 'drought and famine are regularly represented as seven-year scourges in the Ugaritic texts', since there are only four references to seven-year periods in the entire Ugaritic literature, and only one of these refers unambiguously to drought and famine (see n. 8). Second, although seven is certainly a significant number in Ugaritic texts, as also in the Old Testament and elsewhere in the ancient Near East,[12] it is often used as a round number rather than a precise measurement of time, as shown by the fact that in three of the four Ugaritic texts cited the phrase containing 'seven' is supplemented by a parallel phrase with 'eight'.[13] Third, almost all the cited texts refer to periods of seven (or eight) years rather than six-year

---

6. As in the Baal Myth: 'The days turn into months, the months into years. In the seventh year, Môtu, son of 'Ilu, [comes] to Mighty Ba'lu' (*COS:* 1.86 p. 272; *CTA:* 6 v 7-10). Cf. Gray (1965: 73-74).

7. Also in the Baal Myth: 'Seven years the god is abundant. . . . Even eight cycles' (*CTA:* 12 ii 45-46; Gordon 1949b: 55; Caquot et al. 1974: 348).

8. In the Aqhat Legend: 'Seven years has Ba'lu failed, eight [years] he who rides upon the clouds: No dew, no showers, no upsurging [of water] from the deeps, no goodly voice of Ba'lu' (*COS:* 1.103 p. 351; *CTA:* 19 i 42-46).

9. In Dawn and Dusk (also known as The Birth of the Gods) lines 64-67: 'O women whom I have wedded, O sons whom I have begot, Take up [your belongings], prepare [yourselves a place] in the holy steppe-land; There you must dwell as aliens among the stones and trees, For seven full years, eight revolutions of time' (*COS:* 1.87).

10. Tablet VI, lines 103-12 (Kovacs 1989: 54; George 1999: 51).

11. This inscription was probably written in the second century B.C., though it purports to be a decree of King Djoser, who lived in the twenty-sixth century (*COS:* 1.53 p. 131).

12. On the latter, see Lewy and Lewy (1942: 3, 96).

13. Cf. Kapelrud (1968); de Moor (1971: 33-34).

periods followed by a fallow year, so a closer biblical parallel is to be found in the seven years of plenty followed by seven years of famine in the Joseph story (Genesis 41; cf. 2 Kgs 8:1) rather than in the sabbatical year laws.[14] The association of agriculture with religious belief was common to both Israel and Canaan, and the number 'seven' was significant in both cultures, but apart from these general similarities the Israelite sabbatical year remains a distinctive institution unparalleled elsewhere.[15]

b. Book of the Covenant

> *Six years you shall sow your land, and gather its produce; but the seventh [year] you shall let it rest*[16] *and lie fallow so that the poor among your people may eat, and what they leave the wild animals may eat. You shall do the same with your vineyard and your olive grove.*
>
> Exod 23:10-11

There are two laws about the seventh year in the Book of the Covenant, one concerning slavery and the other concerning agriculture. The former has already been discussed above (6.1), so here I focus on the latter. The land is to rest in the seventh year, by lying fallow (vv. 10-11), just as human beings and animals rest on the seventh day (v. 12).[17] Although regular fallow years would have been essential to preserve the fertility of the land before the introduction of artificial fertilisers, efficient agriculture is not the main purpose of the present law, at least in its canonical context. The stated purpose is rather to alleviate the needs of the poor, and the implied purpose is also to honour God as the ultimate owner of the land (cf. Lev

---

14. Periods of seven years are also mentioned in Gen 29:18, 27 and Ezek 39:9. The possibility of a seven-year famine is referred to in the MT of 2 Sam 24:13, but LXX has 'three years', as does MT in 1 Chr 21:12, and most translations follow this reading in 2 Sam 24 too.

15. Cf. Wacholder (1976); Wright (1992b). A related question is whether the sabbath day has an ancient Near Eastern origin, since the sabbatical year is apparently patterned on the sabbath day, as will become evident in the texts to be studied below. Andreasen (1972: 94-121) and Dressler (1982: 22-24) survey various theories, finding all of them wanting and concluding that it is much more likely that the sabbath originated in ancient Israel (cf. Eichrodt 1959: 131-33 esp. n. 4). On the sabbath day, see further below, 11.1.

16. The verb שׁמט ('let rest') is also used in Deut 15:1-3 for the remission of debts in the seventh year.

17. On which, see below, 11.1.

25:2, 4, 23).[18] It may also be seen as a return of the land to its natural state, before human beings disturbed it by agriculture, when nomadic people and wild animals would have wandered freely to look for food.[19] The mention of wild animals is a reminder of God's provision for all his creatures, not only human beings (cf. Gen 1:30; Ps 36:6; 104:21-28; Matt 10:29; Luke 12:24).

It is uncertain whether the intention is for the sabbatical year to be observed simultaneously throughout the whole land, or whether each field would follow a separate cycle. If it were done on a field-by-field basis it would be more practical for the owner and of greater value to the poor who had special gleaning privileges during the fallow year (Exod 23:11). On the other hand, the comparison with the weekly sabbath suggests that it is intended to be fixed on a national basis, and later laws about the seventh year in Leviticus 25:1-8 and Deuteronomy 15:1-11 (cf. 31:10-11) make this explicit.[20] The needs of the poor would be particularly acute in a sabbatical year since the cessation of regular agriculture would mean less opportunity for casual labour. However it is reckoned, the produce of the land which grows of its own accord during the sabbatical year becomes the property of the poor, not of the owner of the land, and the owner is expected to eat the produce which has been put aside from the previous year (cf. Lev 25:20-22).[21]

---

18. Von Rad (1943: 85).

19. Noth (1959: 189-90; cf. 1962: 183). More theologically, Phillips (1970: 75-76) suggests that the sabbatical year was an attempt to recall Israel to her origins by reenacting the conditions of the exodus when the people were fed by Yhwh himself, while Habel (1995b: 102) sees the sabbatical year as a return of the land to its divine owner, whereby the Israelites acknowledge their status as tenants who do not have absolute rights over the land.

20. See also 1 Maccabees 6:49, 53. Wellhausen (1883: 116-18) and Ginzberg (1932: 352-54) suggested that it was originally fixed separately by different landowners, but in due course became fixed (cf. Vesco 1968: 252-53; Lemche 1976: 42-43; Houtman 1996: 251-52). More recently Chirichigno (1993: 306-11) has discussed the matter at some length, concluding that the sabbatical year was intended to be observed simultaneously from the beginning.

21. A few interpreters understand this stipulation differently, arguing that it is only harvesting that is forbidden during the sabbatical year, not sowing, and thereby a whole crop is provided for the benefit of underprivileged members of the community, not just the aftergrowth of the previous year's harvest (e.g. Wellhausen 1883: 116-17; Cazelles 1946: 92). Yet another suggestion is that the prohibition on sowing and reaping only applies to the owner of the land, and the poor are allowed to use the land for farming (cf. Gnuse 1985b: 32-33). However, neither of these interpretations fits well with the text as it stands.

c. Holiness Code

The sabbatical year law of Leviticus is interspersed with the jubilee law in chapter 25.[22] It is an elaboration of the law of Exodus 23:10-11,[23] in three sections:

- the sabbath principle applied to the land (vv. 1-4)
- provision for the seventh year (vv. 5-7)
- promise of divine blessing (vv. 18-22)

The Sabbath Principle Applied to the Land

The LORD spoke to Moses on Mount Sinai, saying: 'Speak to the people of Israel and say to them: "When you enter the land which I am giving to you, the land shall observe a sabbath to the LORD. Six years you shall sow your field, and six years you shall prune your vineyard; and you shall gather its produce. And in the seventh year there shall be a sabbath of complete rest[24] *for the land, a sabbath to the LORD; you shall not sow your field, and you shall not prune your vineyard.*

Lev 25:1-4

The basic law here is identical to that in the Book of the Covenant, though the terminology and accompanying explanations are distinctive. In both cases the parallelism between the seventh year and the seventh day is made clear: in Exodus 23 by the juxtaposition of the two laws, and in Leviticus 25 by the use of the term 'sabbath' (שבת) with reference to the seventh year. In Exodus the stated purpose of the sabbatical year is for the benefit of the poor — and the wild animals — whereas here the primary purpose is to allow the land to rest and to honour the LORD in so doing, assuming that to be the meaning of the phrase 'sabbath to the LORD' (vv. 2, 4).[25] The people are reminded that God is the giver of the land (v. 2) and continues to be

---

22. On which, see above, 4.1.

23. Paran (1989: vi-vii, 29-34); Chirichigno (1993: 303-11); Milgrom (2001: 2154-56); Bergsma (2007: 48-50).

24. Lit. 'sabbath of sabbath rest'; cf. 16:31; 23:3.

25. The phrase is also found in Exod 16:25; 20:10; Lev 23:3; Deut 5:14; cf. Exod 31:15; 35:2 — all with reference to the sabbath day. Cf. Hartley (1992); Chirichigno (1993: 305-6); Milgrom (2001: 2152-53); Lefebvre (2003: 77-79).

its ultimate owner (v. 23). Just as human beings and domestic animals rest every seventh day, this law extends the sabbath principle by stipulating that agricultural land must rest every seventh year. So the sabbath is for the whole of creation, not just human beings, and in the sabbatical year even the land celebrates and is refreshed.[26]

Provision for the Seventh Year

You shall not reap the after-growth of your [previous] harvest, and you shall not harvest the grapes of your unpruned vines; it shall be a year of complete rest for the land. Yet the sabbath [yield] of the land shall be food for you: for yourself and your male and female slaves; for your hired worker and your temporary resident[27] who live with you; and for your livestock and for the wild animals in your land; all its produce shall be to eat.

Lev 25:5-7

Whereas Exodus 23:11 allocates the produce which grows of its own accord during the fallow year to the poor and the wild animals, here the owner of the land is allowed to eat it together with the poor. Seven categories of people and animals are enumerated as beneficiaries of the spontaneous harvest, but this does not mean that other categories are excluded. These seven function as a merism[28] and are intended to encompass all human beings and animals who may wish to eat the produce of the fallow year.[29] Thus the people of Israel return temporarily to the nomadic lifestyle which had been theirs before they entered the promised land (Wenham 1979). They may eat what they find (v. 6), as the poor always do (cf. Lev 19:9-10;

---

26. Moltmann (1985: 289).

27. According to Milgrom (2001: 2161), 'your hired worker and your temporary resident' is a hendiadys, which he translates 'your resident hirelings' (cf. Lev 22:10; 25:40; Exod 12:45).

28. A figure of speech in which a single thing is denoted by a phrase that enumerates two or more of its parts, or which lists several synonyms for the same thing, e.g. 'the heavens and the earth' (Gen 1:1), which refers to one thing — the universe — not two.

29. Cf. Hartley (1992); contra Milgrom (2001: 2160), who argues that Leviticus deliberately changes the law of Exodus in favour of the landowner, excluding the poor from the list of beneficiaries, in order to make a utopian law workable. Milgrom also argues that married children and resident aliens, who do not 'live with you', are deliberately excluded from the list (p. 2161).

Deut 23:24-25), but they are not to reap (v. 5), nor by implication to store any produce in barns or sell any surplus.

Promise of Divine Blessing

> *You shall observe my statutes, and my judgements you shall keep and observe them; and you will live in the land in security. And the land will give its fruit, and you will eat and be satisfied; and you will live in security there. But you may ask, 'What will we eat in the seventh year, if we may not sow, and we may not gather our produce?' Well, I will order my blessing for you, in the sixth year; and [the land] will yield its produce, [enough] for three years. You shall sow in the eighth year, while you eat from the old produce; until the ninth year when its produce comes in, you shall eat the old.*
>
> Lev 25:18-22

First of all there is a general exhortation, assuring the people of the benefits of keeping God's laws, specifically security and sustenance (vv. 18-19). The threat of marauding bands would be particularly great at harvest time (cf. Judg 6:3-6), but obedience will bring protection from such dangers, as the twice-repeated phrase 'you will live in security' emphasises.[30] Moreover, the land will be productive and the people will have enough to eat.

Then the law anticipates a likely objection to the sabbatical year, concerning whether it is a realistic practice (v. 20).[31] Since it was normal in the ancient Near East, including Palestine, to leave fields fallow on a rotational basis, the objection is not concerned with the idea of fallowing in itself but with the simultaneous observance of a fallow year throughout the country. The objection is answered by a divine promise of a bumper harvest in the sixth year, sufficient to last until the normal agricultural cycle is underway again (vv. 21-22),[32] which may be supplemented by any produce that grows spontaneously during the sabbatical year as men-

---

30. Judges 6:7-10 interpret the destruction of Israelite harvests by the Midianites as divine punishment for disobedience.

31. An objection echoed more recently by Gerstenberger (1993: 376-77) and Lowery (2000: 59-60).

32. The text seems to assume a calendar year beginning in autumn, as in the Gezer Calendar, so that crops sown during the winter of the eighth year are reaped during the following summer, and the harvest is complete in the autumn at the beginning of the ninth.

tioned previously (vv. 6-7). This may be compared with the double provision of manna on the sixth day in the wilderness (Exodus 16), and the seven years of plenty which precede the seven-year famine in Joseph's Egypt (Gen 41:47-57). How far this answer is deemed adequate depends on the perspective of the reader, and indications that the sabbatical year was not consistently observed in ancient Israel[33] suggest that a significant number of objectors were unconvinced.[34]

d. Conclusion

The idea that the produce of the land is God's gift to his people, to be shared with all, is distinctive to the Old Testament, as is the specific application of this idea to the observance of the sabbatical year. Although fallowing of land for agricultural reasons was common in the ancient Near East, no law outside the Old Testament specifies doing this for the benefit of the poor, nor as a religious observance.

The basic meaning of sabbath is 'rest'. According to the story of creation, God himself rested on the seventh day because he had finished his work (Gen 2:1-3); and according to the laws, human beings and domestic animals are expected to follow God's example and take regular rest on that day too (Exod 20:8-11; 31:12-17). It is a 'holy day' (Gen 2:3; Exod 20:8, 11; 31:14-15), set apart from ordinary working days (cf. the modern word 'holiday'). The sabbatical year regulations also emphasise the idea of rest, in particular for the land (Exod 23:10-11; Lev 25:2, 4, 5; cf. 26:34-35).[35] For six years the land serves mankind, but in the seventh year it is given a rest. At the same time, of course, this would result in a prolonged rest for agricultural workers.

In this way men and women acknowledge that they do not have absolute rights over the land.[36] They may not exploit the land indiscriminately for their own profit, driven by the pressures of consumerism, because they

---

33. For details, see below, 9.1.d.

34. The primary reference of these verses is to the sabbatical year rather than the jubilee year, as is clear from the reference to sowing in the eighth year (v. 22). The eighth year would have been a fallow year in the case of the jubilee, unless the jubilee was reckoned as the forty-ninth year, in which case it was simultaneous with the seventh sabbatical year, and therefore *was* a sabbatical year. On the calculation of the jubilee year, see above, 4.1.b.

35. Cf. Andreasen (1972: 104-13, 213-25).

36. Cf. Tsevat (1972: 453, 455).

have been permitted to live there and enjoy its produce only as a privilege granted by the owner of the land himself, the LORD God (Exod 15:17; Lev 25:23; Deut 8:7-18). A similar point is made in Psalms: 'The earth is the LORD's, and everything in it' (Ps 24:1); and the Babylonian Talmud: 'The Holy One, blessed be He, said to Israel: sow your seeds six years, but omit the seventh so that you may know that the earth is Mine' (*Sanhedrin* 39a).[37]

Despite all the careful legislation, it seems the sabbatical year was not in fact observed consistently in Old Testament times.[38] There is no direct evidence of its observance before the exile, though it may have been observed in the reign of Josiah[39] and 2 Kings 19:29 might be an allusion to a jubilee year. Israel's failure to keep the regulation about rest for the land is mentioned as one of the sins which resulted in their eventual exile from the promised land (see Lev 26:34-35, 43; 2 Chr 36:21). During the governorship of Nehemiah various economic reforms were enacted, including a sabbatical rest for the land plus remission of debts (Neh 10:31). Later still there is a record of the land sabbatical being observed during the Maccabean period (1 Maccabees 6:49, 53), in spite of the war which made it particularly difficult to do so.[40]

9.2 Gleaning

If the sabbatical year laws were implemented there would be some relief for the poor, but only every seven years. The laws concerning gleaning are designed to ensure that they receive sustenance every harvest,[41] not just intermittently.[42]

37. Translation by Loewenberg (2001: 103).

38. On the observance of the sabbatical year *after* Old Testament times, see Rothkoff (1972); Wacholder (1973; 1975; 1976; 1983); Blosser (1981); Gnuse (1985b: 35); Grabbe (1991: 60-63); Loewenberg (2001: 103-6). It was certainly observed in New Testament times, and is the subject of a whole tractate in the Mishnah (Instone-Brewer 2004: 221-58). In modern Israel the institution is continued by orthodox Jews and the most recent sabbatical year fell in the year 2007/08 (Jewish year 5768).

39. Kaufman (1984).

40. For reflections on the contemporary relevance of the sabbatical year law, see Baker (1998: 55-57).

41. For a study of harvesting in ancient Israel, including gleaning, see Borowski (1987: 57-69).

42. This section is abbreviated and revised from a previously published article (Baker 2006b), with kind permission of the publisher.

a. Ancient Near East

None of the extant laws from the ancient Near East deal with gleaning, and it is rarely mentioned in other texts.

In the Sumerian 'Disputation between the Hoe and the Plough', the Plough claims:

> I fill the storehouses of Mankind;
> Even the orphans, the widows and the destitute
> Take their reed baskets
> And glean my scattered grains.[43]

On the ninth-century statue of Hadad-yith'i from Tell Fekheriye there is a bilingual inscription — in Assyrian and Aramaic — which ends with a list of curses, including the following:

> May his men glean barley from a refuse pit to eat.[44]

Gleaning was clearly a familiar concept, but this text tells us nothing about gleaning in fields.

The Instruction of Amenemope refers implicitly to gleaning:

> Do not pounce on a widow when you find her in the fields
> And then fail to be patient with her reply. . . .
> God prefers him who honours the poor
> To him who worships the wealthy.[45]

---

43. *COS* (1.181 lines 48-51, cf. 179-80); cf. *ETCSL* (5.3.1 lines 45-48, cf. 178-78a). According to Kramer (1963: 108, 341), there is also a reference to gleaning in the harvest section of the Sumerian Farmer's Almanac (lines 79-86):

> The gleaners must do no damage; they must not tear apart the sheaves. During your daily harvesting, as in 'days of need', make the earth supply the sustenance of the young and the gleaners according to their number, [and] let them sleep [in your field] as [in] the [open] marshland. [If you do so] your god will show everlasting favour.

The first sentence assumes there will be gleaners at harvesttime, and sets limits to their activity, while the next two sentences specifically encourage the practice. The harvester is exhorted to leave fallen ears of barley on the ground for needy children and gleaners, and this is considered a charitable deed for which he will receive divine blessing. However, more recent editions of the work translate this section quite differently, so that it does not refer to gleaning at all (*ETCSL*: 5.6.3; Civil 1994: 91).

44. *COS* (2.34).
45. Chapter 28 (*COS*: 1.47 lines xxvi.8-14).

This advice fits with what is known from other Egyptian sources, which indicate that gleaning was commonplace, though not too popular with the landowners.[46]

b. Holiness Code

> *When you reap the harvest of your land, you shall not reap to the very edge*[47] *of your field; or gather the gleanings of your harvest. You shall not strip your vineyard bare, and the fallen grapes of your vineyard you shall not glean; you shall leave them for the poor and the resident alien. I am the* LORD *your God.*
>
> Lev 19:9-10

> *When you reap the harvest of your land, you shall not reap to the very edge of your field, or gather the gleanings of your harvest; you shall leave them for the poor and the resident alien. I am the* LORD *your God.*
>
> Lev 23:22

The two laws on gleaning in Leviticus are almost identical, except that the former deals with fields and vineyards, the latter only with fields.

The first begins a series of laws with an ethical focus (vv. 9-18), several of which concern wealth and poverty.[48] The law is formulated with a pair of double prohibitions, concerning fields and vineyards respectively. The first part of each prohibition instructs the farmer to deliberately leave part of his crop unharvested; the second part forbids him to go back after harvesting to gather grain or grapes which have been unintentionally missed. The law is concluded with an explanation of its purpose — to provide for the poor and the resident alien — and the characteristic theological refrain of the Holiness Code: 'I am the LORD your God'. The relevance of the re-

---

46. Montet (1958: 116).

47. Or 'corner'. Hebrew פאה. A number of texts from Nuzi mention the *kaška* or *kašku*, part of a field that was considered sacred and retained if at all possible by the owner even though the rest was pawned (*CAD* 8: 290; Jankowska 1969: 250). Speiser (1932: 354, 362-66) has suggested a connection with the 'edge' of a field that was to be left for the poor according to Lev 19:9, but this is far from certain.

48. See also 2.1.d; 8.2.c; 11.2.b.

frain here may be clarified by Proverbs 22:23: 'For the LORD will plead their cause; and rob of life those who rob them'.[49]

It is not specified exactly how much of the 'edge' of the field should left for the poor, or how many grapes should be left on the vine, and this provided considerable scope for rabbinic discussion with a whole tractate of the Mishnah being devoted to harvest leftovers. In the case of grain, according to an early tradition, harvest leftovers are one of those things which have no measure, like firstfruits, offerings, deeds of charity, and study of Torah (*Pe'ah* 1:1); but later a minimum of one sixtieth of the crop is stipulated, and more if necessary to supply the needs of the poor (*Pe'ah* 1:2).[50]

The second law is placed immediately after instructions for celebrating the festival of Weeks, in the context of sequential legislation about the various religious festivals. At that point in the year it would be much too early to harvest grapes, which may explain why gleaning of vineyards is not mentioned.[51] The purpose of repeating the law in this context may be to teach the people that fulfilling religious obligations by giving to God does not excuse them from fulfilling social obligations to give to the poor.[52]

c. Deuteronomic Laws

> *When you reap your harvest in your field and you forget a sheaf in the field, you shall not go back to get it; it shall be for the resident alien and the orphan and the widow, so that the LORD your God may bless you, in all the work of your hands. When you beat your olive trees, you shall not go over the branches again; [what is left] shall be for the resident alien and the orphan and the widow. When you gather the grapes in your vineyard, you shall not strip it bare afterwards; [what is left] shall be for the resident alien and the orphan and the widow. Remember that you were a slave in the land of Egypt; that is why I am commanding you to do this.*
>
> Deut 24:19-22

---

49. According to Rashi (cited by Milgrom 2000: 1629).
50. On rabbinic discussions concerning harvest leftovers, see further Levine (1989); Tigay (1996); Milgrom (2000: 1625-28); Loewenberg (2001: 92-96); Instone-Brewer (2004: 121-67).
51. Wenham (1979).
52. Hartley (1992).

The essence of the Deuteronomic law is the same as that in the Holiness Code, but the wording and details are different. Some interpreters assume the Deuteronomic version to be earlier on the basis of standard historical-critical theory,[53] but in fact several features of this text suggest it to be later.[54]

In the Holiness Code the harvest leftovers are reserved for the poor and the resident alien, whereas in Deuteronomy they are for the resident alien, orphan, and widow. This fits with the Deuteronomic context, where the law is part of a longer section beginning with verse 17 on resident aliens, orphans, and widows.[55] Although such people have no land of their own, this law entitles them to a share of the harvest.

Concerning grain (v. 19), the law prohibits returning to collect a forgotten sheaf. This is supplementary to the instructions in Leviticus that the 'edge' of the field should be deliberately left unharvested and grain which accidentally falls to the ground should be left for the poor to glean. A practical question arises here. How can a gleaner distinguish a sheaf that has been forgotten from one that has been deliberately left behind because the harvest has not yet been completed? The Mishnah answers the question with an extended definition of a forgotten sheaf (*Pe'ah* 5:7–6:6).[56]

Concerning grapes (v. 21), the regulation here is essentially the same as the first part of the law in Leviticus: a prohibition of going over the vines a second time to collect clusters that were not fully formed when the main harvest took place.

The law concerning olives (v. 20) is unique to Deuteronomy, but the principle is the same as that for grain and grapes. It was usual to beat olive trees and then gather the fruit which fell to the ground (cf. Isa 17:6; 24:13), and the law instructs the owner to do this only once, leaving it to those without land to come later and gather any remaining fruit. By making this addition, Deuteronomy includes all three characteristic

---

53. E.g. Kilian (1963: 42); Tampubolon (1999: 243-49).

54. For discussion, see Feucht (1964: 120-21); Nielsen (1975: 100-102); Cholewiński (1976: 270); cf. Merendino (1969: 307); Seitz (1971: 180); Grünwaldt (1999: 231-32).

55. On vv. 17-18, see above, 7.2.

56. Carmichael (1997: 74) thinks the Deuteronomic law was impractical, because it helped the poor only if the harvester happened to forget a sheaf, and so the Priestly law revised it to make regular provision for the poor by deliberately leaving part of the field unharvested. If, however, these laws are intended to be complementary rather than comprehensive, the regulations in Deuteronomy may be understood as a partial recapitulation together with a supplement to those of Leviticus (which are assumed to be known by the readers).

crops of the promised land in the gleaning law (cf. Num 18:12; Deut 7:13; 11:14; 12:17; 14:23; etc.).

Two theological reasons are given for the observance of this law. First, looking to the future, those who are generous to others are promised the blessing of God in their own lives (v. 19b; cf. 14:29; 15:10, 18; 23:20). The second reason, looking to the past, is remembrance of slavery in Egypt (v. 22; cf. v. 18; also 15:15; 16:12). The LORD had mercy on the people of Israel, giving them freedom and a land to call their own; so they must always remember that the land and its harvest is theirs not by right but by grace. It follows that they too should be merciful to people in need, sharing the blessing they receive with others. The first reason tends towards 'prosperity theology', while the second is more closely related to the concerns of 'liberation theology', and the combination of these two emphases in one text suggests that neither of these theological approaches should be adopted uncritically without reference to the other.

d. Conclusion

The right of the landless to glean, and the duty of the landowner to facilitate this, is stipulated in both the Holiness Code and the Deuteronomic Laws.[57] This provision for the poor involves the recipients in the work of gleaning, maintaining a balance between generosity and dignity. The landowner is not burdened with extra work in being generous to the poor, and the poor have the privilege of working to supply their needs.[58] This is unique in ancient Near Eastern law.

It is notable that donors do not decide who will receive their donations, as would normally happen with modern charitable giving, but it is left to the poor to come and collect produce from the fields as needed. Some commentators have suggested that this passivity on the part of the donor is intended to emphasise that the land belongs to God, who has entrusted it to the whole covenant community for their sustenance, and

---

57. Gleaning is not mentioned in the Book of the Covenant, except in connection with the fallow year. Wright (1990: 146) suggests that this is because the continuous availability of fallow land had previously made adequate provision for the poor, and it was the transition to a universal fallow year which necessitated annual charity of this kind. However, this is far from certain because there are indications that the fallow year was intended to be observed on a national basis from the beginning (see above, 9.1.b).

58. Craigie (1976); Hartley (1992).

therefore the landless have as much right to benefit from it as the landowners (cf. Lev 25:23).[59] They are entitled to a share of the harvest, not as charity but because it is intended by God for them. In practice, however, most owners of land are likely to view its produce as their personal property, and the gleaning laws encourage them to be generous in sharing their harvest with those who have no land.

It has been frequently suggested that these laws originally had a religious function, probably to placate the spirits of the land, and later the focus moved to social concern, but this suggestion is purely conjectural.[60] No doubt there were such practices in the ancient world, as there still are in parts of the world today, for example the ritual of the last sheaf in Kabylia, Algeria,[61] and the Javanese practice of making offerings *(sajian)* to the spirits at key points in the agricultural year, including harvest.[62] However, this does not prove that the Israelites took over animistic practices and refashioned them as social regulations. There is no indication in the biblical text that this was the case, and the ancient Near Eastern references to gleaning cited above are concerned with social rather than religious issues. So there is no good reason to doubt that from the beginning these laws were formulated for the sake of the poor.[63]

The classic biblical example of gleaning in practice is found in Ruth 2.[64] After obtaining permission from the harvest supervisor (vv. 5-7), Ruth gleaned in the field of Boaz, a relative of her father-in-law. The story emphasises the generosity of Boaz, who not only allowed her freedom to do this in accordance with the law, but ordered protection and sustenance

---

59. Loewenberg (2001: 93-94).

60. Noth (1962), von Rad (1964a), Boecker (1976: 91), Mayes (1979), Fishbane (1985: 299 n. 21), and Gerstenberger (1993) suggest this, but none offer any evidence. It seems the idea was first proposed by von Gall (1910), followed by Beer (1911) and Steuernagel (1923), on the basis of a developmental view of the history of religion. Cf. Nielsen (1975: 100).

61. Bourdieu (1977: 133-35). Canaan (1928: 141) describes a similar [obsolescent] custom in Palestine, of burying the last sheaf in the place where it had been reaped while reciting the Islamic creed. Frazer (1922: 463-77) describes various superstitions in Northern Europe related to the last sheaf.

62. Geertz (1960: 41-42).

63. Cf. Milgrom (2001: 2011). Carmichael (1981) also rejects the conjecture that in some early period of Israelite history a sheaf might have been deliberately left in the field as a propitiatory offering, and that the lawgiver incorporated it here without awareness of its original significance, though his own interpretation of this text in the light of the Joseph story is far from convincing.

64. Gleaning is also mentioned in Judg 8:2 and Jer 6:9; 49:9.

(vv. 8-14) and ensured that there was plenty of grain 'left' to glean (vv. 15-16). Ruth herself belonged to all three vulnerable groups mentioned in Deuteronomy 24:19-22 — she was a resident alien, an orphan,[65] and a widow.[66]

9.3 Triennial Tithes

Every three years there was to be an extra share of the harvest for those who did not own land, specifically the familiar trio of resident aliens, orphans, and widows, and also the Levites. This was provided by means of a tithe of agricultural produce.

a. Tithes in the Ancient Near East

None of the extant laws deal with tithing, though other documents show that it was a widespread practice in the ancient Near East. This is also implied in the Bible when the people of Israel ask Samuel to appoint a king — 'like other nations' — and he warns them of the financial implications, including paying a tithe of crops and flocks to such a leader (1 Sam 8:5, 15, 17). In Genesis 14:20 Abram gives a tithe of the booty to the priest-king Melchizedek, as a voluntary offering rather than a tax, presumably in accordance with royal expectations at the time.[67]

The oldest known references to tithes are from Ur, in the twenty-first century B.C., and there are more from the nineteenth century, but the majority of Mesopotamian texts date to the Neo-Babylonian period (sixth century).[68] Tithes were given to gods and their temples in the form of money, agricultural produce, animals, and manufactured goods. Apparently this was an obligation from which no one was exempt, not even priests and kings, and the temples prospered greatly as a result. It would not be surprising if such wealth was viewed with envy by others, and in

---

65. In the sense that she had left her parents behind in Moab (Christensen 2002: 597).
66. On gleaning today, see Baker (2006b: 409-10).
67. Averbeck (1997).
68. More than 130 Mesopotamian documents refer to tithes. For further discussion, see Johns (1904: 206); Eissfeldt (1918); Leemans (1960a: 24-27, 31-35); Dandama[y]ev (1969); Salonen (1972); Pagolu (1998: 172-78); Stevens (2006: 96-98); cf. Jagersma (1981: 116); North (1988).

view of the fact that many temples were royal establishments it may well be that revenue was sometimes passed on to the palace.[69] There are also occasional references to secular tithes: for example, merchants in Cappadocia paid a 10 percent tax to the local ruler.

Tithes were also known in Ugarit, as taxes paid to the king or one of his officials, consisting primarily of grain, olive oil, and wine, but sometimes silver.[70] They are mentioned specifically in two thirteenth-century Akkadian texts concerning royal land grants:

> Ammistamru, son of Niqmepa, king of Ugarit, has given to Yaṣiranu, son of Ḥuṣanu, the village E[--]ish with everything it has forever, to his sons and grandsons. The grain [and] beer of its tithe, and the sheep [of] its pasturing tax, shall be for Yaṣiranu.
>
> Niqmadu, son of Ammistamru king of Ugarit gave the village Uḫnappu to Kar-Kushuh, son of Ana[nu], and to Apapa, the king's daughter, with its tithe and custom-duties and gifts.[71]

In each case the king grants one or more individuals the right to receive the tithe and other duties from the village. A third Akkadian text lists several kinds of revenue, including a tithe.[72] There are several references to exemption from taxes payable to the palace, and it has been suggested these are also referring to tithes, even though the term is not used.[73] Yet another text lists taxes of grain, wine, and oxen paid by various villages in the kingdom of Ugarit, which may be tithes.[74] In all cases the village was collectively responsible for payment of the tithe rather than individual farmers.

---

69. Cf. Olmstead (1948: 75-76, 418). For biblical examples of kings making use of temple funds for political purposes, see 1 Kgs 15:18-19; 2 Kgs 12:18; 18:15-16.

70. On tithes in Ugarit, see Cazelles (1951); Mendelsohn (1956); Heltzer (1975; 1976: 35-40); Anderson (1987: 78-80); Pagolu (1998: 175-77). According to Heltzer and Anderson, tithes were the central means of tax collection in ancient Canaan, though it seems to me the evidence is too limited to draw such a firm conclusion.

71. *COS* (3.110; 3.82). I have made small alterations to the translations of these texts by *COS*, after comparison with *PRU* 3 (16.153, pp. 46-47; 16.276, pp. 69-70) and Anderson (1987: 80).

72. *PRU* 3 (16.244 p. 93).

73. So Mendelsohn (1956: 20). For the texts, see *PRU* 3 (16.132, lines 22-24, p. 41; 16.238, lines 7-8, p. 107; 16.269, lines 19-20, p. 69).

74. *COS* (3.83); cf. the comments of Heltzer, who edited this text for *COS*.

b. Tithes in Biblical Law

Before discussing the triennial tithe, designated for those in Israel without land, it will be helpful to set it in the context of all the biblical laws on tithes:

- Leviticus 27:30-33 prescribes tithes of grain, fruit, and livestock which are set apart as 'holy to the Lord'.
- Numbers 18:21-32 allocates tithes to the Levites in return for their service in the tent of meeting, and in compensation for not receiving an allotment of land, and instructs them to set apart a tithe of the tithe as 'an offering to the Lord', to be given to Aaron (i.e. the priests).[75]
- Deuteronomy 12:5-19 instructs the people to take tithes (of grain, wine, and oil) to the central sanctuary and eat them 'in the presence of the Lord', together with the Levites.
- Deuteronomy 14:22-27 substantially repeats the instructions of 12:5-19, adding an option for anyone who lives too far away to transport the tithes to the central sanctuary, to sell them and use the proceeds to purchase food and drink for the sacred feast, together with a reminder not to neglect the needs of the Levites.
- Deuteronomy 14:28-29 and 26:12-13 further supplement these instructions by stipulating that every third year the tithe should be stored in the towns and made available for use of the Levites — and also resident aliens, orphans, and widows — after which the head of the family should go to the sanctuary[76] and make a declaration that the obligation has been fulfilled.

It is clear that there are significant differences between these texts, particularly concerning the recipients of the tithes. Rabbinic Judaism understands the texts synchronically as referring to two separate tithes: Numbers is concerned with a tithe for the Levites; while Deuteronomy introduces a second tithe to be consumed by the worshipper at the central sanctuary, except in the third year when it is to be used for charitable purposes.[77]

---

75. It is not specified what this tithe consists of, though grain and wine are mentioned in vv. 27 and 30. It is unclear whether it includes livestock as in Lev 27.

76. Probably the central sanctuary (see below: n. 96).

77. See Instone-Brewer (2004: 305-60); cf. Hoffmann (1913: 219); Oppenheimer (1977: 23-51). Some Reformed theologians have followed this view too (Verhoef 1974: 119).

Some even understood the triennial tithe as a third tithe over and above the others (Deut 26:12, LXX; Tob 1:6-8; Josephus, *Antiquities* 4:240-43).[78]

Modern scholars, however, generally believe there was one tithe, with a development in the legislation due to changing historical circumstances. In accordance with his postexilic dating of the Priestly material, Wellhausen (1883: 156-57) reconstructs a progression from an earlier practice of consuming the tithe in a sacrificial meal at the central sanctuary, later amended so that every third year it is kept in the towns and given to those without land (including the Levites), to a tithe which is devoted entirely to the maintenance of the Levites and priests.[79] Eissfeldt (1917) agrees with this basic reconstruction, but modifies it in several ways. In particular he points out the unlikelihood of the worshippers consuming the entire tithe in their feasting (and that therefore part of it may well have gone to the priests), and that the word 'holy' is used to describe the tithe in Deuteronomy 26:13, which suggests that at least part of it was offered to God, that is to the priests on his behalf.[80]

A very different picture is proposed by Kaufmann (1961: 189-93), who believes the priestly material to predate Deuteronomy. He rejects Wellhausen's idea that the law of Numbers 18, which allocates tithes to the Levites, is postexilic because after the exile there were very few Levites compared with priests (Ezra 2:36-40; cf. 8:15-20) and the priests who were dominant at that time would have been unlikely to create a law which was to their own disadvantage. Kaufmann himself argues for three distinct tithe laws, applying in different historical periods. The earliest, in Leviticus, deals with a freewill offering to the priests which is entirely holy (cf. Gen 14:20; 28:22). The second is in Numbers and originates from a time when the Levites were numerous, which was not the case after the exile. It is also a freewill offering but considered profane, as wages paid to the Le-

---

78. Gitlin (1963: 580) argues for two separate tithes in Deuteronomy, so that the triennial tithe is in addition to the annual sacred feasts, but explains the differences between Numbers and Deuteronomy in terms of different origins (southern and northern kingdoms respectively).

79. Cf. Smith (1894: 244-54); Driver (1902: 168-73); Guthrie (1962); Hawthorne (1978).

80. See pp. 40, 49-50, 54-55. Similar views of the development are held by Eichrodt (1959: 153), de Vaux (1961: 381), von Rad (1964a: 103), and Jagersma (1981: 118-19, 122). Crüsemann (1985; 1992: 215-19) also assumes the Deuteronomic law to be older than those in Leviticus and Numbers, and argues that it abolishes the tithe as a state tax (which he supposes the tithe to have been in the early monarchy, as in other contemporary cultures) and changes it into a sacral meal (for two years) and a contribution to a social programme (in the third year).

vites for their services, except for the tenth part which is holy and given to the priests. The third law is in Deuteronomy, which introduces an obligatory annual tithe, to be eaten at the central sanctuary and designed to link the people with the chosen city. Weinfeld (1972b) has a similar view, though he considers the tithe in Numbers 18 to be an obligatory gift to the Levites, as are the dues to the priests in the earlier part of the chapter. He also emphasises the role of the Deuteronomic tithe as an obligatory gift to the poor, and that the historical development of the tithe reflects a trend towards secularisation rather than the sacralisation argued by Wellhausen. As a consequence of the abolition of the provincial sanctuaries, many Levites were made redundant as sacred officials. Instead of receiving wages, they were now counted among the destitute who were in need of welfare. On this view, the centralisation of worship eliminated the need to maintain a large number of sanctuary personnel, and so Deuteronomy transforms the tithe to become a sacrificial meal eaten by the farmer and his family at the central sanctuary, together with the Levites, and in the third year given to those without land in the various towns. In short, there is a movement from support of sanctuaries towards support of the poor.[81]

If Deuteronomy is the latest of the biblical law collections,[82] the approach of Kaufmann and Weinfeld is an advance over that of Wellhausen and Eissfeldt. Nevertheless, there are problems. First, Milgrom (1976a: 55-63) shows that in all cases the tithe is understood as an obligation rather than a voluntary offering, comparable to the temple tithe in Babylonia. Second, McConville (1984: 73-74) argues convincingly that Deuteronomy — like Numbers — recognises the levitical right to receive the tithe and therefore portrays the Levites as recipients of a regular income rather than poor people who were dependent on welfare.[83] Third, Weinfeld's idea of progression from sacred to secular in the practice of tithing is questionable. It is difficult to reconcile with the postexilic references to tithing in Nehemiah and Malachi, which are entirely concerned with contributions to the temple, in particular for the benefit of the Levites (Neh 10:35-39;

---

81. Hoppe (2004: 38). Haran (1978: 109, 116-17, 127) and Zevit (1982: 485-93, 509) agree with Kaufmann and Weinfeld that the levitical tithe law of Num 18 is older than that of Deuteronomy, though Haran believes it refers to a voluntary offering whereas Zevit argues it is compulsory.

82. On which, see above, 1.2.d.

83. A similar point is made by Bennett (2002: 86-87), though some of his argument is quite speculative.

12:44; 13:5, 12-13; Mal 3:8-10).[84] Also, such a secularisation process does not fit well with Deuteronomy itself, where the law insists that the tithe be eaten in the sanctuary, in the 'presence of the Lord' and with the object of educating the people to 'fear the Lord' (14:23). Further, concerning the poor tithe in the third year — explicitly described as a 'holy portion' — a declaration has to be made at the sanctuary that it has been disposed of in accordance with the law and none of it defiled by handling in a state of impurity (26:13-14; cf. Lev 7:20-21).

None of these attempts to differentiate the tithe laws on the basis of historical development has yielded a consensus. Without denying that there were historical and theological developments in Old Testament law, resulting in different emphases in different situations, it may be more helpful to look at the problem from a canonical perspective and take a holistic approach.[85] It would seem that the final editor of the Pentateuch did not consider the three laws to be contradictory, even though he must have been aware of the differences. An important factor to bear in mind is that the laws are not comprehensive, but rather 'each law only gives a partial picture, omitting much that would have been taken for granted by contemporaries'.[86] Some things would have been taken for granted because of earlier laws that were assumed to be known, others because of common law or common sense. There are in fact several common features in the tithe laws:

- The tithe is understood as an obligation, calculated as one tenth of certain commodities and so effectively a tax, though according to Deuteronomy part of it is consumed in a sacrificial feast by the family who offers it.
- The tithe consists primarily of agricultural produce — especially grain, wine, and oil — though Leviticus also mentions livestock.
- Agricultural tithes can be converted into money in some circumstances.

---

84. The same is true of 2 Chr 31:4-21, which was probably written after the exile, although it concerns the reign of Hezekiah. Weinfeld explains that by the time of Ezra the Pentateuch had become a unity with all the laws considered equally binding, and as a result the older practice was revived alongside the newer one, leading to the Jewish practice of two separate tithes. However, McConville (1984: 75-76) shows that Nehemiah knows the legislation of both Numbers and Leviticus, yet insists on only one tithe, and argues that the idea of multiple tithes was a later development.
85. Cf. McConville (1984: 68-87); Herman (1991: 39-100).
86. McConville (1984: 77).

- The tithe is dedicated to the LORD, which means it is intended for the temple (or tabernacle) rather than the palace, though Deuteronomy stipulates that in the third year it be distributed to the poor.
- The practical implications of dedication to the LORD are that a celebration or declaration is to take place at the sanctuary, and at least part of the tithe is to be used for the support of the Levites.

So it may be concluded that, in spite of the differences, there is an essential unity in the laws and all the relevant texts may be understood as referring to one basic tithe institution in the Old Testament.

A possible reference to the collection of tithes in the late Israelite monarchy occurs in a letter discovered at Arad, but the text is uncertain.[87] From the Second Temple period there is evidence that tithing was practised in Egypt, Carthage, and South Arabia, and it was common among the Jews, as shown by references in the Apocrypha, Dead Sea Scrolls, and Mishnah.[88] The tithe was often 10 percent, in accordance with its etymology, but it seems the term sometimes had a broader reference and included other religious taxes.[89]

c. The Triennial Tithe

> *At the end of [every] three years*[90] *you shall bring out all the tithe of your produce in that year; and you shall store it in your towns. Then the Levites may come, for they have no portion or inheritance with you, and the resident aliens and the orphans and the widows in your towns, and they shall eat and be satisfied; so that the LORD your God may bless you, in all the work of your hands which you do.*
>
> Deut 14:28-29

> *When you finish tithing all the tithe of your produce in the third year, the year of the tithe, you shall give [it] to the Levites, the resi-*

---

87. Aharoni et al. (1975: 20, 143); Pardee (1982: 38); Renz (1995: 365 n. 3).
88. North (1988); Averbeck (1997). On tithing in Second Temple and Talmudic Judaism, see Jaffee (1981); Loewenberg (2001: 96-101); Instone-Brewer (2004: 305-60).
89. Baumgarten (1984).
90. So ESV; NIV; NJB; cf. 'at the end of the third year' (REB; TEV). Alternatively the word 'end' may refer to the last year of the three-year period, i.e. 'in the third year' (NRSV; Meek 1960: 330). Cf. Deut 15:1 (on which, see below, ch. 10 n. 113).

> dent aliens, the orphans, and the widows, and they shall eat in your towns and be satisfied. Then you shall say before the LORD your God, 'I have removed the holy portion from [my] house and furthermore I have given it to the Levites and the resident aliens, to the orphans and the widows, according to all your commandment which you have commanded me; I have not passed over any of your commandments nor have I forgotten [them]'.
>
> Deut 26:12-13

As mentioned in the previous section, the Deuteronomic Law stipulates that every third year the tithe is not to be taken to the central sanctuary, but stored in the towns (14:28) and enjoyed by those who do not have land to grow their own food, specifically Levites, resident aliens, orphans, and widows (v. 29a).[91] The reference to storing implies that farmers would not distribute the whole tithe immediately, but rather keep it separate from their own supplies, perhaps in a public storehouse, and distribute it as required. In the arid climate of Palestine grain could be stored for several years (cf. Gen 41:47-57; Lev 25:20-22), likewise wine and olive oil.[92] Thus the poor would have provisions during the three-year period until the next 'year of the tithe'. As with other expressions of kindness to the poor in Deuteronomy, the people are assured that obedience to this rule will bring blessing in their own lives (v. 29b; cf. 15:4-5, 10, 18; 23:20; 24:19; 26:15).[93]

It is explicitly stated in 26:13 that the tithe is holy (cf. Lev 27:30; Num 18:24), and this is further implied by the use of the verb 'remove' (בער). This is a strong term which often means 'purge' (e.g. Deut 13:5; 17:7), and indicates just how important it is for this portion to be separated from the rest of the farmer's produce. The holy character of the tithe is in accord with its normal allocation to the sanctuary and its personnel, and yet here it is to be given away to ordinary people — some of whom are not even Is-

---

91. The Deuteronomic Laws do not refer explicitly to the sabbatical year, though it is probably assumed (see below, 10.3.b). If that is the case, the triennial tithe would take place in the third and sixth years of the seven-year cycle, since in the sabbatical year there would be no harvest and therefore no tithes. Cf. Craigie (1976); Oppenheimer (1977: 23); McConville (1984: 69).

92. Tigay (1996: 369 n. 43). On storage of grain, see Borowski (1987: 71-83).

93. Herman (1991: 101-46) draws on anthropological studies to interpret the tithe as a gift-exchange (prestation), particularly in terms of the covenant. In Deuteronomy, for example, the tithe is given in response to divine blessing and in anticipation of continued blessing in the future.

raelites! (The Levites were not quite ordinary, perhaps, but those who were in the towns rather than at the central sanctuary were presumably not in active service.[94])

Perhaps to avoid the impression of secularisation, this extraordinary law is supplemented by a stipulation that once the farmer has fulfilled the requirements of the law (26:12),[95] he must make a solemn declaration in the presence of God, probably at the central sanctuary on his next pilgrimage (v. 13).[96] It is emphasised that the tithe is a gift by the worshipper (vv. 12-13), just as the land is God's gift to his people (vv. 1-3, 9-11, 15). The declaration is completed by an assurance that the tithe has not been contaminated by improper handling (v. 14),[97] and a prayer for God's continued blessing on his people as they live in the promised land (v. 15).

d. Conclusion

The triennial tithe was a major innovation compared with the conventional understanding of tithes in the ancient Near East and the Bible. In

---

94. If there was a rota system for service in the temple, as in later times (cf. Millard 2004: 47-48), Levites would no doubt have received remuneration while in Jerusalem (Deut 18:6-8), but they could scarcely take home sufficient provisions to last their family throughout the year.

95. Deut 26:12 refers back to the law of 14:28-29, repeating the essence with close verbal similarity (Skweres 1979: 47-49).

96. Some scholars believe this is intended to take place at the central sanctuary (e.g. Thompson 1974; McConville 2002a), though others have suggested that 'before the LORD your God' (v. 13) could refer to a declaration in the farmer's home or at a local assembly (e.g. Craigie 1976; Christensen 2002). Support for the latter view is found in the fact that references to the central sanctuary in Deuteronomy are usually accompanied by the phrase 'the place which the LORD your God will choose as a dwelling for his name' (e.g. 12:11; 16:6; 26:2), and the absence of the phrase here could suggest that a local ceremony is envisaged. However, the declaration in the preceding passage (26:1-11) is explicitly stated to be made at the central sanctuary, and in the absence of indications to the contrary it would seem likely that the same context is intended here, particularly in view of Deuteronomy's general policy concerning centralisation of worship (cf. Hulst 1938: 103). This is further supported by the research of Wilson (1995: 145-46, 185-87, 197), who argues that the phrase 'before the LORD' in Deut 12–26 generally refers to the divine presence, localised at the one sanctuary (cf. Zakovitch 1974: 346 n. 1).

97. The declaration of innocence in 26:13-14 may be compared with the 'Negative Confession' in chapter 125 of the Egyptian Book of the Dead (*ANET*: 34-36; *COS*: 2.12); also Num 16:15; 1 Sam 12:3; Job 31; Ps 26:4-5 (Beyerlin 1975: 64; Havice 1978: 174-83). Cazelles (1948) interprets v. 14 in particular as a declaration that the worshipper has abstained from Canaanite agricultural rites.

the ancient Near East tithes were taxes payable to the palace (Ugarit) or temple (Babylon), and none of the extant documents picture them as welfare. Likewise all the other biblical references to tithing are concerned with gifts or payments to sanctuaries and their personnel (Gen 14:20; 28:22; Lev 27:30-33; Num 18:21-32; 2 Chr 31:4-21; Neh 10:35-39; 12:44; 13:5, 12-13; Amos 4:4; Mal 3:8-10), with the exception of Samuel's warning about royal tithe-taxes which are portrayed negatively and should not in any case be equated with the tithes prescribed in the laws (1 Sam 8:15, 17). But once every three years there is to be something quite different, for the tithe becomes the first known tax instituted for the purpose of social welfare.[98]

The use of the tithe for social purposes should not be understood as secularisation, but rather as recognition that one way of serving God is to serve the poor. (Of course it does not follow that service to the poor is *ipso facto* service to God, since many spend much effort in such service for humanitarian or other reasons.) Like other tithes and offerings, the triennial tithe in Deuteronomy is closely bound to the faith of Israel, even though it has no link with formal worship. So those who give the tithe thereby acknowledge God as the giver of the land; whereas those without an inheritance receive — as their share in the produce of the land — the 'holy portion' normally devoted to God.[99]

9.4 'Scrumping'

It appears the illicit childhood pastime of 'scrumping' (entering an orchard without permission and helping oneself to fruit, usually apples) is actually encouraged in the Bible! There is no reference to it in the ancient Near Eastern laws, nor am I aware of any other contemporary documents that mention the subject, so I turn immediately to Deuteronomy.

a. Deuteronomic Laws

> *When you go into your neighbour's vineyard, you may eat as many grapes as you wish to satisfy your hunger; but you shall not put [any]*

---

98. Crüsemann (1985: 218).

99. On tithes in the Christian church, especially in England, see the article in *ODCC* (1380-81), which includes further bibliography. For a reflection on tithing at the beginning of the third millennium, see Goldingay (2002).

into your bag[100]. *When you go into your neighbour's standing grain, you may pluck ears with your hand; but you shall not put a sickle to your neighbour's standing grain.*

Deut 23:24-25 [Hebrew 23:25-26]

Permission is given to eat what is growing in a neighbour's vineyard or cornfield, to satisfy hunger (cf. Ps 107:9; Prov 13:25; Isa 58:11; also Deut 12:20) but not to take produce home. As usual, the word 'neighbour' refers to a fellow-Israelite, another member of the covenant community. The law assumes the right to pass through others' fields and vineyards, and simply clarifies the matter of eating along the way. It seems trespass was not an issue, so long as no damage was caused (cf. Exod 22:5-6).

This law is unique to Deuteronomy, like that on the triennial poor tithe. I have found no other evidence of the custom from the ancient Near East, though in more recent times it has been reported as common law in Palestine and Arabia.[101] A similar regulation is found in Plato's *Laws* (8:844-45), permitting a resident alien who passes by to eat grapes and figs — excluding those types which are dried, stored, or used for wine — also pears, apples, and pomegranates.

For whose benefit is this law? On the one hand, it may be seen as provision for the needy.[102] Landless groups are given the right to eat as much as they want in the fields and vineyards, so long as they don't use a sickle or fill a vessel to remove produce from the field. In this way all the riches of the land are made available to them, and all should have enough to eat. The needs of the hungry take precedence over the rights of private property, though not without limits. 'Theft is not defined strictly according to ownership; right of access to satisfy human need is also part of the definition.'[103]

On the other hand, the law gives protection to property owners.[104] It prescribes limits to the practice of showing hospitality to passersby, so that people do not take advantage of such hospitality to rob their neighbour. Privileges can be exploited, and this law forbids the removal of food from the vineyard or field, thus recognising the farmer's property rights: he has

100. Hebrew כלי is translated by NRSV and TEV as 'container', NIV as 'basket', and NJPS as 'vessel'. But in this context it more probably refers to a bag or sack carried by travellers for food and other necessities (Tigay 1996; cf. 1 Sam 9:7; 17:22 [cf. 17-18], 40, 49).

101. Robinson (1856: 493); Doughty (1921: 2:171).

102. Crüsemann (1992: 233); Wright (2004a: 313-14).

103. Gnuse (1985b: 29).

104. Thompson (1974); Craigie (1976); Rofé (1985b: 60).

worked hard to produce the harvest, and should be generous with it, but not deprived of the bulk of it.

So the law is for the benefit of the whole covenant community. The law regulates the practice of helping oneself to food from fields and vineyards belonging to others by permitting wayfarers to enjoy a nibble or satisfy their hunger as they pass by, but forbidding them to harvest crops. It is not intended to imply that whenever someone is hungry all they need to do is to go to the nearest field or vineyard for a meal. But those who are blessed with fruitful land should be willing to share it with others; and those without land, or on a journey without provisions, should be able to enjoy some of that blessing without causing hardship to the land owner.

b. Conclusion

There are two biblical narratives that connect with this law. During their wandering in the wilderness, the people of Israel want to pass through Edom but are denied passage, even though they promise *not* to take any produce on the way through (Num 20:17-20; cf. 21:21-23). This incident does not prove that it was customary for travellers to 'scrump', and it precedes the Deuteronomic law permitting the practice, but in any case it merely refers to a possibility of this happening which is not realised. In the New Testament, Jesus' disciples pluck grain on the sabbath and are reprimanded by the Pharisees (Matt 12:1-8//). This incident assumes the right of a passerby to pluck grain from someone else's field, and the dispute with the Pharisees concerns not the plucking itself but the fact that it is done on the sabbath. Apparently the Pharisees treated plucking as a kind of reaping, and so defined it as work. However, this goes against the point of the Deuteronomic law that forbids passersby to reap, by using a bag or sickle, and only permits them to eat — an activity not forbidden on the sabbath.

Ancient Jewish interpreters discussed this law at length. According to Josephus (*Antiquities* 4:234-37), it applies to any passerby at harvesttime, and those who are reticent in asking should be offered a share of the fruits of the season. In contrast, the Mishnah (*Bava Metsiʿa* 7:2-8) restricts it to workers who are harvesting the field or vineyard for the owner and those who guard the gathered produce. Likewise, the Jerusalem Talmud (*Maʿaserot* 2:6) restricts permission to harvest workers, comparing the rule to that forbidding the muzzling of an ox while it is treading out the grain (Deut 25:4) and refuting the dissenting opinion of Rabbi Isi ben Aqabiah, who argued that Scripture permits anyone who wanders into a field to snack on what they find growing there. According to Rofé (1985b: 61-62), this restriction was due to concern for the agricultural economy after the Jewish War and the Bar Kokhba Revolt, when Jewish society in Palestine was seriously impoverished and farmers needed protection from passers-by depleting the produce of their fields.

Like many of the laws relating to wealth and poverty, this is a compassionate law rather than strict legislation and was probably not intended to be enforced in court. It emphasises both compassion for the poor and respect for private property, both hospitality to travellers and restraint in taking advantage of such hospitality.

As with the other laws, the practicalities are humanitarian but the motivation is theological. The freedom to eat the produce of a neighbour's land is an illustration of the principle that the fruit of the land is a divine gift rather than a human right. The generosity expected of landowners is appropriate for members of the covenant community who have received their land from God and are dependent on his grace for its fruitfulness. As he blesses them, they are expected to share the blessing with others, and in doing so they reflect something of God's own character.

Chapter 10

GENEROUS LOANS

One of the most serious socioeconomic problems in today's world is the escalation of debt. In Britain, for example, personal debt is presently increasing by 10 percent each year, several times the rate of inflation. Personal insolvency has reached an all-time high, while 90 percent of new credit cards are issued without the lender checking whether applicants can afford to repay the debt. The situation is even worse in a third-world country like Indonesia, with static wages, rampant inflation, high interest rates, and dealers ready to take advantage of the situation by offering unsecured loans at extortionate rates. On a global scale, international debt grew enormously during the last two decades of the twentieth century. The Jubilee 2000 Campaign responded to this with a call to leaders of the richest countries to give hope to the impoverished people of the world, by cancelling their backlog of unpayable debts and taking steps to prevent such high levels of debt from building up again. A petition with twenty-four million signatures from sixty countries was presented to the G7 Summit in 1999, who responded with a commitment to write off $100 billion of poor country debts. Nevertheless, developing countries transferred almost $200 billion to the wealthier countries in 2002, four times as much as they received in international aid.[1]

    1. Barrett (2000); UN News Centre (2003); Credit Action (2006); Shah (2006). Further progress on debt relief was made at the G8 Summit in 2005, with a particular focus on Africa, though it is likely that much of this relief will be given with conditions imposed by the rich countries, and it will be many years yet before even the modest United Nations target of 0.7% of Gross National Income as Official Development Assistance set in 1970 is achieved in most developed countries (Development Finance Group 2005).

Generous Loans

It can be a very profitable business to lend to the poor. When people are hungry and desperate to obtain what they need for survival, they may well accept a loan irrespective of the rate of interest, without much thought about the cost of repayment. Even if they escape the worst excesses of loan sharks, the poor are in a weak position to negotiate for good terms on a loan because they have little security to offer. Very probably they will pay much higher rates of interest than rich people who borrow to expand their business or pay for a luxury holiday. Frequently poor people find themselves unable to repay their loans and have to borrow even more to cover interest payments, taking them into a spiral of debt. This is clearly the case today, and was also true of ancient societies (cf. 1 Sam 22:2; 2 Kgs 4:1; Neh 5:1-5; Ps 109:11; Prov 22:7).

10.1 Interest

First I shall look at interest on loans, a matter on which the Old Testament has a significantly different perspective than other parts of the ancient Near East.

a. Ancient Near East

Several law collections deal with the subject of loans, and often refer to interest. The Laws of Eshnunna and Hammurabi stipulate interest of 20% on loans of money and 33⅓% on loans of grain (LE §§18A, 20, 21; CH §§ gap t, u).[2] The same rates of interest are found in *Ana ittišu* (§§B2, 4),[3] the Laws of X (§§m-n), and loan documents from the Ur III and Old Babylonian periods with some variations.[4] The rates for monetary loans at Mari are

---

2. The interest is sometimes specified as annual (e.g. CH § gap u), but often the period is unspecified, perhaps because loans were normally repaid at harvest (cf. LE §§19-20; CH § gap l). A higher interest rate is charged on grain, probably because it would be borrowed when it was scarce and the price relatively high, and returned at harvest when the price would be relatively low (Leemans 1950b: 28). For a detailed discussion of these clauses, see Driver and Miles (1952: 173-77); Yaron (1988: 235-46). On whether the interest rates were annual, see van de Mieroop (1995). On the origin of the concept of interest, see Steinkeller (1981).

3. Cf. Maloney (1974: 4).

4. E.g. *ANET* (p. 217); *COS* (3.136B, F, G); cf. Driver and Miles (1952: 174-76); Simmons (1959: 83-84); Harris (1960: 132); Maloney (1974: 12-15); Skaist (1994: 104-18).

generally higher, often 33⅓% or 50%;[5] the rate at Nuzi is almost always 50%;[6] while Neo-Assyrian tablets specify interest from 12½ to 50% per annum on money and 20% to 100% on grain.[7] Interest rates in the Neo-Babylonian period appear to have been relatively low, usually 20% for both money and grain.[8] Some documents indicate that interest would be charged, but do not specify how much.[9]

Sometimes the debtor gave a pledge[10] to the creditor instead of interest. In one twenty-first-century-B.C. transaction a slave was appointed to work for a creditor during the period of the loan.[11] According to several documents from the seventh century, members of a man's family were given as pledge for his loan and no doubt worked for the creditor during that time.[12] A deadline for repayment of the loan was set in one of the documents, and interest would accrue as well if the debtor failed to meet the deadline. Fields were also given as pledges, in which case the creditor had full use of the land in lieu of interest until the debtor repaid the capital.[13] Occasionally a creditor was granted use of a house or rooms instead of interest.[14]

The use of fields and orchards as pledges is referred to in the Laws of Hammurabi (§§49-50), but here it seems there is a deliberate change from an older practice whereby the creditor had full use of the land and took the whole crop, to one in which the creditor holds the field until harvesttime, when the owner takes the produce and uses it to repay the capital, interest, and any expenses incurred by the creditor for cultivation, keeping any surplus for himself. If, however, the creditor fails to produce a crop, then the

---

5. ARM 8 (nos. 22-61, plus commentary on pp. 199-216).

6. Jordan (1991: 83); Zaccagnini (2002: 180-81).

7. E.g. *ANET* (p. 221); SAA 6 (nos. 26, 36, 43, 64, 71, 74, 75, 97, 104, 170, 189, 235, 237); SAA 14 (no. 163); *COS* (3.57, 58); cf. Driver and Miles (1952: 176-77); Parker (1954; 1957); Maloney (1974: 16); Postgate (1976: 40-43); Radner (1997: 379-80). Some monetary loans fixed on a monthly basis had even higher interest rates, which could amount to 80% or more over a year (e.g. SAA 6: nos. 107, 108, 139; Kohler and Ungnad 1913: 252; cf. Postgate 1976: 40).

8. Petschow (1956: 20 n. 43a); Maloney (1974: 16-18); Homer and Sylla (1991: 30); Jursa (2002: 198-201); Wunsch (2002: 230-31, 234-38).

9. E.g. SAA 14 (no. 103, 201).

10. The issue of pledges will be discussed further under the topic of 'Security' (see below, 10.2).

11. *COS* (3.136E).

12. Wife and sister (*COS*: 3.116); son (SAA 14: no. 108); others whose relationship is unspecified, probably family slaves (SAA 6: no. 307; SAA 14: nos. 209, 216). Cf. Postgate (1976: 48). This is clearly similar in some ways to debt-slavery, on which see above, 6.1.

13. *COS* (3.136F); SAA 6 (no. 223); SAA 14 (no. 122). Cf. Postgate (1976: 51).

14. SAA 14 (no. 440); cf. *COS* (3.136G).

law reverts to the old practice and the creditor bears the loss (§52). Normally a monetary loan is to be repaid in cash (cf. §§50, gap a),[15] but the laws provide for repayment in grain or other commodities in some circumstances (§§49, 51; gap l, u, z; cf. AI §§B1-5). The Laws of Hammurabi also contain several clauses to protect the debtor against fraud or other misbehaviour on the part of the creditor (§§ gap u-y; cf. EAS §5). All these stipulations tend to protect a debtor who could otherwise be at the mercy of an unscrupulous creditor.[16]

There were various kinds of loan contracts in the ancient Near East, one of which is called ḫubuttatu in Akkadian. The ḫubuttatu contracts do not mention interest, and it was once thought that they concern interest-free loans.[17] However, more recent research has shown that the reason interest is not mentioned is that it is included in the total sum stated on the contract, which is the amount to be paid back, not the amount actually received by the borrower.[18] In other words, interest is added to the principal at the beginning of the loan period so it is unnecessary to specify this in the contract, though sometimes there is a stipulation about extra interest if the borrower should be late in making the repayment. For example:

> Shamash-nasu the governor . . . received 133⅓ gur of grain as a ḫubuttatu-loan; for two years no interest shall accrue. . . .

This refers to a real loan of 100 gur, with 33⅓% interest for the two years paid in advance.[19] According to Lipiński (1979: 138-40), most loans which are apparently granted without interest fall into this category. Shiff (1988) shows that the same applies to Neo-Babylonian promissory notes, where clauses prohibiting interest serve to protect the debtor against further

---

15. Likewise a loan of grain would normally be repaid with grain (e.g. LE §20).

16. My interpretation of the clauses discussed in this paragraph is based on that of Driver and Miles (1952: 145-50, 177-85). Cf. also Maloney (1974: 5-10).

17. E.g. Kohler et al. (1904-23: vol. 3, nos. 176, 200, 203); Schorr (1913: 67); Driver and Miles (1952: 210). This meaning is still found in *CDA* (119) and Stevens (2006: 151).

18. This was first suggested by Bilgiç (1947: 451-52), and followed by Kraus (1951: 53 n. 17), Harris (1955: 61), Petschow (1956: 15-16 n. 31), Simmons (1959: 84-85), and Kienast (1978: 62); cf. *CAD* (6: 221-22); Edzard (1970: 30-34, 42 n. 1, 45-49); Eichler (1973: 88); van de Mieroop (1995: 359-60). This view was challenged by Leemans (1960b: 15-16, 23-24), arguing for a wider sense on the basis of two texts of Samsuiluna where ḫubuttatu refers to a purchase on credit, and so effectively an interest-free loan. Skaist (1994: 52-56) also questions it, but does not give an alternative suggestion of his own.

19. Saggs (1988: 248-49).

charges but do not mean that the loan was without profit to the creditor. It may also be that seven Anatolian loan documents which do not mention interest are of the *ḫubuttatu* type, though the word is not actually used in these texts.[20]

In second-millennium Egypt, there are indications of an economic system based on social solidarity and mutual aid, whereas the first millennium saw a movement towards a more commercial system in which the charging of interest became normal.[21] The 'Negative Confession' in the Egyptian Book of the Dead appears to include a claim that the reciter has not committed usury, though the translation is uncertain.[22] This suggests that taking interest was viewed negatively in ancient Egypt, but does not prove it was considered a serious wrongdoing since several of the offences listed in this text are quite trivial. Loans known from Demotic sources appear at first sight to be divided into those with and without interest, but it seems that only a small minority of the latter were entirely interest-free. In a few cases the creditor expected a return on his investment in some way other than interest, but most often the interest was already calculated with the principal, as in the Babylonian *ḫubuttatu* loans.[23]

Two twenty-first-century tablets from Nippur record loans of silver, and a third records the loan of sheep fat.[24] In each case it is stated that interest is not required, though there is a strict deadline for repayment and a substantial penalty in case of default. A number of loan contracts from the Old Babylonian period include a phrase indicating that no interest is to be charged.[25] And there are three Neo-Assyrian documents which record loans — of silver, animals, and grain respectively — where interest is only required in the case of late payment.[26] However, it is difficult to be certain

---

20. So Veenhof (1978: 282-84). Another type of loan contract, called *šu-lá* (Sumerian) or *qīptu* (Akkadian), has been considered by some scholars to be interest-free, and by others to be a synonym of *ḫubuttatu*. CAD (13: 260-63) defines it as 'an amount of silver entrusted to an agent for buying goods to be sold on consignment', which is interest-free for a limited period. For further details, see Skaist (1994: 41-51), who rejects all three views and concludes that it is a commercial interest-bearing loan, in which for some unknown reason the amount of interest is not noted.

21. Bleiberg (2002).

22. Chapter 125 (*ANET*: 35 §B14; *COS*: 2.12 p. 61).

23. Pestman (1971). On loans in legal papyri of the Ptolemaic period, see Rupprecht (1967).

24. *COS* (3.136A, C, D).

25. Sumerian *máš nu-me-a* or *máš nu-tuk* (Skaist 1994: 44, 131-33).

26. SAA 6 (nos. 208, 296); SAA 14 (no. 458); cf. Postgate (1976: 40).

whether these loans were genuinely interest-free, or whether remuneration for the creditor was included in the stated capital sum or provided for in some other way.

It seems that making loans without either interest or alternative remuneration to the creditor was quite rare in the ancient Near East. The Laws of Hammurabi stipulate that interest payments be suspended for a year in the case of devastation of crops by storm, flood, or drought (§48). An Assyrian merchant colony in Cappadocia is known to have had a practice of interest-free loans between members of the same colony.[27] On the whole, however, it is very clear from the laws and loan dockets which have been discovered that it was standard practice to charge interest in the ancient Near East, at rates which would be considered quite high compared with many modern societies.[28]

b. Book of the Covenant

> *If you lend*[29] *money to my people, to one of the poor among you,*[30] *you shall not be like a moneylender: you shall not charge him interest.*
>
> Exod 22:25 [Hebrew 22:24]

In contrast to the common practice of the ancient Near East, the Book of the Covenant prohibits lending money at interest to other members of the covenant people, specifically the poor (cf. Isa 3:15). Any loans should be made as one family member lending to another, not as a moneylender seeking to profit from a business arrangement.[31] Clearly the sort of loan

---

27. Saggs (1988: 249).

28. Leemans (1950b: 32-33) argues that the rates were not excessive in the circumstances, since a field of grain could be expected to yield 30 to 40 times as much seed as that sown, and considerable profits could also be made by investment of money in trading. Maloney (1974: 13) agrees, though he points out that the yield depended on good conditions, and drought or flood could wipe out an entire harvest, leaving a debtor helpless. It may be noted, however, that CH §48 shows awareness of this risk and gives some relief to a debtor in such circumstances by freeing him from interest payments in that year.

29. Lit. 'cause [someone] to borrow'.

30. Cassuto (1951) draws attention to a wordplay between עמי ('my people') and עמך ('among you').

31. The term 'moneylender' (נשה) refers to a professional Canaanite moneylender, according to Hejcl (1907: 67-70). Neufeld (1955: 375-76) disputes this and gives various references to show that it refers to Israelites, not Canaanites or foreigners (e.g. Deut 24:11; 2 Kgs

envisaged is to help a poor person facing a shortage of basic supplies, not a loan sought by someone wanting to raise capital. This law addresses social need by an appeal to the conscience of more affluent Israelites: no one should make a profit by taking advantage of another's need. Like the warnings against abusing resident aliens, widows, and orphans in verses 21-24,[32] the instructions about loans to the poor in verses 25-27 are formulated in the first and second person — a direct address by God to his people — in contrast to the third person used in most of the preceding clauses of the Book of the Covenant. In this way God places himself directly in the role of special protector to the poor.[33]

c. Holiness Code

And when your brother[34] *becomes poor, and cannot support himself*[35] *beside you,*[36] *you shall strengthen*[37] *him; [as] a resident*

4:1; Ps 109:11), though it seems to me far from conclusive that these are necessarily Israelites. Neufeld further argues that neither in Canaan nor Israel were moneylenders professional, but rather rich people who had money to spare and lent it in a commercial way. On moneylenders in Old Babylonia, see Leemans (1950a: 11-21).

32. On which, see above, ch. 7.

33. Childs (1974: 478). Propp (2006) suggests that interest on seed grain is permitted, since the law only refers to monetary loans. But the absence of a prohibition does not mean something is permitted, and the parallel laws in Lev 25:37 and Deut 23:19 specifically include loans of food in the ban on interest.

34. I.e. a fellow-Israelite; cf. v. 25 (on which, see above, ch. 4 n. 42).

35. Lit. 'his hand has failed'.

36. עמך is usually translated 'with you' (e.g. vv. 6, 35b, 36, 40), but in vv. 35a, 39, and 47 'beside you' is more appropriate. NIV renders it 'among you', though this is problematic since the 'you' here is singular. NJPS translates it 'under your authority', followed by Milgrom (2001: 2205-6, 2208-9) who argues for this meaning in almost every occurrence of עם with a pronominal suffix in Lev 25 (cf. Speiser 1960: 38-39). Cf. the discussion of Lefebvre (2003: 228-34).

37. Speiser (1960: 38-39) and Milgrom (2001: 2206-07) argue that החזקת means 'hold', 'seize', 'take control of', and forms part of the protasis. Combined with their translation of עמך referred to in the previous footnote, this results in the sense: 'And when [one of] your brother[s] becomes poor, and falls under your authority, and you hold him [as though] a resident alien or temporary resident, let him live under your authority/in your household.' (Speiser delays the apodosis even further to v. 36, translating as follows: '. . . and he lives in your household, he shall remain with you as your brother.') While these proposals are possible linguistically, there seems to be no conclusive objection to the usual understanding of these terms as found in the majority of translations and commentaries. See Lefebvre (2003: 234-35) for a discussion, concluding in favour of the majority view.

alien or temporary resident[38] *he shall live with you. Do not take from him interest or increase,*[39] *but fear your God; so your brother can live with you. You shall not lend him your money at interest, or increase the price when you lend him food. I am the* LORD *your God, who brought you out from the land of Egypt; to give to you the land of Canaan, to be your God.*

Lev 25:35-38

The phrase 'when your brother becomes poor' (v. 35a) marks the second of three stages in a descent into poverty described in this chapter (cf. vv. 25 and 39).[40] A farmer in difficulty, who may have already mortgaged part of his land to release funds (v. 25), cannot make ends meet and turns to another more wealthy Israelite for help. In such a situation, a member of the covenant community should respond by strengthening his 'brother', allowing him to live with him as he would a resident alien or temporary resident who had no land of his own (v. 35b).[41] Just as ethnic minorities should be cared for, all the more so one's own kith and kin.

To 'strengthen' in this context is not just to give moral and spiritual support but to provide practical help, such as making an interest-free loan or selling food on credit without increasing the price (vv. 36-37). In practice, this would probably mean that the farmer's remaining land acts as security for the loan and he effectively becomes a tenant under the authority of his creditor, but he still remains legally a free person. It might be tempting for someone with surplus funds to invest them elsewhere and make a profit, so it is made clear that there is a responsibility to strengthen the weak brother even though that might not be to one's personal advantage (v. 35; cf. Deut 15:9-11).

Two different terms for interest are used in verses 36-37 (as also in Prov 28:8; Ezek 18:8, 13, 17; 22:12): 'interest' (נשׁך) and 'increase' (תרבית). The ancient versions understand the two terms to be virtually synonymous, as

---

38. Milgrom (2001: 2207) treats these two nouns as a hendiadys, which he translates 'resident alien' (cf. vv. 23, 47). For further discussion, see above, 7.1.b.

39. נשׁך ותרבית. These terms will be discussed below.

40. See above, 4.1.b.

41. Schenker (1998: 29-31) understands this to mean that impoverishment has forced someone to migrate to another area within the land of Israel, so that he effectively becomes an immigrant. This may well have been true in some cases, but the wording of the law could also include someone who appeals for help to another Israelite in his own locality.

does the Talmud,[42] though more recent interpreters have attempted to distinguish their meanings.

The term 'interest' in Hebrew means literally 'bite', and Rashi comments that 'it resembles the bite of a snake . . . inflicting a small wound in a person's foot which he does not feel at first, but all at once it swells, and distends the whole body up to the top of his head'.[43] On the basis of this etymology, 'interest' has been understood as a deduction from money lent ('bitten off' the principal), whereas 'increase' is the extra amount by which the debtor has to increase the amount of a loan on repayment.[44] Thus NJPS translates the two terms as 'advance interest' and 'accrued interest' (cf. REB; NRSV). The former is effectively the same as the *ḫubuttatu* loan in Mesopotamia, where the interest was added up front to the repayment sum in the contract.[45]

Loewenstamm (1969) questions this distinction, arguing that the idea of biting does not necessarily mean interest is exacted at the beginning of the loan. He suggests that the two terms refer to interest on money and produce respectively, on the basis of their usage elsewhere in the Old Testament.[46] He acknowledges that Deuteronomy 23:19 uses the term 'interest' in relation to all kinds of loans, not just money, and explains this exception as an abstract and comprehensive formulation with the dominant term being used to designate interest in general.

This fits well with Leviticus 25:36-37, and the use of the term in relation to monetary loans in Exodus 22:25 and Psalm 15:5. So — at least in the present context — it may be concluded that:

- 'Interest' refers to interest on loans of money.
- 'Increase' refers to an additional amount to be repaid on a loan of food.

In the case of money, there should be no interest; in the case of food, no profit. A loan of food should be repaid in kind, or with the monetary value

---

42. Loewenstamm (1969); Tigay (1996: 217).

43. Childs (1974: 479).

44. Buhl (1897: 730-31). This distinction is followed and elaborated by Stein (1953: 163); Neufeld (1955: 355-57); Speiser (1960: 44-45); cf. Lipiński (1979).

45. See above, 10.1.a. Cf. Speiser (1960: 44), who mistakenly uses the word *ḫubullu* ('debt, interest') instead of *ḫubuttatu;* and Lipiński (1979: 140), who suggests that the biblical prohibition may have resulted in greater use of the נשׁך formulation since it had the advantage of concealing the real nature of the transaction.

46. So also Noth (1962); Gamoran (1971: 131-32); Hartley (1992). Loewenstamm also questions the etymological basis for the assumed link between נשׁך and proto-Semitic *ntk* ('bite').

of the food at the *end* of the loan.[47] Otherwise, to repay the monetary value applying at the beginning of the loan would mean that, if the price of food drops during the period of the loan, the creditor would make a profit. It is quite likely that this would happen, since it is generally during food shortages when prices are high that poor people need to borrow. If on the other hand the price of food should rise between the beginning and end of the loan, the creditor would incur a loss, and this is also an undesirable outcome.

However, to understand the two terms to refer to loans of money and loans of food respectively is not necessarily contradictory to the distinction between advance and accrued interest. It may well be that interest on monetary loans would be calculated and deducted at the beginning of the loan, whereas interest on food might be left until the end of the loan because of the fluctuation in prices mentioned above.[48]

This law is grounded in biblical theology. First, it is linked with fear of God (v. 36), one of the most basic premises of biblical faith (cf. 19:14, 32; 25:17; Deut 15:8-9). Taking interest was not so much illegal (enforceable by human authorities) as immoral (punishable by God).

Second, the law concludes with the self-identification of Yhwh, a frequent refrain in the Holiness Code (v. 38). This underlines the authority of the laws as it reminds Israel of the exodus from Egypt and the covenant relationship by which he became their God and they became his people (cf. 19:36; 22:33; 26:12-13, 45). At the same time, another stated purpose of the exodus is to give Israel the land of Canaan, emphasising the divine ownership of the land (cf. v. 23) and that by ceding it to his people God expects them to obey his laws about land, such as the sabbatical and jubilee years. This combination of Yhwh as Israel's God and land as a divine gift to Israel is also found in Genesis 17:8 and Ezekiel 36:28. Further, God's prior generosity to his people may be understood as an example to them to treat others in a generous way (cf. 19:2; 1 John 4:11).

---

47. Milgrom (2001: 2211).

48. Cf. Milgrom (2001: 2209-10). For further discussion of the meaning of these two terms, see Klingenberg (1977: 38-52); Lefebvre (2003: 248-52).

d. Deuteronomic Laws

> *You shall not charge interest [on loans] to your brother,*[49] *whether interest on money or interest on food, or interest on anything that may earn interest. [On loans] to a foreigner you may charge interest, but [on loans] to your brother you may not charge interest; so that the* LORD *your God may bless you in everything you put your hand to, in the land which you are entering to possess.*
>
> Deut 23:19-20 [Hebrew 23:20-21]

The Deuteronomic Law opens by prohibiting interest on loans to another member of the Israelite covenant community — including loans of money, food, and anything else (v. 19). Some scholars suggest that this law in Deuteronomy is the first to protect all Israelite borrowers, rather than just the poor, but it seems unlikely that it was ever acceptable to exact interest from other Israelites, regardless of whether they were solvent, since nonlegal passages consistently consider it to be wrong.[50] It is true that Exodus and Leviticus specify the poor, but this is probably because they were the ones who most often needed loans in ancient Israel and the law is concerned with the relief of poverty caused by hardship, not with commerce. In any case, it is doubtful whether there was a significant money market in the agrarian economy of ancient Israel.[51] Among the 'children of Israel', members regarded each other as brothers and sisters, and the logical consequence of this would be abolition of economic differences in the community; so although the laws in Exodus and Leviticus explicitly prohibit only interest on loans to the poor, it may be assumed that this was one of those things that was 'not done' between any members of the covenant society.[52]

Concerning the substance of the loans, a development is discernible from the law in Exodus (money), to Leviticus (money and food), to Deuteronomy (money, food, and anything else).[53] A similar generalisation may be

---

49. I.e. fellow-Israelite, as often in Deuteronomy (see above, ch. 2 n. 87); cf. Lev 25:35 (on which, see above, n. 34).

50. Tigay (1996).

51. Gnuse (1985b: 19); Tigay (1996); Christensen (2002: 555); contra Silver (1983: 65-68; 1995: 187).

52. Neufeld (1955: 401-7).

53. For the arguments in favour of this order for the laws see Lewy (1957: 322-24); Gamoran (1971: 132-33); Seeligmann (1978); Fishbane (1985: 175); Braulik (1996: 33-50); Milgrom (2001: 2210); contra Cholewiński (1976: 301-02); Klingenberg (1977: 23). Stein (1953:

seen in Deuteronomy 22:3, compared to the earlier version of that law in Exodus 23:4.[54] Neufeld (1955: 366) sees this as a 'judicial amplification' which shows that jurisprudence in Israel was on a higher plane than in the time of the Book of the Covenant, but it is probably better to understand it simply as a later law closing a loophole in an earlier one. The primary object of the prohibition is money, which is included in all three laws and first in all three, but it was certainly common to lend food as well and none of the laws intend to exclude other items, so Deuteronomy's 'anything' is only making explicit what is already implicit in the earlier formulations.[55]

Next, the law gives permission to charge interest on a loan to a foreigner (נכרי, v. 20a). Although only explicit in Deuteronomy, this is probably implied in Exodus and Leviticus as well. Unlike the resident alien (גר), foreigners are not part of the covenant community and non-members are not subject to the law — either to keep or to benefit — so they are not treated in exactly the same way as fellow-Israelites (cf. 14:21; 15:3; 17:15).[56] Assuming the risk of lending, as well as forgoing interest, is an obligation towards another Israelite within the community but not towards someone who has no reciprocal obligation.[57] Many foreigners would be travelling for trade (cf. Neh 10:31; 13:16) or as mercenaries (e.g. 2 Sam 15:19), and not living at subsistence level, so there is no moral responsibility to forgo interest on loans to such people. The word 'Canaanite' actually means 'trader' in some contexts (Job 41:6; Prov 31:24; Isa 23:8; Zech 14:21). It is not a matter of racial discrimination, but if Israelites get involved in international trade, they can expect both to pay and to receive interest.[58] Ideally, if they are obedient to God and he blesses them, the people of Israel will not need to borrow but will be in a position to 'lend to many nations' (Deut 15:6; 28:12).

Finally the law turns to theology (v. 20b). As an incentive to obey this law, hearers are promised that God will bless them in the land (cf. 7:12-13; 14:29; 15:4-5, 10, 18; 24:19; 28:1-14; 30:16), just as he has done in the past (2:7; 12:7). This is not only a personal benefit, but intended for the whole cove-

---

166-68) argues that the law in the Book of the Covenant is the oldest, but the other laws are also ancient, and he suggests that they are complementary legal traditions — each authoritative — which were incorporated into the Torah.

54. See above, 2.3.c. Also Deut 24:19-22 compared with Lev 19:9-10 (see above, 9.2.c).
55. Gamoran (1971: 129-30).
56. On the terms גר and נכרי, see above, 7.1.b. Cf. Neufeld (1955: 361-62, 383-88).
57. Tigay (1996).
58. McConville (2002a).

nant community, as those who receive the blessing are encouraged to share it with others (15:14) and celebrate it in worship (16:10, 15).

e. Conclusion

There is a marked contrast between the laws of the ancient Near East and those of Israel on the subject of interest. In the ancient Near East, interest is assumed to be the right of a lender, and several law collections set rates for loans of money and grain; whereas the Israelite laws forbid charging interest on loans to other members of the covenant people, particularly the poor. Nonlegal passages in the Old Testament also refer to the giving of loans without interest as characteristic of a righteous person (Ps 15:5; cf. 37:26; 112:5; Prov 28:8; Ezek 18:8, 13, 17; cf. Sirach 29:1-2). This may be compared with the loan of animals without payment, as discussed above (3.3).

However, although none of the ancient Near Eastern law collections prohibit interest on loans, we should not draw the conclusion that other nations had no concern at all for the poor. For example, the Laws of Hammurabi include several clauses intended to restrain creditors who might be inclined to fraud and to prevent exploitation of debtors, and the laws which set interest rates were probably intended to limit the greed of those with capital to spare rather than to insist that those who borrow must pay back more than they receive. Several kings issued decrees wiping out debt and making various social reforms.[59] Also, we cannot assume that the people of Israel always observed the prohibition on charging interest — in fact there are indications to the contrary in the prophets and historical books (e.g. Neh 5:6-11; Ezek 22:12).[60] Documents from the Second Temple period indicate that at least some Jews charged interest on loans to fellow Jews.[61]

---

59. See below, 10.3.a.
60. Cf. Neufeld (1955: 379-82).
61. E.g. a fifth-century Aramaic papyrus from Egypt specifies monthly interest of 5% on a monetary loan (*COS*: 3.69, lines 2-5). Stein (1953: 169) gives further examples (see also Neufeld 1955: 411-12; Porten 1968: 77). However, the Jews in question lived in Egypt, where few of the laws were observed, so these examples do not prove that the law against taking interest was violated in Israel (Gamoran 1971: 133-34). There is also evidence of interest-free loans between Jews in Egypt in the same period (Neufeld; Gamoran; cf. *COS*: 3.81). Philo (*Laws* 2:74-78; *Virtues* 82-87) and Josephus (*Antiquities* 4:266) were strongly opposed to charging interest on loans to fellow Jews, and encouraged creditors to consider the gratitude of needy debtors as sufficient reward for their generosity.

These laws have caused much debate in Judaism, Christianity, and Islam, and have had a significant influence on history, influencing the economic structures of many European countries before the Renaissance, and more recently those of modern Israel and some Islamic countries.[62] There was also antagonism to interest in ancient Greece and Rome, influenced by thinkers such as Plato (*Laws* 5:742-43) and Aristotle (*Politics* 1:3:23), but it was primarily the three monotheistic religions that perpetuated the biblical idea of making loans for the benefit of the borrower rather than the lender.

Lending at interest is forbidden in the Bible because it tends to increase the poverty of the poor and the wealth of the rich. Members of the covenant community who are wealthy enough to make loans should realise that all they have comes from God and any surplus should be used to help others rather than to become even wealthier. The context of these laws in the Book of the Covenant and Holiness Code is exploitation of the poor, so it does not follow that it is forbidden to lend at interest to the *rich*. From ancient times there has been a distinction between productive loans, providing capital for trade or investment, and unproductive loans, which are made to supply immediate need.[63] The Deuteronomic formulation prohibits lending at interest to Israelites while permitting it to foreigners, who would often have been traders. In later times, Jesus' parable of the talents assumes that interest was normal on commercial loans (Matt 25:27),[64] but he instructed his followers to give to the poor and to make generous loans, expecting nothing in return (Luke 6:30-35). Mohammed prohibited the taking of interest, but again the context of the prohibition is aid for the poor rather than commerce (Qur'an 2:270-80).[65] In modern terms, it may be reasonable to charge interest on loans to people who borrow to develop a profit-making business, or to purchase a house which is likely to increase substantially in value by the time the loan is repaid. In Britain students are given loans with interest at approximately the rate of inflation, which is effectively the same as an interest-free loan in real terms.

---

62. See Stein (1953: 161, 169-70; 1956); Noonan (1957); Nelson (1969); Cohn (1972); Gamoran (1973; 1981); Gottfried (1985); Lewis (1985); Mills (1989: 9-23); Homer and Sylla (1991: 69-81); Langholm (1992); Rasor (1993: 167-75); and article 'Usury' in *ODCC* (p. 1420).

63. Hudson (2002: 51-52).

64. This is disputed by Mills (2005b: 203-4).

65. Cf. Neufeld (1955: 408-9) on the relationship of the references in the Qur'an to Jewish customs and to pre-Islamic tribal sentiments.

It may be suggested that a contemporary application of these laws would not necessarily lead to a blanket ban on all kinds of interest, as attempted by some Islamic banks, but rather to provision of interest-free or low-interest loans to those in real need, both on an individual basis and at the international level. Concerning individual loans, banks and finance companies often charge higher interest rates to the poor than to the rich, because they have less security to offer, or refuse them credit completely, so diverting them to private moneylenders who charge even higher rates. Concerning international loans, it has been calculated that at the beginning of the third millennium, when overall world prosperity is higher than at any time in history, the debt repayments of many poor countries to wealthy countries amount to more than the aid grants they receive, resulting in an ongoing flow of funds from the poor to the rich.[66] A relatively new problem on the individual level is that of consumerism, with people borrowing to finance consumption rather than to alleviate poverty or provide capital for business. Many banks and companies tempt people to incur unnecessary debt, sometimes with initial interest-free periods followed by high rates of interest for those who do not pay on time, and there is an urgent need for legislation to combat this, for instance to prohibit or regulate the advertising of consumer credit.[67]

10.2 Security

Any effective system of borrowing and lending has to ensure that loans are readily available for those who need them and that they are promptly repaid to the lender at the end of the agreed period. Security is important for responsible borrowers as well as lenders, because if lenders cannot rely on getting back what is lent they may be inclined to refuse loans. However, insistence on excessive security can be a bad thing if it deters honest borrowers or limits their ability to generate resources and thereby repay their loans. Overall, a healthy economy is one which facilitates the welfare of both creditors and debtors, and many societies have laws to this end.

66. Jubilee Debt Campaign (n.d.).
67. For a contemporary approach to the relevance of these laws, including proposals for a relational financial system based on sharing profit and risk rather than charging interest, see Mills (1989: 30-50; 1993; 2005a; 2005b). Cf. Sutherland (1982); Schluter (1985); Rasor (1993: 167-75); Ballard (1994); Paris (1998). For a critical analysis of consumerism from a Christian perspective, see Bartholomew and Moritz (2000).

a. Ancient Near East

A thorough and up-to-date study of security for debt in ancient Near Eastern law has recently been published. The present section draws mainly on the conclusions of that study.[67]

The most basic kind of security in this context is a pledge, property either given or assigned to a creditor, to be forfeited if the load is not repaid. In legal terminology, a pledge which is given is 'possessory' while an assigned pledge is 'hypothecary'. It appears that the former was more common in the ancient Near East, in which case the property would be held by the creditor as a pawn during the term of the loan, and the right of use would often take the place of interest.[69] The latter was like a mortgage, where the creditor had a charge on the property but it was retained by the debtor and handed over only in the event of nonpayment. Pledges usually took the form of productive assets, primarily land (CH §§49-50), dependents or slaves of the debtor (SLHF §8:3-15; MAL §§A39, 44, 48; C2-3), and occasionally animals (MAL §C4).[70] There are hints that nonproductive assets could also be pledged (MAL §C7), but they are not recorded in the extant contracts. It was not permitted to pledge land linked to a service obligation (CH §38), since the owner did not have ultimate right of disposal over such land.

Another important kind of security was surety, a third party who

---

68. *SDANEL* (2001). There are many detailed studies of security for loans in the periods relevant to the present work: Ur III (Steinkeller 2001); Old Babylonian (ARM 8: 217-27; Koschaker 1911: 1-31; Driver and Miles 1952: 145-50, 208-21, 435-36; Eichler 1973: 49-88; Kienast 1978: 66-103; Skaist 1994: 202-37; Westbrook 2001); Old Assyrian (Eichler 1973: 95-101; Veenhof 2001); Middle Assyrian (Koschaker 1928: 96-116; Driver and Miles 1935: 271-90, 323-30; Eichler 1973: 88-95; Abraham 2001); Nuzi (Eichler 1973; Zaccagnini 2001); Ugarit, Emar, and Middle Babylonian Alalakh (Hoftijzer and van Soldt 1991; Skaist 2001); Neo-Assyrian (Koschaker 1911: 237-50; Postgate 1976: 47-55; Radner 1997: 368-90; 2001); old Aramaic (Lipiński 1998); Neo-Babylonian (Koschaker 1911: 32-236; Petschow 1956; Oelsner 2001; Wunsch 2002: 238-44); Demotic Egyptian (Rupprecht 1967; Pierce 1972: 110-32; Manning 2001).

69. Cf. above, 10.1.a.

70. For examples of loan contracts with land as pledge, see SAA 6 (nos. 95, 97, 146, 268, 295). For examples of loan contracts with persons as pledge, see *AT* (nos. 18-28, 36, 41, 43-44, 53). For more recent translations and discussion of most of these Old Babylonian Alalakh texts, see Eichler (1973: 63-75) and *COS* (3.102). In a few cases the debtor himself acts as pledge, and in one text a whole village is pledged. Neo-Assyrian examples may be found in SAA 6 (nos. 272, 317) and SAA 14 (nos. 93, 97, 101, 159, 181); also SAA 6 (nos. 81, 91, 245), which record pledges consisting of both land and persons.

guarantees payment of a debt and is legally obliged to pay if the debtor defaults. Although none of the extant laws mention surety, there are many references in loan contracts.[71] There are also records of loans to joint debtors which were secured by making each one liable for the whole debt in case of default by any one of them.[72] Punctual repayment was often encouraged by charging punitive interest beyond the agreed loan period.[73] Finally, even if adequate security was not agreed in advance, a creditor could fall back on the possibility of distraint (or 'distress'), whereby persons or property belonging to a defaulting debtor was seized and held to enforce repayment (CH §§114-16). Most often it was a female member of the household who was distrained, and she would work in the creditor's house to cover her maintenance and give some compensation for the late payment.[74] Certain kinds of property were not to be distrained, however, such as grain and oxen (CH §§113, 241).[75]

It appears that there were two parallel systems of credit: subsistence and commercial. The former concerned loans to small farmers, to provide capital for sowing their fields or to survive until harvest. In this case either the farmer's land or members of his household would become security for the loan. The majority of extant sources concerning security refer to this sort of situation. However, there was also a commercial system functioning among merchants, who took out loans to finance their business. The security in this case more often took the form of surety, punitive interest, or a charge on business assets.

The failure to repay a loan would clearly lead to serious consequences for the debtor. If land or other property had been pledged, it would be forfeited to the creditor, though in some periods there was the possibility of redemption at a later date if the debtor found the resources for this.[76] In the case of a human pledge, the person in question would probably be-

---

71. E.g. Balawat tablet no. 100 (Parker 1963: 89); document no. 49 in Postgate (1976: 54-55, 168-70); SAA 6 (nos. 26, 206, 221, 222); SAA 14 (nos. 32, 33, 70, 171, 172). Cf. Porten (1969).

72. E.g. COS (3.99A, lines 17-20). It goes without saying that husbands and wives are liable for each other's debts (CH §152; MAL §A32), and this liability could extend to antenuptial debts as well unless an agreement to the contrary has been made (§151). For discussion of this, see Driver and Miles (1952: 230-33).

73. E.g. SAA 6 (nos. 46, 63, 67, 97, 143, 150, 157, 167, 214, 216, 221, 234).

74. Jackson and Watkins (1984).

75. Distraint is also mentioned in LE §§22-24, but only with reference to persons being distrained illegally, without there being a legitimate claim against the head of the household (cf. Szlechter 1956; Yaron 1988: 246-47, 275-78).

76. Cf. above, 4.1.a.

come a slave in the house of the creditor, and even without a prior pledge there was the possibility that a member of the household — or even the debtor himself — would become a slave to settle the debt.[77]

b. Book of the Covenant

> *If you ever take your neighbour's cloak as a pledge [for a loan], you shall return it to him by sunset; for his cloak [may be] the only covering for his body*[78]; *in what [else] can he sleep? So it will be, if he cries out to me, I will listen, for I am compassionate.*[79]
>
> Exod 22:26-27 [Hebrew 22:25-26]

The law assumes that it is legitimate for a lender to require security, so long as this is balanced with compassion, not allowing a borrower to be deprived of the basic essentials for survival. God is compassionate (v. 27), as Israel herself had experienced in former days (v. 21). Just as God hears the cries of widows and orphans who are abused (vv. 22-24),[80] so he hears the cries of the poor who are abused by their creditors (vv. 25-27). They are *his* people (v. 25), a reminder of the covenant relationship with God which should rule out exploitation of the weak.

The particular matter at issue here is taking a pledge for a loan, which in the case of a very poor person might be his or her cloak. The cloak would be worn on cold days, and could be used to carry things too (Exod 12:34), but at night it would absolutely necessary as a blanket and therefore must be returned to its owner. In the Mishnah the law is expanded by stipulating that a pillow which is pledged must be returned at night, while a plough must be returned during the day (*Bava Metsiʿa* 9:13). It might be thought that having access to the pledge when needed would reduce the borrower's incentive to repay the loan, but the inconvenience and embarrassment of having to collect and return it each day would encourage him to settle the matter as soon as possible.[81]

77. Cf. Veenhof (1978: 289-92). See also above, 6.1.a.
78. Lit. 'skin'.
79. The adjective חנון, here translated 'compassionate', is elsewhere paired with רחום ('merciful') and translated 'gracious': e.g. Exod 34:6; Neh 9:17, 31; Ps 86:15; 103:8; 111:4; 112:4; 116:5; 145:8; Joel 2:13; Jon 4:2.
80. See above, 7.2.b.
81. Cairns (1986b: 188); Tigay (1996: 226).

It seems the significance of the pledge in this case is not in its potential cash value to the creditor, which would probably be much less than the amount of the loan, but that the surrender of such an important item by the borrower would guarantee repayment of the loan as quickly as possible.[82] In practice, it is doubtful whether a compassionate lender would take a pledge at all in such circumstances, and the law may be seen more as a theoretical acknowledgement of the right to security, which has to be foregone if the borrower is not in a position to do without the property.

There has been some discussion about the Hebrew verb which is commonly translated 'take as a pledge' (חבל).[83] It is concerned with security on loans in Exodus 22:26 and Deuteronomy 24:6, 17, as well as in several nonlegal passages.[84] A few scholars argue that the verb actually means 'distrain' and refers to seizure of property belonging to a defaulting debtor.[85] It is true that in some cases it seems to refer to property being taken at the end of a loan period rather than at its beginning (e.g. Job 24:9; Prov 20:16[86]), and this is how it is understood by Josephus (*Antiquities* 4:267-70). However, this may simply mean that the pledge is hypothecary, agreed at the beginning of the loan period but kept by the borrower and handed over to the lender only in the event of failure to repay the loan.[87] It does not prove that distraint (forcible seizure of a debtor's property) is involved. In fact, Deuteronomy 24:10-11 effectively rules out the latter.

---

82. Cf. Judah's pledge in Gen 38:17-18 (Houston 2006: 111).

83. The majority of dictionaries and translations understand the verb to mean 'take as a pledge', including BDB; *DCH;* Hoffner (1976); Wakely (1997a); cf. *HALOT;* also NIV; NJB; NRSV; REB; TEV.

84. The word חבל is related to Akkadian *ḫubullu* ('debt'). In Deut 24:10-13 the verb עבט and related noun עבוט are used, which are synonymous in this context with חבל (Tigay 1996; contra David 1943). A third word is ערב/ערבון, which generally means 'surety' but has the meaning 'pledge' in Gen 38:17-18 and Neh 5:3 (cf. Loewenstamm 1961; Lipiński 1988).

85. Especially David (1943) and Milgrom (1976a: 95-98). A similar suggestion was made long ago by Buhl (1897: 728-29), but apparently not taken up by other scholars at that time. Recent scholars who follow this view include Paul (1991: 83-86) and Tigay (1996: 223).

86. Prov 27:13 is almost identical. According to Dahood (1961), this text — like Amos 2:8 — refers to a garment pawned for the services of a prostitute (cf. Gen 38:16-18).

87. Cf. Frymer-Kensky (2001: 253). For an example, see Kraeling (1953: no. 11 lines 9-11).

c. Deuteronomic Laws

The matter of security for a loan is dealt with in some detail in Deuteronomy 24, covering four specific matters relating to pledges:

- millstones (v. 6)
- respect for the borrower (vv. 10-11)
- cloaks (vv. 12-13)
- widows (v. 17b)

Millstones

No one shall take a pair of millstones, or an upper millstone, as a pledge; for that would be taking a life in pledge.

Deut 24:6

First, the people of Israel are forbidden to take millstones in pledge, because they are essential for survival and the purpose of loans is to help the poor, not to destroy them. A mill consisted of two stones, the upper one held in the hand and moved backwards and forwards over the larger concave stone below. The upper stone was much lighter, and would be more practical to take away as a pledge, but to do so would obviously render the whole mill useless. It was normal to grind flour and bake bread each day, so even the poorest home would have owned a pair of millstones, and to lose either or both would be a disaster (cf. Jer 25:9-11). The Mishnah expands the prohibition to include other utensils needed to prepare essential food, and stipulates that if there are two utensils only one should be taken (*Bava Metsiʿa* 9:13). This law may be compared with the prohibition of distraining an ox in the Laws of Hammurabi (§241) and Job's complaint against those who take a widow's ox for a pledge (24:3), since the ox was a working animal and fundamental to the running of a homestead.

Respect for the Borrower

When you make a loan of any kind to your neighbour, you shall not go into his house to take his pledge. You shall stand outside; and the person to whom you are making the loan shall bring the pledge out to you.

Deut 24:10-11

Second, the purpose of a loan to a poor person is to help him or her, not the lender. So, although it is reasonable for lenders to ask for security, they have no right to seize a pledge but must allow the borrower to give one freely. Daube (1969: 34), in his study of shame-culture in Deuteronomy, suggests that the reason for not entering the house to collect the pledge is to avoid unnecessary embarrassment for the householder. No-one has the right to enter someone else's home without invitation, even if owed money by that person. This both protects the family who live there and gives people in financial difficulty the opportunity to resolve their problems without the use of external force. 'The creditor's "right" to his money is of far less significance than the basic respect he owes a fellow human being.'[88] A corollary of this law is that a creditor is not entitled to take whatever he pleases from the debtor's home.

Cloaks

And if the person is poor, you shall not sleep in his [cloak given to you as a] pledge. Be sure to return the pledge to him at sunset, so that he may sleep in his cloak and bless you; and you will be in the right[89] *before the* LORD *your God.*

Deut 24:12-13

Third, if someone is so poor that they give their cloak as a pledge, it must be returned at nightfall. This is essentially the same as the law of Exodus 22:26-27, already discussed above, but with several changes in wording. In the first sentence, the creditor is prohibited from sleeping in the pledged cloak (v. 12). Rabbinic interpretation points out that a creditor would be unlikely to literally sleep in a poor person's pledge, and suggests that the text means he should not go to sleep at night with the pledge in his possession.[90] The

---

88. Biddle (2003).
89. Lit. 'it will be righteousness to you'. Cf. Deut 6:25; contrast 15:9; 23:21-22; 24:15 — 'you will incur guilt' (lit. 'it will be guilt to you').
90. E.g. *Sifre* 277; cf. Tigay (1996).

motive clause is rephrased positively: such consideration will be rewarded by the gratitude of the poor person and the approval of God (v. 13). Human gratitude will be expressed by a prayer for divine blessing, which is the meaning of 'that he may bless you'; and those who obey God's commandment will be 'in the right' and implicitly can expect the blessing which God promises to the righteous (cf. 2:7; 6:24-25; 28:1-14). McConville (2002a) comments: 'The effect is to extend the concept of being in the right legally beyond the reach of the court. Yahweh himself is judge, and the person who respects the spirit of the law receives the verdict of innocent. . . . The aim is to foster an attitude of deep respect for the principles of the covenant, which protect the interests of all in Israel.'

Widows

And you shall not take a widow's garment as a pledge.

Deut 24:17b[91]

Fourth, the law forbids a lender to take in pledge any widow's 'garment' (בגד; cf. Job 22:6; Prov 20:16; Amos 2:8), a more general word than the 'cloak' (שמלה) mentioned in verses 12-13 (//Exod 22:26-27). This may be due simply to compassion for the plight of the widow, responsible for a home and family without a husband to provide for her (cf. 1 Kgs 17:12; 2 Kgs 4:7), though there is also a rabbinic suggestion that the law is intended to protect her reputation, which might be sullied if her clothes were to be held by a creditor, particularly if she was meeting him every day to deliver and collect them (*Sifre* 281). The Mishnah goes further still in protecting widows, by stipulating that no pledge at all should be taken from them, whether they are rich or poor (*Bava Metsi'a* 9:13).

d. Conclusion

The taking of a pledge for an interest-free loan is permitted in biblical law, so long as it does not cause severe discomfort to the poor person whom the loan is intended to help. However, since the poor who ask for loans are

---

91. This is part of a longer section dealing with widows, orphans, and resident aliens (vv. 17-18), already discussed above (7.1.e; 7.2.c).

likely to own little or nothing that they can easily do without, these laws would have the effect of severely limiting the practice of requiring security on loans. Why should creditors be disadvantaged in this way? Because God cares for the poor (Exod 22:27; Deut 24:13).

It is notable that these laws do not even contemplate the surrender of a family member as a pledge, which was so common in other ancient Near Eastern laws, though this did happen from time to time (Job 24:9; Neh 5:2[92]; cf. 2 Kgs 4:1). Nor do they mention the possibility of pledging land, also common in the ancient Near East, though Nehemiah records the occurrence of this oppressive practice in the postexilic community (5:3-5). The reason for this is probably that persons and land are productive assets, and for a creditor to hold either or both as a pledge would be equivalent to taking interest, which is specifically forbidden to Israelites.[93] Only in the case of someone being unable to repay a loan does the question of 'sale' of persons or land arise. Even then, it is only to be a temporary measure and there are laws to ensure the eventual freedom of persons and restoration of ancestral land.[94]

There are hints in the Old Testament that the laws restricting the use of garments as pledges were not always observed (Job 22:6; Amos 2:8), and the pledging of a widow's ox was clearly against the spirit if not the letter of the law (Job 24:3). Ideally a righteous person would exact no pledge at all (Ezek 18:16), at least from another member of the covenant community, but if he does, then he will certainly restore it on repayment of the debt (v. 7). However, there were wicked creditors in Israel who took pledges and refused to restore them (Ezek 18:12; 33:15). Neufeld emphasises that the creditor acts as a trustee of the object, obtaining control but no right of disposal, with an obligation to keep the object available for redemption in perpetuity.[95]

None of the laws deal with the matter of surety, but it is often specified in loan documents from the ancient Near East, and several nonlegal texts in the Bible suggest that the practice was not uncommon in Israel too. Proverbs warns against giving surety for debts (Prov 22:26-27), whether for a neighbour (6:1-5; 17:18) or a stranger (11:15; cf. 20:16=27:13).

---

92. If the emendation of רבים to ערבים is accepted (BHS; *HALOT*; NJB; REB; Clines 1984; Blenkinsopp 1988; Wakely 1997c); though Williamson (1985a) follows MT, as do NIV and NRSV.

93. See above, 10.1.

94. See above, 4.1; 6.1; 6.3.

95. Neufeld (1958: 82-86; 1962).

The idea is used in a more general sense in the Joseph narrative, where Judah offers to be surety for Benjamin (Gen 43:9; 44:32), and in prayers where God is asked to guarantee his servant's well-being (Ps 119:122; Isa 38:14; cf. Job 17:3).

In 1960 Israeli archaeologists discovered an ostracon from the time of Josiah which has at least a superficial connection with this matter. Written in classical Hebrew, it is a letter by a farm worker who claims that his garment has been seized by an official for no reason and appeals to the commander for assistance in recovering it.[96] We do not know the official's side of the story, of course, and whether he has taken the garment in order to enforce repayment of a loan or because he considers the worker to have failed in his obligations. Nevertheless, even if he has grounds for grievance against the worker — which is strongly disputed by the worker and his companions — it is clearly against the spirit of Israelite law, wisdom, and prophecy for an official to confiscate the garment of a poor person in this way.

To sum up, the principle of security for loans is assumed in the ancient Near Eastern laws and is clearly intended to be enforced quite strictly, with only a few concessions to protect the borrower. The biblical laws do not disagree with the basic principle of security but adopt a much lighter touch, showing more concern for the needs of the poor who borrow than the rights of the rich who lend, though not completely neglecting the latter.[97]

10.3 Debt Relief

In recent years there has been much discussion about debt relief, particularly in relation to the world's poorest nations. It is by no means a new idea, however.

---

96. *ANET* (568); *COS* (3.41); *KAI* (no. 200); Naveh (1960); Lindenberger (2003: 107-10); Dobbs-Allsopp et al. (2005: 357-70). Cf. Tigay (1993).

97. On security for loans in Jewish law, see Elon (1972a; 1972b). For a wide-ranging survey of the pledge idea in different cultures, see Wigmore (1897-98). For a comparison with security in modern consumer credit law, see Rasor (1993: 175-84).

a. Ancient Near East

While none of the law collections refer to debt relief,[98] we know from a number of royal decrees from Mesopotamia that this did happen periodically. Two key words used in these decrees are *andurāru* ('freedom, liberation [of slaves], remission [of debts]') and *mīšaru* ('justice, equity').[99] Although the stated purpose of such decrees was to help the poor, it would also have been beneficial to rulers to minimise discontent in society and avoid widespread poverty, so their motives may not have been purely altruistic.[100]

The earliest known decree was made by Enmetena, king of Lagash, about 2400 B.C., as we learn from the following statement:

> He cancelled obligations for Lagash. . . . He cancelled obligations regarding interest-bearing grain loans.[101]

There is also a brief mention of debt relief in the Reforms of Uru-inimgina fifty years later:

> A citizen of Lagash living in debt, [or] who had been condemned to its prison for impost, hunger, robbery, [or] murder — their freedom he established.[102]

During the Old Babylonian period such decrees became more frequent, often being issued in the year of accession to the throne.[103] A good

---

98. In the prologues to their laws, Ur-Namma, Lipit-Ishtar, and Hammurabi claim that they have established justice in the land. The first is most detailed, listing various specific measures including reform of trade, standardisation of weights and measures, improved security for transport, liberation of oppressed populations, and protection for widows, orphans, and the poor. The reform of trade may have involved debt relief, but the interpretation of this section is uncertain (Renger 2002: 144).

99. The former is related to Hebrew דרור ('freedom, liberation', especially in relation to the jubilee), and the latter to מישרים ('straightness, justice, integrity', especially in Psalms, Proverbs, and Isaiah). See *CAD* (1.2: 115-17); Lewy (1957); Larsen (1976: 71-75); Lemche (1979); Charpin (1987: 36-41); Hamilton (1992b: 48-56); Hudson (1993: 17-42); Weinfeld (1995: 25-44); Otto (1997).

100. On the logic of clean slates, see Hudson (2002); cf. Chaney (1991: 130-32).

101. Cooper (1986: 58, cf. 67).

102. *COS* (2.152). Cf. the translation of Cooper (1986: 73): 'He cleared and cancelled obligations for those indentured families, citizens of Lagash living as debtors because of grain taxes, barley payments, theft or murder.'

103. Finkelstein (1961; 1965); Wiseman (1962; 1973: 11-12); Kraus (1984); Lieberman (1989); Weinfeld (1995: 75-96); Simonetti (2000); Renger (2002).

example is the 1646 Edict of Ammi-saduqa, which has detailed regulations to help weaker members of society.[104] Arrears of farmers, shepherds, fellmongers, porters, alewives, and other palace tenants are remitted (§§1-2, 11-14, 16-17). Some tithes are not to be collected (§15), and some obligations of military personnel are reduced (§19). The basis for all these concessions is that 'the king established equity *(mīšaru)* for the land' (§§2, 12, 14, 15, 16, 19). The king's establishment of equity also has implications for private creditors. An outstanding loan of barley or silver to an Akkadian or Amorite does not have to be repaid (§3; cf. §6), unless it is a business loan or advance (§8). If anyone has collected a loan repayment outside the collection season, he has to refund it (§4). Penalty interest on advances to traders is to be cancelled (§9). Finally, obligations to surrender family members for the payment of debt or as security are cancelled, granting their freedom (*andurāru*, §20).

During the same period in Anatolia there were edicts to wipe out debt, probably modelled on those of Mesopotamia, while in the thirteenth century the Hittite king Tudhaliya IV is known to have made an edict which included measures for debt relief.[105] Some scholars have seen evidence of periodic remissions of debt at Nuzi, though this is uncertain.[106] Various documents from the Neo-Assyrian period mention remission of debts, one of which includes a clause to ensure repayment of a particular loan in the event of a general remission.[107] There is no clear evidence of debt remissions during the Neo-Babylonian and Persian periods,[108] however, nor in pre-Hellenistic Egypt.[109] In sixth-century Athens, the σεισαχθεια ('shaking-off of burdens') of Solon included cancellation

---

104. *COS* (2.134). For the original text and a detailed commentary, see Kraus (1984). See also Finkelstein (1961; 1969); Charpin (1987: 41-44); Olivier (1997b).

105. Balkan (1974); Westbrook and Woodard (1990).

106. *CAD* (1.2: 116); Weinfeld (1995: 93-94); Maidman (1996: 157, 164-70); Zaccagnini (2002: 181-89).

107. E.g. SAA 6 (nos. 221, 226, 259); SAA 14 (no. 64). No. 226 concludes: 'If a remission of debts takes place, S[illim-Aššur] shall retrieve his silver.' Other documents refer to the possibility that slaves might be liberated in an amnesty, stipulating that if this happens their purchase price must be refunded (Postgate 1973: nos. 10 line 8, 248 lines 13-16; 1976: 21-22).

108. There may be some indirect evidence, but it is not at all certain (Jursa 2002: 212-13; Wunsch 2002: 245-47).

109. Goelet (2002) argues that, although there do not seem to have been decrees comparable to those of Mesopotamia, the concept of debt renewal was not unknown in ancient Egypt. For example, the Instruction of Amenemope (ch. 13) advises forgiving two thirds of the large debt of a poor man (*COS*: 1.47).

of debts and liberation of debt-slaves, together with various economic reforms.[110]

b. Deuteronomic Laws

The first part of Deuteronomy 15 legislates for debt relief on a seven-yearly basis. The rules are stated succinctly (vv. 1-3), then expanded with an assurance of God's blessing on the people if they follow his commandment (vv. 4-6) and an exhortation to be generous to the poor (vv. 7-11).[111]

Remission of Debts in the Seventh Year

At the end of [every] seven years[112] you shall grant a remission [of debts[113]]. And this is the manner of the remission: every creditor shall remit his claim,[114] [on] whatever he has lent to his neighbour; he shall not exact it from his neighbour or his brother,[115] for a remission has been proclaimed in the name of the LORD.[116] From a foreigner you may exact it; but you shall remit your claim on whatever of yours is with your brother.

Deut 15:1-3

---

110. Yamauchi (1980: 276-84); Chaney (1991: 132-33); Gomme, Cadoux, and Rhodes (1996).

111. For a detailed rhetorical study of the passage, see Hamilton (1992b: 7-43).

112. This may simply mean the last year of the seven-year period, in which case it could be translated 'In the seventh year' (NJPS) or 'Every seventh year' (NIV; NRSV). This is supported by comparison with the same expression in Deut 31:10 and Jer 34:14 (Driver 1902; Wallenstein 1954), and by Deut 15:9, which refers to the seventh year as the year of remission (Meek 1960: 330). On the other hand, Wright (1990: 167) points out that loans would normally be repaid after harvest, at the end of a year, and suggests that the phrase is to be understood here as a literal reference to the *end* of the seventh year (so RSV). According to Durham (1987), there is a Jewish tradition that the remission took place at sunset on the last day of the seventh year. Cf. above, ch. 9 n. 90.

113. A number of interpreters have argued that it is pledges which are released rather than the debts themselves (e.g. Horst 1930: 61; North 1954b). For a detailed discussion and refutation of this argument, see Chirichigno (1993: 265-72).

114. Lit. 'his hand'. On the somatic vocabulary in this text ('hand', vv. 2, 3, 7, 8, 10, 11; 'heart', vv. 7, 9, 10; 'eye', v. 9), see Hamilton (1992b: 31-34). On the syntax of this clause, and other possible translations, see North (1954b); Wright (1990: 169-73).

115. Both terms are frequently used as synonyms for 'fellow-Israelite'. On their pairing in the present law, see Hamilton (1992b: 34-40); Houston (1995: 304-7; 2006: 181-83).

116. Lit. 'a remission to the LORD has been proclaimed'.

A simple apodictic law (v. 1) is supplemented by details of how it is to be implemented (vv. 2-3).[117] There are a number of similarities to the Mesopotamian royal decrees discussed above, both in content and style.[118] For example, the phrase 'a remission has been proclaimed in the name of the LORD' states the authority for the action to be taken, in a similar way to the Mesopotamian formula, 'the king established equity for the land'. Here God, the King of Israel, establishes a remission of debts.[119]

The fact that this law takes effect every seven years raises the question of its relationship to the sabbatical year of Exodus and Leviticus.[120] Some of the terminology is similar. First, the word 'leave' (שמט) is used in Exodus 23:11 to denote rest for the land, and here for the remission of debts. Second, the expression 'remission in the name of the LORD' (lit. 'remission to the LORD') is parallel to the description of the sabbatical year in Leviticus 25:2, 4 as a 'sabbath to the LORD'. Third, the use of the word 'proclaim' (קרא) — unique with this meaning in Deuteronomy but relatively common in priestly writings — gives a solemnity to the event as an official proclamation, as for the sabbath, jubilee, and other festivals in Leviticus 23:2-4 and 25:10.[121] The similarities suggest that the Deuteronomic lawmaker is aware of the earlier laws concerning the sabbatical year, which are neither cancelled nor changed but assumed to have continuing validity and supplemented by a further measure to help those who have got themselves into serious financial difficulty.[122]

What is new in Deuteronomy is the stipulation that at the end of seven years all debts of fellow Israelites are to be cancelled. In this seventh year, money that has been lent is to return to its natural state like the fallow fields in the earlier laws.[123] The object of this radical measure is not to encourage borrowers to be negligent about repaying their debts, but to provide a way out for needy people who have tried hard to repay them but

---

117. Various theories of the composition of this passage have been proposed (e.g. Horst 1930: 55-56; Morrow 1990), but they do not significantly affect the interpretation of the canonical form of the law.

118. Weinfeld (1990: 43-53; 1995: 162-67).

119. Tigay (1996).

120. On which, see above, 9.1.

121. Cf. Exod 12:16; Num 28:18–29:12; Isa 61:1-2; Jer 34:8.

122. It is generally agreed that the oldest law is that of Exodus, and there is good reason to consider the Deuteronomic law to be later than that in the Holiness Code (Weinfeld 1972a: 223-24; Wright 1990: 167-69; Milgrom 2001: 2245).

123. Clines (n.d.: 4-5).

been unable to do so. Elsewhere there is strong condemnation of the wicked who refuse to repay loans (Ps 37:21). The law is intended to help the poor, not to be a license for irresponsibility. As pointed out in the Mishnah, it does not free employers from the obligation of settling unpaid wages, nor purchasers from the obligation of settling unpaid bills for merchandise, nor criminals from the obligation of paying fines imposed by a court (*Shevi'it* 10:1-2).

Several commentators have suggested that the law intends the deferring of debts only during the sabbatical year, not their cancellation,[124] but it would appear from verses 7-11 that cancellation is intended.[125] Comparison with practice in Mesopotamia also points to cancellation rather than deferment.[126] Josephus and the rabbis agree that it means cancellation of debts, and that is the understanding in NIV, NJB, and NRSV. Presumably the repayment of debts would be scheduled to be complete by the sabbatical year, and cancellation would only be necessary in the case of a poor person who was genuinely unable to repay. As discussed above (9.1.b), it is uncertain whether the land sabbatical is intended to be observed simultaneously throughout the land or field by field, but it is clear that the remission of debts is to take place every seven years on a national basis (Deut 15:9; 31:10-11).

There is a separate rule for foreigners (v. 3), as in the case of charging interest on loans (23:20).[127] It is not a question of discrimination *against* foreigners, but simply that they are not included in these special measures to help members of the covenant community facing hardship. The emphasis throughout this chapter is on care for fellow-Israelites (vv. 2, 3, 7, 9, 11, 12). In any case, foreigners would often be traders on relatively brief visits rather than poor people needing help. They are to be distinguished from resident aliens, who were often needy and were given special protection in Israelite society.[128]

---

124. Keil and Delitzsch (1865); Driver (1902); Craigie (1976); Wakely (1997d); cf. Wright (1990: 172-73).

125. So von Rad (1964a); Clines (n.d.); Phillips (1970: 77-78); Thompson (1974); Mayes (1979); Braulik (1986); Robinson (1988: 122); Chirichigno (1993: 272-74); Houston (1995: 303-4; 2006: 180-81).

126. Weinfeld (1995: 167-68; cf. 75-96).

127. Discussed above, 10.1.d.

128. See above, 7.1.

Promise of Divine Blessing

However, there should not be any poor among you; for the LORD *will certainly bless you, in the land which the* LORD *your God is giving you to possess as an inheritance, if only you listen obediently to the voice of the* LORD *your God, by being careful to observe all this commandment, which I am commanding you today. When the* LORD *your God blesses you, as he has promised you: you will lend to many nations, but you will not borrow; you will rule over many nations, but they will not rule over you.*

Deut 15:4-6

Obedience to the commandment will result in God's blessing (vv. 4-5, 10, 18; cf. Ps 27:25-26), just as it is God's blessing that makes generosity possible (vv. 6, 14). Whereas the preceding and following sections are concerned with individual wealth and poverty, here national prosperity is the main issue. There will be enough for all, if the people listen to the voice of their God; indeed more than enough, so that they can lend to other nations who have not been blessed in this way and rule over them (cf. Deut 28:1-14; contrast vv. 43-44). However, this should not be interpreted as an encouragement of passivity and complacency, nor to have an uncritical attitude towards economic structures in society. On the contrary, 'there should not be any poor among you' is an imperative, demanding action to ensure that this is true of the covenant community.[129] In the present context, the specific action required is redistribution of wealth from the rich to the poor by the remission of unpaid debts, recognising that the blessings of the promised land are the gift of God rather than the result of human achievement. But the expression 'all this commandment' (v. 5; cf. Deut 19:9) is broader in scope than just this one law, making a connection between obedience to the whole law and enjoyment of divine blessing (cf. Lev 26:3-13).[130]

---

129. McConville (2002a); cf. Houston (2006: 183-84).

130. These verses, together with Deut 28:1-14 and similar texts, have been understood by proponents of prosperity theology to encourage those who are faithful to God today to expect material blessings in this world. For discussion of the issues, see the references cited above, ch. 4 n. 66.

Generosity to the Poor

When one of your brothers becomes poor among you, in one of your towns in your land which the LORD *your God is giving to you, you shall not be hard-hearted or tight-fisted toward your poor brother. Rather, open your hand generously to him: lend him freely, sufficient for his need, whatever he lacks. Be careful you do not entertain an evil thought, thinking, 'The seventh year, the year of remission, is near,' so that you close your eyes to the need of*[131] *your poor brother, and do not give to him; then he may cry to the* LORD *against you, and you will be found guilty of sin. Give generously to him, and do not be grudging as you give to him; for on account of this the* LORD *your God will bless you in all you do, in everything you put your hand to. Since there will always be poor people in the midst of the land,*[132] *that is why I am commanding you, as follows: 'Open your hand generously to your brother, to the poor and needy in your land.'*

Deut 15:7-11

In an ideal situation, there should not be poverty among the people of God, if they are faithful and obedient to him (vv. 4-6). But this legislation is realistic rather than idealistic, recognising the reality of human sin, as a result of which 'there will always be poor people in the midst of the land' (v. 11). In this situation it is the duty of Israelites to help the poor by providing loans, as much as is needed, even though the sabbatical year is near and the prospect of being repaid is slim (vv. 7-10; cf. Lev 25:35-38). This is not charity in the sense of an outright gift, and it is expected that those who receive loans will repay them if possible; nevertheless creditors are not to make calculations about the likelihood of debts being repaid but rather to be generous to those in need and trust God for their own future (cf. Prov 14:21; Luke 6:34-35; 14:12-14; 2 Cor 9:6-15). The style changes from law to sermon, as the people are exhorted to show open-handed generosity to the poor, whoever they may be. It would be difficult to enforce generosity in a law court, which is why a poor person feeling hard done by is likely to appeal to God for justice (v. 9).[133] If this happens, the reader is warned,

---

131. Lit. 'and your eye is evil toward'.

132. NRSV translates ארץ here as 'earth', but there is no good reason to translate it differently here from the second occurrence of the word at the end of the verse, where it is correctly translated 'land' (Hamilton 1992a).

133. Cf. Deut 24:13, 15; Exod 22:21-27. On this, see above (ch. 7.2.b) and Kessler (1992). As

God will not acquit the miser. Hard hearts and tight fists have no place in the covenant community (cf. Prov 3:27-28; 1 John 3:17).

c. Conclusion

The sabbatical year regulations in Exodus and Leviticus are concerned with rest for the land, while those in Deuteronomy prescribe the remission of unpaid debts. This contrast could suggest that the older regulations are designed for a simple agrarian society, before the time of the monarchy, whereas Deuteronomy 15:1-11 is intended for a later period in the history of Israel, when a larger proportion of the population live in towns and social equalities have become greater.[134] However, the problem of debt is not confined to urban societies, and in any case it is agricultural rather than commercial debt that is envisaged in the Deuteronomic context.[135] It is more likely that Deuteronomy assumes the earlier regulations as a basis and supplements them with an extra regulation to help the poor.[136]

Apart from these agricultural and economic measures, the seventh year has a special place in the religion of Israel. In Deuteronomy 31:9-13 it is linked with the public reading of the Law (תורה). When a covenant was made in ancient times, it was usual for an official document to be kept in a mutually agreed place and read publicly from time to time. So also the Law, as the official document of the covenant between God and Israel, is to be read every seven years to the whole people of Israel; and the time specified for this public reading is during the festival of Booths in the year of remission of debts.[137]

Houston (2006: 183) points out, the text does not assume a social revolution, but issues a call for moral revolution.

134. Cf. Kraus (1962: 72-73); Botterweck (1970: 30); Lemche (1976: 45); Cairns (1986b: 52); Tigay (1996: 466). There are very different views of the development of ancient Israel's social and economic structure (e.g. Robinson 1932: 355-67; de Vaux 1961: 164-67; Gottwald 1976; Bendor 1996), which cannot be discussed here, though broadly speaking it may be agreed that there was a movement from a relatively egalitarian society based on the family during the early period of the settlement in Palestine to one with greater differentiation in wealth and weaker family bonds during the latter years of the monarchy.

135. Wright (1990: 173).

136. Milgrom (2001: 2245).

137. It is difficult to be certain about the extent of the Law that is to be read, but it is probably substantially the book of Deuteronomy (cf. Deut 1:5; 4:8, 44; 28:58; 31:24). It is also unclear whether it is envisaged that all Israel would literally gather in one place at one time,

As shown above, debt relief was known elsewhere in the ancient Near East, and in certain periods it was quite common for a king on accession to the throne to make a proclamation instituting reforms of injustices and granting favours to the poor. Some Israelite kings may also have issued proclamations of this kind, for example David — who is recorded as having 'established justice and equity for all his people' (2 Sam 8:15) — and Josiah (2 Kgs 22:1-2; Jer 22:15-16).[138] Zedekiah once ordered the release of slaves, but not long afterwards many of them were enslaved again (Jer 34:8-22). Nehemiah, though not a king, insisted on the restoration of mortgaged land and freedom for debt-slaves, and prohibited interest on loans (Neh 5:1-13).[139] However, the Deuteronomic Law requires this to be done every seven years, without waiting for royal orders, which might never be issued unless there was a pious king on the throne or a politically opportune moment arose.

This pattern would foster stability in the economy, compared with the Mesopotamian situation where a remission of debts could be announced without warning. On the other hand, it would make credit more difficult to obtain during the period immediately preceding the year of remission, because the number of people willing to make loans would tend to be fewer as the likelihood of repayment decreased (cf. Deut 15:9). It is even possible that some unscrupulous people would deliberately take out loans at that time with no intention of repaying them. Clearly, the law would work well only if people were both honest and generous, which is why it appeals to the conscience of the covenant community rather than stipulating sanctions for disobedience.

The observance of the sabbatical year — including rest for the land and relief for debtors — should have functioned to reduce the gap between rich and poor which developed after Israel settled in Palestine. However, it would not have been easy to implement laws which benefited the poor at the expense of the rich, since those with power and influence in society would inevitably oppose them.[140] Only after the exile do we find a record

---

or whether just representatives would attend. For further discussion of this text, see Thompson (1974); Craigie (1976); Tigay (1996); Christensen (2002); McConville (2002a). Two other texts refer to a seventh year, in connection with liberation of Hebrew slaves (Exod 21:2-11; Deut 15:12-18). However, this seventh year is reckoned on an individual basis for each slave, not simultaneously throughout the land (see above, 6.1).

138. Weinfeld (1972a: 152-55; cf. 1992); Wiseman (1973: 5-6, 12-14).
139. Cf. Yamauchi (1980: 285-91); Baltzer (1987); Weinfeld (1990: 53-58); Croatto (1997).
140. Amit (1992: 50-53).

of remission of debts in the seventh year actually taking place, under Nehemiah's leadership, which was accompanied by rest for the land (Neh 10:31). The reading of the Law to the whole people is mentioned just once, towards the end of the Old Testament period, by the priest Ezra (Nehemiah 8). In later Judaism, seeing that people were reluctant to make loans shortly before the sabbatical year, the rabbis provided a way round this rule by instituting the *prozbul*. This was a legal fiction designed to circumvent the remission of debts by inserting a clause in loan contracts which permitted a court to collect unpaid debts on behalf of the creditor at any time, irrespective of the seven-year cycle.[141]

---

141. *Mishnah Shevi'it* 10:3-7; *Sifre* 113. On this, see Goodman (1982); Instone-Brewer (2004: 248-51). For a comparison of debt forgiveness in biblical law and modern consumer credit law, see Rasor (1993: 184-89). For two very different reflections on the international debt crisis in the light of the Bible, both by African writers, see Nebo (1998) and Mosala (2002). For reflections on the contemporary relevance of the biblical laws on debt relief, see Hudson (1993: 55-62); Schweitzer (1999).

Chapter 11

FAIR TRADE

According to the laws examined in the previous three chapters, justice and generosity are to characterise the life of the covenant community, specifically in relation to the practice of law, agriculture, and finance. In this final chapter, it will become clear that this is also true in relation to employment and trade. People should work hard, but not be overworked, for all are entitled to free time for rest and worship. A fair wage should be paid for a day's work, without delay, and a fair deal given when people buy goods and services.

There are also various Old Testament laws governing the treatment of animals and plants, but I do not discuss them in this book unless they are concerned with wealth and poverty in human society as well.[1]

In ancient Near Eastern law there are two regulations concerning fair trade which have no Old Testament parallels, and so will be simply mentioned here without discussion. First, the Laws of Hammurabi devote several clauses to fair dealing in trade partnerships (§§ gap cc, 100-107, 112; cf. EAS §8).[2] Second, there are stipulations in the Hittite Laws dealing with

---

1. On concern for working animals, see Exod 20:10; 23:12; Lev 25:6-7; Deut 5:14; 22:10; 25:4; cf. Prov 12:10; on wild animals, see Exod 23:10-11; Lev 25:6-7; on birds, see Deut 22:6-7; on trees, see Lev 19:23-25 (cf. CH §60); Deut 20:19-20. Some of these laws are discussed above in connection with the sabbatical year (9.1) and below under 'holidays' (11.1). Several other laws refer to rights and responsibilities in connection with animals belonging to other people (Exod 21:33-36; 22:1, 10-15; 23:4-5; Deut 22:1-4), but the concern is primarily for the owners rather than the animals themselves (see above, 2.1; 2.3; 3.1; 3.3). For a discussion of laws relating to animals, see Phillips (1995).

2. For discussion of these clauses in the Laws of Hammurabi, see Driver and Miles (1952: 186-202, 208).

unfair competition, which prohibit interference in sales of property, people, and livestock (§§146-48).[3] In any case, although these are of interest in relation to fair trading practice, they do not impinge directly on matters of wealth and poverty.[4]

11.1 Holidays

Holidays in ancient Israel were indeed 'holy-days', and their primary function was to provide the opportunity for religious ceremonies and celebrations. However, holidays are also relevant to wealth and poverty. Of particular interest is the divine right of workers, as well as the privileged classes, to take regular times of rest and recreation.

a. Ancient Near East

None of the ancient Near Eastern laws make provision for holidays. There is an incidental reference to a holiday[5] in a clause on marriage in the Middle Assyrian Laws (§A42), but no further details. From the third millennium, there is a liturgy for the New Year festival which reads as follows: 'During seven days no grain was [ground], the maidservant made herself equal to her mistress, the manservant walked side by side with his master.'[6] However, by the first millennium Babylonian slaves had to work all year, and there is no evidence of their being given regular free time.[7]

There may be an etymological link between the Hebrew word for 'sab-

---

3. The precise meaning of the clauses is uncertain, as may be seen from the three different translations by Hoffner (in *COS*; Hoffner 1997; Roth 1997). For discussion, see Neufeld (1951: 177); Hoffner (1997: 206-8). In the prologue to his laws (lines 114-24), Ur-Namma refers to various trade reforms which he claims to have made, but the information is too brief to tell us a great deal.

4. On trade and commerce in the ancient Near East, see further Johns (1904: 281-86); Leemans (1950a; 1960a); Hawkins (1977); Yoffee (1981); Archi (1984); Silver (1985); Saggs (1988: 233-53); Kemp (1989: 232-60); Postgate (1992: 191-222); Dercksen (1999); King and Stager (2001: 189-200); Monroe (2005).

5. So *COS* and *ANET*; lit. 'empty day' (*CAD* 14: 176); contra Driver and Miles (1935: 411, 482), who translate *ra-a-ki* as 'anointing' (cf. Cardascia 1969: 209). The same word occurs in the Middle Assyrian Palace Decrees §3 (Roth 1997: 198), but the text is incomplete and insufficient to draw any conclusion about the nature of the holiday.

6. Andreasen (1974a: 281-82).

7. Dandama[y]ev (1984: 248).

bath' (שבת) and Akkadian *šapattu,* which denotes the fifteenth day of the month (i.e. day of the full moon). There is no semantic connection, however, since the sabbath consistently refers to a weekly day of rest that is quite independent of the lunar cycle.[8] Nor is there any evidence that *šapattu* was a day of rest at all.[9] The number seven occurs in various Ugaritic texts and may have had a special significance in ancient Canaan, as in Israel, but there is no evidence of a connection with holidays or religious celebrations.[10]

b. Decalogue

Exod 20:8-11

Remember *the sabbath day, to keep it holy.*

Six days you shall labour, and do all your work. But the seventh day is a sabbath to the Lord *your God; you shall not do any work, you or your son or your daughter, your male or female slave*

or your livestock, or your resident alien who is in your town.[11]

For [in] six days the Lord made heaven and earth, the sea, and all that is in them, and he rested [on] the seventh day;

that is why the Lord *blessed the sabbath day* and made it holy.

Deut 5:12-15

Observe *the sabbath day, to keep it holy;* as the Lord *your God has commanded you.*[12]

Six days you shall labour, and do all your work. But the seventh day is a sabbath to the Lord *your God; you shall not do any work, you or your son or your daughter, or your male or female slave,* or your ox or your donkey *or any of your livestock, or your resident alien who is in your town, so that your male or female slave may rest as you do.*

Remember that you were a slave in the land of Egypt, and the Lord your God brought you out from there, with a strong hand and an outstretched arm;

that is why the Lord *your God has commanded you to keep*[13] *the sabbath day.*

---

8. *CAD* (17.1: 449-50); *HALOT* (1410); Haag (1993: 389); cf. *COS* (1.130 line 1:206); Stamm (1967: 90-92); Dressler (1982: 22-24).

9. Phillips (1970: 65); Robinson (1988: 160).

10. Cf. above, 9.1.a.

11. Lit. 'within your gates'.

12. On the basis of a newly published Hebrew ostracon from the seventh century B.C., Lang (1998) suggests that this phrase does not refer to divine commandments given earlier, but is intended to introduce what follows and so should be rendered 'thus the Lord your God commands you'. However, the authenticity of this ostracon is doubtful (see above, ch. 4 n. 48). In any case, even if this should prove to be genuine, it does not affect the essential meaning of the fourth commandment.

13. Lit. 'make'. Eder (2006) prefers the literal translation, arguing that the use of this particular word is significant for the meaning of the commandment.

The essence of the fourth commandment is the same in both versions of the Decalogue. The basic principle, expressed in the first sentence, is that the sabbath must be kept holy (Exod 20:8//Deut 5:12). It is not simply a matter of work and rest, whether seen negatively as the prohibition of work or positively as the command to rest. The sabbath is first of all a holy-day, and only secondly a holiday.

Second, the institution of the sabbath creates a regular pattern of six days' work (Exod 20:9//Deut 5:13) followed by a day of rest (Exod 20:10//Deut 5:14). Positively, the seventh day is 'a sabbath to the LORD' (cf. 16:25; 31:15; 35:2; Lev 23:3, 38); negatively, it is a day when all work is forbidden. It is made very clear that the sabbath is not an option, but a fundamental rule for all members of the covenant community. According to the older version in Exodus,[14] seven groups are specifically told to observe the sabbath, no doubt intended as a merism to indicate 'everyone': old and young, male and female, slave and free, natives and resident aliens. Even domestic animals are included!

However, while these essential points are the same in the two traditions, there are several differences. Exodus begins with the command to 'remember' (זכור, v. 8), a word which refers not merely to mental activity but to observance of an obligation (cf. 13:3), also used in connection with God keeping his covenant (2:24; 6:5; 32:13). Deuteronomy prefers the term 'observe' (שמור, v. 12), which has a wide meaning and can mean simply 'keep' but is frequently used to denote the observance of covenant obligations (e.g. 4:2, 6, 40; 5:1, 10, 29; 6:2, 17; 7:11; 13:4; 16:1). The word 'remember' may have been avoided here because of its use with a different meaning in verse 15. The Deuteronomic version inserts twice its characteristic refrain '[as] the LORD your God has commanded you' (vv. 12 and 15; cf. 4:5; 5:16, 32, 33; 6:17, 25; 13:5; 20:17; 26:13, 14; 28:45). It also gives greater emphasis to the sabbath as a day of rest for slaves and working animals (v. 14), to avoid any risk that free Israelites might think they alone are entitled to the benefits of membership in the covenant community, though it should be noted that Exodus does emphasise this point in a separate law (23:12).[15] The expression 'as you do' is significant in granting equal rights to all human beings with respect to this weekly holiday.[16]

---

14. The reference to livestock is expanded in Deuteronomy so that a total of nine groups is mentioned: six human and three animal.
15. Cf. below, 11.1.c.
16. Wolff (1973: 139-40).

The Exodus commandment ends with a statement of its theological basis, namely the imitation of God (v. 11; cf. 31:17). As God rested after his six days' work of creation, and blessed the seventh day, so human beings are to consider the seventh day holy (cf. Gen 2:2-3). The sabbath is 'built into the very structure of the universe'.[17] However, it is distinct from all other festivals and seasons, which occur in relation to the sun (yearly) and moon (monthly), because it creates an independent rhythm of its own (weekly).

Deuteronomy 5:15 also gives a theological basis for the commandment, but it is quite different. The stated reason is remembrance of the exodus from Egypt, though the connection of this with sabbath observance is not immediately clear. The same reason is given elsewhere for freeing slaves in the seventh year (15:15), and caring for widows, orphans, and resident aliens (24:18, 22). In view of the specific mention of slaves and resident aliens in the sabbath law (v. 14), it seems that the intention is to remind Israel of their previous hardship as slaves in a foreign land and to encourage them to care for those in their own land who suffer similar hardships, in particular by allowing them regular time for rest and worship.[18] The same reason is given for celebrating the festival of Weeks (16:12), which also specifically includes these vulnerable people in the occasion.

On the one hand, Exodus explains why the sabbath is a holy day on the basis of the story of creation; on the other, Deuteronomy is concerned with why the sabbath is to be kept on the basis of the story of salvation. The former directs attention to the God of the covenant, the latter to the people of the covenant. These different theological bases for the sabbath are complementary, not contradictory.[19]

---

17. Childs (1974: 416); cf. Sarna (1991).

18. Cf. Driver (1902); Sarna (1991); Tigay (1996); Christensen (2001); Biddle (2003); Kahn (2004); contra Childs (1974: 417), who argues that the concern of the Deuteronomist is theological, not humanitarian: Israel is commanded to observe the sabbath in order to remember her own deliverance from slavery.

19. I do not enter here into the debates on the origin of the sabbath and on the Hebrew terminology, nor wider questions of its significance for ancient Israel and in the Old Testament. For further discussion of these matters, see Lewy (1942); North (1955a); Jenni (1956); de Vaux (1961: 475-83); Andreasen (1972; 1974b); Tsevat (1972); Negretti (1973); Hallo (1977); Siker-Gieseler (1981); Dressler (1982); Robinson (1980; 1988); Hasel (1992); Haag (1993); Bosman (1997).

c. Book of the Covenant

Six days you shall do your work, but on the seventh day you shall stop; so that your ox and your donkey may rest, and your homeborn slave[20] *and the resident alien may catch their breath.*[21]

Exod 23:12

This repetition of the fourth commandment, between the institution of the sabbatical year (vv. 10-11) and the annual festivals (vv. 14-17), focuses on the weekly pattern of work and rest. It emphasises that sabbath rest is to include slaves, resident aliens, and beasts of burden. A similar emphasis is found in the Deuteronomic version of the fourth commandment, which adds 'your ox or your donkey' to the list of beneficiaries of the sabbath, and also includes a clause stating the purpose of the institution: 'so that your male or female slave may rest as you do' (Deut 5:14). The 'homeborn slave' would be a permanent slave, whose parents had also been slaves, and of relatively low status, so this qualification probably means that even homeborn slaves are allowed to rest. Other chattel slaves and temporary slaves would no doubt be included in the sabbath rest as well. The distinctive closing verb, translated here as 'catch their breath', is also used of God's rest on the seventh day after completing the creation of the world (Exod 31:17).[22]

Outside the Book of the Covenant, there are several other passages in Exodus that deal with the sabbath. It is recounted how the provision of manna on the sixth day of the week was twice the normal amount to allow for rest on the seventh day (16:5, 22-30). A detailed law on the sabbath is recorded in the context of instructions for building the tabernacle, perhaps to emphasise that even the work of creating a place for worship was not important enough in the sight of God to override his principle of regular rest and refreshment (31:12-17). In this passage the sabbath is described as a sign of the covenant, a theme taken up later by the prophet Ezekiel (20:12, 20; cf. Isa 56:2, 4, 6; Jer 17:19-27), who decried the profaning of sabbath as

---

20. Lit. 'son of your maidservant/concubine'. Frey (2006: 5-7) suggests an allusion to Gen 21:10, 13.

21. So Durham (1987); cf. NJB; Cazelles (1946); lit. 'may take breath'. Several translations have 'may be refreshed' (NIV; NJPS; NRSV; Childs 1974; cf. REB). Cf. Akkadian *napāšu*, 'breathe freely, relax' (*CAD* 11.1: 288-91).

22. The only other occurrence of ינפש in the Old Testament is in 2 Sam 16:14. Cassuto (1951) and Frey (2006: 4-5) suggest this verb alludes to the 'soul' (נפש) of a resident alien in v. 9 (translated above as 'how it feels to be [a resident alien]': see 7.1.c).

rebellion against God (20:13, 16, 21, 24; 22:8, 26; cf. Neh 13:17-18). There are also two brief laws on sabbath observance in later chapters of Exodus (34:21; 35:2-3).

d. Deuteronomic Laws

> *You shall rejoice before the* LORD *your God — you, and your sons and your daughters, and your male and female slaves; and the Levites who [are] in your towns, because they have no portion or inheritance among you.*
>
> Deut 12:12

> *You shall eat them[23] before the* LORD *your God, in the place which the* LORD *your God chooses, you, and your son and your daughter, and your male and female slave, and the Levite who [is] in your town; and you shall rejoice before the* LORD *your God in everything you put your hand to.*
>
> Deut 12:18

> *You shall rejoice before the* LORD *your God — you, and your son and your daughter, and your male and female slave, and the Levite who [is] in your town, and the resident alien and the orphan and the widow who [are] in your midst — in the place which the* LORD *your God chooses as a dwelling for his name.*
>
> Deut 16:11

> *You shall rejoice in your festival — you, and your son and your daughter, and your male and female slave, and the Levite, and the resident alien and the orphan and the widow who [are] in your town.*
>
> Deut 16:14

> *You shall rejoice in all the good [things] that the* LORD *your God has given to you and to your household — you, and the Levite, and the resident alien who [is] in your midst.*
>
> Deut 26:11

---

23. Referring to the tithes of produce, firstborn of livestock, and offerings described in the previous verse.

As the texts above show clearly, the Deuteronomic Laws emphasise that the whole community is to be involved in celebrating holidays and festivals: male and female, old and young, slave and free, clergy and laity, native-born and resident alien. In every case there is an emphasis on rejoicing, which includes both worship of God and a hearty communal meal (see also 12:7; 14:23, 26; 15:20; 27:7).[24] Whereas Leviticus focuses primarily on the religious significance of sacrifices and festivals, Deuteronomy is particularly concerned with their social benefits.[25] Holidays are not only for the elite, but to be enjoyed by slaves and other marginal people such as resident aliens, orphans, and widows. There is a particular concern for the Levites in outlying towns, who have no allotment of agricultural land (10:9; 18:1-2) and are dependent on the generosity of others for their livelihood (cf. 12:19; 14:27, 29; 26:12), unlike the levitical priests at the central sanctuary who are provided for in the sacrificial system (18:1-8).

The specific celebrations mentioned are the bringing of firstfruits of the harvest (26:1-11); tithes of produce, firstborn of livestock, and other offerings (12:10-12, 17-18); and the festivals of Weeks (16:9-12) and Booths (16:13-15). Sabbath has already been covered in some detail in the Decalogue, as a holiday for everyone, including underprivileged members of the household. The main celebration which does not include specific reference to marginal people is Passover (16:1-8), though it is evident from the institution of this festival in Exodus that it was intended to include all members of the covenant community (12:3, 47; cf. Num 9:10-13), including resident aliens and household slaves so long as they have been circumcised (Exod 12:19, 44, 48-49; cf. Num 9:14). This omission may be explained by the different character of Passover as a solemn remembrance of the founding of the nation, compared with the joy and celebration which characterise the festivals of Weeks and Booths. For the former it was assumed that all who identified themselves as Israelites would take part in the occasion, whereas for the latter it was felt important to emphasise that such times of celebration are to be enjoyed by all members of society.[26]

---

24. Cf. Lev 23:40; Num 10:10; Neh 8:17; Ps 16:11; 27:6; 42:4; 63:5; Isa 9:3; 30:29; Hos 2:11. For a discussion of eating and drinking as a component of rejoicing in the Lord, see Anderson (1991: 19-26).

25. Weinfeld (1972a: 210-24).

26. Van Houten (1991: 88-91). The Day of Atonement is also a day of rest for the whole community, including resident aliens, but observed as a fast rather than a feast (Lev 16:29). This solemn day is called a 'sabbath of complete rest' (שבת שבתון, v. 31), and its function is purely religious (v. 30).

e. Conclusion

The sabbath is unique in the ancient Near East. Elsewhere times and seasons are reckoned on the basis of solar and lunar phases, but in Israel the most important institution of all is independent of the natural order. It is based simply on the command of God, and therefore denoted 'sabbath to the Lord'. All the major law collections deal with the sabbath, and it stands at the head of the calendar of festivals in Leviticus 23.[27]

Two main purposes are stated for sabbath observance. First, it is a holy day, dedicated to God, and so has a religious function. From this perspective, the cessation of work ensures that no one is distracted from divine worship by other activities. Second, it is a holiday, providing rest and refreshment for tired workers, and so has a social function. Looked at in this way, work is stopped so that all may take a break from their labours and be renewed for the coming week. This aspect is designed primarily for the benefit of the poor, who need to work to earn a living or are forced to do so because of their status as slaves, rather than the wealthy who are free to choose when they work and how much time they spend on leisure activities. Because of this, the sabbath has been described as 'perhaps . . . the greatest social revolution in the history of mankind'.[28]

Several texts indicate that the death penalty was standard for breaking the sabbath rule, as for most of the Ten Commandments, which is an indication of how seriously this institution was taken in ancient Israel (Exod 31:14; 35:2; Num 15:32-36). The fourth commandment is the longest in the Decalogue, perhaps because it is so distinctive and therefore required explanation and justification to persuade people to keep it. However, it is noteworthy that it is one of only two commandments which are formulated positively, and this may suggest that the intended emphasis is on celebration rather than abstinence, joy rather than duty (cf. Isa 58:13-14).[29]

---

27. This important chapter is not discussed here, because its focus is entirely religious and it does not deal with the social implications of the festivals.

28. Eder (2006: 108).

29. Some scholars have argued that the fourth commandment was originally phrased negatively, but this is little more than speculation based on an assumption that the original form of the Decalogue was ten uniform, brief prohibitions (cf. Baker 2005b: 11-14). Most of the other sabbath laws are also phrased positively, emphasising the observance of sabbath as a day of rest rather than prohibition of work (e.g. Exod 23:12; 31:12-17; 34:21; Lev 19:3, 30). In any case, it makes more sense to begin positively with the pattern of six days' work followed

Exactly what is meant by the 'work' (מלאכה) which is prohibited is not specified, but elsewhere it is understood to include gathering and preparing food (Exod 16:22-30; but cf. 12:16), ploughing and harvesting (Exod 34:21), gathering wood and lighting fires (Exod 35:3; Num 15:32-36), shopping (Neh 10:31), and transporting goods (Jer 17:21, 24, 27). In the eighth century, we read of traders who were anxious for the sabbath to end so that they could get back to their business (Amos 8:5). By the time of Nehemiah, people in Judah were treading winepresses and holding markets on the sabbath (Neh 13:15-18; cf. Isa. 58:3). No doubt they would have liked today's 24/7 shopping culture!

Several fifth-century Aramaic documents refer to the sabbath or other Jewish holidays. For example, one of the Elephantine ostraca is a letter referring to the delivery of vegetables, apparently to take place on the sabbath. It is likely that the boatman would have been Egyptian and so does not prove that Jews themselves were breaking the sabbath at this time, though it would still go against the principle of allowing employees to rest.[30] The so-called 'Passover Papyrus' from Elephantine consists of a letter dated 419 B.C. instructing Jedaniah and his colleagues to observe the festivals of Passover and Unleavened Bread.[31] The celebration of Passover is also mentioned in an informal family letter from about 475 B.C.[32]

It is evident from the biblical laws examined above that both the weekly sabbath and the annual festivals are intended for the well-being of all members of the covenant community, alongside their primary purpose of facilitating the worship of God. There is a clear contrast in this matter between Israel and other parts of the ancient Near East. Although people would presumably have stopped work for the purpose of religious observance, no extant law collection outside the Old Testament actually legislates for holidays. Without such legislation, it is likely that many poor peo-

---

by one day's rest, rather than by simply prohibiting work on the sabbath day without an explanation of what that day is intended to be (cf. Phillips 1970: 66).

30. *COS* (3.87G). Differently, Lindenberger (2003: 50) translates the word בשבה as 'on account of the sabbath' and understands the letter to be instructing the recipient to arrive in good time to take the delivery before the sabbath begins. The sabbath day is also mentioned in several other Aramaic texts (Hasel 1992: 853; Lindenberger 2003: 44, 54). Another possible mention is in a seventh-century Hebrew letter found near Yavneh Yam, if לפני שבת is understood as 'before the sabbath' (*ANET*: 568); however, most translators understand the phrase here to mean 'before stopping [work]' (*COS*: 3.41; *KAI*: no. 200; Renz 1995: 317-19, 325; Lindenberger 2003: 110; Dobbs-Allsopp et al. 2005: 359, 362).

31. *COS* (3.46); *DOTT* (258-60); Lindenberger (2003: 61-62, 65-67).

32. Lindenberger (2003: 48).

ple would have continued to work while the wealthy enjoyed their celebrations, perhaps taking a short break to watch or join processions.[33]

11.2 Wages

One common way in which the rich exploit the poor is by unfair payment of wages. Sometimes the rate of pay is too low in the first place; other times the wages are paid late or subjected to unreasonable deductions.

a. Ancient Near East

Several ancient Near Eastern law collections refer to wages. The Laws of Eshnunna stipulate the standard rate of pay for harvesters and winnowers (§§7-8), donkey drivers and hired men (§§10-11), fullers (§14), and caregivers to children (§32). A hired man who accepts advance payment for harvesting but does not keep himself available to work at the required time is liable to pay a hefty fine (§9). Similarly, the Laws of Hammurabi lay down payments for agricultural labourers and ox drivers (§§257-58; cf. 271), herdsmen (§261), seasonal workers (§273), and various kinds of craftsmen (§274). Fees of doctors and veterinarians are specified in considerable detail, as well as professional liability in the event of a patient's death or serious injury (§§215-25; cf. LX §§f-i). Likewise rates of pay for builders (CH §228) and boatmen (LE §4; CH §§234, 239; cf. SLHF §5:37-44) are accompanied by detailed rules about compensation in the case of poor workmanship and negligence (LE §5; CH §§229-33, 235-38). There are also clauses in the Hittite Laws to fix wages for hired workers (§§150, 158) and smiths (§§160-61).[34]

The main concern in these laws appears to be the standardisation of wages and fees, in several cases supplemented by clarification of the

---

33. For discussions of the observance of the sabbath in Judaism, the relationship between the Old Testament sabbath and the Christian Sunday, and reflection on the relevance of these biblical institutions in today's world, see Heschel (1951a; 1951b); Rordorf (1962); Lee (1966); Jewett (1971); Bacchiocchi (1977; 1980); Lohfink (1977b: 203-21); Beckwith and Stott (1978); Carson (1982); Gordis (1982); Swartley (1983: 65-95); Moltmann (1985: 276-96); Eskenazi, Harrington, and Shea (1991); Ratzinger (1994); Sales (1994); Greene-McCreight (1995); Beckwith (1996: 10-50); Harrelson (1997: 67-77); Doering (1999); Lowery (2000: 79-152); Weiss (2003); Bockmuehl (2005); Brashler and Balentine (2005).

34. On remuneration for tenant farmers and shepherds, see above, 3.3.a.

worker's responsibility to do a satisfactory job. There is only one reference to the employer's responsibility with respect to payment of wages (CH §264), in a clause which seems to imply that an owner of livestock can only make a claim against a shepherd for default in his duties if he has paid his wages in full.[35]

b. Holiness Code

You shall not hold back the wage of a hired worker[36] till the next morning.

Lev 19:13b

This terse law is grouped with laws on gleaning (vv. 9-10), and theft and fraud (vv. 11a, 13a).[37] All three laws concern rights and responsibilities with respect to property:

- Landowners should be generous with their harvest, sharing it with the landless.
- The right to hold personal property should not be infringed by others.
- Wages should be paid promptly once work has been completed.

To withhold wages is an example of fraud, mentioned in the first half of the verse, since once wages have been earned they become the property of the worker. 'Fraud' is a strong word, with overtones of oppression and violence (cf. Deut 28:29, 33; 1 Sam 12:3-4; Ps 62:11; 72:4, 14; 103:6; Prov 14:31; Eccl 4:1; 5:8; Mic 2:2), indicating that unfair treatment of workers is by no means a trivial matter.[38]

---

35. Driver and Miles (1952: 456-57). For further discussion of the above-mentioned laws, see Driver and Miles (1952: 416-21, 425-35, 448-49, 453-54, 469-78); Yaron (1988: 224-26); Hoffner (1997: 209-10); cf. Johns (1904: 271-74). On contracts and other information relating to wages in the ancient Near East, see Sollberger (1965: text 72); Garelli (1969: 281-87); Dandama[y]ev (1987: 272-76); Dosch (1987: 232); Eyre (1987: 178-79, 201-03); Waetzoldt (1987).

36. Lit. 'the wage of a hired worker shall not spend the night with you'. Milgrom (2000: 1637-38) takes אתך ('with you') with שכיר ('hired worker') to mean 'your hired worker', but this phrase is not found elsewhere in the Old Testament, and it is more natural in this sentence to understand אתך as a qualification of the verb 'spend the night'.

37. On gleaning, see above, 9.2.b; on theft and fraud, see 2.1.d.

38. Cf. Milgrom (1976a: 98-102); Pons (1981: 67-83); Hanks (1983: 5-8); Gerstenberger (1988).

c. Deuteronomic Laws

> *You shall not defraud a hired worker, [one who is] poor and needy;*[39] *whether one of your brothers*[40] *or a resident alien who is in your land, in your town. You shall pay his wage on the same day, before the sun goes down, because he is poor, and his life is dependent on it.*[41] *Otherwise he may cry to the* LORD *against you, and you will be found guilty of sin.*
>
> Deut 24:14-15

The essence of this law is identical to that in Leviticus, though it is formulated positively and expanded substantially. In both traditions the law concerning prompt payment of wages to hired workers is linked with a prohibition of fraud or oppression. Deuteronomy adds the qualification 'poor and needy' to clarify the reason why hired workers should not be defrauded by delaying their wages, though not of course implying that fraud is permissible in other circumstances (v. 14a). It further emphasises that the rule applies to both Israelites and resident aliens (v. 14b). Next, the main point of the law is expressed positively — wages are to be paid at the end of the working day — and once again the worker's poverty is mentioned as the reason for this policy (v. 15a). The deadline for payment (sunset) is the same as that for returning a poor person's pledge stipulated in the preceding section (v. 13). Finally, there is a warning that oppressed workers, even though unable to do much about their plight on a human level, can 'cry to the LORD' and are assured of a hearing in the divine court (v. 15b; cf. Jas 5:4).[42]

---

39. The verb עשק ('defraud') is variously translated 'oppress' (ESV; RSV), 'take advantage of' (NIV), 'exploit' (NJB), or 'abuse' (NJPS). On the basis of a Qumran text, Craigie (1976) reads שׂכר ('wage') instead of שׂכיר ('hired worker'), yielding the translation: 'You shall not withhold the wage of the poor and needy' (cf. LXX; NRSV; REB; Christensen 2002). Although this is not impossible, it is unlikely because the verb עשק generally takes a person as object rather than a thing (cf. Talmon 1960: 154; Tigay 1996: 390 n. 50). There is actually no problem with MT and inadequate reason to emend it (cf. Mayes 1979).

40. I.e. fellow-Israelites.

41. Lit. 'he sets his life on it'.

42. Cf. Deut 15:9; also Exod 22:21-27 (on which, see above, 7.2.b).

d. Conclusion

There is neither commonality nor conflict between Old Testament and other ancient Near Eastern laws on the matter of wages, so they cannot be compared directly. One thing is clear, however: their emphases are quite different. The nonbiblical laws are concerned primarily with setting standard rates of pay, and compensation for employers if employees fail to work well; the biblical laws are concerned simply with prompt payment for workers. The one is interested in the rights of the [relatively rich] employer, whereas the other focuses on the rights of the [relatively poor] employee.

Prompt payment of wages is a very simple principle, which was assumed by Jesus (Matt 20:8; cf. Luke 10:7; 1 Tim 5:18) and is taken for granted by most people in prosperous countries today. There are of course situations where an employer in financial difficulty is genuinely unable to pay on time, and employees may well be able to accept this if there is genuine transparency on the issues. But that is not the situation addressed by the laws discussed above. Rather they are concerned for workers who are paid late without due cause, whether because of deliberate policy or simple inefficiency on the part of the employer (cf. Prov 3:27-28; Jer 22:13). Intentional or not, such a delay is effectively an unauthorised loan extracted by the wealthy from the poor. In ancient Israel — as in many places today — hired workers were among the poorest and weakest members of society, with no unions to demand their rights and no savings to keep them going through hard times (cf. Job 7:2). To take advantage of such people by withholding their wages is a serious offence, according to biblical law, which will not be ignored by God (cf. Mal 3:5; Tobit 4:14; Sirach 34:22; Jas 5:4).

11.3 Weights and Measures

As mentioned above (2.1.e), various kinds of indirect theft are condemned by Old Testament law. One of these is the manipulation of weights and measures by a seller in order to take advantage of a customer.

a. Ancient Near East

One of the political and economic reforms carried out by the Sumerian king Ur-Namma, according to the prologue to his laws, was the standardisation of weights and measures (lines 135-49).[43] There are also two clauses in the Laws of Hammurabi dealing with this matter:

> If a merchant gives grain or silver as an interest-bearing loan and when he gives it as an interest-bearing loan he gives the silver according to the small weight or the grain according to the small *sūtu*-measure but when he receives payment he receives the silver according to the large weight or the grain according to the large *sūtu*-measure, [that merchant] shall forfeit [anything that he gave]. (§ gap x)
>
> If a tapster should refuse to accept grain for the price of beer but accepts [only] silver measured by the large weight, thereby reducing the value of beer in relation to the value of grain, they shall charge and convict that tapster and they shall cast her into the water. (§108)

In each case the concern is evidently to protect anyone involved in trade from cheating by unscrupulous dealers. Various standards for weights and measures were used in ancient Babylonia, and traders were expected to apply them fairly. Dishonesty in business dealing, such as deceiving a customer in quantities of goods supplied, was considered a serious offence.[44]

These are the only references to justice in weights and measures in the law collections, but it is also a matter of concern in wisdom literature. For example, the Babylonian hymn to Shamash, god of justice, contrasts at length the honest merchant who uses balances fairly and the trickster who uses different sets of weights for buying and selling, for making loans and demanding repayment.[45] Similarly, the Egyptian Amenemope advises: 'Do not move the scales nor alter the weights, nor diminish the fractions of the

---

43. An Ur III text implies that standardisation of weights also took place at the beginning of the reign of Amar-Sin, Ur-Namma's grandson (Finkel 1987).

44. For detailed discussion of these clauses in the Laws of Hammurabi, see Driver and Miles (1952: 148, 180-84, 202-5). According to Saggs (1988: 250), roguery was forestalled in some contracts by including a regulation that payment should be made according to a particular standard. For a very thorough study of weights and measures in Mesopotamia, see Powell (1990). A briefer survey is provided by Postgate (1976: 63-72).

45. Lines 107-21 (*BWL:* 132-33; *COS:* 1.117; *DOTT:* 109). Cf. the hymn to Nanshe lines 142-43 (*COS:* 1.162; Heimpel 1981: 90-91); and the Shurpu incantations tablets 2:37, 42-43 and 8:64-67 (Reiner 1958). There is also a Sumerian proverb which appears to express the complaint of a housewife over being cheated in the marketplace (Gordon 1959: 1.165), and another which implies that merchants tend to use scales to their own advantage (Civil 1976: 74).

measure';[46] and the 'Negative Confession' in the Book of the Dead assures the Lord of Justice that the reciter has done no such thing.[47]

b. Holiness Code

You shall not act corruptly[48] in judging [measures],[49] whether of length, weight, or capacity.[50] Fair scales, fair weights, a fair ephah, and a fair hin — that is what you shall have. I am the LORD *your God, who brought you out of the land of Egypt.*

Lev 19:35-36

The general prohibition of judicial corruption in verse 15, where it refers to lawsuits, is here repeated with reference to business ethics (v. 35). In the everyday activities of buying and selling, everything must be just right (צדק, here translated 'fair'): scales and weights, dry and liquid measures (v. 36a). It is not primarily a matter of instrumental accuracy, but of refusing the common ploy in unregulated markets of increasing profits by using non-standard measures without informing the customer. This too has a theological basis, in the nature of God, who saved his people from unfair treatment as slaves in Egypt and expects them to treat each other fairly (v. 36b; cf. Exod 20:2; Lev 25:38; 26:13; Num 15:41). He has made it possible for Israel to live and work in the promised land, free from foreign oppression, and it would be a grave misuse of this freedom to oppress others. This law is quite general, with no reference to a 'brother' or 'neighbour', so it may be assumed that it is intended to cover dealings with fellow-members of the covenant community and also with outsiders.

46. Chapter 16, expanded in chapter 17 (*COS*: 1.47 lines xvii.17-19; xviii.15-xix.7; *DOTT*: 182).
47. Chapter 125 (*ANET*: 34 lines A22-26; *COS*: 2.12 p. 60).
48. On the meaning of עול, see above: ch. 8 n. 46.
49. Lit. 'in judgement'.
50. So most translations, though Milgrom (2000: 1595, 1708-9), following an unpublished Hebrew dissertation by Schwartz which argues that מדה is a general term for all measures, proposes: '. . . in judgement, [namely,] in measures of weight or capacity'. In support of this proposal, it may be noted that both v. 36 and the expansion of the law in Deut 25:13-15 refer to measures of weight and capacity but not to length. Nevertheless, use of the word מדה elsewhere suggests that it refers to length and breadth, rather than weight or capacity (e.g. Exod 26:2, 8; 36:9, 15; Josh 3:4; Jer 31:9; Ezek 40:20-21; 41:13). Also, the syntax of this verse in Hebrew suggests three items in sequence rather than two. I therefore follow the conventional translation here.

c. Deuteronomic Laws

> *You shall not have in your bag differing weights*[51], *large and small. You shall not have in your house differing measures*[52], *large and small. A full and fair weight is what you shall have, and a full and fair measure is what you shall have, so that your days may be long in the land which the* LORD *your God is giving to you. For anyone doing these things, anyone acting corruptly, is an abomination to the* LORD *your God.*
>
> Deut 25:13-16

This appears to be an expansion of the shorter law in the Holiness Code, taking up the key phrases 'fair weight', 'fair ephah/measure', 'is what you shall have', and 'acting corruptly'.[53] The Deuteronomic version may also have been influenced by ancient Israelite proverbs, as suggested by the terms 'bag' (cf. Prov 16:11), 'differing weights' and 'differing measures' (cf. Prov 20:10, 23), 'full weight' (cf. Prov 11:1), and 'abomination to the LORD' (cf. Prov 11:1; 20:10, 23).[54]

Deuteronomy makes the same point as Leviticus but in greater detail, prohibiting the use of differing weights and measures for buying and selling (vv. 13-14) and insisting on one standard for both (v. 15a). In fact the text goes further, because it is not only the use of false weights and measures which is outlawed but even possession of such means of deception (cf. *Sifre* 294). The standards are to be 'full and fair', both adjectives that have theological overtones. The former (שׁלמה) includes the ideas of wholeness, prosperity, and peace; the latter (צדק) denotes righteousness and justice.

Finally, two theological incentives are provided for keeping the law. Positively, the covenant people are assured that honesty in trading will lead to longevity in the promised land (v. 15b), as promised earlier to all who obey God's commandments (4:40; 5:33; 6:1-2), especially those who honour their parents (5:16) and practise justice (16:20). Negatively, corruption is abhorrent to God, and it follows that people who act dishon-

---

51. Lit. 'stone and stone' or 'weight and weight'.
52. Lit. 'ephah and ephah' or 'measure and measure'.
53. Milgrom (2000: 1707).
54. Cf. Weinfeld (1972a: 265-69). Carmichael (1967; 1974: 241-43) also sees wisdom influence in this passage, and argues further — though much less convincingly — for a link with the just and careful provision of manna in Exod 16.

estly will have to face his judgement (v. 16), like those who indulge in idolatry, child sacrifice, and magic (7:25-26; 12:31; 13:14; 17:4; 18:9-12; 20:18; 27:15; cf. 4:25-26).[55]

d. Conclusion

The principle of fair dealing in matters of weights and measures was clearly recognised in the common law and wisdom of the ancient Near East, so the Old Testament is not innovating here. The point of the law is not to say something new, but to emphasise the importance of a principle that was widely ignored in ancient Israel according to the prophets — at least in the eighth century (Hos 12:7; Amos 8:5; Mic 6:10-11). The same principle is affirmed in the wisdom literature, where false weights and measures are castigated as an 'abomination to the LORD' as in Deuteronomy (Prov 11:1; 20:10, 23; cf. 16:11). It also reappears in the shape of a law in Ezekiel 45:10, which quotes Leviticus 19:36 and adds a new measure: 'Fair scales, and a fair ephah, and a fair bath — that is what you shall have.' The following verses clarify that the bath and ephah are in fact the same, standardised at one tenth of a homer (v. 11), and stipulate the ratio between a gerah, a shekel, and a mina (v. 12).

Several hundred inscribed weights from ancient Judah have been found by archaeologists and have been the subject of detailed study. The recent work of Kletter (1991; 1998) concludes that they indicate the existence of a standard system for weights based on a shekel of about 11.33 grams, probably equivalent to the ordinary shekel of the Old Testament rather than the sanctuary shekel (Exod 30:13, 24). This contrasts with the view of earlier scholars, who argued for the existence of several different standards.[56]

In many developing countries, there are still market-sellers who take advantage of customers by doctoring their scales or using nonstandard weights and measures which benefit their owner. At first sight this may seem quite outrageous to foreign visitors who expect consistent enforce-

---

55. On the term תועבה ('abomination'), and its significance in the Old Testament against its ancient Near Eastern background, see Humbert (1960); L'Hour (1964); Hallo (1985); Grisanti (1997).

56. Especially Scott (1959a; 1959b; 1964; 1965; 1970; 1985). On weights and measures in ancient Israel, see further COS (2.81); DOTT (227-30); de Vaux (1961: 195-209); Sellers (1962); Powell (1992); Goldstein et al. (2001); Röllig (2003); Dobbs-Allsopp et al. (2005: 623-38).

ment of trading standards. However, a closer look at marketing tactics in 'developed' countries shows that there is no reason for complacency. For example, a great deal of modern advertising and packaging is designed to make potential customers think the product on sale is bigger and better than it really is, even if nothing is said or written that is strictly inaccurate. Though not a literal breaking of the biblical law on weights and measures, the intention is similar. Worse still, in sourcing produce from poorer countries, multinational corporations and other powerful companies are in a position to exert enormous leverage on suppliers, forcing selling-prices far below 'fair' levels, often with disastrous consequences for the livelihood of local workers. In the light of this, it has been encouraging in the past few years to see the growth of the 'fair trade' movement, which aims to provide a better deal for producers and to encourage consumers to be more aware of the working conditions of those who produce the goods they purchase, though this is still a relatively small sector in the vast global markets of the third millennium.

Biblical law has something to say to all of these situations, from the individual trader who uses traditional weights and measures to the international business with sophisticated technology and thousands of employees. Whatever the scale, wherever the location, all forms of trade should be governed by the fundamental principle of justice.[57]

---

57. For current information, see the websites of the Fairtrade Foundation <www.fairtrade.org.uk> and the Trade Justice Movement <www.tjm.org.uk>. On business ethics, see the websites of the Institute for Business Ethics <www.ibe.org.uk>, the Jewish Association for Business Ethics <www.jabe.org>, and Transforming Business <www.transformingbusiness.net>. Another modern issue which merits consideration in the light of these laws is that of inflation, which may be seen as the creation of excess currency or credit beyond the real wealth of a country (Larkin 1982). The biblical laws assume payment in silver or goods, which are relatively stable in value, but a new issue arises when the value of the currency itself varies due to inflation or devaluation. This is particularly relevant when money takes the form of bank-notes or electronic transfers, where it is possible to create extra money by simply printing more of it. This effectively reduces the value of the currency, and therefore infringes the principle of justice in buying and selling. It is particularly serious for the poor who live at subsistence level, and the elderly who rely on their savings for retirement income.

Chapter 12

CONCLUSION

From my own perspective, this study has proved even more enlightening than expected. As I have examined the Old Testament laws relating to wealth and poverty in their ancient Near Eastern context, it has become clear that they are not only of interest in themselves, but express principles which are fundamental in other parts of the Old Testament too. Many of them are assumed or developed further by New Testament and rabbinic writers, and by other thinkers throughout the centuries. There is a great deal which is of practical relevance to economic and social problems today and has the potential to encourage and challenge those who are trying in different ways to mend our damaged world. Although detailed study of practical implications has not been possible within the scope of this book, at various points I have given pointers to their ongoing theological and ethical significance.

To conclude, it remains to draw out the key similarities between Old Testament and other ancient Near Eastern laws, followed by an outline of the distinctive features of Old Testament law. As will quickly become apparent, the differences far outnumber the similarities. Finally, I will summarise some of the theological and ethical implications of the study, relating to each of the three major themes covered: property and land, marginal people, justice and generosity.

12.1 Biblical Law in Its Ancient Near Eastern Context

a. Similarities

Although it is doubtful whether the compilers of the Old Testament laws were familiar with the Mesopotamian and Hittite law collections as such, it is likely that they were aware of legal principles common throughout the ancient Near East.

(1) For example, it is generally accepted that owners are entitled to protection from theft or damage to their *property*. In the case of theft, punishment is stipulated, as well as replacement of the stolen goods. In the case of damage, the person responsible is required to make good any loss, which includes indirect responsibility laid on the owner of an uncontrolled animal or unsafe structure, or someone who carelessly allows damage by fire or flood. The same applies if loss or damage occurs when someone entrusts his property to another for safekeeping, borrowing, rental, or in the course of employment. Two further property matters have parallels in other ancient Near Eastern law. With respect to lost property, the finder is expected to return it to the owner, and failure to do this is considered equivalent to stealing. Concerning boundary markers, the violation of land boundaries is treated as a serious offence, also in the category of theft.

(2) On the borderline between the laws of property and those of persons is the institution of *slavery*. The existence of chattel slavery is taken for granted in Old Testament, as elsewhere in the ancient Near East, and readers today often wonder why it is not more clearly condemned. While the kidnapping of free citizens is illegal, war captives are enslaved, and other slaves are bought and sold, given and inherited, and their children become slaves as well. These practices are only true of chattel slaves, however, in contrast to temporary slaves who work for a limited period of service, probably with somewhat better terms and conditions, and whose status is more like that of bonded labourers.

(3) A healthy community requires *justice* in the legal system, so attempts to undermine this — for instance by giving false testimony — are punished. Fair dealing is also important for a stable trading economy, and the need for honesty in weights and measures is recognised in the common law and wisdom of the ancient Near East, so the Old Testament instructions on this matter are simply reminding people of a principle that was well-enough known but frequently ignored in practice.

b. Differences

Alongside the basic similarities with other ancient Near Eastern laws mentioned above, there are many distinctive features of Old Testament law.

(1) The penalties for infringing *property rights* in the Bible are much more humane than elsewhere, and never involve mutilation, beating, or death. In the case of theft, the culprit is simply required to make multiple restitution to the person whose goods have been stolen. Another Old Testament distinctive is that one rule applies for all, whereas in some other laws the severity of the punishment depends on whose property is stolen as well as the social status or gender of the thief. The widespread principle of returning lost property to its owner is accepted, and taken a step further. Even enemies should be helped in this way, by returning their lost property and helping when their beast of burden is in difficulty. Moreover, in a law which has absolutely no parallel in the ancient Near East, the Decalogue extends the prohibition of theft into the thought-life of the covenant community, forbidding members even to think about depriving someone else of their legitimate possessions.

(2) The Old Testament laws on *owner liability* for animals and buildings are distinctive when it comes to loss of another person's life. Whereas the Mesopotamian laws deal with the economic aspect, and provide compensation for the victim's family, biblical law is concerned first of all with bloodguilt, because human life is of inestimable value. A goring ox must therefore be stoned, and its owner is also to be executed if there is evidence of culpable negligence. Another distinctive feature is seen in the regulations of the Book of the Covenant for loaning animals to the poor without charge, a matter which is not even mentioned in the other laws with their extensive treatment of rental.

(3) According to the Old Testament, *ancestral land* is God's gift to his chosen people, allocated equitably to each one of them. This sacred inheritance is to be enjoyed, preserved, and passed on to one's descendants. In the jubilee year anyone who has lost ancestral land is to receive it back, while bonded labourers are to regain their freedom and return home. Such reforms are known to have occurred elsewhere on an occasional basis, but the idea of practising them every fifty years is distinctive to Israel. Restoration of land is to take place on a regular cycle, irrespective of political or economic convenience. There is a clear contrast here with Old Babylonian and Middle Assyrian law, where land belongs to the king. He may grant a portion of land to a subject in return for an obligation of service, but in the

event of failure to render that service — whether deliberately or because of capture in battle — the land reverts to the crown.

(4) Although *chattel slavery* is not abolished completely in the Old Testament, it is limited to non-Israelites and the laws provide significant protection for slaves. For example, masters must not abuse their slaves, fugitive slaves are to be given asylum rather than returned to their masters, and slaves are entitled to holidays. Elsewhere in the ancient Near East slaves are subject to property law, which focuses on the rights of slave-owners over their property. In Israel the slaves themselves have rights, and the laws are concerned with the slave as a person, emphasising compassion for someone in a vulnerable position.

(5) There are several distinctive features of Old Testament law concerning *semi-slaves*. For example, temporary slaves are given the option of becoming permanent members of the household at the end of their six years' service, implying that slaves are to be looked after so well that they might prefer to continue in that status rather than claim their freedom. If they do choose freedom, however, they are to be provided with capital to enable a successful return to an independent life. Another possibility for paying off a debt is bonded labour, also for a limited term, made realistic by the Old Testament policy of interest-free loans. Elsewhere high interest rates would often mean that bonded labour merely covered interest payments and resulted in lifelong bondage for unfortunate debtors. Concubines, too, are given a degree of protection in the biblical laws and entitled to some of the rights of a wife or daughter, including conjugal rights in the case of the former. If a prisoner of war becomes a concubine, she is to be treated kindly and allowed time to mourn her parents before taking on this role. If a master wants to end the relationship with his concubine, he may not sell her as a slave but must grant her freedom. This kindness towards concubines is in notable contrast to their utilitarian treatment in Mesopotamia.

(6) In principle, the protection of *vulnerable people* in the ancient Near East is considered to be the divine will and a royal responsibility. In practice, however, the legal rights of widows and orphans are quite limited, whereas Old Testament law is more concerned to ensure that widows and orphans are not abused, nor exploited in law courts or financial dealings. They are also beneficiaries of several other laws, especially those on gleaning, the triennial tithe, and celebrations. Old Testament law also reflects a concern for ethnic minorities within the covenant community, not found in the other law collections, on the basis of Israel's own experience as slaves in a foreign land.

(7) Biblical law also has distinctive emphases in relation to *just lawsuits*. While the principle of impartiality may well have been assumed elsewhere, it is only explicitly stated in the biblical law collections. This principle is particularly important for the poor, since it is most often the wealthy who have the resources to influence judges and courts in their favour. However, partiality towards the poor is also forbidden. Justice must be administered impartially to all, without exception. On the matter of bribery, Old Testament law is also distinctive in its categorical prohibition of all payments to judges. Elsewhere it was common for judges to receive fees and gifts, which was not considered improper unless intended to pervert the course of justice, but in practice that would be difficult to prove and such payments would inevitably influence those who received them.

(8) Another Old Testament distinctive is the idea that *agricultural produce* is God's gift to his people, to be shared with all. This is made specific in several laws for the benefit of the poor, concerning the sabbatical year, gleaning, the triennial tithe, and 'scrumping'. In other parts of the ancient Near East, fallowing takes place for agricultural purposes and tithes are paid to palace or temple, but neither of these practices is designed as social welfare. The biblical laws on gleaning and 'scrumping' are unique, having no parallel elsewhere. However, it is probable that these harvest laws were not intended as strict legislation to be enforced in court, but rather as a reminder to the covenant community that they live on the land and enjoy its crops by the grace of God. They should therefore be generous to others just as the ultimate Owner of the land has been to his tenants.

(9) There is a marked contrast between the laws of the ancient Near East and those of the Old Testament on the subject of *loans*. Mesopotamian law is concerned with standardising rates of interest, assumed to be the right of a lender; whereas Israelite law forbids interest on loans to fellow-members of the covenant community, especially the poor. While all the laws assume the principle of security for loans, Exodus and Deuteronomy are more concerned with the needs of the poor who borrow than the rights of the rich who lend. A pledge is allowed so long as it does not cause hardship to the borrower but — since the poor are likely to own very little that they do not need — this law virtually eliminates security in practice. The biblical laws do not even contemplate the surrender of a family member or ancestral land as a pledge, which is common in other ancient Near Eastern laws, probably because persons and land are productive assets, so that to hold them as security would be equivalent to taking interest. There is Babylonian evidence for occasional debt relief, in the context of eco-

nomic and judicial reform, but the Deuteronomic law is distinctive in requiring remission of debts on a regular basis, every seventh year.

(10) Finally, the brief Old Testament laws on terms and conditions for *employment* are unparalleled in the other law collections. The concept of sabbath is unique in the ancient Near East, both in its independence of lunar and solar cycles, and in its emphasis that regular rest and recreation is a fundamental right for all — including slaves, resident aliens, and livestock. The same emphasis is clear in connection with several other biblical festivals. Although people elsewhere would no doubt have stopped work for religious observances, no other law collection specifically legislates for holidays. There is also a contrast in the laws on wages, between the extrabiblical laws, which seem designed primarily to protect the rights of employers, and the biblical laws, which are more concerned with the right of employees to prompt payment for their work.

12.2 Theological and Ethical Implications

a. Property and Land

The ownership of property is obviously a key issue in politics and economics, whether in feudalism, capitalism, or communism. Although the Bible does not discuss the issue at length, there are two clear implications from the theft laws. First, property ownership is a divinely given right and responsibility, and therefore members of the covenant community may not deprive someone else of their personal property. Second, the Bible values human life much more highly than material possessions, and as a result offences against property are punished less severely than those against the life and dignity of other people. The former are dealt with by compensation to the victim, whereas offences against persons are punished physically in proportion to the seriousness of the crime, often with the death penalty. This distinction applies both to direct offences such as theft and murder and to indirect ones caused by negligence.

Most societies have laws and customs relating to the ownership of land, and ancient Israel was no exception. The Old Testament laws are based on the conviction that the land belongs to God, who has entrusted it to his chosen people. They live in this land as stewards or tenants, not owners, and therefore have no right to sell it to others. In case of need, the law allows landholders to lease a plot to someone else until the jubilee year, but at that point it must revert to the original holder or his descendants. How far the jubilee year was observed in practice is uncertain, but its values were not forgotten. Naboth was aware of his right to hold onto ancestral land, and Isaiah uses jubilee images to challenge and encourage his hearers. A related matter is the Old Testament's generous attitude to exemption from military service, which emphasises that participation in warfare should be undertaken willingly. In some circumstances, responsibilities related to ancestral land take precedence over the responsibility to serve one's country, specifically for those who are involved in building houses, planting vineyards, and getting married.

Those who are privileged to own property have responsibilities as well as rights. For example, community members are expected to help others in need by lending an animal without making a profit, just as they are expected to lend money without interest to a needy person. Other ancient Near Eastern laws are commercial in orientation, specifying conditions for renting out animals and lending money at interest, so that the owner's rights are protected. In contrast, biblical law emphasises compassion, encouraging positive action to supply the needs of the poor rather than simply fulfilling minimal legal requirements. People of God should take the initiative to help others, whether or not they deserve it, as expressed by the principle of loving one's neighbour as oneself.

Nevertheless, even good deeds are not sufficient to keep the law perfectly. The tenth commandment takes us beyond visible action to consider our thoughts, with a reminder that God is concerned with the whole of human life, including areas which are invisible to others. In relation to wealth and poverty, this commandment points to the dangers of greed, advocating contentment and gratitude. Many methods used by the powerful to enrich themselves at the expense of others may not be technically illegal, but they are unacceptable because they derive from covetous ambitions or self-interest. The nature of the covenant community requires that members focus their attention not on their own prosperity but on the worship of God and service of neighbour.

b. Marginal People

Old Testament tradition portrays the origin of Israel as a people who have experienced famine in their own land, followed by marginalisation and eventually slavery in a foreign country, and who therefore should be sympathetic to others in a similar position. As God has shown mercy to them, they must be merciful to others. It is characteristic of Old Testament law to benefit those at the margins of society rather than the wealthy and powerful. For example, a fugitive slave is invited to choose a place to live in the land of Israel and given protection from his master. Resident aliens are integrated into the covenant community, and are to be loved like Israelites, imitating God's love for vulnerable people. In a close-knit community like ancient Israel it would be easy for a newcomer to feel marginalised, so compassion for strangers is repeatedly emphasised in the laws, even more frequently than love of God and observance of the sabbath. Such laws do not originate from a struggle between competing interest groups, as claimed by some scholars, since they protect those without the social influence to have laws produced for their benefit. Old Testament laws are designed not for the benefit of the lawmaker but for that of the whole covenant community.

Israel's memory of slavery is inextricably linked with the conviction that God has freed his chosen people from this desperate situation, and it follows from this that slavery is strongly discouraged in the covenant community. Those whom God has liberated are not to be enslaved again. If in exceptional circumstances no other way can be found to pay off a debt, temporary slavery and bonded labour may be permitted, so long as it is strictly limited in term, with conditions like those of an employee. Compared with today's world, where slavery is illegal yet there are more slaves than at any other time in history, it is arguable that Old Testament law is simply being realistic. Rather than outlawing the institution of slavery completely, it establishes various principles to ameliorate the condition of the poor and needy, emphasising the individual worth of every human being and treating slaves as persons rather than property. If all these principles had been practised consistently, slavery would probably have disappeared many centuries before Wilberforce.

The problem with many of these principles is that compassion cannot be enforced, since it is impractical to punish those who are not compassionate unless they can be proved to have broken a specific law. Even memory of his or her own suffering in the past is no guarantee that someone will spare others similar suffering in the present. Perhaps because of this, many laws are supplemented with a motive clause. Various motives are given, falling into two main categories: warnings of divine judgement on those who abuse the weak and fail to help the needy; and promises of divine blessing for those who treat others fairly and kindly. There is also a good deal of implicit motivation in the context, for example in the repeated assertions of the Holiness Code that the laws have divine authority ('The LORD spoke to Moses', 'I am the LORD', etc.) and the frequent exhortations of Deuteronomy to obedience, reminding the people that these laws are an integral part of their covenant with God and to ignore them would be disastrous for their relationship with him.

c. Justice and Generosity

Members of the covenant community are expected to give truthful testimony, with a reminder that — even if they can lie successfully in a human court — nothing is hidden from God. 'In the end truth will out.' The Old Testament also emphasises the importance of truth in the form of integrity in public life, particularly criticising religious leaders who take advantage of their respected position in society to propagate lies and half-truths. God is depicted as the source of justice, an impartial judge who is immune to bribery, who expects his delegates to implement his judicial policy with integrity. Justice and righteousness are absolutely fundamental for the health of the covenant community, so all attempts to pervert the legal system by means of wealth and influence are ruled out. Since the poor are unable to pay for justice, the prohibition of bribes and gifts to judges is essential to ensure just lawsuits for all.

In a predominantly agricultural society, the highlight of the year is harvest. It affects religion, with joyful celebrations at home and in sanctuaries; it also affects economics, with the price of grain and fruit peaking beforehand, then returning to normal. For those without land, however, there is little reason for rejoicing. Though prices may be lower than immediately before harvest, there is also less work available. So the biblical laws encourage landholders to be generous, sharing harvest blessings with less fortunate members of the community through regulations for the sabbatical year, gleaning, tithing, and 'scrumping'. In this way Israelites are reminded that they do not have absolute rights over the land and its produce, but have been privileged to live there by the divine owner and are dependent on him for its fertility. The use of the triennial tithe for social purposes is also a recognition that one way of serving God is to serve the poor. By means of this tithe, landholders acknowledge God as the giver of the land, while the landless receive a share in its produce — the 'holy portion' which in other years is given to God.

One of the most serious problems in ancient and modern societies is debt, and Old Testament law addresses this problem with several radical proposals. The prohibition of interest on loans has caused much debate throughout the ages and influenced the economic structures of both European and Islamic countries at different points in their history. Members of the covenant community with surplus resources are reminded that all they have comes from God, and surpluses should be used for the benefit of others rather than to enrich themselves further. So loans to the poor must always be interest-free, though this does not necessarily exclude the possibility of making a profit on business loans which provide capital for trade or investment. A pledge may be required only if it does not cause hardship to the borrower, and the poor must not be refused loans if they are unable to provide security. Regular debt relief should foster stability in the economy, and reduce the risk of people remaining in abject poverty. Unfortunately, as the eighth-century prophets make clear, such generosity on the part of the wealthy was the exception rather than the rule in ancient Israel, and the gap between rich and poor grew ever wider.

Employment rights do not feature in other ancient Near Eastern law collections, but the biblical laws include two important principles. The first is regular rest for all, following God's own example of resting on the seventh day of creation. Both the weekly sabbath and the annual festivals are intended to benefit everyone in the covenant community, alongside their primary purpose for divine worship. Even domestic animals are included, and the sabbatical year regulations extend it to the land as well. This is particularly significant for employees who do not have the freedom to determine their working conditions, and might otherwise be compelled to work without adequate breaks. However, it also applies to employers and the self-employed, who may need encouragement to take a break from their daily activities for their own good. The second principle is prompt payment, countering the reality that workers in many places are paid late without due cause, either because of deliberate policy or inefficiency. To take advantage of hired workers in this way, perhaps depending on their reluctance to protest for fear of losing their job, is serious wrongdoing according to the Bible. Similarly, for a merchant to take advantage of a customer by manipulating weights and measures is quite contrary to the fundamental principle of trade justice.

d. Postscript

> *You shall not be hard-hearted or tight-fisted toward your poor brother. Rather, open your hand generously to him.*
>
> Deut 15:7b-8a

Tight fists or open hands? Are property and land to be grasped and exploited to maximise profit, or enjoyed as the gift of God and shared with others? Are marginal people to be utilised or ignored, depending on their economic potential, or embraced as fellow-members of the community and enabled to live their lives to the full? Are justice and generosity the guiding principles of our economic activity, or greed and jealousy? The Old Testament laws on wealth and poverty leave us in no doubt about their vision for the life of the people of God. The Old Testament historians and prophets give us some idea of how far ancient Israel realised — and failed to realise — this vision. It remains for us to consider whether we are willing and able to make the vision a reality in the twenty-first century.

Bibliography

Aaron, David H. 2006. *Etched in Stone: The Emergence of the Decalogue.* New York: T. & T. Clark.

Abraham, Kathleen. 2001. 'The Middle Assyrian Period'. Pp. 161-221 in *SDANEL*.

Adamiak, Richard. 1985. *Justice and History in the Old Testament: The Evolution of Divine Retribution in the Historiographies of the Wilderness Generation.* 2nd ed. Cleveland: Zubal.

Aejmelaeus, Anneli. 1975. 'What Can We Know About the Hebrew *Vorlage* of the Septuagint?' *ZAW* 99:58-89.

Aharoni, Yohanan et al. 1975. *Arad Inscriptions.* Judean Desert Studies. Jerusalem: Israel Exploration Society, 1981. (trans. from Hebrew)

Albeck, Shalom. 1972. 'Lost Property'. *EncJud* 11:504-6.

———. 1985. 'The Ten Commandments and the Essence of Religious Faith'. Pp. 261-89 in *The Ten Commandments in History and Tradition,* ed. Ben-Zion Segal and Gershon Levi. Publications of the Perry Foundation for Biblical Research. Jerusalem: Magnes, 1990. (trans. from Hebrew)

Alcorn, Randy. 2003. *Money, Possessions, and Eternity.* Rev. ed. Wheaton: Tyndale House.

Alt, Albrecht. 1934. 'The Origins of Israelite Law'. Pp. 79-132 in *Essays on Old Testament History and Religion.* Oxford: Blackwell, 1966. (trans. from German)

———. 1949. 'Das Verbot des Diebstahls im Dekalog'. Pp. 333-40 in *Kleine Schriften zur Geschichte des Volkes Israel,* vol. 1. Munich: Beck, 1953. Repr. from unpublished paper.

———. 1952. 'Zu hitʿammēr'. *VT* 2:153-59.

Altman, Amnon. 2002. 'On Some Basic Concepts in the Law of People Seeking Refuge and Sustenance in the Ancient Near East'. *ZABR* 8:323-42.

Amit, Yairah. 1992. 'The Jubilee Law — An Attempt at Instituting Social Justice'. Pp. 47-59 in *Justice and Righteousness: Biblical Themes and Their Influence,* ed. Henning Graf Reventlow and Yair Hoffmann. JSOTSup 137. Sheffield: Sheffield Academic.

Amusin, Joseph D. 1981. 'Die Gerim in der sozialen Legislatur des *Alten Testaments*'. *Klio* 63:15-23.

Andersen, Francis I. 1969. 'Israelite Kinship Terminology and Social Structure'. *BT* 20:29-39.

Anderson, Cheryl B. 2004. *Women, Ideology, and Violence*. JSOTSup 394. London: T. & T. Clark.
Anderson, Gary A. 1987. *Sacrifices and Offerings in Ancient Israel: Studies in Their Social and Political Importance*. HSM 41. Atlanta: Scholars.
———. 1991. *A Time to Mourn, a Time to Dance: The Expression of Grief and Joy in Israelite Religion*. University Park: Pennsylvania State University Press.
Andreasen, Niels-Erik. 1972. *The Old Testament Sabbath: A Tradition-Historical Investigation*. SBLDS 7. Missoula: Scholars.
———. 1974a. 'Festival and Freedom: A Study of an Old Testament Theme'. *Int* 28:281-97.
———. 1974b. 'Recent Studies of the Old Testament Sabbath: Some Observations'. *ZAW* 86:453-69.
Andrew, Maurice Edward. 1963. 'Falsehood and Truth: An Amplified Sermon on Exodus 20:16'. *Int* 17:425-38.
Anti-Slavery International. 1996. *'This Menace of Bonded Labour': Debt Bondage in Pakistan*. London: Anti-Slavery International.
———. [1998]. *Debt Bondage*, ed. Margaret O'Grady. London: Anti-Slavery International.
———. 2005. 'Web-Site' <www.antislavery.org>.
Archi, Alfonso. 2002. '"Debt" in an Archaic Palatial Economy: The Evidence from Ebla'. Pp. 95-108 in *DERANE*.
———, ed. 1984. *Circulation of Goods in Non-Palatial Context in the Ancient Near East: Proceedings of the International Conference Organized by the Istituto per gli studi Micenei ed Egeo-Anatolici*. Incunabula Graeca 82. Rome: Ateneo.
Armerding, Carl E. 2001. 'Borrowing and Lending: Is There Anything Christian About Either?' *Transformation* 18:146-54.
Ashmore, James Philip. 1995. 'The Social Setting of the Law in Deuteronomy'. Ph.D. diss., Duke University.
Astour, Michael C. 1976. 'Habiru'. Pp. 382-85 in *IDBSup*.
Ateek, Naim S. 1989. *Justice, and Only Justice: A Palestinian Theology of Liberation*. Maryknoll: Orbis.
Avalos, Hector. 1990. 'Exodus 22:9 and Akkadian Legal Formulae'. *JBL* 109:116-17.
Averbeck, Richard E. 1997. '5130 מעשר'. Pp. 1035-55 in *NIDOTTE*, vol. 2.
———, Mark W. Chavalas, and David B. Weisberg, eds. 2003. *Life and Culture in the Ancient Near East*. Bethesda, MD: CDL.
Baab, Otto J. 1962. 'Marriage'. Pp. 278-87 in *IDB*, vol. 3.
Bacchiocchi, Samuele. 1977. *From Sabbath to Sunday: A Historical Investigation of the Rise of Sunday Observance in Early Christianity*. Rome: Pontifical Gregorian University.
———. 1980. *Divine Rest for Human Restlessness: A Theological Study of the Good News of the Sabbath for Today*. Rome: private publication.
Bailey, Kenneth C. 1963. 'The Decalogue as Morality and Ethics'. *ThTo* 20:183-95.
Bailey, Lloyd R. 2005. *Leviticus-Numbers*. SHBC. Macon: Smyth & Helwys.
Baker, David L. 1998. 'The Jubilee and the Millennium'. *Themelios* 24/1:44-69.
———. 2005a. 'Covenant: An Old Testament Study'. Pp. 21-53 in *The God of Covenant: Biblical, Theological and Contemporary Perspectives*, ed. Jamie A. Grant and Alistair I. Wilson. Leicester: Apollos.
———. 2005b. 'The Finger of God and the Forming of a Nation: The Origin and Purpose of the Decalogue'. *TynBul* 56/1:1-24.

———. 2005c. 'Last but Not Least: The Tenth Commandment'. *HBT* 27:3-24.

———. 2005d. 'Ten Commandments, Two Tablets: The Shape of the Decalogue'. *Themelios* 30/3: 6-22.

———. 2006a. 'Safekeeping, Borrowing, and Rental'. *JSOT* 31:27-42.

———. 2006b. 'To Glean or Not to Glean . . .' *ExpTim* 117:406-10.

———. 2007a. 'Finders Keepers? Lost Property in Ancient Near Eastern and Biblical Law'. *BBR* 17:207-14.

———. 2007b. 'Concubines and Conjugal Rights: ענה in Exodus 21:10 and Deuteronomy 21:14'. *ZABR* 13:87-101.

———. 2009. 'Protecting the Vulnerable — The Law and Social Care'. Pp. 15-32 in *Transforming the World: The Gospel and Social Theology,* ed. Jamie A. Grant and Dewi Hughes. Nottingham: Inter-Varsity.

Bakir, Abd el-Mohsen. 1952. *Slavery in Pharaonic Egypt.* Supplément aux Annales du Service des Antiquités de l'Égypte 18. Cairo: Institut français d'archéologie orientale.

Balentine, Samuel E. 2002. *Leviticus.* Interpretation. Louisville: John Knox.

Bales, Kevin. 1999. *Disposable People: New Slavery in the Global Economy.* Berkeley: University of California Press.

Balkan, Kemal. 1974. 'Cancellation of Debts in Cappadocian Texts from Kültepe'. Pp. 29-41 in *Anatolian Studies,* ed. Kurt Bittel, Ph. H. J. Houwink ten Cate, and Erica Reiner. Hans Gustav Güterbock Festschrift. Uitgaven van het Nederlands Historisch-Archaeologisch Instituut te Istanbul 35. Istanbul: Nederlands Historisch-Archaeologisch Instituut in het Nabije Oosten.

Ballard, Bruce. 1994. 'On the Sin of Usury: A Biblical Economic Ethic'. *Christian Scholar's Review* 24:210-28.

Baltzer, Klaus. 1987. 'Liberation from Debt Slavery after the Exile in Second Isaiah and Nehemiah'. Pp. 477-84 in *Ancient Israelite Religion,* ed. Patrick D. Miller, Paul D. Hanson, and S. Dean McBride. Frank Moore Cross Festschrift. Philadelphia: Fortress.

Barbiero, Gianni. 1991. *L'asino del nemico: Rinuncia alla vendetta e amore del nemico nella legislazione dell' Antico Testamento (Es 23,4-5; Dt 22,1-4; Lv 19,17-18).* AnBib 128. Rome: Pontifical Biblical Institute.

Barclay, John M. G. 2007. '"Am I Not a Man and a Brother?" The Bible and the British Anti-Slavery Campaign'. *ExpTim* 119:3-14.

Barkay, Gabriel. 1991. '"Your Poor Brother": A Note on an Inscribed Bowl from Beth Shemesh'. *IEJ* 41:239-41.

———. 1992. 'The World's Oldest Poorbox'. *BAR* 18/6:48-50.

Barker, P. A. 2003. 'Sabbath, Sabbatical Year, Jubilee'. Pp. 695-706 in *DOTP.*

Barr, James. 1984. '*Migraš* in the Old Testament'. *JSS* 29:15-31.

Barrett, Marlene, ed. 2000. *The World Will Never Be the Same Again.* Report, Jubilee 2000 Coalition.

Barrois, Georges Augustin. 1962. 'Wages'. P. 795 in *IDB,* vol. 4.

Bartholomew, Craig, and Thorsten Moritz, eds. 2000. *Christ and Consumerism: A Critical Analysis of the Spirit of the Age.* Carlisle: Paternoster.

Baumgarten, Joseph M. 1984. 'On the Non-Literal Use of *ma'aser/dekate*'. *JBL* 103:245-51.

Bazak, Jacob. 1987. 'Judicial Ethics in Jewish Law'. Pp. 27-40 in *Jewish Law Association Studies III: The Oxford Conference Volume,* ed. A. M. Fuss. Atlanta: Scholars.

Bechtel, Lyn M. 1991. 'Shame as a Sanction of Social Control in Biblical Israel: Judicial, Political, and Social Shaming'. *JSOT* 49:47-76.

Beckman, Gary. 1999. *Hittite Diplomatic Texts*. 2nd ed. SBLWAW 7. Atlanta: Scholars.

———. 2003. 'International Law in the Second Millennium: Late Bronze Age'. Pp. 753-74 in *HANEL*, vol. 1.

Beckwith, Roger T. 1980. 'The Significance of the Calendar for Interpreting Essene Chronology and Eschatology'. *RevQ* 10:167-202.

———. 1996. *Calendar and Chronology, Jewish and Christian: Biblical, Intertestamental and Patristic Studies*. AGJU 33. Leiden: Brill.

———, and Wilfrid Stott. 1978. *This Is the Day: The Biblical Doctrine of the Christian Sunday in Its Jewish and Early Church Setting*. London: Marshall, Morgan & Scott. Repr. as *The Christian Sunday: A Biblical and Historical Study*. Grand Rapids: Baker, 1980.

Beer, Georg. 1911. 'Das Stehenlassen der Pe'a Lev 19 9'. *ZAW* 31:152.

Bendor, Shunya. 1996. *The Social Structure of Ancient Israel*. Jerusalem Biblical Studies 7. Jerusalem: Simor.

Ben-Dov, Jonathan. 2006. 'The Poor's Curse: Exodus xxii 20-26 and Curse Literature in the Ancient World'. *VT* 56:431-51.

Bennett, Harold V. 2002. *Injustice Made Legal: Deuteronomic Law and the Plight of Widows, Strangers, and Orphans in Ancient Israel*. BIW. Grand Rapids: Wm. B. Eerdmans.

Bergsma, John S. 2003. 'The Jubilee: A Post-Exilic Priestly Attempt to Reclaim Lands?' *Bib* 84:225-46.

———. 2005. 'Once Again, the Jubilee, Every 49 or 50 Years?' *VT* 55:121-25.

———. 2007. *The Jubilee from Leviticus to Qumran: A History of Interpretation*. VTSup 115; Leiden: Brill.

Berlin, Adele. 1984. 'Jeremiah 29:5-7: A Deuteronomic Allusion'. *HAR* 8:3-11.

Bess, Stephen Herbert. 1963. 'Systems of Land Tenure in Ancient Israel'. Ph.D. diss., University of Michigan.

Beyerlin, Walter, ed. 1975. *Near Eastern Religious Texts Relating to the Old Testament*. OTL. Philadelphia: Westminster/London: SCM. (trans. from German)

Beyse, Karl-Martin. 1986. 'עָבַט'. Pp. 405-7 in *TDOT*, vol. 10 (1999). (trans. from German)

———. 1993. 'שָׁחַד'. Pp. 555-58 in *TDOT*, vol. 14 (2004). (trans. from German)

Bianchi, Enzo. 1979. 'The Status of Those without Dignity in the Old Testament'. Pp. 3-11 in *The Dignity of the Despised of the Earth*, ed. Jacques Pohier and Dietmar Mieth. Concilium 130. New York: Seabury.

Bianchi, Francesco. 2000. 'Das Jobeljahr in der hebräischen Bibel und in den nachkanonischen jüdischen Texten'. Pp. 55-104 in *Das Jobeljahr im Wandel: Untersuchungen zu Erlassjahr- und Jobeljahrtexten aus vier Jahrtausenden*, ed. Georg Scheuermann. FB 94. Würzburg: Echter.

Bickerman, Elias J. 1956. 'Two Legal Interpretations of the Septuagint'. *RIDA* 3/3:81-104.

Biddle, Mark E. 2003. *Deuteronomy*. SHBC. Macon: Smyth & Helwys.

Bilgiç, Emin. 1947. 'Die wichtigsten Ausdrücke über Schulder und Darlehen in den Keilschrifttexten'. *Dil ve Tarih-Coğrafya Fakültesi Dergisi* 5:419-45 (Turkish); 47-54 (German summary).

Birch, Bruce C. 1991. *Let Justice Roll Down: The Old Testament, Ethics, and Christian Life*. (Louisville: Westminster John Knox).

———. 1995. 'Moral Agency, Community, and the Character of God in the Hebrew Bible'. *Semeia* 66:23-41.
Black, Jeremy A. et al., eds. 2004. *The Literature of Ancient Sumer*. Oxford: Oxford University Press.
Bleiberg, Edward. 2002. 'Loans, Credit and Interest in Ancient Egypt'. Pp. 257-76 in *DERANE*.
Blenkinsopp, Joseph. 1986. 'Yahweh and Other Deities: Conflict and Accommodation in the Religion of Israel'. *Int* 40:354-66.
———. 1988. *Ezra-Nehemiah*. OTL. Philadelphia: Westminster/London: SCM.
———. 1992. *The Pentateuch: An Introduction to the First Five Books of the Bible*. ABRL. New York: Doubleday/London: SCM.
Block, Daniel I. 2000. *The Gods of the Nations: Studies in Ancient Near Eastern National Theology*. 2nd ed. Evangelical Theological Society Studies. Grand Rapids: Baker/Leicester: Apollos.
Blosser, D. 1981. 'The Sabbath Year Cycle in Josephus'. *HUCA* 52:129-39.
Bockmuehl, Markus. 2005. '"Keeping It Holy": Old Testament Commandment and New Testament Faith'. Pp. 95-124 in *I Am the Lord Your God: Christian Reflections on the Ten Commandments*, ed. Carl E. Braaten and Christopher R. Seitz. Grand Rapids: Wm. B. Eerdmans.
Boecker, Hans Jochen. 1976. *Law and the Administration of Justice in the Old Testament and Ancient East*. London: SPCK, 1980. (trans. from German)
de Boer, P. A. H. 1948. 'Some Remarks on Exodus XXI 7-11: The Hebrew Female Slave'. Pp. 162-66 in *Orientalia Neerlandica: A Volume of Oriental Studies*, ed. Netherlands' Oriental Society. Leiden: Sijthoff.
Bordreuil, Pierre, Felice Israel, and Dennis Pardee. 1996. 'Deux ostraca paléo-hébreux de la collection Sh. Moussaïeff: Ostracon no. 2: Réclamation d'une veuve auprès d'un fonctionnaire'. *Sem* 46:61-76.
———. 1998. 'King's Command and Widow's Plea: Two New Hebrew Ostraca of the Biblical Period'. *NEA* 61:2-13.
Borger, Rykle et al. 1982. *Rechtsbücher*. TUAT I/1. Gütersloh: Mohn.
Borowski, Oded. 1987. *Agriculture in Iron Age Israel*. Winona Lake: Eisenbrauns.
Bosman, Hendrik L. 1997. 'Sabbath'. Pp. 1157-62 in *NIDOTTE*, vol. 4.
Bothwell, John. 1982. 'Coveting amid Affluence'. Pp. 117-26 in *Voice from the Mountain: New Life for the Old Law*, ed. Philip Jefferson. Toronto: Anglican Book Centre.
Bottéro, Jean. 1954. *Le problème des Ḫabiru à la 4e Rencontre assyriologique internationale*. Cahiers de la Société asiatique 12. Paris: Imprimerie Nationale.
———. 1982. 'The "Code" of Ḥammurabi'. Pp. 156-84 in *Mesopotamia: Writing, Reasoning, and the Gods*. Chicago: University of Chicago Press, 1992. (trans. from French; originally published in Italian)
Botterweck, G. Johannes. 1970. 'אֶבְיוֹן'. Pp. 27-41 in *TDOT*, vol. 1 (rev. ed. 1977). (trans. from German)
Bourdieu, Pierre. 1977. *Outline of a Theory of Practice*. Cambridge Studies in Social Anthropology 16. Cambridge: Cambridge University Press. (trans. from French, rev. for translation)
Bovati, Pietro. 1994. *Re-Establishing Justice: Legal Terms, Concepts and Procedures in the Hebrew Bible*. JSOTSup 105. Sheffield: Sheffield Academic.

Boyce, Richard Nelson. 1988. *The Cry to God in the Old Testament*. SBLDS 103. Atlanta: Scholars.

Braaten, Carl E. 2005. 'Sins of the Tongue'. Pp. in 206-17 *I Am the Lord Your God: Christian Reflections on the Ten Commandments*, ed. Carl E. Braaten and Christopher R. Seitz. Grand Rapids: Wm. B. Eerdmans.

———, and Christopher R. Seitz, eds. 2005. *I Am the Lord Your God: Christian Reflections on the Ten Commandments*. Grand Rapids: Wm. B. Eerdmans.

Brashler, James A., and Samuel E. Balentine, eds. 2005. 'Sabbath'. *Int* 59:3-63.

Braulik, Georg. 1986. *Deuteronomium 1–16,17*. NEchtB 15. Würzburg: Echter.

———. 1991. *Die deuteronomischen Gesetze und der Dekalog: Studien zum Aufbau von Deuteronomium 12–26*. Stuttgarter Bibelstudien 145. Stuttgart: Katholisches Bibelwerk.

———. 1995. 'Die dekalogische Redaktion der deuteronomischen Gesetze: Ihre Abhängigkeit von Levitikus 19 am Beispiel von Deuteronomium 22,1-12; 24,10-22; 25,13-16'. Pp. 1-25 in *Bundesdokument und Gesetz: Studien zum Deuteronomium*. Herders biblische Studien 4. Freiburg im Breisgau: Herder. Repr. in *Studien zum Buch Deuteronomium*. Stuttgart: Katholisches Bibelwerk, 1997.

———. 1996. 'Weitere Beobachtungen zur Beziehung zwischen dem Heiligkeitsgesetz und Deuteronomium 19–25'. Pp. 23-55 in *Das Deuteronomium und seine Querbeziehungen*, ed. Timo Veijola. Schriften der Finnischen Exegetischen Gesellschaft 62. Göttingen: Vandenhoeck & Ruprecht.

Brichto, Herbert Chanan. 1973. 'Kin, Cult, Land and Afterlife — A Biblical Complex'. *HUCA* 44:1-54.

Bright, John. 1973. 'The Apodictic Prohibition: Some Observations'. *JBL* 92:185-204.

Brin, Gershon. 1994. *Studies in Biblical Law: From the Hebrew Bible to the Dead Sea Scrolls*. JSOTSup 176. Sheffield: Sheffield Academic. (trans. from Hebrew)

Britannica. 2003a. 'Slavery'. In *Encyclopædia Britannica* (electronic ed.).

———. 2003b. 'Slavery in the 21st Century'. In *Encyclopædia Britannica* (electronic ed.).

Brown, Raymond. 1993. *The Message of Deuteronomy: Not by Bread Alone*. Bible Speaks Today. Downers Grove: InterVarsity.

Brown, William P., ed. 2004. *The Ten Commandments: The Reciprocity of Faithfulness*. Library of Theological Ethics. Louisville: Westminster John Knox.

Broyde, Michael J., and Michael Hecht. 1995. 'The Return of Lost Property According to Jewish and Common Law: A Comparison'. *JLR* 12:225-53.

Brubacher, Gordon. 1999. 'Principles of Jubilee in the Old Testament, and for the Enduring Community of Faith'. Pp. 33-54 in *Holy Land, Hollow Jubilee: God, Justice and the Palestinians*, ed. Naim S. Ateek and Michael Prior. London: Melisende.

Brueggemann, Walter. 1975. 'Reflections on Biblical Understandings of Property'. *International Review of Mission* 64:354-61.

———. 1994. 'The Book of Exodus'. Pp. 675-981 in *NIB*, vol. 1.

———. 1997. 'Truth-Telling as Subversive Obedience'. Pp. 291-300 in *The Ten Commandments: The Reciprocity of Faithfulness*, ed. Willliam P. Brown. Library of Theological Ethics. Louisville: Westminster John Knox. Repr. from *Journal for Preachers* (1997): 2-9.

———. 2002. *The Land: Place as Gift, Promise, and Challenge in Biblical Faith*. 2nd ed. OBT. Minneapolis: Fortress.

de Bruin, W. M. 1999. 'Die Freistellung vom Militärdienst in Deut. xx 5-7: Die Gattung der

Wirkungslosigkeitssprüche als Schlüssel zum Verstehen eines alten Brauches'. *VT* 49:21-33.

Budde, Karl. 1899. *Religion of Israel to the Exile*. American Lectures on the History of Religions, 1898-99. New York: Knickerbocker. (trans. from German)

Buhl, Frants. 1897. 'Some Observations on the Social Institutions of the Israelites'. *AJT* 1:728-40.

———. 1899. *Die socialen Verhältnisse der Israeliten*. Berlin: Reuther & Reichard.

du Buit, M. 1959. 'Quelques contacts bibliques dans les archives royales de Mari'. *RB* 66:576-81.

Bultmann, Christoph. 1992. *Der Fremde im antiken Juda: Eine Untersuchung zum sozialen Typenbegriff gerund seinem Bedeutungswandel in der alttestamentlichen Gesetzgebung*. FRLANT 153. Göttingen: Vandenhoeck & Ruprecht.

Burnside, Jonathan P. 2001. 'The Status and Welfare of Immigrants: The Place of the Foreigner in Biblical Law and Its Relevance to Contemporary Society'. Jubilee Centre, Cambridge.

Bush, Frederic W. 1996. *Ruth, Esther*. WBC 9. Dallas: Word.

Cairns, I. J. 1986a. *Kitab Ulangan: Fasal 1–11 [Deuteronomy: Chapters 1–11]*. Tafsiran Alkitab. Jakarta: BPK Gunung Mulia.

———. 1986b. *Kitab Ulangan: Fasal 12–34 [Deuteronomy: Chapters 12–34]*. Tafsiran Alkitab. Jakarta: BPK Gunung Mulia.

Campbell, Ronald Michael. n.d. 'The Tithe in the Old Testament'. M.Th. thesis, Calvin Theological Seminary. Not available to me; abstract in *CTJ* 22 (1987): 378-79.

Canaan, Tawfiq. 1928. 'Plant-Lore in Palestinian Superstition'. *JPOS* 8:129-68.

———. 1933. 'The Palestinian Arab House: Its Architecture and Folklore'. *JPOS* 13:1-83; continuation of article in vol. 12 (1932).

Caquot, André et al. 1974. *Textes ougaritiques: Tome 1. Mythes et légendes*. LAPO 7. Paris: Cerf.

———. 1989. *Textes ougaritiques: Tome 2. Textes religieux et rituels; correspondance*. LAPO 14. Paris: Cerf.

Cardascia, Guillaume. 1958. 'Le statut de l'étranger dans la Mésopotamie ancienne'. Pp. 105-17 in *L'étranger*. Recueils de la Societe Jean Bodin 9. Brussels.

———. 1969. *Les lois assyriennes*. LAPO 2. Paris: Cerf.

Cardellini, Innocenzo. 1981. *Die biblischen 'Sklaven'-Gesetze im Lichte des keilschriftlichen Sklavenrechts: Ein Beitrag zur Tradition, Überlieferung und Redaktion der alttestamentlichen Rechtstexte*. BBB 55. Bonn: Hanstein.

Carmichael, Calum M. 1967. 'Deuteronomic Laws, Wisdom, and Historical Traditions'. *JSS* 12:198-206.

———. 1974. *The Laws of Deuteronomy*. Ithaca: Cornell University Press.

———. 1981. 'The Law of the Forgotten Sheaf'. *SBLSP* 20:35-37.

———. 1985a. 'Biblical Laws of Talion'. *HAR* 9:107-26.

———. 1985b. *Law and Narrative in the Bible: The Evidence of the Deuteronomic Laws and the Decalogue*. Ithaca: Cornell University Press.

———. 1992. *The Origins of Biblical Law: The Decalogues and the Book of the Covenant*. Ithaca: Cornell University Press.

———. 1994. 'Laws of Leviticus 19'. *HTR* 87:239-56.

———. 1997. *Law, Legend, and Incest in the Bible: Leviticus 18–20*. Ithaca: Cornell University Press.

---. 1999. 'The Sabbatical/Jubilee Cycle and the Seven-Year Famine in Egypt'. *Bib* 80:224-39.

---. 2000. 'The Three Laws on the Release of Slaves (Ex 21,2-11; Dtn 15,12-18; Lev 25,39-46)'. *ZAW* 112:509-25.

---. 2006. *Illuminating Leviticus: A Study of Its Laws and Institutions in the Light of Biblical Narratives*. Baltimore: Johns Hopkins University Press.

Carpenter, Eugene. 1997. '6268 עבד'. Pp. 304-9 in *NIDOTTE*, vol. 3.

Carroll Rodas, M. Daniel. 2003a. 'Orphan'. Pp. 619-21 in *DOTP*.

---. 2003b. 'Widow'. Pp. 890-93 in *DOTP*.

Carson, Donald A., ed. 1982. *From Sabbath to Lord's Day: A Biblical, Historical, and Theological Investigation*. Grand Rapids: Zondervan.

Cassuto, Umberto. 1951. *A Commentary on the Book of Exodus*. Jerusalem: Magnes, 1967. (trans. from Hebrew)

Cazelles, Henri. 1946. *Études sur le Code de l'Alliance*. Paris: Letouzey et Ané.

---. 1948. 'Sur un rituel du Deutéronome (Deut. xxvi, 14)'. *RB* 55:54-71.

---. 1951. 'La dîme israélite et les textes de Ras Shamra'. *VT* 1:131-34.

---. 1954. 'La mission d'Esdras'. *VT* 4:113-40.

Ceresko, Anthony R. 1988. 'The Challenge of the Tenth Commandment'. Pp. 237-39 in *Psalmists and Sages: Studies in Old Testament Poetry and Religion*. Indian Theological Studies Supplements 2. Bangalore: St Peter's Institute, 1994. Repr. from *Compass*.

Černý, Jaroslav. 1937. 'Restitution of, and Penalty Attaching to, Stolen Property in Ramesside Times'. *JEA* 23:186-89.

Chaney, Marvin L. 1991. 'Debt Easement in Israelite History and Tradition'. Pp. 127-39 in *The Bible and the Politics of Exegesis*, ed. David Jobling, Peggy L. Day, and Gerald T. Sheppard. Norman Gottwald Festschrift. Cleveland: Pilgrim.

Charles, R. H. 1926. *The Decalogue*. 2nd ed. Warburton Lectures, 1919-23. Edinburgh: T. & T. Clark.

Charpin, Dominique. 1987. 'Les décrets royaux à l'époque paléo-babylonienne, à propos d'un ouvrage récent'. *AfO* 34:36-44.

Childs, Brevard S. 1974. *The Book of Exodus*. OTL. Philadelphia: Westminster/London: SCM.

Chirichigno, Gregory C. 1981. 'A Theological Investigation of Motivation in Old Testament Law'. *JETS* 24:303-13.

---. 1993. *Debt-Slavery in Israel and the Ancient Near East*. JSOTSup 141. Sheffield: JSOT.

de Chirico, Leonardo. 1999. 'The Biblical Jubilee'. *Evangelical Review of Theology* 23:347-62.

Cholewiński, Alfred. 1976. *Heiligkeitsgesetz und Deuteronomium: Eine vergleichende Studie*. AnBib 66. Rome: Pontifical Biblical Institute.

Christensen, Duane L. 2001. *Deuteronomy 1:1–21:9*. Rev. ed. WBC 6A. Nashville: Thomas Nelson.

---. 2002. *Deuteronomy 21:10–34:12*. WBC 6b. Nashville: Thomas Nelson.

Civil, Miguel. 1976. 'Enlil, the Merchant: Notes to Ct 15 10'. *JCS* 28:72-81.

---. 1994. *The Farmer's Instructions: A Sumerian Agricultural Manual*. AuOrSup 5. Sabadell-Barcelona: AUSA.

Clay, Rachel. 1938. *The Tenure of Land in Babylonia and Assyria*. University of London Institute of Archaeology Occasional Paper 1. London: Institute of Archaeology.

Clines, David J. A. 1984. *Ezra, Nehemiah, Esther*. NCB. Grand Rapids: Wm. B. Eerdmans/London: Marshall, Morgan & Scott.

———. 1995. 'The Ten Commandments, Reading from Left to Right'. Pp. 26-45 in *Interested Parties: The Ideology of Writers and Readers of the Hebrew Bible*. JSOTSup 205. Sheffield: Sheffield Academic. Rev. from earlier version in John F. A. Sawyer Festschrift (1995).

———. n.d. 'Social Responsibility in the Old Testament'. Unpublished paper, Shaftesbury Project.

———, and Stephen D. Moore, eds. 1998. *Auguries: The Jubilee Volume of the Sheffield Department of Biblical Studies*. JSOTSup 269. Sheffield: Sheffield Academic.

Coats, George W. 1972. 'Widow's Rights: A Crux in the Structure of Genesis 38'. *CBQ* 34:461-72.

Cohen, Chaim. 1978-79. 'Studies in Extrabiblical Hebrew Inscriptions I: The Semantic Range and Usage of the Terms אמה and שפחה'. *Shnaton* 5-6:xxv-liii.

Cohen, Matty. 1990. 'Le "ger" biblique et son statut socio-religieux'. *RHR* 207:131-58.

Cohn, Haim Hermann. 1972. 'Slavery'. Pp. 1655-60 in *EncJud*, vol. 14.

Cole, H. R. 2000. 'The Sabbath and the Alien'. *AUSS* 38:223-29.

Cole, R. Alan. 1973. *Exodus: An Introduction and Commentary*. TOTC. Downers Grove: InterVarsity/London: Tyndale.

Contenau, Georges. 1954. *Everyday Life in Babylon and Assyria*. London: Edward Arnold. (trans. from French)

Cooper, Alan. 1988. 'The Plain Sense of Exodus 23:5'. *HUCA* 59:1-22.

Cooper, Jerrold S. 1986. *Sumerian and Akkadian Royal Inscriptions*. Vol. 1: *Presargonic Inscriptions*. AOSTS 1. New Haven: American Oriental Society.

———. 2003. 'International Law in the Third Millennium'. Pp. 241-51 in *HANEL*, vol. 1.

Cornell, Tim J. 1989. 'The Recovery of Rome'. Pp. 309-50 in *The Rise of Rome to 220 B.C.*, ed. F. W. Walbank et al. CAH, 2nd ed. 7/2. Cambridge: Cambridge University Press.

———. 1995. *The Beginnings of Rome: Italy and Rome from the Bronze Age to the Punic Wars (c. 1000-264 BC)*. London: Routledge.

Cowley, A. E., ed. 1923. *Aramaic Papyri of the Fifth Century B.C.* Oxford: Clarendon.

Craigie, Peter C. 1976. *The Book of Deuteronomy*. NICOT. Grand Rapids: Wm. B. Eerdmans.

Credit Action. 2006. 'Debt Statistics'. http://www.creditaction.org.uk/debtstats.htm.

Cripps, Eric L. 2007. *Land Tenure and Social Stratification in Ancient Mesopotamia: Third Millennium Sumer before the Ur III Dynasty* (BAR International Series, 1676; Oxford: Archaeopress).

Croatto, José Severino. 1997. 'The Debt in Nehemiah's Social Reform: A Study of Nehemiah 5:1-19'. Pp. 39-59 in *Subversive Scriptures: Revolutionary Readings of the Christian Bible in Latin America*, ed. Leif E. Vaage. Valley Forge: Trinity Press International.

Crüsemann, Frank. 1985. 'Der Zehnte der israelitischen Königszeit'. *WD* 18:21-47.

———. 1987. '"Auge um Auge . . ." (Ex 21,24f): Zum sozialgeschichtlichen Sinn des Talionsgesetzes im Bundesbuch'. *EvT* 47:411-26.

———. 1992. *The Torah: Theology and Social History of Old Testament Law*. Edinburgh: T. & T. Clark, 1996. (trans. from German)

Dahood, Mitchell. 1961. '"To Pawn One's Cloak"'. *Bib* 42:359-66.

Dalley, Stephanie. 1989. *Myths from Mesopotamia: Creation, the Flood, Gilgamesh, and Others*. World's Classics. Oxford: Oxford University Press.

Dam, Cornelis van. 1997. '8509 שכר'. Pp. 1244-46 in *NIDOTTE*, vol. 3.

Dandama[y]ev, Muhammad A. 1969. 'Der Tempelzehnte in Babylonien während des 6.-4. Jh.

v. u. Z.'. Pp. 82-90 in *Beiträge zur alten Geschichte und deren Nachleben*, ed. Ruth Stiehl and Hans Erich Stier. Franz Altheim Festschrift. Berlin: de Gruyter.
———. 1984. *Slavery in Babylonia: From Nabopolassar to Alexander the Great (626-331 BC)*. DeKalb: Northern Illinois University Press. (rev. trans. from Russian, 1974)
———. 1987. 'Free Hired Labor in Babylonia During the Sixth through Fourth Centuries BC'. Pp. 272-79 in *Labor in the Ancient Near East*, ed. Marvin A. Powell. AOS 68. New Haven: American Oriental Society.
———. 1992a. 'Slavery: Ancient Near East'. Pp. 58-62 in *ABD*, vol. 6.
———. 1992b. 'Slavery: Old Testament'. Pp. 62-65 in *ABD*, vol. 6.
Daube, David. 1947. *Studies in Biblical Law*. Cambridge: Cambridge University Press.
———. 1956. *The New Testament and Rabbinic Judaism*. School of Oriental and African Studies, Jordan Lectures in Comparative Religion 2. London: Athlone.
———. 1961. 'Direct and Indirect Causation in Biblical Law'. *VT* 11:246-69.
———. 1963. *The Exodus Pattern in the Bible*. London: Faber.
———. 1969. 'The Culture of Deuteronomy'. *Orita: Ibadan Journal of Religious Studies* 3:27-52.
———. 1973. 'The Self-Understood in Legal History'. *Juridical Review* 18:126-34.
David, M. 1943. 'Deux anciens termes bibliques pour le gage'. *OtSt* 2:79-86.
———. 1948. 'The Manumission of Slaves under Zedekiah (A Contribution to the Laws About Hebrew Slaves)'. *OtSt* 5:63-79.
———. 1950. 'The Codex Hammurabi and Its Relation to the Provisions of Law in Exodus'. *OtSt* 7:149-78.
———. 1951. 'Hit'amer (Deut xxi 14; xxiv 7)'. *VT* 1:219-21.
Davies, Eryl W. 1981. 'Inheritance Rights and the Hebrew Levirate Marriage'. *VT* 31:138-44, 257-68.
———. 1989. 'Land: Its Rights and Privileges'. Pp. 349-69 in *The World of Ancient Israel: Sociological, Anthropological and Political Perspectives*, ed. Ronald E. Clements. Cambridge: Cambridge University Press.
———. 1999. 'Walking in God's Ways: The Concept of *Imitatio Dei* in the Old Testament'. Pp. 99-115 in *True Wisdom*, ed. Edward Ball. JSOTSup 300. Sheffield: Sheffield Academic.
Davies, Graham I. 1991. *Ancient Hebrew Inscriptions: Corpus and Concordance*, vol. 1. Cambridge: Cambridge University Press.
———. 2004a. *Ancient Hebrew Inscriptions: Corpus and Concordance*, vol. 2. Cambridge: Cambridge University Press.
———. 2004b. 'Was There an Exodus?' Pp. 23-40 in *In Search of Pre-Exilic Israel: Proceedings of the Oxford Old Testament Seminar*, ed. John Day. JSOTSup 406. London: T. & T. Clark.
———. 2005. 'Some Uses of Writing in Ancient Israel in the Light of Recently Published Inscriptions'. Pp. 155-74 in *Writing and Ancient Near Eastern Society*, ed. Piotr Bienkowski, Christopher Mee, and Elizabeth Slater. Alan Millard Festschrift. LHB/OTS 426. New York: T. & T. Clark.
Davies, W. D. 1974. *The Gospel and the Land: Early Christianity and Jewish Territorial Doctrine*. Berkeley: University of California Press.
le Déaut, Roger. 1972. 'Critique textuelle et exégèse: Exode XXII 12 dans la Septante et le Targum'. *VT* 22:164-75.

Dercksen, Jan Gerrit, ed. 1999. *Trade and Finance in Ancient Mesopotamia: Proceedings of the First MOS Symposium (Leiden 1997)*. Uitgaven van het Nederlands Historisch-Archaeologisch Instituut te Istanbul 84. Istanbul: Nederlands Historisch-Archaeologisch Instituut.

Development Finance Group. 2005. 'Heavily Indebted Poor Countries Debt Analysis and Strategy'. *Strategies for Financing Development* 24:1-12, 16.

Diakonoff, I. M. 1987. 'Slave-Labour Vs. Non-Slave Labour: The Problem of Definition'. Pp. 1-3 in *Labor in the Ancient Near East*, ed. Marvin A. Powell. AOS 68. New Haven: American Oriental Society.

Diamond, A. S. 1957. 'An Eye for an Eye'. *Iraq* 19:151-55.

Diepold, Peter. 1972. *Israels Land*. BWANT 95. Stuttgart: Kohlhammer.

Dietrich, Manfried, and Oswald Loretz. 1986. "*DB* und *D̠B* im Ugaritischen". *UF* 17:105-16.

Dobbs-Allsopp et al. 2005. *Hebrew Inscriptions: Texts from the Biblical Period of the Monarchy with Concordance*. New Haven: Yale University Press.

Doering, Lutz. 1999. *Schabbat*. TSAJ 78. Tübingen: Mohr Siebeck.

Dohmen, Christoph. 2004. *Exodus 19–40*. HTKAT. Freiburg im Breisgau: Herder.

Domeris, William R. 1997. '4575 מוּךְ'. P. 868 in *NIDOTTE*, vol. 2.

———. 2007. *Touching the Heart of God: The Social Construction of Poverty among Biblical Peasants*. LHB/OTS 466. London: T. & T. Clark.

Dommershausen, Werner. 1977. 'חָנֵף'. Pp. 19-21 in *TDOT*, vol. 5 (1986). (trans. from German)

Doron, Pinchas. 1978. 'Motive Clauses in the Laws of Deuteronomy: Their Forms, Functions and Contents'. *HAR* 2:61-77.

Dosch, Gudrun. 1987. 'Non-Slave Labor in Nuzi'. Pp. 223-35 in *Labor in the Ancient Near East*, ed. Marvin A. Powell. AOS 68. New Haven: American Oriental Society.

Doughty, Charles M. 1921. *Travels in Arabia Deserta*. 2 vols. 3rd ed. London: Lee Warner. Repr. New York: Dover, 1979.

Douglas, Mary. 1999. 'Justice as the Cornerstone: An Interpretation of Leviticus 18–20'. *Int* 53:341-50.

Draffkorn, Anne E. 1957. '*Ilani/Elohim*'. *JBL* 76:216-24.

Dreher, Carlos A. 1993. 'Las uvas del vecino'. *Revista de Interpretación Bíblica Latinoamericana* 14:23-39. Not available to me; abstract in *OTA* 16 (1993): 1861.

Dressler, Harold H. P. 1982. 'The Sabbath in the Old Testament'. Pp. 21-41 in *From Sabbath to Lord's Day: A Biblical, Historical, and Theological Investigation*, ed. Donald A. Carson. Grand Rapids: Zondervan.

Driver, G. R., and John C. Miles, eds. 1935. *The Assyrian Laws*. Ancient Codes and Laws of the Near East. Oxford: Clarendon.

———, ed. 1952. *The Babylonian Laws*. Vol. 1: *Legal Commentary*. Ancient Codes and Laws of the Near East. Oxford: Clarendon. Repr. with minor corrections 1960.

———, ed. 1955. *The Babylonian Laws*. Vol. 2: *Transliterated Text, Translation, Philological Notes, Glossary*. Ancient Codes and Laws of the Near East. Oxford: Clarendon. Repr. with minor corrections 1960.

Driver, S. R. 1902. *A Critical and Exegetical Commentary on Deuteronomy*. 3rd ed. ICC. Edinburgh: T. & T. Clark. Repr. 1996.

———. 1911. *The Book of Exodus*. Cambridge Bible for Schools and Colleges. Cambridge: Cambridge University Press.

Durham, John I. 1987. *Exodus*. WBC 3. Waco: Word.

Ebeling, Erich. 1916. 'Die "7 Todsünden" bei den Babylonieren'. *OLZ* 19:296-98.

———, ed. 1919. *Keilschrifttexte aus Assur religiösen Inhalts,* vol. 1. Ausgrabungen der Deutschen Orientgesellschaft in Assur, E: Inschriften, 2/28. Leipzig: Hinrichs.

Eder, Asher. 2006. 'The Sabbath: To Remember, to Observe, to Make'. *JBQ* 34:104-9.

Edzard, Dietz Otto. 1970. *Altbabylonische Rechts- und Wirtschaftsurkunden aus Tell ed-Dēr im Iraq Museum, Baghdad.* ABAW 72. Munich: Bayerische Akademie der Wissenschaften.

Ehrlich, Arnold B. 1908. *Randglossen zur Hebräischen Bibel: Textkritisches, sprachliches und sachliches,* vol. 1. Leipzig: Hinrichs. Repr. Hildesheim: Olms, 1968.

Eichler, Barry L. 1973. *Indenture at Nuzi: The Personal Tidennūtu Contract and Its Mesopotamian Analogues.* Yale Near Eastern Researches 5. New Haven: Yale University Press.

———. 1987. 'Literary Structure in the Laws of Eshnunna'. Pp. 71-84 in *Language, Literature, and History,* ed. Francesca Rochberg-Halton. Erica Reiner Festschrift. AOS 67.

Eichrodt, Walther. 1959. *Theology of the Old Testament,* vol. 1. OTL. Philadelphia: Westminster, 1961. (trans. from German, 6th ed.)

Eissfeldt, Otto. 1917. *Erstlinge und Zehnten im Alten Testament: Ein Beitrag zur Geschichte des Israelitisch-jüdischen Kultus.* BWAT 22. Leipzig: Hinrichs.

———. 1918. 'Zum Zehnten bei den Babyloniern'. Pp. 163-74 in *Abhandlungen zur semitischen Religionskunde und Sprachwissenschaft,* ed. Wilhelm Frankenberg and Friedrich Küchler. Wolf Wilhelm Graf von Baudissin Festschrift. BZAW 33. Giessen: Töpelmann.

Ellens, Deborah L. 2008. *Women in the Sex Texts of Leviticus and Deuteronomy: A Comparative Conceptual Analysis.* LHB/OTS 458. London: T. & T. Clark.

Ellison, H. L. 1973. 'The Hebrew Slave: A Study in Early Israelite Society'. *EvQ* 45:30-35.

Elman, Pearl. 1997. 'Deuteronomy 21:10-14: The Beautiful Captive Woman'. *Women in Judaism* 1/1.

Elon, Menachem. 1972a. 'Pledge'. Pp. 636-44 in *EncJud,* vol. 13.

———. 1972b. 'Suretyship'. Pp. 524-29 in *EncJud,* vol. 15.

Engelhard, David H. 1980. 'The Lord's Motivated Concern for the Underprivileged'. *CTJ* 15:5-26.

Engelken, Karen. 1988. 'פִּלֶגֶשׁ'. Pp. 549-51 in *TDOT,* vol. 11 (2001). (trans. from German)

———. 1990. *Frauen im Alten Israel: Eine begriffsgeschichtliche und sozialrechtliche Studie zur Stellung der Frau im Alten Testament.* BWANT 130. Stuttgart: Kohlhammer.

Ennew, Judith. 1981. *Debt Bondage — A Survey.* London: Anti-Slavery Society.

Enns, Peter. 1997. '5477 מִשְׁפָּט'. Pp. 1142-44 in *NIDOTTE,* vol. 2.

Ephʿal, Israel, and Joseph Naveh. 1998. 'Remarks on the Recently Published Moussaieff Ostraca'. *IEJ* 48:269-73.

Epstein, T. Scarlett. 1962. *Economic Development and Social Change in South India.* Manchester: Manchester University Press.

Epsztein, Léon. 1983. *Social Justice in the Ancient Near East and the People of the Bible.* London: SCM, 1986. (trans. from French)

Eskenazi, Tamara C., Daniel J. Harrington, and William H. Shea, eds. 1991. *The Sabbath in Jewish and Christian Traditions.* New York: Crossroad.

Eyre, Christopher J. 1987. 'Work and the Organisation of Work in the New Kingdom'. Pp. 167-221 in *Labor in the Ancient Near East,* ed. Marvin A. Powell. AOS 68. New Haven: American Oriental Society.

Fabry, Heinz-Josef. 1974. 'דַּל'. Pp. 208-30 in *TDOT,* vol. 3 (1978). (trans. from German)

———. 1997. 'Deuteronomium 15: Gedanken zur Geschwister-Ethik im Alten Testament'. *ZABR* 3:92-111.
Fager, J. A. 1987. 'Land Tenure in the Biblical Jubilee: A Moral World View'. *HAR* 11:59-68.
———. 1993. *Land Tenure and the Biblical Jubilee: Uncovering Hebrew Ethics through the Sociology of Knowledge*. JSOTSup 155. Sheffield: Sheffield Academic.
Falk, Ze'ev W. 1959. 'Exodus xxi 6'. *VT* 9:86-88.
———. 1967.'Hebrew Legal Terms: II'. *JSS* 12:241-44.
———. 1970. Review of Reuven Yaron, *The Laws of Eshnunna* (1969). *Bib* 51:130-33.
———. 1992. 'Law and Ethics in the Hebrew Bible'. Pp. 82-90 in *Justice and Righteousness: Biblical Themes and Their Influence*, ed. Henning Graf Reventlow and Yair Hoffmann. JSOTSup 137. Sheffield: Sheffield Academic.
———. 2001. *Hebrew Law in Biblical Times: An Introduction*. 2nd ed. Provo: Brigham Young University Press/Winona Lake: Eisenbrauns.
Falkenstein, Adam, and Wolfram von Soden, eds. 1953. *Sumerische und akkadische Hymnen und Gebete*. Bibliothek der alten Welt, Reihe der alte Orient. Zurich: Artemis.
Farbridge, Maurice H. 1923. *Studies in Biblical and Semitic Symbolism*. Trubner's Oriental Series. London: Kegan Paul.
Faulkner, Raymond D., and Carol A. R. Andrews, eds. 1985. *The Ancient Egyptian Book of the Dead*. Rev. ed. London: British Museum.
Feeley-Harnik, Gillian. 1982. 'Is Historical Anthropology Possible? The Case of the Runaway Slave'. Pp. 95-126 in *Humanizing America's Iconic Book: Society of Biblical Literature Centennial Addresses 1980*, ed. Gene M. Tucker and Douglas A. Knight. SBLBSNA 6. Chico: Scholars.
Feliks, Jehuda. 1972. 'Agricultural Methods and Implements in Ancient Erez Israel; Agriculture in the Land of Israel'. Pp. 374-98 in *EncJud*, vol. 2.
Fensham, F. Charles. 1959. 'New Light on Exodus 21:6 and 22:7 from the Laws of Eshnunna'. *JBL* 78:160-61.
———. 1962a. '*'d* in Exodus xxii 12'. *VT* 12:337-39.
———. 1962b. 'Widow, Orphan, and the Poor in Ancient Near Eastern Legal and Wisdom Literature'. *JNES* 21:129-39. Repr. Pp. 161-71 in *Studies in Ancient Israelite Wisdom*, ed. James L. Crenshaw. New York: Ktav, 1976.
———. 1976. 'The Rôle of the Lord in the Legal Sections of the Covenant Code'. *VT* 26:262-74.
———. 1978. 'Liability in Case of Negligence in the Old Testament Covenant Code and Ancient Legal Traditions'. Pp. 183-94 in *Acta Juridica* 1976. Ben Beinart Festschrift, vol. 1.
———. 1981. 'The Root *b'r* in Ugaritic and in Isaiah in the Meaning "to Pillage"'. *JNSL* 9:67-69.
———. 1988. 'Liability of Animals in Biblical and Ancient Near Eastern Law'. *JNSL* 14:85-90.
Feucht, Christian. 1964. *Untersuchungen zum Heiligkeitsgesetz*. Theologische Arbeiten 20. Berlin: Evangelische Verlagsanstalt.
Finkel, Irving L. 1987. 'An Issue of Weights from the Reign of Amar-Sin'. *ZA* 77:192-93.
Finkelstein, Jacob J. 1952. 'The Middle Assyrian Šulmānu-Texts'. *JAOS* 72:77-80.
———. 1961. 'Ammiṣaduqa's Edict and the Babylonian "Law Codes"'. *JCS* 15:91-104.
———. 1965. 'Some New Misharum Material and Its Implications'. *AS* 16:233-46.
———. 1969. 'The Edict of Ammiṣaduqa: A New Text'. *RA* 63:45-64.
———. 1970. 'On Some Recent Studies in Cuneiform Law'. Review of J. A. Ankum,

R. Feenstra, and W. F. Leemans, eds., *Symbolae Iuridicae et Historicae*. Martino David Festschrift (1968). *JAOS* 90:243-56.

———. 1973. 'The Goring Ox: Some Historical Perspectives on Deodands, Forfeitures, Wrongful Death and the Western Notion of Sovereignty'. *Temple Law Quarterly* 46:169-290.

———. 1981. *The Ox That Gored*. Transactions of the American Philosophical Society 71/2. Philadelphia: American Philosophical Society.

Finley, Moses I. 1973. *The Ancient Economy*. Berkeley: University of California Press.

———. 1981. 'Debt-Bondage and the Problem of Slavery'. Pp. 150-66 in *Economy and Society in Ancient Greece*, ed. Brent D. Shaw and Richard P. Saller. London: Chatto & Windus.

———, ed. 1960. *Slavery in Classical Antiquity: Views and Controversies*. Cambridge: Heffer.

Fishbane, Michael. 1985. *Biblical Interpretation in Ancient Israel*. Oxford: Clarendon.

Fitzpatrick-McKinley, Anne. 1999. *The Transformation of Torah from Scribal Advice to Law*. JSOTSup 287. Sheffield: Sheffield Academic.

Fleishman, Joseph. 2000. 'Does the Law of Exodus 21:7-11 Permit a Father to Sell His Daughter to Be a Slave?' *JLA* 13:47-64.

Fohrer, Georg. 1965. 'Das sogenannte apodiktisch formulierte Recht und der Dekalog'. *KD* 11:49-74.

Foster, Benjamin R. 2005. *Before the Muses: An Anthology of Akkadian Literature*. 3rd ed. Bethesda, Maryland: CDL.

Frazer, James George. 1922. *The Golden Bough: A Study in Magic and Religion*. Abridged ed. New York: Macmillan. Repr. 1958.

Freedman, David Noel. 2000. *The Nine Commandments: Uncovering a Hidden Pattern of Crime and Punishment in the Hebrew Bible*. ABRL. New York: Doubleday.

Fretheim, Terence E. 1991. *Exodus*. Interpretation. Louisville: John Knox.

———. 2003. 'Law in the Service of Life: A Dynamic Understanding of Law in Deuteronomy'. Pp. 183-200 in *A God So Near: Essays on Old Testament Theology*, ed. Brent A. Strawn and Nancy R. Bowen. Patrick Miller Festschrift. Winona Lake: Eisenbrauns.

Frevel, Christian, Michael Konkel, and Johannes Schnocks, eds. 2005. *Die Zehn Worte: Der Dekalog als Testfall der Pentateuchkritik*. QD 212. Freiburg im Breisgau: Herder.

Frey, Hellmuth. 1957. *Das Buch der Verbindung Gottes mit seiner Gemeinde: Kapitel 19–24 des zweiten Buches Mose*. 2nd ed. BAT 6/1. Stuttgart: Calwer. 1st ed. 1952.

Frey, Mathilde. 2006. 'The Sabbath Commandment in the Book of the Covenant: Ethics on Behalf of the Outcast'. *Journal of Asia Adventist Seminary* 9:3-11.

Frick, Frank S. 1977. *The City in Ancient Israel*. SBLDS 36. Missoula: Scholars.

Fried, Lisbeth S., and David Noel Freedman. 2001. 'Was the Jubilee Year Observed in Preexilic Judah?' Pp. 2257-70 in Jacob Milgrom, *Leviticus 23–27*. AB 3B. New York: Doubleday.

Fritz, Volkmar. 1995. *The City in Ancient Israel*. Sheffield: Sheffield Academic.

Frymer-Kensky, Tikva. 1980. 'Tit for Tat: The Principle of Equal Retribution in Near Eastern and Biblical Law'. *BA* 43:230-34.

———. 2001. 'Israel'. Pp. 251-63 in *SDANEL*.

———. 2003. 'Anatolia and the Levant: Israel'. Pp. 975-1046 in *HANEL*, vol. 2.

von Gall, August Freiherrn. 1910. 'Die Entstehung der humanitären Forderungen des Gesetzes: I. Ein vergessenes Baalsopfer'. *ZAW* 30:91-98.

Galpaz-Feller, Pnina. 2008. 'The Widow in the Bible and Ancient Egypt', *ZAW* 120:231-53.

Galvão, Henrique de Noronha. 1994. 'The Messianic Sabbatical Year and the Social Mission of the Church'. *Comm* 21:49-68.

Gamoran, Hillel. 1971. 'The Biblical Law against Loans on Interest'. *JNES* 30:127-34.

———. 1973. 'Talmudic Controls on the Purchase of Futures'. *JQR* 64:48-66.

———. 1981. 'The Talmudic Law of Mortgages in View of the Prohibition against Lending on Interest'. *HUCA* 52:153-62.

García López, Felix, and Heinz-Josef Fabry. 1995. 'תּוֹרָה'. Pp. 609-46 in *TDOT*, vol. 15 (2006). (trans. from German)

Garelli, Paul. 1969. *Le Proche-Orient asiatique: Des origines aux invasions des peuples de la mer*. Nouvelle Clio: L'histoire et ses problèmes 2. Paris: Presses universitaires de France.

Garrett, D. A. 2003. 'Levi, Levites'. Pp. 519-22 in *DOTP*.

Geertz, Clifford. 1960. *The Religion of Java*. Glencoe, IL: Free Press. Repr. Chicago: University of Chicago Press, 1976.

Geiger, Abraham. 1857. *Urschrift und Uebersetzungen der Bibel: In ihrer Abhängigkeit von der innern Entwicklung des Judenthums*. Breslau: Hainauer. Repr. Frankfurt: Madda, 1928 (with new introduction and appendix).

Gelb, Ignace J., Piotr Steinkeller, and Robert M. Whiting, Jr. 1991. *Earliest Land Tenure Systems in the Near East: Ancient Kudurrus*. OIP 104. Chicago: Oriental Institute of the University of Chicago.

Gemser, Berend. 1953. 'The Importance of the Motive Clause in Old Testament Law'. Pp. 50-66 in *Congress Volume: Copenhagen 1953*. In Memoriam Aage Bentzen. VTSup 1. Leiden: Brill.

George, Andrew, ed. 1999. *The Epic of Gilgamesh: The Babylonian Epic Poem and Other Texts in Akkadian and Sumerian*. New York: Barnes & Noble.

Gerleman, Gillis. 1977. 'Nutzrecht und Wohnrecht: Zur Bedeutung von אחזה und נחלה'. *ZAW* 89:313-25.

Gerstenberger, Erhard S. 1965. *Wesen und Herkunft des 'Apodiktischen Rechts'*. WMANT 20. Neukirchen-Vluyn: Neukirchener.

———. 1986. 'עָזַב'. Pp. 584-92 in *TDOT*, vol. 10 (1999). (trans. from German)

———. 1987. 'עָנָה II'. Pp. 230-52 in *TDOT*, vol. 11 (2001). (trans. from German)

———. 1988. 'עָשַׁק'. Pp. 412-17 in *TDOT*, vol. 11 (2001). (trans. from German)

———. 1993. *Leviticus*. OTL. Louisville: Westminster John Knox, 1996. (trans. from German)

———. 2001. *Theologies in the Old Testament*. Edinburgh: T. & T. Clark, 2002. (trans. from German)

Gertz, Jan Christian. 1994. *Die Gerichtsorganisation Israels im deuteronomischen Gesetz*. FRLANT 165. Göttingen: Vandenhoeck & Ruprecht.

Gevirtz, Stanley. 1961. 'West-Semitic Curses and the Problem of the Origins of Hebrew Law'. *VT* 11:137-58.

Gibb, H. A. R., and J. H. Kramers, eds. 1961. *Shorter Encyclopaedia of Islam*. Royal Netherlands Academy, Leiden: Brill/London: Luzac.

Giles, Kevin. 1994. 'The Biblical Argument for Slavery: Can the Bible Mislead? A Case Study in Hermeneutics'. *EvQ* 66:3-17.

Gilmer, Harry W. 1975. *The If-You Form in Israelite Law*. SBLDS 15. Missoula: Scholars.

Ginsberg, H. Louis. 1982. *The Israelian Heritage of Judaism*. Texts and Studies of the Jewish

Theological Seminary of America 24. New York: Jewish Theological Seminary of America.

Ginzberg, E. 1932. 'Studies in the Economics of the Bible'. *JQR* 22:343-408.

Gitlin, Emmanuel M. 1963.'The Tithe in Deuteronomy'. *Religion in Life* 32:574-85.

Glancy, Jennifer A. 2002. *Slavery in Early Christianity.* Oxford: Oxford University Press, Repr. Minneapolis: Fortress, 2006.

Glass, Zipporah G. 2000. 'Land, Slave Labor and Law: Engaging Ancient Israel's Economy'. *JSOT* 91:27-39.

Glassner, Jean-Jacques. 2004. *Mesopotamian Chronicles.* SBLWAW 19. Atlanta: SBL.

Glessmer, Uwe. 1991. 'Der 364-Tage-Kalender und die Sabbatstruktur seiner Schaltungen in ihrer Bedeutung für den Kult'. Pp. 379-98 in *Ernten, Was Man Sät,* ed. Dwight R. Daniels, Uwe Glessmer, and Martin Rösel. Klaus Koch Festschrift. Neukirchen-Vluyn: Neukirchener.

Gnuse, Robert. 1985a. 'Jubilee Legislation in Leviticus: Israel's Vision of Social Reform'. *BTB* 15:43-48.

——. 1985b. *You Shall Not Steal: Community and Property in the Biblical Tradition.* Maryknoll: Orbis.

Goelet, Ogden, Jr. 2002, 'Fiscal Renewal in Ancient Egypt: Its Language, Symbols, and Metaphors'. Pp. 277-322 in *DERANE.*

Goetze, Albrecht. 1966. 'On §§163, 164/5 and 176 of the Hittite Code'. *JCS* 20:128-32.

Goldberg, Michael L. 1984. 'The Story of the Moral: Gifts or Bribes in Deuteronomy?' *Int* 38:15-25.

Goldingay, John. 2002. 'Jubilee Tithe'. *Transformation* 19:198-205.

Goldstein, A. M. et al., eds. 2001. *Measuring and Weighing in Ancient Times.* Haifa: Reuben and Edith Hecht Museum.

Gomme, A. W., T. J. Cadoux, and P. J. Rhodes. 1996. 'Solon'. Pp. 1421-22 in *OCD.*

Goodman, Martin. 1982. 'The First Jewish Revolt: Social Conflict and the Problem of Debt'. *JJS* 33:417-27.

Gordis, Robert. 1974. 'Love, Marriage, and Business in the Book of Ruth'. Pp. 241-64 in *A Light unto My Path,* ed. Howard N. Bream, Ralph D. Heim, and Carey A. Moore. Jacob Myers Festschrift. Gettysburg Theological Studies 4. Philadelphia: Temple University Press.

——, ed. 1982. 'The Sabbath Is Forever — A Symposium'. *Judaism* 31:6-98.

Gordon, Barry. 1982a. 'Lending at Interest: Some Jewish, Greek, and Christian Approaches, 800 BC-AD 100'. *History of Political Economy* 14:406-26.

Gordon, Cyrus H. 1935. 'אלהים in Its Reputed Meaning of *Rulers, Judges'. JBL* 54:139-44.

——. 1936. 'Nuzi Tablets Relating to Theft'. *Or* 5:305-30.

——. 1949a. 'Azitawadd's Phoenician Inscription'. *JNES* 8:108-15.

——. 1949b. *Ugaritic Literature: A Comprehensive Translation of the Poetic and Prose Texts.* Scripta Pontificii Instituti Biblici 98. Rome: Pontifical Biblical Institute.

——. 1953. 'Sabbatical Cycle or Seasonal Pattern?' Review of A. S. Kapelrud, *Baal in the Ras Shamra Texts* (1952). *Or* 22:79-81.

——. 1982b. 'The Biblical Sabbath, Its Origin and Observance in the Ancient Near East'. *Judaism* 31:12-16.

Gordon, Edmund I. 1959. *Sumerian Proverbs: Glimpses of Everyday Life in Ancient Mesopotamia.* Museum Monographs 19. Philadelphia: University Museum.

Gossai, Hemchand. 1993. *Justice, Righteousness and the Social Critique of the Eighth-Century Prophets*. American University Studies, Ser. VII/141. New York: Lang.
Gottfried, Paul E. 1985. 'The Western Case against Usury'. *Thought* 60:89-98.
Gottstein, Moshe H. 1953. 'Du sollst nicht stehlen'. *TZ* 9:394-95.
Gottwald, Norman K. 1976. 'Israel, Social and Economic Development of'. Pp. 465-68 in *IDBSup*.

———. 1979. *The Tribes of Yahweh: A Sociology of the Religion of Liberated Israel: 1250-1050 B.C.E.* Maryknoll: Orbis.

———. 1993. 'Recent Studies of the Social World of Premonarchic Israel'. *CurBS* 1:163-89.

Gowan, Donald E. 1981. 'Reflections on the Motive Clauses in Old Testament Law'. Pp. 111-27 in *Intergerini Parietis Septum (Eph. 2:14)*, ed. Dikran Y. Hadidian. Markus Barth Festschrift. Pittsburgh: Pickwick.

———. 1987. 'Wealth and Poverty in the Old Testament: The Case of the Widow, the Orphan, and the Sojourner'. *Int* 41:341-53.

Grabbe, Lester L. 1991. 'Maccabean Chronology: 167-164 or 168-165 BCE'. *JBL* 110:59-74.
Gray, John. 1965. *The Legacy of Canaan: The Ras Shamra Texts and Their Relevance to the Old Testament*. 2nd ed. VTSup 5. Leiden: Brill.
Gray, Mary P. 1958. 'The Ḫâbīru-Hebrew Problem in the Light of the Source Material Available at Present'. *HUCA* 29:135-202.
Greenberg, Moshe. 1955. *The Ḫab/piru*. AOS 39. New Haven: American Oriental Society.

———. 1960. 'Some Postulates of Biblical Criminal Law'. Pp. 5-28 in *Yehezkel Kaufmann Jubilee Volume: Studies in Bible and Jewish Religion Dedicated to Yehezkel Kaufmann on the Occasion of His Seventieth Birthday*, ed. Menahem Haran. Jerusalem: Magnes.

———. 1962a. 'Avenger of Blood'. P. 321 in *IDB*, vol. 1.

———. 1962b. 'Crimes and Punishments'. Pp. 733-44 in *IDB*, vol. 1.

———. 1972. 'Sabbatical Year and Jubilee: Ancient Near Eastern Legal Background'. P. 578 in *EncJud*, vol. 14.

———. 1986. 'More Reflections on Biblical Criminal Law'. Pp. 1-17 in *Studies in Bible, 1986*, ed. Sara Japhet. ScrHier 31. Jerusalem: Magnes.

Greene-McCreight, Kathryn. 1995. 'Restless Until We Rest in God: The Fourth Commandment as Test Case in Christian "Plain Sense" Interpretation'. Pp. 223-36 in *The Ten Commandments: The Reciprocity of Faithfulness*, ed. Willliam P. Brown. Library of Theological Ethics. Louisville: Westminster John Knox. Repr. from *ExAud* 11 (1995): 29-41.

Greenfield, Jonas C. 1967. 'Some Aspects of Treaty Terminology in the Bible'. Pp. 117-19 in *Fourth World Congress of Jewish Studies: Papers*, vol. 1. Jerusalem: World Union of Jewish Studies.

———. 1991. 'Asylum at Aleppo: A Note on Sfire III, 4-7'. Pp. 272-78 in *Ah, Assyria . . . : Studies in Assyrian History and Ancient Near Eastern Historiography*, ed. Mordechai Cogan and Israel Eph'al. Hayim Tadmor Festschrift. ScrHier 33. Jerusalem: Magnes.

Greengus, Samuel. 1992. 'Law: Biblical and ANE Law'. Pp. 242-52 in *ABD*, vol. 4.

———. 1994. 'Some Issues Relating to the Comparability of Laws and the Coherence of the Legal Tradition'. Pp. 60-87 in *Theory and Method in Biblical and Cuneiform Law*, ed. Bernard M. Levinson. JSOTSup 181. Sheffield: Sheffield Academic.

———. 1995. 'Legal and Social Institutions of Ancient Mesopotamia'. Pp. 469-84 in *CANE*, vol. 1.

———. 1997. 'The Selling of Slaves: Laws Missing from the Hebrew Bible?' *ZABR* 3:1-11.
Greidanus, Sidney. 1984. 'Human Rights in Biblical Perspective'. *CTJ* 19:5-31.
Grisanti, Michael A. 1997. 'תעב'. Pp. 314-18 in *NIDOTTE*, vol. 4.
Grünwaldt, Klaus. 1999. *Die Heiligkeitsgesetz Leviticus 17–26: Ursprüngliche Gestalt, Tradition und Theologie*. BZAW 271. Berlin: de Gruyter.
Gurewicz, S. B. 1958. 'The Deuteronomic Provisions for Exemption from Military Service'. *ABR* 6:111-21.
Gurney, O. R. 1949. 'Texts from Dur-Kurigalzu'. *Iraq* 11:131-49.
Guthrie, H. H., Jr. 1962. 'Tithe'. Pp. 654-55 in *IDB*, vol. 4.
Haag, Ernst. 1993. 'שָׁבַת, שַׁבָּת'. Pp. 381-97 in *TDOT*, vol. 14.
Haas, G. H. 2003. 'Slave, Slavery'. Pp. 778-83 in *DOTP*.
Haase, Richard. 1957. 'Zur Anzeigepflicht des Finders nach hethitischem Recht'. *WO* 2:378-81.
———. 1967. 'Die Behandlung von Tierschäden in den Keilschriftrechten'. *RIDA* 14:11-65.
———. 1997. 'Talion und spiegelnde Strafe in den keilschriftlichen Rechtscorpora'. *ZABR* 3:195-201.
Habel, Norman C. 1995a. 'The Future of Social Justice Research in the Hebrew Scriptures: Questions of Authority and Relevance'. Pp. 277-91 in *Old Testament Interpretation: Past, Present, and Future*, ed. James Luther Mays, David L. Petersen, and Kent Harold Richards. Gene Tucker Festschrift. Nashville: Abingdon/Edinburgh: T. & T. Clark.
———. 1995b. *The Land Is Mine: Six Biblical Land Ideologies*. OBT. Minneapolis: Fortress.
Halbe, Jörn. 1975. *Das Privilegrecht Jahwes: Ex 34, 10-26: Gestalt und Wesen, Herkunft und Wirken in vordeuteronomischer Zeit*. FRLANT 114. Göttingen: Vandenhoeck & Ruprecht.
Hallo, William W. 1977. 'New Moons and Sabbaths: A Case-Study in the Contrastive Approach'. *HUCA* 48:1-18.
———. 1985. 'Biblical Abominations and Sumerian Taboos'. *JQR* 76:21-40.
———. 1995. 'Slave Release in the Biblical World in Light of a New Text'. Pp. 79-93 in *Solving Riddles and Untying Knots: Biblical, Epigraphic, and Semitic Studies*, ed. Ziony Zevit, Seymour Gitin, and Michael Sokoloff. Jonas C. Greenfield Festschrift. Winona Lake: Eisenbrauns.
Hamel, Édouard. 1969. *Les dix paroles: Perspectives bibliques*. Essais pour notre temps, Section de théologie 7. Brussels: Desclée de Brouwer/Montreal: Bellarmin.
Hamilton, Jeffries M. 1992a. '*Hā'āreṣ* in the Shemitta Law'. *VT* 42:214-22.
———. 1992b. *Social Justice and Deuteronomy: The Case of Deuteronomy 15*. SBLDS 136. Atlanta: Scholars.
Hamilton, Victor P. 1997. '3846 יָתוֹם'. Pp. 570-71 in *NIDOTTE*, vol. 2.
Hamp, Vinzenz. 1974. 'גָּנַב'. Pp. 39-53 in *TDOT*, vol. 3 (1978). (trans. from German)
Hanks, Thomas D. 1983. *God So Loved the Third World: The Biblical Vocabulary of Oppression*. Maryknoll: Orbis. (trans. from Spanish, rev.)
Hanson, Paul D. 1977. 'The Theological Significance of Contradiction within the Book of the Covenant'. Pp. 110-31 in *Canon and Authority: Essays in Old Testament Religion and Theology*, ed. George W. Coats and Burke O. Long. Philadelphia: Fortress.
Haran, Menahem. 1978. *Temples and Temple-Service in Ancient Israel: An Inquiry into the Character of Cult Phenomena and the Historical Setting of the Priestly School*. Oxford: Clarendon.
Harland, P. J. 2000. 'בצע: Bribe, Extortion or Profit?' *VT* 50:310-22.

Harrelson, Walter J. 1997. *The Ten Commandments and Human Rights*. Rev. ed. Macon: Mercer University Press. 1st ed. 1980.
Harris, Rivkah. 1955. 'The Archive of the Sin Temple in Khafajah (Tutub)'. *JCS* 9:31-88, 91-120.
———. 1960. 'Old Babylonian Temple Loans'. *JCS* 14:126-37.
Harrison, R. K. 1980. *Leviticus*. TOTC. Downers Grove: InterVarsity.
Hartley, John E. 1992. *Leviticus*. WBC 4. Dallas: Word.
Hasel, Gerhard F. 1992. 'Sabbath'. Pp. 849-56 in *ABD*, vol. 5.
Hattu, Donna Efrina. 2002. 'Ketaatan kepada Allah: Karena atau Supaya? Pemahaman Ulangan 28:1-14 dan Relevansinya dengan Teologi Kemakmuran [Obedience to God: Because of or So that? The Meaning of Deuteronomy 28:1-14 and Its Relevance to Prosperity Theology]'. M.Th. thesis, STT Jakarta.
Havice, Harriet K. 1978. 'The Concern for the Widow and the Fatherless in the Ancient Near East: A Case Study in Old Testament Ethics'. Ph.D. diss., Yale University.
Hawkins, John David, ed. 1977. *Trade in the Ancient Near East*. Papers of the XXIIIrd. Rencontre Assyriologique Internationale, Birmingham 1976. London: British School of Archaeology in Iraq. Repr. from *Iraq* 39 (1977): 1-231.
Hawthorne, Gerald F. 1978. 'Tithe'. Pp. 851-55 in *NIDNTT*, vol. 3. (trans. from German)
Heaton, E. W. 1946. 'Sojourners in Egypt'. *ExpTim* 58:80-82.
Heger, Paul. 2005. 'Source of Law in the Biblical and Mesopotamian Law Collections'. *Bib* 86:324-42.
Heimpel, W. 1981. 'The Nanshe Hymn'. *JCS* 33:65-139.
Heinemann, Joseph. 1974. 'Early Halakhah in the Palestinian Targum'. *JJS* 25:117-19.
Hejcl, Johann. 1907. *Das alttestamentliche Zinsverbot: im Lichte der ethnologischen Jurisprudenz sowie des altorientalischen Zinswesens*. BibS(F) 12/4. Freiburg im Breisgau: Herder.
Heltzer, Michael. 1975. 'On Tithe Paid in Grain in Ugarit'. *IEJ* 25:124-28.
———. 1976. *The Rural Community in Ancient Ugarit*. Wiesbaden: Reichert.
———. 2004. 'New Evidence About the Judge in Pre-Exilic Judah'. *ZABR* 10:287-91.
Herlianto. 1992. *Teologi Sukses: Antara Allah dan Mamon [Theology of Success: Between God and Mammon]*. Jakarta: BPK Gunung Mulia.
Herman, Menahem. 1991. *Tithe as Gift: The Institution in the Pentateuch and in Light of Mauss's Prestation Theory*. Distinguished Dissertation Series. San Francisco: Mellen Research University Press.
Hermisson, Hans Jürgen. 1985. 'Gottes Freiheit — Spielraum des Menschen: Alttestamentliche Aspekte eines biblisch-theologischen Themas'. *ZTK* 82:129-52.
Herrmann, Johannes. 1927. 'Das zehnte Gebot'. Pp. 69-82 in *Beiträge zur Religionsgeschichte und Archäologie Palästinas*, ed. Anton Jirku. Ernst Sellin Festschrift. Leipzig: Deichertsche.
Herrmann, Wolfram. 1958. 'Das Aufgebot aller Kräfte: Zur Interpretation von 1 K II$_{96-103}$ = IV$_{184-191}$ und Dtn 20$_{5-7}$'. *ZAW* 70:215-20.
Heschel, Abraham J. 1951a. 'A Palace in Time'. Pp. 214-22 in *The Ten Commandments: The Reciprocity of Faithfulness*, ed. Willliam P. Brown. Library of Theological Ethics. Louisville: Westminster John Knox. Repr. from *The Sabbath: Its Meaning for Modern Man*, 13-24.
———. 1951b. *The Sabbath: Its Meaning for Modern Man*. New York: Farrar, Straus & Young.

Hiebert, Paula S. 1989. '"Whence Shall Help Come to me?" The Biblical Widow'. Pp. 125-41 in *Gender and Difference in Ancient Israel*, ed. Peggy L. Day. Minneapolis: Fortress.

Hoenig, S. B. 1969. 'Sabbatical Years and the Year of Jubilee'. *JQR* 59:222-36.

Hoffmann, David. 1905. *Das Buch Leviticus*, vol. 1. Berlin: Poppelauer.

———. 1913. *Das Buch Deuteronomium*. Vol. 1: *Deut. I–XXI,9*. Berlin: Poppelauer.

———. 1922. *Das Buch Deuteronomium*. Vol. 2: *Deut. XXI,16–XXXI*. Berlin: Poppelauer.

Hoffmeier, James K. 1997. *Israel in Egypt: The Evidence for the Authenticity of the Exodus Tradition* (Oxford: Oxford University Press).

Hoffner, Harry A. 1972. 'אַלְמָנָה'. Pp. 287-91 in *TDOT*, vol. 1 (rev. ed. 1977). (trans. from German)

———. 1976. 'חָבַל II'. Pp. 185-88 in *TDOT*, vol. 4 (1980). (trans. from German)

———. 1995. 'Legal and Social Institutions of Hittite Anatolia'. Pp. 555-69 in *CANE*, vol. 1.

———. 1997. *The Laws of the Hittites: A Critical Edition*. Studies in Near Eastern Archaeology and Civilisation 23. Leiden: Brill.

Hoftijzer, Jacob. 1957. 'Ex. xxi 8'. *VT* 7:388-91.

Hoftijzer, Jacob, and W. H. van Soldt. 1991. 'Texts from Ugarit Concerning Security and Related Akkadian and West Semitic Material'. *UF* 23:189-216.

Hogg, James Edward. 1926. 'The Meaning of לצמתת in Lev. 25:23-30'. *AJSL* 42:208-10.

Holladay, William L. 1971. *A Concise Hebrew and Aramaic Lexicon of the Old Testament: Based upon the Lexical Work of Ludwig Koehler and Walter Baumgartner*. Grand Rapids: Wm. B. Eerdmans.

Homer, Sidney, and Richard Sylla. 1991. *A History of Interest Rates*. 3rd ed. New Brunswick: Rutgers University Press.

Hopkins, David C. 1985. *The Highlands of Canaan: Agricultural Life in the Early Iron Age*. SWBA 3; Sheffield: Almond.

———. 1987. 'Life on the Land: The Subsistence Struggles of Early Israel'. *BA* 50:178-91.

Hoppe, Leslie J. 2004. *There Shall Be No Poor among You: Poverty in the Bible*. Nashville: Abingdon. Rev. and expansion of *Being Poor: A Biblical Study*. Wilmington: Michael Glazier, 1987.

Horst, Friedrich. 1930. *Das Privilegrecht Jahwes: Rechtsgeschichtliche Untersuchungen zum Deuteronomium*. FRLANT 45. Göttingen: Vandenhoeck & Ruprecht. Repr. pp. 17-154 in *Gottes Recht: Gesammelte Studien zum Recht im Alten Testament*. TB 12. Munich: Kaiser, 1961.

———. 1935. 'Der Diebstahl im Alten Testament'. Pp. 19-28 in *Festschrift Paul Kahle*. Leiden: Brill. Repr. pp. 167-75 in *Gottes Recht: Gesammelte Studien zum Recht im Alten Testament*. TB 12. Munich: Kaiser, 1961.

———. 1956. 'Recht und Religion im Bereich des Alten Testaments'. *EvT* 16: 49-75. Repr. pp. 260-91 in *Gottes Recht: Gesammelte Studien zum Recht im Alten Testament*. TB 12; Munich: Kaiser, 1961.

———. 1957. 'Der Eid im Alten Testament'. *EvT* 17:366-84. Repr. pp. 292-314 in *Gottes Recht: Gesammelte Studien zum Recht im Alten Testament*. TB 12. Munich: Kaiser, 1961.

———. 1961. 'Zwei Begriffe für Eigentum (Besitz): נחלה und אחזה'. Pp. 135-56 in *Verbannung und Heimkehr*, ed. Arnulf Kuschke. Wilhelm Rudolph Festschrift. Tübingen: Mohr.

Hossfeld, Frank-Lothar. 2004. 'Der Stand der Dekalogforschung'. Pp. 57-65 in *Recht und*

Ethik im Alten Testament, ed. Bernard M. Levinson and Eckart Otto. Altes Testament und Moderne 13. Münster: Lit.

Houston, Walter J. 1995. '"You Shall Open your Hand to Your Needy Brother": Ideology and Moral Formation in Deut. 15:1-18'. Pp. 296-314 in *The Bible in Ethics: The Second Sheffield Colloquium,* ed. John W. Rogerson, Margaret Davies, and M. Daniel Carroll Rodas. JSOTSup 207. Sheffield: Sheffield Academic.

———. 2004. Review of Harold V. Bennett. *Injustice Made Legal* (2002). *VT* 54:132.

———. 2006. *Contending for Justice: Ideologies and Theologies of Social Justice in the Old Testament.* LHB/OTS 428. London: T. & T. Clark.

Houten, Christiana van. 1991. *The Alien in Israelite Law.* JSOTSup 107. Sheffield: Sheffield Academic.

———. 1992. 'Remember That You Were Aliens: A Traditio-Historical Study'. Pp. 224-40 in *Priests, Prophets and Scribes,* ed. Eugene Ulrich et al. Joseph Blenkinsopp Festschrift. JSOTSup 149. Sheffield: JSOT.

Houtman, Cornelis. 1986. *Exodus.* Vol. 1: *Chapters 1:1–7:13.* Historical Commentary on the Old Testament. Kampen: Kok, 1993. (trans. from Dutch)

———. 1996. *Exodus.* Vol. 3: *Chapters 20–40.* Historical Commentary on the Old Testament. Leuven: Peeters, 2000. (trans. from Dutch)

———. 1997. *Das Bundesbuch: Ein Kommentar.* Studies in Near Eastern Archaeology and Civilisation 24. Leiden: Brill.

Hubbard, Robert L., Jr. 1991. 'The Go'el in Ancient Israel: Theological Reflections on an Israelite Institution'. *BBR* 1:3-19.

———. 1997. '1457 גאל'. Pp. 789-94 in *NIDOTTE,* vol. 1.

Hudson, Michael. 1993. *The Lost Tradition of Biblical Debt Cancellations.* New York: Social Science Forum, Henry George School of Social Science.

———. 1999. '"Proclaim Liberty Throughout the Land": The Economic Roots of the Jubilee'. *BRev* 15/1:26-33, 44.

———. 2002. 'Reconstructing the Origins of Interest-Bearing Debt and the Logic of Clean Slates'. Pp. 7-58 in *DERANE.*

Huehnergard, John. 1987. *Ugaritic Vocabulary in Syllabic Transcription.* HSS 32. Atlanta: Scholars.

Huffmon, Herbert B. 1974. 'Exodus 23:4-5: A Comparative Study'. Pp. 271-78 in *A Light unto My Path,* ed. Howard N. Bream, Ralph D. Heim, and Carey A. Moore. Jacob Myers Festschrift. Gettysburg Theological Studies 4. Philadelphia: Temple University Press.

Huggler, Justin. 2006. 'The Price of Being a Woman: Slavery in Modern India'. *Independent* 3 April 2006.

Hulst, Alexander Reinard. 1938. *Het Karakter van den Cultus in Deuteronomium.* Wageningen: Veenman & Zonen.

Hulst, Alexander Reinard et al. 1960. *Old Testament Translation Problems.* Helps for Translators 1. Leiden: Brill/United Bible Societies.

Humbert, Paul. 1960. 'Le substantif *to'ēbā et le verbe tʿb* dans l'Ancien Testament'. *ZAW* 72:217-37.

Hurowitz, Victor Avigdor. 1992. '"His Master Shall Pierce His Ear with an Awl" (Exodus 21.6) — Marking Slaves in the Bible in the Light of Akkadian Sources'. *PAAJR* 58:47-77.

———. 1997. *Divine Service and Its Rewards: Ideology and Poetics in the Hinke Kudurru.* Beer-Sheva 10. Beer-Sheva: Ben-Gurion University of the Negev Press.

Hurvitz, Avi. 1974. 'The Evidence of Language in Dating the Priestly Code: A Linguistic Study in Technical Idioms and Terminology'. *RB* 81:24-56.

———. 1982. *A Linguistic Study of the Relationship between the Priestly Source and the Book of Ezekiel: A New Approach to an Old Problem*. CahRB 20. Paris: Gabalda.

Hütter, Reinhard. 2005. 'The Tongue — Fallen and Restored: Some Reflections on the Three Voices of the Eighth Commandment'. Pp. 189-205 in *I Am the Lord Your God: Christian Reflections on the Ten Commandments*, ed. Carl E. Braaten and Christopher R. Seitz. Grand Rapids: Wm. B. Eerdmans.

Hyatt, J. Philip. 1971. *Exodus*. NCB. Grand Rapids: Wm. B. Eerdmans/London: Marshall, Morgan & Scott.

ILO. 2005. *A Global Alliance against Forced Labour: Global Report under the Follow-up to the ILO Declaration on Fundamental Principles and Rights at Work, Report I (B)*. International Labour Conference, 93rd Session. Geneva: International Labour Office.

Instone-Brewer, David. 2002. *Divorce and Remarriage in the Bible: The Social and Literary Context*. Grand Rapids: Wm. B. Eerdmans.

———. 2004. *Traditions of the Rabbis from the Era of the New Testament*. Vol. 1: *Prayer and Agriculture*. Grand Rapids: Wm. B. Eerdmans.

Irani, K. D., and Morris Silver, eds. 1995. *Social Justice in the Ancient World*. Contributions in Political Science 354. Westport, CT: Greenwood.

Jackson, Bernard S. 1971. 'Liability for Mere Intention in Early Jewish Law'. *HUCA* 42:197-225.

———. 1972. *Theft in Early Jewish Law*. Oxford: Clarendon.

———. 1974. 'The Fence-Breaker and the *Actio de Pastu Pecoris* in Early Jewish Law'. *JJS* 25:123-36.

———. 1975a. 'Foreign Influence in the Early Jewish Law of Theft'. Pp. 235-49 in *Essays in Jewish and Comparative Legal History*. SJLA 103. Leiden: Brill.

———. 1975b. 'The Goring Ox'. Pp. 108-52 in *Essays in Jewish and Comparative Legal History*. SJLA 103. Leiden: Brill. Repr. with minor revisions from 'The Goring Ox Again', *JJP* 18 (1972): 55-93.

———. 1975c. 'Principles and Cases: The Theft Laws of Hammurabi'. Pp. 64-74 in *Essays in Jewish and Comparative Legal History*. SJLA 103. Leiden: Brill. Repr. with minor revisions from *Irish Jurist* (1972).

———. 1975d. 'The Problem of Exodus 21:22-5 *(Ius Talionis)*'. Pp. 75-107 in *Essays in Jewish and Comparative Legal History*. SJLA 103. Leiden: Brill. Repr. with minor revisions from *VT* 23 (1973):273-304.

———. 1975e. 'Reflections on Biblical Criminal Law'. Pp. 25-63 in *Essays in Jewish and Comparative Legal History*. SJLA 103. Leiden: Brill. Repr. with minor revisions from *JJS* (1973).

———. 1975f. '"Two or Three Witnesses"'. Pp. 153-71 in *Essays in Jewish and Comparative Legal History*. SJLA 103. Leiden: Brill.

———. 1976. 'A Note on Exodus 22:4 (MT)'. *JJS* 27:138-41.

———. 1978. 'Travels and Travails of the Goring Ox: The Biblical Text in British Sources'. Pp. 41-56 in *Studies in Bible and the Ancient Near East*. Samuel E. Loewenstamm Festschrift. Jerusalem: Rubinstein.

———. 1989a. 'Ideas of Law and Legal Administration: A Semiotic Approach'. Pp. 185-202 in

The World of Ancient Israel: Sociological, Anthropological and Political Perspectives, ed. Ronald E. Clements. Cambridge: Cambridge University Press.

———. 1998a. 'Justice and Righteousness in the Bible: Rule of Law or Royal Paternalism?' *ZABR* 4:218-62.

———. 1998b. "Law' and 'Justice' in the Bible'. *JJS* 49:218-29.

———. 2000. *Studies in the Semiotics of Biblical Law*. JSOTSup 314. Sheffield: Sheffield Academic.

———. 2002. 'Models in Legal History: The Case of Biblical Law'. *JLR* 18:1-30.

———. 2005. 'Revolution in Biblical Law: Some Reflections on the Role of Theory in Methodology'. *JSS* 50:83-115.

———. 2006. *Wisdom-Laws: A Study of the Mishpatim of Exodus 21:1–22:16*. Oxford: Oxford University Press.

———, ed. 1995. 'Modelling Biblical Law: The Covenant Code'. *Chicago-Kent Law Review* 70:1745-1827.

———, and T. F. Watkins. 1984. 'Distraint in the Laws of Eshnunna and Hammurabi'. Pp. 409-19 in *Studi in onore di Cesare Sanfilippo*, vol. 5. Università di Catania, Pubblicazioni della Facoltà di Giurisprudenza 96. Milan: Giuffrè.

Jackson, Robert. 1989b. 'Prosperity Theology and the Faith Movement'. *Them* 15/1:16-24.

Jacob, Benno. 1923. 'The Decalogue'. *JQR* 14:141-87.

———. 1945. *The Second Book of the Bible: Exodus*. Hoboken: Ktav, 1992. (trans. from German)

Jaffee, Martin S. 1981. *Mishnah's Theology of Tithing: A Study of Tractate Maaserot*. BJS 19. Chico: Scholars.

Jagersma, H. 1981. 'The Tithes in the Old Testament'. Pp. 116-28 in *Remembering All the Way . . .* , ed. A. S. van der Woude. OtSt 21. Leiden: Brill.

Jankowska, N. B. 1969. 'Communal Self-Government and the King of the State of Arrapḫa'. *JESHO* 12:233-82.

Janzen, Waldemar. 1992. 'Land'. Pp. 143-54 in *ABD*, vol. 4.

Japhet, Sara. 1978. 'The Relationship between the Legal Corpora in the Pentateuch in Light of Manumission Laws'. Pp. 63-89 in *Studies in Bible*. ScrHier 31. Jerusalem: Magnes, 1986. (trans. from Hebrew article in *Studies in Bible and the Ancient Near East*. Samuel E. Loewenstamm Festschrift. Jerusalem: Rubinstein, 1978)

———. 1992. 'The Israelite Legal and Social Reality as Reflected in Chronicles: A Case Study'. Pp. 79-91 in *Sha'arei Talmon: Studies in the Bible, Qumran, and the Ancient Near East*, ed. Michael Fishbane and Emanuel Tov. Shemaryahu Talmon Festschrift. Winona Lake: Eisenbrauns.

Jas, Remko. 1996. *Neo-Assyrian Judicial Procedures*. SAAS 5. Helsinki: Neo-Assyrian Text Corpus Project.

Jasnow, Richard. 2003a. 'Egypt: Middle Kingdom and Second Intermediate Period'. Pp. 255-88 in *HANEL*, vol. 1.

———. 2003b. 'Egypt: New Kingdom'. Pp. 289-359 in *HANEL*, vol. 1.

———. 2003c. 'Egypt: Old Kingdom and First Intermediate Period'. Pp. 93-140 in *HANEL*, vol. 1.

———. 2003d. 'Egypt: Third Intermediate Period'. Pp. 777-818 in *HANEL*, vol. 2.

Jenni, Ernst. 1956. *Die theologische Begründung des Sabbatgebotes im Alten Testament*. ThSt 46. Zurich: Evangelischer.

Jepsen, Alfred. 1927. *Untersuchungen zum Bundesbuch*. BWANT 41. Stuttgart: Kohlhammer.
———. 1958. ''Ama[h] und Schiphcha[h]'. *VT* 8:293-97, 425.
———. 1967. 'Beiträge zur Auslegung und Geschichte des Dekalogs'. *ZAW* 79:275-304.
Jermyn, Leslie. 2002. 'Slavery Now!' http://www.globalaware.org/Articles_eng/slave_art_eng.htm.
Jewett, Paul K. 1971. *The Lord's Day: A Theological Guide to the Christian Day of Worship*. Grand Rapids: Wm. B. Eerdmans.
Jirku, Anton. 1929. 'Das israelitische Jobeljahr'. Pp. 169-79 in *Reinhold Seeberg Festschrift*, vol. 2, ed. W. Koepp. Leipzig: Scholl. Repr. pp. 319-29 in *Von Jerusalem nach Ugarit: Gesammelte Schriften*. Graz: Akademische, 1966.
Johns, C. H. W. 1904. *Babylonian and Assyrian Laws, Contracts and Letters*. Library of Ancient Inscriptions 6. Edinburgh: T. & T. Clark.
Johnson, Bo. 1984. 'מִשְׁפָּט'. Pp. 86-98 in *TDOT*, vol. 9 (1998). (trans. from German)
Johnston, Philip, and Peter Walker, eds. 2000. *The Land of Promise: Biblical, Theological and Contemporary Perspectives*. Downers Grove: InterVarsity/Leicester: Apollos.
Joosten, Jan. 1996. *People and Land in the Holiness Code: An Exegetical Study of the Ideational Framework of the Law in Leviticus 17–26*. VTSup 67. Leiden: Brill.
Jordan, Gregory D. 1991. 'Usury, Slavery, and Land-Tenure: The Nuzi *Tidennūtu* Transaction'. *ZA* 80:76-92.
Josephus. *The Works of Josephus: Complete and Unabridged*. Trans. by William Whiston. Rev. ed. Peabody: Hendrickson, 1987.
Jubilee Debt Campaign. n.d. 'The Debt Crisis: Facts & Figures'. http://www.jubileedebtcampaign.org.uk/?lid=247.
Jursa, Michael. 2002. 'Debts and Indebtedness in the Neo-Babylonian Period: Evidence from the Institutional Archives'. Pp. 197-220 in *DERANE*.
Kahle, Paul E. 1959. *The Cairo Geniza*. 2nd ed. Oxford: Blackwell. 1st ed. 1947.
Kahn, Pinchas. 2004. 'The Expanding Perspectives of the Sabbath'. *JBQ* 32:239-44.
Kaiser, Otto. 1992. 'The Law as Center of the Hebrew Bible'. Pp. 93-103 in *Sha'arei Talmon: Studies in the Bible, Qumran, and the Ancient Near East*, ed. Michael Fishbane and Emanuel Tov. Winona Lake: Eisenbrauns.
Kapelrud, Arvid S. 1968. 'The Number Seven in Ugaritic Texts'. *VT* 18:494-99.
———. 1986. 'נָשַׁךְ, נֶשֶׁךְ'. Pp. 61-65 in *TDOT*, vol. 10 (1999). (trans. from German)
Kaufman, Stephen A. 1979. 'The Structure of the Deuteronomic Law'. *Maarav* 1:105-58.
———. 1984. 'A Reconstruction of the Social Welfare Systems of Ancient Israel'. Pp. 277-86 in *In the Shelter of Elyon: Essays on Ancient Palestinian Life and Literature in Honor of G. W. Ahlström*, ed. W. B. Barrick and J. R. Spencer. JSOTSup 31. Sheffield: Sheffield Academic.
———. 1985. 'Deuteronomy 15 and Recent Research on the Dating of P'. Pp. 273-76 in *Das Deuteronomium: Entstehung, Gestalt und Botschaft*, ed. Norbert L. Lohfink. BETL 68 Leuven: Leuven University Press.
Kaufmann, Yehezkel. 1961. *The Religion of Israel: From Its Beginnings to the Babylonian Exile*. London: Allen & Unwin. (abridged trans. from Hebrew, 1937-56)
Kawashima, Robert S. 2003. 'The Jubilee, Every 49 or 50 Years?' *VT* 53:117-20.
Keil, Carl F., and Franz Delitzsch. 1864. *The Pentateuch*, vol. 2. Biblical Commentary on the Old Testament. Grand Rapids: Wm. B. Eerdmans/Edinburgh: T. & T. Clark. (trans. from German)

———. 1865. *The Pentateuch*, vol. 3. Biblical Commentary on the Old Testament. Grand Rapids: Wm. B. Eerdmans/Edinburgh: T. & T. Clark. (trans. from German)

Kellermann, Dieter. 1973a. 'בצע'. Pp. 205-8 in *TDOT*, vol. 2 (rev. ed. 1977). (trans. from German)

———. 1973b. 'גור'. Pp. 439-49 in *TDOT*, vol. 2 (rev. ed. 1977). (trans. from German)

Kemp, Barry J. 1989. *Ancient Egypt: Anatomy of a Civilization*. London: Routledge.

Kennett, R. H. 1920. *Deuteronomy and the Decalogue*. Cambridge: Cambridge University Press.

Kessler, Martin. 1971. 'The Law of Manumission in Jeremiah 34'. *BZ* 15:105-8.

Kessler, Rainer. 1992. 'Die Rolle des Armen für Gerechtigkeit und Sünde des Reichen: Hintergrund und Bedeutung von Dtn 15,9; 24,13.15'. Pp. 153-63 in *Was ist der Mensch . . . ? Beiträge zur Anthropologie des Alten Testaments*, ed. Frank Crüsemann, Christof Hardmeier, and Rainer Kessler. Hans Walter Wolff Festschrift. Munich: Kaiser.

———. 2002. 'Die Sklavin als Ehefrau: Zur Stellung der 'āmāh'. *VT* 52:501-12.

Keszler, Werner. 1957. 'Die literarische, historische und theologische Problematik des Dekalogs'. *VT* 7:1-16.

Kienast, Burkhart. 1978. *Die altbabylonischen Briefe und Urkunden aus Kisurra*, vol. 1. Freiburger altorientalische Studien 2. Wiesbaden: Steiner.

Kilian, Rudolf. 1963. *Literarkritische und formgeschichtliche Untersuchung des Heiligkeitsgesetzes*. BBB 19. Bonn: Hanstein.

King, Leonard W., ed. 1912. *Babylonian Boundary-Stones and Memorial-Tablets in the British Museum*. London: British Museum.

King, Philip J., and Lawrence E. Stager. 2001. *Life in Biblical Israel*. Library of Ancient Israel. Louisville: Westminster John Knox.

Kinsler, F. Ross, and Gloria Kinsler. 1999. *The Biblical Jubilee and the Struggle for Life: An Invitation to Personal, Ecclesial, and Social Transformation*. Maryknoll: Orbis.

Kippenberg, Hans G. 1983. 'Die Entlassung aus Schuldknechtschaft im antiken Judäa: Eine Legitimitätsvorstellung von Verwandtschaftsgruppen'. Pp. 74-104 in *'Vor Gott sind alle gleich': Soziale Gleichheit, soziale Ungleichheit und die Religionen*, ed. Günter Kehrer. Düsseldorf: Patmos.

Kitchen, Kenneth A. 2003. *On the Reliability of the Old Testament*. Grand Rapids: Wm. B. Eerdmans.

Kittel, Rudolf. 1925. *The Religion of the People of Israel*. London: Allen & Unwin. (trans. from German)

Kiuchi, Nobuyoshi. 2007. *Leviticus*. Apollos Old Testament Commentary. 3. Nottingham: Apollos.

Klein, H. 1976. 'Verbot des Menschendiebstahls im Dekalog? Prüfung einer These Albrecht Alts'. *VT* 26:161-69.

Kletter, Raz. 1991. 'The Inscribed Weights of the Kingdom of Judah'. *TA* 18:121-63.

———. 1998. *Economic Keystones: The Weight System of the Kingdom of Judah*. JSOTSup 276. Sheffield: Sheffield Academic.

Kline, Meredith G. 1963. *Treaty of the Great King: The Covenant Structure of Deuteronomy*. Grand Rapids: Wm. B. Eerdmans.

Klingenberg, Eberhard. 1977. *Das israelitische Zinsverbot in Torah, Mišnah und Talmud*. Abhandlungen der Geistes- und Sozialwissenschaftlichen Klasse, 1977/1. Mainz: Akademie der Wissenschaften und der Literatur/Wiesbaden: Steiner.

Klopfenstein, Martin A. 1964. *Die Lüge nach dem Alten Testament: Ihr Begriff, ihre Bedeutung und ihre Beurteilung*. Zurich: Gotthelf.
Knauth, R. J. D. 2003. 'Alien, Foreign Resident'. Pp. 26-33 in *DOTP*.
Knierim, Rolf P. 1995. *The Task of Old Testament Theology: Substance, Method, and Cases*. Grand Rapids: Wm. B. Eerdmans.
Knight, Douglas A. 2000. 'Village Law and the Book of the Covenant'. Pp. 163-79 in *"A Wise and Discerning Mind"*, ed. Saul M. Olyan and Robert C. Culley. Burke Long Festschrift. BJS 325. Providence: Brown University.
Knohl, Israel. 1995. *The Sanctuary of Silence: The Priestly Torah and the Holiness School*. Minneapolis: Fortress. (rev. trans. from Hebrew, 1992)
Knox, D. B. 1996. 'Wealth'. In *New Bible Dictionary*, ed. D. R. W. Wood. 3rd ed.; electronic ed. Downers Grove: InterVarsity.
Knudtzon, J. A., ed. 1915. *Die el-Amarna-Tafeln, mit Einleitung und Erläuterungen*. Vorderasiatische Bibliothek. Aalen: Otto Zeller; repr. 1964.
Koenig, John. 1992. 'Hospitality'. Pp. 299-301 in *ABD*, vol. 3.
Kohler, Josef, et al. 1904-23. *Hammurabi's Gesetz*. Leipzig: Eduard Pfeiffer.
Kohler, Josef, and Arthur Ungnad. 1913. *Assyrische Rechtsurkunden in Umschrift und Uebersetzung nebst einem Index der Personen-Namen und Rechtserläuterungen*. Leipzig: Eduard Pfeiffer.
Köhler, Ludwig. 1953. *Hebrew Man: Lectures Delivered at the Invitation of the University of Tübingen, December 1-16, 1952*. London: SCM, 1956/Nashville: Abingdon, 1957. (trans. from German)
Konkel, August H. 1997. '1591 גור'. Pp. 836-39 in *NIDOTTE*, vol. 1.
Koopmans, William T. 1997. '299 אחזה'. Pp. 358-60 in *NIDOTTE*, vol. 1.
Kooy, V. H. 1962. 'Hospitality'. P. 654 in *IDB*, vol. 2.
Koschaker, Paul. 1911. *Babylonisch-assyrisches Bürgschaftsrecht: Ein Beitrag zur Lehre von Schuld und Haftung*. Leipzig: Teubner.
———. 1928. *Neue keilschriftliche Rechtsurkunden aus der El-Amarna-Zeit*. ASAW 39/5. Leipzig: Hirzel.
Kovacs, Maureen Gallery. 1989. *The Epic of Gilgamesh*. Stanford: Stanford University Press.
Kraeling, Emil G., ed. 1953. *The Brooklyn Museum Aramaic Papyri: New Documents of the Fifth Century B.C. from the Jewish Colony at Elephantine*. Publications of the Department of Egyptian Art. New Haven: Yale University Press.
Kramer, Samuel Noah. 1963. *The Sumerians: Their History, Culture, and Character*. Chicago: University of Chicago Press.
Krapf, Thomas. 1984. 'Traditionsgeschichtliches zum deuteronomischen Fremdling-Waise-Witwe-Gebot'. *VT* 34:87-91.
Kraus, F. R. 1951. 'Nippur und Isin nach altbabylonischen Rechtsurkunden'. *JCS* 3:1-209.
———. 1958. *Ein Edikt des Königs Ammi-ṣaduqa von Babylon*. Studia et documenta ad iura orientis antiqui pertinentia 5. Leiden: Brill.
———. 1976. 'Akkadische Wörter und Ausdrücke, X'. *RA* 70:165-72.
———. 1984. *Königliche Verfügungen in altbabylonischer Zeit*. SDIO 11. Leiden: Brill. (Replaces *Ein Edikt des Königs Ammi-ṣaduqa von Babylon*. SDIO 5, 1958)
Kraus, Hans-Joachim. 1962. *Worship in Israel: A Cultic History of the Old Testament*. Oxford: Blackwell.
Krauss, Stuart. 2006. 'The Word *"Ger"* in the Bible and Its Implications'. *JBQ* 34:264-70.

Kugler, Franz Xaver. 1922. *Von Moses bis Paulus: Forschungen zur Geschichte Israels, nach biblischen und profangeschichtlichen insbesondere neuen keilinscriftlichen Quellen.* Münster: Aschendorffschen.

Kuntz, Paul Grimley. 2004. *The Ten Commandments in History: Mosaic Paradigms for a Well-Ordered Society.* Ed. Thomas D'Evelyn. Emory University Studies in Law and Religion. Grand Rapids: Wm. B. Eerdmans.

L'Hour, Jean. 1964. 'Les interdits toʿeba dans le Deutéronome'. *RB* 71:481-503.

Lafont, Bertrand, and Raymond Westbrook. 2003. 'Mesopotamia: Neo-Sumerian Period (Ur III)'. Pp. 183-226 in *HANEL*, vol. 1.

Lafont, Sophie. 1994. 'Ancient Near Eastern Laws: Continuity and Pluralism'. Pp. 91-118 in *Theory and Method in Biblical and Cuneiform Law*, ed. Bernard M. Levinson. JSOTSup 181. Sheffield: Sheffield Academic.

———. 2003. 'Mesopotamia: Middle Assyrian Period'. Pp. 521-63 in *HANEL*, vol. 1.

Lalleman, Hetty. 2004. *Celebrating the Law? Rethinking Old Testament Ethics.* Milton Keynes: Paternoster.

Landes, David S. 1998. *The Wealth and Poverty of Nations: Why Some Are So Rich and Some So Poor.* New York: Norton.

Landsberger, Benno. 1939. 'Die babylonischen Termini für Gesetz und Recht'. Pp. 219-34 in *Symbolae ad iura orientis antiqui pertinentes Paulo Koschaker dedicatae*, ed. Theunis Folkers et al. SDIO 2. Leiden: Brill.

———. 1968. 'Jungfräulichkeit'. Pp. 41-105 in *Symbolae iuridicae et historicae*, ed. J. A. Ankum, R. Feenstra, and W. F. Leemans. Martino David Festschrift, vol. 2. Leiden: Brill.

Lang, Bernhard. 1983. "כָּפַר". Pp. 288-303 in *TDOT*, vol. 7 (1995). (trans. from German)

———. 1986. 'נכר'. Pp. 423-31 in *TDOT*, vol. 9 (1998). (trans. from German)

———. 1998. 'The Decalogue in the Light of a Newly Published Palaeo-Hebrew Inscription (Hebrew Ostracon Moussaïeff no. 1)'. *JSOT* 77:21-25.

Langholm, Odd. 1992. *Economics in the Medieval Schools: Wealth, Exchange, Value, Money and Usury according to the Paris Theological Tradition, 1200-1350.* Studien und Texte zur Geistesgeschichte des Mittelalters 29. Leiden: Brill.

Larkin, William J., Jr. 1982. 'The Ethics of Inflation: A Biblical Critique of the Causes and Consequences'. *Grace Theological Journal* 31:89-105.

Larsen, Mogens Trolle. 1976. *The Old Assyrian City-State and Its Colonies.* Mesopotamia 4. Copenhagen: Akademisk.

Lee, Francis Nigel. 1966. *The Covenantal Sabbath.* London: Lord's Day Observance Society.

Leemans, W. F. 1950a. *The Old-Babylonian Merchant: His Business and His Social Position.* SDIO 3. Leiden: Brill.

———. 1950b. 'The Rate of Interest in Old Babylonian Times'. *RIDA* 5:7-34.

———. 1960a. *Foreign Trade in the Old Babylonian Period: As Revealed by Texts from Southern Mesopotamia.* SDIO 6. Leiden: Brill.

———. 1960b. *Legal and Administrative Documents of the Time of Hammurabi and Samsuiluna (Mainly from Lagaba).* Studia ad tabulas cuneiformes collectas a F. M. Th. de Liagre Böhl pertinentia 1/3. Leiden: Brill.

Leeuwen, Cornelis van. 1997. '530 אַלְמָנָה'. Pp. 413-15 in *NIDOTTE*, vol. 1.

Lefebvre, Jean-François. 2003. *Le jubilé biblique: Lv 25 — exégèse et théologie.* OBO 194. Fribourg: University Press/Göttingen: Vandenhoeck & Ruprecht.

Leggett, Donald A. 1974. *The Levirate and Goel Institutions in the Old Testament: With Special*

Attention to the Book of Ruth. Cherry Hill, NJ: Mack. Repr. of doctoral thesis, Free University: Amsterdam, 1974.

Lehmann, Manfred R. 1969. 'Biblical Oaths'. *ZAW* 81:74-92.

Lemche, Niels Peter. 1975. 'The "Hebrew Slave": Comments on the Slave Law Ex. xxi 2-11'. *VT* 25:129-44.

———. 1976. 'The Manumission of Slaves — The Fallow Year — The Sabbatical Year — The Jobel Year'. *VT* 26:38-59.

———. 1979. '*Andurārum* and *Mīšarum:* Comments on the Problem of Social Edicts and Their Application in the Ancient Near East'. *JNES* 38:11-22.

———. 1984. 'The Hebrew and the Seven Year Cycle'. *BN* 25:65-75.

———. 1992. 'Habiru, Hapiru'. Pp. 6-10 in *ABD,* vol. 3.

Levine, Baruch A. 1989. *Leviticus.* JPS Torah Commentary. Philadelphia: JPS.

Levine, Etan. 1999. 'On Exodus 21,10 '*Onah* and Biblical Marriage'. *ZABR* 5:133-64.

Levinson, Bernard M. 1997. *Deuteronomy and the Hermeneutics of Legal Innovation.* New York: Oxford University Press.

———. 2004. 'Is the Covenant Code an Exilic Composition? A Response to John Van Seters'. Pp. 272-325 in *In Search of Pre-Exilic Israel: Proceedings of the Oxford Old Testament Seminar,* ed. John Day. JSOTSup 406. London: T. & T. Clark.

———. 2005a. 'The Birth of the Lemma: The Restrictive Reinterpretation of the Covenant Code's Manumission Law by the Holiness Code (Leviticus 25:44-46)'. *JBL* 124:617-39.

———. 2005b. 'Deuteronomy's Conception of Law as an "Ideal Type": A Missing Chapter in the History of Constitutional Law'. *Maarav* 12:83-119.

———. 2006a. 'The "Effected Object" in Contractual Legal Language: The Semantics of "If You Purchase a Hebrew Slave" (Exod. xxi 2)'. *VT* 56:485-504.

———. 2006b. 'The Manumission of Hermeneutics: The Slave Laws of the Pentateuch as a Challenge to Contemporary Pentateuchal Theory'. Pp. 281-324 in *Congress Volume: Leiden 2004,* ed. André Lemaire. VTSup 109. Leiden: Brill.

———, ed. 1994. *Theory and Method in Biblical and Cuneiform Law.* JSOTSup 181. Sheffield: Sheffield Academic.

Lévy, Edmond, ed. 2000. *La codification des lois dans l'antiquité: Actes du Colloque de Strasbourg 27-29 Novembre 1997.* Travaux du Centre de Recherche sur le Proche-Orient et la Grèce Antiques 16. Paris: De Boccard.

Lewis, Philip. 1985. 'Can Mammon Submit? The Economics of Islam'. *Third Way* 8/9:16-18.

Lewy, Immanuel. 1957. 'Dating of Covenant Code Sections on Humaneness and Righteousness (Ex. xxii 20-26; xxiii 1-9)'. *VT* 7:322-26.

Lewy, Julius. 1939. 'Ḫābirū and Hebrews'. *HUCA* 14:587-623.

———. 1958. 'The Biblical Institution of d^{e}rôr in the Light of Akkadian Documents'. *ErIsr* 5:21-31.

———, and Hildegard Lewy. 1942. 'The Origin of the Week and the Oldest West Asiatic Calendar'. *HUCA* 17:1-152.

Lieberman, Stephen J. 1989. 'Royal "Reforms" of the Amurrite Dynasty'. *BO* 46:241-59.

Liedke, Gerhard. 1971. *Gestalt und Bezeichung alttestamentlicher Rechtssätze: Eine formgeschichtlich-terminologische Studie.* WMANT 39. Neukirchen-Vluyn: Neukirchener.

Limet, Henri. 1995. 'L'émigré dans la société mésopotamienne'. Pp. 165-79 in *Immigration and Emigration within the Ancient Near East,* ed. Karel van Lerberghe and Antoon Schoors. Edward Lipiński Festschrift. OLA 65. Leuven: Peeters.

Lindars, Barnabas. 1973. 'Imitation of God and Imitation of Christ'. *Theology* 76:394-402.
Lindenberger, James M. 1991. 'How Much for a Hebrew Slave? The Meaning of *Mišneh* in Deut 15:18'. *JBL* 110:479-82.
———. 2003. *Ancient Aramaic and Hebrew Letters,* ed. Kent Harold Richards 2nd ed. SBLWAW 14. Atlanta: SBL.
Lindgren, James. 1995. 'Measuring the Value of Slaves and Free Persons in Ancient Law'. *Chicago-Kent Law Review* 71:149-215.
Lipiński, Edward. 1976. 'L'"esclave hébreu"'. *VT* 26:120-24.
———. 1979. '*Nešek* and *Tarbit* in the Light of Epigraphic Evidence'. *OLP* 10:133-41.
———. 1982. 'Sale, Transfer, and Delivery in Ancient Semitic Terminology'. Pp. 173-85 in *Gesellschaft und Kultur im alten Vorderasien,* ed. Horst Klengel. Schriften zur Geschichte und Kultur des alten Orients 15 Berlin: Akademie.
———. 1984. 'מכר'. Pp. 291-96 in *TDOT,* vol. 8 (1997). (trans. from German)
———. 1986a. 'נָקַם'. Pp. 1-9 in *TDOT,* vol. 10 (1999). (trans. from German)
———. 1986b. 'נָחַל'. Pp. 319-35 in *TDOT,* vol. 9 (1998). (trans. from German)
———. 1988. 'עָרַב I'. Pp. 326-30 in *TDOT,* vol. 11 (2001). (trans. from German)
———. 1990. 'קָנָה'. Pp. 58-65 in *TDOT,* vol. 13 (2004). (trans. from German)
———. 1992. 'שָׁכַר'. Pp. 128-35 in *TDOT,* vol. 14 (2004). (trans. from German)
———. 1998. 'Old Aramaic Contracts of Guarantee'. Pp. 39-44 in *Written on Clay and Stone,* ed. Jan Braun et al. Szarzyńska Festschrift. Warsaw: Agade.
Lochman, Jan Milič. 1979. *Signposts to Freedom: The Ten Commandments and Christian Ethics*. Minneapolis: Augsburg, 1982. (trans. from German)
Lockshin, Martin I., ed. 1997. *Rashbam's Commentary on Exodus: An Annotated Translation.* BJS 310. Atlanta: Scholars. (trans. from Hebrew, 12th century, with commentary)
Loewenberg, Frank M. 2001. *From Charity to Social Justice: The Emergence of Communal Institutions for the Support of the Poor in Ancient Judaism.* New Brunswick: Transaction.
Loewenstamm, Samuel E. 1961. '?ערב = עבט'. *Leš* 25:111-14.
———. 1969. 'נשך and מ/תרבית'. *JBL* 88:78-80.
———. 1971. 'Law'. Pp. 231-67 in *The World History of the Jewish People.* Vol. 3: *Judges,* ed. Benjamin Mazar. Tel-Aviv: Massada.
———. 1977. 'Exodus xxi 22-25'. *VT* 27:352-60.
Lohfink, Norbert L. 1977a. 'חָפְשִׁי'. Pp. 114-18 in *TDOT,* vol. 5 (1986). (trans. from German)
———. 1977b. *Great Themes from the Old Testament.* Edinburgh: T. & T. Clark, 1982. (trans. from German)
———. 1986. 'The Kingdom of God and the Economy in the Bible'. *Comm* 13:216-31.
———. 1991. 'Poverty in the Laws of the Ancient Near East and of the Bible'. *TS* 52:34-50.
———. 1996a. 'Fortschreibung? Zur Technik von Rechtsrevisionen im deuteronomischen Bereich, erörtert an Deuteronomium 12, Ex 21,2-11 und Dtn 15,12-18'. Pp. 127-71 in *Das Deuteronomium und seine Querbeziehungen,* ed. Timo Veijola. Schriften der Finnischen Exegetischen Gesellschaft 62. Helsinki: Finnische Exegetische Gesellschaft.
———. 1996b. 'The Laws of Deuteronomy: A Utopian Project for a World without Any Poor'. *Scripture Bulletin* 26:2-19.
Long, Burke O. 1982. 'The Social World of Ancient Israel'. *Int* 36:243-55.
Loretz, Oswald. 1960. 'Ex 21,6; 22,8 und angebliche Nuzi-Parallelen'. *Bib* 41:167-75.
———. 1962. 'Ugaritisches samatu und hebräisches sm(y)tt'. *BZ* 6:269-79.

———. 1984. *Habiru-Hebräer: Eine sozio-linguistische Studie über die Herkunft des Gentiliziums ʿibrî vom Appellativum ḫabiru*. BZAW 160. Berlin: de Gruyter.
Lorton, David. 1995. 'Legal and Social Institutions of Pharaonic Egypt'. Pp. 345-62 in *CANE*, vol. 1.
Lowery, Richard H. 2000. *Sabbath and Jubilee*. Understanding Biblical Themes. St. Louis: Chalice.
Luciani, Didier. 1999. 'Le jubilé dans Lévitique 25'. *RTL* 30:456-86.
Lumbantobing, Bonar H. 1984. 'Pinjaman pada Orang Miskin: Pemahaman Fungsi *ʿbt* dalam Ulangan 15:1-11'. M.Th. thesis, Jakarta Theological Seminary.
Lurje, I. M. 1971. *Studien zum altägyptischen Recht des 16. bis 10. Jahrhunderts v. u. Z.* Forschungen zum römischen Recht 30. Weimar: Böhlaus. (trans. from Russian, 1960)
Macholz, Georg Christian. 1972. 'Zur Geschichte der Justizorganisation in Juda'. *ZAW* 84:314-40.
Mafico, Temba L. J. 1992. 'Just, Justice'. Pp. 1127-29 in *ABD*, vol. 3.
Maidman, Maynard P. 1996. '"Privatization" and Private Property at Nuzi: The Limits of Evidence'. Pp. 153-63 in *Privatization in the Ancient Near East and Classical World*, ed. Michael Hudson and Baruch A. Levine. Peabody Museum Bulletin 5. International Scholars Conference on Ancient Near Eastern Economics 1. Cambridge, MA: Peabody Museum of Archaeology and Ethnology.
Malchow, Bruce V. 1996. *Social Justice in the Hebrew Bible: What Is New and What Is Old*. Collegeville: Liturgical.
Malfroy, Jean. 1965. 'Sagesse et Loi dans le Deuteronome'. *VT* 15:49-65.
Maloney, Robert P. 1974. 'Usury and Restrictions on Interest-Taking in the Ancient Near East'. *CBQ* 36:1-20.
Malul, Meir. 1990. *The Comparative Method in Ancient Near Eastern and Biblical Legal Studies*. AOAT 227. Kevelaer: Butzon & Bercker/Neukirchen-Vluyn: Neukirchener.
Manning, Joseph G. 2001. 'Demotic Papyri (664-30 BCE)'. Pp. 307-26 in *SDANEL*.
———. 2003. 'Egypt: Demotic Law'. Pp. 819-62 in *HANEL*, vol. 2.
Marcus, Ralph, and Ignace J. Gelb. 1949. 'The Phoenician Stele Inscription from Cilicia'. *JNES* 8:116-20.
Margalit, Baruch. 1987. 'Ugaritic Contributions to Hebrew Lexicography'. *ZAW* 99:391-404.
Marshall, I. Howard. 1980. 'Justice in the Bible'. *Third Way*, February: 9-12.
Marshall, Jay W. 1993. *Israel and the Book of the Covenant: An Anthropological Approach to Biblical Law*. SBLDS 140. Atlanta: Scholars.
———. 2003. 'Decalogue'. Pp. 171-82 in *DOTP*.
Martin, James D. 1989. 'Israel as a Tribal Society'. Pp. 95-117 in *The World of Ancient Israel: Sociological, Anthropological and Political Perspectives*, ed. Ronald E. Clements. Cambridge: Cambridge University Press.
Marx, Alfred. 1988. 'Sacrifice de réparation et rites de levée de sanction'. *ZAW* 100:183-98.
Matlock, Michael D. 2007. 'Obeying the First Part of the Tenth Commandment: Applications from the Levirate Marriage Law'. *JSOT* 31:295-310.
Mattha, Girgis, and George R. Hughes. 1975. *The Demotic Legal Code of Hermopolis West*. Bibliothèque d'étude 45. Cairo: Institut français d'archéologie orientale.
Matthews, Victor H. 1994. 'The Anthropology of Slavery in the Covenant Code'. Pp. 119-35 in *Theory and Method in Biblical and Cuneiform Law*, ed. Bernard M. Levinson. JSOTSup 181. Sheffield: Sheffield Academic.

———, and Don C. Benjamin. 1993. *Social World of Ancient Israel 1250-587 B.C.E.* Peabody: Hendrickson.
Mauch, T. M. 1962. 'Sojourner'. Pp. 397-99 in *IDB*, vol. 4.
Mauss, Marcel. 1950. *The Gift: The Form and Reason for Exchange in Archaic Societies*. London: Routledge, 1990. (trans. from French)
Mayes, Andrew D. H. 1979. *Deuteronomy*. NCB. Grand Rapids: Wm. B. Eerdmans/London: Oliphants.
———. 1989. *The Old Testament in Sociological Perspective*. London: Marshall Pickering.
Mays, James Luther. 1983. 'Justice: Perspectives from the Prophetic Tradition'. *Int* 37:5-17.
McConville, J. Gordon. 1984. *Law and Theology in Deuteronomy*. JSOTSup 33. Sheffield: JSOT.
———. 1998. 'King and Messiah in Deuteronomy and the Deuteronomistic History'. Pp. 271-95 in *King and Messiah in Israel and the Ancient Near East: Proceedings of the Oxford Old Testament Seminar*, ed. John Day. JSOTSup 270. Sheffield: Sheffield Academic.
———. 2002a. *Deuteronomy*. Apollos Old Testament Commentary 5. Leicester: Apollos/Downers Grove: InterVarsity.
———. 2002b. 'Singular Address in the Deuteronomic Law and the Politics of Legal Administration'. *JSOT* 97:19-36.
———. 2006. 'Old Testament Laws and Canonical Intentionality'. Pp. 259-81 in *Canon and Biblical Interpretation,* ed. Craig Bartholomew et al. Scripture and Hermeneutics 7. Milton Keynes: Paternoster/Grand Rapids: Zondervan.
McKane, William. 1963. 'Ruth and Boaz'. *TGUOS* 19:29-40.
McKay, J. W. 1971. 'Exodus XXIII 1-3, 6-8: A Decalogue for the Administration of Justice in the City Gate'. *VT* 21:311-25.
McKeating, Henry. 1963. 'Vengeance Is Mine: A Study of the Pursuit of Vengeance in the Old Testament'. *ExpTim* 74:239-45.
McKeown, James. 2003. 'Land, Fertility, Famine'. Pp. 487-91 in *DOTP*.
Meek, Theophile J. 1930. 'The Translation of *Gêr* in the Hexateuch and Its Bearing on the Documentary Hypotheses'. *JBL* 49:172-80.
———. 1960. 'Translating the Hebrew Bible'. *JBL* 79:328-35.
Meier, Ernst. 1846. *Die ursprüngliche Form des Dekalogs*. Mannheim: Bassermann.
Meinhold, Arndt. 1985. 'Zur Beziehung Gott, Volk, Land im Jobel-Zusammenhang'. *BZ* 29:245-61.
Meislin, Bernard J., and Morris L. Cohen. 1964. 'Backgrounds of the Biblical Law against Usury'. *Comparative Studies in Society and History* 6:250-67.
Meissner, Bruno. 1936. *Warenpreise in Babylonien*. Abhandlungen der Preussischen Akademie der Wissenschaften, 1936/1. Berlin: de Gruyter.
Mendelsohn, Isaac. 1935. 'The Conditional Sale into Slavery of Free-Born Daughters in Nuzi and the Law of Ex. 21:7-11'. *JAOS* 55:190-95.
———. 1949. *Slavery in the Ancient Near East: A Comparative Study of Slavery in Babylonia, Assyria, Syria, and Palestine, from the Middle of the Third Millennium to the End of the First Millennium*. New York: Oxford University Press.
———. 1955. 'On Slavery in Alalakh'. *IEJ* 5:65-72.
———. 1956. 'Samuel's Denunciation of Kingship in the Light of the Akkadian Documents from Ugarit'. *BASOR* 143:17-22.
———. 1962. 'Slavery in the OT'. Pp. 383-91 in *IDB*, vol. 4.

Mendenhall, George E. 1954. 'Ancient Oriental and Biblical Law'. *BA* 17:26-46.

———. 1973. *The Tenth Generation: The Origins of the Biblical Tradition.* Baltimore: Johns Hopkins University Press.

Merendino, Rosario Pius. 1969. *Das deuteronomische Gesetz: Eine literarkritische, gattungs- und überlieferungsgeschichtliche Untersuchung zu Dt 12–26.* BBB 31. Bonn: Hanstein.

Merz, Erwin. 1916. *Die Blutrache bei den Israeliten.* BWAT 20. Leipzig: Hinrichs.

Mieroop, Marc van de. 1995. 'Old Babylonian Interest Rates: Were They Annual?' Pp. 357-64 in *Immigration and Emigration within the Ancient Near East,* ed. Karel van Lerberghe and Antoon Schoors. Edward Lipiński Festschrift. OLA 65. Leuven: Peeters.

———. 2002. 'A History of Near Eastern Debt?' Pp. 59-94 in *DERANE.*

Mikliszanski, Jacques K. 1947. 'The Law of Retaliation and the Pentateuch'. *JBL* 66:295-303.

Milgrom, Jacob. 1976a. *Cult and Conscience: The Asham and the Priestly Doctrine of Repentance.* SJLA 18. Leiden: Brill.

———. 1976b. 'Profane Slaughter and a Formulaic Key to the Composition of Deuteronomy'. *HUCA* 47:1-17.

———. 1983. 'The Ideological and Historical Importance of the Judge in Deuteronomy'. Pp. 129-39 in *Isac Leo Seeligmann Volume: Essays on the Bible and the Ancient World,* vol. 3, ed. Alexander Rofé and Yair Zakovitch. Jerusalem: Rubinstein.

———. 1991. *Leviticus 1–16.* AB 3. New York: Doubleday.

———. 1993. 'Sweet Land and Liberty'. *BRev* 9/4:8, 54.

———. 1995. 'The Land Redeemer and the Jubilee'. Pp. 66-69 in *Fortunate the Eyes That See: Essays in Honor of David Noel Freedman,* ed. Astrid B. Beck et al. Grand Rapids: Wm. B. Eerdmans.

———. 2000. *Leviticus 17–22.* AB 3A. New York: Doubleday.

———. 2001. *Leviticus 23–27.* AB 3B. New York: Doubleday.

———. 2004. *Leviticus.* CC. Minneapolis: Fortress.

Millard, Alan R. 2004. 'Zechariah Wrote (Luke 1:63)'. Pp. 46-55 in *The New Testament in Its First-Century Setting: Essays on Context and Background.* Bruce Winter Festschrift. Grand Rapids: Wm. B. Eerdmans.

———. 2005. 'Only Fragments from the Past: The Role of Accident in Our Knowledge of the Ancient Near East'. Pp. 301-19 in *Writing and Ancient Near Eastern Society,* ed. Piotr Bienkowski, Christopher Mee, and Elizabeth Slater. Alan Millard Festschrift. LHB/OTS 426. New York: T. & T. Clark.

Miller, Geoffrey P., ed. 1995. 'The Development of Law in the Ancient Near East'. *Chicago-Kent Law Review* 70:1621-847.

Miller, Patrick D. 1969. 'The Gift of God: The Deuteronomic Theology of the Land'. *Int* 23:451-65.

———. 1980. 'Studies in Hebrew Word Patterns'. *HTR* 73:79-89.

Mills, Paul. 1989. 'Interest in Interest: The Old Testament Ban on Interest and Its Implications for Today'. Unpublished paper, Jubilee Centre, Cambridge.

———. 1993. 'The Ban on Interest: Dead Letter or Radical Solution?' *Cambridge Papers.* March 1993.

———. 2005a. 'Economy'. Pp. 216-33 in *Jubilee Manifesto: A Framework, Agenda & Strategy for Christian Social Reform,* ed. Michael Schluter and John Ashcroft. Downers Grove: InterVarsity.

———. 2005b. 'Finance'. Pp. 196-215 in *Jubilee Manifesto: A Framework, Agenda & Strategy for Christian Social Reform,* ed. Michael Schluter and John Ashcroft. Downers Grove: InterVarsity.

Miranda, José Porfirio. 1971. *Marx and the Bible: A Critique of the Philosophy of Oppression.* Maryknoll: Orbis, 1974. (trans. from Spanish)

Möller, Hans. 1978. 'Lösungsvorschlag für eine Crux interpretum (Lev 25:33)'. *ZAW* 90:411-12.

Moloney, Francis J. 2000. 'The Scriptural Basis of Jubilee'. *ITQ* 65:99-110, 231-44.

Moltmann, Jürgen. 1985. *God in Creation: An Ecological Doctrine of Creation.* Gifford Lectures, 1984-85. San Francisco: Harper & Row/London: SCM.

Monroe, Christopher M. 2005. 'Money and Trade'. Pp. 155-68 in *A Companion to the Ancient Near East,* ed. Daniel C. Snell. Blackwell Companions to the Ancient World. Malden, MA: Blackwell.

Montet, Pierre. 1958. *Everyday Life in Egypt in the Days of Ramesses the Great.* London: Arnold. (trans. from French)

Montgomery, David J. 2000. '"A Bribe Is a Charm": A Study of Proverbs 17:8'. Pp. 134-49 in *The Way of Wisdom,* ed. James I. Packer and Sven K. Soderlund. Bruce Waltke Festschrift. Grand Rapids: Zondervan.

Moo, Douglas J., ed. 1988. 'The "Health and Wealth Gospel"'. *TJ* 9:129-220.

de Moor, Johannes C. 1971. *The Seasonal Pattern in the Ugaritic Myth of Ba'lu: According to the Version of Ilimilku.* AOAT 16. Kevelaer: Butzon & Bercker.

Moran, William L. 1967. 'The Conclusion of the Decalogue (Ex 20,17 = Dt 5,21)'. *CBQ* 29:543-54.

Morgenstern, Julian. 1928. *The Book of the Covenant.* Cincinnati, 1968. Repr. from *HUCA* 5 (1928).

———. 1962a. 'Jubilee, Year of'. Pp. 1001-2 in *IDB,* vol. 2.

———. 1962b. 'Sabbatical Year'. Pp. 141-44 in *IDB,* vol. 4.

Morrow, William S. 1990. 'The Composition of Deut. 15:1-3'. *HAR* 12:115-31.

———. 1994. 'A Generic Discrepancy in the Covenant Code'. Pp. 136-51 in *Theory and Method in Biblical and Cuneiform Law,* ed. Bernard M. Levinson. JSOTSup 181. Sheffield: Sheffield Academic.

———. 1995. *Scribing the Center: Organization and Redaction in Deuteronomy 14:1–17:3.* SBLMS 49. Atlanta: Scholars.

Mosala, Itumeleng. 2002. 'The Politics of Debt and the Liberation of the Scriptures'. Pp. 77-84 in *Tracking The Tribes of Yahweh: On the Trail of a Classic,* ed. Roland Boer. JSOTSup 351. Sheffield: Sheffield Academic.

Motyer, Alec. 2005. *The Message of Exodus: The Days of Our Pilgrimage.* The Bible Speaks Today. Downers Grove: InterVarsity.

Moucarry, Georges Chawkat. 1988. 'The Alien according to the Torah'. *Them* 14:17-20.

Na'aman, Nadav. 1986. 'Ḫabiru and Hebrews: The Transfer of a Social Term to the Literary Sphere'. *JNES* 45:271-88.

Nardoni, Enrique. 2004. *Rise Up, O Judge: A Study of Justice in the Biblical World.* Peabody: Hendrickson. (rev. trans. from Spanish, 1997)

Nasuti, Harry P. 1986. 'Identity, Identification, and Imitation: The Narrative Hermeneutics of Biblical Law'. *JLR* 4:9-23.

Naudé, Jackie A. 1997. '2852 חנך'. Pp. 200-201 in *NIDOTTE,* vol. 2.

Naveh, Joseph. 1960. 'A Hebrew Letter from the Seventh Century B.C.' *IEJ* 10:129-39.

Nebo, Chinedu. 1998. 'International Debt and Christian Responsibility'. *Transformation* 15/2:28-31.

Negretti, Nicola. 1973. *Il settimo giorno: Indagine critico-teologica delle tradizioni presacerdotali e sacerdotali circa il sabato biblico.* AnBib 55. Rome: Pontifical Biblical Institute.

Nel, Philip J. 1994. 'The Talion Principle in Old Testament Narratives'. *JNSL* 20/1:21-29.

———. 2000. 'Social Justice as Religious Responsibility in Near Eastern Religions: Historic Ideal and Ideological Illusion'. *JNSL* 26/2:143-53.

Nelson, Benjamin N. 1969. *The Idea of Usury: From Tribal Brotherhood to Universal Otherhood.* 2nd ed.; Chicago: University of Chicago Press. 1st ed. 1949.

Nelson, Richard D. 2002. *Deuteronomy.* OTL. Louisville: Westminster John Knox.

Neufeld, Edward. 1954. 'The Rate of Interest and the Text of Nehemiah 5.11'. *JQR* 44:194-204.

———. 1955. 'The Prohibitions against Loans at Interest in Ancient Hebrew Laws'. *HUCA* 26:355-412.

———. 1958. 'Socio-Economic Background of *yōbēl* and *šᵉmiṭṭā*'. *RSO* 33:53-124.

———. 1961. '*Ius redemptionis* in Ancient Hebrew Law'. *RIDA* 8:29-40.

———. 1962. 'Inalienability of Mobile and Immobile Pledges in the Laws of the Bible'. *RIDA* 9:33-47.

Neufeld, Ephraim. 1944. *Ancient Hebrew Marriage Laws: With Special References to General Semitic Laws and Customs.* London: Longmans, Green.

———. 1951. *The Hittite Laws: Translated into English and Hebrew with Commentary.* London: Luzac.

Niehr, Herbert. 1995. 'שָׁפַט'. Pp. 411-31 in *TDOT*, vol. 15 (2006). (trans. from German)

———. 1997. 'The Constitutive Principles for Establishing Justice and Order in Northwest Semitic Societies with Special Reference to Ancient Israel and Judah'. *ZABR* 3:112-30.

Nielsen, Eduard. 1975. '"You Shall Not Muzzle an Ox While It Is Treading Out the Corn", Dt. 25,4'. Pp. 94-105 in *Law, History and Tradition: Selected Essays.* Copenhagen: Gads, 1983. (trans. from Danish)

Nihan, Christophe. 2004. 'The Holiness Code between D and P: Some Comments on the Function and Significance of Leviticus 17–26 in the Composition of the Torah'. Pp. 81-122 in *Das Deuteronomium zwischen Pentateuch und Deuteronomistischem Geschichtswerk,* ed. Eckart Otto and Reinhard Achenbach. FRLANT 206. Göttingen: Vandenhoeck & Ruprecht.

Noonan, John T., Jr. 1957, *The Scholastic Analysis of Usury.* Cambridge, MA: Harvard University Press.

North, Robert G. 1954a. *Sociology of the Biblical Jubilee.* AnBib 4. Rome: Pontifical Biblical Institute.

———. 1954b. '*Yâd* in the Shemitta-Law'. *VT* 4:196-99.

———. 1955a. 'The Derivation of Sabbath'. *Bib* 36:182-201.

———. 1955b. 'Flesh, Covering, and Response, Ex. xxi 10'. *VT* 5:204-6.

———. 1975. 'דְּרוֹר'. Pp. 265-69 in *TDOT*, vol. 3 (1978). (trans. from German)

———. 1980. 'יוֹבֵל'. Pp. 1-6 in *TDOT*, vol. 6 (1990). (trans. from German)

———. 1988. 'עֶשֶׂר'. Pp. 404-9 in *TDOT*, vol. 11 (2001). (trans. from German)

———. 2000. *The Biblical Jubilee: After Fifty Years.* AnBib 145. Rome: Pontifical Biblical Institute.

Noth, Martin. 1940. 'The Laws in the Pentateuch: Their Assumptions and Meaning'. Pp. 1-107 in *The Laws in the Pentateuch and Other Studies*. Edinburgh: Oliver & Boyd, 1966/Philadelphia: Fortress, 1967. (trans. from German)

———. 1959. *Exodus*. OTL. Philadelphia: Westminster/London: SCM, 1962. (trans. from German)

———. 1962. *Leviticus*. OTL. Philadelphia: Westminster/London: SCM, 1965. (trans. from German)

Nurmela, Risto. 1998. *The Levites: Their Emergence as a Second-Class Priesthood*. South Florida Studies in the History of Judaism 193. Atlanta: Scholars.

O'Brien, David P. 2001. 'A Comparison between Early Jewish and Early Christian Interpretations of the Jubilee Year'. Pp. 436-42 in *Historica, biblica, theologica et philosophica*, ed. M. F. Wiles and E. J. Yarnold. StPatr 34. Louvain: Peeters.

Oelsner, Joachim. 2001. 'The Neo-Babylonian Period'. Pp. 289-305 in *SDANEL*.

———, Bruce Wells, and Cornelia Wunsch. 2003. 'Mesopotamia: Neo-Babylonian Period'. Pp. 911-74 in *HANEL*, vol. 2.

Ohler, Annemarie. 1979. *Israel, Volk und Land: Zur Geschichte der wechselseitigen Beziehungen zwischen Israel und seinem Land in alttestamentlicher Zeit*. Stuttgart: Katholisches Bibelwerk.

Olivier, Johannes P. J. 1997a. '2002 דרור'. Pp. 986-89 in *NIDOTTE*, vol. 1.

———. 1997b. 'Restitution as Economic Redress: The Fine Print of the Old Babylonian *mēšarum*-Edict of Ammiṣaduqa'. *ZABR* 3:12-25.

Ollenburger, Ben C. (2001). 'Jubilee: "The Land Is Mine; You Are Aliens and Tenants with Me."' Pp. 208-34 in *Reclaiming the Old Testament*, ed. Gordon Zerbe. Janzen Festschrift. Winnipeg: Canadian Mennonite Bible College.

Olmstead, A. T. 1948. *History of the Persian Empire*. Chicago: University of Chicago Press.

Olson, Dennis T. 1994. *Deuteronomy and the Death of Moses: A Theological Reading*. OBT. Minneapolis: Fortress.

Ominsky, Harris. n.d. 'Finders Keepers? First Impressions and Ancient Wisdom'. *Jewish Law* http://www.jlaw.com/Articles/finderskeepers.html.

Oosthuizen, Martin J. 1997. 'Deuteronomy 15:1-18 in Socio-Rhetorical Perspective'. *ZABR* 3:64-91.

Oppenheim, A. Leo. 1964. *Ancient Mesopotamia: Portrait of a Dead Civilization*. Chicago: University of Chicago Press.

———. 1967. *Letters from Mesopotamia: Official, Business, and Private Letters on Clay Tablets from Two Millennia*. Chicago: University of Chicago Press.

Oppenheimer, Aharon. 1977. *The 'am ha-aretz: A Study in the Social History of the Jewish People in the Hellenistic-Roman Period*. ALGHJ 8. Leiden: Brill.

Osborne, Thomas P., and Joseph Stricher. 1999. *L'année jubilaire et la remise des dettes: Repères bibliques*. Paris: Bayard.

Osgood, S. Joy. 1992. 'Women and the Inheritance of Land in Early Israel'. Pp. 29-52 in *Women in the Biblical Tradition*, ed. George J. Brooke. Studies in Women and Religion 31. Lewiston: Mellen.

Osumi, Yuichi. 1991. *Die Kompositionsgeschichte des Bundesbuches Exodus 20,22b–23,33*. OBO 105. Fribourg: University Press/Göttingen: Vandenhoeck & Ruprecht.

———. 1992. 'Brandmal für Brandmal: Eine Erwägung zum Talionsgesetz im Rahmen der Sklavenschutzbestimmungen'. *AJBI* 18:3-30.

Otto, Eckart. 1988a. 'Die rechtshistorische Entwicklung des Depositenrechts in altorientalischen und altisraelitischen Rechtskorpora'. *Zeitschrift der Savigny-Stiftung für Rechtsgeschichte* 105:1-31.

———. 1988b. *Wandel der Rechtsbegründungen in der Gesellschaftsgeschichte des antiken Israel: Eine Rechtsgeschichte des 'Bundesbuches' Ex XX 22–XXIII 13*. Studia biblica 3. Leiden: Brill.

———. 1989. *Rechtsgeschichte der Redaktionen im Kodex Ešnunna und im 'Bundesbuch': Eine redaktionsgeschichtliche und rechtsvergleichende Studie zu altbabylonischen und altisraelitischen Rechtsüberlieferungen*. OBO 85. Fribourg: University Press/Göttingen: Vandenhoeck & Ruprecht.

———. 1991a. 'Die Geschichte der Talion im Alten Orient und Israel'. Pp. 101-30 in *Ernten, Was Man Sät,* ed. Dwight R. Daniels, Uwe Glessmer, and Martin Rösel. Klaus Koch Festschrift. Neukirchen-Vluyn: Neukirchener.

———. 1991b. *Körperverletzungen in den Keilschriftrechten und im Alten Testament: Studien zum Rechtstransfer im Alten Testament*. AOAT 226. Kevelaer: Butzon & Bercker/Neukirchen-Vluyn: Neukirchener.

———. 1993a. 'Town and Rural Countryside in Ancient Israelite Law: Reception and Redaction in Cuneiform and Israelite Law'. *JSOT* 57:3-22.

———. 1993b. 'Vom Bundesbuch zum Deuteronomium: Die deuteronomische Redaktion in Dtn 12–26'. In *Biblische Theologie und gesellschaftlicher Wandel,* ed. Georg Braulik, Walter Gross, and Sean E. McEvenue. Norbert Lohfink Festschrift. Freiburg im Breisgau: Herder.

———. 1994a. 'Aspects of Legal Reforms and Reformulations in Ancient Cuneiform and Israelite Law'. Pp. 160-96 in *Theory and Method in Biblical and Cuneiform Law,* ed. Bernard M. Levinson. JSOTSup 181. Sheffield: Sheffield Academic.

———. 1994b. 'Das Heiligkeitsgesetz Leviticus 17–26 in der Pentateuchredaktion'. Pp. 65-80 in *Altes Testament: Forschung und Wirkung,* ed. Peter Mommer and Winfried Thiel. Henning Graf Reventlow Festschrift. Frankfurt: Lang.

———. 1994c. *Theologische Ethik des Alten Testaments*. Theologische Wissenschaft 3/2. Stuttgart: Kohlhammer.

———. 1995a. 'On Aims and Methods in Hebrew Bible Ethics'. *Semeia* 66:161-72.

———. 1995b. 'Rechtsreformen in Deuteronomium xii–xxvi und im Mittelassyrischen Kodex der Tafel A (KAV 1)'. Pp. 239-73 in *Congress Volume: Paris 1992,* ed. John A. Emerton. VTSup 61. Leiden: Brill.

———. 1996a. 'Diachronie und Synchronie im Depositenrecht des "Bundesbuches": Zur jüngsten literatur- und rechtshistorischen Diskussion von Ex 22,6-14'. *ZABR* 2:76-85.

———. 1996b. 'The Pre-Exilic Deuteronomy as a Revision of the Covenant Code'. Pp. 112-22 in *Kontinuum und Proprium: Studien zur Sozial- und Rechtsgeschichte des Alten Orients und des Alten Testaments*. Orientalia biblica et christiana 8. Wiesbaden: Harrassowitz.

———. 1997. 'Programme der sozialen Gerechtigkeit: Die neuassyrische *(an-)durāru*-Institution sozialen Ausgleichs und das deuteronomische Erlassjahr in Dtn 15'. *ZABR* 3:26-63.

———. 1999a. *Das Deuteronomium: Politische Theologie und Rechtsreform in Juda und Assyrien*. BZAW 284. Berlin: de Gruyter.

———. 1999b. 'Innerbiblische Exegese im Heiligkeitsgesetz Levitikus 17–26'. Pp. 125-96 in *Levitikus als Buch,* ed. Heinz-Josef Fabry and Hans-Winfried Jüngling. BBB 119. Berlin: Philo.

---. 2001. *Die Tora des Mose: Die Geschichte der literarischen Vermittlung von Recht, Religion und Politik durch die Mosegestalt*. Berichte aus den Sitzungen der Joachim Jungius-Gesellschaft der Wissenschaften 19/2. Hamburg: Joachim Jungius-Gesellschaft der Wissenschaften/Göttingen: Vandenhoeck & Ruprecht.

---. 2004. Review of John Van Seters, *A Law Book for the Diaspora* (2003). RBL http://www.bookreviews.org/pdf/3929_801.pdf.

Ottosson, Magnus. 1973. 'גְּבוּל'. Pp. 361-66 in *TDOT*, vol. 2 (rev. ed. 1977). (trans. from German)

Otwell, John H. 1977. *And Sarah Laughed: The Status of Woman in the Old Testament*. Philadelphia: Westminster.

Owen, David I. 1980. 'Widows' Rights in Ur III Sumer'. *ZA* 70:170-84.

Pagolu, Augustine. 1998. *The Religion of the Patriarchs*. JSOTSup 277. Sheffield: Sheffield Academic.

Paradise, Jonathan. 1997. 'What Did Laban Demand of Jacob: A New Reading of Genesis 31:50 and Exodus 21:10'. Pp. 91-98 in *Tehillah le-Moshe*, ed. Mordechai Cogan, Barry L. Eichler, and Jeffrey H. Tigay. Moshe Greenberg Festschrift. Winona Lake: Eisenbrauns.

Paran, Meir. 1989. *Forms of the Priestly Style in the Pentateuch: Patterns, Linguistic Usages, Syntactic Structures*. Publications of the Perry Foundation for Biblical Research. Jerusalem: Magnes. (Hebrew, with English summary)

Pardee, Dennis. 1982. *Handbook of Ancient Hebrew Letters: A Study Edition*. SBLSBS 15. Chico: Scholars.

Paris, Dov. 1998. 'An Economic Look at the Old Testament'. Pp. 39-103 in *Ancient and Medieval Economic Ideas and Concepts of Social Justice*, ed. S. Todd Lowry and Barry Gordon. Leiden: Brill.

Parker, Barbara. 1954. 'The Nimrud Tablets, 1952 — Business Documents'. *Iraq* 16:29-58.

---. 1957. 'Nimrud Tablets, 1956 — Economic and Legal Texts from the Nabu Temple'. *Iraq* 19:125-38.

---. 1963. 'Economic Tablets from the Temple of Mamu at Balawat'. *Iraq* 25:86-103.

Paterson, Robert M. 1994. *Kitab Imamat [Leviticus]*. Tafsiran Alkitab. Jakarta: BPK Gunung Mulia.

Patrick, Dale (1973). 'Casuistic Law Governing Primary Rights and Duties', *JBL* 92:180-84.

---. 1985. *Old Testament Law*. Atlanta: John Knox/London: SCM, 1986.

---. 1994. 'Who Is the Evolutionist?' Pp. 152-59 in *Theory and Method in Biblical and Cuneiform Law*, ed. Bernard M. Levinson. JSOTSup 181. Sheffield: Sheffield Academic.

---. 1995. 'The Rhetoric of Collective Responsibility in Deuteronomic Law'. Pp. 421-36 in *Pomegranates and Golden Bells*, ed. David P. Wright, David Noel Freedman, and Avi Hurvitz. Jacob Milgrom Festschrift. Winona Lake: Eisenbrauns.

---. 2002. Review of Christiana van Houten, *The Alien in Israelite Law* (1991). *JLR* 17:413-17.

---, ed. 1989. 'Thinking Biblical Law'. *Semeia* 45:1-109.

Patterson, Richard D. 1973. 'The Widow, the Orphan, and the Poor in the Old Testament and Extra-Biblical Literature'. *BSac* 130:223-34.

Paul, Shalom M. 1969. 'Exod. 21:10 a Threefold Maintenance Clause'. *JNES* 28:48-53.

---. 1970. *Studies in the Book of the Covenant in the Light of Cuneiform and Biblical Law*. VTSup 18. Leiden: Brill.

---. 1991. *Amos*. Hermeneia. Minneapolis: Fortress.

Payer, Cheryl. 1974. 'The International Monetary Fund and Indonesian Debt Slavery'. Pp. 50-70 in *Remaking Asia: Essays on the American Uses of Power,* ed. Mark Selden. New York: Pantheon.

Pedersen, Johannes. 1920. *Israel: Its Life and Culture.* Vols I-II. London: Oxford University Press, 1926. (trans. from Danish)

Peels, H. G. L. 1995. *The Vengeance of God: The Meaning of the Root NQM and the Function of the NQM-Texts in the Context of Divine Revelation in the Old Testament.* OtSt 31. Leiden: Brill.

———. 1997. '5933 נקם'. Pp. 154-56 in *NIDOTTE,* vol. 3.

Perriman, Andrew, ed. 2003. *Faith, Health and Prosperity.* Carlisle: Paternoster.

Pestman, P. W. 1971. 'Loans Bearing No Interest?' *JJP* 16–17:7-29.

Petschow, Herbert. 1956. *Neubabylonisches Pfandrecht.* ASAW 48/1. Berlin: Akademie.

Petuchowski, Jakob J. 1957. 'A Note on W. Kessler's "Problematik des Dekalogs"'. *VT* 7:397-98.

Phillips, Anthony. 1970. *Ancient Israel's Criminal Law: A New Approach to the Decalogue.* Oxford: Blackwell.

———. 1973. 'Some Aspects of Family Law in Pre-Exilic Israel'. *VT* 23:349-61.

———. 1983. 'The Decalogue — Ancient Israel's Criminal Law'. *JJS* 34:1-20.

———. 1984. 'The Laws of Slavery: Exodus 21.2-11'. *JSOT* 30:51-66. Repr. pp. 96-110 in *Essays on Biblical Law.* JSOTSup 344 (2002).

———. 1995. 'Animals and the Torah'. *ExpTim* 106:260-65. Repr. pp. 127-38 in *Essays on Biblical Law.* JSOTSup 344 (2002).

———. 2004. Review of Harold V. Bennett, *Injustice Made Legal* (2002). *JTS* 55:177-78.

Philo. *The Works of Philo: Complete and Unabridged.* Trans. by C. D. Yonge. New ed. Peabody: Hendrickson, 1993.

Piattelli, Daniela. 1987. 'The Enfranchisement Document on Behalf of the Fugitive Slave'. Pp. 59-85 in *Jewish Law Association Studies III: The Oxford Conference Volume,* ed. A. M. Fuss. Atlanta: Scholars.

———. 1995. 'Zedaqà: Pursuit of Justice and the Instrument of "Ius Talionis"'. *ILR* 29:65-78.

Pierce, Richard H. 1972. *Three Demotic Papyri in the Brooklyn Museum: A Contribution to the Study of Contracts and Their Instruments in Ptolemaic Egypt.* SOSup 24. Oslo: Universitetsforlaget.

Pirenne, Jacques. 1958. 'Le statut de l'étranger dans l'ancienne Egypte'. Pp. 93-103 in *L'étranger.* Recueils de la Societe Jean Bodin 9. Brussels: Librairie Encyclopédique.

Pitard, Wayne T. 1982. 'Amarna *ekēmu* and Hebrew *nāqam*'. *Maarav* 3:5-25.

Pleins, J. David. 1992. 'Poor, Poverty (Old Testament)'. Pp. 401-14 in *ABD,* vol. 5.

———. 2001. *The Social Visions of the Hebrew Bible: A Theological Introduction.* Louisville: Westminster John Knox.

Ploeg, J. P. M. van der. 1951. 'Studies in Hebrew Law: IV. The Religious Character of the Legislation'. *CBQ* 13:164-71.

———. 1972. 'Slavery in the Old Testament'. Pp. 72-87 in *Congress Volume: Uppsala 1971.* VTSup 22. Leiden: Brill.

Pons, Jacques. 1981. *L'oppression dans l'Ancien Testament.* Paris: Letouzey et Ané.

Porten, Bezalel. 1968. *Archives from Elephantine: The Life of an Ancient Jewish Military Colony.* Berkeley: University of California Press.

———. 2003. 'Egypt: Elephantine'. Pp. 863-81 in *HANEL,* vol. 2.

———, and Jonas C. Greenfield. 1969. 'The Guarantor at Elephantine-Syene'. *JAOS* 89:153-57.
Porteous, Norman W. 1966. 'The Care of the Poor in the Old Testament'. Pp. 27-36 in *Service in Christ,* ed. James I. McCord and T. H. L. Parker. Karl Barth Festschrift. London: Epworth. Repr. pp. 143-55 in *Living the Mystery.* Oxford: Blackwell, 1967.
Portugali, Juval. 1984. ''*Arim, Banot, Migrashim* and *Haserim:* The Spatial Organization of Eretz-Israel in the 12th-10th Centuries BCE according to the Bible'. *ErIsr* 17:282-90. (Hebrew, with English summary)
Postgate, J. Nicholas. 1971. 'Land Tenure in the Middle Assyrian Period: A Reconstruction'. *BSOAS* 34:496-520.
———. 1973. *The Governor's Palace Archive.* Cuneiform Texts from Nimrud 2. London: British School of Archaeology in Iraq.
———. 1976. *Fifty Neo-Assyrian Legal Documents.* Warminster: Aris & Phillips.
———. 1992. *Early Mesopotamia: Society and Economy at the Dawn of History.* London: Routledge.
Powell, Marvin A. 1990. 'Masse und Gewichte'. Pp. 457-517 in *Reallexikon der Assyriologie und Vorderasiatischen Archäologie,* ed. Dietz Otto Edzard. Berlin: de Gruyter, vol. 7. (English)
———. 1992. 'Weights and Measures'. Pp. 897-908 in *ABD,* vol. 6.
———, ed. 1987. *Labor in the Ancient Near East.* AOS 68. New Haven: American Oriental Society.
Premnath, D. N. 1988. 'Latifundialization and Isaiah 5.8-10'. *JSOT* 40:49-60.
Pressler, Carolyn. 1993. *The View of Women Found in the Deuteronomic Family Laws.* BZAW 216. Berlin: de Gruyter.
———. 1998. 'Wives and Daughters, Bond and Free: Views of Women in the Slave Laws of Exodus 21.2-11'. Pp. 147-72 in *Gender and Law in the Hebrew Bible and the Ancient Near East,* ed. Victor H. Matthews, Bernard M. Levinson, and Tikva Fryma-Kensky. JSOTSup 262. Sheffield: Sheffield Academic.
Price, Ira M. 1929. 'The Oath in Court Procedure in Early Babylonia and the Old Testament'. *JAOS* 49:22-29.
Propp, William H. C. 2006. *Exodus 19-40.* AB 2A. New York: Doubleday.
Rabast, Karlheinz. 1949. *Das apodiktische Recht im Deuteronomium und im Heiligkeitsgesetz.* Berlin: Heimatdienst.
Rabinowitz, J. J. 1958. 'A Biblical Parallel to a Legal Formula from Ugarit'. *VT* 8:95.
———. 1959. 'Exodus xxii 4 and the Septuagint Version Thereof'. *VT* 9:40-46.
von Rad, Gerhard. 1943. 'The Promised Land and Yahweh's Land in the Hexateuch'. Pp. 79-93 in *The Problem of the Hexateuch and Other Essays.* Edinburgh: Oliver & Boyd, 1966. (trans. from German)
———. 1964a. *Deuteronomy.* OTL. Philadelphia: Westminster/London: SCM, 1966. (trans. from German)
———. 1964b. *Das fünfte Buch Mose: Deuteronomium.* ATD. Göttingen: Vandenhoeck & Ruprecht.
Radner, Karen. 1997. *Die neuassyrischen Privatrechtsurkunden als Quelle für Mensch und Umwelt.* SAAS 6. Helsinki: Neo-Assyrian Text Corpus Project.
———. 2001. 'The Neo-Assyrian Period'. Pp. 265-88 in *SDANEL.*
———. 2003. 'Mesopotamia: Neo-Assyrian Period'. Pp. 883-910 in *HANEL,* vol. 2.

Rainey, Anson, et al. 1972. 'Concubine'. Pp. 862-65 in *EncJud*, vol. 5.
Ramírez Kidd, José E. 1999. *Alterity and Identity in Israel: The גר in the Old Testament*. BZAW 283. Berlin: de Gruyter.
Rankin, Oliver Shaw. 1930. *The Origins of the Festival of Hanukkah: The Jewish New-Age Festival*. Edinburgh: T. & T. Clark.
Rasor, Paul B. 1993. 'Biblical Roots of Modern Consumer Credit Law'. *JLR* 10:157-92.
Ratzinger, Joseph. 1994. 'The Meaning of Sunday'. *Comm* 21:5-26.
Redford, Donald B. 2001. 'The So-Called "Codification" of Egyptian Law under Darius I'. Pp. 135-59 in *Persia and Torah: The Theory of Imperial Authorization of the Pentateuch*, ed. James W. Watts. SBLSymS 17. Atlanta: SBL.
Rehm, Merlin D. 1992. 'Levites and Priests'. Pp. 297-310 in *ABD*, vol. 4.
Reif, Stefan C. 1972. 'Dedicated to חנך'. *VT* 22:495-501.
Reimer, David J. 1997. '7405 צדק'. Pp. 744-69 in *NIDOTTE*, vol. 3.
Reiner, Erica. 1958. *Šurpu: A Collection of Sumerian and Akkadian Incantations*. AfOB 11. Repr. Osnabrück: Biblio-Verlag, 1970.
Rendtorff, Rolf. 1996. 'The *Gēr* in the Priestly Laws of the Pentateuch'. Pp. 77-87 in *Ethnicity and the Bible*, ed. Mark G. Brett. Biblical Interpretation Series 19. Leiden: Brill.
Renger, Johannes. 1994. 'Noch einmal: Was war der 'Kodex' Ḥammurapi — ein erlassenes Gesetz oder ein Rechtsbuch?' Pp. 27-59 in *Rechtskodifizierung und soziale Normen im interkulturellen Vergleich*, ed. Hans-Joachim Gehrke and Eckhard Wirbelauer. Scripta Oralia 66, Altertumswissenschaftliche Reihe 15. Tübingen: Narr.
———. 2002. 'Royal Edicts of the Old Babylonian Period — Structural Background'. Pp. 139-62 in *DERANE*.
Renkema, Johan. 1995. 'Does Hebrew *Ytwm* Really Mean "Fatherless"?' *VT* 45:119-22.
Reno, R. R. 2005. 'God or Mammon'. Pp. 218-36 in *I Am the Lord Your God: Christian Reflections on the Ten Commandments*, ed. Carl E. Braaten and Christopher R. Seitz. Grand Rapids: Wm. B. Eerdmans.
Renz, Johannes. 1995. *Die althebräischen Inschriften: Teil 1. Text und Kommentar*. Handbuch der althebräischen Epigraphik 1. Darmstadt: Wissenschaftliche Buchgesellschaft.
Reuter, Eleonore. 1995. 'שִׁפְחָה'. Pp. 405-10 in *TDOT*, vol. 15 (2006). (trans. from German)
Reventlow, Henning Graf. 1961. *Das Heiligkeitsgesetz: Formgeschichtlich Untersucht*. WMANT 6. Neukirchen-Vluyn: Neukirchener.
———. 1962. *Gebot und Predigt im Dekalog*. Gütersloh: Mohn.
———, and Yair Hoffmann, eds. 1992. *Justice and Righteousness: Biblical Themes and Their Influence*. JSOTSup 137. Sheffield: Sheffield Academic.
Richardson, M. E. J. 2000. *Hammurabi's Laws: Text, Translation and Glossary*. Biblical Seminar 73. Sheffield: Sheffield Academic.
Riesener, Ingrid. 1979. *Der Stamm עבד im Alten Testament: Eine Wortuntersuchung unter Berücksichtigung neuerer sprachwissenschaftlicher Methoden*. BZAW 149. Berlin: de Gruyter.
Ringe, Sharon H. 1985. *Jesus, Liberation, and the Biblical Jubilee: Images for Ethics and Christology*. Philadelphia: Fortress.
Ringgren, Helmer. 1971a. 'אָיַב'. Pp. 212-18 in *TDOT*, vol. 1 (rev. ed. 1977). (trans. from German)
———. 1971b. 'אָח'. Pp. 188-93 in *TDOT*, vol. 1 (rev. ed. 1977). (trans. from German)
———. 1973. 'גָּאַל'. Pp. 350-55 in *TDOT*, vol. 2 (rev. ed. 1977). (trans. from German)
———. 1982. 'יָתוֹם'. Pp. 477-81 in *TDOT*, vol. 6 (1990). (trans. from German)

———, Udo Rüterswörden, and Horacio Simian-Yofre. 1986. 'עָבַד'. Pp. 376-405 in *TDOT*, vol. 10 (1999). (trans. from German)

———, and Bo Johnson. 1989. 'צָדַק'. Pp. 239-64 in *TDOT*, vol. 12 (2003). (trans. from German)

Ro, Bong Rin, ed. 1996. 'Prosperity Theology and Theology of Suffering'. *Evangelical Review of Theology* 20:3-94.

Robinson, Edward, et al. 1856. *Biblical Researches in Palestine and the Adjacent Regions: A Journal of Travels in the Years 1838 & 1852*. vol. 1. 2nd ed. London: Murray.

Robinson, Gnana. 1980. 'The Idea of Rest in the Old Testament and the Search for the Basic Character of Sabbath'. *ZAW* 92:32-42.

———. 1988. *The Origin and Development of the Old Testament Sabbath: A Comprehensive Exegetical Approach*. BBET 21. Frankfurt: Lang.

———. 1991. 'Das Jobel-Jahr: Die Lösung einer sozial-ökonomischen Krise des Volkes Gottes'. Pp. 471-94 in *Ernten, Was Man Sät*, ed. Dwight R. Daniels, Uwe Glessmer, and Martin Rösel. Klaus Koch Festschrift. Neukirchen-Vluyn: Neukirchener.

Robinson, T. H. 1932. *A History of Israel*. Vol. 1: *From the Exodus to the Fall of Jerusalem, 586 B.C.* Oxford: Clarendon.

Rodd, Cyril S. 2001. *Glimpses of a Strange Land: Studies in Old Testament Ethics*. OTS. Edinburgh: T. & T. Clark.

Rofé, Alexander. 1985a. 'The Laws of Warfare in the Book of Deuteronomy: Their Origins, Intent and Positivity'. *JSOT* 32:23-44.

———. 1985b. 'The Tenth Commandment in the Light of Four Deuteronomic Laws'. Pp. 45-65 in *The Ten Commandments in History and Tradition*, ed. Ben-Zion Segal and Gershon Levi. Publications of the Perry Foundation for Biblical Research. Jerusalem: Magnes, 1990. (trans. from Hebrew)

Rogerson, John W. 1986. 'Was Early Israel a Segmentary Society?' *JSOT* 36:17-26.

Röllig, Wolfgang. 2003. *Althebräische Schriftsiegel und Gewichte*. Handbuch der althebräischen Epigraphik 2/2. Darmstadt: Wissenschaftliche Buchgesellschaft, pp. 79-456.

Rollston, Christopher A. 2003. 'Non-Provenanced Epigraphs I: Pillaged Antiquities, Northwest Semitic Forgeries, and Protocols for Laboratory Tests'. *Maarav* 10:135-93.

Rordorf, Willy. 1962. *Sunday: The History of the Day of Rest and Worship in the Earliest Centuries of the Christian Church*. London: SCM, 1968. (trans. from German)

Rosoli, Gianfausto, and Lydio F. Tomasi. 1979. 'The Attitude of Rich Western Christian Societies toward Immigrants'. Pp. 95-103 in *The Dignity of the Despised of the Earth*, ed. Jacques Pohier and Dietmar Mieth. Concilium 130. New York: Seabury.

Roth, Martha T. 1991-93. 'The Neo-Babylonian Widow'. *JCS* 43–45:1-26.

———. 1997. *Law Collections from Mesopotamia and Asia Minor*. 2nd ed. SBLWAW 6. Atlanta: Scholars. (with a contribution by Harry A. Hoffner)

Rothenbusch, Ralf. 2000. *Die kasuistische Rechtssammlung im 'Bundesbuch' (Ex 21,2-11.18-22,16) und ihr literarischer Kontext im Licht altorientalischer Parallelen*. AOAT 259. Münster: Ugarit.

Rothkoff, Aaron. 1972. 'Sabbatical Year in Post-Biblical Times'. Pp. 582-85 in *EncJud*, vol. 14.

Rowbotham, Michael. 1998. *The Grip of Death: A Study of Modern Money, Debt Slavery and Destructive Economics*. Charlbury: Jon Carpenter.

Rowe, Ignatius Márquez. 1999. 'The Legal Texts from Ugarit'. Pp. 390-422 in *Handbook of*

Ugaritic Studies, ed. Wilfred G. E. Watson and Nicolas Wyatt. Handbook of Oriental Studies, Near and Middle East 39. Leiden: Brill.

———. 2003a. 'Anatolia and the Levant: Alalakh'. Pp. 693-717 in *HANEL*, vol. 1.

———. 2003b. 'Anatolia and the Levant: Ugarit'. Pp. 719-35 in *HANEL*, vol. 1.

Rowley, H. H. 1952. 'The Marriage of Ruth'. Pp. 77-99 in *The Servant of the Lord and Other Essays on the Old Testament*. London: Lutterworth. Rev. version of article originally published in *HTR* 40 (1947): 77-99.

Rudolph, Wilhelm. 1962. *Das Buch Ruth, das Hohe Lied, die Klagelieder*. KAT 17/1-3. Gütersloh: Mohn.

Rupprecht, Hans-Albert. 1967. *Untersuchungen zum Darlehen im Recht der graeco-aegyptischen Papyri der Ptolemäerzeit*. MBPF 51. Munich: Beck.

Rüterswörden, Udo. 1987. *Von der politischen Gemeinschaft zur Gemeinde: Studien zu Dt 16,18–18,22*. BBB 65. Frankfurt: Athenäum.

Ruwe, Andreas. 1999. *'Heiligkeitsgesetz' und 'Priesterschrift': Literaturgeschichtliche und rechtssystematische Untersuchungen zu Leviticus 17,1–26,2*. FAT 26. Tübingen: Mohr Siebeck.

Sacks, Jonathan. 1999. *Morals and Markets*. Occasional Paper 108. London: Institute of Economic Affairs. (with commentaries by Norman Barry, Robert Davidson, and Michael Novak)

Safrai, Shmuel. 1972. 'Jubilee in the Second Temple Period'. Pp. 578-82 in *EncJud*, vol. 14.

Saggs, H. W. F. 1988. *The Greatness That Was Babylon: A Survey of the Ancient Civilization of the Tigris-Euphrates Valley*. 2nd ed. London: Sidgwick & Jackson. 1st ed. 1962.

Sales, Michel. 1994. 'The Fulfillment of the Sabbath: From the Holiness of the Seventh Day to God's Resting in God'. *Comm* 21:27-48.

Salonen, Erkki. 1972. *Über den Zehnten im alten Mesopotamien: Ein Beitrag zur Geschichte der Besteuerung*. Studia orientalia 43/4. Helsinki: Finnish Oriental Society.

Sanders, James A. 1992. 'Sins, Debts and Jubilee Release'. Pp. 273-81 in *Text as Pretext: Essays in Honor of Robert Davidson*, ed. Robert P. Carroll. JSOTSup 138. Sheffield: Sheffield Academic.

Sarna, Nahum M. 1973. 'Zedekiah's Emancipation of Slaves and the Sabbatical Year'. Pp. 143-49 in *Orient and Occident*, ed. Harry A. Hoffner. Cyrus Gordon Festschrift. Kevelaer: Butzon & Bercker.

———. 1991. *Exodus*. JPS Torah Commentary. Philadelphia: JPS.

Scaria, K. J. 1978. 'Social Justice in the Old Testament'. *Bible Bhashyam* 4:163-92.

Schaeffer, Henry. 1922. *Hebrew Tribal Economy and the Jubilee: As Illustrated in Semitic and Indo-European Village Communities*. Leipzig: Hinrichs.

Schelbert, Georg. 1958. 'Exodus xxii 4 im Palästinischen Targum'. *Baptist Review of Theology* 8:253-63.

Schenker, Adrian. 1988. 'Affranchissement d'une esclave selon Ex 21,7-11'. *Bib* 69:547-56.

———. 1990. *Versöhnung und Widerstand: Bibeltheologische Untersuchung zum Strafen Gottes und der Menschen, Besonders im Lichte von Exodus 21–22*. SBS 139. Stuttgart: Katholisches Bibelwerk.

———. 1998. 'The Biblical Legislation on the Release of Slaves: The Road from Exodus to Leviticus'. *JSOT* 78:23-41.

Scherer, Andreas. 1997. 'Is the Selfish Man Wise? Considerations of Context in Proverbs 10.1–22.16 with Special Regard to Surety, Bribery and Friendship'. *JSOT* 76:59-70.

Schiffman, Lawrence H. 1998. 'The Prohibition of Judicial Corruption in the Dead Sea

Scrolls, Philo, Josephus and Talmudic Law'. Pp. 155-78 in *Hesed Ve-Emet*, ed. Jodi Magness and Seymour Gitin. Ernest S. Frerichs Festschrift. BJS 320. Atlanta: Scholars.

Schluter, Michael. 1985. 'The Saved and Their Savings'. *Third Way* 8/9:20-23.

———. 2005. 'Welfare'. Pp. 175-95 in *Jubilee Manifesto: A Framework, Agenda & Strategy for Christian Social Reform*, ed. Michael Schluter and John Ashcroft. Downers Grove: InterVarsity.

Schneider, Théo R. 1982. 'Translating Ruth 4.1-10 among the Tsonga People'. *BT* 33:301-8.

Schoneveld, J. 1973. 'Le sang du cambrioleur: Exode XXII 1,2'. Pp. 335-40 in *Symbolae biblicae et Mesopotamicae*, ed. Martinus A. Beek et al. F. M. T. de Liagre Böhl Festschrift. Studia Francisci Scholten Memoriae Dicata 4. Leiden: Brill.

Schorr, Moses. 1907-10. *Altbabylonische Rechtsurkunden aus der Zeit der I. babylonischen Dynastie (ca. 2300-2000 v. Chr.): Umschrift, Übersetzung und Kommentar.* 3 vols. SÖAW 155/2, 160/5, 165/2. Vienna: Holder.

———. 1913. *Urkunden des altbabylonischen Zivil- und Prozessrechts*. VAB 5. Leipzig: Hinrichs.

von Schuler, Einar. 1957. *Hethitische Dienstanweisungen für höhere Hof- und Staatsbeamte: Ein Beitrag zum antiken Recht Kleinasiens.* AfO 10. Graz: private publication.

Schultz, Richard. 1997a. '563 אָמָה'. Pp. 418-21 in *NIDOTTE*, vol. 1.

———. 1997b. '9149 שפט'. Pp. 213-20 in *NIDOTTE*, vol. 4.

———. 1997c. 'Justice'. Pp. 837-46 in *NIDOTTE*, vol. 4.

Schunck, Klaus-Dietrich. 1984. 'Das 9. und 10. Gebot — Jüngstes Glied des Dekalogs?' *ZAW* 96:104-9.

———. 1992. 'Wanting and Desiring'. Pp. 866-67 in *ABD*, vol. 6.

Schwally, Friedrich. 1891. 'Miscellen'. *ZAW* 11:169-83.

Schweitzer, Alexander M., ed. 1999. 'The Year of Jubilee and the Remission of Debt: From the Biblical-Pastoral Perspective'. *Bulletin Dei Verbum* 51/2:1-31.

Schwendemann, Wilhelm. 1995. 'Eine Untersuchung von Ex 21,2-11 im Rahmen theologischer Anthropologie'. *BN* 77:34-40.

Schwienhorst-Schönberger, Ludger. 1990. *Das Bundesbuch (Ex 20,22–23,33): Studien zu seiner Entstehung und Theologie.* BZAW 188. Berlin: de Gruyter.

Scott, R. B. Y. 1959a. 'The Shekel Sign on Stone Weights'. *BASOR* 153:32-35.

———. 1959b. 'Weights and Measures of the Bible'. *BA* 22:22-40.

———. 1964. 'Shekel-Fraction Markings on Hebrew Weights'. *BASOR* 173:53-64.

———. 1965. 'The Scale-Weights from Ophel, 1963-64'. *PEQ* 97:128-39.

———. 1970. 'The N-Ṣ-P Weights from Judah'. *BASOR* 200:62-66.

———. 1985. 'Weights from the 1961-1967 Excavations'. Pp. 197-212 in *Excavations in Jerusalem 1961-1967*, ed. A. D. Tushingham. Toronto: Royal Ontario Museum, vol. 1.

Seebass, Horst. 1993. 'Noch einmal zum Depositenrecht Ex 22,6-14'. Pp. 21-31 in *Gottes Recht als Lebensraum*, ed. Peter Mommer et al. Hans Jochen Boecker Festschrift. Neukirchen-Vluyn: Neukirchener.

———. 1999. 'Zum Sklavenrecht in Ex 21,28-32 und der Diskrepanz zwischen Ersatzrecht und Todesrecht'. *ZABR* 5:179-85.

Seeligmann, I. L. 1978. 'Lending, Pledge and Interest in Biblical Law and Biblical Thought'. Pp. 209-10 in *Studies in Bible and the Ancient Near East*. Samuel E. Loewenstamm Festschrift. Jerusalem: Rubinstein. (also Hebrew abstract)

Segal, Ben-Zion, and Gershon Levi, eds. 1985. *The Ten Commandments in History and Tradi-*

tion. Publications of the Perry Foundation for Biblical Research. Jerusalem: Magnes, 1990. (trans. from Hebrew)

Segal, Moses H. 1967. *The Pentateuch: Its Composition and Its Authorship and Other Biblical Studies*. Jerusalem: Magnes.

Seitz, Gottfried. 1971. *Redaktionsgeschichtliche Studien zum Deuteronomium*. BWANT 93. Stuttgart: Kohlhammer.

Sellers, Ovid R. 1962. 'Weights and Measures'. Pp. 828-39 in *IDB*, vol. 4.

Selms, Adrianus van. 1950. 'The Goring Ox in Babylonian and Biblical Law'. *ArOr* 18:321-30.

———. 1976. 'Jubilee, Year of'. Pp. 496-98 in *IDBSup*.

Seux, Marie-Joseph. 1976. *Hymnes et prières aux dieux de Babylonie et d'Assyrie*. LAPO. Paris: Cerf.

Shah, Anup. 2006. 'The US and Foreign Aid Assistance' (Global Issues). http://www.globalissues.org/TradeRelated/Debt/USAid.asp.

Shanks, Hershel. 1997. 'Three Shekels for the Lord'. *BAR* 23/6:28-32.

Shead, Andrew G. 2002. 'An Old Testament Theology of the Sabbath Year and Jubilee'. *RTR* 61:19-33.

Shemesh, Yael. 2005. 'Punishment of the Offending Organ in Biblical Literature'. *VT* 55:343-65.

Shiff, Laurence. 1988. 'Neo-Babylonian "Interest-Free" Promissory Notes'. *JCS* 40:187-94.

Shupak, Nili. 1993. *Where Can Wisdom be Found? The Sage's Language in the Bible and in Ancient Egyptian Literature*. OBO 130. Fribourg: Universitätsverlag/Göttingen: Vandenhoeck & Ruprecht.

Sider, Ronald J. 1977. *Rich Christians in an Age of Hunger: A Biblical Study*. Downers Grove: InterVarsity/London: Hodder, 1978.

Siker, Jeffrey S. 1981. 'The Theology of the Sabbath in the Old Testament: A Canonical Approach'. *Studia biblica et theologica* 11:5-20.

Silver, Morris. 1983. *Prophets and Markets: The Political Economy of Ancient Israel*. Boston: Kluwer-Nijhoff.

———. 1985. *Economic Structures of the Ancient Near East*. London: Croom Helm/Totowa: Barnes & Noble, 1986.

———. 1995. 'Prophets and Markets Revisited'. Pp. 179-98 in *Social Justice in the Ancient World*, ed. K. D. Irani and Morris Silver. Westport: Greenwood.

Simian-Yofre, Horacio. 1986. 'עוד'. Pp. 495-515 in *TDOT*, vol. 10 (1999). (trans. from German)

Simmons, Stephen D. 1959. 'Early Old Babylonian Tablets from Ḥarmal and Elsewhere'. *JCS* 13:71-93, 105-19.

Simonetti, Cristina. 2000. 'Die Nachlassedikte in Mesopotamien und im antiken Syrien'. Pp. 5-54 in *Das Jobeljahr im Wandel: Untersuchungen zu Erlassjahr- und Jobeljahrtexten aus vier Jahrtausenden*, ed. Georg Scheuermann. FB 94. Würzburg: Echter.

Sivan, Hagith. 2004. *Between Woman, Man and God: A New Interpretation of the Ten Commandments*. JSOTSup 401. London: T. & T. Clark.

Skaist, Aaron. 1994. *The Old Babylonian Loan Contract: Its History and Geography*. Bar-Ilan Studies in Near Eastern Languages and Culture. Ramat Gan: Bar-Ilan University Press.

———. 2001. 'Emar'. Pp. 237-50 in *SDANEL*.

Skaist, Aaron, and Bernard M. Levinson, eds. 2005. 'Judge and Society in Antiquity'. *Maarav* 12:1-173.

Skweres, Dieter Eduard. 1979. *Die Rückverweise im Buch Deuteronomium*. AnBib 79. Rome: Pontifical Biblical Institute.

Slanski, Kathryn E. 2003a. *The Babylonian Entitlement narûs (kudurrus): A Study in Their Form and Function*. ASOR Books 9. Boston: ASOR.

———. 2003b. 'Mesopotamia: Middle Babylonian Period'. Pp. 485-520 in *HANEL*, vol. 1.

Smith, Morton. 1987. *Palestinian Parties and Politics That Shaped the Old Testament*. 2nd ed. London: SCM. 1st ed. 1971.

Smith, W. Robertson. 1894. *Lectures on the Religion of the Semites: The Fundamental Institutions*. New ed. Burnett Lectures, 1st series, 1888. London: Black, 1894. Repr. New Brunswick: Transaction, 2002.

Sneed, Mark R. 1999a. 'Israelite Concern for the Alien, Orphan, and Widow: Altruism or Ideology?' *ZAW* 111:498-507.

———, ed. 1999b. *Concepts of Class in Ancient Israel*. South Florida Studies in the History of Judaism 201. Atlanta: Scholars.

Snell, Daniel C. 1997. *Life in the Ancient Near East, 3100-332 B.C.E*. New Haven: Yale University Press.

———. 2001. *Flight and Freedom in the Ancient Near East*. Culture and History of the Ancient Near East 8. Leiden: Brill.

———, ed. 2005. *A Companion to the Ancient Near East*. Blackwell Companions to the Ancient World. Malden: Blackwell.

Sollberger, Edmond. 1965. *Royal Inscriptions, Part 2*. Ur Excavations, Texts 8. London: Joint Expedition of the British Museum and of the University Museum, University of Pennsylvania, Philadelphia, to Mesopotamia.

Sonsino, Rifat. 1980. *Motive Clauses in Hebrew Law: Biblical Forms and Near Eastern Parallels*. SBLDS 45. Chico: Scholars.

———. 1992. 'Law: Forms of Biblical Law'. Pp. 252-54 in *ABD*, vol. 4.

Soss, Neal M. 1973. 'Old Testament Law and Economic Society'. *JHI* 34:323-44.

Sparks, Kenton L. 1998. *Ethnicity and Identity in Ancient Israel: Prolegomena to the Study of the Ethnic Sentiments and Their Expression in the Hebrew Bible*. Winona Lake: Eisenbrauns.

Speiser, E. A. 1932. 'New Kirkuk Documents relating to Security Transactions'. *JAOS* 52:350-67.

———. 1960. 'Leviticus and the Critics'. Pp. 29-45 in *Yehezkel Kaufmann Jubilee Volume: Studies in Bible and Jewish Religion Dedicated to Yehezkel Kaufmann on the Occasion of His Seventieth Birthday*, ed. Menahem Haran. Jerusalem: Magnes.

Spina, Frank A. 1983. 'Israelites as *gērîm*, "Sojourners," in Social and Historical Context'. Pp. 321-35 in *The Word of the Lord Shall Go Forth*, ed. Carol L. Meyers and M. O'Connor. David Noel Freedman Festschrift. Winona Lake: Eisenbrauns/ASOR.

Sprinkle, Joe M. 1994. *'The Book of the Covenant': A Literary Approach*. JSOTSup 174. Sheffield: JSOT.

———. 2003. 'Theft and Deprivation of Property'. Pp. 841-45 in *DOTP*.

Staalduine-Sulman, Eveline van. 2006. 'Between Legislative and Linguistic Parallels: Exodus 21:22-25 in Its Context'. Pp. 207-24 in *The Interpretation of Exodus*, ed. Riemer Roukema. Cornelis Houtman Festschrift. Leuven: Peeters.

Stackert, Jeffrey (2007). *Rewriting the Torah: Literary Revision in Deuteronomy and the Holiness Legislation*. FAT 52. Tübingen: Mohr Siebeck.

Stager, Lawrence E. 1985. 'The Archaeology of the Family in Ancient Israel'. *BASOR* 260:1-35.

Stamm, Johann Jakob, and Maurice Edward Andrew. 1967. *The Ten Commandments in Recent Research*. SBT, 2nd ser. 2. London: SCM. (trans. from German 2nd ed., 1962, with additions by Andrew)

Steele, Francis Rue. 1943. *Nuzi Real Estate Transactions*. AOS 25. New Haven: American Oriental Society.

Stein, Siegfried. 1953. 'The Laws on Interest in the Old Testament'. *JTS* 4:161-70.

———. 1956. 'Interest Taken by Jews from Gentiles: An Evaluation of Source Material (Fourteenth to Seventeenth Centuries)'. *JSS* 1:141-64.

Steinberg, Naomi. 2004. 'Romancing the Widow: The Economic Distinctions between the *'almana*, the *'iššā-'almana* and the *'ešet-hammet'*. Pp. 327-46 in *God's Word for Our World*, ed. J. Harold Ellens et al. Simon John DeVries Festschrift. JSOTSup 388. London: T. & T. Clark, vol. 1.

Steinkeller, Piotr. 1981. 'The Renting of Fields in Early Mesopotamia and the Development of the Concept of "Interest" in Sumerian'. *JESHO* 24:113-45.

———. 2001. 'The Ur III Period'. Pp. 47-62 in *SDANEL*.

———. 2002. 'Money-Lending Practices in Ur III Babylonia: The Issue of Economic Motivation'. Pp. 109-37 in *DERANE*.

Steuernagel, Carl. 1923. *Das Deuteronomium*. 2nd ed. HKAT 3/1. Göttingen: Vandenhoeck & Ruprecht.

Stevens, Marty E. 2006. *Temples, Tithes, and Taxes: The Temple and the Economic Life of Ancient Israel*. Peabody: Hendrickson.

Stoebe, Hans Joachim. 1952. 'Das Achte Gebot (Exod. 20 v. 16)'. *WD* 3:108-26.

Strecker, Georg, ed. 1983. *Das Land Israel in biblischer Zeit: Jerusalem-Symposium 1981 der Hebräischen Universität und der Georg-August-Universität*. GTA 25. Göttingen: Vandenhoeck & Ruprecht.

Strenge, Irene. 2006. *Codex Hammurapi und die Rechtsstellung der Frau*. Würzburg: Königshausen & Neumann.

Sulzberger, Mayer. 1923. 'The Status of Labor in Ancient Israel'. *JQR* 13:245-302, 397-459.

Sutherland, John. 1982. 'Usury: God's Forgotten Doctrine'. *Crux* 18/1:9-14.

Swanson, Dwight D. 1995. *The Temple Scroll and the Bible: The Methodology of 11QT*. STDJ 14. Leiden: Brill.

Swartley, Willard M. 1983. *Slavery, Sabbath, War, and Women: Case Issues in Biblical Interpretation*. Scottdale: Herald.

Swartzback, Raymond H. 1952. 'A Biblical Study of the Word "Vengeance"'. *Int* 6:451-57.

Szlechter, Émile. 1954. *Les lois d'Ešnunna: Transcription, traduction, et commentaire*. Publications de l'Institut de Droit Romain de l'Université de Paris 12. Paris: Recueil Sirey.

———. 1955. 'Le prêt dans l'Ancien Testament et dans les codes mésopotamiens d'avant Hammourabi'. *RHPR* 35:16-25.

———. 1956. 'La saisie illégale dans les lois d'Ešnunna et dans le code de Hammurabi'. Pp. 271-81 in *Studi in onore di Pietro de Francisci*. Milan: Giuffrè, vol. 1.

Taber, Charles R. 1976. 'Marriage'. Pp. 573-76 in *IDBSup*.

Talmon, Shemaryahu. 1960. 'Double Readings in the Massoretic Text'. *Text* 1:144-84.

———. 1981. 'The Ancient Hebrew Alphabet and Biblical Text Criticism'. Pp. 497-530 in *Mélanges Dominique Barthélemy: Études bibliques offertes à l'occasion de son 60e* anniversaire, ed. Pierre Casetti, Othmar Keel, and Adrian Schenker. OBO 38. Fribourg: Universitätsverlag/Göttingen: Vandenhoeck & Ruprecht.

Talmon, Shemaryahu, and Weston W. Fields. 1989. 'The Collocation נשתין בקיר ועצור ועזוב and Its Meaning'. *ZAW* 101:85-112.

Tampubolon, R. O. M. 1999. 'Keadilan Sosial menurut Hukum di dalam Pentateukh [Social Justice according to Law in the Pentateuch]'. D.Th. diss., South-East Asia Graduate School of Theology.

Tavares, A. Augusto. 1987. 'L'*Almanah* hébraïque et l'*Almattu* des textes akkadiens'. Pp. 155-62 in *La femme dans le Proche-Orient antique: Compte rendu de la XXXIIIe Rencontre Assyriologique Internationale (Paris, 7-10 Juillet 1986)*, ed. Jean-Marie Durand. Paris: Éditions recherche sur les civilisations.

Teicher, J. L. 1951. 'A Sixth-Century Fragment of the Palestinian Targum?' *VT* 1:125-29.

Thiel, Winfried. 1985. *Die soziale Entwicklung Israels in vorstaatlicher Zeit*. 2nd ed. Neukirchen-Vluyn: Neukirchener.

Thompson, J. A. 1974. *Deuteronomy*. TOTC. Downers Grove: InterVarsity.

Tidball, Derek. 2005. *The Message of Leviticus: Free to Be Holy*. Bible Speaks Today. Downers Grove: InterVarsity.

Tigay, Jeffrey H. 1993. 'A Talmudic Parallel to the Petition from Yavneh-Yam'. Pp. 328-33 in *Minḥah le-Naḥum: Biblical and Other Studies*, ed. Marc Zvi Brettler and Michael Fishbane. Nahum M. Sarna Festschrift. JSOTSup 154. Sheffield: Sheffield Academic.

———. 1995. 'Some Archaeological Notes on Deuteronomy'. Pp. 373-80 in *Pomegranates and Golden Bells*, ed. David P. Wright, David Noel Freedman, and Avi Hurvitz. Jacob Milgrom Festschrift. Winona Lake: Eisenbrauns.

———. 1996. *Deuteronomy*. JPS Torah Commentary. Philadelphia: JPS.

———. n.d. 'Shmitah: Remission of Debts Every Seven Years'. *Jewish Heritage Online Magazine*. http://www.jhom.com/topics/seven/shmita.html.

Tinsley, E. J. 1960. *The Imitation of God in Christ: An Essay on the Biblical Basis of Christian Spirituality*. Library of History and Doctrine. Philadelphia: Westminster/London: SCM.

Toorn, Karel van der. 1994. *From Her Cradle to Her Grave: The Role of Religion in the Life of the Israelite and the Babylonian Woman*. Biblical Seminar 23. Sheffield: Sheffield Academic.

Tsevat, Matitiahu. 1958. 'Alalakhiana'. *HUCA* 29:109-34.

———. 1972. 'The Basic Meaning of the Biblical Sabbath'. *ZAW* 84:447-59.

———. 1994. 'The Hebrew Slave According to Deuteronomy 15:12-18: His Lot and the Value of His Work, with Special Attention to the Meaning of מִשְׁנֶה'. *JBL* 113:587-95.

Turkowski, Lucian. 1969. 'Peasant Agriculture in the Judaean Hills'. *PEQ* 101:21-33, 101-12.

Turnham, Timothy John. 1987. 'Male and Female Slaves in the Sabbath Year Laws of Exodus 21:1-11'. *SBLSP* 26:545-49.

Ucko, Hans, ed. 1997. *The Jubilee Challenge: Utopia or Possibility? Jewish and Christian Insights*. Geneva: WCC.

UNHCHR. 1991. 'Contemporary Forms of Slavery'. *Fact Sheet No. 14*. Office of the High Commissioner for Human Rights. http://www.unhchr.ch/html/menu6/2/fs14.htm.

UN News Centre. 2003. 'Development Funds Moving from Poor Countries to Rich Ones, Annan Says'. 30 October. http://www.un.org/apps/news/story.asp?NewsID=8722&Cr=financing&Cr1=development.

UNODC. 2006. 'Trafficking in Persons: Global Patterns'. United Nations Office on Drugs and Crime. http://www.unodc.org/unodc/en/trafficking_persons_report_2006-04.html.

VanderKam, James C. 1992. 'Calendars: Ancient Israelite and Early Jewish'. Pp. 813-20 in *ABD*, vol. 1.

Vannoy, J. Robert. 1974. 'The Use of the Word *ha'elohim* in Exodus 21:6 and 22:7, 8'. Pp. 225-41 in *The Law and the Prophets*, ed. John H. Skilton. Oswald Allis Festschrift. Nutley, NJ: Presbyterian and Reformed.

Van Seters, John. 1996. 'The Law of the Hebrew Slave'. *ZAW* 108:534-46.

———. 1999. 'Some Observations on the Lex Talionis in Exod 21:23-25'. Pp. 27-37 in *Recht und Ethos im Alten Testament: Gestalt und Wirkung*, ed. Stefan Beyerle, Günter Mayer, and Hans Strauss. Horst Seebass Festschrift. Neukirchen-Vluyn: Neukirchener.

———. 2003. *A Law Book for the Diaspora: Revision in the Study of the Covenant Code*. Oxford: Oxford University Press.

———. 2007. 'Law of the Hebrew Slave: A Continuing Debate'. *ZAW* 119:169-83.

Vargyas, Peter. 1995. 'Immigration into Ugarit'. Pp. 395-402 in *Immigration and Emigration within the Ancient Near East,* ed. Karel van Lerberghe and Antoon Schoors. Edward Lipiński Festschrift. OLS 65. Leuven: Peeters.

Vasholz, Robert I. 1987. 'You Shall Not Covet Your Neighbor's Wife'. *WTJ* 49:397-403.

———. 1991. 'A Legal "Brief" on Deuteronomy 23:15-16'. *Presb* 17:127.

Vaux, Roland de. 1961. *Ancient Israel: Its Life and Institutions*. London: Darton, Longman & Todd. Repr. BRS. Grand Rapids: Wm. B. Eerdmans/Livonia: Dove, 1997. (rev. trans. from French, 1958-60)

Veenhof, Klaas R. 1978. 'An Ancient Anatolian Money-Lender: His Loans, Securities and Debt-Slaves'. Pp. 279-311 in *Festschrift Lubor Matouš*, ed. B. Hruška and Géza Komoróczy. Budapest: Eötvös Loránd Tudományegyetem, vol. 2.

———. 2001. 'The Old Assyrian Period'. Pp. 93-159 in *SDANEL*.

———. 2003. 'Mesopotamia: Old Assyrian Period'. Pp. 431-83 in *HANEL,* vol. 1.

Verhoef, Pieter A. 1974. 'Tithing — A Hermeneutical Consideration'. Pp. 115-27 in *The Law and the Prophets*, ed. John H. Skilton. Oswald Allis Festschrift. Nutley, NJ: Presbyterian and Reformed.

Vermeylen, Jacques. 1997. 'Un programme pour la restauration d'Israël: Quelques aspects de la loi dans le Deutéronome'. Pp. 45-80 in *La loi dans l'un et l'autre Testament*, ed. Camille Focant. LD 168. Paris: Cerf.

Vesco, Jean-Luc. 1968. 'Les lois sociales du Livre de l'Alliance (Exode, xx, 22–xxiii, 19)'. *RThom* 68:241-64.

Vink, J. G. 1969. 'The Date and Origin of the Priestly Code in the Old Testament'. *OtSt* 15:1-144.

Vliet, Hendrik van. 1958. *No Single Testimony: A Study on the Adoption of the Law of Deut. 19:15 Par. into the New Testament*. Studia Theologica Rheno-Traiectina 4. Utrecht: Kemink & Zoon.

Volz, Paul. 1932. *Mose und sein Werk*. 2nd ed. Tübingen: Mohr.

Wacholder, Ben Zion. 1973. 'The Calendar of Sabbatical Cycles During the Second Temple and the Early Rabbinic Period'. *HUCA* 44:153-96.

———. 1975. 'Chronomessianism: The Timing of Messianic Movements and the Calendar of Sabbatical Cycles'. *HUCA* 46:201-18.

———. 1976. 'Sabbatical Year'. Pp. 762-63 in *IDBSup*.

———. 1983. 'The Calendar of Sabbath Years During the Second Temple Era: A Response'. *HUCA* 54:123-33.
Waetzoldt, Hartmut. 1987. 'Compensation of Craft Workers and Officials in the Ur III Period'. Pp. 117-41 in *Labor in the Ancient Near East*, ed. Marvin A. Powell. AOS 68. New Haven: American Oriental Society.
Wafawanaka, Robert. 2000. 'African Perspectives on Poverty in the Hebrew Law Codes'. Pp. 490-97 in *The Bible in Africa: Transactions, Trajectories, and Trends*, ed. Gerald O. West and Musa W. Dube. Leiden: Brill.
Wagenaar, Jan A. 2004. 'The Annulment of a "Purchase" Marriage in Exodus 21,7-11'. *ZABR* 10:219-31.
Wagner, Volker. 1969. 'Zur Systematik in dem Codex Ex 21:2–22:16'. *ZAW* 81:176-82.
Wakely, Robin. 1997a. '2471 חבל'. Pp. 6-11 in *NIDOTTE*, vol. 2.
———. 1997b. '6292 עבט'. Pp. 310-13 in *NIDOTTE*, vol. 3.
———. 1997c. '6842 ערב'. Pp. 512-20 in *NIDOTTE*, vol. 3.
———. 1997d. '9023 שמט'. Pp. 155-60 in *NIDOTTE*, vol. 4.
Waldow, H. Eberhard von. 1970. 'Social Responsibility and Social Structure in Early Israel'. *CBQ* 32:182-204.
———. 1974. 'Israel and Her Land: Some Theological Considerations'. Pp. 493-508 in *A Light unto My Path*, ed. Howard N. Bream, Ralph D. Heim, and Carey A. Moore. Jacob Myers Festschrift. Gettysburg Theological Studies 4. Philadelphia: Temple University Press.
Wallace, Ronald S. 1965. *The Ten Commandments: A Study of Ethical Freedom*. Grand Rapids: Wm. B. Eerdmans/Edinburgh: Oliver & Boyd.
Wallenstein, M. 1954. 'Some Lexical Material in the Judean Scrolls'. *VT* 4:211-14.
Walton, John H. 1989. *Ancient Israelite Literature in Its Cultural Context: A Survey of Parallels between Biblical and Ancient Near Eastern Texts*. Library of Biblical Interpretation. Grand Rapids: Zondervan.
———. 2006. *Ancient Near Eastern Thought and the Old Testament: Introducing the Conceptual World of the Hebrew Bible*. Grand Rapids: Baker.
Warhaftig, Shillem. 1972. 'Labor Law'. Pp. 1325-30 in *EncJud*, vol. 10.
Washington, Harold C. 1997. 'Violence and the Construction of Gender in the Hebrew Bible: A New Historicist Approach'. *BibInt* 5:324-63.
Waterman, Anthony. 1982. 'Private Property, Inequality, Theft'. Pp. 96-108 in *Voice from the Mountain: New Life for the Old Law*, ed. Philip Jefferson. Toronto: Anglican Book Centre.
Watts, James W. 1999. *Reading Law: The Rhetorical Shaping of the Pentateuch*. Biblical Seminar 59. Sheffield: Sheffield Academic.
Weber, Max. 1921. *Ancient Judaism*. Glencoe: Free Press, 1952. (trans. from German)
Wehmeier, Gerhard. 1977. 'The Prohibition of Theft in the Decalogue'. *IJT* 26:181-91.
Weiler, Ingomar. 1980. 'Zum Schicksal der Witwen und Waisen bei den Völkern der alten Welt'. *Saeculum* 31:157-93.
Weinfeld, Moshe. 1972a. *Deuteronomy and the Deuteronomic School*. Oxford: Clarendon.
———. 1972b. 'Tithe'. Pp. 1156-62 in *EncJud*, vol. 15.
———. 1973. 'The Origin of the Apodictic Law: An Overlooked Source'. *VT* 23:63-75.
———. 1977. 'Judge and Officer in Israel and in the Ancient Near East'. *IOS* 7:65-88.
———. 1990. 'Sabbatical Year and Jubilee in the Pentateuchal Laws and Their Ancient Near Eastern Background'. Pp. 39-61 in *The Law in the Bible and in Its Environment*, ed. Timo

Veijola. Publications of the Finnish Exegetical Society 51. Göttingen: Vandenhoeck & Ruprecht. Repr. pp. 152-78 in Weinfeld 1995.

———. 1991. *Deuteronomy 1–11*. AB 5. New York: Doubleday.

———. 1992. '"Justice and Righteousness" — משפט וצדקה — The Expression and Its Meaning'. Pp. 228-46 in *Justice and Righteousness: Biblical Themes and Their Influence*, ed. Henning Graf Reventlow and Yair Hoffmann. JSOTSup 137. Sheffield: Sheffield Academic.

———. 1993. *The Promise of the Land: The Inheritance of the Land of Canaan by the Israelites*. Berkeley: University of California Press.

———. 1995. *Social Justice in Ancient Israel and in the Ancient Near East*. Jerusalem: Magnes/Minneapolis: Fortress. (rev. trans. from Hebrew)

———. 2004. *The Place of the Law in the Religion of Ancient Israel*. VTSup 100. Leiden: Brill.

Weingreen, Jacob. 1976. *From Bible to Mishna: The Continuity of Tradition*. Manchester: Manchester University Press/New York: Holmes & Meier.

Weippert, Manfred. 1967. *The Settlement of the Israelite Tribes in Palestine: A Critical Survey of Recent Scholarly Debate*. SBT, 2nd ser. 21. Naperville: Allenson/London: SCM, 1971. (trans. from German)

Weisberg, Dvora E. 2004. 'The Widow of Our Discontent: Levirate Marriage in the Bible and Ancient Israel'. *JSOT* 28:403-29.

Weiss, Herold. 2003. *A Day of Gladness: The Sabbath among Jews and Christians in Antiquity*. Columbia: University of South Carolina Press.

Welch, Adam C. 1924. *The Code of Deuteronomy: A New Theory of Its Origin*. London: Clarke.

Welch, John W. 2005. *Biblical Law Cumulative Bibliography*. Updated electronic ed. Provo: Brigham Young University Press. 1st ed. *Bibical Law Bibliography*. Lewiston: Mellen, 1990. Supplements in *ZABR* 3 (1997): 207-46; 9 (2003): 279-318.

Wellhausen, Julius. 1883. *Prolegomena to the History of Israel*. Edinburgh: Black, 1885. (trans. from German)

Wells, Bruce. 2006. 'The Covenant Code and Near Eastern Legal Traditions: A Response to David P. Wright'. *Maarav* 13:85-118.

Wenham, Gordon J. 1971. 'Legal Forms in the Book of the Covenant'. *TynBul* 22:95-102.

———. 1978a. 'Grace and Law in the Old Testament'. Pp. 3-23 in *Law, Morality and the Bible*, ed. Bruce N. Kaye and Gordon J. Wenham. Downers Grove: InterVarsity.

———. 1978b. 'Law and the Legal System in the Old Testament'. Pp. 24-52 in *Law, Morality and the Bible*, ed. Bruce N. Kaye and Gordon J. Wenham. Downers Grove: InterVarsity.

———. 1978c. 'Leviticus 27 $_{2\text{-}8}$ and the Price of Slaves'. *ZAW* 90:264-65.

———. 1979. *The Book of Leviticus*. NICOT. Grand Rapids: Wm. B. Eerdmans.

———. 1996. 'Law'. In *New Bible Dictionary*, ed. D. R. W. Wood. 3rd ed.; electronic ed. Downers Grove: InterVarsity.

———. 1997. 'The Gap between Law and Ethics in the Bible'. *JJS* 48:17-29.

———. 1999. 'The Priority of P'. *VT* 49:240-58.

———. 2000. *Story as Torah: Reading the Old Testament Ethically*. OTS. Edinburgh: T. & T. Clark.

Westbrook, Raymond. 1971a. 'Jubilee Laws'. *ILR* 6:209-25. Repr. pp. 36-57 in *Property and the Family in Biblical Law*. JSOTSup. 113. Sheffield: Sheffield Academic, 1991.

———. 1971b. 'Purchase of the Cave of Machpelah'. *ILR* 6:29-38. Repr. pp. 24-35 in *Property and the Family in Biblical Law*. JSOTSup 113. Sheffield: Sheffield Academic, 1991.

———. 1971c. 'Redemption of Land'. *ILR* 6:367-75. Repr. pp. 58-68 in *Property and the Family in Biblical Law*. JSOTSup 113. Sheffield: Sheffield Academic, 1991.

———. 1977. 'The Law of the Biblical Levirate'. *RIDA* 24:65-87. Repr. pp. 69-89 in *Property and the Family in Biblical Law*. JSOTSup 113. Sheffield: Sheffield Academic, 1991.

———. 1985a. 'Biblical and Cuneiform Law Codes'. *RB* 92:247-64.

———. 1985b. 'The Price Factor in the Redemption of Land'. *RIDA* 32:97-127. Repr. pp. 90-117 in *Property and the Family in Biblical Law*. JSOTSup 113. Sheffield: Sheffield Academic, 1991.

———. 1986. 'Lex Talionis and Exodus 21, 22-25'. *RB* 93:52-69.

———. 1988a. *Old Babylonian Marriage Law*. AfOB 23. Horn: Berger.

———. 1988b. *Studies in Biblical and Cuneiform Law*. CahRB 26. Paris: Gabalda.

———. 1989. 'Cuneiform Law Codes and the Origins of Legislation'. *ZA* 79:201-22.

———. 1991. 'The Dowry'. Pp. 142-64 in *Property and the Family in Biblical Law*. JSOTSup 113. Sheffield: Sheffield Academic.

———. 1994a. 'The Deposit Law of Exodus 22,6-12'. *ZAW* 106:390-403.

———. 1994b. 'The Old Babylonian Term *napṭarum*'. *JCS* 46:41-46.

———. 1994c. 'What Is the Covenant Code?' Pp. 15-36 in *Theory and Method in Biblical and Cuneiform Law*, ed. Bernard M. Levinson. JSOTSup 181. Sheffield: Sheffield Academic.

———. 1995a. 'Slave and Master in Ancient Near Eastern Law'. *Chicago-Kent Law Review* 70:1631-76.

———. 1995b. 'Social Justice in the Ancient Near East'. Pp. 149-63 in *Social Justice in the Ancient World*, ed. K. D. Irani and Morris Silver. Westport, CT/London: Greenwood.

———. 1998. 'The Female Slave'. Pp. 214-38 in *Gender and Law in the Hebrew Bible and the Ancient Near East*, ed. Victor H. Matthews, Bernard M. Levinson, and Tikva Frymer-Kensky. JSOTSup 262. Sheffield: Sheffield Academic.

———. 2001. 'The Old Babylonian Period'. Pp. 63-92 in *SDANEL*.

———. 2003a. 'Anatolia and the Levant: Emar and Vicinity'. Pp. 657-91 in *HANEL*, vol. 1.

———. 2003b. 'The Character of Ancient Near Eastern Law'. Pp. 1-90 in *HANEL*, vol. 1.

———. 2003c. 'Mesopotamia: Old Babylonian Period'. Pp. 361-430 in *HANEL*, vol. 1.

———, and Roger D. Woodard. 1990. 'The Edict of Tudhaliya IV'. *JAOS* 110:641-59.

Westermann, William L. 1955. *The Slave Systems of Greek and Roman Antiquity*. Philadelphia: American Philosophical Society.

Wigmore, John H. 1897-98. 'The Pledge Idea: A Study in Comparative Legal Ideas'. *Harvard Law Review* 10:321-50, 389-417; 11:18-39.

Wijk-Bos, Johanna W. H. van. 2005. *Making Wise the Simple: The Torah in Christian Faith and Practice*. Grand Rapids: Wm. B. Eerdmans.

Wilcke, Claus. 2003. 'Mesopotamia: Early Dynastic and Sargonic Periods'. Pp. 141-81 in *HANEL*, vol. 1. Abridged version of Wilcke 2007.

———. 2007. *Early Ancient Near Eastern Law: A History of Its Beginnings: The Early Dynastic and Sargonic Periods*. Rev. ed. Winona Lake: Eisenbrauns. Originally published as SBAW 2003, vol. 2. Abridged version published as Wilcke 2003.

Williamson, H. G. M. 1985a. *Ezra, Nehemiah*. WBC 16. Waco: Word.

———. 1985b. 'A Reconsideration of עזב II in Biblical Hebrew'. *ZAW* 97:74-85.

Willis, Timothy M. 2004. Review of Harold V. Bennett, *Injustice Made Legal* (2002). *CBQ* 66:437-38.

Wilson, Ian. 1995. *Out of the Midst of the Fire: Divine Presence in Deuteronomy.* SBLDS 151. Atlanta: Scholars.

Wiseman, Donald J. 1962. 'Laws of Hammurabi Again'. *JSS* 7:161-72.

———. 1973. 'Law and Order in Old Testament Times'. *VE* 8:5-21.

Wolff, Hans Walter. 1973. *Anthropology of the Old Testament.* Philadelphia: Fortress/London: SCM, 1974. (rev. trans. from German)

Wright, Christopher J. H. 1979. 'The Israelite Household and the Decalogue: The Social Background and Significance of Some Commandments'. *TynBul* 30:101-24.

———. 1984. 'What Happened Every Seven Years in Israel? Old Testament Sabbatical Institutions for Land, Debts and Slaves'. *EvQ* 56:129-38, 193-201.

———. 1990. *God's People in God's Land: Family, Land, and Property in the Old Testament.* Grand Rapids: Wm. B. Eerdmans/Exeter: Paternoster.

———. 1992a. 'Jubilee, Year of'. Pp. 1025-30 in *ABD*, vol. 3.

———. 1992b. 'Sabbatical Year'. Pp. 857-61 in *ABD*, vol. 5.

———. 1996. *Deuteronomy.* NIBCOT 4. Peabody: Hendrickson/Carlisle: Paternoster.

———. 1997. '5706 נחל'. Pp. 77-81 in *NIDOTTE*, vol. 3.

———. 2004a. *Old Testament Ethics for the People of God.* Downers Grove: InterVarsity. Rev. and integrated ed. of *Living as the People of God.* Leicester: Inter-Varsity/*An Eye for an Eye.* Downers Grove: InterVarsity, 1983; and *Walking in the Ways of the Lord.* Downers Grove: InterVarsity, 1995.

———. 2006a. *The Mission of God: Unlocking the Bible's Grand Narrative.* Downers Grove: InterVarsity.

———. 2006b. 'Response to Gordon McConville'. Pp. 282-90 in *Canon and Biblical Interpretation,* ed. Craig Bartholomew et al. Scripture and Hermeneutics 7. Milton Keynes: Paternoster/Grand Rapids: Zondervan.

Wright, David P. 2003. 'The Laws of Hammurabi as a Source for the Covenant Collection (Exodus 20:23–23:19)'. *Maarav* 10:11-87.

———. 2004b. 'The Compositional Logic of the Goring Ox and Negligence Laws in the Covenant Collection (Ex 21:28-36)'. *ZABR* 10:93-142.

———. 2006c. 'The Laws of Hammurabi and the Covenant Code: A Response to Bruce Wells'. *Maarav* 13:211-60.

Wunsch, Cornelia. 2002. 'Debt, Interest, Pledge and Forfeiture in the Neo-Babylonian and Early Achaemenid Period: The Evidence from Private Archives'. Pp. 221-55 in *DERANE.*

Yamauchi, Edwin M. 1980. 'Two Reformers Compared: Solon of Athens and Nehemiah of Jerusalem'. Pp. 269-92 in *The Bible World,* ed. Gary Rendsburg et al. Cyrus Gordon Festschrift. New York: Ktav/New York University Institute of Hebrew Culture and Education.

Yaron, Reuven. 1959. 'Redemption of Persons in the Ancient Near East'. *RIDA* 6:155-76.

———. 1960. 'A Document of Redemption from Ugarit'. *VT* 10:83-90.

———. 1966. 'The Goring Ox in Near Eastern Laws'. *ILR* 1:396-406. Repr. pp. 50-60 in *Jewish Law in Ancient and Modern Israel,* ed. Haim H. Cohn. New York: Ktav, 1971.

———. 1980. 'Biblical Law: Prolegomena'. Pp. 27-44 in *Jewish Law in Legal History and the Modern World,* ed. Bernard S. Jackson. Jewish Law Annual Supplement 2. Leiden: Brill.

———. 1988. *The Laws of Eshnunna.* Rev. ed. Jerusalem: Magnes/Leiden: Brill. 1st ed. 1969.

———. 1993. 'Social Problems and Policies in the Ancient Near East'. Pp. 19-41 in *Law, Poli-*

tics and Society in the Ancient Mediterranean World, ed. Baruch Halpern and Deborah W. Hobson. Sheffield: Sheffield Academic.

Yoffee, Norman. 1981. *Explaining Trade in Ancient Western Asia*. Monographs on the Ancient Near East 2/2. Malibu: Undena.

Younker, Randall W. 2003. 'Social Structure'. Pp. 783-87 in *DOTP*.

Zaccagnini, Carlo. 2001. 'Nuzi'. Pp. 223-36 in *SDANEL*.

———. 2002. 'Debt and Debt Remission at Nuzi'. Pp. 175-96 in *DERANE*.

———. 2003. 'Mesopotamia: Nuzi'. Pp. 565-617 in *HANEL*, vol. 1.

Zakovitch, Yair. 1974. 'Some Remnants of Ancient Laws in the Deuteronomic Code'. *ILR* 9:346-51.

Zeitlin, Solomon. 1962. *The Rise and Fall of the Judaean State: A Political, Social and Religious History of the Second Commonwealth*, vol. 1. Philadelphia: JPS.

Zevit, Ziony. 1982. 'Converging Lines of Evidence Bearing on the Date of P'. *ZAW* 94:481-511.

Zimmerli, Walther. 1970. 'Das "Gnadenjahr des Herrn"'. Pp. 321-32 in *Archäologie und Altes Testament*, ed. Arnulf Kuschke and Ernst Kutsch. Kurt Galling Festschrift. Tübingen: Mohr Siebeck. Repr. pp. 222-34 in *Studien zur alttestamentlichen Theologie und Prophetie*. TB 51. Munich: Kaiser, 1974.

Index of Subjects

Aaron, 8, 156, 241
Abdihiba, 29
Abigail, 163, 194
Abraham, 15, 75, 76, 86, 119, 141, 178, 239
abuse, 120, **121-30**, 155, 191-94, 207, 211, 269, 298, 308, 312
adoption, 87, 115, 151
Advice to a Prince, 216
agriculture, 18, 58, 60, 63, 64, 75, 82, 83, 86, 92, 100, 105, 113, 176, 224-31, 238, 239, 244, 247, 251, 283, 286, 293, 296, 309, 313
Ahab, 158
Akkadians, 177
Alalakh, 19, 48, 132, 138, 202, 267
Amalekites, 135, 181
Amarna letters, 29
Amar-Sin, 300
Amenemhet I, 191
Amenemope. *See* Instruction of Amenemope
Ammi-saduqa. *See* Edict of Ammi-saduqa
Ammistamru, 240
amnesty, 78, 277
Amorites, 177
Amurru, 132
Ana ittišu, 4
Anatolia, 111, 277

ancient Near Eastern laws, **1-6**
  history, 2
  nature and purpose, 2
  relation to Bible, 2, 6, 27, 28, 39, 53, 73, 120, **306-10**
  unsystematic character, 3
animals, 19-22, 26, 27, 31, 37-46, 49, 50, 53-74, 113, 116, 180, 186, 224-31, 239, 256, 264, 267, 271, 286, 289, 306, 307, 311, 314
ass, 39, 63
bear, 70
beast of burden, 23, 39, 40, 307
bull, 19, 37, 45, 47, 52, 55
dog, 45, 53, 55, 57
donkey, 22, 30-32, 36-43, 49, 67, 68, 288, 291
goat, 57, 58, 61, 70
horse, 19, 37, 63
lion, 63, 65, 70
livestock, 31, 39, 59-61, 65, 92, 177, 229, 241, 244, 287-89, 292, 293, 297, 310
mule, 37, 63
ox, 19, 22, 23, 27, 30-32, 36-42, 45-56, 63, 67, 68, 121, 123, 125, 127, 130, 240, 250, 268, 271, 274, 288, 291, 307
sheep, 22, 23, 27, 40, 41, 57-61, 65-70, 81, 97, 145, 167, 240, 256
snake, 260

369

INDEX OF SUBJECTS

wild beast, 69, 70, 72
wolf, 63, 65
apostasy, 206, 207
Aqhat Legend, 191, 225
Arabia, 245, 249
Arad-Sin, 78
Araunah the Jebusite, 76
Aristotle, 265
Arrapha, 152
Ashhur, 158
Assur, 5
Assyria, 1, 5, 15, 29, 152, 202
asylum, 133, 135, 177, 308
Athens, 178, 277
Augustine, 31
avenge, vengeance, 123-28, 207. *See also* blood: blood vengeance
Azatiwada Inscription, 30

Baal, 225
Babylon, 4, 105, 120, 133, 149, 177-79, 216, 248
Babylonia, 1, 4, 15, 17, 58, 78, 106, 111, 114, 115, 138, 147, 152, 179, 202, 243, 256, 287, 300, 309
Babylonian Seisachtheia. *See* Edict of Ammi-saduqa
bankruptcy, 150
barley, 79, 93, 233, 276, 277
beast of burden, 39, 291
Bedouin, 23
beer, 97, 240, 300
Beeroth, 179
benefactor, 190
Benjamin, 275
Benjaminites, 158
biblical laws, 6-11, 101, 195
    relation to other laws. *See* ancient Near Eastern laws: relation to Bible
blasphemy, 9, 185
blessing, 96, 143, 145, 147, 167, 168, 203, 223, 228, 230, 232, 233, 235, 237, 245-47, 250, 251, 262-64, 272, 273, 278, 281, 282, 288, 290, 312
blood, 40, 88, 163, 186, 220
    blood vengeance, 123, 126, 127

bloodguilt, 51, 52, 56, 307
boat, 17, 18, 63, 64, 72, 73
Boaz, 89, 90, 200, 238
bonded labour/labourer, 80, 93, 95, 112, 120, 136, 140, 143, 149, **159-74**, 306-08, 312
Book of the Covenant, **8-9**, 10, 11, 28, 53, 140, 168, 183, 258, 263
Book of the Dead, 29, 247, 256, 301
borrowing, 62, 63, 71-74, 266, 306
boundary, 9, 26, 34, 75, 76, **97-102**, 191, 192, 306
bribe, bribery, 187, 200, 214, **215-22**, 309, 313
brother, 40-42, 78, 87, 88, 117, 118, 134, 143, 144, 162-64, 167, 170, 179, 186, 206, 209, 214, 258, 259, 262, 278, 282, 298, 301, 315
burglary. *See* theft
buying. *See* purchase

Cain, 42
Caleb, 158
Canaan, land of, 75, 106, 179, 259, 261. *See also* Palestine
Canaanites, 1, 35, 76, 91, 119, 178, 179, 181, 182, 184, 226, 240, 247, 257, 263, 288
canal, 36, 57
capital, 31, 137, 145, 148, 164, 254, 257, 258, 264-68, 308, 314
Cappadocia, 240, 257
Carthage, 245
charity, 56, 89, 90, 157, 164, 180, 188, 190, 233, 235, 237, 238, 241, 282
childless wife/widow, 151, 194
children, 32, 79, 93, 105, 106, 113, 114, 118, 119, 124, 126, 137-41, 149-52, 156, 162-68, 171, 172, 175, 189, 191, 229, 233, 292, 306
circumcision, 179, 188, 293
city, 27, 30, 75, 80, 86, 87, 90-92, 95, 130, 131, 175, 179, 188, 191, 243, 283
clan, 81, 88, 93, 111, 133, 162-64, 167, 188
clean slate, 276
Clement of Alexandria, 31
cloak, 269, 271-73

clothing, 40, 42, 67, 146, 153, 154, 160, 172, 187
Code of Hammurabi. *See* Laws of Hammurabi
compassion, 16, 74, 134, 185, 187, 193, 210, 211, 251, 269, 273, 308, 311, 312
compensation, 17-19, 22, 23, 26, 27, 37, 45, 46, 48-51, 54-64, 79, 84, 97, 98, 113, 121, 122, 126-30, 154, 155, 168, 200, 241, 268, 296, 299, 307, 310
concubine, 112, 115, 119, 120, 136, 137, 144, **150-59**, 166, 291, 308
constitution, 8
construction, 46, 51, 113
consumerism, 231, 266
contentment, 35, 311
contract, 17, 63, 73, 113-15, 132, 138, 140, 149, 151, 152, 154, 160, 174, 255, 256, 260, 267, 268, 285, 297, 300
corruption, 18, 212, 216, 221, 301, 302
covenant community, 16, 28, 31, 36, 39, 40, 42, 43, 74, 85, 101, 117, 118, 120, 123, 127, 129, 133, 136, 144, 149, 156, 162, 173, 176, 179-81, 188, 195, 202, 204, 208, 220, 221, 237, 249-51, 257, 259, 261-65, 269, 274, 280-86, 289, 293, 295, 301, 302, 307-14
covenant formula, 162
coveting, 9, 17, 20, **28-36**, 101, 149, 155, 199, 202, 311
creditor, 80, 136, 138, 144, 147, 148, 151, 154, 166, 172, 254-57, 259, 261, 267-74, 278, 285
cultivation, 64, 65, 72
curse, 10, 11, 105, 187, 220, 233

damage, 17, 44, 52, 53, 56, **57-62**, 63-65, 72, 122, 129, 233, 249, 306
damages, 19, 56, 59, 62
Daniel, 191
David, 70, 73, 76, 127, 135, 158, 284
Dawn and Dusk, 225
Day of Atonement, 80, 81, 179, 293
Dead Sea Scrolls, 83, 96, 245, 298
death, 22, 37, 45-56, 63, 69-72, 107, 115, 123, 125, 130, 135, 141, 194, 208, 210, 211, 225, 296, 307
death penalty. *See* punishment: capital punishment
debt, debtor, 3, 23, 78, 120, 134-39, 143-54, 160, 168, 170-74, 252-55, 257, 260, 264, 266-77, 283, 284, 308, 312, 314
  debt relief, 78, 137, 143, 147, 177, 180, 224, 226, 232, 252, **275-85**, 309, 310, 314
  debt-slave/slavery, 123, 127, 134, 149, 151, 154, 278, 284
Decalogue, **7-9**, 11, 16, 20, 21, 31, 33, 34, 100, 101, 140, 183, 202, 203, 294
deceit, 203, 212
Demotic period, 1, 138, 256, 267
deodand, 56
deposit, 24, 25, 73
descent into poverty, 80, 162, 259
desire. *See* coveting
Deuteronomic Laws, 9, **10-11**, 40, 86, 169, 179, 194
dignity, 28, 121, 123, 128, 212, 237, 310
Disputation between the Hoe and the Plough, 233
distraint, 268, 270
divorce, 157, 175, 189
Djoser, 225
Doeg the Edomite, 165
drink, 241, 293

ear-piercing, 142, 146
economics, 35, 310, 313
Edict of Ammi-saduqa, 5, 277
Edom, 250
Egypt, 1, 19, 29, 30, 80, 98, 111, 114, 116, 117, 131, 132, 134, 135, 140, 141, 145, 146, 149, 160-62, 165-67, 168, 173, 177, 178, 181-87, 191-93, 202, 209, 216, 231, 234, 235, 237, 245, 247, 256, 259, 261, 264, 267, 277, 288, 290, 295, 301
El, 225
elder, 37, 104, 127, 200, 213, 218
Elephantine, 114, 216, 295
Elimelech, 88, 90
Elisha, 76

INDEX OF SUBJECTS

Elkanah, 158
Eloquent Peasant, 29, 191, 192, 209
Emar, 267
employee, 18, 73, 162, 295, 299, 304, 310, 312, 314
employer, 18, 176, 280, 297, 299, 310, 314
employment, 28, 62, 65, 72, 73, 121, 174, 176, 286, 306, 310
enemy, 38-43, 70, 72, 102, 131, 190
Enmetena, 276
ephah, 301-03
Ephron the Hittite, 76
epidemic, 65, 72
equality, 95, 151, 181, 185
equity, 276, 277, 279, 284. *See also* justice
Eshnunna, 4, 36. *See also* Laws of Eshnunna
ethnic minority, 112, 133, 176, 182-84, 187-89, 259, 308
exile, 10, 178, 179, 232, 242, 244, 284
exodus, 140, 145-47, 162, 166, 179, 181, 187, 192, 227, 261, 290
exploitation, 35, 85, 101, 130, 182, 187, 189, 231, 264, 265, 269, 296
extradition, 132, 134, 135
Ezra, 244

face, 212
fallowing, 82, 83, 224, 226, 227, 229-31, 237, 279
family, 16, 21, 27, 32, 40, 48, 52, 55, 56, 76, 78, 80, 81, 88-90, 93, 95, 99, 105-07, 111, 123, 126, 127, 133, 134, 139, 142, 144, 150-55, 158, 162, 164, 166, 169, 171, 172, 180, 188-90, 194, 195, 241, 243, 244, 247, 254, 257, 272-74, 277, 283, 295, 307, 309
famine, 76, 80, 88, 188, 225, 226, 231, 311
Famine Stela, 225
farmer, 65, 80, 99, 224, 234, 243, 246, 247, 249, 259, 268
favouritism. *See* partiality
fear of God, 84, 85, 162, 166, 167, 259, 261
feast, 241, 242, 244, 293
fee, 200, 216-18, 220, 221, 296, 309

festival, 176, 179, 186, 235, 279, 283, 290-95, 310, 314. *See also* Day of Atonement, sabbath
  Booths, 186, 283, 293
  New Year, 287
  Passover, 82, 176, 179-81, 186, 293, 295
  Unleavened Bread, 295
  Weeks, 235, 290, 293
field, 16, 30-32, 37, 57-61, 64, 65, 72, 78, 79, 81, 91, 93, 94, 97-100, 102, 103, 224, 227, 228, 230, 233-38, 249-51, 254, 257, 268, 279, 280
fiftieth year, 79-82, 95, 168, 172
fire, 17, 28, 57-61, 306
flood, 57-58, 61, 65, 72, 257, 306
food, 80, 83, 86, 102, 153, 154, 160, 172, 177, 187, 224, 227, 229, 241, 246, 249, 250, 258-63, 271, 293, 295
forced labour, 98, 119, 120
foreigner, 114, 117, 118, 126, 134, 160, 164-66, 169, 173, 176, 177, 179, 180, 182, 184, 257, 262, 263, 265, 278, 280
forty-ninth year, 82, 231
fraud, 24, 25, 63, 78, 211, 255, 264, 297, 298
free citizen, 21, 111, 112, 114-16, 119-23, 125, 128-30, 136, 137, 142, 144, 145, 149, 153, 154, 157, 169, 182, 259, 306
freedom, 23, 47, 77, 78, 80, 81, 93, 111, 116, 129, 134, 135, 137, 138, 140-44, 148, 149, 151, 154, 157, 159, 160, 166, 169, 172-74, 178, 187, 237, 238, 251, 274, 276, 277, 284, 301, 307, 308, 314
fruit, fruit tree, 15, 58, 105, 241, 249, 313. *See also* orchard

generosity, 133, 145-47, 167, 172, 223, 237, 238, 251, 261, 264, 281, 282, 286, 293, 305, **313-14**, 315
Gezer Calendar, 230
Gibeon, 178, 179, 184
Gideon, 119, 158
gift, 16, 75, 85, 86, 90, 94, 101, 107, 113, 142, 145, 213, 216-18, 220, 231, 243, 246, 247, 251, 261, 281, 282, 307, 309, 315
Gilgamesh, 106

Index of Subjects

Gilgamesh Epic, 225
gleaning, 188, 193, 227, **232-39**, 308, 309, 313
grain, 57, 58, 60, 63-65, 68, 73, 145, 200, 224, 234-36, 239-41, 244, 246, 249, 250, 253-58, 264, 268, 276, 287, 300, 313
gratitude, 35, 145, 264, 273, 311
grazing, 57-61
Greece, 23, 99, 112, 206, 265
greed, 35, 36, 264, 311, 315

Hadad-yith'i, 233
Hagar, 135
Hammurabi, 4, 5, 199, 276. *See also* Laws of Hammurabi
Hamor, 76
Hanamel, 89
hard hearts, 283
Harem Edicts. *See* Middle Assyrian Palace Decrees
harvest, 58, 59, 64, 81, 82, 96, **223-51**, 253, 254, 257, 268, 278, 293, 295, 296, 297, 309, 313
Hatti, 29
Hattusha, 5
Hebrews, 116, 120, 123, 127, 133, 139, 140, 143, 149, 165, 167, 170, 171
hire, 70, 113, 147
hired worker, 147, 148, 161, 163, 167, 168, 171-73, 175, 176, 188, 189, 229, 296-99, 314
Hittite Laws, 5
Hittites, 1, 5, 29, 76, 111, 132, 165, 177, 202, 209, 216, 277
holiday, 83, 120, 188, 193, 231, 253, **287-96**, 308, 310
Holiness Code, **9-10**, 11, 86, 169, 234, 261, 313
holy, 8, 9, 77, 79, 81, 94, 96, 134, 225, 231, 241-44, 246, 248, 287-90, 294, 313
homer, 93, 303
homicide. *See* murder
Horemheb, 216
hospitality, 133, 158, 177, 179, 249, 251
house, 16-19, 22, 23, 28, 30-32, 36, 40, 41, 46, 48, 51-53, 55, 58, 61-63, 65-67, 69, 72, 73, 77-80, 86, 90-92, 95, 103-06, 111, 114, 119, 131, 137, 142, 155, 158, 171, 172, 190, 246, 254, 265, 268, 269, 271, 272, 302, 311
household, 17, 30-32, 66, 80, 112, 113, 126, 136, 142, 146, 148, 151, 162-64, 167, 172, 180, 194, 258, 268, 269, 292, 293, 308
humane treatment, 27, 120, 130, 142, 161, 165, 169, 174, 307
hunger, 248-50, 276
Hymn to the Sun God. *See* Shamash Hymn

imitation of God, 188, 214, 220, 290, 312
immigrant. *See* resident alien
impartiality. *See* partiality
impoverishment, 80, 162, 259
inclusive language, 6, 25
inclusive reckoning, 82, 83
indenture. *See* bonded labour
inheritance, 75, 86, 90, 93, 95, 97, 99, 100, 107, 151, 164, 179, 190, 194, 245, 248, 281, 292, 307
injury, 55, 56, 63, 69, 70-73, 122, 123, 125, 128, 129, 296
Installation of the Vizier Rekhmire, 209
Instruction for Merikare, 29, 209
Instruction of Amenemope, 98, 101, 191, 202, 209, 216, 233, 277, 300
Instruction of Ptah-hotep, 29, 192
Instructions to Commanders of Border Garrisons, 177, 209, 216
Instructions to Priests and Temple Officials, 177
Intef the Royal Herald, 191
integrity, 101, 276, 313
intention, 33, 34, 44, 68, 116, 124, 128, 146, 218, 220, 284, 290, 304
interest, 26, 74, 80, 137, 138, 148, 162, 173, 180, 252, **253-66**, 267, 268, 273, 274, 276, 277, 280, 284, 300, 308, 309, 311, 314
interests, 21, 82, 91, 122, 194, 195, 273, 312
irrigation, 57, 60
Isaac, 178
Isin, 3, 4

Islamic law, 221

Jacob, 15, 70, 73, 76, 100, 141, 146, 178, 187
Jarha, 141
Java, 238
Jedaniah, 295
Jeremiah, 88, 89, 105, 149, 178
Jesus, 34, 174, 192, 206, 208, 215, 250, 265, 299
Jethro, 221
jewellery, 146
Joash, 158
John the Baptist, 15
Joseph, 80, 116, 156, 226, 231, 238, 275
Josephus. *See* Index of Authors
Josiah, 11, 232, 275, 284
jubilee, **76-97**, 112, 141, 160-70, 172, 173, 228, 231, 232, 261, 276, 279, 307, 310, 311
Judah, 270, 275
Judas Maccabaeus, 106
judge, 66-68, 78, 104, 125, 127, 158, 186, 191, 200, 204-07, 210-21, 273, 309, 313
judgement, 191, 211-15, 219, 221
  judgement of God, 67-69, 98, 100, 101, 127, 200, 209, 215, 312
  judgements, 8, 230
justice, 2, 53, 73, 78, 95, 118, 127, 183, 186, 187, 190-94, **199-222**, 223, 276, 282, 284, 286, 300, 302, 304-06, 309, **313-14**, 315

Kabylia, 238
Karatepe, 30
kidnapping, 20, 21, 24, 33, 113, 116, 117, 119, 306
kindness, 43, 133, 158, 159, 188, 246, 308
king, 2, 27, 30, 37, 56, 76, 78, 79, 86, 87, 98, 103, 106, 107, 111, 112, 118, 157, 163, 190, 191, 199, 200, 214, 221, 239, 240, 277, 279, 284, 307, 308
Kirta Epic, 75, 106, 141
Ktesias, 160
Kupanta-Kurunta, 29

Laban, 70, 100, 141, 146

labour, 79, 113, 124, 138, 149, 159, 162, 166, 172, 174, 227, 288, 308
Lagash, 3, 78, 276
Lamech, 158
land, 16, 26, 29, 30, 35, 54, 57-59, 63, 64, 73, 75, 76, 78-82, 84-95, 97-103, 105-07, 111, 112, 116, 118, 127, 135, 138, 142, 145, 159, 161, 162, 164-69, 171-73, 175-77, 179, 181, 182, 184, 186-88, 192, 194, 199, 213, 219, 223, 224, 226-32, 234-43, 246-51, 254, 259, 262, 263, 267, 268, 274, 276, 277, 279, 280, 281-85, 288, 290, 293, 297, 298, 302, 305, 306, 308-15
  ancestral land, **75-107**, 112, 163, 169, 172, 173, 274, 307, 309, 311
  dedicated land, 93, 94
  landholder, 171
  promised land, 75, 82, 86, 91, 99, 100, 105, 178, 180, 219, 229, 232, 237, 247, 281, 301, 302
  real estate, 16, 75, 87
Larsa, 160
law
  apodictic law, 7, 9, 24, 41, 101, 192, 279
  casuistic law, 9, 41, 101
  common law, 2, 43, 177, 244, 249, 303, 306
  law and ethics, 7
  law collections, 1-3, 6, 53, 101, 177
  law court, 68, 183, 193, 200, 204, 213, 214, 282
  lawsuit, 38, 52, 92, 114, 186, **199-222**, 301, 309, 313
  lawyers, 2, 203, 205
  legal document, 1, 52, 85, 201, 206
  legal personality, 151
  legal procedure, 200
  legal system, 208, 214, 218, 221, 306, 313
  maritime law, 43
Laws about Rented Oxen, 4
Laws of Eshnunna, 4, 53
Laws of Hammurabi, 4, 53, 147, 190
Laws of Lipit-Ishtar, 3
Laws of Ur-Namma, 3
Laws of X, 4
lease, 84, 85, 87, 161, 310

Index of Subjects 375

Legend of King Keret. *See* Kirta Epic
Levites, 80, 92, 95, 112, 158, 175-76, 179, 189, 200, 239, 241-43, 245-47, 292, 293
Leviticus, date of, 169
lex talionis. See talion
liability, 18, 19, **44-56**, 57, 59, 61, 70, 125, 163, 185, 200, 268, 296, 307
liberation, 78, 81, 149, 166, 237, 276, 278, 283
life-style, 15, 97, 229
Lipit-Ishtar, 3, 199, 276. *See also* Laws of Lipit-Ishtar
livestock. *See* animals: livestock
loan, 18, 26, 62, 79, 80, 85, 90, 92, 137, 138, 162, 173, 180, 186, 192, **252-85**, 299, 300, 308, 309, 314
looting, 17, 28
loss, 18, 19, 22, 23, 27, 44, 46, 49-51, 54, 55-58, 60, 61, 63-65, 67, 69-74, 96, 112, 122, 125, 129, 171, 210, 255, 261, 306, 307
Lot, 158
lot, sacred, 68, 200
Louvre, 4
love, 8, 39, 42, 43, 141, 142, 149, 167, 184, 185, 187, 188, 192, 193, 311, 312
lying, 24, 63, 203, 208, 313

Maccabean period, 232
Mahlon, 90
manslaughter, 52, 124, 125
manumission, 115, 119, 137, 168-70, 172
marginal people, 112, 129, 133, 175, 176, 188, 189, 221, 293, 305, **311-13**, 315
Mari, 106, 132, 156, 253
marriage, 32, 90, 104-06, 114, 141, 149, 151, 152, 156, 157, 287
  bride-price, 104, 115, 152
  conjugal relations, 155. *See also* rights: conjugal rights
  dowry, 31, 190
  levirate marriage, 90, 105, 194
  monogamy, 150
  polygamy, 150, 157
  secondary wife, 150, 151, 155
  wife, 15, 18, 29-33, 79, 103, 104, 106, 107, 115, 120, 126, 137, 138, 140-42, 149-52, 154-58, 166, 167, 172, 177, 191, 194, 209, 225, 268, 308
master, 47, 48, 79, 111, 112, 115, 121-35, 137, 140-42, 144-46, 149, 151-55, 158, 162, 164, 165, 167-69, 172, 287, 308, 312
materialism, 15
Melchizedek, 239
memory, remembrance, 145, 184, 186, 192, 193, 235, 237, 288-290, 293, 312
Mentuhotep, 191
Mered, 158
Merikare, 191
Mesopotamia, 4, 48, 52, 53, 55, 70, 76, 78, 87, 95, 99, 121, 137, 140, 159, 160, 168, 177, 200, 239, 260, 276, 277, 279, 280, 284, 300, 307-09
messianic age, 97, 192
Middle Assyrian Laws, 5, 27
Middle Assyrian Palace Decrees, 6, 287
Middle Assyrian period, 86, 107, 267, 307
Middle Babylonian period, 19, 131, 201
middle chronology, 1
Midian, 230
military service, 76, **102-07**, 311
millstone, 271
Mira-Kuwaliya, 29
Mishnah, 117, 170, 205, 221, 232, 235, 236, 245, 250, 269, 271, 273, 280, 285
Moab, 75, 88, 99, 239
Moabite Stone, 75
Mohammed, 265
money, 19, 45, 47-51, 55, 56, 58, 62-64, 74, 78, 84, 115, 116, 119, 121, 122, 124, 126, 127, 130, 131, 143, 153, 155, 239, 244, 253-55, 257-64, 272, 279, 304, 311
moneylender, 257, 266
mortgage, 97, 103, 162, 171, 259, 267, 284
Moses, 7-11, 33, 99, 106, 156, 199, 200, 214, 221, 228, 313
Mot, 225
motive, motivation, 31, 36, 138, 142, 147, 183, 184, 187, 188, 192, 193, 211, 218, 251, 273, 302, 312, 313
mourning, 156, 158

INDEX OF SUBJECTS

murder, 9, 22, 24, 27-29, 44, 48, 51, 52, 56, 100, 123-27, 206, 207, 276, 310
Mursili II, 29
mutilation. *See* punishment: mutilation

Naaman, 120
Naboth, 76, 200, 206, 208, 311
Nanshe, 191, 300
Naomi, 76, 88, 89, 90
native, 179, 180, 185, 289
Nebuchadnezzar, 120
Negative Confession, 29, 247, 256, 301
negligence, 44, 51, 52, 54, 56, **57-62**, 64, 65, 70, 73, 131, 279, 296, 307, 310
Nehemiah, 97, 232, 244, 284, 285, 295
neighbour, 24, 26, 29-36, 39, 40, 42, 50, 54, 57, 59, 66-71, 84, 85, 97-101, 129, 134, 202, 207, 248, 249, 251, 269, 271, 274, 278, 301, 311
Neo-Assyrian period, 6, 111, 114, 115, 138, 152, 201, 254, 256, 267, 277
Neo-Babylonian Laws, 5
Neo-Babylonian period, 19, 114, 131, 132, 137, 160, 201, 239, 254, 255, 267, 277
Neo-Sumerian period, 19, 132
New Testament, 15, 35, 159, 193, 206, 215, 222, 232, 250, 305
next-of-kin, 87-90
Nin-girsu, 189
Ninurta, 191
Nippur, 4, 256
Nuzi, 19, 48, 52, 86, 132, 147, 151, 152, 160, 165, 216, 217, 234, 254, 267, 277

oath, 24, 26, 63, 66-69, 71, 73, 100, 114, 131, 132, 142, 200, 203
Obed, 90
offering, 176, 235, 238, 239, 241, 243, 248, 292, 293
    freewill offering, 242
    grain offering, 68
    guilt offering, 25, 71, 130
    sin offering, 25
oil, 240, 241, 244, 246. *See also* olive, olive grove
Old Aramaic period, 267

Old Assyrian Laws, 6
Old Assyrian period, 151, 160, 201, 267
Old Babylonian period, 2, 78, 107, 111, 148, 160, 201, 253, 256, 258, 267, 276, 307
Old Testament laws, **6-11**
    relation to other laws. *See* ancient Near Eastern laws: relation to Bible
olive, olive grove, 226, 235, 236. *See also* oil
Omri, 76
open hands, 282, 315
oppress, oppression, 24, 84, 85, 97, 98, 102, 132, 155, 173, 182-84, 188-92, 221, 276, 297, 298, 301
oracle, 68
orchard, 16, 65, 98, 102, 223, 248. *See also* fruit, fruit tree
orphan, 85, 112, 133, 171, 175, 177, 183, 186-88, **189-95**, 213, 233, 235, 236, 239, 241, 245, 246, 258, 269, 273, 276, 290, 292, 293, 308
ownership, 15-17, 22-28, 37-91, 94-95, 98, 103, 107, 113-14, 130-31, 151, 168, 173, 226-29, 232-37, 249-50, 254, 261, 267, 269, 297, 303, 306-07, 310, 313
ox. *See* animals: ox

palace, 6, 18, 19, 36, 103, 113, 131, 159, 240, 245, 248, 277, 309
Palestine, 22, 60, 61, 83, 135, 224, 230, 238, 246, 249, 251, 283, 284. *See also* Canaan, land of
parapet, 51, 52, 55
partiality, 187, 200, **209-15**, 309, 313
Passover papyrus, 295
pasture, 92, 95, 175
payment, 17, 19, 27, 47-49, 55, 56, 62-66, 71, 95, 104, 114, 115, 125, 126, 139, 145, 148, 153, 154, 167, 218, 220, 221, 240, 256, 264, 267-77, 296-300, 304, 310, 314
people of God, 8, 20, 26, 28, 34, 35, 40, 100, 104-06, 133, 180, 188, 203, 219, 282, 311, 315
perfection, 34, 35, 311
perjury, 200, 201, 202

Index of Subjects

Persian period, 114, 277
persons, 21, 56, 119, 123, 129, 150, 267, 268, 274, 306, 309, 310, 312
perversion of justice, 186, 187, 192, 193, 204, 206, 209-11, 213, 215, 219, 220, 309, 313
Pharisees, 250
Philistines, 135, 139
Philo. *See* Index of Authors
Phoenicia, 30
pit, 46, 49, 53, 54, 233
plague, 188
Plato, 249, 265
pledge, 114, 115, 160, 254, 267-75, 278, 298, 309, 314
Prayer of Kantuzilis, 202
Prayer Stele of Nefer-abu to Ptah, 202
priest, 69, 93, 111, 112, 127, 177, 195, 200, 206, 207, 239, 241-43, 293
prisoner, 102, 158, 190, 308
property, 15-18, 20-25, 27-29, 32, 34, 37, 43, 44, 46, 48, 50, 54, 56, 57, 62, 66-69, 72-75, 77, 78, 81, 84-89, 91-95, 98, 99, 102, 103, 107, 111-14, 116, 118-25, 127, 129, 130, 134, 140, 141, 150, 151, 155, 158, 161, 162, 167, 173, 180, 190, 191, 194, 201, 211, 223, 227, 238, 249, 267, 268, 270, 287, 297, 305, 306, 308, **310-11**, 312, 315
    care of property, 44, **62-74**
    lost property, 17, 24-26, **36-43**, 67, 306, 307
    private property, 21, 249, 251
    property rights. *See* rights: property rights
    stolen property, 17-20, 22, 27, 63, 66, 69, 306, 307
prophecy, 7, 20, 208, 275
prosperity, 75, 96, 237, 266, 281, 302, 311
prosperity theology, 96, 237, 281
prostitute, 115, 120, 152, 157, 174, 175, 270
Ptolemaic period, 256
punishment, 18, 22, 26, 27, 34, 35, 37, 45, 46, 49, 51, 54-56, 61, 98, 100, 113, 116, 117, 122, 124-26, 128, 132, 139, 192, 200, 205, 207, 211, 216, 306, 307
    beating, 18, 19, 27, 98, 122-25, 128, 132, 307
    capital punishment, 9, 16-19, 21-24, 27, 34, 36, 45-49, 51, 52, 55, 56, 65, 73, 102, 116-18, 123, 125-27, 130, 131, 133, 200, 205-07, 211, 221, 294, 310
    composition, 17, 27
    corporal punishment, 128
    divine punishment, 230. *See also* judgement: judgement of God
    lenience, 207
    mutilation, 18, 19, 27, 58, 98, 128, 307
    restitution, 17-19, 22, 23, 25-27, 37, 49, 50, 59-61, 63, 65, 67-71, 73, 98, 139, 307
    vicarious punishment, 48, 127
purchase, 76, 79, 84, 88, 89-92, 97, 103, 113, 118, 119, 139, 144, 152, 165, 167, 180, 207, 256, 286, 300-302, 304

quid pro quo, 217
Qumran. *See* Dead Sea Scrolls
Qur'an, 265

Rameses III, 191
ransom, 47, 48, 56, 116, 125
rape, 155, 156, 201
reaping. *See* harvest
Rechabites, 15, 179
recreation, 287, 310
redemption, 47, 48, 55, 56, 76-79, 84, 85, 87-89, 93-95, 115, 163-66, 170, 171, 268, 274. *See also* rights: right of redemption
Reforms of Uru-inimgina, 3
refugee, 175, 182
Rehoboam, 158
remembrance. *See* memory, remembrance
rental, 37, 62-64, 66, 70-74, 88, 306, 307, 311
resident alien, 24, 80, 85, 95, 117, 118, 163, 165, 167, 175, **176-89**, 192, 193, 195, 213, 214, 229, 234-36, 239, 241, 245, 246, 249, 258, 259, 263, 273, 280, 288-93, 298, 310

responsibilities, 26, 28, 44, 57, 105-07, 112, 177, 185, 286, 297, 311
  property responsibilities, **44-74**
rest, 83, 105, 223, 224, 226, 228, 229, 231, 232, 279, 283-91, 293-95, 310, 314
restitution. *See* punishment: restitution
restoration, 77, 80-82, 84, 93, 95, 97, 98, 139, 164, 179, 274, 284
righteousness, 199, 210, 212, 213, 217, 219-21, 223, 264, 272-74, 302, 313
rights, 64, 75, 112, 117, 118, 126, 129, 144, 153, 154, 158, 172, 177, 178, 182, 185, 210, 227, 231, 275, 286, 287, 289, 299, 308-10, 313
  conjugal rights, 153, 154, 159, 308
  employment rights, 314
  family rights, 140
  human rights, 112, 119-21, 125, 129
  inheritance rights, 151, 157, 164, 190, 194
  legal rights, 165, 177, 193, 223, 308
  ownership rights, 121, 134, 140, 151, 160, 164, 311
  property rights, **15-43**, 44, 74, 78, 129, 163, 249, 297, 307, 311
  right of disposal, 16, 86, 112, 136, 223, 267, 274
  right of redemption, 77, 78, 85, 88, 90-93, 95, 103, 137, 153, 154, 161, 163, 164, 167, 173
robbery. *See* theft
Rome, 23, 99, 112, 137, 149, 206, 265
roof, 51-53, 55
Ruth, 88, 90, 238, 239

sabbath, 8, 32, 76, 81, 179, 188, 223, 226-29, 231, 250, 279, **287-96**, 310, 312, 314
sabbatical year, 79, 81-83, 96, 140, 188, **223-32**, 246, 279, 280, 282-85, 291, 309, 313, 314
sacralisation, 243
sacrifice, 176, 179, 186, 293
sacrificial meal, 242, 243
safekeeping, 17, 62, 63, 66-73, 306
safety, 20, 51, 121
sale, 20, 22, 36, 75-79, 84, 86-88, 90, 91, 95, 103, 113-15, 119, 137, 138, 143, 152-54, 157, 160-64, 171, 179, 259, 274, 300-302, 304
Samson, 120
Samuel, 27, 221, 239, 248
sanctions, 20, 35, 284
sanctity of life, 207
sanctuary, 67-69, 94, 142, 146, 207, 241-48, 293, 313
Saul, 127, 135, 156, 158, 181
scrumping, **248-51**, 309, 313
secularisation, 243, 244, 247, 248
security, 24, 54, 63, 70, 72, 75, 80, 86, 96, 186, 188, 192, 193, 230, 253, 259, **266-75**, 276, 277, 309, 314
Sefire, 132, 218
serf, 111, 136, 159
seventh year, 23, 76, 83, 138, 140, 143-45, 149, 166, 167, 170, 180, 223-31, 246, 278, 279, 282, 283, 285, 290, 310
severance pay, 145
sexual intercourse, 155, 157, 181. *See also* marriage: conjugal relations
Shaharaim, 158
Shamash Hymn, 29, 31, 192, 209, 216, 300
Shamash-nasu, 255
shame, 212, 272
sheep. *See* animals: sheep
Shemer, 76
shepherd, 58, 60, 65, 66, 70, 297
Sheshan, 141
Shimei, 127, 135
Shunammite, 76
Shurpu incantations, 98, 202, 300
silver, 16-19, 23, 29, 33, 45, 47, 64, 66, 73, 84, 93, 121, 130, 200, 240, 256, 277, 300, 304
sin, 26, 199, 205, 282, 298
Sippar, 5
Sirach, 192
sister, 42, 143, 167, 170, 254, 262
slander, 201, 203, 204
slave, slavery, 17-19, 22, 23, 30-32, 36, 45, 47, 48, 51, 55, 58, 78, 80, 81, 85, 88, 92, **111-35**, 175, 177, 186, 192, 193, 226, 229,

Index of Subjects

235, 237, 254, 267, 269, 276, 277, 283, 284, 287-94, 301, 306, 308, 310-12
   chattel slave, 21, 111, **112-21**, 123, 134, 136, 142, 147-50, 154-56, 158, 160, 291, 306, 308
   debt-slave. *See* debt: debt-slave/slavery
   fugitive slave, 36, 85, 120, **130-35**, 175, 308, 312
   semi-slave, 120, **136-74**, 150, 308
   slave abuse, **121-30**
   slave-mark, 131-32
   temporary slave, 112, 114, 115, 120, **136-50**, 153, 154, 159, 161, 166, 170-72, 174, 291, 306, 308, 312
social concern, 293. *See also* welfare
social revolution, 130, 135, 282, 294
social structure, 81, 111, 112, 283
sojourner. *See* resident alien
soldier, 102, 103, 107
Solomon, 120, 135, 158, 181
Solon, 277
sowing, 82, 227, 231, 268
Sparta, 178
spirits, 238
squatter, 64
standardisation, 276, 296, 299, 300, 309
State Archives of Assyria, 6, 224
status, 18-21, 27, 32, 48, 55, 87, 112, 114, 115, 119, 123, 130, 134, 136, 137, 139, 140, 148, 150-52, 155-57, 159, 160, 165, 166, 168, 169, 171, 173, 177, 178, 180, 181, 185, 189, 214, 227, 291, 294, 306-08
status quo, 169
stealing. *See* theft
Stephen, 206
stewardship, 16
stoning, 48, 55
storm, 65, 72, 257
stranger. *See* resident alien
student exercise, 2, 4
subordinate citizen. *See* serf
Sumer, 1-4, 78, 111, 190, 199
Sumerian Family Laws. *See Ana ittišu*
Sumerian Farmer's Almanac, 233
Sumerian Laws Exercise Tablet, 4
Sumerian Laws Handbook of Forms, 4

surety, 267, 268, 270, 274, 275
Susanna, 206
sustenance, 91, 106, 142, 145, 188, 194, 230, 232, 233, 237, 238

tabernacle, 245, 291
taboo, 48, 49
talion, 56, 128, 129, 192, 200, 207
Talmud, 232, 250, 260
tattoo, 173
tax, 239, 240, 242, 244, 245, 248, 276
Tell Fekheriye, 233
temple, 17, 18, 19, 36, 63, 93, 99, 103, 113, 133, 159, 181, 239, 240, 243, 245, 247, 248, 309
temporary resident, 85, 95, 118, 161, 163, 164, 165, 167, 181, 188, 229, 258, 259
temporary slave. *See* slave, slavery: temporary slave
Ten Commandments. *See* Decalogue
tenant, 64, 65, 80, 111, 259, 296
testimony. *See* witness
theft, 9, **16-28**, 29, 33, 35-37, 43, 44, 46, 56, 60, 63, 65-70, 72, 73, 100, 113, 114, 116, 117, 131, 139, 188, 201, 202, 235, 249, 276, 299, 306, 307, 310
third party, 69, 88, 129, 267
third year, 45, 241-46
thoughts, 30, 33-35, 311
tight fists, 282, 283, 315
tithe, tithing, 176, **239-45**, 246-48, 277, 292, 293, 309, 313
   triennial tithe, 179, 188, 193, **239-48**, 249, 308, 309, 313
trade, trader, 91, 113, 263, 265, 276, 277, 280, 286, 287, 295, 300, 304, 314
   fair trade, 92, **286-304**
   sex trade, 121
   slave trade, 149
tribe, 81, 95, 111
trumpet, 80, 81
truthfulness, 206, 208
Tudhaliya, 209, 277
Tutub, 78

INDEX OF SUBJECTS

Ugarit, 1, 32, 76, 85, 86, 132, 148, 177, 191, 202, 225, 240, 248, 267, 288
United Nations, 121, 252
Ur, 3, 160, 190, 239, 253, 267, 300
Uriah the Hittite, 165, 181
Ur-Namma, 189, 199, 276, 299. *See also* Laws of Ur-Namma
Ur-Nammu. *See* Ur-Namma
Uru-inimgina, 78, 189. *See also* Reforms of Uru-inimgina
Uru-kagina. *See* Uru-inimgina

veil, 115, 152, 201
vengeance. *See* avenge, vengeance
victim, 47, 48, 52, 54, 55, 127, 205, 307, 310
vine, vineyard, 15, 58-61, 81, 104-06, 223, 226, 228, 229, 234-36, 248-50, 311. *See also* wine
vision, 95, 96, 218, 315
vulnerable people, 164, 176, 183, 188, 190, 193, 195, 213, 290, 308, 312

wages, 24, 70, 147, 148, 188, 242, 243, 252, 280, **296-99**, 310
wall, 45, 46, 51, 53-55, 91, 201
war, 27, 104-06, 113, 117, 119, 127, 150, 155, 156, 158, 181, 188, 232, 306, 308
weights and measures, 276, **299-304**, 306, 314

welfare, 39, 42, 189, 243, 248, 266, 309
widow, 85, 88, 89, 98, 112, 115, 133, 163, 171, 175, 177, 183, 186-88, **189-95**, 213, 233, 235, 236, 239, 241, 245, 246, 258, 269, 271, 273, 274, 276, 290, 292, 293, 308
wife. *See* marriage: wife
Wilberforce, 174, 312
wine, 145, 167, 240, 241, 244, 246, 249, 295. *See also* vine, vineyard
wisdom, 9, 11, 20, 29, 30, 101, 130, 194, 208, 216, 220, 221, 275, 300, 302, 303, 306
witness, 17, 36, 46, 50, 63, 69, 73, 114, 125, 152, 199, 200, **201-08**, 210, 211, 217, 218, 306, 313
work, 65, 66, 85, 87, 90, 91, 113, 121, 136, 140, 144, 145, 151, 153, 154, 157, 171, 172, 176, 181, 231, 235, 237, 245, 250, 254, 268, 286-91, 294-97, 299, 301, 306, 310, 313, 314. *See also* bonded labour/labourer
worship, 8, 36, 51, 120, 181, 241, 247, 248, 264, 286, 290, 291, 293-95, 311, 314
centralisation of, 146, 243, 247

Zedekiah, 149, 158, 284
Zelek the Ammonite, 165
Ziba, 120

Index of Foreign Words

HEBREW

אביון	176, 209	גור	178	מדה	301		
אוה	31	גזל	20, 24	מהר	104		
אזרח	179	גנב	20	מוך	87, 176		
אח	87, 144, 179	גר	178-82, 263	מות	124, 125, 127		
אחזה	86, 119	דברי	217	מיטב	59		
איב	38	דל	176, 210, 212	מישרים	276		
אלהים	66, 67	דרור	81, 96, 276	מכר	84, 87, 89, 139, 143, 161, 172		
אליו	87	הרג	210				
אלמנה	194	הקים	41	מלאכה	295		
אמה	152	התעמר	117, 155	מנוחה	105		
ארץ	282	זכור	289	משנה	147		
אשה־אלמנה	194	זר	180	משפחה	81		
אשת־המת	194	חבל	270	משפט	199, 213, 219		
אתך	297	חזק	147, 258	משפטים	8		
בגד	273	חמד	31	מתן/מתנה	217, 218		
בית	31, 32	חנון	269	נחל	100		
בני	118	חנך	104	נחלה	86, 100		
בן־נכר	180	חפשי	139	נטה	204, 209		
בעה	59	חרם	27	נכרי	153, 180, 263		
בער	59, 246	יבל	81	נפש	291		
בפרך	162	ינה	84, 85, 182-84	נקם	123, 126, 127		
בצע	217	יעדה	153	נשה	257		
גאל	165	יצא	140, 165, 166	נשך	259, 260		
גבול	99, 100	יתום	191	סרה	206		
גבל	100	כבד	147	עבד	112, 152		
גדל	210	כלי	249	עבט	270		
גדול	212	כפר	217	עברי	139, 140		
		לחץ	182, 184	עד	69, 202		
		לקח	20	עול	212, 301		

INDEX OF FOREIGN WORDS

עזב	38, 39, 41	שוא	203	ḫabiru	139, 160
עזר	38	שופר	81	ḫubullu	260, 270
עם	104	שחד	217, 219	ḫubuttatu	255, 256, 260
עמד	124, 125	שטרים	104	kaška	234
עמי	257	שלום	217	kudurru	99
עמך	161, 257, 258	שלח	146	máš nu-me-a	256
ענה	155	שלם	49	máš nu-tuk	256
עני	176	שלמה	302	mazzazānūtu	160
ענק	146	שלמן	217	mīšaru	78, 276, 277
ערב/ערבון	270	שמד	47	muškēnu	111
ערכך	25, 93	שמור	289	napāšu	291
עשיר	212	שמט	223, 224, 226, 279	napṭaru	62
עשק	24, 298	שמר	47	narû	99
פאה	234	שפט	8, 199, 213, 219	nexum	137
פילגש	152	שקר	203, 206, 211	prozbul	285
פקד	126	תועבה	303	qīptu	256
פקחים	217, 218	תורה	283	ra-a-ki	287
פשע	67	תושב	181	rēdû	102
צדיק	219	תחת	128	shublugal	79
צדק	199, 213, 219, 301, 302	תצא אש	60	šapattu	288
		תרבית	259	šarāku	18
קדש	9	תרפים	66	šu-lá	256
קנה	84, 139, 165			šulmānu	216
קרא	279	**OTHER ANCIENT LANGUAGES**		ṭātu	216
קשה	147			tidennu/ūtu	160
רבים	204, 274			ubaru	177
רחום	269			wardu	111, 112
ריקם	146	'bd 'lm	141		
שכיר	70, 297, 298	abbuttu	131	αφεσις	81
שכר	298	amtu	111	δωρον	217
שמלה	273	andurāru	78, 81, 276, 277	μετοικοι	178
שבה	295	awīlu	45, 111	περιοικοι	178
שבט	213	bā'iru	102	σεισαχθεια	277
שבת	223, 228, 288, 293, 295	bel madgalti	177	συνεγερεις	39
		esirtu	152		

Index of Scripture

OLD TESTAMENT/ HEBREW BIBLE		14:13	139	24:31-32	41
		14:14	119, 141	24:53	104
		14:20	239, 240, 242, 248	25:6	104, 157
Genesis				25:21	175
1:1	229	15:2-3	141	26:3	178
1:30	227	15:3	119, 141	27:37	213
2:1-3	231	15:7-21	75	27:41–28:5	175
2:2-3	223, 290	15:13	178	28:4	178
2:3	231	16	151	28:13-15	75
2:7	126	16:6	135	28:22	242, 248
2:24	157	17:8	86, 178, 261	29–31	141, 175
3:6	31	17:12	84, 86, 119, 141	29:18	226
3:14-24	199	17:13	119, 141	29:21-30	141, 157
4:9	42	17:23	119, 141	29:27	226
4:9-15	127, 199	17:27	119, 141	29:31	175
4:10	127	18:1-8	179	30:1-13	151
4:15	127	19:1-8	179	31:14-16	32
4:19	158, 207	19:8	158	31:15	180
4:23-24	199, 207	20:1	178	31:33	152
6:1-8	199	20:13	67, 152	31:38-39	70
6:5	35	20:17	152	31:41-42	146
7:1	31	21:10	152, 291	31:45	100
9:3-4	186	21:13	152, 291	31:46-48	100
9:5-6	48, 56, 126, 199	22:20-24	157	31:49	100
9:25	119, 126	23	15, 76	31:51-52	100
11:30	175	23:4	178, 181	31:53	67
12:1-9	75	23:10	200	32:4	178
12:10	178	23:15	76, 181, 200	32:5	15
13:2	15	23:18	178, 200	33:18-20	76

383

33:19	15	4:23	147	18:13-26	220
34:2	155	5:3	140	18:16	200
34:12	104	6:1	147	18:21	217, 221
34:29	119	6:4	178	18:22	200
35:2	156	6:5	289	18:23	217
35:7	67	6:6-7	162	18:26	200
35:27	178	6:11	147	19:4-6	162
36:2-3	157	7:3	147	19:5	85
36:12	157	7:13-14	147	19:13	81
37:25-28	118	7:16	140	20	31
37:28	48, 147	7:22	147	20:1	8
38:1-11	194	8:15	147	20:2	117, 301
38:16-18	270	8:19	147	20:2-17	7
39:5	32	8:32	147	20:5-6	34
39:14	139	9:1	140	**20:8-11**	112, 179, 180, 228, 214, 231, 286, **288-90**, 294-96
39:17	32, 139	9:7	147		
40:15	20, 116, 139	9:12	147		
41	226	9:13	140	20:12	75
41:12	139	9:34-35	147	**20:15**	**20-21**, 26-28, 116
41:47-57	231, 246	10:3	140	**20:16**	69, 200, **202-03**, 208, 211
43:9	275	11:2-3	146		
43:18	139	12:3	293	20:16-17	24
44:4-17	139	12:6	295	**20:17**	30-33, 33-36, 157
44:32	275	12:16	279	20:22—21:1	8
47:4	178	12:19	179, 185, 293	21:2—22:17	8-9
47:6	59	12:34	269	**21:2**	8, 23, 138, **139-40**, 143-45, 148-50, 153, 166-71
47:11	59	12:35-36	146		
47:13-26	80	12:37	293		
50:10	156	12:38	181	21:2-11	120, 283
		12:43	180	**21:3-4**	138, **140-41**, 143, 148-50, 153, 166-71
Exodus		12:44	84, 119, 293		
1:13-14	162	12:45	70, 161, 176, 181, 229		
1:15-16	139			**21:5-6**	66, 67, 138, **141-42**, 143, 148-50, 153, 166-71
1:19	139	12:47	293		
2:6-7	139	12:47-48	186		
2:13	24	12:48	180, 181	**21:7-11**	144, **152-54**, 155-59, 166
2:22	178	12:48-49	179, 185, 293		
2:23-25	192	13:3	289	21:12	34, 125, 126
2:24	289	13:15	147	21:12-13	156
3:7-8	192	15:17	232	21:12-14	124
3:9	183, 184	16	231, 295, 302	21:12-17	116
3:18	140	16:5	291	21:12-27	122
3:20	147	16:10	145	21:13	156
3:21-22	146	16:17	145	21:13-14	124, 145
4:21	147	16:22-30	291, 295	21:14	24, 156
4:22-23	192	16:25	228, 289	21:15	34, 125

Index of Scripture

21:16	20, 24, 113, **116-18**, 119-21, 125	22:25-27	183, 258, 269	31:15	228, 289
21:17	34, 125	**22:26-27**	8, 192, **269-70**, 272, 273-75	31:17	290, 291
21:18-19	125	22:28-31	183	32:1-5	34
21:20-21	120, 122, **123-28**, 129-30, 205	**23:1-2**	69, 200, **204-05**, 206, 208	32:13	289
21:23-25	56, 125, 128, 192, 207	23:1-3	183, 201	32:29	175
21:24-27	128	23:1-9	183	34:6	269
21:26-27	125, **128-29**, 129-30, 144	**23:3**	**209-11**, 212, 214-15	34:6-7	26
21:28-32	**46-49**, 52-56, 120, 125, 130, 145, 147	**23:4-5**	**38-39**, 40, 42-43, 211, 263, 286	34:21	292, 294, 295
		23:6-7	**209-11**, 212-15	35:2	228, 289, 295
21:32-36	126	23:6-8	183, 201, 204	35:2-3	292
21:33-34	46, **49-50**, 52-56, 286	**23:8**	**217-18**, 220-22	35:3	295
21:35-36	46, **50-51**, 52-56, 286	**23:9**	117, **182-84**, 186-89	36:9	301
21:36–22:15	49	**23:10-11**	210, 223, **226-27**, 228, 229, 231-32, 279, 286, 291	36:15	301
22:1-4	**22-24**, 26-28, 34, 113, 116, 126, 139, 143, 286	23:10-12	8, 183	**Leviticus**	
		23:10-19	8	4:1–5:13	25
22:5-6	**59-61**, 61-62, 249	**23:12**	152, 179, 180, 223-27, 286, 289, **291-92**, 294-96	5:1	208
22:7-9	22, 41, 43, **66-68**, 69, 71-74, 141, 217			5:7-13	176
22:7-11	200	23:13	8	5:14-19	25
22:10-11	25	23:13-33	8	6	26
22:10-13	66, **68-70**, 71-74, 203, 286	23:14-17	291	6:2-5	67
22:14-15	66, **70-71**, 71-74, 286	23:14-19	8	6:2-7	24-25, 43, 71, 73
		23:20-26	75	6:2-11	25
22:18–23:12	8	23:20-33	10	7:20-21	244
22:20	8, 34, 182	23:34	184	9:24	60
22:21–23:9	173, 183	24:1	8	10:2	60
22:21	85, 117, 133, 178, **182-84**, 187-89, 269	24:3	8	10:6	87
		24:7	8	14:8-9	156
22:21-23	191	24:14	217	14:21-32	176
22:21-24	258	26:2	301	16:29	179, 181, 185, 293
22:21-27	183, 282, 298	26:8	301	16:30-31	293
22:22-24	117, 127, 183, **191-92**, 193-95, 269	28:15	200	16:31	228
		28:30	200	17–26	9
		30:13	303	17	9, 10, 186
		30:15	212	17:3-7	186
		30:24	303	17:8	179
		31:12-17	214, 231, 291, 294	17:8-9	181, 186
22:25	210, **257-58**, 260, 264-66, 269	31:14	294	17:8-10	181, 185
		31:14-15	34, 231	17:10	186
				17:10-16	179
				17:11	186
				17:12-14	869
				17:12-16	185
				17:15	180
				18–26	9-10
				18	9

386 INDEX OF SCRIPTURE

18:1-5	9	22:11	84, 119, 141		227, **230-31**, 232, 246
18:8	154	22:13	175, 189, 229		
18:15	154	22:18	179, 181, 185	25:23-24	16, 79, **85-87**, 95-97, 143, 161, 163-66, 180, 181, 227, 229, 232, 238, 261
18:24-30	86	22:33	261		
18:26	179, 185	23	294		
19:2	214, 261	23:2-4	279		
19:3	294	23:3	228, 289		
19:9-10	188, 229, **234-35**, 237-39, 263, 297	23:8	82	25:24-25	86, 88
		23:9	82	25:25-28	80, 86, **87-90**, 91, 94-97, 118, 161, 162, 164, 259
19:9-18	234	23:9-18	234		
19:11	**24-26**, 26-28, 203, 297	23:11	229		
		23:15-16	82	25:29-31	80, **90-92**, 95-97, 161
19:11-13	24, 202	**23:22**	188, **234-35**, 237-39		
19:12	203			25:29-32	119
19:13	**24-26**, 26-28, 43, 70, **297**, 299	23:38	289	25:32-34	80, 86, **92**, 95-97, 143, 161, 175
		23:40	293		
19:14	85, 162, 261	23:42	186		
19:15	201, 210, **212-13**, 214-15, 219, 301	24:10	181	25:35-38	75, 80, 87, 91, 94, 161-63, 173, 179, 185, **258-61**, 262, 264-66, 282, 301
		24:10-14	185		
19:16	203, 211, 212, 213, 215	24:15-22	185		
		24:16	34, 179, 181		
19:17-18	24, 43	24:18-20	128, 207		
19:18	127, 185, 188	24:19-20	56	25:39-43	75, 80, 86, 87, 91, 93, 117, 119, 140, 143, 144, 159, 160, **161-63**, 164-74, 229, 259
19:20-22	130	24:21	34		
19:23-25	104, 105, 286	**24:22**	117, 165, 179, 181, **185-86**, 187-89		
19:28	119, 173				
19:30	294	24:23	185	25:44-46	81, 86, 88, **118-19**, 119-21, 162, 165, 181
19:32	261	25	79-80, 96, 143, 160, 166, 168-70, 171, 228, 258		
19:33-34	24, 81, 85, 117, 133, 164, 178, 179, **184-85**, 187-89			25:47-52	9, 87, 88, 91, 140, 143, 161, **163-65**, 166-74, 188
		25:1-4	75, 227, **228-29**, 231-32, 279		
19:35-36	261, **301**, 302-04, 325	25:1-7	79		
		25:1-8	227	25:47-55	80, 93, 159, 160
20:2	127, 179, 185	25:1-12	170	25:53-55	140, 161-163, **165-66**, 166-74
20:4	127, 218	25:2-6	223		
20:7	214	**25:5-7**	161, 188, **229-30**, 231-32, 286	26:3-12	75
20:9-10	34			26:3-13	96, 281
20:11-12	154	**25:8-12**	79, 81-82, 86, **80-83**, 94-97, 279	26:13	301
20:22-23	86			26:12-13	261
20:24	75			26:14-39	86
20:26	214	**25:13-17**	79, **84-85**, 86, 94-97, 133, 162, 164, 184, 261	26:25	126
21:2-3	87			26:34-35	96, 231, 232
21:7	175			26:34-39	168
21:8	214				
21:14	175, 189	**25:18-22**	79, 82, 83, 96,	26:43	96, 232
22:10	161, 229				

Index of Scripture

26:45	99, 261	27:1-11	194	4:6	289
26:46	9	27:9-11	88, 164	4:8	283
27	241	27:11	87	4:25-26	303
27:2-5	148	28:18—29:12	279	4:40	289, 302
27:8	87	31:2-3	126	4:42	24
27:16-19	93-94	31:3	126	4:44	283
27:16-24	80	31:7-12	119	5:1	289
27:20-24	94	31:17-18	156	5:6-21	7
27:27	143	32—36	75	5:10	289
27:30	246	32:5	86	**5:12-15**	31, 75, 146, 179,
27:30-33	241, 248	32:18-20	86		187, 228, 286,
		35:1-8	92, 175		289, 291, **288-90**,
Numbers		35:2-5	92		294-96, 302
3:41	175	35:8	86	**5:19**	20-21, 26-28, 272
3:45	175	35:15	181, 185, 188	**5:20**	**202-03**, 208
5:5-8	25	35:16-21	207	**5:21**	**30-33**, 33-36, 101
5:11-31	68, 200	35:16-28	124	5:29	289
6:9	156	35:19	126	5:32	289
8:7	156	35:20	124	5:33	220, 289, 302
9:10-13	293	35:30	206	6:1-2	302
9:13-14	186	35:30-31	126	6:2	289
9:14	179, 185, 293	35:31	48	6:4-9	134
10:10	293	35:31-33	125	6:17	289
11:4	181	35:31-34	207	6:18	220
15	25	36:1-12	95	6:24	220
15:13-16	179, 185	36:6-9	194	6:24-25	273
15:26	179, 185			6:25	220, 272, 289
15:29-30	179, 185	**Deuteronomy**		7:2	134
15:32-36	294, 295	1—4	100	7:6	134
15:41	301	1:5	283	7:9-11	134
16:15	247	1:8	75	7:11	289
18:12	237	1:13	213, 220	7:12-13	263
18:20	92	1:13-15	214	7:12-16	75
18:21-24	176	1:15	104, 213	7:13	237
18:21-32	241-43, 248	1:16	179, 186	7:16	207
18:23-24	92, 175	1:16-17	212, 214	7:25	33
18:24	246	1:17	215, 220	7:25-26	303
19:10	179, 185	1:21	75	8:1	220
20:17-20	250	1:25	75	8:1-10	75
20:29	156	2:7	263, 273	8:10-14	35
21:5-6	127	2:35	27	8:11-20	86
21:21-23	48	3:7	27	8:17-18	15, 16, 232
22:27	38	3:20	105	10:8	175
26	75	4:1	220	10:9	175, 178, 293
26:62	175	4:2	289	10:14	85
27:1-8	95	4:5	289	10:17	214, 215, 220, 221

INDEX OF SCRIPTURE

10:17-18	193	15:1-11	144, 227, 278, 283	17:4	207, 218, 303
10:17-19	187, 188, 193	15:3-12	40	**17:6**	**205-06**, 208
10:18-19	214	**15:4-6**	75, 246, 263, 278,	17:7	118, 207, 246
10:19	178, 187		**281**, 282-85	17:8-13	200, 207
11:6	31	**15:7-11**	40, 96, 133, 134,	17:9	200
11:14	237		147, 192, 210, 237,	17:12	118
12—26	10, 247		246, 259, 261,	17:15	40, 180
12:1	75		263, 272, 278,	17:17	157, 246, 263
12:3	293		280, 281, **282-83**,	17:18-20	27, 112, 200
12:5	135		283-85, 298, 315	17:20	207
12:5-19	176, 241	**15:12**	134, 139, **143-44**,	18:1-2	175, 293
12:7	263, 293		147-50, 280	18:1-8	176, 293
12:8-12	75	15:12-18	120, 143, 148, 166,	18:6	179
12:9-10	105		167, 169-71, 283	18:6-8	247
12:10-12	293	**15:13-15**	117, 140, **145-46**,	18:9-12	303
12:11	135, 247		147-50, 162, 171,	18:15	40
12:12	**292-93**, 294-96		187, 214, 237, 264,	19—25	10
12:14	135		281, 290	19:1-13	75, 100
12:17	237	**15:16-17**	134, 144, **146**,	19:3	100
12:17-18	293		147-50	19:4-5	124
12:18	**292-93**, 294-96	**15:18**	40, 145, **147-48**,	19:6	126
12:19	293		148-50, 237, 246,	19:8	100
12:20	249		263, 281	19:9	281
12:23	207	15:20	293	19:10	100
12:31	303	16:1	289	19:11-13	124
12:47	293	16:1-8	293	19:12	126
13:1	133	16:6	247	19:13	118, 207
13:4	206, 289	16:9-12	293	**19:14**	33, **99-101**, 101-
13:5	118, 206, 207,	16:10	145, 264		02, 134
	246, 289	**16:11**	133, 176, 179,	**19:15**	125, **205-06**, 208
13:6-9	207		**292-93**, 294-96	19:15-21	186, 201
13:11	207	16:12	146, 187, 237, 290	**19:16-21**	34, 40, 118, 128,
13:14	207, 218, 303	16:13-14	218		200, 204, **206-07**,
14:1	156	16:13-15	293		208, 211, 218
14:21	180, 263	**16:14**	176, 179, **292-93**,	20	104, 105
14:22-27	241		294-96	20:1-4	106
14:22-29	176	16:15	264	**20:5-7**	**104-06**, 106-07
14:23	237, 244, 293	16:17	145	20:5-10	106
14:26	293	**16:18-20**	104, 145, 186,	20:10-14	119
14:27	293		200, 201, 212,	20:13	156
14:28-29	147, 179, 189,		**213-14**, 214-15,	20:14	27, 155
	237, 241, **245-47**,		217, **219-20**, 220-	20:15-18	119
	247-48, 263, 293		22, 302	20:17	289
15:1-3	118, 134, 180, 224,	17:2	133	20:18	303
	226, 245, 263,	17:2-5	206	20:19-20	286
	278-80, 283-85	17:2-7	34	21:1-9	127

Index of Scripture

21:2-4	188, 200	24:14-15	40, 134, 188, 192, 272, 282, **298**, 299	28:1-14	75, 96, 263, 273, 281
21:5	200			28:7-14	105
21:6-8	200	24:16	48, 127	28:12	263
21:8	207	**24:17-18**	117, 146, **186-87**, 187-89, **192-93**, 193-95, 237	28:15-68	86
21:10-14	84, 117, 119, **155-57**, 157-59			28:29	297
				28:30	104, 105
21:15-17	157, 194	**24:17b**	186, 193, 213, 236, 270, 271, **273**, 273-75	28:33	297
21:18-21	34			28:43	165, 188
21:19-20	200			28:43-44	281
21:21	118	24:18-22	290	28:45	289
22:1-4	38, 39, **40-42**, 42-43, 87, 134, 263, 286	**24:19-22**	117, 146, 147, 187, 226, **235-37**, 237-39, 246, 263	28:58	283
				28:65	105
22:6-7	286			28:68	161
22:8	**51-52**, 52-56	25:1-2	200	29:9-12	187
22:10	286	25:3	40, 105, 124	29:10	104
22:15-21	200	25:4	250, 286	29:10-12	179
22:17	203	25:5-10	90, 105, 106, 194	29:11	181
22:21	118	25:7-9	200	29:22	180
22:22	34, 118	25:11-12	207	30:15-20	126
22:23-24	104	**25:13-16**	301, **302-03**, 303-04	30:16	263
22:23-27	130			30:19	135
22:24	118, 155	26:1-3	75, 247	30:19-20	220
22:29	155	26:1-11	247, 293	31:8	104
23:7	178	26:2	247	31:9-13	283
23:12	289	26:5	178	31:10	278
23:15-16	85, **132-34**, 133-35, 183, 184	26:7	183, 184	31:10-11	227, 280
		26:9-11	247	31:12	179, 187
23:19-20	40, 134, 147, 180, 237, 246, 258, 260, **262-64**, 264-66, 280	**26:11**	176, 179, **292-93**, 294-96	31:24	283
				31:28	104
		26:12-13	179, 176, 241, 242, **245-47**, 247-48, 289, 293	32:4	212, 223
				32:8	85
23:21-22	272			32:35	127
23:24-25	24, 31, 230, **248-51**	26:13-14	244, 247	32:36	162
		26:14	247, 289	32:39	126
24:5	105, 157	26:15	246, 247	32:41	127
24:6	270, **271**, 273-75	26:17	179	32:43	127
24:7	20, 24, 40, 113, **116-18**, 119-21, 134, 155	26:29	246	33:8-10	175, 200
		27–28	10	34:8	156
		27:7	293		
24:10-11	34, 118, 134, 165, 257, 270, **271-72**, 273-75	27:15	34, 303	**Joshua**	
		27:17	100	1:2-6	75
		27:19	187, 193, 213	2:6	51
24:10-14	270	27:25	211, 220	3:4	301
24:12-13	220, 271, **272-73**, 273-75, 282, 298	28	105	6:4-13	81
				7:10-20	200

INDEX OF SCRIPTURE

7:11	27
7:14	213
7:20	200
7:21	27
8:32-35	179, 187
9:17	179
9:21-27	181
9:23	119
10:13	126
13–21	75
13:14	179
14:4	92
15:16-19	32
16:10	119, 181
17:13	119, 181
20:4	217
20:9	179, 188
21	92
21:2-3	92
22:19	85, 86
23:4	213
23:14-16	86
24:1	67

Judges

1:28-35	119, 181
2:18	184
4:3	181, 184, 200
4:4-5	200
5:2	106
5:17	106
5:23	106
6:1	230
6:3-6	230
6:7-10	230
6:9	184
6:27	120
7:1-8	106
7:11	27
8:2	238
8:30-31	158
9:4	176
10:12	184
11:1	175
11:36	126
15:5	61

15:7	126
16:21	120, 155
17:2	200
17:7-9	179
19	158
19:1	179
19:1-3	158
19:12	180
19:16-23	179
19:21	41
19:23	158
19:24	158
19:25	158
19:27-28	158
21	158

Ruth

1:1	178
1:8-11	194
1:21	88
2	176, 238
2:2	88
2:5-7	238
2:8-14	239
2:15-16	239
3:12-13	90
4:1-9	76
4:1-12	194, 200
4:3	88
4:3-12	90
4:5	88, 194
4:10	84
4:17	90
4:20	90

1 Samuel

1:1-2	158
1:1-3	151
2:5	176
4:6	139
4:9	139
6:3	146
7:15-17	200
8:1-3	221
8:3	215, 217, 218
8:5	200, 239

8:11-17	27
8:15	239, 248
8:17	239, 248
9:3-20	41
9:7	249
9:25	51
10:18	184
10:19	213
10:20-24	200
12:1-5	27
12:3	217, 247
12:3-4	297
12:3-5	221
12:9	84
13:19-20	139
14:11	139
14:21	139
14:36	67
14:38-42	200
14:50	158
16:7	35
17:17-18	249
17:22	249
17:34-35	70
17:40	249
17:49	249
18:25	104
18:29	38
19:4-5	200
20:42	68
21:4-5	181
21:7	165
22:2	253
24	127
25	163, 194
25:10	135
25:39-44	158
26	127
27:1-4	175
27:12	141
28:24	41
29:3	139
30:11-15	135
31:13	156

Index of Scripture

2 Samuel					
1:13	181	4:7-19	91	4:8	212
3:7	158	4:25	15	4:8-10	163
3:14	104	5:13-14	120	5:2	120
4:3	179	5:15-16	181	8:1	226
5:13	158	7:7	200	8:1-2	178
7:14	124	7:14	194	8:1-6	76, 163
8:15	200, 284	8:31-32	68, 200	8:3	32
9:10	120	8:32	211	8:3-6	200
10:6	176	8:36	85	8:5	32
11	181	8:41	180	11:2	20
11:2	51	9:15-21	119, 181	12:18	240
11:3	165	9:16	32	13:4	184
12:1-6	21	9:19	91	16:8	217
12:1-14	200	9:22	120	18:15-16	240
12:6	22	11:3	158	18:31	15
12:8	158	11:26	194	19:29	83, 96, 232
12:13	26	11:28	120	22:1-2	284
13:12	155	11:40	158, 175	25:26	175
13:14	155	12:4	120		
13:22	155	12:18	120	**1 Chronicles**	
13:32	155	15:5	217	2:12	90
14:4-7	194	15:18-19	240	2:18	158
14:4-11	200	15:19	217	2:34-35	141
14:5	194	15:22	106	2:46	158
14:30	61	16:24	76	2:48	158
15:2-6	200	17:9-10	194	3:1-9	158
15:3	217	17:10-12	194	4:5	158
15:6	20	17:12	273	4:17-19	158
15:19	263	17:20	194	5:21	70
16:5-14	127	19:10	204	6:54-81	92
16:14	291	20:3	158	7:14	157
19:3	20	20:34	91	8:8	158
19:18-23	127	21	27	21:12	226
19:32	212	21:1-4	76	22:2	181
19:41	20	21:3	76	29:10-15	180
21:7	68	21:7-10	202	29:12	226
23:37	165	21:8-14	200	29:15	86, 181
24:13	226	21:10	203, 206		
24:18-25	76	21:13	203, 206	**2 Chronicles**	
		21:20	38, 84	2:17-18	181
1 Kings		21:25	84	7:20	85
2:36-46	135			11:21	158
2:42-43	68	**2 Kings**		14:11	204
3:6-8	200	4:1	171, 253, 257, 274	14:15	70
3:9	200	4:1-7	139, 163	15:9	179
		4:7	273	19:5-8	200

INDEX OF SCRIPTURE

19:6-7	215, 220, 221	1:17	70	26:4-5	247
19:8-11	200	3:19	130	26:10	218, 221
22:11	20	4:12	20	27:6	293
24:3	158	6:22	217	27:12	203
24:12	158, 176	7:1-2	176	27:12-14	208
28:8-15	120, 155	7:2	299	27:25-26	281
30:25	179	9:24	218	35:10	26
31:4-21	244, 248	9:27	39	35:11	203
33:10-13	26	10:1	39	36:6	227
36:21	96, 232	17:3	275	37:21	280
		19:15	153, 180	37:26	264
Ezra		20:13	39	39:12	86, 180, 181
1:4	178	21:8	20	39:21	280
2:36-40	242	22:6	273, 274	40:6-8	142
2:64-65	120	22:9	146, 189	42:4	293
8:15-20	242	24:3	194, 271, 274	42:6	175
		24:3-4	102, 189	43:1	212
Nehemiah		24:9	102, 189, 270, 274	45:10	157
3:8	39	24:14	23	45:11	31
3:34	39	24:16	23	50:12	85
5:1-5	97, 253	24:21	175	50:18	26
5:1-13	284	27:20	20	50:19-20	203
5:2	274	29:7	200	51	26
5:3	270	29:12-13	189, 200	52:7	15
5:3-5	274	31	247	53:1	212
5:5	139, 171	31:13-15	129, 130	61:4	86
5:6-11	264	31:16-21	189	62:10	26, 35
5:8	143, 149, 165	31:29	43	62:11	297
5:9-13	149	31:32	179	63:5	293
5:11-12	97	34:10	212	68:5	192
8	285	34:19	215	68:16	192
8:16	51	35:9	204	69:4	26
8:17	293	37:23	223	69:4-33	208
9:17	269	41:4	141	69:8	153, 180
9:31	269	41:6	263	72:1-2	200, 215
10:31	232, 263, 285, 295			72:2	210
10:35-39	243, 248	**Psalms**		72:4	297
12:44	248	10:14	192	72:14	297
13:5	248	10:16	85	74:2	162
13:12-13	248	10:18	192	78:47	210
13:15-18	295	12:3-4	203	82:2-4	215
13:16	263	15:2	203, 208	82:3-4	192
13:17-18	292	15:5	218, 221, 260, 264	85:1	85
		16:11	293	86:15	260
Job		24:1	85, 232	89:14	223
1:15	70	24:4	203, 208	92:5	212

Index of Scripture

94:1	127	12:4	157	23:10-11	101, 192
94:6	175	12:6	203	23:13-14	124
94:16-23	208	12:10	286	23:23	84
96:13	208	12:13-22	203	24:17	43
99:8	127	12:17	208	24:23-26	215
100:3	162	13:3	203	25:18	208
103:6	297	13:24	124	25:21	43
103:8	269	13:25	249	26:3	124
104:21-28	227	14:3	203	26:18-28	203
105:17	143	14:5	208	27:13	270, 274
105:23	178	14:21	282	28:8	259, 264
106:42	184	14:25	203, 208	28:16	217, 221
107:9	249	14:31	297	28:21	215
107:42	212	15:18	208	29:14	200
109:11	253, 257	15:25	101, 192, 194	29:19	130
111:4	269	15:27	217, 221	29:21	130
112:4	269	16:1-5	208	29:24	208
112:5	264	16:10	200	29:27	212
116:5	269	16:11	302, 303	30:7-9	35
119:19	180	16:33	200	30:10	130
119:122	275	17:8	217, 221	30:21-22	130
122:5-6	217	17:15	211	31:10-31	32
128	157	17:18	217, 274	31:23	200
132:13-14	31	17:23	218, 220, 221	31:24	263
139	35	18:5	215		
144:7	180	18:6-8	203	**Ecclesiastes**	
145:8	269	18:16	217, 218, 221	2:7	119, 141
146:9	84, 175, 192	18:17-18	200	3:16-17	208
		18:22	157	4:1	297
Proverbs		19:5	208	5:8	297
3:27-28	283, 299	19:6	217, 221	7:7	217, 220, 221
4:5	84	19:9	208	8:9	130
5:15-19	157	19:10	130	9:9	157
6:1-5	274	19:25	124	10:5-7	130
6:17	203	20:10	302, 303	12:7	126
6:19	208	20:16	270, 273, 274		
6:25	31	20:23	302, 303	**Isaiah**	
6:35	217	21:14	217	1:5	206
7:26	210	21:28	208	1:7	180
8:15-16	220	22:7	253	1:17	188, 189, 194
10:13	124	22:15	124	1:23	188, 189, 194, 217, 218, 221
10:15	212	22:16	212	2:6	180
10:18-21	203	22:22-23	192	3:14	59
11:1	303	22:23	235	3:15	257
11:11	302	22:26-27	274	5:5	59
11:15	274	22:28	101		

5:8	32, 35, 99	56:4	291	29:5-7	106
5:8-10	96	56:6	291	29:7	43
5:18	208	58	96, 97	29:32	206
5:18-23	211	58:3	295	30:8	180
5:20	208	58:7	40	31:5	104
5:23	218, 221	58:11	249	31:9	81, 301
8:2	206	58:13-14	294	32	88
9:3	293	59:3	212	32:7-10	76
9:6	219	60:10	180	32:7-14	89
9:6-7	217	61	96, 97	32:9-12	206
10:2	188, 189, 213, 215	61:1	81	34	96, 149
11:4	219	61:1-2	279	34:8	81, 279
11:11	84	61:5-7	180	34:8-10	149
14:1	179	61:8	212	34:8-22	284
14:2	85, 119	62:8	180	34:9	139, 144
14:25	85			34:11	149
16:3-4	133	**Jeremiah**		34:12-14	149
16:14	147	1:5	35	34:14	143, 145, 278
17:6	236	2:7	85	34:15-16	168
19:20	184	2:14	141	34:17	144, 149, 168
23:8	263	2:25	180	35:7	179
24:13	236	5:19	180	38:23	158
25:2	180	5:28	188, 194, 221	40:11-12	175
25:5	180	6:9	238	42:15	178
29:21	215	6:13-14	208	42:17	178
30:9-11	208	7:6	188, 175, 194	42:22	178
30:29	293	7:9	26, 208	43:2	178
31:6	206	8:10-11	208	43:5	178
32:7	208	9:4-5	203	43:5-7	175
33:15	217, 218, 221	11:19	204	44:8	178
34:8	126	16:18	85	44:12	178
37:30	83, 96	17:19-27	291	44:14	178
38:14	275	17:21	295	44:28	178
43:1-3	162	17:24	295	46:21	176
43:9	203	17:27	295	49:9	238
43:10	203	18:18	200	50:28	175
43:12	203	19:13	51	51:51	180
44:5	180	21:11-12	200		
45:13	217	22:3	85, 133, 175, 184, 188, 194	**Lamentations**	
47:1-2	115	22:13	176, 299	3:35-36	215
47:3	126	22:15-16	200, 284	3:40	215
50:1	143, 154, 171	23:9-40	208	3:55-66	215
52:3	143	23:30	20	5:2	180
52:4	178	25:9-11	271	5:3	189
55:12	81	28:16	206		
56:2	291				

Index of Scripture

Ezekiel
3:20	212
7:21	180
11:19	180
13	208
14:7	179
16:33	218
16:49	188
18:7	26, 85, 133, 184
18:8	259, 264
18:12	26, 85, 133, 184, 274
18:13	259, 264
18:16	26, 85, 133, 184, 274
18:17	259, 264
18:18	26
18:24	212
18:26	212
20:12	291
20:20	291
22:7	85, 133, 175, 184, 188, 194
22:10-11	155
22:12	218, 221, 259, 264
22:29	85, 133, 184, 188
27:13	119
28:7	180
28:10	180
28:15	212
30:13	303
30:24	303
31:12	180
33:13	212
33:15	274
33:18	212
34:4	41, 162
34:6	41
34:8	41
34:10	41
34:11	41
34:16	41
36:5	85
36:20	85
36:28	261
39:9	226
40:20-21	301
41:13	301
44:22	175
44:28	86
45:8	85, 133, 184
45:10	303
46:16-18	96
46:17	81, 173
46:18	85, 133, 184
47:22-23	179
48:13-14	92

Hosea
2:11	293
4:2	26, 203
5:10	102
7:9	180
9:3	85
10:13	212
12:7	303

Joel
1:6	85
2:1	81
2:13	269
2:15	81
2:18	85
3:3	119
3:6	119

Amos
1:6	119
1:9	119
2:6	84, 139
2:7	154
2:8	270, 273, 274
3:12	70
4:4	248
5:10	200, 208
5:12	200, 213, 215, 217, 221
5:15	200
5:24	213, 219
6:14	184
8:4	188
8:5	295, 303

Obadiah
1:11	180

Jonah
1:7	200
1:9	139
4:2	269

Micah
2:1-2	35
2:1-4	96
2:2	26, 32, 100, 101, 297
3:9-11	221
3:9-12	208
3:11	218
4:4	15
6:10-11	303
7:3	217
7:30	221

Zechariah
3:10	15
5:3-4	26, 68
7:10	175, 188, 189, 194
8:10	176
8:16	200, 217
14:21	263

Malachi
2:6	212
2:7	200
2:9	215
2:14	157
3:1-5	211
3:5	175, 176, 188, 189, 192, 215, 299
3:8-10	244, 248

NEW TESTAMENT

Matthew
5:33-37	203
5:44	43
6:24	15

10:29	227	8:27	35	**1 Peter**	
12:1-8	250	12:19	127	1:17	215
15:19	35, 203				
18:16	206, 214	**1 Corinthians**		**1 John**	
18:23-25	214	7:21-23	135	3:17	283
22:24	194	12:13	135	4:11	214, 261
25:27	265				
26:15	222, 265	**2 Corinthians**		**Revelation**	
26:59-60	206	9:6-15	282	3:17	15
28:12-15	222	13:1	206		

Mark
12:14	215

Luke
4:18	174
6:20-21	16
6:24-25	15
6:30-35	265
6:34-35	282
7:12	194
10:7	299
10:25-37	43
10:31-32	43
12:16-21	15
12:24	227
14:12-14	282
18:18-30	34
18:20	34
18:21	34

John
2:24-25	35
8:31-32	203
8:44	203
20:26	82

Acts
4:32-37	15
5:4	15
6:11-14	206
10:9	51
10:34	215
24:26	222

Romans
2:11	215

Galatians
3:28	135, 215

Ephesians
4:25	203
6:9	215

Colossians
3:9	203
3:11	135
3:22	135
3:25	215
4:1	135

1 Timothy
5:18	299
5:19	206, 299
6:6-8	35
6:9-10	15
6:10	35
6:17	15
6:18	15

Philemon
8-21	135

Hebrews
6:17	15
11:13	86
13:5	35

James
1:27	193
2:1-13	215
3:1-12	203
5:4	298, 299

APOCRYPHA/ DEUTEROCANONICAL BOOKS

Tobit
1:6-8	242
1:14	73
4:1	73
4:14	299
4:20	73
5:1-3	73
9:3-7	73

1 Maccabees
3:41	119
3:56	106
6:49	227, 232
6:53	227, 232

2 Maccabees
8:10-11	119

Sirach (Ecclesiasticus)
4:22	215
20:29	220
29:1-2	264
33:24-28	130
33:29-31	130
33:31	134
34:22	299
35:12	220
35:12-15	215
35:13-20	192

Susanna (Daniel 13)
13:28-41	206

Index of Ancient Near Eastern Laws

Ana ittišu tablet 7		26-30	102	gap t	253
A1	132	31	103	gap u-y	255
A7	113	32	103, 114	gap u	253, 255
B1-5	253	33	102	gap x	300
B2	255	36-37	103	gap z	255
B4	255	38-39	103	gap cc	286
		38	267	100-107	286
Laws of Hammurabi		40	103	108	300
1-4	207	41	103	112	286
5	216	42-44	64	113	268
6	18, 27	46	72	114-16	268
7	17, 27, 114	48	257	116	121, 127, 128, 147,
8	17, 23, 27	49-51	255		207, 210
9-13	36	49-50	254, 267	117	137, 138, 147, 148,
9-10	22	52	254		151
9	17	53	50	118	151
10	17, 27	54	113	119	151, 154
11-13	17	55-56	57	120-21	63
14	20, 113	56	58	120	68, 73
15	131	57	45, 58	122-23	63, 73
16-19	131	58	58	124	63, 68, 73
17	114, 131	59	17	125	63, 72
18	131	60-61	65	126	63, 68, 73
20	131	60	286	129	18
21-22	17	62-63	64	130	130
23-24	17	64-65	65	136	177
23	27, 68	gap a	255	144	151
24	28	gap e	46, 50, 201	145-47	151
25	17, 28	gap l	253, 255	146	131

INDEX OF ANCIENT NEAR EASTERN LAWS

150	190	274	296	77	72
152	268	275-77	64	79	37
167	190	278	113	80	65
170-74	190	279	113, 114	81-85	19
170-71	151	280-81	114, 133	81	5
175-76	114	282	114, 122, 128, 132	86	37
176	45, 190			90	57
177	190	**Edict of Ammi-saduqa**		91-92	5, 19
196-98	122	1-3	277	93-99	27
196-97	128, 207	4	177, 255, 277	93-97	19
199	121, 129	6	177	93	19
200	128, 207	8	177, 286	94	5
205	122	9	227	98	58
209-12	122	11-17	277	100	58
210	48	19	277	101-04	19
213	121	20	115, 177, 277	105-07	58, 60
214	121, 147, 210	21	115, 177	108-10	19
215-25	296			113	19
219	121	**Hittite Laws**		119-33	19
220	121	1-4	122	142-43	19
226-27	132	6	122	144	65
228	296	7-8	122	146-48	287
229-33	46, 296	11-12	122	150	296
229-32	128, 207	11	122	158	296
230	48	14	122	160-61	296
234	296	16-18	122	166-67	57
235-38	64, 296	19-21	113, 117	168	97
239	296	19	20	169	97
240	64, 68	22-23	114, 131	173b	132
241	268, 271	24	131	175	115
244	63, 70, 72	31-32	114	176	45, 47
245-48	63	33-36	115	198	18
249	63, 72	35	201		
250	45, 49	40-41	115	**Laws of Eshnunna**	
251-52	45	45	37	3	70
251	47, 121, 210	57-70	19	4	296
252	121, 147, 210	57-59	5	5	64, 296
253-56	18, 28	57	19, 45	6	17
257-58	148, 296	60-62	37	7-11	296
259-60	18	63	5, 27	12-13	16
261	148, 296	66	37	13	23
262-64	65	67-69	5	14	296
264	297	69-70	27	18-20	253
266	70, 72	71	37, 41	20	255
271	70, 296	74-75	63, 72	21	253
273	148, 296	77-78	63	22-24	268

Index of Ancient Near Eastern Laws   399

26	130	6	63	A52	128, 207
30	177	7-9	72	B6	86
31	121, 130	7-8	63	B8	98
32	296			B12	207
33-35	115	**Laws of Ur-Namma**		B14-15	18
36-37	62-63	Prologue	276, 287, 299,	C2-3	114, 267
37	67, 72, 142		300	C4	267
39	77	4	115, 140	C5	18
40	17, 114	5	114	C7	267
41	177	17	114, 130	C8-11	18
49-50	131	28-29	201	F1-2	18
50	36	30	64	L5	216
51-52	131	31	57	M3	65
53-55	45	32	64		
53	50, 53			**Neo-Babylonian Laws**	
54	47	**Laws of X**		3	57
55	48	f-i	296	6	113
56-57	45	m-n	253	12-13	190
58	45, 50			15	190
60	65, 73	**Middle Assyrian Laws**			
		A1	18	**Reforms of**	
Laws of		A3-6	18	**Uru-inimgina**	
Lipit-Ishtar		A10	207		78-79, 189, 276
d	121	A12	201		
f	121	A17	201	**Sumerian Laws Exercise**	
5	64	A25-26	190	**Tablet**	
7-8	65	A28-29	190	3	64
9-10	16	A32	268	9-10	63
11	46	A34-35	190		
12-13	131	A36	177	**Sumerian Laws**	
13	48	A39	267	**Handbook of Forms**	
14	137, 148	A40-41	115, 152	2:1-13	137
17	201, 207	A40	201	3:10-15	18
24-27	190	A41	190	4:35-41	57
25-26	151	A42	287	4:42–5:36	64
31	190	A44	122, 267	5:37-44	64, 296
34-37	63	A45	103, 190	6:11-15	63
		A46	86, 190	6:16-22	63, 72
Laws about Rented		A47	201	6:23-31	63
Oxen		A48	267	6:32-36	63, 72
1-5	63	A50	128, 207	8:3-15	267

Index of Authors

Aaron, 8, 156, 241
Abraham, 15, 75, 76, 86, 119, 141, 178, 267
Adamiak, 199
Aejmelaeus, 59
Aharoni et al., 245
Albeck (1972), 43; (1985), 214
Alcorn, 96
Alt (1934), 7, 68, 139, 171; (1949), 20, 30, 33; (1952), 117
Altman, 175
Amit, 83, 284
Amusin, 178
Andersen, 81
Anderson, G. A. (1987), 240; (1991), 293
Andreasen (1972), 223, 226, 231, 290; (1974a), 287; (1974b), 290
Andrew, 208
Anti-Slavery International (1996), 149; (1998), 149; (2005), 121
Archi (1984), 287
Ashmore, 11
Astour, 139
Ateek, 199
Averbeck (1997), 239, 245; (2003), 2

Bacchiocchi (1977), 296; (1980), 296
Bailey, K. C. (1963), 7
Bailey, L. R. (2005), 212
Baker (1998), 96, 97, 232; (2005a), 162; (2005b), 7, 8, 31, 294; (2005c), 28, 31, 33; (2005d), 8, 20, 31, 34; (2006a), 62; (2006b), 232, 239; (2007a), 36; (2007b), 153, 155, 157; (2009), 193
Bakir, 112, 131, 132
Bales, 121
Balkan, 277
Ballard, 266
Baltzer, 284
Barbiero, 43
Barclay, 119
Barkay (1991), 87; (1992), 87
Barr, 92
Barrett, 252
Bartholomew, 266
Baumgarten, 245
Bazak, 221
Bechtel, 212
Beckman (1999), 1, 29; (2003), 132
Beckwith (1980), 83; (1996), 83, 296
Beckwith and Stott, 296
Beer, 238
Bendor, 112, 283
Ben-Dov, 192
Bennett, 178, 182, 194, 243
Bergsma (2005), 83; (2007), 78, 79, 80, 83, 96, 139, 169, 170, 228
Berlin, 106
Bess, 76

Beyerlin, 1, 98, 177, 202, 216, 247
Beyse (1993), 218
Bianchi, E. (1979), 182
Biddle, 11, 100, 212, 272, 290
Bilgiç, 255
Birch (1991), 199; (1995), 214
Black, 1, 317
Bleiberg, 256
Blenkinsopp (1986), 185; (1988), 274; (1992), 10
Block, 75, 86
Blosser, 232
Bockmuehl, 296
Boecker, 2, 7, 91, 122, 123, 124, 126, 133, 142, 143, 153, 194, 199, 238
Bordreuil et al. (1996), 89; (1998), 89
Borger, 3, 4, 5
Borowski, 224, 232, 246
Bosman, 223, 290
Bothwell, 36
Bottéro (1954), 139, 160; (1982), 2, 4
Botterweck, 176, 283
Bourdieu, 238
Bovati, 199, 200, 217, 218
Boyce, 192
Braaten, 208
Braaten and Seitz, 8
Brashler and Balentine, 296
Braulik (1986), 280; (1991), 8, 11; (1995), 10, 40; (1996), 10, 262
Brichto, 88
Bright, 7
Brin, 7, 210
Britannica (2003a), 121; (2003b), 121
Brown, R. (1993), 100
Brown, W. P. (2004), 8
Brubacher, 97
Brueggemann (1975), 16; (1994), 21, 129, 202; (1997), 208; (2002), 76
de Bruin, 105
Budde, 68
Buhl (1897), 87, 260, 270; (1899), 87
Bultmann, 178, 179
Burnside, 178, 180, 181, 182, 189
Bush, 88, 90

Cairns (1986b), 220, 269, 283
Canaan (1928), 238; (1933), 22, 41
Caquot (1974), 1, 225; (1989), 1
Cardascia (1958), 177; (1969), 2, 5, 18, 98, 103, 287
Cardellini, 112, 123, 143, 168
Carmichael (1967), 100, 302; (1974), 11, 105, 204, 302; (1981), 238; (1985a), 207; (1985b), 8, 11; (1992), 8, 9, 141; (1997), 236; (1999), 80; (2000), 141, 146; (2006), 80
Carpenter, 112
Carson, 296
Cassuto, 22, 32, 39, 59, 66, 68, 70, 71, 125, 140, 154, 202, 204, 209, 210, 211, 257, 291
Cazelles (1946), 9, 123, 153, 204, 210, 217, 227, 291; (1948), 247; (1951), 240; (1954), 178, 179
Ceresko, 35
Chaney, 276, 278
Charpin, 276, 277
Childs, 9, 38, 59, 67, 70, 123, 125, 139, 153, 202, 204, 210, 217, 258, 260, 290, 291
Chirichigno, 170, 171; (1981), 188; (1993), 125, 136, 159
de Chirico, 97
Cholewiński, 10, 11, 168, 236, 262
Christensen (2001), 11, 100, 104, 143, 217, 219, 290; (2002), 52, 117, 155, 156, 239, 247, 262, 283, 298
Civil (1976), 300; (1994), 233
Clay, 78
Clines (1984), 274; (1995), 21; (n.d.), 279, 280
Coats, 194
Cohen, C. (1978-79), 152
Cohen, M. (1990), 178, 179
Cohn, 265
Cole (1973), 68, 70, 116, 140, 152, 169, 210
Contenau, 2, 112
Cooper, A. (1988), 38, 39
Cooper, J. S. (1986), 3, 78, 79, 276; (2003), 132
Cornell, 137
Cowley, 1, 318

Craigie, 11, 21, 52, 104, 133, 140, 143, 147, 155, 205, 206, 237, 246, 247, 249, 280, 283, 298
Credit Action, 252
Cripps, 111
Croatto, 284
Crüsemann (1985), 242, 248; (1987), 207; (1992), 7, 9, 10, 11, 42, 70, 141, 153, 154, 183, 204, 249

Dahood, 270
Dalley, 1
van Dam, 176
Dandama[y]ev (1969), 239; (1984), 111, 112, 113, 114, 115, 131, 132, 136, 137, 160, 172, 287; (1987), 297; (1992a), 112, 119; (1992b), 112
Daube (1947), 7, 22, 49, 50, 60, 116, 207; (1956), 89; (1961), 52, 53, 125; (1963), 146; (1969), 212, 272; (1973), 7
David (1943), 270; (1948), 143, 149; (1950), 2, 4, 53, 123; (1951), 117
Davies, E. W. (1981), 194; (1989), 76; (1999), 214
Davies, G. I. (1991), 1; (2004a), 1, 89; (2004b), 179
Davies, W. D. (1974), 76
le Déaut, 69
Dercksen, 287
Development Finance Group, 252
Diakonoff, 111
Diamond, 207
Diepold, 76
Dietrich, 39
Dobbs-Allsopp et al., 1, 89, 275, 295, 303
Doering, 296
Domeris (1997), 176
Dommershausen, 104
Doron, 188
Dosch, 297
Doughty, 249
Draffkorn, 66
Dressler, 226, 288, 290
Driver and Miles (1935), 5, 6, 18, 98, 103, 115, 152, 190, 194, 201, 267, 287; (1952), 4, 17, 18, 36, 46, 48, 57, 58, 60, 63, 65, 68, 70, 103, 112, 113, 114, 115, 123, 131, 132, 133, 137, 148, 151, 172, 201, 216, 253, 254, 255, 267, 268, 286, 297, 300; (1955), 3, 4, 5, 103
Driver, S. R. (1902), 11, 40, 99, 117, 133, 143, 144, 168, 207, 242, 278, 280, 290; (1911), 125, 142
du Buit, 156
Durham, 9, 21, 31, 38, 39, 42, 59, 67, 68, 70, 123, 142, 153, 154, 183, 202, 203, 204, 210, 217, 278, 291

Ebeling (1916), 29; (1919), 29
Eder, 288, 294
Edzard, 255
Ehrlich, 66, 71, 211
Eichler (1973), 160, 173, 255, 267; (1987), 2, 4
Eichrodt, 90, 226, 242
Eissfeldt (1917), 242, 243; (1918), 239
Ellens, 156, 194
Ellison, 139, 170
Elman, 157
Elon (1972a), 275; (1972b), 275
Engelhard, 188
Engelken (1988), 152; (1990), 152
Ennew, 149
Enns, 199
Eph'al and Naveh, 89
Epstein, 149
Epsztein, 199
Eskenazi et al., 296
Eyre, 297

Fabry (1974), 176, 210
Fager (1993), 83, 86
Falk (1959), 142; (1967), 84, 139, 143; (1992), 7; (2001), 7, 176, 200
Falkenstein and von Soden, 1, 191
Farbridge, 156
Faulkner and Andrews, 1
Feeley-Harnik, 135
Feliks, 224
Fensham (1959), 67, 142; (1962a), 69; (1962b), 191; (1963), 66; (1976), 66; (1978), 53, 63; (1981), 59; (1988), 48

Feucht, 236
Finkel, 300
Finkelstein (1952), 216, 217; (1961), 2, 5, 276, 277; (1965), 276; (1969), 277; (1970), 62; (1973), 56; (1981), 2, 22, 27, 46, 48, 49, 50, 52, 54, 56
Finley (1960), 112; (1973), 111, 119; (1981), 137-38
Fishbane, 238, 262
Fitzpatrick-McKinley, 2, 7
Fleishman, 153
Fohrer, 8
Foster, 1, 29, 191
Frazer, 238
Fretheim (2003), 11
Frevel et al., 8
Frey, H. (1957), 204
Frey, M. (2006), 291
Frick and Freedman, 91
Fried, 97
Fritz, 91
Frymer-Kensky (1980), 207; (2001), 270; (2003), 7, 39, 200

von Gall, 238
Galpaz-Feller, 191, 194
Galvão, 97
Gamoran (1971), 260, 262, 263, 264; (1973), 265
García López and Fabry, 7
Garelli, 148, 297
Garrett, 176
Geertz, 238
Geiger, 70
Gelb et al., 99
Gemser, 7, 188
George, 1, 106, 225
Gerleman, 86
Gerstenberger (1965), 7; (1986), 39; (1987), 176; (1988), 297; (1993), 212, 230, 238
Gertz, 200, 213
Gevirtz, 7
Gibb and Kramers, 221
Giles, 119
Gilmer, 7

Ginsberg, 169
Ginzberg, 82, 83, 168, 227
Gitlin, 242
Glancy, 112
Glassner, 1
Glessmer, 83
Gnuse (1985a), 82, 83, 144; (1985b), 21, 27, 76, 133, 168, 227, 232, 249, 262
Goelet, 277
Goetze, 45
Goldberg, 217
Goldingay, 97, 248
Goldstein et al., 303
Gomme et al., 278
Goodman, 285
Gordis (1974), 88; (1982), 296
Gordon, C. H. (1935), 66; (1936), 19; (1949a), 30; (1949b), 1, 225; (1953), 225
Gordon, E. I. (1959), 1, 300
Gossai, 199
Gottfried, 265
Gottstein, 20
Gottwald (1976), 283; (1979), 81, 112; (1993), 112
Gowan (1981), 188
Grabbe, 232
Gray, M. P. (1958), 139
Gray, J. (1965), 225
Greenberg (1955), 139; (1960), 27, 48, 54; (1962a), 126; (1962b), 123, 127; (1972), 87; (1986), 47, 48, 123, 125, 127
Greene-McCreight, 296
Greenfield (1967), 217, 218; (1991), 132, 133
Greengus (1992), 2, 7; (1994), 2; (1995), 113; (1997), 113, 120
Grisanti, 303
Grünwaldt, 10, 236
Gurewicz, 105
Gurney, 131
Guthrie, 242

Haag, 223, 288, 290
Haas, 112
Haase (1957), 37; (1967), 46, 57, 58; (1997), 207

Habel (1995a), 199; (1995b), 76, 227
Halbe, 8, 39
Hallo (1977), 95, 290; (1985), 303; (1995), 137
Hamel, 8
Hamilton, J. M. (1992a), 282; (1992b), 143, 144, 199, 276, 278
Hamp, 20, 21
Hanks, 297
Hanson, 9
Haran, 10, 243
Harland, 217
Harrelson, 21, 208, 296
Harris (1955), 78, 255; (1960), 253
Harrison, 93, 169, 212
Hartley, 10, 25, 82, 83, 89, 91, 92, 93, 94, 96, 118, 130, 161, 162, 163, 169, 170, 182, 185, 212, 228, 229, 235, 237, 260
Hasel, 290, 295
Hattu, 96
Havice, 190, 191, 247
Hawkins, 287
Hawthorne, 242
Heger, 2
Heimpel, 300
Heinemann, 59
Hejcl, 257
Heltzer (1975), 240; (1976), 240; (2004), 200
Herlianto, 96
Herman, 244, 246
Herrmann, J. (1927), 33
Herrmann, W. (1958), 106
Heschel (1951a), 296; (1951b), 296
Hiebert, 190, 194
Hoenig, 82
Hoffmann (1905), 9; (1913), 142, 241
Hoffmeier, 179
Hoffner (1972), 191; (1976), 270; (1995), 111; (1997), 5, 27, 63, 65, 98, 113, 115, 131, 194, 201, 216, 287, 297
Hoftijzer (1991), 132
Hoftijzer and von Soldt, 153, 267
Hogg, 85
Holladay, 67
Homer and Sylla, 254, 265

Hopkins (1985), 83, 224
Hoppe, 243
Horst (1930), 143, 278, 279; (1956), 126; (1957), 69; (1961), 86
Hossfeld, 8
Houston (1995), 278, 280; (2004), 195; (2006), 95, 199, 210, 270, 280, 281, 282
van Houten (1991), 178, 179, 181, 182, 195; (1992), 188
Houtman (1996), 9, 21, 22, 31, 38, 48, 50, 59, 66, 67, 70, 100, 116, 123, 125, 127, 142, 179, 182, 204, 209, 210, 211, 217, 227
Hubbard (1991), 164; (1997), 89
Hudson (1993), 276, 285; (1999), 78; (2002), 265, 276
Huehnergard, 85
Huffmon, 38, 39, 42, 43
Huggler, 121
Hulst (1938), 247
Hulst et al. (1960), 117
Humbert, 303
Hurowitz (1992), 142; (1997), 99
Hurvitz (1974), 10; (1982), 10
Hütter, 208
Hyatt, 21, 33

ILO, 121
Instone-Brewer (2002), 175; (2004), 232, 235, 241, 245, 285
Irani and Silver, 199

Jackson, B. S. (1971), 21, 33; (1972), 20, 22, 25, 67, 68; (1974), 61; (1975a), 100; (1975b), 47, 48, 49, 50, 53; (1975c), 18; (1975d), 128; (1975e), 48, 126; (1975f), 125, 205; (1976), 59, 60; (1978), 56; (1989a), 7; (1995), 9; (1998a), 199; (1998b), 200; (2000), 7, 8, 153; (2002), 207; (2005), 195; (2006), 9
Jackson and Watkins (1984), 268
Jackson, R. (1989b), 96
Jacob (1923), 33; (1945), 211
Jaffee, 245
Jagersma, 239, 242
Jankowska, 234

Janzen, 76
Japhet (1978), 10, 80, 143, 162, 169; (1992), 141
Jas, 200
Jasnow (2003a), 1, 19, 202; (2003b), 1, 19, 150, 202, 216; (2003c), 1, 202; (2003d), 1
Jenni, 290
Jepsen (1927), 9; (1958), 152; (1967), 8, 31
Jermyn, 121
Jewett, 296
Jirku, 83
Johns, 1, 201, 216, 239, 287, 297
Johnson (1984), 199, 200
Johnston and Walker, 76
Joosten, 10, 76, 91, 178, 179, 181, 182
Jordan, 254
Josephus, 31, 47, 81, 117, 156, 169, 221, 242, 250, 264, 270, 280
Jubilee Debt Campaign, 266
Jursa, 254, 277

Kahle, 59
Kahn, 290
Kaiser, 7
Kapelrud (1968), 225
Kaufman (1979), 11; (1984), 82, 232; (1985), 169
Kaufmann, 10, 143, 169, 242, 243
Kawashima, 83
Keil and Delitzsch (1864), 169; (1865), 280
Kellermann (1973a), 217; (1973b), 178, 181
Kemp, 287
Kennett, 11
Kessler, M. (1971), 149
Kessler, R. (1992), 282; (2002), 152
Keszler, 8
Kienast, 255, 267
Kilian, 9, 236
King, L. W., 99
King and Stager, 194, 287
Kinsler and Kinsler, 97
Kitchen, 48
Kittel, 68
Klein, 21

Kletter (1991), 303; (1998), 303
Kline (1963), 11
Klingenberg, 261, 262
Klopfenstein, 203
Knauth, 178, 182
Knierim, 199
Knight, 9
Knohl, 10, 83
Knudtzon, 30
Koenig, 177
Kohler and Ungnad, 1, 6, 254
Kohler et al., 4, 255
Köhler, L. (1953), 200
Konkel, 178
Koopmans, 86
Kooy, 177
Koschaker (1911), 267; (1928), 1, 267
Kovacs, 1, 225
Kraeling, 270
Kramer, 3, 78, 79, 233
Krapf, 175
Kraus, F. R. (1951), 255; (1958), 5; (1976), 62, 76; (1984), 5, 276, 277
Kraus, H.-J. (1962), 283
Krauss, 178
Kugler, 82
Kuntz, 8

L'Hour, 303
Lafont and Westbrook, 19, 132
Lafont, S. (1994), 2; (2003), 18, 150
Lalleman, 7
Landes, 27
Landsberger (1939), 2; (1968), 62
Lang (1983), 217; (1998), 288
Langholm, 265
Larkin, 304
Larsen, 276
Lee, 296
Leemans (1950a), 257, 287; (1950b), 253, 257; (1960a), 239, 287; (1960b), 1, 255
Lefebvre, 81, 82, 83, 86, 87, 92, 161, 163, 170, 171, 172, 181, 228, 258, 261
Leggett, 78, 89, 164, 172, 181, 182, 194
Lehmann, 69
Lemche (1975), 139; (1976), 78, 140, 227,

283; (1979), 276; (1984), 143; (1992), 139
Levine, B. A. (1989), 89, 164, 212, 235
Levine, E. (1999), 153, 175
Levinson (1994), 7; (1997), 11; (2004), 9, 53; (2005b), 11; (2006a), 139; (2006b), 143, 169
Lévy, 2
Lewis, 265
Lewy, I. (1957), 9, 183, 262, 276
Lewy, J. (1939), 139; (1958), 83
Lewy and Lewy (1942), 225, 290
Lieberman, 276
Liedke, 7, 123, 126
Limet, 177
Lindars, 214
Lindenberger (2003), 1, 89, 131, 132, 147, 216, 275, 295
Lindgren, 113
Lipiński (1976), 139; (1979), 255, 260; (1982), 84, 143; (1984), 84, 143; (1986a), 123, 126, 127; (1986b), 86, 100; (1988), 270; (1990), 84, 139; (1992), 70, 172, 176; (1998), 267
Lochman, 21
Loewenberg, 97, 199, 232, 235, 238, 245
Loewenstamm (1961), 270; (1969), 260; (1971), 133, 168, 176; (1977), 128
Lohfink (1977a), 139, 142; (1977b), 296; (1991), 183; (1996a), 143; (1996b), 175
Long, 112
Loretz (1960), 66, 142; (1962), 85; (1984), 139, 143
Lorton, 111
Lowery, 97, 139, 147, 150, 230, 296
Lurje, 1, 19

Macholz, 200
Mafico, 199
Maidman, 277
Malchow, 199
Malfroy, 11
Maloney, 253, 254, 255, 257
Malul, 2, 53
Manning (2001), 267; (2003), 1
Marcus and Gelb, 30

Margalit, 39
Marshall, I. H. (1980), 199
Marshall, J. W. (1993), 9, 38, 60, 68, 125, 204, 210; (2003), 8
Martin, 112
Marx, 26
Matlock, 32, 194
Mattha and Hughes, 1
Mauch, 178
Mauss, 217
Mayes (1979), 21, 133, 144, 147, 156, 206, 217, 238, 280, 298; (1989), 112
Mays, 199
McConville (1984), 147, 243, 244, 246; (1998), 11; (2002a), 11, 21, 99, 104, 105, 133, 139, 143, 147, 155, 206, 213, 217, 247, 263, 273, 281, 283; (2002b), 11, 214; (2006), 6
McKane, 90
McKay, 210, 219
McKeating, 126
Meek (1930), 178, 182; (1960), 245, 278
Meier, 33
Meissner, 78, 148
Mendelsohn (1935), 152; (1949), 112, 113, 114, 115, 131, 133, 135, 136, 148, 152, 170, (1955), 48; (1956), 240; (1962), 107, 112, 123, 142, 147, 164
Mendenhall (1954), 2, 7, 9, 29; (1973), 128
Merendino, 11, 236
Merz, 126
van de Mieroop (1995), 253, 255
Mikliszanski, 207
Milgrom (1976a), 243, 270, 297; (1976b), 10; (1983), 214; (1995), 88; (1991), 10, 169; (2000), 10, 119, 130, 173, 178, 179, 182, 186, 209, 212, 235, 297, 301, 302; (2001), 10, 78, 80, 81, 82, 83, 85, 86, 87, 89, 91, 92, 93, 94, 119, 161, 162, 163, 164, 165, 169, 170, 171, 173, 181, 228, 229, 238, 258, 259, 261, 262, 279, 283; (2004), 25, 26, 80, 89
Millard, 102; (2004), 247; (2005), 3
Miller, P. D. (1969), 86; (1980), 175
Miller, G. P. (1995), 2

Mills (1989), 265, 266; (2005a), 266; (2005b), 265, 266
Miranda, 199
Möller, 92
Moloney, 97
Moltmann, 229, 296
Monroe, 287
Montet, 234
Montgomery, 217, 218
Moo, 96
de Moor, 225
Moran, 29, 30, 32, 33
Morgenstern (1928), 9
Morrow (1990), 279; (1994), 9; (1995), 213, 219
Mosala, 285
Moucarry, 189

Na'aman, 139
Nardoni, 199
Nasuti, 214
Naudé, 104
Naveh, 275
Nebo, 285
Negretti, 290
Nel (1994), 207; (2000), 199
Nelson, B. N. (1969), 265
Nelson, R. D. (2002), 105, 117, 156
Neufeld, Edward (1955), 40, 180, 257, 260, 262, 263, 264, 265; (1958), 78, 83, 97, 274; (1961), 164
Neufeld, Ephraim (1944), 152, 153; (1951), 5, 115, 287
Niehr (1995), 199, 200; (1997), 199
Nielsen, 236, 238
Nihan, 10
Noonan, 265
North (1954a), 82, 83; (1954b), 278; (1955a), 223, 290; (1955b), 153; (1975), 81; (1980), 81; (1988), 239, 245; (2000), 83, 91
Noth (1940), 7; (1959), 21, 38, 124, 127, 142, 154, 210, 227; (1962), 82, 89, 91, 212, 227, 238, 260
Nurmela, 176

O'Brien, 96
Oelsner (2001), 19, 113, 131, 201, 267
Oelsner et al. (2003), 19, 131, 201
Ohler, 76
Olivier (1997a), 81; (1997b), 277
Olmstead, 240
Olson, 8, 11
Ominsky, 43
Oppenheim (1964), 99; (1967), 106
Oppenheimer, 241, 246
Osborne, 96
Osgood, 194
Osumi (1991), 9, 138, 153; (1992), 128
Otto (1988a), 65; (1988b), 8; (1989), 4, 9, 46, 51, 65; (1991a), 207; (1991b), 51; (1993a), 9; (1993b), 11; (1994a), 2, 9, 11; (1994b), 10; (1994c), 7, 9, 10, 11, 207; (1995a), 195; (1995b), 11; (1996b), 11; (1997), 276; (1999a), 11; (1999b), 10; (2001), 7; (2004), 9
Otwell, 175, 194
Owen, 190

Pagolu, 239, 240
Paradise, 153, 154
Paran, 228
Pardee, 245
Paris, 266
Parker (1954), 254; (1957), 254; (1963), 268
Paterson, 82, 212
Patrick (1973), 7; (1986), 7; (1989), 7; (1994), 9; (1995), 11; (2002), 179
Paul (1969), 152, 153; (1970), 2, 9, 22, 27, 48, 54, 59, 67, 68, 71, 116, 122, 123, 128, 139, 140, 142, 153; (1991), 270
Payer, 149
Pedersen, 59, 89, 91, 178
Peels (1995), 123, 124, 126, 127; (1997), 127
Perriman, 96
Pestman, 256
Petschow, 254, 255, 267
Petuchowski, 20
Phillips (1970), 21, 52, 125, 127, 168, 203, 207, 227, 280, 288, 294; (1973), 129;

(1983), 32; (1984), 2, 139, 144, 145, 147, 153; (1995), 286; (2004), 195
Philo, 22, 23, 31, 39, 117, 149, 169, 210, 221, 264
Piattelli (1987), 135; (1995), 207
Pierce, 267
Pirenne, 177
Pitard, 128
Pleins (1992), 176
van der Ploeg (1951), 83; (1972), 112, 123
Pons, 297
Porten (1968), 114, 131, 264; (2003), 1
Porten and Greenfield, 268
Portugali, 92
Postgate (1971), 86, 103; (1973), 277; (1976), 1, 6, 76, 201, 254, 256, 267, 268, 277, 300; (1992), 2, 287
Powell (1987), 112; (1990), 300; (1992), 93, 303
Premnath, 35
Pressler (1993), 155, 156, 194; (1998), 139, 153
Price, 69
Propp, 21, 23, 31, 32, 59, 66, 70, 139, 142, 153, 202, 258

Rabast, 7
Rabinowitz (1958), 85; (1959), 59
von Rad (1943), 76; (1964a), 21, 33, 133, 143, 220, 238, 242, 280; (1964b), 213
Radner (1997), 111, 112, 113, 254, 267; (2001), 267; (2003), 150
Ramírez Kidd, 178
Rankin, 104
Rasor, 265, 266, 275, 285
Ratzinger, 296
Redford, 1
Rehm, 176
Reif, 104
Reimer, 199
Reiner, 300
Rendtorff, 178
Renger (1994), 2; (2002), 276
Renkema, 191
Reno, 36
Renz, 245, 295

Reuter, 152
Reventlow (1961), 10; (1962), 8
Reventlow and Hoffmann, 199
Richardson, 4, 102, 103
Riesener, 112, 139, 152, 162
Ringe, 97
Ringgren (1971a), 38; (1971b), 40; (1982), 191
Ringgren and Johnson (1989), 199
Ringgren et al. (1986), 112
Ro, 96
Robinson, E. et al. (1856), 249
Robinson, G. (1980), 223, 290; (1988), 144, 280, 288, 290; (1991), 83
Robinson, T. H. (1932), 283
Rodd, 7, 182, 214
Rofé (1985a), 104, 105; (1985b), 33, 101, 249, 251
Rogerson, 112
Röllig, 303
Rollston, 89
Rordorf, 296
Rosoli, 189
Roth (1991-93), 190; (1997), 1, 3, 4, 5, 6, 98, 103, 287
Rothenbusch, 9, 51
Rothkoff, 232
Rowbotham, 149
Rowe (1999), 1; (2003a), 19, 131, 132, 202; (2003b), 177, 202
Rowley, 90
Rudolph, 89
Rupprecht, 256, 267
Rüterswörden, 213
Ruwe, 10

Sacks, 16, 27
Saggs, 255, 257, 287, 300
Sales, 296
Salonen, 239
Sarna (1973), 149; (1991), 23, 39, 48, 59, 60, 66, 70, 122, 123, 127, 140, 141, 153, 154, 169, 211, 290
Sasson, 2
Schaeffer, 82, 83
Schelbert, 59

Schenker (1990), 9, 51; (1998), 80, 143, 161, 170, 171, 172, 259
Scherer, 218
Schiffman, 216, 221
Schluter (1985), 266; (2005), 174
Schneider, 88
Schoneveld, 23
Schorr (1907-10), 1; (1913), 1, 255
von Schuler, 177, 209, 216
Schultz (1997a), 152; (1997b), 199; (1997c), 199
Schwally, 66
Schweitzer, 97, 285
Schwienhorst-Schönberger, 9, 48, 50, 59, 126, 183
Scott (1959a), 303; (1959b), 303; (1964), 303; (1965), 303; (1970), 303; (1985), 303
Seeligmann, 262
Segal and Levi (1985), 8
Segal, M. H. (1967), 11, 106
Seitz, 236
Sellers, 303
van Selms (1950), 48, 53; (1976), 82
Seux, 1, 29, 191
Shah, 252
Shanks, 89
Shemesh, 207
Shiff, 255
Shupak, 30
Siker-Gieseler, 290
Silver (1983), 262; (1985), 2, 287
Simian-Yofre, 202
Simmons, 253, 255
Simonetti, 78, 276
Sivan, 21
Skaist (1994), 253, 255, 256, 267; (2001), 267
Skaist and Levinson, 200
Skweres, 247
Slanski (2003a), 99; (2003b), 19, 131, 201
Smith, W. R. (1894), 242
Sneed (1999a), 194; (1999b), 112
Snell (1997), 2; (2001), 135; (2005), 2
Sollberger, 297
Sonsino (1980), 7, 188; (1992), 7

Soss, 6
Sparks, 143, 180, 181, 194
Speiser (1932), 234; (1960), 80, 161, 258, 260
Spina, 178, 179, 182
Sprinkle (1994), 9, 22, 23, 38, 39, 43, 48, 50, 59, 60, 66, 68, 70, 71, 126, 128, 138, 140, 142, 153, 183, 188, 204, 210, 217; (2003), 25, 60
van Staalduine-Sulman, 128
Stackert, 10
Stager, 22, 41
Stamm, 288
Steele, 87
Stein (1953), 83, 260, 262, 264, 265; (1956), 265
Steinberg, 194
Steinkeller (1981), 253; (2001), 267; (2002), 138, 149
Steuernagel, 238
Stevens, 239, 255
Strecker, 76
Strenge, 2, 4
Sulzberger, 178
Sutherland, 266
Swanson, 221
Swartley, 119, 296
Swartzback, 128
Szlechter (1954), 4; (1956), 268

Talmon (1960), 298; (1981), 60
Talmon and Fields (1989), 39
Tampubolon, 236
Tavares, 194
Teicher, 59
Thiel, 112
Thompson, 11, 117, 133, 220, 247, 249, 280, 283
Tidball, 97
Tigay (1993), 275; (1995), 22, 41; (1996), 11, 21, 40, 52, 101, 104, 105, 106, 133, 135, 141, 143, 144, 145, 156, 170, 205, 207, 214, 218, 235, 246, 249, 260, 262, 263, 269, 270, 272, 279, 283, 290, 298
Tinsley, 214
van der Toorn, 194

Tsevat (1958), 147; (1972), 231, 290; (1994), 147
Turkowski, 224
Turnham, 138

Ucko, 97
UN News Centre, 252
UNHCHR, 121
UNODC, 121

Vannoy, 66, 67
Van Seters (1996), 143, 153; (2003), 9
Vargyas, 177
Vasholz (1987), 32
de Vaux, 83, 89, 93, 112, 126, 133, 140, 168, 172, 174, 177, 178, 181, 188, 194, 200, 242, 283, 290, 303
Veenhof (1978), 256, 269; (2001), 151, 267; (2003), 201
Verhoef, 241
Vermeylen, 11
Vesco, 9, 124, 227
Vink, 179
Vliet, 206
Volz, 33

Wacholder (1973), 83, 232; (1975), 232; (1976), 226, 232; (1983), 232
Waetzoldt, 297
Wafawanaka, 7
Wagenaar, 153
Wakely (1997a), 270; (1997c), 274; (1997d), 224, 280
von Waldow (1970), 112; (1974), 76
Wallace, 36
Wallenstein, 278
Walton (1989), 2; (2007), 2
Warhaftig, 172
Washington, 156
Waterman, 16
Watts, 7, 188
Weber, 178, 179, 195
Wehmeier, 21
Weinfeld (1972a), 10, 11, 101, 133, 147, 169, 186, 207, 219, 279, 284, 293, 302; (1972b), 133, 243-44; (1973), 7; (1977), 177, 200, 209, 216; (1990), 78, 279, 284; (1991), 21, 32; (1992), 284; (1993), 76; (1995), 83, 199, 276, 277, 279, 280; (2004), 10, 168, 169
Weingreen, 139, 143, 169
Weippert, 139
Weisberg, 194
Weiss, 296
Welch, A. C. (1924), 11
Wellhausen, 168, 227, 242, 243
Wells, 2, 9
Wenham (1971), 22; (1978a), 7; (1978b), 7; (1978c), 148; (1979), 9, 25, 82, 83, 93, 94, 130, 139, 161, 162, 169, 182, 185, 212, 229, 235; (1997), 7; (1999), 10; (2000), 174
Westbrook (1971a), 83; (1971b), 15; (1971c), 88, 90; (1977), 194; (1985a), 2; (1985b), 77, 88; (1986), 128; (1988a), 114, 150, 151; (1988b), 2, 20, 22, 45, 48, 114, 116, 127; (1989), 2; (1991), 32; (1994a), 68; (1994b), 62; (1994c), 9; (1995a), 112; (1995b), 199; (1998), 114, 115, 151, 152, 153, 154, 157; (2001), 267; (2003a), 190; (2003b), 2, 32, 111, 112, 177, 190, 216; (2003c), 122, 131, 132, 177, 201
Westbrook and Woodard, 277
Westermann, 112, 113, 133
Wigmore, 275
van Wijk-Bos, 187
Wilcke (2003), 150; (2007), 112
Williamson (1985a), 274; (1985b), 39
Willis, 195
Wilson, 207, 247
Wiseman (1962), 4, 276; (1973), 2, 276, 284
Wolff, 43, 112, 289
Wright, C. J. H. (1990), 21, 32, 35, 48, 49, 51, 76, 80, 81, 86, 89, 91, 100, 122, 126, 129, 139, 168, 170, 171, 173, 237, 278, 279, 280, 283; (1992a), 83; (1992b), 226; (1997), 86, 100; (2004a), 7, 35, 76, 199, 200, 249; (2006a), 97; (2006b), 6, 9

Wright, D. P. (2003), 2, 9, 53; (2004b), 51; (2006c), 2, 9
Wunsch, 254, 267, 277

Yamauchi, 278, 284
Yaron (1959), 164; (1960), 89; (1966), 53; (1988), 3, 4, 45, 46, 50, 53, 62, 65, 77, 78, 131, 253, 268, 297
Yoffee, 287

Younker, 112

Zaccagnini (2001), 267; (2002), 254, 277; (2003), 19, 132
Zakovitch, 147, 247
Zeitlin, 82
Zevit, 10, 243
Zimmerli, 96